A Cumulative Index to
the Grammar and Syntax of Biblical Hebrew

A Cumulative Index
to the
Grammar and Syntax
of
Biblical Hebrew

Compiled by

Frederic Clarke Putnam

Winona Lake, Indiana
EISENBRAUNS
1996

Library of Congress Cataloging in Publication Data

Putnam, Frederic C.
    A cumulative index to the grammar and syntax of Biblical Hebrew /
compiled by Frederic Clarke Putnam.
        p.   cm.
    ISBN 1-57506-001-9 (cloth)
    ISBN 1-57506-007-8 (pbk.)
    1. Hebrew language—Grammar—Indexes.   2. Bible. O.T.—
Language, style—Indexes.   I. Title.
PJ4553.P87   1995
016.4924'7—dc20   95-33708
                                                            CIP

The paper used in this publication meets the minimum requirements of the
American National Standard for Information Sciences—Permanence of Paper for
Printed Library Materials, ANSI Z39.48-1984. ⊛

To Emilie, my crown
(Proverbs 12:4a)

Lydia and Abigail, my delights
(Proverbs 10:1a)

TABLE OF CONTENTS

INTRODUCTION

Purpose and Scope

Wanting to encourage my students at Biblical Seminary to examine the original languages of Scripture carefully and with the benefit of the insights of others, I combined the Scripture indexes of five English works on the grammar and syntax of Biblical Hebrew. The original index covered only Ruth, but the positive response of my colleagues and students encouraged me to extend it to the Megillot and Minor Prophets. I sent this to Jim Eisenbraun, who encouraged me over the next several years to compile what you now hold in your hands, asking only that I include works in German, which I was happy to do.

The works indexed are standard reference works (e.g., GKC, Bergsträsser), those commonly used in schools (e.g., Davidson, Williams, Gibson's revision of Davidson), and some that have stretched our understanding of Biblical Hebrew (e.g., GAHG, Schneider).

This index compiles and collates the various Scripture indexes (although Bergsträsser and GAHG were indexed exclusively for this work). All indexes are cited in full, but references to the exercises in Jenni's *Lehrbuch* have been omitted, since they simply contain the biblical text without comment or analysis.

References to Works Cited

Citations are either to paragraph (§) or page (no siglum), according to each author's style. Some indexes (e.g., Bauer-Leander) cite references by both page and paragraph, a practice that I followed in indexing Bergsträsser. Commas separate references within a work; semicolons separate works. Works in English are cited first, followed by those in German, roughly following the order in which they were compiled (it is far easier to add references to the end of a list than to insert them within it). Footnotes are referred to by "n" followed by the number (or letter) of the note. Volume numbers are followed by a period and the page or paragraph number, etc. Examples:

GAHG 3.78 n 208   GAHG, volume 3, page 78, footnote 208
Berg 2.78k   Bergsträsser, volume 2, page 78, section k
GKC §16b, 21b   *Gesenius' Grammar*, paragraphs 16b and 21b
IBHS 274   Waltke and O'Connor, IBHS, page 274

Publications in English are cited first and are separated from German works by □. Many entries have only English or only German references.

Errors

Errors discovered in the *indexes* of the works cited are corrected without comment. These lists therefore do not fully agree with the *indexes* of the works cited. A number of incorrect Scripture citations in the *text* of the books indexed were also discovered as we worked. Where the correct citation has been recovered, we have marked it in this index with ‡. I cast no stones, however, for compiling this index has made me realize how likely I am to make errors in my own work. I would solicit the readers' help in alerting me to any that are discovered.

Scripture References

The order of the biblical books follows the order of *Biblia Hebraica Stuttgartensia*. Bergsträsser used / to distinguish different textual traditions (in, e.g., Exodus 20, Deuteronomy 5).
Scripture references followed by "f." ("and the following verse") have been expanded (e.g., 27.16-17 rather than 27.16f.), but "ff." references are not, since it is often difficult to determine the author's intended *terminus*. References to more than one verse are listed in ascending order; for example:

Genesis 1.1–8
Genesis 1.1–2
Genesis 1.1
Genesis 1:2
etc.

Acknowledgments

My thanks to Jim Eisenbraun for his unflagging support and to his staff, especially Jim Kinney and Beverly Fields, whose careful attention to detail caught many errors (those remaining are my own). I thank also my students and colleagues at Biblical, and especially my family, whose prayers and encouragement have enabled me to persevere. The Lord who sees what is done in secret will reward them openly.

Frederic Clarke Putnam
Biblical Theological Seminary
Hatfield, Pennsylvania
August, 1995

ABBREVIATIONS

B-L	Hans Bauer and Pontus Leander. *Historische Grammatik der hebräischen Sprache des Alten Testamentes.* Halle: Niemeyer. Reprinted, Hildesheim: Olms, 1962.
B-M	Georg Beer. *Hebräische Grammatik.* 1915. Reprinted in four volumes, edited by D. Rudolf Meyer. Sammlung Göschen. Berlin: de Gruyter, 1972.
Berg	Gotthelf Bergsträsser. *Hebräische Grammatik.* 29th ed. 2 volumes in 1. Leipzig: Hinrichs. Reprinted, Hildesheim: Olms, 1962.
Brock	Carl Brockelmann. *Hebräische Syntax.* Neukirchen: Neukirchener Verlag, 1956.
Dav	A. B. Davidson. *Hebrew Syntax.* 3d ed. Edinburgh: T. & T. Clark, 1901.
GAHG	Wolfgang Richter. *Grundlagen einer althebräischen Grammatik.* 3 vols. St. Ottilien: EOS, 1978–80.
Gib	J. C. L. Gibson, *Davidson's Introductory Hebrew Grammar ~ Syntax.* 4th ed. Edinburgh: T. & T. Clark, 1994.
GKC	E. Kautzsch. *Gesenius' Hebrew Grammar.* 2d English ed., edited by A. E. Cowley. Oxford: Clarendon, 1910.
IBHS	Bruce K. Waltke and M. O'Connor. *An Introduction to Biblical Hebrew Syntax.* Winona Lake, Ind.: Eisenbrauns, 1990; 5th printing with corrections, 1995.
Jen	Ernst Jenni. *Lehrbuch der hebräischen Sprache des Alten Testaments.* Basel: Helbing und Lichtenhahn, 1981.
J-M	Paul Joüon. *Grammaire de l'hébreu biblique.* Rome: Pontifical Biblical Institute, 1923. Translated and edited by T. Muraoka as *A Grammar of Biblical Hebrew,* 1991.
Ros	Franz Rosenthal. *A Grammar of Biblical Aramaic.* Porta Linguarum Orientalium 5. Wiesbaden: Harrassowitz, 1961. 3d printing, 1968. Indexed by Gerald H. Wilson, "An Index to the Biblical Passages Cited in Franz Rosenthal, *A Grammar of Biblical Aramaic.*" *Journal of Semitic Studies* 24 (1979) 21–24.
Sch	Wolfgang Schneider. *Grammatik des biblischen Hebräisch: Ein Lehrbuch.* Munich: Claudius, 1974.
Wms	R. J. Williams. *Hebrew Syntax: An Outline.* Toronto: University of Toronto Press, 1967. 2d ed., 1976.

GENESIS

1.1–8	Jen §15.2
1.1–5	Sch §44.1
1.1–2	IBHS 129 □ B-M 2.93
1.1	GKC §5n, 15b n 2, 21b, 103b, 117a, 125f, 142g, 145h; J-M §112c, 129p(3), 137k; Wms §162, 475, 489; IBHS 156 n 38, 250, 633; Gib 12, 116, 150 □ B-L 636i; B-M 1.69, 1.72f, 3.73; Sch §50.1.1; Berg 1.5l, 2.26c
1.2	GKC §15f n 1 (p. 60), 104g, 125g, 141c n 2, 141i, 142c; J-M §31d, 104d, 154m; Wms §72, 495; IBHS 64, 113, 138, 241, 483; Gib 37, 46, 167, 168 □ GAHG 3.80 n 219, 3.162 n 488; B-L 189s, 521c, 649l; B-M 1.72, 2.45, 2.181; Berg 1.105a, 2.26c, 2.71f; Sch §49.1.1, 44.3; Brock §14bε
1.3ff.	IBHS 473
1.3–4	GKC §126d, IBHS 242 □ Brock §21bα
1.3	GKC §109b, 145h; J-M §114h, 118c n 1, 155l; IBHS 274, 486, 546; Gib 56, 81, 167 □ B-L 274j; B-M 3.47; Sch §51.4.1; Berg 2.48f, 2.163g
1.4	GKC §15b n 2, 53n, 117h; J-M §157d, 177i; Wms §58, 475; Gib 111 □ B-L 426, 645g"; B-M 1.97, 2.124; Sch §50.3.3
1.4a	B-M 2.93
1.5	Dav §47; GKC §29e, 98a, 111c; J-M §31c, 112c, 118f; Wms §273, 430, 575; IBHS 274, 486, 546; Gib 99, 171 □ B-L 188p, 276t, 629z; B-M 1.91, 1.97, 2.93, 3.51, 3.80; Berg 1.79m, 1.130c, 2.26c

1.6	GKC §102h, 109b, 116r; J-M §103c, 121e; Wms §273; IBHS 212, 629; Gib 105, 138, 148 □ B-L 638w, 645g"; B-M 3.69; GAHG 2.45 n 195, 3.80 n 219; Berg 2.73k; Brock §44e
1.7	GKC §15f, 16b, 21b, 138b, 140b; J-M §19c, 158a*; IBHS 200, 331; Gib 141 □ B-L 188o; B-M 1.72, 1.97; Berg 1.70b, 1.105a, 2.163g; Brock §120a
1.8	GKC §126w; IBHS 274
1.9	GKC §75t, 107n, 109a n 2, 109a n 2b; J-M §79m, 114g n 1; IBHS 501, 509, 566; Gib 105 □ B-L 416v'; Berg 2.161b; Brock §119a
1.10	Wms §273, 451 □ B-L 588l; B-M 3.94; Sch §53.3.2
1.11–12	Ros §186 □ Berg 2.103d*
1.11	GKC §16h, 20f, 29f, 53n, 109b, 117r; J-M §18j, 94h, 125p, 154f, 154fa; Wms §274; IBHS 166, 207, 443 n 27; Gib 9, 150 □ B-L 189r, 534; B-M 1.72, 3.75; Berg 1.66r, 1.130c, 2.106m; Brock §92a
1.12	GKC §20f, 91d; J-M §94h, 125p, 154fa □ B-L 199n, 534; Berg 1.66r
1.13	IBHS 274
1.14	Dav §55a, 113; GKC §112q, 145o, 145s; Wms §228, 278; IBHS 530; Gib 21, 94 □ B-M 3.20; Berg 2.41f; Brock §50a
1.15	IBHS 443 □ B-L 276h
1.16	GKC §133f; J-M §142c; Wms §277; IBHS 234, 245, 258 n 6; Gib 47 □ Brock §66b
1.17	Berg 2.123d
1.18	J-M §9c(5) □ B-L 208r, 636m; B-M 1.112; Berg 1.124w
1.20–21	GKC §117z

B-L: Bauer and Leander, *Historische Grammatik* **B-M**: Beer, *Grammatik* **Berg**: Bergsträsser, *Grammatik*
Brock: Brockelmann, *Syntax* **Dav**: Davidson, *Syntax* **GAHG**: Richter, *Grammatik*
Gib: Gibson, *Davidson's Syntax, 4th ed.* **GKC**: *Gesenius' Grammar* **IBHS**: Waltke and O'Connor, *Syntax*
Jen: Jenni, *Lehrbuch* **J-M**: Joüon and Muraoka, *Grammar* **Ros**: Rosenthal, *Grammar*
Sch: Schneider, *Grammatik* **Wms**: Williams, *Syntax*

1.20	GKC §15m; Wms §286; Gib 113, 171	2.4	Dav §32R2; GKC §5n, 20f, 114q, 117a; J-M §143b; Wms §109, 241; IBHS 250, 611; Gib 29, 128, 129, 178 □ B-M 3.58, 3.74; GAHG 3.199 n 745; Jen §10.3.1.3; Sch §50.1.2; Berg 1.5l
1.21	Dav §101Rd; GKC §87a, 91c, 91k, 117c, 126x; J-M §94h, 125h, 138d, 155m; IBHS 122 n 14, 180; Gib 44, 113, 116, 135 □ B-L 252r, 534; Brock §96		
		2.4–6	Gib 167
1.22	GKC §64g; Wms §475 □ B-L 189s; GAHG 3.213 n 803; Berg 2.46c, 2.116b, 2.163f	2.5	Dav §22R3, 90, 91a; GKC §106f, 107c, 142a, 152k, 152r; J-M §113j, 160h; Wms §408; IBHS 216, 443; Gib 57, 73, 149, 181 □ B-L 188o, 633t; B-M 2.124, 2.129, 2.174, 3.8, 3.43; GAHG 3.173 n 549, 3.173 n 562; Berg 2.27d, 2.31c, 2.57l; Brock §32d, 35a, 42a, 145bα
1.24–25	GKC §90o; Jen §25.3.2.4		
1.24	Dav §32R2, 99R1; J-M §93r; Gib 24, 29 □ B-L 525i, 598; GAHG 1.126 n 403		
1.25	J-M §93r, 94h; IBHS 179 □ B-L 598; GAHG 1.126 n 403		
1.26–27	GKC §119h		
1.26	GKC §75l, 122s, 124g n 2; J-M §79o, 114e; IBHS 203, 654; Gib 19, 105, 150 □ B-L 409m, 636m, 650q; Brock §61	2.6	Dav §44b, 54b, 105; GKC §107b, 107d, 112e, 142b; J-M §113f, 119c, 119u; IBHS 503, 527; Gib 73, 94, 173 □ B-L 276z; Brock §135d
1.27	GKC §117kk, 122g; J-M §149a; Wms §50, 572; IBHS 74, 108; Gib 178 □ Jen §25.3.3	2.7	Dav §76; GKC §70a, 117hh, 125f; J-M §103d, 125v; Wms §53, 322; IBHS 174, 209 n 81; Gib 114, 143, 144, 150, 167 □ B-L 123t, 380x; B-M 2.139; Jen §27.3.3; Berg 2.128e; Brock §106a, 107iγ
1.28	GKC §15f, 110c, 126x; J-M §138d; IBHS 304; Gib 105, 135 □ B-L 636m		
1.29	GKC §16a, 106m, 141n; J-M §125p, 154f, 154fa; IBHS 209; Gib 59 □ B-L 188o; B-M 3.74; Jen §11.3.3, 24.3.3.3; Berg 1.70b, 2.27e	2.8	Dav §39c; Wms §572; IBHS 179; Gib 9, 66, 143, □ B-M 3.99; Jen §28.3.3; Brock §152, d
		2.9	Dav §19; GKC §115d, 127b; J-M §124d n 2, 124j, 134n, 139h; Wms §105; IBHS 105, 138, 602; Gib 17 □ Berg 2.55e, 2.69d, 2.113h; Brock §16d, 99b, 106i
1.30	J-M §125h		
1.31	Dav §22R3; GKC §126w, 126w n 2, 131q; J-M §112c, 138b, 167l n 2, 177i; IBHS 260 n 16, 268; Gib 44, 98, 141 □ B-M 2.93; GAHG 2.21 n 77, 3.204 n 775; Sch §47.1.5; Berg 2.26d, 2.70e; Brock §81g		
		2.10	Dav §54b, 97R1, 100b; GKC §107d, 107f, 112e, 141a; J-M §111i, 119u, 121h n 1, 153, 154d; IBHS 625; Gib 136 □ B-M 2.9, 2.67; Berg 2.71g; Brock §14cβ, 44c
2.1	GKC §111k; J-M §118i; IBHS 250, 419 n 4, 550; Gib 96		
2.2	GKC §106f, 138a, 138b; J-M §138b; Gib 150 □ Jen §25.3.3; Berg 2.26d, 2.164i; Brock §41h		
2.3	GKC §114o, 126w; J-M §124o n 2, 138b □ Berg 2.26d, 2.27d, 2.60p, 2.62c; Brock §60a		
2.4–7	Jen §19.5.6		

B-L: Bauer and Leander, *Historische Grammatik*   **B-M**: Beer, *Grammatik*   **Berg**: Bergsträsser, *Grammatik*
Brock: Brockelmann, *Syntax*   **Dav**: Davidson, *Syntax*   **GAHG**: Richter, *Grammatik*
Gib: Gibson, *Davidson's Syntax, 4th ed.*   **GKC**: *Gesenius' Grammar*   **IBHS**: Waltke and O'Connor, *Syntax*
Jen: Jenni, *Lehrbuch*   **J-M**: Joüon and Muraoka, *Grammar*   **Ros**: Rosenthal, *Grammar*
Sch: Schneider, *Grammatik*   **Wms**: Williams, *Syntax*

2.11	Dav §19R3, 22d, 38R1; GKC §98a, 116q, 126k, 134k, 141n; J-M §137ia, 137l, 142m, 158j; IBHS 131, 245 n 12, 248, 274, 623; Gib 28, 55, 179 □ B-M 3.99; Jen §26.3.2; Brock §21cβ, 21cε, 152b
2.12	Dav §102, 103; GKC §10g, 104e, 141b; J-M §8a n 4, 9d, 39c; IBHS 138, 145, 261, 306; Gib 53, 54, 168 □ B-L 183c', 208r; B-M 1.76, 1.112; GAHG 3.85 n 230; Berg 1.124w
2.13	GKC §26o n 1; J-M §154fc n 1; IBHS 274; Gib 55, 179 □ GAHG 3.69 n 177
2.14	Dav §106d; GKC §118g; J-M §154j; IBHS 103, 274, 297 n 27; Gib 52, 55, 179 □ Brock §116a
2.15	Dav §24a, 72, 96Obs; GKC §122l; Wms §110; IBHS 104, 153, 164; Gib 17, 32, 115, 131 □ Berg 2.124f; Brock §16g
2.16–17	GKC §26o n 1, 113p; Gib 173, 182; □ Berg 2.63c
2.16	GKC §107s; J-M §113l, 123h, 123p; Wms §170; IBHS 165, 582; Gib 125 ⊔ B-M 3.43; Berg 2.35i, 2.119a, 2.164i
2.17	Dav §90, 106b, 155; GKC §61d, 113n, 113v, 114b, 135c n 1, 143c; J-M §65c, 123e, 124d, 124d n 2; Wms §194, 205, 396, 431, 575; IBHS 75, 511, 586, 651 n 12; Gib 79, 81, 124, 128, 181 □ B-L 277d'; B-M 3.14; Berg 2.55e, 2.62c, 2.63c, 2.82n, 2.114i, 2.119a, 2.147g; Brock §93a, 123e
2.18	GKC §75l, 114a; J-M §124b, 124h, 154B; Wms §192, 399; IBHS 133, 601; Gib 39, 52, 128, 167 □ B-L 123t, 278i', 409m; GAHG 3.78 n 208, 3.175 n 582; Sch §49.3.2; Berg 2.54d; Brock §15f, 16e, 27d
2.19	Dav §43b, 44b, 73R5; GKC §70a, 107k, 131n n 1, 145m; J-M §146i; Wms §588; IBHS 213, 513; Gib 4, 8, 37, 74, 79, 110, 147, 167 □ B-L 380x, 445p; B-M 3.43; Berg 2.30a, 2.128e, 2.157b, 2.149m; Brock §143c
2.20	GKC §111c; J-M §172a; IBHS 26; Gib 167, 173
2.21	GKC §103d; J-M §103e n 1; Gib 46 □ B-L 645d"
2.22	Dav §78R5; IBHS 209 n 81, 222; Gib 19, 113, 150 □ B-M 2.102, 3.80; Berg 2.162f; Brock §107iγ
2.23	Dav §21R1, 38R5, 81R2; GKC §10h, 20c, 52d, 102g, 125i, 126b, 141a; J-M §103c, 143b, 143i; Wms §87, 273; IBHS 110, 307, 308, 310, 384; Gib 5, 6, 28, 51, 119 □ B-L 199o, 212j, 366t; B-M 2.117, 2.121, 3.10; Berg 1.126aa, 2.87c, 2.97h; Brock §23d
2.24	GKC §107g, 112m, 117a; IBHS 145, 527; Gib 93, 115 □ B-L 276z, 312t; B-M 3.53; Berg 2.77c; Brock §106a, 110e, 135d
2.25	Dav §44b; GKC §9o, 72m, 85t, 93pp, 107b, 111d, 134d; J-M §111i; IBHS 276, 303, 431; Gib 74 □ B-M 3.37; Berg 1.45e, 2.98b; Brock §42d, 139b
3.1	Dav §11Rb, 19, 33, 127a; GKC §111a, 119w, 141i, 142c, 152b; J-M §118c, 154m, 157a n 2, 160k; Wms §487; IBHS 69, 270, 652 n 15; Gib 14, 45, 55, 65, 85, 98, 140, 141, 166, 175 □ GAHG 3.80 n 219, 3.177 n 605; Berg 2.26c, 2.26d; Brock §30c, 159a
3.2	Dav §43b; GKC §107s, 127a; J-M §130c; IBHS 241; Gib 79 □ B-M 2.137, 3.30; Berg 2.35i
3.3–4	GKC §72u; Gib 173

B-L: Bauer and Leander, *Historische Grammatik*   **B-M**: Beer, *Grammatik*   **Berg**: Bergsträsser, *Grammatik*
Brock: Brockelmann, *Syntax*   **Dav**: Davidson, *Syntax*   **GAHG**: Richter, *Grammatik*
Gib: Gibson, *Davidson's Syntax, 4th ed.*   **GKC**: *Gesenius' Grammar*   **IBHS**: Waltke and O'Connor, *Syntax*
Jen: Jenni, *Lehrbuch*   **J-M**: Joüon and Muraoka, *Grammar*   **Ros**: Rosenthal, *Grammar*
Sch: Schneider, *Grammatik*   **Wms**: Williams, *Syntax*

3.3	Dav §9R2, 43b, 43c; J-M §130fa, 168g, 172a; Wms §175, 461; IBHS 333, 511, 517 n 61; Gib 9, 79, 160 □ B-M 3.102; Brock §123e, 175
3.4	Dav §43a, 86b; GKC §113v; J-M §123e, 123o; Wms §205; Gib 124 □ B-M 2.137; GAHG 2.64 n 271; Berg 2.63c
3.5	Dav §39c, 56, 98b, 100b, 104b; GKC §61d, 112oo, 116n; J-M §154fa, 176a; Wms §109, 213, 440; IBHS 203, 303, 537, 624; Gib 31, 87, 128, 134, 136, 150, 174 □ B-M 3.67; GAHG 3.192 n 704; Berg 2.42g, 2.82n, 2.114l; Brock §44d
3.6	GKC §35g, 116e, 131t; J-M §132a, 157c, 158p, 177i; Wms §378; IBHS 74, 240; Gib 30, 38, 170, 175 □ B-L 263g; B-M 3.67; GAHG 2.49 n 230, 2.63 n 267, 3.192 n 704; Berg 2.69d, 2.119a, 2.163f; Brock §160a
3.7	GKC §85t, 93pp; IBHS 70, 263, 416; Gib 13 □ B-L 274o, 588l
3.8	Dav §70a, 114; GKC §118p, 146f; J-M §127a; IBHS 70, 114, 172 n 19, 206, 427; Gib 13, 19, 22, 56, 114 □ B-M 2.156; GAHG 3.34 n 100, 3.102 n 289; Berg 1.71e, 1.127cc, 2.156b; Brock §103a, 132
3.9	J-M §102k; IBHS 327; Gib 4, 185 □ Brock §80e
3.10	Dav §11a, 104b; GKC §142f; J-M §154fa; Wms §574; IBHS 239, 366; Gib 12 □ Brock §27d, 122i
3.11	Dav §95, 146; GKC §106b, 114s, 150e; J-M §124e, 157c, 160k n 1, 161b; Wms §120, 423; IBHS 239, 317, 603; Gib 7, 62, 64, 110, 132 □ B-L 349q; B-M 3.87, 3.103; Berg 1.161f, 2.25b, 2.58n, 2.114i, 2.119a; Brock §41g, 152c, 155b
3.12	Dav §106; GKC §44g, 68e, 135c; J-M §156e; Wms §573; IBHS 129; Gib 62 □ B-L 315n'; Jen §15.6.1; Berg 2.14a; Brock §155b
3.13ff.	GKC §106b
3.13	Dav §7c, 48a, 105, 144R1; GKC §136c, 142a, 148b; J-M §143g, 143g n 2, 153 n 2; Wms §32, 118, 573; IBHS 110, 128, 313 n 19, 323, 555; Gib 3, 8, 11, 100 □ B-M 3.10, 3.14, 3.89; Berg 2.25b, 2.151q; Brock §48
3.14	Dav §68, 100R1, 110; GKC §116r n 1, 118k, 119w, 158b; J-M §126i, 163b, 170d, 170n; Wms §56, 173, 444; IBHS 75, 110, 171, 270, 640; Gib 55, 62, 77, 144, 170, 178, 185 □ B-M 1.68, 3.106; Jen §11.3.3; Sch §53.3.3.1; Brock §5b, 7c, 16e
3.15	Dav §71, 71R3; GKC §117ll; J-M §126g, 146a; IBHS 129, 172, 295; Gib 2, 77, 145, 172, 178 □ Berg 1.71e, 1.127cc; Brock §94c
3.16	GKC §113o, 154a n 1, 154a n 1b; J-M §88Mb, 123p, 154ff.; Wms §72, 438; IBHS 69, 582; Gib 77, 125, 177 □ B-L 80t, 188o, 426, 499iθ, 539i; B-M 1.91, 2.59, 2.162 Anm 1; Berg 1.101m, 2.63e, 2.161c; Brock §27e
3.17	Dav §48b; GKC §10g, 106b; J-M §9c(3), 158i, 170d, 170l, 170n; IBHS 207; Gib 101, 118, 178 □ Berg 1.124w, 2.25b, 2.26d, 2.35i, 2.119a; Brock §27d
3.18	B-M 2.116; Gib 143
3.19	Dav §91a, 92; GKC §29e, 95e, 141l; J-M §31c, 39a, 154fa; Wms §311, 575; Gib 128, 130, 147, 149 □ B-L 188p, 326n; B-M 2.55, 3.9; GAHG 3.192 n 704; Sch §44.3; Berg 1.130c, 1.161f, 2.87c; Brock §27c, 108a, 122l
3.20	GKC §135a; □ GAHG 3.162 n 488; Gib 29

B-L: Bauer and Leander, *Historische Grammatik*   **B-M**: Beer, *Grammatik*   **Berg**: Bergsträsser, *Grammatik*
Brock: Brockelmann, *Syntax*   **Dav**: Davidson, *Syntax*   **GAHG**: Richter, *Grammatik*
Gib: Gibson, *Davidson's Syntax, 4th ed.*   **GKC**: *Gesenius' Grammar*   **IBHS**: Waltke and O'Connor, *Syntax*
Jen: Jenni, *Lehrbuch*   **J-M**: Joüon and Muraoka, *Grammar*   **Ros**: Rosenthal, *Grammar*
Sch: Schneider, *Grammatik*   **Wms**: Williams, *Syntax*

3.21	GKC §15f, 60g, 128o; Gib 32 □ B-L 636k
3.22–23	GKC §152w
3.22	Dav §35R2, 39b, 56, 93, 127c; GKC §76i, 96 (p. 283), 106b, 107q, 112p, 114o, 124g n 2, 130a, 130g, 167a; J-M §129o; IBHS 139, 155 n 35, 483, 529, 609; Gib 46, 59, 63, 91, 93, 131, 160, 174 □ B-L 423, 521i, 622b; B-M 3.37, 3.51, 3.60; GAHG 3.206 n 786; Sch §54.1.1; Berg 2.25b, 2.40b, 2.60p, 2.132a*
3.23	Dav §9d, 39c; GKC §138c; IBHS 334, 374; Gib 10 □ B-M 1.106, 2.117; Berg 2.26d; Brock §152b
3.24	Dav §20, 23; GKC §128h; IBHS 138, 148; Gib 31□ B-M 3.33; Berg 2.116b
4.1	GKC §111a, 117a; J-M §118c; Wms §345; IBHS 129, 164, 195, 548, 652 n 15; Gib 3, 97, 100, 148, 166, 168 □ Berg 2.26c, 2.163g; Brock §122n
4.2	Dav §29a, 105; GKC §131h, 142d; J-M §131i; Wms §70, 562, 573; IBHS 232; Gib 40 □ B-M 2.140, 3.35; Jen §6.3.1.6; Sch §46.1.4; Berg 2.127e; Brock §65a
4.3–4	Gib 174
4.3	GKC §111f; Dav §51; Wms §324
4.4–5	Gib 65, 99
4.4	Dav §47; GKC §91c, 91k, 106d, 106e, 154a n 1b; J-M §94h, 94j n 1, 146e n 3; Wms §381, 434; Gib 37 □ Berg 2.26c, 2.163g
4.5	Dav §47, 48a, 109; Wms §395, 575; IBHS 555; Gib 173 □ B-M 2.158; Berg 2.163g; Brock §35b
4.6	Dav §39b; GKC §20f, 144b; J-M §112a n 5, 112e, 152d; IBHS 324, 484; Gib 61, 62, 63 □ Berg 2.28g
4.7	GKC §132 n 2, 141l n 2, 145u, 159t; J-M §154h, 167h; Wms §106, 515; IBHS 205; Gib 150, 154, 183 □ B-L 441c; GAHG 3.79 n 215, 3.173 n 549; Berg 2.123c; Brock §107a, 121c
4.8	Dav §29a, 51, 92, 101Rb; GKC §111f; J-M §131j, 166l; Wms §70, 303; IBHS 74, 232, 604; Gib 4, 40, 130, 147, 157 □ B-M 2.102; Brock §64a, 108c
4.9–12	Gib 179
4.9	Dav §100b, 122; GKC §106g, 141b, 141l, 150d; Wms §163, 581; IBHS 327; Gib 136, 183, 185 □ B-L 633s; B-M 3.87; Sch §13.3, 51.3.1; Berg 2.28g; Brock §54b
4.10	Dav §7b, 39b, 100c; GKC §146b, 148b; J-M §112c, 136b, 154fc, 162d n 1; Wms §124; IBHS 120, 134, 145, 317, 323, 487, 626; Gib 3, 7, 20, 30, 62, 136 □ Berg 2.71g; Brock §14cα, 124a
4.11	J-M §158a*; Gib 115 □ Berg 2.74 n 1, 2.124f
4.12	Dav §63R3; GKC §109d, 114m, 164d; J-M §75f, 121f n 1, 124c; IBHS 602; Gib 82, 87 □ B-L 109 n 2; B-M 3.114; Berg 2.52 n n, 2.54d*, 2.79h, 2.123d, 2.143 n b; Brock §5a
4.13	Dav §34R2, 96R5, 104a; GKC §76b, 133c, 141m; J-M §141i; Wms §579; IBHS 266, 604 n 25; Gib 45, 132 □ B-L 441c; Berg 2.56f, 2.84q, 2.157b; Brock §27d
4.14	Dav §57; GKC §112p, 112y, 116g; J-M §112f, 121f n 1, 121k, 137f; IBHS 246, 618; Gib 14, 90, 134 □ B-L 276z; B-M 3.55, 3.69; Berg 2.36i, 2.36k, 2.92h, 2.143 n b

B-L: Bauer and Leander, *Historische Grammatik*   **B-M**: Beer, *Grammatik*   **Berg**: Bergsträsser, *Grammatik*
Brock: Brockelmann, *Syntax*   **Dav**: Davidson, *Syntax*   **GAHG**: Richter, *Grammatik*
Gib: Gibson, *Davidson's Syntax, 4th ed.*   **GKC**: *Gesenius' Grammar*   **IBHS**: Waltke and O'Connor, *Syntax*
Jen: Jenni, *Lehrbuch*   **J-M**: Joüon and Muraoka, *Grammar*   **Ros**: Rosenthal, *Grammar*
Sch: Schneider, *Grammatik*   **Wms**: Williams, *Syntax*

4.15   Dav §38R5, 95, 148; GKC §97h,
       114s, 115k, 116w, 117e, 134r;
       J-M §100o, 124g, 125e, 139h,
       160k n 2, 168c; Wms §524;
       IBHS 286, 375 n 33; Gib 51,
       129, 132, 159, 180 □ B-L
       286m′, 629c′; B-M 3.59, 3.61,
       3.74; GAHG 3.177 n 603; Berg
       2.68c, 2.88c; Brock §45, 88, 99b,
       101
4.16   GKC §118g, 119c; J-M §126h □
       B-L 188p, 442h; B-M 2.164;
       Berg 1.71e, 2.125c; Brock §116a
4.17   GKC §29e; J-M §121f; Gib 138
       □ Sch §49.1.1; Berg 1.130c,
       2.73i*, 2.125c
4.18   Dav §79, 81R3; GKC §121b;
       J-M §128b; IBHS 178, 182, 385;
       Gib 117 □ B-L 524h; GAHG
       3.120 n 330, 3.122 n 332; Brock
       §35d
4.19   Dav §38R1; J-M §142m; IBHS
       388; Gib 12 □ B-M 3.85; Brock
       §21cε, 107d
4.20   GKC §117bb; Gib 31, 179 □
       GAHG 3.162 n 488; Brock §17
4.21   Gib 179
4.22   GKC §127b; IBHS 301; Gib 2 □
       B-M 1.96
4.23   GKC §44o, 46f; J-M §44d n 2;
       IBHS 206 n 65, 303, 482; Gib 3
       □ B-L 303d′, 362a′; B-M 2.114;
       Berg 2.20a, 2.29h, 2.118c; Brock
       §77a
4.24   GKC §29g, 134r, 159bb, 159dd;
       J-M §100o, 142q; IBHS 375;
       Gib 51, 118 □ B-L 286m′; Berg
       2.36k, 2.88c
4.25   GKC §9u, 16f, 26o n 1, 157b;
       J-M §14c(7); IBHS 220; Gib 58,
       149 □ B-L 175t, 183i′; B-M
       1.75; GAHG 3.170 n 532,
       3.171 n 534; Berg 1.71e,2.27d

4.26   Dav §1, 39a, 73R6, 105, 109;
       GKC §107c, 135h, 144k; J-M
       §124b, 146c, 155a; Wms §177;
       IBHS 71, 301, 374 n 30; Gib 2,
       72, 119, 120 □ B-L 636h; B-M
       3.22; GAHG 1.186 n 640,
       3.120 n 329; Berg 2.87c,
       2.138n, 2.157b; Brock §34a
5   Dav §37c; Gib 49
5.ff. GKC §119h
5.1   GKC §115i, 119h, 125f; J-M
       §143b; Gib 178 □ Jen §6.3.1.1;
       Berg 2.156b
5.2   B-M 1.94
5.3   GKC §134d □ Berg 2.164g
5.4   GKC §115d, 115h; IBHS 447
5.5   Dav §116R2; GKC §146c; IBHS
       482; Gib 23 □ B-L 423; Berg
       2.132a*
5.6   GKC §134h; Gib 117
5.10   B-M 3.38
5.15   Dav §37c; Gib 49
5.20   GKC §134h; Wms §97; IBHS
       280 □ Brock §84c
5.21   B-L 524h
5.22   IBHS 278, 427
5.23   GKC §145q, 146c
5.24   Dav §127b; GKC §152m; J-M
       §155m; IBHS 427 □ Brock
       §13b, 80e, 122e
5.26   Berg 1.124w
5.29   GKC §125i; Gib 5; □ B-L 435p′,
       539i; B-M 2.59
5.32   GKC §154a n 1; Gib 36 □
       Brock §74c
6.1   GKC §164d; J-M §135c n 2;
       Wms §445; Gib 97, 100, 120,
       167 □ B-M 1.69, 2.147, 3.109;
       GAHG 3.122 n 332; Berg 2.27d,
       2.87c, 2.136f
6.2   Dav §101Rc; GKC §117h,
       119w n 2, 128v; J-M §129j,
       133e, 157d; Wms §326; IBHS
       242, 365; Gib 32 □ B-L 521g;
       Berg 2.124f
6.3   GKC §67p, 72r; J-M §38 n 6,
       80k, 155m □ B-L 264b, 398h″;
       Berg 2.135 n f, 2.152 n t; Brock
       §150c

B-L: Bauer and Leander, *Historische Grammatik*   **B-M**: Beer, *Grammatik*   **Berg**: Bergsträsser, *Grammatik*
Brock: Brockelmann, *Syntax*   **Dav**: Davidson, *Syntax*   **GAHG**: Richter, *Grammatik*
Gib: Gibson, *Davidson's Syntax, 4th ed.*   **GKC**: *Gesenius' Grammar*   **IBHS**: Waltke and O'Connor, *Syntax*
Jen: Jenni, *Lehrbuch*   **J-M**: Joüon and Muraoka, *Grammar*   **Ros**: Rosenthal, *Grammar*
Sch: Schneider, *Grammatik*   **Wms**: Williams, *Syntax*

6.4	Dav §9c, 44R1, 54b; GKC §107e, 112e, 128t; J-M §129j; Wms §360; IBHS 221; Gib 6, 9, 37, 73, 94 □ B-L 274g; B-M 2.148, 3.16, 3.99; Berg 2.31d, 2.32d
6.5	GKC §153, 157b; J-M §139g; Wms §75, 391, 490, 563; IBHS 261, 645, 669 n 91; Gib 39, 53, 100, 142 □ B-L 267f; Brock §27d
6.6	Dav §39c; Gib 66, 98, 110 □ B-L 131; Berg 2.91g
6.7	Dav §9b, 43a; Gib 9, 62, 110 □ B-M 3.51; Berg 2.25b, 2.122a
6.8	GKC §142b; Wms §432, 573; Gib 167, 173
6.9ff.	GKC §111a
6.9	GKC §16b; IBHS 427, 429 n 18; Gib 52, 178 □ B-L 119 n 2, 188o; B-M 1.76, 2.122; GAHG 3.229 n 879; Berg 1.131d, 2.99e; Brock §28bδ
6.10	GKC §117a; Wms §68; IBHS 231 □ B-M 3.37; Sch §47.3.3
6.11	GKC §117z
6.12–13	Wms §444
6.12	B-M 1.75; GAHG 3.204 n 775; Gib 29, 98
6.13	GKC §117z; Wms §343, 376, 533; IBHS 221; Gib 148 □ B-L 79t, 636l; B-M 3.74; Jen §11.3.3, Berg 2.72h
6.14	Dav §55a; GKC §112r, 117ii, 126n 128o; IBHS 152, 530; Gib 32, 94 □ B-L 643u′; Berg 2.53q
6.15	J-M §143a; Wms §486; IBHS 134, 312, 644; Gib 5, 54, 56 □ B-M 3.93
6.16	GKC §117ii, 142f □ B-L 217g; B-M 1.69, 2.149; Berg 2.152t
6.17	Dav §29b; GKC §112t, 116p, 131k n 2, 158n; J-M §119n, 126c; Wms §68, 214; IBHS 300 n 39, 300 n 40, 627; Gib 40, 178, 181 □ B-M 3.69; GAHG 3.203 n 766; Berg 2.72h
6.18	GKC §49l, 72w; J-M §119n, 146c; Wms §111, 298; IBHS 74; Gib 147, 148 □ Berg 2.16d, 2.148k, 2.150n; Brock §108a
6.19	GKC §35f; J-M §35d, 154m; Gib 178 □ B-L 263i; B-M 2.19; Berg 2.114l; Brock §30c
6.20	J-M §124s
6.21	Dav §44a; GKC §107g; J-M §119c; Wms §168; IBHS 507 □ Berg 2.35i, 2.53q, 2.124f; Brock §135d
6.22	GKC §117b; Gib 178
7.1	Dav §72R1, 76, 114; GKC §117e, 117h, 117ii; J-M §146l; Wms §57, 372; IBHS 194, 221, 294, 309; Gib 2,114, 116
7.2	Dav §9R2, 29R8, 38R4; GKC §119w n 2, 138b; J-M §142p, 145a, 158e, 160b, 160i; IBHS 116 n 6, 276, 289, 333, 660; Gib 9, 42, 51, 52 □ B-L 629b′; GAHG 3.173 n 549; Brock §87, 129a, 152a
7.3	Dav §29R8; Gib 37, 51
7.4	Dav §68; GKC §112t, 116p, 118k, 141a, 141f; J-M §119n, 121e; IBHS 206, 630; Gib 50, 58, 137, 144 □ Berg 2.72h*; Brock §35a, 44b
7.5	GKC §117b; IBHS 165 □ Berg 2.162d
7.6	GKC §131k n 2, 164a; J-M §166g; Gib 167 □ Brock §14cβ
7.7	Dav §114; GKC §146f; Gib 22 □ B-L 444m
7.7–9	Gib 178
7.8–9	IBHS 289
7.8	J-M §160b, 160i; Gib 148
7.9	Dav §29R8; GKC §106f, 134q; J-M §142p; Wms §100; IBHS 165; Gib 51, 116, 149 □ B-L 629b′; B-M 2.91; Berg 2.27d
7.10	Dav §51R1; Gib 99, 171 □ Berg 2.96g
7.11ff.	GKC §16b

B-L: Bauer and Leander, *Historische Grammatik*   **B-M**: Beer, *Grammatik*   **Berg**: Bergsträsser, *Grammatik*
Brock: Brockelmann, *Syntax*   **Dav**: Davidson, *Syntax*   **GAHG**: Richter, *Grammatik*
Gib: Gibson, *Davidson's Syntax, 4th ed.*   **GKC**: *Gesenius' Grammar*   **IBHS**: Waltke and O'Connor, *Syntax*
Jen: Jenni, *Lehrbuch*   **J-M**: Joüon and Muraoka, *Grammar*   **Ros**: Rosenthal, *Grammar*
Sch: Schneider, *Grammatik*   **Wms**: Williams, *Syntax*

7.11	Dav §28R5; GKC §106e, 126y, 129f, 134o; J-M §142o, 143k, 176h; Wms §99; IBHS 286, 311, 381; Gib 6, 36, 171 □ B-L 624h, 629y; B-M 1.76; Berg 2.26c; Brock §60a, 86	8.5	GKC §113u, 129f, 134p; J-M §123s n 3; Wms §206; Gib 50, 126 □ B-L 629z; B-M 3.32; Sch §50.4.3.2; Berg 2.65h; Brock §93g
7.12	Gib 171	8.6	GKC §111f □ Brock §123h
7.13	Dav §11c, 36R3; GKC §97c, 104g, 139g; J-M §100d n 1, 143k, 147a; Wms §95; Gib 13, 48 □ B-L 521c, 623d, 650l; B-M 2.45, 3.51; Jen §12.3.3; Berg 2.26c; Brock §84a*	8.7–8	GKC §126r n 1t
		8.7	Dav §22c, 86c; GKC §45e, 70a n 2, 113s; J-M §75i, 123m, 124h; Wms §92; IBHS 590; Gib 27, 125, 149 □ B-L 382; B-M 2.106, 3.28, 3.64; GAHG 2.69 n 302; Sch §50.4.3.1; Berg 2.65h, 2.83p, 2.126d
7.14	Gib 29		
7.15	Dav §29R8; GKC §127c, 134q; J-M §154f, 154fa; Wms §100; Gib 51	8.8–9	B-M 3.44, 3.95
		8.8	Dav §125; GKC §150i; Gib 27 □ Berg 2.134c; Brock §143c
7.16	Gib 148	8.9	GKC §135i; J-M §125ia, 129f, 146k, 170d, 170n; IBHS 152, 153, 194, 305, 555, 640; Gib 4, 32, 158 □ GAHG 3.192 n 704; Berg 2.26c; Brock §80c, 122c
7.17	B-L 441c; Berg 2.122b		
7.18–19	Gib 171		
7.18	Gib 142		
7.19	GKC §106d, 106e, 133k, 142a; Wms §178, 349; IBHS 220, 555 □ Brock §93k, 129b		
		8.10	GKC §114m □ GAHG 3.171 n 534; Sch §50.5.2; Berg 2.54d*, 2.118b, 2.173 n f; Gib 128
7.20	Dav §69c; GKC §118h; J-M §126j; IBHS 171; Gib 65, 144 □ B-M 3.77; Berg 2.96g; Brock §101	8.11	Dav §146; IBHS 206; Gib 110, 150 □ B-L 588l
7.21–22	Gib 178	8.12	GKC §69t, 114m; □ B-L 382; GAHG 3.171 n 534; Berg 2.128 n g
7.21	GKC §119i; Wms §250; IBHS 198 □ Brock §60a		
7.22	Dav §101Rc; GKC §119w n 2; J-M §133e; Wms §326 □ Brock §152a	8.13	GKC §15l, 72t, 72aa, 111f; J-M §177i □ B-M 2.93; Berg 1.153c, 2.149m
		8.14	GKC §129f
7.23	Dav §10; GKC §51n, 75o, 153; IBHS 334, 384 n 18; Gib 10, 38 □ B-L 321k; B-M 2.158; Berg 2.91g, 2.163g, 2.164 n	8.15	GKC §114o n 1 □ Berg 2.60p
		8.16	Berg 2.125c
		8.17	GKC §69v, 70b, 112r, 119i, 142f □ B-L 443i; Berg 2.128 n h
7.24	GKC §118k; Gib 144	8.18–19	Gib 178
8.1	IBHS 436 □ Jen §29.3.3; Berg 2.134d	8.18	GKC §15g, 146f □ B-M 1.74
		8.19	Gib 65
8.3	Dav §86R4; GKC §63f, 113u; J-M §123s; Wms §206; IBHS 590; Gib 126 □ B-L 277e'; GAHG 2.69 n 308; Sch §50.4.3.2; Berg 2.65h, 2.111c; Brock §93a	8.20	Berg 2.165k
		8.21	Dav §11c; GKC §72aa, 117e; J-M §124h; Wms §395; Gib 13, 120 □ GAHG 3.171 n 537; Jen §12.3.3; Berg 1.153c, 2.79h, 2.149m; Brock §116m, 121a
8.4	GKC §124o □ B-L 95 n 2, 564; Berg 1.122t, 2.144c; Brock §86		

B-L: Bauer and Leander, *Historische Grammatik*   **B-M**: Beer, *Grammatik*   **Berg**: Bergsträsser, *Grammatik*
Brock: Brockelmann, *Syntax*   **Dav**: Davidson, *Syntax*   **GAHG**: Richter, *Grammatik*
Gib: Gibson, *Davidson's Syntax, 4th ed.*   **GKC**: *Gesenius' Grammar*   **IBHS**: Waltke and O'Connor, *Syntax*
Jen: Jenni, *Lehrbuch*   **J-M**: Joüon and Muraoka, *Grammar*   **Ros**: Rosenthal, *Grammar*
Sch: Schneider, *Grammatik*   **Wms**: Williams, *Syntax*

8.22	GKC §104g, 146d; J-M §104d; Wms §431; IBHS 22; Gib 21, 58 □ B-L 649l; Brock §122s
9.2	GKC §135m; Gib 178 □ B-L 95 n 4, 547
9.3–4	IBHS 670
9.3	Dav §9a, 9R2; GKC §117c, 138b; J-M §158g; Gib 9 □ Brock §96, 152a
9.4	GKC §119n, 131k; Wms §248, 388, 559; Gib 176 □ GAHG 3.173 n 549
9.5	Dav §11Rd; GKC §139c, 139c n 1; J-M §147d; Gib 14, 178 □ B-L 119 n 2
9.6	Dav §81, 101Ra, 132R2; GKC §116w, 121f, 143b; J-M §96Cc, 121m, 132e, 156g; Wms §245; IBHS 197, 385, 621; Gib 119, 150, 157 □ B-M 3.84; Berg 2.69c; Brock §106e
9.7	GKC §135a □ B-M 3.15
9.8	Brock §69
9.9–16	Gib 90
9.9	GKC §143a; J-M §154h; IBHS 195, 303; Gib 181 □ GAHG 3.203 n 766; Berg 2.72h; Brock §69, 121a
9.10	Dav §32R2, 98R1, 101Rc; GKC §116h, 119i, 126x, 143e; J-M §121n, 133e, 138d; Wms §326; IBHS 617; Gib 31, 44, 134 □ B-L 118 n 3; Brock §31a, 89
9.11	Dav §81, 101Rc; GKC §121f, 152b; J-M §132d, 160k; Wms §320; IBHS 213, 385, 392 n 33; Gib 119 □ B-M 3.84; GAHG 3.171 n 534, 171 n 537; Berg 1.45e; Brock §42f, 111h
9.12	B-M 3.16; Berg 2.72h*; Gib 148
9.13	Dav §51R2;GKC §142f; Gib 61, 102, 178 □ Berg 2.27e; Brock §122i
9.14–15	IBHS 539 □ B-M 3.113
9.14	GKC §52d, 112y, 117r; J-M §125p; IBHS 166, 412, 634; Gib 87, 90, 115 □ B-L 220m, 437; Berg 2.97h; Brock §123h
9.15	GKC §159g □ GAHG 3.171 n 534
9.16–17	IBHS 312
9.16	GKC §131t, 159g; J-M §132a; Gib 86
9.17	J-M §143b; Gib 5
9.18	Dav §106d; J-M §154j; IBHS 298 □ Berg 2.68c
9.19	Dav §36R4; GKC §67dd, 134k; J-M §142l, 143b; IBHS 129; Gib 48 □ Brock §85b
9.20	Dav §20R2, 83R2; GKC §120b; J-M §126c; IBHS 149 n 27, 241; Gib 26, 121 □ B-M 2.147; Brock §103a
9.21	GKC §75bb, 91e; J-M §94h □ B-L 252k; Berg 2.162f, 2.164i; Brock §106i
9.22	GKC §117f; J-M §146i
9.23	Dav §21e; GKC §117f, 141e, 146f; J-M §150q, 154d; IBHS 134; Gib 22, 27 □ B-M 3.8; Brock §25cβ, 132, 137
9.24	Dav §10, 34; GKC §70a, 133g; J-M §76d, 125g; Wms §77; IBHS 180; Gib 10, 45, 116 □ B-L 380x; B-M 3.99; Jen §8.3.3.2; Berg 2.126 n d
9.25	Dav §34R4; GKC §133i; J-M §141l, 154e n 3; Wms §80; IBHS 134, 154, 267; Gib 46, 55, 178
9.26–27	GKC §103f n 3
9.26	GKC §116r n 1; J-M §103f, 154e, 163b; IBHS 569; Gib 82 □ Berg 2.49h
9.27	GKC §75gg, 103f n 3; J-M §103f; IBHS 654 □ B-L 108g'; Berg 2.49h(bis), 2.165k
9.28	Wms §360 □ Brock §116c
10	Berg 1.1d
10.1	GKC §154a n 1a; Gib 178 □ GAHG 3.122 n 332
10.2	Wms §430
10.3	B-L 510v
10.5	GKC §139b
10.6ff.	GKC §1a n 2
10.6	GKC §1a n 2; J-M §177o n 1 □ B-L 2b, 35j'
10.7	B-L 118 n 3; B-M 1.70; Berg 1.69x, 2.132a*

B-L: Bauer and Leander, *Historische Grammatik* **B-M**: Beer, *Grammatik* **Berg**: Bergsträsser, *Grammatik*
Brock: Brockelmann, *Syntax* **Dav**: Davidson, *Syntax* **GAHG**: Richter, *Grammatik*
Gib: Gibson, *Davidson's Syntax, 4th ed.* **GKC**: *Gesenius' Grammar* **IBHS**: Waltke and O'Connor, *Syntax*
Jen: Jenni, *Lehrbuch* **J-M**: Joüon and Muraoka, *Grammar* **Ros**: Rosenthal, *Grammar*
Sch: Schneider, *Grammatik* **Wms**: Williams, *Syntax*

10.8	Dav §83R2; Gib 121 ☐ Berg 2.59n*, 2.132a*		11.4	Dav §138a; GKC §107q, 141f, 152w; Wms §494; IBHS 575 n 22, 651; Gib 82, 105, 167, 179 ☐ B-L 188o, 409m; B-M 1.67, 2.157, 2.159; GAHG 3.76 n 199; Jen §7.3.1.3; Berg 2.47e, 2.125c; Brock §25d
10.9–10	GKC §111a			
10.9	Dav §34R6, 44a; GKC §107g; Gib 46 ☐ B-L 320g			
10.10	IBHS 104 ☐ Berg 2.163g			
10.11	GKC §118f ☐ B-M 1.13			
10.12	GKC §126u, 141b ☐ B-M 3.8; Sch §47.1.3; Brock §28bδ		11.5	GKC §114g, 165c; IBHS 607 ☐ B-L 278i'; B-M 3.59; Berg 2.56k
10.14	B-L 131, 148 n 5, 149 n 1; Brock §20b, 148		11.6	Dav §4R1, 35; GKC §67w, 67dd, 133d, 147b; J-M §82j, 82n; IBHS 601; Gib 46, 59 ☐ B-L 183f', 436; Berg 2.54d, 2.139 n o, 2.139p; Brock §4
10.15	GKC §1a n 2			
10.16	J-M §135c			
10.17	GKC §35g			
10.18	IBHS 392 n 33 ☐ Brock §17		11.7	Dav §149; GKC §67dd, 107q, 124g n 2, 165b; J-M §82j, 114e, 168f; Wms §132, 191; IBHS 575, 639; Gib 82, 160, 179 ☐ B-L 435p'; B-M 3.102; Jen §10.4.8, 19.3.4; Berg 2.47e, 2.53q, 2.139p
10.19	Dav §108R3; GKC §91d, 144h; J-M §155h; Gib 14, 149 ☐ B-L 444o			
10.20	Gib 178			
10.21ff.	GKC §, 1a, 1a n 2			
10.21	Dav §1, 27, 34; GKC §2b, 135h; IBHS 269 n 29; Gib 2, 45 ☐ B-L 2b, 13d; GAHG 1.186 n 640		11.8	Dav §82; GKC §63f; Gib 120, 128 ☐ B-M 2.128; Sch §50.5.2; Berg 2.111c
10.22	B-L 118 n 3		11.9	Dav §108; GKC §144d; J-M §155e; Wms §160; IBHS 71, 104; Gib 13 ☐ Jen §14.3.3; Berg 2.148l; Brock §36d
10.24	B-L 13d			
10.25ff.	GKC §2b			
10.25	J-M §142m; Gib 12 ☐ B-L 13d; B-M 3.37; GAHG 3.122 n 332; Brock §21cι		11.10	GKC §118i; J-M §142g; IBHS 281; Gib 49, 178
10.26	GKC §35m		11.11–25	Dav §37c
10.30	Dav §108R3; GKC §144h; J-M §155h; IBHS 302; Gib 14 ☐ B-M 2.10		11.12ff.	GKC §111a
			11.13–25	Gib 49
			11.13	B-M 3.37
10.32	IBHS 245		11.14	GKC §2b ☐ B-L 13d
11.1	Dav §29e, 35; GKC §141b; J-M §142b, 147a, 154e; IBHS 228, 273, 275; Gib 42, 47, 100 ☐ B-L 622b; Brock §83a, 14bε		11.16	B-L 13d
			11.17	B-L 13d
			11.24	IBHS 280; Gib 49
			11.26	GKC §154a n 1
11.2	GKC §111f ☐ B-L 363h; Berg 2.123c; Brock §20b		11.27ff.	GKC §111a
			11.28	GKC §125h; J-M §131n; Gib 40
11.3	Dav §11Rc, 22d, 62; GKC §69o, 108b, 117r; J-M §32f, 105e, 114e, 115c, 118f, 119j, 125p; Wms §132, 191; IBHS 245 n 12, 575 n 22, 578; Gib 14, 28, 82, 179 ☐ B-L 535f, 653f; Berg 2.47e, 2.53q; Brock §6a		11.29	GKC §146f; J-M §150q; IBHS 127 n 7; Gib 12, 35, 55 ☐ B-L 512d'; B-M 2.49; Sch §44.6.2, 53.1.1
			11.30	GKC §24a n 1, 152o; J-M §160h; Gib 57, 178 ☐ B-L 192i, 512d', 633t; B-M 1.97
			11.31	GKC §20f; Wms §309; IBHS 215; Gib 34, 40, 149
			12.1–4	IBHS 395 n 38

B-L: Bauer and Leander, *Historische Grammatik*   **B-M**: Beer, *Grammatik*   **Berg**: Bergsträsser, *Grammatik*
Brock: Brockelmann, *Syntax*   **Dav**: Davidson, *Syntax*   **GAHG**: Richter, *Grammatik*
Gib: Gibson, *Davidson's Syntax, 4th ed.*   **GKC**: *Gesenius' Grammar*   **IBHS**: Waltke and O'Connor, *Syntax*
Jen: Jenni, *Lehrbuch*   **J-M**: Joüon and Muraoka, *Grammar*   **Ros**: Rosenthal, *Grammar*
Sch: Schneider, *Grammatik*   **Wms**: Williams, *Syntax*

12.1–2	IBHS 578 □ Sch §53.1.3.2		12.13	GKC §110d, 112p, 141l, 157a,
12.1	Dav §101, 101Rb; GKC §110a,			165b; J-M §119f, 157b, 157ca,

12.1–2   IBHS 578 □ Sch §53.1.3.2
12.1   Dav §101, 101Rb; GKC §110a,
         119s, 121c; J-M §114m, 132g,
         133d; Wms §238, 272; IBHS
         222, 242; Gib 9, 150 □ Sch
         §50.3.1.3; Berg 2.131o; Brock
         §94a, 107f, 152d
12.2   Dav §62, 78R5; GKC §63q,
         110i, 141d; J-M §116b, 116h;
         Wms §278; IBHS 209; Gib 82,
         106, 114, 118 □ B-M 2.120;
         Berg 2.46c, 2.49h, 2.114l,
         2.162d; Brock §3, 107iγ
12.3   GKC §, 10g, 116g; IBHS
         391 n 27, 395, 530, 618; Gib 82,
         94, 171 □ B-M 3.69; Sch
         §49.1.3; Berg 2.52o, 2.134d;
         Brock §91, 124a, 138
12.4   GKC §134h; Wms §97; IBHS
         281; Gib 49 □ B-M 2.120; Sch
         §45.4.4; Brock §108a, 151
12.5   IBHS 114; Gib 40, 144 □ Berg
         1.66r
12.6   J-M §154h; Gib 150 □ Berg
         2.34g; Brock §17, 121b
12.7   Dav §99; GKC §116o; Wms
         §90, 218; IBHS 248, 621, 623;
         Gib 135 □ Berg 2.69c, 2.164h
12.8   Dav §140; GKC §91e, 156c; J-M
         §94h, 159b; Wms §323, IBHS
         212; Gib 110, 148 □ B-L 182b′;
         GAHG 2.49 n 228, 2.69,
         3.151 n 415; Berg 2.163g;
         Brock §20b, 89, 139a
12.9   Dav §86R4; GKC §113u; J-M
         §123s; IBHS 590; Gib 126 □ Jen
         §10.3.1.1; Berg 2.65h; Brock §89
12.10   Wms §579; Gib 97 □ B-L 312t;
         Brock §89
12.11–14 Gib 99
12.11–13 Sch §53.2.1
12.11   GKC §111g, 114m; J-M §164a;
         Gib 33, 98 □ B-L 521h; GAHG
         3.170 n 524; Sch §53.4.3; Berg
         2.28g, 2.57k, 1.105a; Brock §51
12.12   Dav §56, 146R1; GKC §112c,
         112y, 112hh, 164d; J-M §119d,
         154fb, 157b; IBHS 401 n 22;
         Gib 77, 111 □ B-M 3.55; Brock
         §27c, 97bα

12.13   GKC §110d, 112p, 141l, 157a,
         165b; J-M §119f, 157b, 157ca,
         168d; Wms §175, 367, 521;
         IBHS 511, 529, 579; Gib 4, 93,
         111, 119, 159 □ B-M 3.94,
         3.102; GAHG 3.200 n 749;
         Berg 2.40b, 2.48g, 2.126d;
         Brock §143b, 145bγ
12.14   Dav §34, 51; GKC §111g, 117h,
         118u; J-M §157d; Wms §58,
         262, 505; IBHS 202 n 49, 205;
         Gib 45, 98 □ Sch §49.3.1; Berg
         2.96e; Brock §160a
12.15   GKC §118f; Gib 118 □ B-L 436;
         Berg 2.87c; Brock §89
12.16   GKC §145o, 154a n 1; J-M
         §177o □ B-M 2.141; Sch
         §44.6.2; Berg 2.26c, 2.129h;
         Brock §116m, 122k
12.17   Dav §67b, 67R2; GKC §117q;
         Gib 115 □ Brock §93k
12.18   GKC §136c, J-M §143g,
         165b n 2; IBHS 207; Gib 62,
         110, 184 □ B-M 3.89; GAHG
         3.173 n 547
12.19   Dav §48a, 73R5; GKC §111m,
         117f, 147b; J-M §118h, 146i,
         161m; Gib 5, 59, 91, 110, 111 □
         GAHG 3.203 n 763,
         3.204 n 772, 3.205 n 779; Berg
         2.53q; Brock §4
12.20   Brock §90b, 97bγ, 110c
13.1–4   Sch §52.5.1 - 52.5.5
13.1   J-M §146c; IBHS 219 n 114,
         295; Gib 22, 148 □ Berg 2.163g
13.2   Dav §22d; GKC §126n,
         154a n 1; J-M §137ia, 159f;
         IBHS 245, 668; Gib 28, 53, 168,
         174 □ B-M 3.28; Sch §53.4.2;
         Brock §21cβ
13.3   Dav §101Rb; GKC §91e, 138c,
         154a n 1, 154a n 1b; J-M §94h,
         129q n 2; IBHS 200, 334; Gib 9,
         148
13.5   Dav §99; GKC §145o; J-M
         §138a; Gib 135, 174 □ B-L
         580u′
13.6   Wms §572; Gib 128 □ B-M
         2.115; Berg 2.125b; Brock §122e

B-L: Bauer and Leander, *Historische Grammatik*   **B-M**: Beer, *Grammatik*   **Berg**: Bergsträsser, *Grammatik*
Brock: Brockelmann, *Syntax*   **Dav**: Davidson, *Syntax*   **GAHG**: Richter, *Grammatik*
Gib: Gibson, *Davidson's Syntax, 4th ed.*   **GKC**: *Gesenius' Grammar*   **IBHS**: Waltke and O'Connor, *Syntax*
Jen: Jenni, *Lehrbuch*   **J-M**: Joüon and Muraoka, *Grammar*   **Ros**: Rosenthal, *Grammar*
Sch: Schneider, *Grammatik*   **Wms**: Williams, *Syntax*

13.7	Dav §22, 103; GKC §126m, IBHS 651 n 14; Gib 28 □ B-L 588l; Brock §139b
13.8	GKC §131b; J-M §131b; Wms §562, 579; Gib 82 □ Berg 2.49h; Brock §8a
13.9	Dav §123, 130R2; GKC §51n, 56, 118f, 159r; J-M §176k; IBHS 571, 579; Gib 183 □ B-M 2.127; Berg 2.48f, 2.91g, 2.129h, 2.110e; Brock §169b
13.10	Dav §29e, 108R3, 145; GKC §115i, 117h, 144h; J-M §125f, 155h, 157d; Wms §371; Gib 14, 42, 129, 131, 144, 157 □ B-L 267f; Brock §107lα
13.11	Dav §11Rc; GKC §139e; J-M §147c; Gib 14 □ B-M 2.131
13.12	GKC §142c; J-M §129f; Wms §310, 573; IBHS 129, 224, 482; Gib 65, 172 □ Berg 1.155f, 2.74a, 2.172 n f
13.13	Dav §103; GKC §140a; Gib 142 □ Brock §77a
13.14	GKC §104g; J-M §104d, 105c n 2, 125f, 129q n 2; Wms §360; IBHS 134 n 19, 193; Gib 157, 179 □ B-L 188o, 441c, 649l; Berg 2.122c
13.15	GKC §142g, 143c; J-M §121h n 2, 154f, 155q, 156c; Wms §574; IBHS 183; Gib 117, 181, 182 □ Brock §123e
13.16	Dav §11Rb, 130a; GKC §139d, 166b; J-M §125w n 2, 147b, 155m, 158h n 1, 169f; Wms §465; Gib 14, 79, 153 □ B-M 3.116; GAHG 3.100; Sch §52.6.3, 53.5.1.1; Berg 2.69d, 2.128e; Brock §24e, 165a
13.17	GKC §120g; Wms §274; IBHS 206 n 67 □ Berg 2.53p
13.18	Berg 2.74a, 2.172 n f
14	B-L 70 n 2
14.1–2	GKC §111f
14.1	GKC §154a n 1a □ Berg 1.4b
14.2	Dav §144R3; IBHS 130; Gib 12
14.3	Dav §101; Wms §114; Gib 12
14.4	Dav §39a, 68; GKC §118i, 118k, 134o; IBHS 486; Gib 144 □ B-L 623e; Brock §86
14.5	GKC §111a, 134o; J-M §118c, 142o; IBHS 119, 284
14.6	Dav §29a; GKC §93aa, 131f; J-M §129u, 131h; IBHS 159; Gib 40 □ B-L 564; B-M 2.65
14.7	J-M §118c □ B-L 588l
14.9	Dav §37R5; GKC §134k; IBHS 278; Gib 48, 119 □ B-M 3.39; Brock §85b
14.10	Dav §28R6, 29R8; GKC §27q, 90c, 90i, 93aa, 123e, 130e; J-M §93c, 93d, 130r, 135e; Wms §16; Gib 36, 42, 167, 171 □ B-L 564; B-M 2.66; Berg 1.152a; Brock §122p
14.12	Gib 168
14.13	Dav §24R3, 28R4, 138b; GKC §2b, 126r, 128u; J-M §129j, 137n; IBHS 150, 243; Gib 35, 168 □ B-L 13c; B-M 1.12; Brock §74b
14.15	B-L 528s; Gib 144
14.16	Brock §130b; Gib 171
14.17–18	Brock §48
14.17	Dav §90, 91R3, 145; GKC §115a; Wms §506; Gib 12, 128, 129, 157
14.18	GKC §129c; J-M §130b; Wms §573; IBHS 127 n 6; Gib 53
14.19	Dav §22R3, 81; GKC §121f, 128a; J-M §129b, 132f, 137h n 2; Wms §29, 82; IBHS 139, 250; Gib 29, 37, 54 □ B-M 3.31; Sch §45.3.4; Berg 2.120a; Brock §7b, 20b, 70f, 107e
14.20	Berg 2.123d
14.21	Berg 2.123d; Gib 171
14.22	GKC §106i; J-M §112f, 165b n 1; Wms §164; IBHS 488; Gib 35, 61 □ Berg 2.28e, 2.148k; Brock §41d
14.23	Dav §101Rb; GKC §102b, 109g, 135a, 149c, 154a n 1b; J-M §103d, 116j, 165i; IBHS 295 □ B-L 643u'; Berg 2.120a
14.24	GKC §135c; IBHS 294 n 22; Gib 38

B-L: Bauer and Leander, *Historische Grammatik*   **B-M**: Beer, *Grammatik*   **Berg**: Bergsträsser, *Grammatik*
Brock: Brockelmann, *Syntax*   **Dav**: Davidson, *Syntax*   **GAHG**: Richter, *Grammatik*
Gib: Gibson, *Davidson's Syntax, 4th ed.*   **GKC**: *Gesenius' Grammar*   **IBHS**: Waltke and O'Connor, *Syntax*
Jen: Jenni, *Lehrbuch*   **J-M**: Joüon and Muraoka, *Grammar*   **Ros**: Rosenthal, *Grammar*
Sch: Schneider, *Grammatik*   **Wms**: Williams, *Syntax*

15.1–2	GKC §111a
15.1	Dav §4R1, 104b; GKC §126r, 131q; J-M §103a; Wms §360, 402; IBHS 129, 193; Gib 98, 147, 177 □ B-L 276t, 426, 521g; B-M 3.8; GAHG 3.43 n 135; Berg 2.50k, 2.65h*, 2.126d; Brock §25cγ, 116c
15.2	Dav §70a, 138b; GKC §116n, 118n, 128v, 135q, 141e; J-M §16f n 2, 159d; IBHS 124; Gib 7, 56, 98, 168 □ B-L 276t; B-M 3.104; Berg 2.72h*
15.3	Dav §100R1; J-M §155q; IBHS 488, 678; Gib 59, 137 □ GAHG 3.173 n 550; Sch §54.1.1; Berg 2.14a, 2.72h
15.4	Dav §106; GKC §135c, J-M §145a, 156k; IBHS 294 n 22; Gib 181 □ Brock §25d, 155b
15.5	GKC §150i; Wms §62; IBHS 185, 245 □ B-L 333z, 443i; GAHG 3.170 n 524; Berg 2.157b; Brock §25cγ, 42e
15.6	Dav §58R1, 80, 109R2; GKC §112ss, 122q, 135p; J-M §119z, 152b; IBHS 175, 305; Gib 103, 114 □ B-M 3.76; Berg 2.43 n b-k; Brock §94dβ
15.7	Dav §9a; GKC §29f, 66i, 138d; J-M §158n; IBHS 333; Gib 9 □ B-L 189r, 638t; Berg 2.123d, 2.127e, 2.157c
15.8	Dav §7b; J-M §16f n 2, 37d; IBHS 317, 325; Gib 7, 32, 185 □ Berg 2.127e
15.9	IBHS 422 □ Berg 2.124f
15.10	Dav §11Rd, 110; GKC §139b, 139c; IBHS 200 n 39, 406; Gib 14 □ B-L 267e; B-M 2.17; Berg 2.26c
15.11	GKC §126r; Wms §287; IBHS 216 n 107
15.12	Dav §51R1, 94, 113; GKC §111f, 114i; J-M §124l, 154d, 166d; Wms §196, 227; IBHS 610; Gib 21, 59, 99, 131, 167 □ Berg 2.60o
15.13	GKC §113o, 118k, 135p, 155e; J-M §113m, 123h, 149a; Wms §540; IBHS 303, 587 n 32; Gib 11, 144, 179 □ B-M 3.96; Berg 2.63e
15.14	GKC §29w, 116p, 119n; J-M §154fe n 1; IBHS 628; Gib 77, 136 □ Berg 1.160a, 2.72h*
15.15	GKC §135a; Wms §252; Gib 78, 150, 178
15.16	Dav §71R1; GKC §118q
15.17	Dav §113, 141; GKC §111g; J-M §150k; IBHS 200; Gib 21, 167 □ B-L 645g″; Berg 2.26d; Brock §4
15.18	Dav §24a, 41a; GKC §106m, 136b; J-M §112g, 129f, 143j, 176h; Wms §42; IBHS 103, 153, 314; Gib 6, 40, 61 □ Berg 2.27e; Brock §41d, 115a
15.19ff.	GKC §154a n 1
15.19–21	GKC §154a n 1a; IBHS 115
15.19	GKC §111a, 126m
15.21	Gib 28
16.1–2	GKC §111a
16.1	Dav §105R1, 113; GKC §142b, 156b; IBHS 232, 652 n 15; Gib 21, 167 □ B-M 3.52; Berg 2.27d
16.2	GKC §51g, 51p, 119x; J-M §105c, 155m, 164a; IBHS 579, 663; Gib 79, 132 □ B-M 3.80; GAHG 3.170 n 524; Berg 2.48g, 2.91f, 2.92h
16.3	Dav §28R5, 29a, 91R2; GKC §102f, 115f, 129f, 142g; J-M §103c, 124g; Wms §70; IBHS 232; Gib 36, 40, 130, 141 □ B-L 638u; B-M 2.139; Berg 2.125b
16.4	GKC §67p; IBHS 392 n 31 □ B-M 2.144; Berg 2.135d, 2.165l
16.5	Dav §2, 23, 101Rd; GKC §5n, 103o, 135a, 135m; J-M §103n, 146a; Wms §110; IBHS 147, 201, 296, 303; Gib 2, 3, 32, 148, 149 □ B-L 79s, 645h″; B-M 2.144; Berg 1.5l, 2.135d; Brock §8a
16.6	Dav §103 □ Brock §107e

B-L: Bauer and Leander, *Historische Grammatik*   **B-M**: Beer, *Grammatik*   **Berg**: Bergsträsser, *Grammatik*
Brock: Brockelmann, *Syntax*   **Dav**: Davidson, *Syntax*   **GAHG**: Richter, *Grammatik*
Gib: Gibson, *Davidson's Syntax, 4th ed.*   **GKC**: *Gesenius' Grammar*   **IBHS**: Waltke and O'Connor, *Syntax*
Jen: Jenni, *Lehrbuch*   **J-M**: Joüon and Muraoka, *Grammar*   **Ros**: Rosenthal, *Grammar*
Sch: Schneider, *Grammatik*   **Wms**: Williams, *Syntax*

16.7	Dav §101Rd; GKC §60d, 127e; J-M §137n; Gib 31 □ GAHG 2.17 n 53; Jen §29.3.3; Berg 2.23g; Brock §73a, 82a, 110a	17.10	Dav §88R5; GKC §113gg; J-M §123v, 130g; Wms §209; Gib 127, 178 □ Berg 2.66k, 2.67l, 2.147i; Brock §28bδ
16.8	Dav §45R1, 100R1; GKC §10k, 76g, 107h, 116n; J-M §121h n 1, 143k; IBHS 328, 329, 504, 626; Gib 76, 137, 185 □ B-M 3.67; Berg 1.49d, 2.71g	17.11	Dav §72R3, 80; GKC §67dd, 112aa, 121d, 144b; J-M §126g; IBHS 181; Gib 117 □ B-L 403, 431t; B-M 3.54; Berg 2.147i, 2.151q; Brock §98a, 102
16.9	Gib 80	17.12	GKC §138b; Dav §9R2, 88R5, 101Rc; J-M §126c, 130g, 158g; IBHS 172; Gib 47 □ GAHG 3.77 n 203
16.10	Dav §101Rc; GKC §166a; J-M §170i; Gib 124 □ Jen §11.3.1.2; Berg 2.63e		
16.11	Dav §117R2; GKC §74g, 80d, 94f, 116n; J-M §89j; Wms §300 □ B-L 198i, 612z; B-M 2.79; Berg 1.49d, 1.137 n g	17.13	GKC §113w, Dav §88R5; J-M §125q □ Berg 1.78m, 2.63d; Brock §93b
16.12	Dav §24a; GKC §127c, 128l, 156b; J-M §129f; Wms §242; IBHS 197; Gib 32, 178 □ B-M 3.9; Brock §14cγ	17.14	Dav §72R3, 80; GKC §29q, 67v, 112mm, 121d, 158a, 167b n 1; J-M §170b; Gib 117, 178, 182 □ B-L 232j; B-M 3.84, 3.105; Berg 2.44i, 2.137k; Brock §133c
16.13	GKC §116o; J-M §118j; IBHS 616; Gib 133, 184 □ B-L 208r, 577i', 577j'; Berg 1.126bb, 2.69c	17.15	GKC §143b; J-M §172c, 172c n 1; Wms §447, 555; IBHS 76, 671; Gib 174, 182 □ B-L 512d'; GAHG 3.120 n 330
16.14	GKC §144d; J-M §155e; Gib 13 □ Brock §36d	17.16	B-L 517w
16.16	GKC §115f; Gib 128, 167	17.17	Dav §24R3, 126R2; GKC §96 (p. 285), 100l, 107t, 134d, 150g, 167b n 1; J-M §102m, 152f, 152fa; IBHS 281; Gib 184 □ B-L 618j, 632h; B-M 2.80; Sch §13.3.1; Berg 1.68v
17.1–2	IBHS 578 □ Berg 2.46c		
17.1	GKC §110f; J-M §111i; IBHS 263 □ B-M 3.38		
17.2	IBHS 654 □ Berg 2.53q		
17.3	GKC §114o n 1 □ Berg 2.60p		
17.4	GKC §96 (p. 282), 143a; J-M §98b; IBHS 677; Gib 91, 181, 182 □ B-L 615a; B-M 2.79; GAHG 3.203 n 766; Berg 2.42g	17.18	Dav §134; GKC §151e; J-M §163c; Wms §460, 548; Gib 79, 186 □ B-M 3.117; GAHG 3.179 n 618; Brock §8b
17.5	Dav §81R3, 155; GKC §117ii, 121b, 163a; J-M §98b, 125w, 128b, 172a, 172c; Wms §59, 552; IBHS 671 n 102; Gib 91, 114, 118, 173 □ B-L 615a; B-M 2.10, 2.79; GAHG 3.120 n 330, 3.171 n 534; Sch §50.1.3	17.19	GKC §49l, 116p; J-M §154fc, 164a n 2; IBHS 630, 672; Gib 137 □ GAHG 3.176 n 598; Berg 2.16d, 2.72h*; Brock §56b
		17.20–21	Brock §135b
		17.20	GKC §106m, 112s; IBHS 207, 490, 532; Gib 59, 93, 102, 150 □ B-M 2.121, 3.54; GAHG 3.199 n 743; Berg 1.93g, 1.107e, 2.27e, 2.28e
17.6	IBHS 305 □ Berg 2.125b; Brock §122p		
17.7	Berg 2.148k		
17.8	GKC §128p; J-M §129f; IBHS 149	17.21	GKC §154a; Wms §268; IBHS 310; Gib 173
17.9	GKC §94f, 142f n 2; J-M §146c □ GAHG 3.106 n 301	17.24	GKC §121d □ Gib 117

B-L: Bauer and Leander, *Historische Grammatik*   **B-M**: Beer, *Grammatik*   **Berg**: Bergsträsser, *Grammatik*
Brock: Brockelmann, *Syntax*   **Dav**: Davidson, *Syntax*   **GAHG**: Richter, *Grammatik*
Gib: Gibson, *Davidson's Syntax, 4th ed.*   **GKC**: *Gesenius' Grammar*   **IBHS**: Waltke and O'Connor, *Syntax*
Jen: Jenni, *Lehrbuch*   **J-M**: Joüon and Muraoka, *Grammar*   **Ros**: Rosenthal, *Grammar*
Sch: Schneider, *Grammatik*   **Wms**: Williams, *Syntax*

17.25	Dav §72R3, 80; GKC §156d n 4; Gib 117, 145
17.26–27	B-M 2.153
17.26	GKC §72ee □ Berg 2.151q
17.27	Berg 2.151q
18.1ff.	Sch §48.2, 54.2.2.4
18.1	Dav §69a, 138b; GKC §116o, 118g, 141e; J-M §126h, 159d, 166h, 166m; IBHS 170; Gib 143, 168 □ B-M 3.12, 3.77, 3.92; Jen §11.3.3; Brock §109b, 139b
18.2–5	Sch §51.4.2
18.2	Dav §101Rd; IBHS 626; Gib 31, 59, 149 □ Berg 2.70e, 2.164i; Brock §89
18.3–4	GKC §105b n 1 (p. 308)
18.3	Dav §60; GKC §135q, 159n; J-M §167h; Wms §511, 515; IBHS 579; Gib 81 □ B-M 3.115; GAHG 3.170 n 526; Berg 2.48g; Brock §164bβ
18.4	Dav §60; GKC §105b n 1 (p. 308); J-M §69c; IBHS 374; Gib 32, 118 □ B-M 3.47; Berg 2.48g(bis), 2.87c, 2.124f
18.5	Dav §151; GKC §158b n 1; J-M §69c, 103a, 170h n 1; IBHS 641; Gib 161 □ B-L 77m, 354c; B-M 2.131, 3.106; Sch §53.4.3; Berg 1.3i, 2.36i, 2.119e; Brock §110a
18.6	Dav §29d, 29R4; GKC §90b n 3, 90c, 90i, 93q, 131d; J-M §69c, 102g, 127b, 131e; IBHS 173, 413; Gib 41 □ B-L 580u′; B-M 1.90, 3.37; GAHG 3.109 n 310; Berg 1.154e; Brock §62c, 89
18.7–8	Wms §83; IBHS 242 □ Brock §137
18.7	Dav §21, 21d, 73R5; GKC §117f, 126r; J-M §137n, 146i; Wms §178, 588; IBHS 243,244; Gib 5, 26, 27, 28, 110 □ B-M 3.33; Jen §26.3.2; Berg 2.26c, 2.59n*
18.8	Dav §138b, 142; GKC §116o, 141e; J-M §137f; Gib 26, 66, 168 □ Brock §110a, 139b
18.9	Dav §117, 117R3; GKC §5n, 147b; J-M §146h; IBHS 328; Gib 59, 185 □ B-L 79s; Berg 1.5l; Brock §29a
18.10	Dav §138b; GKC §113n, 118g, 118u; J-M §123e, 127c; Wms §262; IBHS 586; Gib 124, 143 □ Berg 2.63e, 2.147g; Brock §93a
18.11	GKC §116d, 146d; J-M §148a, 148d; Gib 21, 178 □ B-M 3.22, 3.67; Berg 2.77c
18.12	Dav §11c, 41R2, 92, 121, 138a; GKC §106n, 139f, 141e, 150a, 150b; J-M §112j; Gib 67, 131, 167, 183 □ Jen §24.3.3.1; Brock §41e
18.13	Dav §123R1, 138c; GKC §106g, 136c; J-M §112a, 143g, 155l, 159e; Wms §385; IBHS 324, 662 n 65; Gib 2, 63, 141, 142, 168, 184 □ B-L 232j, 311t, 632i; Jen §7.1; Berg 2.28g; Brock §41b, 139b
18.14	Dav §11Rb, 34R2; GKC §107t, 133c, 139d, 141m; J-M §147b; Wms §262, 318; IBHS 266; Gib 14, 45 □ Brock §81f, 111g
18.15	Dav §118; GKC §106b, 163a; J-M §112c, 172c; Wms §398, 594; IBHS 486; Gib 62, 141, 174 □ B-M 2.104; Jen §7.1; Sch §53.3.1.1; Berg 1.67u, 2.25b
18.16	GKC §116o, 141e □ Berg 2.69c; Brock §110k, 122f
18.17	Dav §100b, 104c, 122; GKC §100l, 142b ; J-M §14c(6), 35c, 102m, 154fe; Gib 136, 183 □ B-L 632h; Jen §9.4.9
18.18	Dav §53a, 67a; GKC §75n, 113n, 142d; J-M §123e, 171f; Wms §179, 495; Gib 92 □ Berg 1.44d, 1.72g, 2.62c, 2.160a; Brock §41f, 135d
18.19	GKC §114o, 165c; J-M §124o, 177j; IBHS 639; Gib 111, 159 □ Berg 2.40b; Brock §107lγ

B-L: Bauer and Leander, *Historische Grammatik* **B-M**: Beer, *Grammatik* **Berg**: Bergsträsser, *Grammatik* **Brock**: Brockelmann, *Syntax* **Dav**: Davidson, *Syntax* **GAHG**: Richter, *Grammatik* **Gib**: Gibson, *Davidson's Syntax, 4th ed.* **GKC**: *Gesenius' Grammar* **IBHS**: Waltke and O'Connor, *Syntax* **Jen**: Jenni, *Lehrbuch* **J-M**: Joüon and Muraoka, *Grammar* **Ros**: Rosenthal, *Grammar* **Sch**: Schneider, *Grammatik* **Wms**: Williams, *Syntax*

18.20   Dav §118; GKC §128h, 148d,
         159ee; J-M §164b; IBHS
         132 n 17, 152, 668; Gib 141, 170
         □ B-M 1.105, 2.115, 3.11, 3.33;
         Jen §9.4.9; Sch §45.4.2, 51.1.1;
         Berg 2.28g; Brock §22d, 51, 77e
18.21   Dav §2, 22R4, 62; GKC §10g,
         48c, 100l, 108b, 135m, 138k;
         J-M §114d, 145e; IBHS
         339 n 32, 579; Gib 3, 29, 82 □
         B-L 208s, 265e, 409m, 632h;
         B-M 2.16; Berg 1.68v, 1.124w,
         2.47d, 2.53q; Brock §6c
18.22   Dav §100f, 145R3; GKC §116o,
         141e; Wms §370; IBHS 221;
         Gib 4, 58, 137, 180 □ B-L 77l;
         B-M 3.6; Berg 1.3i; Brock §89
18.23   Berg 2.121a
18.24ff. GKC §117g
18.24–25 Gib 179
18.24   Dav §37b, 73R5; GKC §122l;
         J-M §134m, 154k; Wms §365,
         477; Gib 49, 57, 110, 149, 175,
         184 □ B-M 3.38; GAHG
         3.175 n 579; Brock §127b
18.25   Dav §93, 123, 151R2; GKC
         §112v, 115b, 161c; J-M §124i,
         174k; Wms §256; IBHS 537,
         642; Gib 79, 131, 183 □ B-L
         654j; GAHG 3.162 n 488,
         3.173 n 547; Berg 1.66r; Brock
         §126a
18.26   Dav §37b; GKC §112ff.; J-M
         §176d; Wms §440, 453; IBHS
         511; Gib 49, 63, 86 □ Brock
         §176a
18.27   GKC §141e; J-M §171f; Wms
         §528; IBHS 133; Gib 1, 168 □
         GAHG 3.170 n 524; Berg
         2.163g
18.28   Dav §37f, 130a; GKC §47m,
         117aa, 119p, 134l, 159n n 1,
         159r; J-M §125d, 167v; Wms
         §96, 247; IBHS 168, 198; Gib
         49, 50, 113, 150, 153 □ Brock
         §85c
18.29   Dav §37R5, 90; GKC §134k;
         Gib 48, 58, 79, 128
18.30ff. GKC §108d

18.30   Dav §63; GKC §159n n 1; J-M
         §114i, 116b, 167v; IBHS 575;
         Gib 82, 106 □ Berg 2.46c,
         2.47e, 2.48g, 2.163g
18.31   GAHG 3.170 n 524
18.32   Dav §153; Wms §388; IBHS
         575, 670 n 93; Gib 39, 142 □
         Berg 2.47e, 2.48g; Brock §176c
18.33   Dav §105; Gib 66, 167 □ B-M
         3.59; Berg 2.27d, 2.59n; Brock
         §122n
19.1   Dav §140R1; GKC §116o, 141e,
         141f, 156c; J-M §121f, 126f,
         166h; Wms §219; IBHS 549;
         Gib 168 □ GAHG 3.148 n 391;
         Sch §47.3.1; Berg 2.164i; Brock
         §89, 102
19.2   Dav §55a; GKC §17e, 20d, 20g,
         100o, 135q, 142g, 150n, 152c;
         J-M §18i n 1, 105c, 119l,
         136d n 5, 155p, 172c; IBHS 124,
         550; Gib 94 □ B-L 653g; B-M
         1.68, 2.125, 2.180; GAHG
         3.170 n 524, 3.205 n 779; Sch
         §53.3.1.1; Berg 1.3i, 1.66t,
         2.48g, 2.152t; Brock §3, 5b, 41f,
         56a
19.3   Brock §138
19.4   Dav §45, 127d; GKC §15l, 107c,
         152r, 154a n 1b, 164c; J-M
         §82h, 113j, 131i; Wms §167,
         313, 327, 509; Gib 73, 149, 167
         □ B-M 3.43, 3.108; Jen
         §24.3.3.7; Brock §42a, 65b
19.5   GKC §29f, 108d; J-M §137f;
         IBHS 246; Gib 185 □ B-L 188p;
         Brock §100b
19.6   GKC §93i; IBHS 180 □ B-L
         569n; Berg 2.26c; Brock §42c,
         122i
19.7–8   GKC §105b n 1 (p. 308)
19.7   Dav §63, 127a; Gib 140 □ Berg
         2.48f, 2.137k

B-L: Bauer and Leander, *Historische Grammatik*   **B-M**: Beer, *Grammatik*   **Berg**: Bergsträsser, *Grammatik*
Brock: Brockelmann, *Syntax*   **Dav**: Davidson, *Syntax*   **GAHG**: Richter, *Grammatik*
Gib: Gibson, *Davidson's Syntax, 4th ed.*   **GKC**: *Gesenius' Grammar*   **IBHS**: Waltke and O'Connor, *Syntax*
Jen: Jenni, *Lehrbuch*   **J-M**: Joüon and Muraoka, *Grammar*   **Ros**: Rosenthal, *Grammar*
Sch: Schneider, *Grammatik*   **Wms**: Williams, *Syntax*

19.8 GKC §34b, 103b, 139d, 158b n 1; GKC §105b n 1 (p. 308); J-M §18i n 1, 147b; Wms §253, 560; IBHS 669; Gib 38, 47, 150, 176 □ B-L 261b; GAHG 3.170 n 524, 3.192 n 693; Berg 2.49i; Brock §97c, 106a

19.9 Dav §33, 86R1; GKC §66c, 113r; J-M §72c n 1; Gib 45 □ B-L 367; B-M 2.135; Berg 2.64g, 2.122c, 2.137k

19.10 Dav §17R4; IBHS 180; Gib 24 □ GAHG 2.31 n 128; Brock §89

19.11 Dav §22R1, 101Rb; GKC §126n, 154a n 1, 154a n 1b; J-M §126h, 136h; IBHS 121, 246; Gib 28 □ B-L 217a; B-M 1.114; Berg 2.157b; Brock §19b, 21cγ

19.12 Berg 2.157b

19.13 Dav §100b, 100c; J-M §121e; Gib 63, 136 □ Berg 2.72h*

19.14 Dav §98b; GKC §20g, 116d, 120g; Gib 134 □ Berg 1.66t, 2.53p, 2.69c, 2.125c; Brock §99a

19.15 Dav §83R4, 145; GKC §107g, 120g, 152w, 164d, 164g; Wms §262, 500; Gib 97, 137, 157 □ B-M 3.109; Berg 2.53p; Brock §133a, 133e, 163b

19.16 Dav §91a, 91b; GKC §15f, 45d, 55g, 115f; J-M §170j; Gib 47, 129 □ B-L 283v, 348i; B-M 3.60; Berg 1.75g, 2.83p, 2.117a; Brock §106a

19.17 GKC §107p, 111g, 126e; Wms §295; Gib 116, 149, 160 □ Jen §29.3.3; Berg 1.75g, 2.52 n n; Brock §5a

19.18 GKC §152g □ Brock §56a

19.19 Dav §53c, 93; GKC §60d, 72n, 105b n 1 (p. 308), 107f, 112p, 152w, 154a; J-M §63a, 125b, 155m; IBHS 579; Gib 36, 93, 131, 160 □ B-L 232j, 273g, 337n; B-M 2.151; GAHG 3.170 n 524; Berg 2.23g, 2.40b, 2.146f; Brock §39bδ, 89, 106l

19.20 Dav §96Obs; GKC §109f; J-M §116d; Gib 106 □ B-M 2.118; GAHG 3.170 n 524; Berg 1.132e, 2.47e, 2.57k, 2.92h; Brock §6c

19.21 Dav §95; GKC §61a; J-M §158i; Gib 132 □ B-L 344e"; B-M 2.167; Berg 2.57k, 2.82n

19.22 Dav §83; GKC §114d, 120g; J-M §155e; Gib 120 □ B-L 444o; Berg 2.111c, 2.156a; Brock §36e

19.23 GKC §164b; J-M §166c; Gib 167, 169 □ B-L 582u'; Brock §122n

19.24 Brock §48

19.25 Berg 2.113e; Gib 31, 134

19.27 Dav §101; GKC §106f; J-M §129q n 2, 133b; Gib 10, 147 □ B-M 3.52

19.28 GKC §126o; J-M §137i; IBHS 245; Gib 66 □ Berg 2.26c

19.29 Dav §91R1; GKC §111g, 115a, 115e n 1, 124o; Wms §586; Gib 129, 130

19.30 GKC §126r; J-M §137n; IBHS 606 □ Berg 2.58n

19.31 GKC §133f, 152o; J-M §104c, 160h □ B-M 3.10f; Berg 2.57l; Brock §110a

19.32 Dav §83R4, 117; GKC §69x, 117cc; J-M §105e, 177f n 1; Wms §191; Gib 179, 188 □ B-L 385h', 653c; Berg 2.47e; Brock §6a, 111h

19.33 Dav §6, 32R3; GKC §5n, 47l, 61c, 93s, 126y; J-M §44d, 65b, 138h; Wms §74; IBHS 313 n 22; Gib 6 □ B-L 79s, 303c', 344d"; B-M 1.82, 2.167, 3.29; GAHG 3.97; Berg 1.5l, 2.19a, 2.82m; Brock §23d, 117b

19.34 GKC §111g, 126b, 133f; Wms §323; IBHS 212 n 97; Gib 59, 99, 148 □ B-L 511v; Jen §28.3.3

19.35 Dav §83R4, 152; J-M §65b □ B-L 344d"; Berg 2.82m

19.36 J-M §44d, 132f n 1 □ B-L 303c'; Berg 1.145 n e, 2.19a; Brock §111h

B-L: Bauer and Leander, *Historische Grammatik*   **B-M**: Beer, *Grammatik*   **Berg**: Bergsträsser, *Grammatik*
Brock: Brockelmann, *Syntax*   **Dav**: Davidson, *Syntax*   **GAHG**: Richter, *Grammatik*
Gib: Gibson, *Davidson's Syntax, 4th ed.*   **GKC**: *Gesenius' Grammar*   **IBHS**: Waltke and O'Connor, *Syntax*
Jen: Jenni, *Lehrbuch*   **J-M**: Joüon and Muraoka, *Grammar*   **Ros**: Rosenthal, *Grammar*
Sch: Schneider, *Grammatik*   **Wms**: Williams, *Syntax*

19.37	Berg 1.145 n e; Brock §115a; Gib 149	20.13	Dav §9d, 31, 116R4; GKC §111g, 119u, 124h n 1, 127e,
20.1–8	Sch §52.3.2, 52.3.3		141f, 145i, 167b; J-M
20.1	GKC §90c □ Berg 2.144c		§158m n 1; IBHS 210, 334; Gib
20.2	Dav §101Rb, 146R1; GKC §141l; Gib 111, 147		5, 10, 23, 43, 111, 150, 178 □ Jen §27.3.3; Berg 2.27d; Brock §50f, 107iα, 152c
20.3	Dav §98b, 138a; GKC §116p, 141e; J-M §121e, 170h; Wms	20.14	J-M §177o; Gib 36 □ Brock §137
	§214, 291; IBHS 218, 627; Gib 58, 134, 137, 168 □ Berg 2.72h	20.15	Dav §103; J-M §125f □ Berg 2.125b
20.4	Dav §39c, 110; GKC §142b; Wms §379, 495; IBHS 367, 402;	20.16	Dav §37R4; GKC §116s, 134n; J-M §142n; Sch §47.3.5; Gib 50
	Gib 65 □ GAHG 2.65 n 279; Berg 2.27d, 2.77c	20.17	Dav §113; GKC §145u; Wms §300; IBHS 184 n 39; Gib 18 □
20.5	Dav §123; GKC §32l; Wms §579; IBHS 132, 241; Gib 4, 183		Berg 2.125b
	□ Brock §122k	20.18	GKC §106f, 113n □ Berg 2.27d, 2.64 n g
20.6	Dav §65d, 107; GKC §66b, 75qq, 114m, 157b n 2; Wms	21.1ff.	GKC §111a
	§193; IBHS 122, 221; Gib 132 □	21.1	IBHS 652 n 15; Gib 110, 171 □
	B-L 363h, 375; Sch §44.5; Berg		Berg 2.27d, 2.95d
	2.28g, 2.32d, 2.59n, 2.123c,	21.2	Dav §9b, 83R4; Gib 9
	2.158d; Brock §107c	21.3	Dav §22R4; GKC §138k; J-M
20.7	Dav §100d, 104b, 127b; GKC		§132c; IBHS 340; Gib 29 □ B-L
	§63q, 110i; J-M §125f, 154l,		265e; Brock §60b
	159v; IBHS 202, 430; Gib 57,	21.5	Dav §81R3; GKC §121b, 128v;
	105, 136, 148 □ Berg 2.50k,		J-M §128b, 129j; Wms §59;
	2.114l, 2.125c, 2.149m; Brock		IBHS 150, 182; Gib 117, 128
	§3, 122k, 164bα	21.6	Dav §87, 101Rb; GKC §10g,
20.8	GKC §147b n 3 □ Sch §47.1.4;		64h, 114c; J-M §124c □ B-L
	Brock §107c		357; Jen §10.3.1.3, 27.3.3; Sch
20.9	Dav §30, 44a; GKC §107g,		§50.5.1; Berg 1.135c, 2.55e;
	107w; J-M §113m, 158f, 169e;		Brock §107h, 137
	Wms §172; IBHS 509; Gib 43,	21.7	Dav §17R3, 41R2, 111; GKC
	68, 79 □ B-L 266g, 445p; Berg		§106p, 124o, 142f, 151a; J-M
	2.35i, 2.148k; Brock §122d,		§112j, 136j; Gib 68
	150c, 161bβ	21.8	Dav §30, 81R3; GKC §51m,
20.10	Dav §150; GKC §107v, 166b;		121b; J-M §51b, 128b; Wms
	J-M §160e; Wms §527; IBHS		§59; IBHS 258; Gib 43, 63 □
	323; Gib 160		B-L 232j, 320g; B-M 2.118;
20.11	Dav §57R1, 127b; GKC §112x,		Berg 2.91g; Brock §99b
	153; J-M §119e, 164a; IBHS	21.9	Dav §70a; GKC §52n; J-M
	534; Gib 39, 57, 88, 176 □		§126b; IBHS 172 n 19; Gib 114
	GAHG 3.175 n 577,		□ B-L 357; GAHG 3.100,
	3.192 n 693; Berg 1.156l, 2.42g;		3.102 n 289; Berg 1.161e,
	Brock §22d, 41f		2.95d; Brock §103a
20.12	GKC §152d; J-M §93h; IBHS	21.10	Dav §29a, 29b; IBHS 219; Gib
	557; Gib 38, 141, 142 □ B-M		40 □ B-M 1.105; Brock §65a
	3.45; Berg 2.37a	21.11	GKC §67p; J-M §152d □ Berg
			2.135d; Brock §110m

B-L: Bauer and Leander, *Historische Grammatik*   **B-M**: Beer, *Grammatik*   **Berg**: Bergsträsser, *Grammatik*
Brock: Brockelmann, *Syntax*   **Dav**: Davidson, *Syntax*   **GAHG**: Richter, *Grammatik*
Gib: Gibson, *Davidson's Syntax, 4th ed.*   **GKC**: Gesenius' *Grammar*   **IBHS**: Waltke and O'Connor, *Syntax*
Jen: Jenni, *Lehrbuch*   **J-M**: Joüon and Muraoka, *Grammar*   **Ros**: Rosenthal, *Grammar*
Sch: Schneider, *Grammatik*   **Wms**: Williams, *Syntax*

21.12	Dav §109; J-M §152d; IBHS 569 □ Berg 2.48f, 2.135d; Brock §35b, 110e
21.13	GKC §143c; J-M §156c; Gib 182 □ Brock §123e
21.14	Dav §24b, 41R3; GKC §95l, 128q, 156d n 4; Wms §287; Gib 32, 65, 178 □ B-L 573x, 583y'; B-M 2.72; Berg 2.163g
21.15	GKC §95l; J-M §137v; IBHS 251
21.16	GKC §75kk, 108b, 113h, 119k, 119s; J-M §114c, 123r, 133d; Wms §184, 204, 272, 401; IBHS 573; Gib 126 □ B-L 420k"; Jen §27.3.3; Berg 2.47d, 2.65h*, 2.107a, 2.168p; Brock §6c, 106a, 111d
21.17	Dav §8R3, 10R3; GKC §138e; J-M §158m; IBHS 134 n 19, 323; Gib 8, 10
21.18	Berg 2.122c; Brock §133a
21.19	GKC §117cc □ Berg 2.165k
21.20	GKC §131b; J-M §121f n 1; Gib 40 □ B-L 438; Berg 2.174 n h
21.22	GKC §111g; J-M §176f; Wms §484, 580; Gib 99 □ B-M 3.93
21.23–24	IBHS 296
21.23	GKC §20f, 44g, 48i, 51o, 149c; J-M §42f, 158j, 165d; Wms §72; Gib 187 □ B-L 134h, 315n'; B-M 2.118; Berg 1.107e, 1.132f (4xx), 1.149g; Brock §106d
21.24	Dav §107R1; GKC §51p, 135a; J-M §146a; IBHS 391; Gib 2 □ B-M 2.118; Berg 2.92h
21.25	Dav §58b; GKC §112rr; J-M §119z; Gib 103
21.26	Dav §8, 125; GKC §162b; IBHS 319; Gib 8, 39, 110 □ GAHG 3.173 n 549; Sch §51.2.1; Berg 2.28g; Brock §41c
21.27	Sch §50.3.1
21.28	GKC §91c, 127e □ B-L 252p, 563x
21.29	GKC §91f, 126x, 134l; J-M §94h, 138b; IBHS 260; Gib 44 □ B-L 252p, 563x

21.30	Dav §72R4; GKC §107q, 117d, 157b; J-M §125h, 150g, 157c, 157ca, 157e, 168e; Wms §522; IBHS 180; Gib 116 □ Berg 1.5l, 2.51m; Brock §145bδ, 161a
21.31	Dav §108; Gib 13 □ Berg 2.27d
21.32	GKC §138f, 146f, 146h; Gib 22
21.34	Dav §68; GKC §118k; Gib 144
22.1	GKC §111f, 111g; Gib 58, 99, 167, 168 □ Sch §48.2.3, 48.6.1.4, 53.2.1, 54.2.2.1, 54.2.2.4; Brock §4, 42c
22.2	Dav §35R2; GKC §131h, 119s; J-M §112a, 113l, 129f(8), 133d, 137v, 142b; IBHS 233, 251, 275, 464, 508 n 29; Gib 46, 63 □ B-L 276w; Brock §41c, 65a
22.3	GKC §135i; J-M §140a, 177a; IBHS 276 □ Berg 2.113g; Brock §73a, 135a, 152d
22.4	Dav §50b; GKC §111b; J-M §125ia, 176h n 1; IBHS 553 □ Brock §123f
22.5	Dav §62, 101Rb; GKC §119s; J-M §16i, 133d; IBHS 573; Gib 82, 150, 171 □ B-M 2.101; GAHG 1.182 n 604; Jen §27.3.3; Berg 2.47d, 2.53q; Brock §107f
22.6	Dav §21d; Wms §85; IBHS 243, 415; Gib 27
22.7	GKC §100o, 147b; J-M §102k; Wms §277; IBHS 677; Gib 185 □ Brock §4, 82b
22.8	Wms §573 □ Brock §48
22.10	J-M §125ia, 146g □ B-L 354e
22.11	J-M §139c □ Berg 1.78m; Brock §73a
22.12	Dav §11Rb, 63, 65R3, 98b, 104b; GKC §116g, 158a; J-M §121l, 147b, 170c; Wms §451; IBHS 617; Gib 14, 54, 62, 107, 134 □ B-M 3.105; Jen §10.3.3; Berg 2.25b, 2.28g, 2.163g; Brock §27d, 111c
22.13	J-M §103a, 125ia, 146i; Wms §352; Gib 135, 140 □ B-M 2.137; Sch §54.2.3.3; Berg 2.70e, 2.121d; Brock §137

B-L: Bauer and Leander, *Historische Grammatik* **B-M**: Beer, *Grammatik* **Berg**: Bergsträsser, *Grammatik*
Brock: Brockelmann, *Syntax* **Dav**: Davidson, *Syntax* **GAHG**: Richter, *Grammatik*
Gib: Gibson, *Davidson's Syntax, 4th ed.* **GKC**: *Gesenius' Grammar* **IBHS**: Waltke and O'Connor, *Syntax*
Jen: Jenni, *Lehrbuch* **J-M**: Joüon and Muraoka, *Grammar* **Ros**: Rosenthal, *Grammar*
Sch: Schneider, *Grammatik* **Wms**: Williams, *Syntax*

22.14	Dav §150; GKC §107g, 130d n 2, 166b; J-M §169f; Wms §492; IBHS 639; Gib 161 □ Jen §19.3.4; Brock §23d	23.10	Dav §98R1; GKC §116h, 141b, 143e; J-M §121n, 125b, 125l; IBHS 148, 617; Gib 31, 134 □ Berg 2.144b; Brock §31a
22.15	GKC §134r, J-M §102f, 142q □ Brock §88	23.11ff.	GKC §106m
22.16	Dav §40b, 120R5, 147; GKC §149a, 157b; J-M §112f, 165i, 170f, 170n; Wms §363, 534; IBHS 640; Gib 61, 87, 158 □ B-L 276x; B-M 3.106; Jen §20.3.3; Berg 2.27e; Brock §41d	23.11	GKC §152c; J-M §112g, 163c n 2; Gib 61, 178 □ B-M 3.50; GAHG 2.33 n 138; Berg 2.27e
		23.13–14	GKC §110, 110e
		23.13	Dav §134; GKC §151e, 167b; J-M §112g, 163c n 2; IBHS 489, 578; Gib 61, 186 □ GAHG 3.179 n 618; Berg 2.27e, 2.48g; Brock §3, 170a
22.17	GKC §75ff., 113n; J-M §123e, 123p; IBHS 395, 582, 586; Gib 125, 170 □ B-L 650p; Berg 2.39 n i, 2.62c	23.14–15	GAHG 2.33 n 138
22.18	GKC §158b; J-M §170g; Wms §534; IBHS 391 n 27, 395, 641; Gib 159 □ Jen §20.3.3	23.15	IBHS 327; Gib 8
		23.16	J-M §158i □ B-L 101u
		23.18	Gib 134
22.20	Dav §29a; J-M §155m; IBHS 232, 554	23.19	Berg 2.26c
		23.20	GKC §111k; J-M §118i; IBHS 550; Gib 96
22.21	Dav §29a	24	Gib 98
22.22	IBHS 127 □ B-L 525h	24.1–2	GKC §111a □ Berg 2.37a
22.23	Dav §36R4; GKC §134k; Gib 48, 178 □ Brock §85b	24.1	GKC §142b; IBHS 492; Gib 63, 98 □ B-M 3.7, 3.108; Berg 2.27d
22.24	Dav §50b, 106a; GKC §111h, 147e; IBHS 553; Gib 97 □ Brock §13b	24.2	GKC §110d; IBHS 571; Gib 98 □ Berg 1.132e, 1.149h, 2.48f
23.1	Dav §37c; GKC §134d, 134h; Gib 30, 49 □ Sch §47.3.4; Brock §84c	24.3–4	Jen §9.3.3.2
		24.3	Dav §9c, 28R4; GKC §128a, 165b; J-M §129b; IBHS 139, 626; Gib 9, 35 □ B-M 3.31, 3.94 □ Jen §15.6.2; Sch §45.3.4; Berg 2.71g; Brock §160b
23.2	Berg 1.5l; Brock §90a		
23.3	GKC §122f□ B-L 278l'		
23.4	GKC §52f, 108d, 128m; J-M §116b, 129f; IBHS 153, 649 n 5 □ Jen §21.3.4; Brock §15b	24.4	Dav §29a; GKC §112q, 131h; Wms §70, 179; IBHS 232, 528; Gib 40 □ B-M 3.48; Berg 2.51m, 2.53q
23.5–6	GAHG 2.33 n 138		
23.5	GKC §110e; J-M §163c n 2	24.5	Dav §9d, 43b, 86a; GKC §100n, 113q; Gib 10, 79, 98, 124, 141 □ B-L 632j; GAHG 3.173 n 548; Berg 2.63d, 2.120a; Brock §152b
23.6	GKC §75qq, 119x, 128r, 139d, 142f n 2, 152b; J-M §78g, 129k; IBHS 124, 154, 268; Gib 26, 46 □ B-L 375; Sch §49.3.1; Berg 2.159g; Brock §24e		
23.7	J-M §131i		
23.8	GKC §61g, 159v; IBHS 609 □ GAHG 3.175 n 580; Berg 2.58m, 2.81k	24.6	Dav §127c; GKC §51n, 152w; J-M §133d; Wms §461; Gib 160 □ B-L 189r; B-M 2.118; Jen §27.3.3; Berg 2.91g; Brock §89, 107f
23.9	GKC §119p; J-M §130c □ B-L 583w'; Berg 1.124w		
23.10–11	IBHS 489		

B-L: Bauer and Leander, *Historische Grammatik* **B-M**: Beer, *Grammatik* **Berg**: Bergsträsser, *Grammatik*
Brock: Brockelmann, *Syntax* **Dav**: Davidson, *Syntax* **GAHG**: Richter, *Grammatik*
Gib: Gibson, *Davidson's Syntax, 4th ed.* **GKC**: *Gesenius' Grammar* **IBHS**: Waltke and O'Connor, *Syntax*
Jen: Jenni, *Lehrbuch* **J-M**: Joüon and Muraoka, *Grammar* **Ros**: Rosenthal, *Grammar*
Sch: Schneider, *Grammatik* **Wms**: Williams, *Syntax*

24.7 Dav §53a, 106; GKC §135c, 138a, 138b; J-M §156e; IBHS 294 n 22 □ Brock §155b

24.8 Dav §32R3, 63R2; GKC §75x, 109d, 112ff, 126y; J-M §79h, 114l, 129e, 138g, 176d; Wms §74, 390; IBHS 310; Gib 6, 82, 154, 176 □ GAHG 3.173 n 549, 3.215 n 814; Berg 2.52 n n; Brock §5a, 23d, 60b

24.9 Dav §4R1; GKC §16h; Gib 5, 98 □ B-L 132c, 184k'; B-M 1.78; Berg 1.71e, 2.117a

24.10 Dav §24R6, 36a, 138a; GKC §127b; J-M §131n; Gib 34, 98, 168 □ B-L 268h; B-M 2.17; Brock §139b

24.11 Dav §22R3, 91a; Gib 29, 128 □ Berg 2.54d; Brock §107a

24.12 Dav §29R2; Wms §70, 331; IBHS 219, 232 n 12; Gib 40 □ Berg 2.48g

24.13 GKC §116p □ Berg 2.72h; Gib 58, 136, 137

24.14 Dav §1R2, 57, 72R1, 148; GKC §112p, 112bb, 135p, 167c; J-M §152b; IBHS 110, 305; Gib 3, 93, 116, 159 □ Brock §16e, 97bα, 152a

24.15–16 Gib 100

24.15 Dav §138a, 141R1; GKC §106f, 107c, 111g, 152r, 164c; J-M §113j; IBHS 651, 678; Gib 98, 120, 167, 169, 181 □ B-L 583y'; GAHG 3.122 n 332; Berg 2.59n, 2.70e; Brock §25d, 42a, 145bα

24.16 Dav §24d, 69b; J-M §159f; IBHS 151; Gib 33. 98. 144 □ B-M 2.158; GAHG 2.24 n 91; Berg 2.163g; Brock §89

24.17 B-L 339y; Gib 98

24.18 Dav §83; GKC §120d; Wms §224; Gib 120

24.19 Dav §41c, 51R1, 145; GKC §106o, 164b; J-M §112i, 166b; Wms §378, 457, 496; Gib 67, 120, 158 □ B-M 3.52, 3.110; Brock §41h, 107e, 163b

24.20 GKC §75bb; IBHS 243; Gib 27, 58 □ B-L 451l; Berg 2.164i

24.21 Dav §100b, 125; GKC §130a, 150i; J-M §160j; IBHS 428; Gib 136, 167 □ Berg 2.115a, 2.161b; Brock §99a

24.22 Dav §24b, 36R3, 37R4, 139R1, 145; GKC §134n, 156b; J-M §142n, 158b, 166n; Wms §500; IBHS 134, 278; Gib 32, 50, 98, 120, 157 □ B-M 2.39; Brock §148, 163b

24.23 Dav §7a, 20, 60, 69a, 122, 126; GKC §37a, 73b, 118g, 137b, 150d; J-M §81b, 126h, 144a; IBHS 170, 317; Gib 7, 143, 183 □ B-L 217a, 265a, 399h"; B-M 1.114, 2.13; Berg 2.152t; Brock §143c

24.24 J-M §154g

24.25 Dav §136; GKC §154a n 1c, 164c; J-M §177q; Wms §330; IBHS 606; Gib 37, 148 □ Berg 2.57l, 2.152t

24.26 GKC §67p □ Berg 2.138o

24.27 Dav §83, 106c; GKC §75ll, 118f, 135e, 143b; IBHS 77; Gib 144, 180, 182 □ B-M 3.14; Berg 1.70b, 2.74 n l

24.29 GKC §115e n 1, 156b; Gib 98, 167 □ GAHG 3.206 n 786

24.30 Dav §91c, 91R1, 100a; GKC §114e, 115e n 1, 116s; J-M §146h, 154c; Wms §587; IBHS 604, 624, 678; Gib 30, 59, 98, 128, 130, 136, 149, 157 □ B-L 101u; B-M 3.58; Jen §15.7.2; Brock §29a

24.31 Dav §98b, 105; GKC §107f, 107h, 116l; J-M §113d, 121p; Gib 134, 168 □ B-M 3.42; Berg 2.167o

24.32 IBHS 145 □ B-L 521g; B-M 3.76; GAHG 3.153 n 423; Berg 2.117a; Brock §89

24.33 GKC §69q, 73f; J-M §112i, 129d; IBHS 143, 375 n 32; Gib 80, 158 □ B-L 286m', 405, 637p; B-M 1.80, 2.151; Berg 2.88c, 2.114i, 2.119a; Brock §163b

24.34 Dav §104b; Gib 26 □ Sch §44.3

B-L: Bauer and Leander, *Historische Grammatik*   B-M: Beer, *Grammatik*   Berg: Bergsträsser, *Grammatik*
Brock: Brockelmann, *Syntax*   Dav: Davidson, *Syntax*   GAHG: Richter, *Grammatik*
Gib: Gibson, *Davidson's Syntax, 4th ed.*   GKC: *Gesenius' Grammar*   IBHS: Waltke and O'Connor, *Syntax*
Jen: Jenni, *Lehrbuch*   J-M: Joüon and Muraoka, *Grammar*   Ros: Rosenthal, *Grammar*
Sch: Schneider, *Grammatik*   Wms: Williams, *Syntax*

24.35	GKC §154a n 1a; J-M §177o; Wms §269; Gib 36 □ Berg 2.95d	24.56	Dav §138c; GKC §108d, 142d; J-M §116b, 159e, 170c; Wms §495; IBHS 651; Gib 168 □ Berg 2.48g
24.36	Berg 2.83p; Gib 157		
24.37	GKC §149c; Gib 136 □ Berg 2.71g	24.57	Dav §62; J-M §114b n 1, 116b; IBHS 565 n 3; Gib 82 □ Berg 2.47d, 2.52o
24.38	Dav §53a □ Brock §169b*, 170c		
24.39	Gib 141	24.58	Dav §122, 126; GKC §150n; J-M §113n, 143d, 161l; Wms §171, 541; IBHS 509; Gib 183, 184 □ B-M 3.86
24.40	Dav §53a □ Jen §15.6.3		
24.41	GKC §95n, 107c n 3, 112ff, 117f, 159s, 159bb, 164d; J-M §146i, 176d □ Berg 2.34g		
		24.59	Gib 40
24.42	Dav §130a, 135R1; GKC §141k, 159v, 167c; J-M §154l; Wms §479; Gib 57, 137, 153, 186 □ GAHG 2.34 n 146, 3.170 n 526; Berg 2.71g, 2.72h*; Brock §80e, 170a	24.60	Dav §107; GKC §63q, 97g, 134g; IBHS 281, 572; Gib 2, 49 □ B-L 627t; Berg 2.46c, 2.49h, 2.115l; Brock §3
		24.61	GKC §69x, 146g, 146h; J-M §150q □ B-L 233j; B-M 2.142; Berg 1.162g, 2.131o(bis); Brock §132
24.43–44	Berg 2.41e, 2.44k		
24.43	GKC §112t; IBHS 539, 623 □ Berg 2.68c, 2.72h		
24.44	GKC §154a n 1, 154a n 1c, 162b; J-M §177q; Gib 38, 174	24.62	Dav §105R1; J-M §170c; Gib 98, 167, 168
24.45	Dav §45, 127d; GKC §107c, 135a, 152r; J-M §113j, 159d; Gib 13, 73, 98, 181 □ B-L 274h; Berg 2.48g, 2.70e; Brock §42a, 139b	24.63	Dav §12; GKC §114f n 1, 122d; J-M §126b n 1; IBHS 107, 608; Gib 16, 98 □ B-M 3.17, 3.70; Berg 2.57k, 2.70e, 2.152 n t
		24.64	Dav §21d; IBHS 243; Gib 27
24.46	B-M 2.158; Berg 2.162f	24.65	Dav §6, 21d, 104c; GKC §34f, 141b, 141l; J-M §36b, 137f; Wms §86, 581; IBHS 131, 196, 243, 307, 308, 318; Gib 1, 7, 26, 27 □ B-L 261f, 265a; B-M 3.8, 3.89; Berg 2.164i; Brock §25b
24.47	Berg 2.21d		
24.48	GKC §75t		
24.49	Dav §152; GKC §, 141k, 159v; J-M §102k, 154l, 160j; Gib 39, 137, 154, 163 □ B-M 3.9; Brock §30b, 80e, 131, 164bα		
24.50	GKC §107f, 114m, 146f; IBHS 602; Gib 22, 39 □ GAHG 3.185 n 656; Berg 2.54d*; Brock §122l	24.67	Dav §20R4, 145R1; GKC §93q, 127f; J-M §146g; Gib 26, 158 □ B-L 131; Berg 2.91g; Brock §73d
24.51	GKC §109f, 117f; J-M §146i; Wms §565 □ Brock §25d, 107lα, 135c	25.1	Dav §83; GKC §120d, 120h; J-M §177c; Wms §224; Gib 120 □ B-M 3.82; Jen §23.3.3
24.52	Brock §89, 163b; Gib 98, 99	25.2	B-L 101u
24.53	Brock §122h	25.3	B-L 101u
24.54	J-M §130fa; Wms §328; IBHS 219; Gib 22 □ Sch §48.4.2	25.5–6	Gib 171
		25.5	GKC §16a □ Berg 1.70b
24.55	GKC §139h, 146f; J-M §147b n 2; IBHS 654; Gib 14, 22, 140 □ B-L 77m; B-M 3.22; Berg 1.3i	25.6	Wms §499; Gib 36, 58 □ B-L 569p; B-M 3.111; Brock §89
		25.7	Dav §37c; GKC §134h; Gib 49 □ B-L 423
		25.8	Dav §70a; J-M §47b; IBHS 171 n 18; Gib 56 □ Berg 2.91g

B-L: Bauer and Leander, *Historische Grammatik*   **B-M**: Beer, *Grammatik*   **Berg**: Bergsträsser, *Grammatik*
Brock: Brockelmann, *Syntax*   **Dav**: Davidson, *Syntax*   **GAHG**: Richter, *Grammatik*
Gib: Gibson, *Davidson's Syntax, 4th ed.*   **GKC**: *Gesenius' Grammar*   **IBHS**: Waltke and O'Connor, *Syntax*
Jen: Jenni, *Lehrbuch*   **J-M**: Joüon and Muraoka, *Grammar*   **Ros**: Rosenthal, *Grammar*
Sch: Schneider, *Grammatik*   **Wms**: Williams, *Syntax*

25.10	IBHS 421	26.8	GKC §111g, Wms §497; Gib 27,
25.11	Wms §329; IBHS 219; Gib 148		99 □ B-L 357; B-M 3.93; Berg
	□ Brock §113		2.70e; Brock §64a, 116b, 117b
25.13	B-L 636m	26.9	Dav §118; GKC §148b, 152w,
25.16	Dav §106R2; GKC §136d □ Jen		157b; IBHS 328; Gib 160, 176,
	§8.3.1.2		185 □ B-M 3.94; GAHG
25.17	GKC §134h; J-M §47b □ Berg		3.204 n 771; Sch §53.3.1; Brock
	2.91g		§110e
25.18	Gib 178	26.10	Dav §39d, 51R2, 57R1; GKC
25.19ff.	GKC §111a		§49l, 106p; J-M §143g; IBHS
25.21	Dav §81; GKC §51n, 121f;		494, 531; Gib 69, 88 □ B-L
	IBHS 390 □ Berg 2.91g		445p; B-M 3.33, 3.37; Berg
25.22	GKC §136c, 159v □ B-L 357,		2.41d
	438; Gib 184	26.11	Dav §98a, 99; J-M §125b; Wms
25.23	GKC §119ff.; J-M §154ff.		§218; IBHS 587, 622; Gib 133,
25.24	GKC §23f; J-M §24fa □ B-L		135 □ Berg 2.63d, 2.64f
	224h, 535f; Berg 1.92e	26.12	Dav §38R5; GKC §134g; J-M
25.25	J-M §126a; IBHS 172, 175; Gib		§126i; Gib 51
	56 □ Brock §103a	26.13	Dav §86R4, 145; GKC §113u,
25.26	Dav §91R3; GKC §93hh, 115a,		164f; J-M §112b, 123s; IBHS
	115c, 115e n 1, 116o, 141e; J-M		481, 589 n 39; Gib 125, 158 □
	§96Bd, 121f; IBHS 166; Gib		B-M 3.110; Berg 2.65 n h, 2.77c;
	130, 167, 168 □ Berg 1.149h;		Brock §93g
	Brock §139b	26.14	GKC §52d □ B-L 376r; Berg
25.28	Dav §98a; GKC §121b; IBHS		2.97h
	616; Gib 133, 171 □ Berg	26.15	Dav §1R3, 75; GKC §60h, 135o,
	2.120b		143b; J-M §125u; IBHS 302;
25.30	J-M §142k		Gib 3, 65 □ B-L 337j, 375; Berg
25.31	GKC §35n, 48i; J-M §35d, 48d,		2.97h
	155t □ B-L 227x, 306l; B-M	26.16	Dav §34R2; GKC §133c; J-M
	2.19, 2.114; Berg 2.81i; Brock		§141i; IBHS 267; Gib 45, 63 □
	§109b		Berg 2.131o
25.32	Dav §100j; J-M §137p; Gib 137,	26.17	B-M 2.158; Berg 2.163g
	184 □ Brock §121a	26.18	Dav §48c; GKC §60h, 111q,
25.33	B-L 132c; GAHG 1.189 n 664		120d, 135o, 144f; J-M
25.34	GKC §75o, 154 n 1a, 154a n 1,		§118d n 1, 155b, 177b; IBHS
	□ GAHG 3.107 n 303; Sch		76, 490; Gib 101 □ B-L 337j;
	§44.5; Berg 2.162f		Berg 2.27d
26.1	IBHS 22	26.20	Dav §104c; GKC §141m; IBHS
26.2	Dav §60; Gib 81 □ Berg 2.119a		73; Gib 14 □ Jen §7.3.1.4
26.3–4	GKC §34b, 142g	26.21	Gib 38
26.3	J-M §155q	26.22	Dav §57R1; GKC §112x; J-M
26.5	GKC §158b; J-M §170g; Gib		§33, 157c; IBHS 531; Gib 62, 88
	159		□ Berg 2.42g*, 2.145e, 2.153t
26.7	Dav §24d, 146R1; GKC	26.23	GKC §118f □ Brock §89
	§114p n 1, GKC §144p n 1,	26.24	Dav §104b; J-M §126i; Wms
	147a n 1; Gib 33, 111, 160 □		§56 □ Brock §117b
	GAHG 2.24 n 91; Berg 2.58n	26.25	GKC §76c □ Berg 2.163g;
			Brock §122f

B-L: Bauer and Leander, *Historische Grammatik*   **B-M**: Beer, *Grammatik*   **Berg**: Bergsträsser, *Grammatik*
Brock: Brockelmann, *Syntax*   **Dav**: Davidson, *Syntax*   **GAHG**: Richter, *Grammatik*
Gib: Gibson, *Davidson's Syntax, 4th ed.*   **GKC**: *Gesenius' Grammar*   **IBHS**: Waltke and O'Connor, *Syntax*
Jen: Jenni, *Lehrbuch*   **J-M**: Joüon and Muraoka, *Grammar*   **Ros**: Rosenthal, *Grammar*
Sch: Schneider, *Grammatik*   **Wms**: Williams, *Syntax*

26.26	GKC §80f □ B-L 510v, 534; Jen §6.3.1.6; Berg 1.147 n d		27.6	Dav §70a, 78; J-M §9d(4); Wms §573; IBHS 172 n 19; Gib 91, 114 □ GAHG 3.102 n 285
26.27	Dav §138c; GKC §142d; Wms §495; Gib 63, 168 □ Berg 2.28g, 2.157c; Brock §133d		27.7	GKC §58g □ B-L 345q"; Brock §176c
26.28–29	Brock §170c		27.8	Dav §98a; Gib 91, 133
26.28	GKC §75n, 103p n 1, 108d, 113n; J-M §103n n 3, 163a; Wms §335; IBHS 201; Gib 63, 82 □ B-L 646h"; B-M 3.63; Jen §11.4.10; Berg 1.160a, 2.28g,2.47d, 2.63e, 2.160a; Brock §112		27.9	Dav §76; GKC §117ii; J-M §48d, 112a, 112b, 116b, 125w; Gib 63, 113, 144 □ Berg 2.77c
			27.10	Dav §149; GKC §49k; 165b; J-M §9c, 168e; Wms §522; IBHS 639; Gib 160 □ B-M 3.102; Berg 2.17d
26.29	GKC §65h, 75hh, 149c; J-M §121p, 125b, 154h; Wms §331, 332, 391; IBHS 166; Gib 39, 52, 109 □ B-L 360t, 360v, 425; B-M 2.133; GAHG 3.173 n 549; Berg 2.118c, 2.118d, 2.161b; Brock §121b		27.11	J-M §154fa; Gib 58, 172
			27.12	Dav §53b; GKC §49l, 112p; IBHS 528; Gib 93 □ B-L 445p; Berg 2.109c, 2.135d
			27.13	Dav §73R5, 133, 153; GKC §10g, 135m, 141f; IBHS 670; Gib 5, 110, 185
26.32–33	Sch §52.4.3		27.14	Dav §73R5; GKC §109f, J-M §112b; Gib 5, 110 □ Berg 2.77c
26.32	GKC §136b; J-M §143j □ Brock §110m			
26.33	GKC §136b; Wms §273, 311		27.15	Dav §27; GKC §133f; Wms §73, 340; IBHS 195 n 23; Gib 35
26.34	B-L 510v		27.16	B-M 2.124
26.35	B-L 598		27.17	Brock §106a
27.1	GKC §111q, 114d, 119y; J-M §169h; Gib 59, 97, 99, 101 □ B-M 3.10; Jen §29.3.3		27.18	J-M §102k
			27.19	Dav §60R4, 126; GKC §60d, 107q; J-M §48d, 63a, 154 □ B-L 871'; Berg 2.53p, 2.125b
27.2–3	Sch §54.1.1; Gib 140			
27.2	Dav §40a; GKC §29l; IBHS 493; Gib 61, 63 □ B-M 3.50; GAHG 3.170 n 524; Berg 2.28g(bis)		27.20	GKC §114n n 2, 136c, 148b, 157b; J-M §124n, 143g; IBHS 312, 326; Gib 8 □ Sch §50.5.2; Berg 2.59n*
27.3	Dav §69b; GKC §118f, 122t; Wms §54; IBHS 170; Gib 91, 102, 144, 175 □ GAHG 3.170 n 522, 3.215 n 815; Berg 1.149g		27.21	Dav §6R2, 124; GKC §67r, 136d, 150a n 1; J-M §82o, 143a, 160j; Wms §118; Gib 6, 106, 184 □ B-L 367, 437; B-M 2.135; Jen §7.3.5.1; Berg 2.122c, 2.140q
27.4	Dav §65a, 145, 149; GKC §20b, 106g, 107q, 108d, 165b; J-M §112a, 116b, 166b n 1; Wms §175, 187, 518, 522; IBHS 493, 575; Gib 63, 72, 106, 131, 160 □ B-M 3.42, 3.102; Brock §6d, 42a		27.22	J-M §153 n 6, 154ea n 3; IBHS 392 n 33; Gib 52 □ Berg 2.135d
			27.23	B-L 650r; GAHG 3.162 n 488
			27.24	Dav §121, 126; GKC §150a, 150a n 1, 150n; J-M §161l; IBHS 132; Gib 183 □ Brock §35d, 54a
27.5–6	Brock §48			
27.5	B-M 3.76; GAHG 3.153 n 423; Brock §106d			

B-L: Bauer and Leander, *Historische Grammatik*   **B-M**: Beer, *Grammatik*   **Berg**: Bergsträsser, *Grammatik*
Brock: Brockelmann, *Syntax*   **Dav**: Davidson, *Syntax*   **GAHG**: Richter, *Grammatik*
Gib: Gibson, *Davidson's Syntax, 4th ed.*   **GKC**: Gesenius' *Grammar*   **IBHS**: Waltke and O'Connor, *Syntax*
Jen: Jenni, *Lehrbuch*   **J-M**: Joüon and Muraoka, *Grammar*   **Ros**: Rosenthal, *Grammar*
Sch: Schneider, *Grammatik*   **Wms**: Williams, *Syntax*

27.25	Dav §149; GKC §29e, 108d, 165b; J-M §116b, 168d; Gib 159 □ B-L 444m; Berg 1.130c, 1.162g, 2.119a
27.26	Dav §60; GKC §10g □ B-L 208r, 368t; Berg 1.124w, 2.122c
27.27	J-M §105d □ Berg 1.124w, 2.53p, 2.149m; Brock §91
27.28	GKC §20m; J-M §177l □ Berg 1.113 n 3, 1.129b, 1.131d
27.29	Dav §98c, 116R1; GKC §116g, 145l; J-M §154e; Wms §104, 580; IBHS 134, 652; Gib 23, 134 □ B-L 423; B-M 3.19; Berg 1.124w, 2.153u; Brock §7c, 26
27.30	Dav §86a, 141R2; GKC §106f, 111f, 111g, 113n, 164b n 1; J-M §111d, 123k, 166c; IBHS 588; Gib 124, 167 □ Berg 2.26d, 2.27d, 2.59n, 2.62c
27.31	GKC §60d, 72t; J-M §6b n 6, 80k □ Berg 2.51 n m
27.32	J-M §154g; Gib 54
27.33	Dav §34, 45, 50a, 99, 100e, 100R4; GKC §107c, 116d, 116x, 117q, 150l, 153; J-M §113j, 121i, 121j; Wms §380, 509; IBHS 75, 514, 561, 631; Gib 38, 45, 73, 135, 137, 185 □ B-M 3.45f; GAHG 3.229 n 880; Berg 2.38e; Brock §42c, 55b
27.34	Dav §1, 51R1, 67b; GKC §111b, 111h n 2, 113m, 117q, 118u, , 135e, 153; J-M §125r, 146c, 146d, 176a; Wms §107, 378; IBHS 301; Gib 2, 38, 115 □ B-L 208s; B-M 3.16; GAHG 1.186 n 640; Jen §11.3.3; Brock §68a
27.35	J-M §155nd
27.36	Dav §6R2, 38R5, 126R3; GKC §63m, 136e, 150e; J-M §143a, 161j; Wms §118; IBHS 287; Gib 6, 51, 178 □ Berg 2.25b, 2.113f; Brock §54e
27.37	GKC §103g, 117ff., 117ii, 142g, 150l; J-M §125u, 125w □ B-L 640f'; B-M 2.177; GAHG 3.106; Brock §94b
27.38	GKC §10g, 16g, 100l, 141h; J-M §102m, 125ia □ B-L 208s, 600j', 632h; B-M 2.158; GAHG 1.186 n 640; Berg 1.124w, 2.162f
27.39	GKC §20m, 119c; Gib 148 □ Berg 1.113 n 3
27:40	Gib 87, 90, 170
27.41	Dav §23; GKC §63f; Gib 32 □ B-M 2.128; Berg 1.124w, 2.112c
27.42	Dav §79, 83, 103; GKC §61a, 121a; J-M §128b; Wms §59, 475; IBHS 182; Gib 118 □ B-M 3.83; GAHG 3.120 n 330; Jen §13.3.3; Berg 2.82n; Brock §35d
27.43	GKC §112r, 112v, 119s, 120g; J-M §119l n 2, 133d; IBHS 208 □ B-M 3.81
27.44	Dav §68, 145; GKC §139h, J-M §112i n 5, 119l n 2, 142b; IBHS 275 n 8; Gib 14, 144, 158 □ B-L 521g; B-M 3.110; Berg 2.53q; Brock §83a
27.45	Dav §43b, 55b, 68, 96, 145; GKC §114d, 114r, 117aa, 118i, 150e, 154a n 1, 154a n 1c; J-M §119g, 119o, 124k, 124q, 125d, 126i; Wms §508; IBHS 508, 537; Gib 79, 94, 113, 131, 144, 158, 184 □ B-M 3.77; Jen §11.3.3; Berg 2.41f, 2.117a
27.46	GKC §159v, J-M §112a, 137p, 154fa, 156h, 170i; Wms §515; Gib 154 □ Berg 1.5l
28.2	GKC §16h, 90i; J-M §93c □ B-L 174l, 184k', 548z; GAHG 2.31 n 130; Jen §14.4.7; Berg 1.151c
28.3	Dav §55a; GKC §75ll, 112q; J-M §155ne; Gib 9, 94
28.4	GKC §95g, 114g, 115d, 165c □ B-L 600j'; Berg 1.129b, 1.131d, 2.57k
28.5	Dav §28R4; Wms §29; Gib 35
28.6ff.	GKC §167c
28.6	GKC §111q, 112pp, 115d; J-M §155m; IBHS 541, 562; Gib 102 □ Berg 2.38g, 2.43 n b-k; Brock §122a
28.8	GKC §111d

B-L: Bauer and Leander, *Historische Grammatik*   **B-M**: Beer, *Grammatik*   **Berg**: Bergsträsser, *Grammatik*
Brock: Brockelmann, *Syntax*   **Dav**: Davidson, *Syntax*   **GAHG**: Richter, *Grammatik*
Gib: Gibson, *Davidson's Syntax, 4th ed.*   **GKC**: *Gesenius' Grammar*   **IBHS**: Waltke and O'Connor, *Syntax*
Jen: Jenni, *Lehrbuch*   **J-M**: Joüon and Muraoka, *Grammar*   **Ros**: Rosenthal, *Grammar*
Sch: Schneider, *Grammatik*   **Wms**: Williams, *Syntax*

28.9	GKC §119aa n 2; Wms §292; IBHS 217 n 110 □ B-L 510v; Jen §5.3.1	29.2	Dav §54b, 101Rd, 108; GKC §107e, 144f; J-M §113e, 119u, 126b, 155b; IBHS 71, 474; Gib 13, 73, 94 □ GAHG 3.146 n 383; Berg 2.70e(bis); Brock §22c
28.11	Dav §21R2, 69a, 101Rc; GKC §126r; J-M §137n; Gib 28, 66, 98, 143 □ B-L 600i′; Berg 2.27d		
28.12	GAHG 3.204 n 775; Berg 2.70e*(bis); Gib 23, 168	29.3	Dav §54b; J-M §119u; Gib 90, 94 □ B-L 276z, 436; Berg 1.124w; Brock §89
28.13–15	Gib 78		
28.13	Dav §9c, 104b, 143b; J-M §156c; IBHS 333; Gib 180, 182 □ Jen §15.6.4; Berg 2.70e*; Brock §123b, 152a	29.4	Dav §104c, 126; J-M §154g; Gib 185 □ GAHG 3.76 n 199; Brock §27e
		29.5–6	GKC §150n □ Sch §13.3.1, 51.3.4
28.14	GAHG 3.162 n 488		
28.15	Dav §41c 145; GKC §106o, 147b, 164f; J-M §112i; Wms §457; IBHS 436, 491; Gib 67, 158 □ B-M 3.110; Berg 2.40c, 2.148k, 2.150n; Brock §41f, 152d, 163b	29.5	J-M §161l; GKC §100l □ B-L 632h; Brock §56a
		29.6	Dav §126; GKC §150n; J-M §161l; Gib 184
28.16	Dav §40a, 118; GKC §106g; J-M §164a; Wms §568; IBHS 492, 670 n 97; Gib 57, 110, 141 □ B-M 3.6; GAHG 2.33 n 133, 3.173 n 561, 3.175 n 579, 3.176 n 599; Berg 2.126d; Brock §12	29.7	GKC §114b, 126i, 152d; J-M §124d; Wms §194; IBHS 601; Gib 58, 128 □ B-M 2.129; GAHG 3.175 n 586, 3.175 n 590, 3.204 n 768; Berg 2.54d; Brock §29b
28.17	Dav §4b, 154; GKC §148b; J-M §154fb; Wms §127; Gib 7, 39, 52, 170, 176 □ Berg 2.69d; Brock §12	29.8	Dav §53b; GKC §107l; Gib 77, 93, 158 □ B-L 436; Berg 1.124w
		29.9	Dav §104b, 141; GKC §116u, 129h; J-M §130e, 166f n 2; Gib 36, 167, 168, 169 □ B-M 3.32, 3.70; GAHG 2.52 n 247; Berg 2.26c, 2.70e*
28.18	Dav §76; GKC §71; J-M §124w □ GAHG 3.103, 3.116; Berg 2.127e, 2.130m		
28.19	IBHS 673	29.10	GKC §67p, 75gg, 106f □ B-M 2.144; Jen §6.3.1.1; Berg 2.27d, 2.80 n h, 2.138 n l
28.20ff.	GKC §159r		
28.20–21	IBHS 526, 527	29.11	J-M §125ia; Gib 59 □ Brock §107c
28.20	Dav §100b, 130c; J-M §167h; Wms §515; Gib 92, 136, 154 □ B-L 115d; B-M 2.135, 2.175; Brock §164bγ	29.12	J-M §157c; Gib 26, 53 □ Brock §160a
		29.13	B-M 2.120; Berg 2.95d; Brock §107c; Gib 33, 99
28.21	GKC §141l □ B-M 3.30		
28.22	J-M §123e, 150m; GKC §113n, 113w, 145u; IBHS 414; Gib 182 □ Berg 2.62c; Brock §93a	29.14	Dav §29d; GKC §131d, 141l; Gib 41, 141, 176 □ Brock §100b
		29.15	Dav §126R3; GKC §112cc, 150e; J-M §161j, 161k, 161m; IBHS 534 □ B-M 3.87; Berg 1.5l, 2.42g*; Brock §54e
29.2–3	GKC §112e; IBHS 527 □ Berg 2.32d; Brock §41f		
		29.16	Dav §104c; GKC §133f, 141m; IBHS 269 n 29; Gib 45 □ Brock §21cα, 83b

---

B-L: Bauer and Leander, *Historische Grammatik*   **B-M**: Beer, *Grammatik*   **Berg**: Bergsträsser, *Grammatik*
Brock: Brockelmann, *Syntax*   **Dav**: Davidson, *Syntax*   **GAHG**: Richter, *Grammatik*
Gib: Gibson, *Davidson's Syntax, 4th ed.*   **GKC**: *Gesenius' Grammar*   **IBHS**: Waltke and O'Connor, *Syntax*
Jen: Jenni, *Lehrbuch*   **J-M**: Joüon and Muraoka, *Grammar*   **Ros**: Rosenthal, *Grammar*
Sch: Schneider, *Grammatik*   **Wms**: Williams, *Syntax*

29.17	Dav §31, 103; GKC §142d, 145n; Wms §563; Gib 33, 43, 53, 168, 172 ☐ B-M 3.19; Brock §28a, 77f	30.3	GKC §51g, 109f ☐ B-M 3.102; Berg 2.91f
29.18	GKC §118k, 119p, 133f ☐ GAHG 2.56; Brock §64b	30.6	GKC §26g, 58i, 59f; J-M §62c, 125v; IBHS 517 n 64 ☐ B-L 402u"; Brock §94dγ, 107d
29.19–20	GKC §115d	30.8	Dav §34R6, 67R2; GKC §85n, 117q, 154a n 1, 154a n 1c; Wms §335; Gib 46 ☐ B-L 486lε; B-M 2.35
29.19	Dav §33, 90, 104a; GKC §133a; J-M §124b, 124s n 1, 141g; Wms §317; Gib 45, 128, 174 ☐ B-M 3.10, 3.12; GAHG 3.78 n 208; Sch §49.3.4.3; Berg 2.54d, 2.123d; Brock §15f, 16e		
		30.9	GKC §164b ☐ B-M 3.108
		30.13	GKC §106n; IBHS 490; Gib 68 ☐ Berg 2.29h
29.20	Dav §11Ra, 72R1; GKC §139h; IBHS 275; Gib 14, 47, 116 ☐ Berg 2.83p; Brock §83a, 99b, 106e	30.14	J-M §136b; IBHS 120; Gib 14, 148, 149 ☐ Berg 2.123d; Brock §106f
29.21	GKC §69o, 108d, 165a; J-M §33, 75k, 116b; IBHS 113, 684; Gib 63 ☐ B-L 653f; Berg 2.28g, 2.125c	30.15	GKC §100l, 114a, 115d; J-M §124b; IBHS 69, 610 n 37; Gib 128 ☐ B-M 3.60; Berg 1.108 n 3, 2.54d, 2.124f
29.23	Jen §6.3.1.4; Sch §54.2.3.2	30.16	Dav §6, 32R3, 101Ra; GKC §119p, 126y, 142g; J-M §138h; Wms §74; IBHS 313 n 22; Gib 6
29.25	GKC §142g; J-M §143g, 177m ☐ Sch §54.2.3.2		
29.26	Dav §44a, 93; GKC §107g, 133f; IBHS 603; Gib 74, 131 ☐ Berg 2.35i, 2.56f, 2.60p, 2.123d; Brock §15g	30.18	Dav §3R2; GKC §17c, 135m, 158b; J-M §170e; Gib 158 ☐ B-M 3.106; Berg 1.3g
		30.19	GKC §96 (p. 285)
29.27	Dav §4, 20; GKC §121b; J-M §143b; Wms §59; IBHS 239, 308; Gib 5, 38, 118, 119, 175 ☐ B-L 613d'; GAHG 3.120 n 330; Brock §35e	30.20	Dav §1; GKC §117bb, 117ff., 152t; IBHS 174; Gib 2, 47, 112 ☐ B-L 236a'; Berg 1.150k; Brock §97bα
		30.21	B-L 618l; B-M 2.80
29.30	Dav §33; GKC §133b; IBHS 265; Gib 45, 175 ☐ Brock §111g	30.23	GKC §135m
		30.24	IBHS 569 ☐ Berg 2.49h
29.31	J-M §154fc, 160k;GKC §164b; Gib 53, 173 ☐ Jen §8.3.4.2	30.25	J-M §116b; GKC §108d; Gib 106, 150, 151
29.32	GKC §60d, 157b; J-M §63a, 155m, 157c ☐ B-L 337n, 371u; Berg 2.23g; Brock §122h	30.26	J-M §116b ☐ GAHG 3.97; Berg 2.123d; Brock §132
29.33	Dav §4, 146R2; J-M §157c; Gib 5, 111 ☐ GAHG 3.171 n 534	30.27	Dav §146R4; GKC §111h n 2, 120f, 159dd; J-M §170l; Gib 111 ☐ B-M 3.94; GAHG 3.170 n 526
29.34	Dav §36a; IBHS 278; Gib 47		
30.1	Dav §51R1, 100b, 104b; GKC §141l, 152k, 159v; J-M §125bc, 160j; Gib 154 ☐ B-L 278l'; GAHG 3.68 n 175, 3.174 n 576; Berg 2.72h*; Brock §106h, 169a	30.28	Dav §132b; Gib 106, 156 ☐ Jen §29.3.3; Berg 2.46c, 2.122c, 2.123d; Brock §110b
		30.29	GKC §157c
		30.30	Dav §145R1, 145R3; IBHS 77; Gib 91, 158, 185 ☐ Brock §107lα, 117d
30.2	J-M §140b n 3 ☐ Brock §106h		

30.31	GKC §120g, 120h, 159t; J-M §177h; Wms §225; IBHS 323; Gib 120, 154 □ B-M 3.114; Berg 2.47d, 2.51m, 2.53q	31.5	Dav §146; J-M §154fd; Gib 111, 173
30.32	Dav §87; GKC §112mm, 113h; J-M §123r; Gib 126	31.6	GKC §32i, 135a; IBHS 296 □ B-L 248i; Jen §8.4.2
30.33	Gib 31, 182	31.7	Dav §38R5, 58a; GKC §15b n 2, 67w, 112h, 134r, 157b n 2; J-M §142q; IBHS 219, 287, 540; Gib 103 □ B-M 2.91; Berg 2.43 n b-k, 2.105 n k, 2.137k, 2.138l; Brock §88, 106h
30.34	Dav §63, 126; GKC §109b, 151e; J-M §163c, 163c n 1; Wms §460, 548; Gib 81, 184 □ B-M 3.86; GAHG 3.179 n 618; Berg 2.50k; Brock §4, 8b, 56b		
		31.8	Dav §54b, 130b; GKC §112gg, 145u, 159r, 159s; J-M §150m; Wms §453; Gib 23, 94, 154 □ B-M 3.109; Berg 2.32d; Brock §50e, 164bγ
30.35	Dav §32R5; IBHS 263; Gib 44 □ B-M 2.71		
30.36	GKC §103o; J-M §103n; Wms §40, 73; Gib 167 □ B-M 3.37; Brock §59b, 112	31.9	GKC §135o; J-M §149b; Gib 3
		31.10	B-M 2.158; Berg 2.54d, 2.125 n a-e, 2.163f
30.37	Dav §32R5, 87; GKC §117r, 123b; J-M §125p; IBHS 263; Gib 44, 126 □ B-L 195a', 493zζ, 512f'; Berg 2.84p; Brock §92a	31.12	Gib 182 □ Berg 1.66q
		31.13	Dav §9d, 20R4; GKC §127f; Wms §82; Gib 10, 26 □ B-L 560p; GAHG 2.17 n 51
30.38	Dav §115; GKC §10g, 47k, 69f, 76g, 95f, 107e, 138c, 145c; J-M §44d; Gib 22 □ B-L 212j, 436, 444p, 615d'; B-M 1.118, 2.100, 2.150, 3.20; Berg 1.124w, 2.19a, 2.20a, 2.31d, 2.33 n e, 2.125 n a-e, 2.146f	31.14	Dav §11R1, 114; GKC §134r, 146g, 146h; J-M §150p, 150q; Wms §230; Gib 22 □ B-M 3.22; GAHG 3.175 n 588
		31.15	Dav §80, 81, 86c; GKC §113r; J-M §123l, 128c, 132f, 132f n 1; Wms §206, 280; IBHS 210, 385, 586; Gib 56, 118, 119, 124 □ GAHG 2.33 n 139, 2.65 n 279, 3.168 n 503; Berg 2.64g, 2.119a
30.39	Dav §113; GKC §69f, 145p, 154a n 1, 154a n 1a; J-M §150c; IBHS 107 □ B-L 436; Berg 2.19a, 2.125 n a-e		
30.40–41	IBHS 534	31.16	J-M §154i; GKC §141m; IBHS 298; Gib 150, 182
30.40	GKC §119aa n 1, 119aa n 2, 142f	31.18	Gib 30
30.41–42	Gib 90	31.19	Dav §28R5, 39c, 105R1; GKC §67cc, 106f; J-M §82k, 130e; IBHS 607; Gib 65 □ B-M 2.145; Jen §29.4.1; Berg 2.27d, 2.133b, 2.156a; Brock §47, 107h
30.41	Dav §57, 90; GKC §91f, 112ee; Gib 128 □ B-L 252p, 382; Berg 2.42g*, 2.125 n a-e(bis)		
30.42–43	GKC §112ee	31.20	GKC §158b; J-M §160m; Wms §291, 418, 489; IBHS 645; Gib 159 □ B-L 23n; B-M 3.106; Berg 2.72h*; Brock §52b*, 145a
30.42	GKC §107e □ Berg 1.155f, 2.102d		
30.43	GKC §132g, 145o; IBHS 257 □ Brock §129f	31.21	Dav §69R2, 114; GKC §118f; Wms §88 □ Berg 2.56 n h
31.1	Dav §10; IBHS 335; Gib 10 □ Brock §151	31.22	GKC §37d
31.2	GAHG 3.204 n 777; Gib 57	31.23	GKC §118h; J-M §126j
31.3	Gib 91		
31.4	Dav §69b, 69R2; GKC §118f; Gib 44		

B-L: Bauer and Leander, *Historische Grammatik*   **B-M**: Beer, *Grammatik*   **Berg**: Bergsträsser, *Grammatik*
Brock: Brockelmann, *Syntax*   **Dav**: Davidson, *Syntax*   **GAHG**: Richter, *Grammatik*
Gib: Gibson, *Davidson's Syntax, 4th ed.*   **GKC**: *Gesenius' Grammar*   **IBHS**: Waltke and O'Connor, *Syntax*
Jen: Jenni, *Lehrbuch*   **J-M**: Joüon and Muraoka, *Grammar*   **Ros**: Rosenthal, *Grammar*
Sch: Schneider, *Grammatik*   **Wms**: Williams, *Syntax*

31.24	Dav §101Rb, 127c; GKC §152w; Gib 132, 160 □ B-L 23n; Brock §107f		31.39	GKC §23f, 74k, 75oo, 75qq, 90l, 107e; J-M §24fa, 93o, 112d n 2, 113e; IBHS 128, 411, 509; Gib 178 □ B-L 346x″, 375, 526k, 598; Berg 1.92e, 2.97h; Brock §77c
31.25	Wms §573			
31.26	Dav §47; GKC §148b; J-M §118j; IBHS 552; Gib 96			
31.27	Dav §82; GKC §63c, 65h, 111m, 114n n 2; J-M §118h, 124n; Wms §226 □ B-L 360v, 375; B-M 2.129; Berg 2.59n*, 2.111b*, 2.157c; Brock §106b		31.40	Dav §83; GKC §67cc, 76a, 104g, 143a n 2, 167b n 1; Gib 182 □ Berg 2.133 n a; Brock §139b
31.28	GKC §75n, 114c; J-M §124c, 124n n 1; IBHS 410, 602, 611 □ B-L 425; B-M 2.124, 2.160; Berg 2.18f, 2.55d*, 2.161c; Brock §93k		31.41	GKC §136d; J-M §143a; IBHS 287; Gib 6 □ Brock §23a, 88
			31.42	Dav §131, 131R2; GKC §106p, 159x, 159ee; J-M §155p, 167s; IBHS 638; Gib 141, 155 □ Jen §16.3.4; Berg 2.117a, 2.129h; Brock §176b
31.29	Dav §96R1; GKC §152i, 165c; J-M §124b, 155ne; Gib 73, 132, 173 □ Berg 2.58m; Brock §15g			
31.30	Dav §86a; GKC §51i, 113p; IBHS 205 n 60, 208, 588; Gib 124 □ B-L 322y; B-M 2.119; Berg 2.63d, 2.92i		31.43	GKC §141m; J-M §154i; Wms §574; Gib 52, 136, 170 □ Brock §155b
			31.44	Dav §55a; GKC §69x; J-M §105e, 119j; Gib 37, 94 □ B-L 385h′, 653c; Berg 2.47e; Brock §133a, 135d
31.31	GKC §152w; Gib 160 □ Berg 2.157c; Brock §119a, 133e			
31.32	Dav §10R1; GKC §37d, 59g, 138f; J-M §37c, 112c, 158m; Wms §162, 330; IBHS 334 n 13, 490 □ B-L 266e; Berg 2.18f; Brock §152c		31.45	GKC §117ii; J-M §125w □ Brock §94dβ
			31.47	GKC §1c; Ros §1; IBHS 5 n 6; Gib 171 □ B-L 23n; B-M 1.11; Berg 1.1d
31.33	Dav §48a; J-M §118d; Gib 65			
31.34	Dav §31, 39c, 48c; GKC §106f, 111q, 124h n 1, 132h n 1, 132h n 2; J-M §118d, 112c, 155n; IBHS 556; Gib 43, 65, 98, 100, 101, 167 □ Berg 2.27d(bis)		31.49	GKC §158b; J-M §170e; Gib 148 □ Berg 2.49h, 2.162f
			31.50	GKC §119aa n 1, 119aa n 2, 159s; J-M §105d, 160h; Gib 149, 154 □ B-M 3.8; Brock §110g
31.35	GKC §106l, 107f; IBHS 140 n 9 □ Berg 2.48g; Brock §22b, 35b, 106l, 161a			
			31.52	Dav §152; GKC §149c, 167b; Wms §551, 580, 596; IBHS 72 □ Brock §27c, 170c
31.36	GKC §37d; J-M §37c, 169e; IBHS 317; Gib 7, 68, 177 □ B-L 266f; B-M 2.14, 3.104; Brock §35b, 97a			
			31.53	GKC §145i □ B-L 132c
			31.54	IBHS 196
31.37	GKC §109f		32.1	GKC §103b, 122g; J-M §149a; IBHS 108 □ B-L 642n′; Brock §107a
31.38	GKC §130d; J-M §125i n 2; Wms §118; Gib 6 □ B-L 582v′; Brock §14bγ, 96			
			32.2	Brock §106a
31.39–40	Berg 2.32e		32.3	GKC §136b; J-M §154fb □ B-M 3.10, 3.110
			32.4	B-L 115d; Brock §89

B-L: Bauer and Leander, *Historische Grammatik* **B-M**: Beer, *Grammatik* **Berg**: Bergsträsser, *Grammatik*
Brock: Brockelmann, *Syntax* **Dav**: Davidson, *Syntax* **GAHG**: Richter, *Grammatik*
Gib: Gibson, *Davidson's Syntax, 4th ed.* **GKC**: *Gesenius' Grammar* **IBHS**: Waltke and O'Connor, *Syntax*
Jen: Jenni, *Lehrbuch* **J-M**: Joüon and Muraoka, *Grammar* **Ros**: Rosenthal, *Grammar*
Sch: Schneider, *Grammatik* **Wms**: Williams, *Syntax*

32.5 Dav §48b; GKC §64h, 68f, 142g; J-M §73g; IBHS 555; Gib 101 □ B-L 371r; Berg 1.91d, 2.120a, 2.120c; Brock §64a

32.6 Dav §51R7; GKC §49e, 104g, 123b, GKC §145o; J-M §134c, 135c; IBHS 114; Gib 102 □ B-M 2.101, 2.113 □ Sch §50.3.1.1; Berg 2.23f; Brock §17, 107d

32.7 Dav §100a; GKC §116s; J-M §154c; Wms §587; IBHS 135; Gib 136 □ Jen §7.3.1.4; Berg 2.71f

32.8 Dav §109; GKC §67p, 144b; J-M §152d □ B-L 428f; B-M 2.144; Berg 2.135d, 2.163g; Brock §35b

32.9 Dav §35; GKC §112p, 145u; J-M §89b n 2, 155m, 176d; Wms §94; IBHS 528; Gib 46, 154 □ Berg 2.162d

32.10 GKC §116o; Wms §331; Gib 63 □ Sch §44.3; Berg 2.46c, 2.69c; Brock §135c

32.11 GKC §106g, 119n, 133c; J-M §112a, 134f, 141a; IBHS 214, 256, 266, 491 □ B-L 276v; B-M 3.36; Jen §24.3.3.2; Berg 1.106c, 2.28g; Brock §14bδ, 41b, 106b, 111g

32.12 Dav §53c, 98a, 127c, 140; GKC §112p, 116n, 119aa n 1, 119aa n 2, 141l, 152w, 156c; J-M §131i, 159b; Wms §461; IBHS 616; Gib 93, 133, 137, 149, 160 □ GAHG 3.151 n 413; Jen §29.3.3; Sch §51.2.5.2; Berg 2.71g, 2.85r; Brock §44d, 65b, 68a, 110g, 133e

32.13 GKC §107w, 142a n 1; Gib 79 □ B-L 650p; Berg 2.35i, 2.63e, 2.105i; Brock §111h

32.15 Dav §36c, 37b; GKC §134c; J-M §142d n 1; Gib 47

32.16 Dav §1R3, 12, 36c, 37b; GKC §28b, 122d, 132e, 135o; J-M §134d, 149b, 150r; IBHS 107, 257, 280; Gib 3, 16, 47, 49 □ B-L 649h; B-M 3.17

32.17 Dav §29R8; GKC §113o, 123d; IBHS 119 n 12; Gib 42 □ Brock §129a

32.18 Dav §7a; GKC §9v, 10g, 60b, 64f, 137b, 159bb; J-M §176a; IBHS 317, 511; Gib 7, 154 □ B-L 346x''; GAHG 3.151 n 413; Berg 2.77c, 1.134c

32.19 GKC §124i; J-M §131i, 176a; Wms §440; IBHS 232; Gib 175 □ Brock §65a

32.20 GKC §15a n 1c, 52n, 61d, 74h, 93q, 154a n 1; J-M §65c, 155p, 177q; Gib 37 □ B-L 328w, 375; Berg 2.83n, 2.156 n a; Brock §106f

32.21 GKC §108b, 153; J-M §114c, 155p; IBHS 574 n 21; Gib 38

32.22 Berg 2.144b

32.23 Dav §6, 37a; GKC §126y; J-M §138h; Wms §74; IBHS 279, 313 n 22; Gib 6, 48

32.24 J-M §125u; Gib 10

32.25–26 IBHS 391

32.25 GKC §51n □ GAHG 3.106 n 301; Berg 2.91g; Brock §113

32.26 Dav §51R1; IBHS 166 □ Berg 2.125b, 2.174 n h

32.27 Dav §154; GKC §60f, 65h, 163c; J-M §173b; Wms §556; IBHS 642; Gib 176 □ Brock §168

32.28 Dav §8R1; IBHS 320; Gib 7, 8

32.29 Dav §155; J-M §172c; Wms §447; IBHS 661 n 59; Gib 141, 148, 174 □ B-L 115d; B-M 2.159; GAHG 3.171 n 537; Brock §168

32.30 Dav §45R1; GKC §20f, 107h; J-M §113d; Gib 76 □ B-L 274i; B-M 2.102; Brock §107c

32.31–32 GKC §90k

32.31 Dav §22R3, 48R1, 140; GKC §111e, 156c, 157b; J-M §93s, 126f, 171f; Wms §299; IBHS 127, 550; Gib 29, 97 □ B-L 525h; B-M 2.49; Brock §103b

32.32 J-M §93s; IBHS 127; Gib 168 □ B-L 524h; B-M 2.49; Brock §139b, 163b

B-L: Bauer and Leander, *Historische Grammatik*   B-M: Beer, *Grammatik*   Berg: Bergsträsser, *Grammatik*
Brock: Brockelmann, *Syntax*   Dav: Davidson, *Syntax*   GAHG: Richter, *Grammatik*
Gib: Gibson, *Davidson's Syntax, 4th ed.*   GKC: *Gesenius' Grammar*   IBHS: Waltke and O'Connor, *Syntax*
Jen: Jenni, *Lehrbuch*   J-M: Joüon and Muraoka, *Grammar*   Ros: Rosenthal, *Grammar*
Sch: Schneider, *Grammatik*   Wms: Williams, *Syntax*

32.33	GKC §107g; J-M §113c; IBHS 164, 506 □ GAHG 3.173 n 549; Brock §42f	33.18	Dav §144R3; GKC §118n □ Brock §106f
33.1	J-M §125ia, 126b n 1; IBHS 135 □ Jen §7.3.1.4; Berg 2.70e; Brock §27b	33.19	GKC §119p, 127e, 134g; Gib 50 □ B-M 2.158; Berg 2.162f
33.2	GKC §146e n 1	34.3	Berg 1.155f
33.3	Dav §107; GKC §66b, 142a n 1; J-M §125t; Gib 2, 51 □ Berg 2.123c; Brock §89, 93h	34.5	Dav §58b; GKC §112ss; J-M §119z; Gib 103 □ Berg 2.27d, 2.43 n b-k
33.4	GKC §5n; J-M §125b □ B-L 79s; B-M 1.82; Berg 1.51	34.7	Dav §44a, 51R1, 93; GKC §45c, 45g, 107g, 114o; J-M §49f; Wms §172; Gib 131 □ B-M 2.116; Berg 2.35i, 2.81m
33.5	Dav §78R1; GKC §37a, 67a, 117ff., 137a; Gib 7 □ B-L 265a; Berg 1.65q, 2.132a*; Brock §90c	34.8	GKC §140d, 143b; J-M §156b, 157d n 2; IBHS 76; Gib 180, 182
33.6	Berg 2.19a	34.9	GKC §117w; J-M §125c
33.7	GKC §146f, 146g, 146h; J-M §150q	34.10	Berg 2.125b
		34.11	J-M §114b n 1, 163a; IBHS 565 n 3 □ Berg 2.52o
33.8	Dav §8R1; GKC §37a, 137a, 147a n 1; J-M §144b; IBHS 140 n 9; Gib 8	34.12	J-M §174a; Wms §256
33.9	Dav §63; Gib 57, 81 □ Berg 2.48f	34.13	GKC §158b; J-M §170e; Wms §468
33.10	Dav §91R1, 128R2; GKC §112gg, 152g, 158b n 1; J-M §105c, 124s, 170h n 1; IBHS 661 n 59; Gib 130 □ GAHG 3.170 n 526; Berg 2.41d; Brock §164bβ, 170c	34.15–17	IBHS 524, 636; Gib 153 □ Jen §9.3.3.2
		34.15	GKC §72h, 114o, 115g, 119p, 153; J-M §130g; Gib 39 □ Berg 2.60p, 2.144b; Brock §23e
		34.16	GKC §44o, 49k; J-M §42e; Gib 171
33.11	GKC §67a, 74g, 148d □ B-L 445p; GAHG 3.175 n 580; Berg 2.132a*, 2.158e; Brock §106h	34.19	GKC §64d, 64h; IBHS 270; Gib 63 □ B-L 354j; Berg 1.152a, 2.115a
33.12	Dav §62; J-M §114c n 1 □ B-L 367; Berg 2.122b	34.20	GKC §146f
33.13	Dav §1R1, 132a; GKC §60h, 104g, 122d, 126i, 135o; J-M §134d, 154f, 154fc; IBHS 107, 531; Gib 136, 156 □ B-L 342w', 649k; Berg 2.44k; Brock §16b, 25a	34.21	Dav §104b, 106d; J-M §154i, 154p, 156e; Wms §579; Gib 53 □ GAHG 3.80 n 219, 3.164 n 498, 3.203 n 766; Brock §30a
		34.22	GKC §72ee; J-M §130g □ B-M 2.153; Berg 2.144b, 2.151q
33.14	Dav §62, 101Rb; J-M §114h, 116i; IBHS 569, 603; Gib 82 □ Jen §10.3.1.3; Berg 2.115a; Brock §89, 117d	34.23	GKC §143a; J-M §154i n 3; IBHS 298; Gib 176 □ Berg 2.144b
33.15	IBHS 140 n 9, 565 n 3 □ B-L 188o; Berg 2.47d, 2.52o	34.24	Dav §98R1; GKC §116h, 145d; J-M §150e; Gib 22, 134
33.16	Gib 6	34.25	GKC §118q, 131q; J-M §126d, 166l; Gib 149 □ B-M 3.78; Berg 2.74l
33.17	Dav §105; GKC §135i; J-M §146k; Gib 13 □ Brock §89	34.26	Brock §107a

B-L: Bauer and Leander, *Historische Grammatik*   **B-M**: Beer, *Grammatik*   **Berg**: Bergsträsser, *Grammatik*
Brock: Brockelmann, *Syntax*   **Dav**: Davidson, *Syntax*   **GAHG**: Richter, *Grammatik*
Gib: Gibson, *Davidson's Syntax, 4th ed.*   **GKC**: *Gesenius' Grammar*   **IBHS**: Waltke and O'Connor, *Syntax*
Jen: Jenni, *Lehrbuch*   **J-M**: Joüon and Muraoka, *Grammar*   **Ros**: Rosenthal, *Grammar*
Sch: Schneider, *Grammatik*   **Wms**: Williams, *Syntax*

34.27	GKC §107q n 1, 144g, 158b; J-M §170e □ B-M 3.80	35.26	Dav §81R3; GKC §121b; Gib 178 □ GAHG 3.122 n 332
34.30	GKC §128n, 141d; J-M §131f; Wms §48 □ B-M 3.34; Berg 2.42g, 2.54c; Brock §14bδ, 17	35.29	J-M §47b □ B-L 557f'; Berg 1.124w
34.31	Dav §101Rd; GKC §107t, 118v; J-M §113m, 125w n 2, 133h; IBHS 508; Gib 150 □ B-L 370p, 632h; Berg 2.36k	36.1	Gib 179
		36.2ff.	GKC §111a
		36.2	J-M §155nd □ Brock §122m
		36.4	J-M §93s
35.1	GKC §65a, 116o; Gib 100, 131 □ Berg 2.83n, 2.125b; Brock §133a, 143b	36.5	GAHG 3.122 n 332
		36.6	GKC §135m; Gib 30
35.2	IBHS 73 □ B-L 198e, 583w'	36.7	GKC §133c; J-M §141i; Wms §76, 318; IBHS 266; Gib 45 □ B-M 2.115; Berg 2.123c
35.3	Dav §50a, 99, 100e; GKC §116d, 116o, 116x; J-M §121i, 121j; IBHS 561, 631; Gib 33, 102, 135, 137 □ Berg 2.38e, 2.53q; Brock §140	36.8	IBHS 131, 297; Gib 1
		36.10	Wms §114, 562
		36.12	GKC §129c; J-M §130b
		36.13	GAHG 3.163 n 493
35.4	Dav §101Rd; IBHS 219 n 116 □ B-M 2.112; Berg 2.80 n h	36.14	GKC §111d, IBHS 551; Gib 96
		36.19	Jen §8.3.4.1
35.5	Dav §113; GKC §144f; Wms §81 □ Brock §22c	36.27	IBHS 309
		36.30	IBHS 134 n 20
35.6	Gib 22	36.31–32	IBHS 551 n 12
35.7	Dav §116R4; GKC §124h n 1, 145i; J-M §133b; Gib 23, 43	36.31	Gib 157 □ B-M 1.104, 2.115
		36.32	GKC §111d
35.8	GKC §126d, 144d; J-M §155e; IBHS 242 □ B-M 3.27; Brock §120a	36.35	GKC §116o □ Berg 2.69c
		36.43	B-L 115d
35.9	GAHG 3.170 n 532, 3.171 n 534	37.2	Dav §32R2, 83R2, 100R2, 138a; GKC §111a, 116r, 126z; J-M §121f, 126a, 154fa; Wms §572; IBHS 293, 629; Gib 44, 97, 138, 167, 168 □ Berg 2.73i*; Brock §103a
35.10	Dav §81R3; J-M §155e; Gib 174 □ GAHG 3.162 n 488, 3.171 n 537		
35.11	GKC §145f	37.3	Dav §54R1; GKC §112h, 133b; J-M §155nc, 159f; IBHS 121, 265, 491 □ B-M 2.115; Berg 2.77c; Brock §111g
35.12	GKC §143c; J-M §156c; Gib 147		
35.13	Dav §9d; GKC §130c, 142g; J-M §158j; Gib 10	37.4	Dav §91R4; GKC §114m, 115c, 142f; Gib 45, 130 □ Berg 2.77c
35.14	GKC §71, 138c □ Berg 2.127e; Brock §92a	37.5ff.	Sch §48.6.1.2
		37.5	GKC §114m; J-M §124c □ B-L 376r; Berg 2.157b; Brock §91, 93k
35.15	J-M §158j; Gib 10 □ Jen §15.6.5		
35.16	B-L 367; Berg 2.125b, 2.164i	37.6	Gib 62 □ B-M 2.133; Berg 2.25b
35.17	Dav §21d; IBHS 243; Gib 27 □ Berg 2.103e		
35.18	Dav §105		
35.19	GKC §121a; IBHS 140 n 10 □ B-L 115 n 2		
35.21	GKC §91e; J-M §94h		
35.22	GKC §15p, 45g □ B-L 210f; B-M 1.74, 2.116; Berg 1.77i, 1.122t		

B-L: Bauer and Leander, *Historische Grammatik*   **B-M**: Beer, *Grammatik*   **Berg**: Bergsträsser, *Grammatik*
Brock: Brockelmann, *Syntax*   **Dav**: Davidson, *Syntax*   **GAHG**: Richter, *Grammatik*
Gib: Gibson, *Davidson's Syntax, 4th ed.*   **GKC**: *Gesenius' Grammar*   **IBHS**: Waltke and O'Connor, *Syntax*
Jen: Jenni, *Lehrbuch*   **J-M**: Joüon and Muraoka, *Grammar*   **Ros**: Rosenthal, *Grammar*
Sch: Schneider, *Grammatik*   **Wms**: Williams, *Syntax*

37.7 Dav §45R1, 98a, 100f; GKC
§47l, 107b, 116o, 116q, 117r,
147b, 154a n 1c; J-M §90e,
113f, 118n, 121f, 125p; Gib 22,
133, 137 □ B-L 303c'; Berg
1.150l, 2.19a, 2.34h(bis), 2.70e*,
2.134c, 2.135d

37.8 Dav §43a, 86a, 124; GKC
§113q, 150h; J-M §123f, 136j,
161e; IBHS 199, 587; Gib 124,
184 □ B-M 3.89; Jen §10.3.1.3;
Berg 2.63d; Brock §93a, 110c,
136b

37.9 Dav §37a; J-M §125a; IBHS
279; Gib 48 □ B-L 426; B-M
3.38; GAHG 3.204 n 769; Berg
2.70e*

37.10 GKC §113q, J-M §123f, 158ha;
IBHS 222; Gib 124 □ Jen
§10.3.1.1; Berg 2.63d; Brock
§106h

37.11 Wms §573; Gib 171 □ B-M
3.90; Sch §48.2.3; Brock §48,
138

37.12 GKC §5n □ B-L 79s; Berg 1.5l

37.13 Dav §123R2; J-M §105e; Gib
55, 184 □ Brock §54c

37.14 Dav §75; Gib 112

37.15 17 Sch §52.4.3.2

37.15 Dav §45R1, 100a; GKC §107f,
116s; J-M §113d, 121d, 146h,
154c; Wms §167, 587; IBHS
113, 624; Gib 59, 136, 137 □
B-M 2.119; GAHG 3.204 n 775;
Brock §29a, 42f

37.16 Dav §111R1; GKC §142f n 1 (p.
457), 142f(d) n 1; J-M §121d,
154h, 155ob; Wms §213; Gib
133, 137, 185 □ Brock §44a,
121c, 143c

37.17 GKC §88c, 117f; J-M §91h,
103a, 114e; Wms §358; IBHS
574, 621 □ GAHG 3.102 n 285,
3.102 n 289; Jen §8.3.2.2; Brock
§116c

37.18 Dav §50a, 73R4, 145; GKC
§107c, 117w; J-M §113j; IBHS
514; Gib 4, 73 □ B-M 3.77; Sch
§48.4.3.5; Brock §98a

37.19–20 IBHS 677

37.19 Dav §24R3; GKC §128u; J-M
§129j; IBHS 149, 306, 307; Gib
33 □ B-L 261f; B-M 3.34; Sch
§45.4.4; Brock §74b

37.20 J-M §105e; IBHS 275, 325; Gib
8, 91

37.21 Dav §51R1, 71, 78; GKC §117ll;
J-M §126g; Wms §57; Gib 145
□ Brock §94c

37.22 Dav §60, 91R4, 149; GKC
§165c, J-M §168d; Wms §367,
520; IBHS 199; Gib 81, 130,
159, 171 □ Brock §107lγ

37.23 Dav §75, 92; GKC §117cc; J-M
§125u, 140b n 1; IBHS 177, 304,
441; Gib 112 □ Brock §163b

37.24 Dav §78, 127b; J-M §124c; Gib
57 □ B-M 2.123; GAHG
3.175 n 577; Jen §10.3.4; Brock
§89

37.25 J-M §96As, 126b n 1; Gib 168
□ B-L 577i'; Berg 2.70e; Brock
§89

37.26 Dav §8R2, 53b; GKC §75z,
112p; J-M §144d, 157a; Wms
§124; IBHS 323 n 16; Gib 8, 93
□ B-M 3.93; Sch §53.3.2; Brock
§159a

37.27 Dav §105; J-M §177s; IBHS
384 n 17; Gib 82 □ Berg 2.47d,
2.47e

37.28 GKC §119p □ B-L 501bι; Brock
§85e

37.29 Dav §127b; GKC §152l; J-M
§154k, 160g; Wms §407; IBHS
677; Gib 57 □ GAHG
3.174 n 564, 3.175 n 578,
3.204 n 777; Brock §32d

37.30 Dav §127b; GKC §116p, 143a;
IBHS 627; Gib 180, 185 □ B-L
631f; Berg 2.72h*

37.32–33 Brock §29a

37.32 GKC §100l, 150i, 150n; J-M
§102m, 154ea n 3; Wms §544 □
Berg 1.68v

37.33 Dav §105; GKC §60d, 113w;
J-M §63a, 146h; IBHS 375 n 31,
584; Gib 125 □ B-L 287n'; Sch
§50.4.2; Berg 2.23g, 2.62c, 2.64f,
2.88c

B-L: Bauer and Leander, *Historische Grammatik*   **B-M**: Beer, *Grammatik*   **Berg**: Bergsträsser, *Grammatik*
Brock: Brockelmann, *Syntax*   **Dav**: Davidson, *Syntax*   **GAHG**: Richter, *Grammatik*
Gib: Gibson, *Davidson's Syntax, 4th ed.*   **GKC**: *Gesenius' Grammar*   **IBHS**: Waltke and O'Connor, *Syntax*
Jen: Jenni, *Lehrbuch*   **J-M**: Joüon and Muraoka, *Grammar*   **Ros**: Rosenthal, *Grammar*
Sch: Schneider, *Grammatik*   **Wms**: Williams, *Syntax*

37.35	Dav §70a; GKC §118n, 157b; J-M §126a, 157c; IBHS 171 n 18, 606; Gib 56, 120 □ B-L 535f; Berg 2.58n	38.25	Dav §9c, 100a, 141; GKC §32l, 74i, 116v, 142e, 164b; J-M §121f, 132f n 1, 166f; IBHS 625; Gib 9, 135 □ B-M 3.68, 3.108; Jen §29.4.1; Berg 1.90b, 2.69d, 2.70e*
37.36	IBHS 240 n 7; Gib 167 □ B-L 501bɩ		
38.5	Dav §58c, 72R1; GKC §112uu, 115d, 120d; J-M §177c; Gib 116 □ Brock §99b	38.26	GKC §133b n 2, 148b, 158b n 1; J-M §170h n 1; IBHS 265 □ B-M 2.139; GAHG 3.171 n 537; Berg 2.125c
38.7	Wms §563		
38.8	IBHS 413	38.27	B-L 224h, 535f
38.9	Dav §54b, 95, 110, 130b; GKC §13c, 66i, 112ee, 112gg, 159o, 164d; J-M §72i, 167g, 168c; IBHS 539; Gib 132, 154 □ B-M 2.136; Berg 1.67u, 2.42g*, 2.123d; Brock §125a	38.28	Dav §21d, 108; GKC §144d; IBHS 243; Gib 13, 27
		38.29	Dav §100R6; GKC §148b, 164g; J-M §166p; Gib 138 □ Berg 2.26c; Brock §163b
38.10	J-M §132a; IBHS 331 □ B-M 3.100; Brock §151	39.1	Dav §69b; GKC §142b; IBHS 240 n 7; Gib 65, 144, 167 □ GAHG 2.59; Berg 2.129i
38.11	Dav §70a, 107, 127c, 145; GKC §118g, 152w, 164d; J-M §126c, 126h; Gib 56, 143, 158, 160 □ B-M 3.109; Brock §64a, 145bζ	39.2	GKC §111l; J-M §118h; IBHS 548 □ B-M 3.103
		39.3	J-M §121f
38.12	Dav §69a; Gib 22	39.4	Dav §143; GKC §130d, 155d, 155n; J-M §129q(a,3), 158d; Gib 11, 171 □ B-M 2.131; Berg 2.116b; Brock §110c
38.13	GKC §67cc; J-M §82k; IBHS 625, 675 □ Jen §29.4.1, 10.4.11; Berg 2.133b, 2.136f; Brock §44a, 89		
		39.5	Dav §143; GKC §111g; 145q, 164d; J-M §150j; Wms §228; IBHS 644; Gib 11, 15, 157 □ GAHG 3.175 n 580; Jen §18.3.4.2; Brock §158
38.14	J-M §61b, 112b; IBHS 140 n 10 □ Berg 2.164i; Brock §81a		
38.15	Dav §78R5		
38.16	J-M §105e; IBHS 565 n 3; Gib 188 □ Berg 1.65q, 2.35i, 2.52o	39.6	Dav §154; GKC §128x; J-M §111i, 121f, 121i; Wms §46; IBHS 151; Gib 33 □ B-M 3.34; Brock §77f
38.17	Dav §107R1; GKC §159dd; J-M §70d, 146a, 167r; Gib 2 □ Sch §53.5.2.3; Berg 2.82n; Brock §54f, 170a		
		39.7	Wms §299
		39.8	GKC §137c; Gib 168 □ GAHG 3.175 n 580, 3.204 n 768
38.18	Dav §2; GKC §107u; 135m; J-M §132f n 1; Gib 5, 110 □ Brock §137, 107e	39.9	Dav §53b, 102; GKC §107t, 112p; 148b; J-M §155pb, 170j; Wms §247, 534; IBHS 528; Gib 52, 57, 93, 159, 185 □ B-M 3.106; Sch §53.4.3; Brock §163a
38.19	Dav §73; Gib 108, 109		
38.21	GKC §88c, 126y; J-M §91h; Gib 185 □ Brock §23e		
38.23	Gib 160	39.10	GKC §123c; J-M §135d; Wms §15, 258, 532; IBHS 116, 195 □ B-M 3.77; Berg 2.59n; Brock §117c, 129a
38.24	GKC §20m, 97c, 109f, 116s, 119y n 3; J-M §154c; Wms §316; Gib 137 □ B-L 623d, 643r'; B-M 2.159; GAHG 3.204 n 771; Berg 1.142f; Brock §84a*, 107a, 135c		
		39.11	GKC §35n, 126s, 139d n 2; IBHS 651; Gib 57, 168 □ B-L 227x; Brock §107h

B-L: Bauer and Leander, *Historische Grammatik*   **B-M**: Beer, *Grammatik*   **Berg**: Bergsträsser, *Grammatik*
Brock: Brockelmann, *Syntax*   **Dav**: Davidson, *Syntax*   **GAHG**: Richter, *Grammatik*
Gib: Gibson, *Davidson's Syntax, 4th ed.*   **GKC**: *Gesenius' Grammar*   **IBHS**: Waltke and O'Connor, *Syntax*
Jen: Jenni, *Lehrbuch*   **J-M**: Joüon and Muraoka, *Grammar*   **Ros**: Rosenthal, *Grammar*
Sch: Schneider, *Grammatik*   **Wms**: Williams, *Syntax*

39.12	Dav §69b; Gib 144 ☐ B-L 581; Brock §106a	40.7	Dav §68; GKC §84^{b}f, 87t ; Gib 144 ☐ B-L 517y; Berg 1.119o; Brock §133d
39.13	Dav §48c; GKC §111g; IBHS 556; Gib 101	40.8	Dav §67b, 127b; GKC §152o; Gib 57, 115, 133, 136 ☐ GAHG
39.14	GKC §2b, 29g, 64g; J-M §69d ☐ B-L 13c, 356s, 376r; Berg 1.130c, 2.116b; Brock §63a, 106h		3.174 n 567; Berg 1.132e; Brock §99a
		40.9	GKC §143d; Gib 59
39.15	Berg 2.148k	40.10	GKC §91e, 164g ☐ B-L 533f, 599h'
39.16	GKC §72ee; IBHS 603 ☐ Jen §10.3.1.3; Berg 2.151q	40.12	IBHS 312; Gib 5, 32, 47 ☐ B-M 3.10; Brock §14bζ, 15b
39.17	GKC §2b, 29g, 64g; J-M §155nd ☐ B-L 13c; Berg 1.130c, 2.116b	40.13	Dav §9c, 53a; GKC §72w, 112p; J-M §155pa; Gib 9, 58, 77 ☐ B-L 276z, 402q'', 564; B-M
39.18	Dav §50a, 91c, 92, 96; GKC §114r, 115h; J-M §118l, 124q, 133g; Gib 102, 128, 129, 130, 131, 157 ☐ Berg 2.38g; Brock §140	40.14	2.170, 3.109; Berg 2.149l GKC §105b n 1 (p. 308), 106n n 2, 151e, 163d; J-M §112k n 3; Wms §347; IBHS 533; Gib 69 ☐ B-M 3.55;
39.19	Brock §35b; Gib 14, 129		GAHG 1.190 n 680,
39.20	Dav §25; GKC §130c; J-M §126h, 129q; Wms §489; IBHS 156, 620, 645; Gib 12 ☐ GAHG 2.52 n 248; Brock §162	40.15	3.169 n 514, 3.215 n 813; Berg 2.41d, 2.126d Dav §39c, 150; GKC §2b, 52r, 113w, 125e; J-M §33, 56b, 123p, 169e; IBHS 419 n 2, 582,
39.21	Dav §3R2; GKC §135m; J-M §129h; IBHS 303; Gib 3		639; Gib 68, 125, 160 ☐ B-L 13c, 326o; B-M 2.109, 3.63; Jen
39.22	Dav §100R2, 108; GKC §116r, 116s; J-M §121f; IBHS 620; Gib 13, 138 ☐ Berg 2.71f, 2.73i		§14.4.3; Sch §31.3.3; Berg 1.151b, 2.62c, 2.96f, 2.145e
39.23	Dav §100d; GKC §116o, 117c, 152l; J-M §160i, 170j; Wms §247, 407, 534; IBHS 641; Gib 136, 159 ☐ Jen §20.3.3; Berg 2.71f; Brock §163a	40.16	GKC §135f; J-M §156b; Wms §384; IBHS 301; Gib 2, 38, 175
		40.17	Gib 133
		40.18	GKC §126i; IBHS 152; Gib 47 ☐ Berg 1.162g
40.1	Dav §27, 51R1, 114; GKC §111f; J-M §129a, 150q; Gib 22, 30, 35, 99 ☐ B-L 538i; GAHG 2.67 n 289; Brock §132	40.19	J-M §137m, 155pa
		40.20	Dav §79; GKC §69w, 71, 121b; J-M §128b; IBHS 448, 601 ☐ B-L 379t; B-M 2.125, 2.142;
40.2	J-M §132g; IBHS 217		GAHG 3.122 n 332; Berg 2.54d,
40.3	Dav §25; GKC §130c; J-M §129q; Wms §489; IBHS 139, 620; Gib 12 ☐ B-L 522j; Brock §152b, 162		2.106n, 2.130m; Brock §99b
		40.21–22	IBHS 651; Gib 65, 171
		40.22	GKC §144n
40.4	GKC §139h; Gib 4, 14, 115 ☐ B-M 2.112	40.23	Dav §47; Gib 96, 173
		41.1–3	Gib 137
40.5	Dav §27; GKC §129h; J-M §126h, 129a; Wms §131; Gib 35	41.1	Dav §29d, 100a, 101Rd; GKC §111f, 116s, 119cc, 131d; J-M §127d, 131e, 154c; Wms §68;
40.6	Gib 137 ☐ Berg 2.70e, 2.85r		Gib 41, 136, 137 ☐ B-M 3.35; Sch §54.2.3.4; Berg 2.70e*

B-L: Bauer and Leander, *Historische Grammatik*   **B-M:** Beer, *Grammatik*   **Berg:** Bergsträsser, *Grammatik*
Brock: Brockelmann, *Syntax*   **Dav:** Davidson, *Syntax*   **GAHG:** Richter, *Grammatik*
Gib: Gibson, *Davidson's Syntax, 4th ed.*   **GKC:** *Gesenius' Grammar*   **IBHS:** Waltke and O'Connor, *Syntax*
Jen: Jenni, *Lehrbuch*   **J-M:** Joüon and Muraoka, *Grammar*   **Ros:** Rosenthal, *Grammar*
Sch: Schneider, *Grammatik*   **Wms:** Williams, *Syntax*

41.2–6	Dav §24d; Gib 33
41.2	GKC §128x, J-M §154h □ B-M 3.13; GAHG 2.60 n 260; Berg 2.70e*; Brock §77f, 121e
41.3	Gib 59, 148 □ Berg 2.70e*; Brock §117c
41.4	GKC §128x; J-M §129i; IBHS 151 □ GAHG 2.60
41.5	Dav §38R5; IBHS 626; Gib 51 □ B-L 614; Berg 1.126bb, 1.160a, 2.70e*; Brock §88
41.6	Dav §98b; GKC §116l; J-M §121p, 177s; IBHS 617; Gib 31, 134 □ Berg 2.70e*
41.7	Gib 43, 137 □ Brock §4
41.8	Dav §27, 100d; GKC §64b, 122i; J-M §129a; Wms §23; Gib 35, 57, 99, 136 □ B-L 321k; GAHG 2.67 n 288; Berg 2.92g
41.9–10	Gib 66
41.9	Dav §111R1; GKC §142f(d) n 1; Gib 133
41.10	Dav §1; J-M §129c; Gib 4
41.11	Dav §51R7; GKC §49e; J-M §47e, 147a; Gib 102 □ Berg 2.23f
41.12	Dav §11Rd, 27, 28R5; GKC §2b, 129c, 139c; J-M §130b, 147d; Gib 14, 35, 178 □ B-L 13c; Brock §137
41.13	Dav §151; GKC §144n; J-M §174b; IBHS 641; Gib 116, 161, 178 □ B-L 564
41.14	GKC §144f, 144n; J-M §155b; Gib 13 □ Berg 2.117a
41.15	Dav §100d, 146R1; GKC §152o, 157a; J-M §157ca; IBHS 218; Gib 136, 149, 173 □ GAHG 3.174 n 567
41.17–18	J-M §155pa
41.17	GKC §116o; J-M §121f □ Berg 2.70e*
41.18	Berg 2.70e*
41.19	Wms §273; IBHS 204 n 58, 207; Gib 150 □ Berg 2.70e*; Brock §107iα
41.20	J-M §100d
41.21	GKC §91f, 93ss □ B-L 252p, 582u'; B-M 2.54; Berg 2.126d, 2.146f
41.23	GKC §135o; J-M §149b, 177s
41.24	Gib 136
41.25–27	Dav §104b
41.25	Dav §106d; GKC §116d, 116p; IBHS 627; Gib 55, 137 □ Berg 2.72h*; Brock §151
41.26–36	Gib 78
41.26	GKC §126i, 126x, 141h; J-M §138b, 154e; IBHS 260; Gib 44 □ GAHG 3.162 n 484; Brock §14bζ
41.27	J-M §121p, 138b; Wms §234 □ Brock §50d, 77d
41.28	GKC §53p, 125k; J-M §152b; Gib 137 □ B-L 426; Berg 2.106l
41.29	GKC §156c □ Berg 2.72h
41.30	GKC §112x □ B-M 3.54
41.31	IBHS 668; Gib 45 □ Berg 2.117a; Brock §111i
41.32	Wms §289; IBHS 218 □ B-L 217d, 425; Brock §159a
41.33–35	Berg 2.53q
41.33	Dav §63; GKC §75p, 75hh; J-M §114h; Gib 81, 149 □ B-L 425; B-M 2.158; GAHG 3.102 n 284; Berg 2.48g, 2.163f
41.34	Dav §63; GKC §75t, 107n; J-M §79m; IBHS 414; Gib 80 □ Berg 2.48g, 2.53q, 2.160b
41.35	Dav §32; Wms §350; IBHS 220, 257; Gib 6 □ Berg 1.133f, 2.53q
41.36	J-M §132e □ Berg 2.19a
41.37	Berg 2.126d
41.38	Wms §256; Gib 14
41.39	Dav §91c, 145R1; GKC §115a; J-M §124f; IBHS 445; Gib 158 □ Brock §99b
41.40	Dav §33, 71; GKC §118h; J-M §126g; Wms §57, 390; IBHS 75, 265, 669 n 91; Gib 39, 45, 145, 170 □ B-L 267f; GAHG 3.156 n 446; Jen §11.3.3; Brock §101
41.41	J-M §105d
41.42	Dav §20R2, 75; GKC §117cc, 126n; J-M §125u; IBHS 176 n 25, 246, 442; Gib 26, 112

B-L: Bauer and Leander, *Historische Grammatik*　**B-M**: Beer, *Grammatik*　**Berg**: Bergsträsser, *Grammatik*
Brock: Brockelmann, *Syntax*　**Dav**: Davidson, *Syntax*　**GAHG**: Richter, *Grammatik*
Gib: Gibson, *Davidson's Syntax, 4th ed.*　**GKC**: *Gesenius' Grammar*　**IBHS**: Waltke and O'Connor, *Syntax*
Jen: Jenni, *Lehrbuch*　**J-M**: Joüon and Muraoka, *Grammar*　**Ros**: Rosenthal, *Grammar*
Sch: Schneider, *Grammatik*　**Wms**: Williams, *Syntax*

41.43	Dav §14, 28R5, 72R1; GKC §85h, 113z, 129h; J-M §123x; Wms §210; Gib 18, 36, 116 □ B-L 277h', 614; Berg 1.148g, 2.62b, 2.67m	42.11	Dav §104b, 106a; GKC §32d, 91f, 141f; IBHS 132; Gib 1, 52, 53, 55, 63, 180, 182 □ B-L 248h, 268j; B-M 3.37; Jen §8.4.2; Berg 2.28g; Brock §30c
41.44	Gib 39 □ Brock §116k	42.12	GAHG 3.192 n 695; Brock §134a
41.46	Wms §504		
41.48	Gib 178	42.13	GKC §133g, 141b, 152m; J-M §151b; IBHS 269, 279; Gib 45, 48, 57, 172 □ Brock §27c, 80e
41.49	Dav §145; GKC §75ff., 131q; Wms §311; Gib 158 □ GAHG 3.174 n 576; Berg 2.65h*	42.14	Dav §4R1; J-M §152b; Gib 133
41.50	GKC §107c; Gib 47, 73 □ B-M 3.111; GAHG 3.122 n 332; Brock §145bα	42.15	Dav §4R1, 119, 120; J-M §152a; IBHS 312; Gib 5, 176, 186, 187 □ B-L 204w; Sch §53.5.3.2; Brock §23e, 170c
41.51–52	GKC §157b; Gib 171		
41.51	Dav §75; GKC §52m; J-M §52a n 6 □ B-L 442e; Berg 2.95 n d	42.16	Dav §125; GKC §110c; J-M §48a n 2, 114o; Wms §449; Gib 167, 187 □ B-M 3.114; Berg 2.50k; Brock §31b
41.52	Dav §75		
41.54	IBHS 651; Gib 171 □ Berg 2.134c, 2.138l	42.18	Dav §64, 132b; GKC §110f; J-M §116f, 117a n 1, 119m, 121l, 152a, 155o n 2, 167u; Wms §190; IBHS 312; Gib 5, 80, 105, 156 □ B-M 3.48; Berg 2.50k, 2.114l; Brock §3
41.56	GKC §122i; IBHS 367; Gib 167		
41.57	Dav §115; GKC §145e; J-M §150e; IBHS 109, 193 n 19; Gib 22 □ Brock §50e		
42.1	GKC §54f; IBHS 431; Gib 57 □ B-L 126z; GAHG 3.175 n 580; Berg 2.115a; Brock §39dβ	42.19	Dav §23, 32R2; GKC §126z, 134d; J-M §114o, 126h, 142m, 154fa; IBHS 259, 375 n 31; Gib 2, 44, 153 □ B-M 2.64; Brock §60b, 164bα
42.2	GKC §109g; J-M §116j; IBHS 578; Gib 106 □ B-M 2.114, 3.102; GAHG 3.106 n 301, 3.175 n 580	42.20	J-M §116e; Gib 107 □ Berg 2.39i, 2.51m
42.4	Dav §111, 127c; GKC §75rr, 152w; Gib 160, 173	42.21	Dav §118; J-M §170e; IBHS 672; Gib 141 □ B-L 437; Berg 2.100h; Brock §56b
42.5–6	IBHS 298		
42.6	Dav §99R3, 106d; GKC §126k; J-M §137l, 154j □ GAHG 3.148 n 391; Brock §30q	42.22	GAHG 3.204 n 771; Brock §106h
42.7	Dav §14; GKC §107h, 122q; J-M §134n; IBHS 194, 505; Gib 13, 17, 76, 185 □ B-L 316c	42.23	GKC §126r; J-M §137n, 154fc; IBHS 243; Gib 2, 136
42.8	Dav §107; J-M §155na; Gib 2	42.24	B-L 120m, 120 n 3; B-M 2.146; Berg 1.154e, 1.157n, 2.111c, 2.112d, 2.136i; Brock §119a
42.9–14	Sch §44.2.2		
42.9	GKC §114g; J-M §154fa, 155r; IBHS 72, 134; Gib 54, 178 □ GAHG 3.67 n 173; Berg 2.57k	42.25	Dav §11Rd, 75, 146R4; GKC §93m, 120f, 124l, 139c; J-M §96Ad, 136b, 177j; Wms §9; IBHS 176; Gib 14, 111, 113, 150 □ B-L 375, 581; B-M 2.69, 3.75; Berg 1.122t
42.10	GKC §152c, 163a; J-M §172a; IBHS 661 n 59; Gib 66, 173		

B-L: Bauer and Leander, *Historische Grammatik*   B-M: Beer, *Grammatik*   Berg: Bergsträsser, *Grammatik*
Brock: Brockelmann, *Syntax*   Dav: Davidson, *Syntax*   GAHG: Richter, *Grammatik*
Gib: Gibson, *Davidson's Syntax, 4th ed.*   GKC: *Gesenius' Grammar*   IBHS: Waltke and O'Connor, *Syntax*
Jen: Jenni, *Lehrbuch*   J-M: Joüon and Muraoka, *Grammar*   Ros: Rosenthal, *Grammar*
Sch: Schneider, *Grammatik*   Wms: Williams, *Syntax*

42.28	Dav §101; GKC §119gg, 147b; J-M §133b, 146h, 154c; Wms §118; IBHS 193 n 19; Gib 147 □ GAHG 3.204 n 771; Brock §29a	43.6	GKC §150i n 3; J-M §161f n 1; Gib 131 □ GAHG 3.175 n 588
42.29	IBHS 616, 621; Gib 133 □ B-M 3.66, 3.68; Brock §99a	43.7	Dav §43b, 86a, 122; GKC §107k, 107t, 113o, 113q, 150d; J-M §113b, 113l, 123h, 123k; Wms §167; IBHS 587; Gib 57, 58, 79, 111, 124, 183 □ B-M 2.131; GAHG 3.175 n 588; Jen §10.3.1.1; Berg 2.63d, 2.63e, 2.30a, 2.36k; Brock §54b, 93a, 110l
42.30	Dav §26, 78R8; GKC §122q, 124i, 126p; IBHS 195; Gib 66 □ Sch §49.1.2; Brock §122d		
42.31	J-M §111i; Gib 63, 178		
42.32	Gib 172		
42.33	GKC §134d; J-M §142m; IBHS 259 n 9; Gib 44, 172 □ Berg 2.124f	43.8	J-M §177q; Gib 22, 37 □ Berg 2.52o; Brock §130b, 135c
42.34	J-M §116b; GKC §108d; Gib 54 □ B-M 3.102; GAHG 3.175 n 582, 3.175 n 583; Brock §32a	43.9	Dav §41c, 51R2, 130b; GKC §159o; J-M §112i, 167h n 1; Gib 2, 153, 154, 177 □ B-L 268g, 346x″; Berg 2.40d, 2.148k
42.35	Dav §11Rd, 141; GKC §93m, 111g, 116u, 139c; J-M §96Ad, 136o, 147d; Wms §9; Gib 14, 20, 167 □ B-L 581; Berg 1.122t, 2.70e*; Brock §72a	43.10	Dav §38R5, 131, 131R2; GKC §106p, 159x, 159ee; J-M §167k, 167s; Wms §118, 166, 449, 516; IBHS 494; Gib 6, 51, 141, 155 □ Berg 2.109c
42.36	Dav §1R2, 127b; GKC §91f, 135p; J-M §94h, 152b; IBHS 395; Gib 3, 170, 178 □ B-L 252p, 268j; B-M 2.121; Brock §32d	43.11	J-M §155o n 2; Gib 178 □ B-L 577i′
		43.12	Dav §38R5; GKC §65d, 72bb, 93pp, 131e; J-M §113m, 119i n 1, 142q; IBHS 286; Gib 51, 52, 135 □ B-L 405
42.37	GKC §107s, 159r; J-M §113l, 167v; Wms §170; IBHS 508; Gib 153, 154 □ Berg 2.35i	43.13	Berg 2.124f
42.38	Dav §132a; GKC §112kk; J-M §32c, 155m; IBHS 171; Gib 144, 156 □ Berg 2.168q; Brock §89	43.14	Dav §32R2, 130R4; GKC §29u, 106o, 126z; J-M §32c, 112i, 138f, 176o n 1; IBHS 260, 364; Gib 44 □ B-L 312v; Berg 1.161e
43.1	Gib 167 □ B-M 3.8		
43.2	Brock §163b	43.15	Dav §38R5; GKC §20c, 131q; J-M §142q; IBHS 286; Gib 51, 171 □ Brock §89
43.3	Dav §86a, 86R1, 140, 140R1, 154; GKC §113n, 113o, 163c; J-M §123j, 129p, 173a; Wms §422, 557; IBHS 588 n 33, 643; Gib 124, 176 □ GAHG 3.169 n 510; Berg 2.63e; Brock §144	43.16	Dav §10; GKC §65b, 72y; J-M §158l; Wms §62; IBHS 185, 335; Gib 10 □ B-L 361a′, 445p; B-M 2.132; Berg 2.117a, 2.149m; Brock §122d, 151
		43.17	GKC §90c; J-M §93d, 129a n 4; Wms §62; IBHS 185; Gib 144 □ B-M 3.31; GAHG 2.31 n 127
43.4	Dav §130a; GKC §131k; J-M §114e, 154l; Wms §479; Gib 57, 136, 137, 153 □ Berg 2.52o, 2.72h*; Brock §30b, 80e	43.18	GKC §116d; J-M §121i; IBHS 623; Gib 135, 137 □ Berg 2.69c; Brock §107iγ
43.5	Dav §100d, 140; GKC §116q, 159g; J-M §154l; IBHS 624; Gib 136, 153 □ Berg 2.52o, 2.72h*	43.20	GKC §113o; J-M §105c, 123k □ Berg 2.63e

B-L: Bauer and Leander, *Historische Grammatik* B-M: Beer, *Grammatik* Berg: Bergsträsser, *Grammatik*
Brock: Brockelmann, *Syntax* Dav: Davidson, *Syntax* GAHG: Richter, *Grammatik*
Gib: Gibson, *Davidson's Syntax, 4th ed.* GKC: *Gesenius' Grammar* IBHS: Waltke and O'Connor, *Syntax*
Jen: Jenni, *Lehrbuch* J-M: Joüon and Muraoka, *Grammar* Ros: Rosenthal, *Grammar*
Sch: Schneider, *Grammatik* Wms: Williams, *Syntax*

43.21 GKC §49e; J-M §47e; IBHS 577 □ B-L 302z; B-M 2.113; Berg 2.23f; Brock §159a

43.22 Dav §8; GKC §137c; J-M §161g □ GAHG 3.97; Brock §143c

43.23 Gib 188 □ B-M 3.9; Berg 1.160a, 2.50k; Brock §7b

43.24 GKC §90c; J-M §93d □ GAHG 2.31 n 127

43.25 Dav §43a; GKC §107k; Wms §167; Gib 77, 149 □ Berg 2.30a; Brock §42g

43.26 GKC §14d; J-M §20a n 1 □ B-L 126z, 445p; B-M 1.68; Berg 1.64n, 1.93h; Brock §89

43.27 GKC §141c n 3; J-M §154h n 1; Wms §67; Gib 183

43.28 Dav §29a; GKC §67g; J-M §154ff. □ Berg 2.139p

43.29 GKC §67n; J-M §63b; IBHS 131; Gib 4, 45, 183 □ B-L 437p'; Berg 2.134 n d; Brock §8a

43.30 IBHS 386 □ Brock §108a

43.31ff. Sch §48.4.3.1

43.31 IBHS 426 □ Berg 2.99e, 2.152t

43.32 GKC §2b, 107g; J-M §154h; Wms §168 ⊔ Brock §121d

43.33 Dav §101; GKC §119gg; J-M §133b; Gib 147

43.34 GKC §134r, 144n; J-M §126j, 141h, 142q; IBHS 287; Gib 51 □ B-L 614; B-M 2.158; Berg 2.163f; Brock §88, 101

44.1 Dav §10; GKC §47m, 138e; J-M §157f, 158l; Gib 10, 116, 171 □ Berg 2.54d*; Brock §94b, 151

44.2 Dav §23; GKC §133g, 135n n 2, 135n n 2; J-M §140b n 1; IBHS 304

44.3-4 Wms §235

44.3 Dav §141; GKC §142e, 144c, 164b; J-M §152e; IBHS 372; Gib 169 □ Berg 2.144b; Brock §35a

44.4 Dav §41R3, 132a; GKC §112kk, 138e, 142e, 156f, 164b; J-M §119l n 2, 125n, 158l, 166b; Wms §55; IBHS 170, 181, 440; Gib 65, 109, 134, 147, 149, 156, 158 □ B-M 3.53; Jen §18.3.4.1; Berg 2.53q; Brock §89, 114c, 139a

44.5 Dav §44a; GKC §119m n 1; J-M §123k; Gib 74, 183 □ B-M 3.100; Brock §106a, 151

44.7 Dav §45R1, 117R1; GKC §107h, 139b n 1; J-M §113d, 147f, 155l, 161a n 1; Wms §256; Gib 14, 76, 188 □ Brock §111f

44.8 Dav §43b, 152; GKC §148b; Gib 39, 79, 185 □ B-L 402r"; Berg 2.148k

44.9 GKC §112ii, 138f; J-M §158m, 176i; IBHS 334 n 13; Gib 79, 174 □ Berg 2.44i; Brock §157

44.10 GKC §153; J-M §152b, 176i; Gib 172 □ GAHG 3.77 n 202; Brock §16e

44.11 Dav §83; Gib 120

44.12 Dav §41R3; GKC §156d; J-M §159c; Gib 65, 178

44.13 J-M §147d n 1

44.14 Gib 22, 34, 58, 168

44.15 J-M §37c, 158f; Wms §256, 572; IBHS 203 n 51; Gib 8, 14, 79 □ B-L 651z

44.16 Dav §136; GKC §20d, 58k; J-M §144e; Wms §126, 378; IBHS 326, 425; Gib 37 □ B-L 197a; B-M 1.107, 1.115, 3.89; Jen §14.4.5

44.17 J-M §165k; IBHS 680; Gib 172, 182 □ B-L 654j

44.18-34 Gib 78

44.18 Dav §151R2; GKC §161c; J-M §105c, 154b, 174i; IBHS 642; Gib 105, 188 □ B-M 3.7; GAHG 3.76 n 202, 3.216 n 815; Berg 1.132e, 2.47e, 2.48g; Brock §8a, 15d, 105b

44.19-20 B-M 3.88

44.19 Gib 39, 66, 183

B-L: Bauer and Leander, *Historische Grammatik* **B-M**: Beer, *Grammatik* **Berg**: Bergsträsser, *Grammatik*
Brock: Brockelmann, *Syntax* **Dav**: Davidson, *Syntax* **GAHG**: Richter, *Grammatik*
Gib: Gibson, *Davidson's Syntax, 4th ed.* **GKC**: *Gesenius' Grammar* **IBHS**: Waltke and O'Connor, *Syntax*
Jen: Jenni, *Lehrbuch* **J-M**: Joüon and Muraoka, *Grammar* **Ros**: Rosenthal, *Grammar*
Sch: Schneider, *Grammatik* **Wms**: Williams, *Syntax*

44.20	J-M §112a; Wms §478; IBHS 492 ☐ GAHG 3.173 n 556; Berg 2.77c; Brock §12	45.6–7	IBHS 550
		45.6	Dav §6R2, 9c, 152; GKC §138c; J-M §158k, 175a; IBHS 22, 334; Gib 6, 9, 39 ☐ GAHG 3.175 n 576, 3.192 n 704; Brock §106i, 152d
44.21	Dav §17R4 ☐ Brock §135c		
44.22	Dav §132a; GKC §GKC §112kk, 159g; J-M §112a, 155m, 167b; Wms §512; IBHS 531; Gib 156 ☐ Berg 2.44k; Brock §135b, 164a		
		45.7	GKC §117n ☐ Berg 2.152t
		45.8	Dav §127a, 155; GKC §119hh; Gib 2, 91, 141 ☐ Brock §97c, 134a
44.23	GKC §137b; J-M §155m		
44.24	Gib 157	45.9	J-M §119l n 2, 155p; Gib 81, 178 ☐ GAHG 2.14 n 37; Berg 2.125b; Brock §64a
44.26	Gib 57, 153, 168 ☐ GAHG 3.175 n 580		
44.27	Dav §107R1; J-M §146a; Gib 2	45.10	Brock §68a, 108b
44.28	GKC §113n, 113w; J-M §123e; Wms §205, 389; IBHS 375 n 31, 670 n 95; Gib 124, 176 ☐ B-L 287n'; GAHG 2.65 n 274, 3.168 n 509; Berg 2.62c, 2.64f, 2.88c; Brock §93c	45.11	Dav §29d; Gib 41 ☐ B-M 1.99, 2.152; GAHG 3.171 n 539, 3.175 n 589; Berg 2.174 n h
		45.12	GKC §112a, 116q, 126k; J-M §137l; IBHS 248, 623 ☐ B-M 3.35; GAHG 3.69 n 177; Brock §64a
44.29	GKC §112kk, 159g; J-M §125g, 167e; IBHS 179; Gib 156 ☐ B-M 2.133; Berg 2.44k, 2.162d; Brock §89		
		45.13	J-M §158e ☐ Berg 2.42i
		45.14	GKC §93pp; Gib 171 ☐ Berg 1.129b
44.30–33	Sch §48.3.4.1		
44.30–31	Gib 87	45.15	B-L 188p; Berg 1.130c; Brock §107c
44.30	Gib 91, 167, 168		
44.31	GKC §112oo; Gib 90 ☐ GAHG 3.174 n 576	45.16	Dav §69a; Gib 143, 167
		45.17	J-M §135o n 2 ☐ Brock §133a
44.32	Berg 2.42h; Brock §22a	45.18	Dav §34R5, 65d; GKC §110i; IBHS 271; Gib 46, 106 ☐ Berg 2.46c, 2.50k; Brock §3
44.33	Dav §60, 70a; GKC §69p, 109b; J-M §114h; Gib 82, 105, 171 ☐ B-M 2.158; GAHG 3.206 n 785, 3.213 n 803, 3.216 n 815; Berg 2.47e, 2.125b, 2.163g		
		45.19	J-M §119l, 135o n 2; Gib 94 ☐ B-M 2.161
		45.20	J-M §154i; Gib 81, 182 ☐ Berg 2.51l
44.34	Dav §43b; GKC §107t, 152w; J-M §159d, 168g n 3; Gib 79, 185		
		45.22	Dav §37R4; Gib 50
		45.23	GKC §102g; Gib 47
45.1	Dav §11Rb, 127a; Gib 13, 14, 140, 157 ☐ B-L 359j; B-M 2.140; Berg 2.118b, 2.129l; Brock §119a	45.25	Dav §69b; IBHS 170; Gib 144 ☐ B-M 3.33
		45.26	Dav §146R2 ☐ GAHG 3.175 n 586
45.3	J-M §154d, 154fa; IBHS 386; Gib 183 ☐ GAHG 3.175 n 588; Jen §8.3.4.1	45.28	J-M §114c; Wms §509; IBHS 573; Gib 72 ☐ B-M 3.101; GAHG 3.175 n 591; Brock §11a
		46.1	B-L 174l; GAHG 2.31 n 130; Brock §91
45.4	Dav §9b; GKC §138d; J-M §158k, 175a; Wms §463; IBHS 334, 486; Gib 9, 62 ☐ B-L 367; B-M 3.99; Brock §153a		
		46.2	GKC §124e, 126r; J-M §136j ☐ B-M 1.78
45.5	GAHG 3.106 n 301; Berg 2.48g	46.3–4	Gib 77

B-L: Bauer and Leander, *Historische Grammatik*   **B-M**: Beer, *Grammatik*   **Berg**: Bergsträsser, *Grammatik*
Brock: Brockelmann, *Syntax*   **Dav**: Davidson, *Syntax*   **GAHG**: Richter, *Grammatik*
Gib: Gibson, *Davidson's Syntax, 4th ed.*   **GKC**: *Gesenius' Grammar*   **IBHS**: Waltke and O'Connor, *Syntax*
Jen: Jenni, *Lehrbuch*   **J-M**: Joüon and Muraoka, *Grammar*   **Ros**: Rosenthal, *Grammar*
Sch: Schneider, *Grammatik*   **Wms**: Williams, *Syntax*

46.3	GKC §69m; IBHS 234 □ B-L 383; Berg 2.50k, 2.126c; Brock §66a		47.6	Dav §106d, 146R4; GKC §128t, 159o; J-M §158l, 177h; Wms §115; Gib 111 □ Brock §76d, 135b, 151
46.4	Dav §86c; GKC §113r, 113w; J-M §123l, 123p; Wms §379; IBHS 582, 586; Gib 124, 125 □ GAHG 2.33 n 139, 3.148 n 503; Berg 2.64f, 2.64g, 2.162d; Brock §93c		47.8	IBHS 325; Gib 185 □ B-L 651w
			47.9	Dav §26; GKC §128a; J-M §129c, 154f; Gib 178 □ B-M 1.103, 3.31; GAHG 2.33 n 144, 3.43 n 135, 3.170 n 526; Sch §45.3.2; Brock §25cγ
46.9	J-M §177o n 1			
46.13	J-M §177o n 1 □ Berg 1.93h			
46.18	J-M §125g □ Brock §84b		47.11	GKC §69v □ B-L 384c'; B-M 2.141; Berg 2.129h
46.19	Jen §8.3.4.1			
46.20	Dav §81R3; J-M §128b		47.12	Dav §75; GKC §117cc; J-M §125u; Gib 113 □ Berg 2.108c; Brock §107lδ
46.22	GKC §121b			
46.25	J-M §134k			
46.26	Dav §98R1; GKC §116h; J-M §121n; Gib 39, 134 □ Brock §84b		47.13	GKC §152o; J-M §160h; Gib 52, 57 □ B-M 2.158; Berg 2.163g
			47.14	IBHS 620 □ Berg 2.69d
46.27	Dav §22R4, 36R3; GKC §121b, 132g, 134e n 1, 138k; J-M §134k, 145e; IBHS 277, 622; Gib 29 □ Berg 1.106c		47.15	Gib 79 □ B-M 2.144; Berg 2.138o
			47.16	GKC §159o □ B-L 653f; Berg 2.125c; Brock §135c
46.29	GKC §144n □ B-L 120m; Berg 1.69x, 1.148g, 2.112d		47.17	GKC §93ss □ Berg 2.115a; Brock §106e
46.30	GKC §108b; J-M §114c n 2 □ GAHG 3.175; Berg 2.49i; Brock §6c		47.18	Dav §154; Wms §56, 98 □ B-L 439p'; Brock §108b
			47.19	GKC §67p; J-M §82h; Gib 37 □ Berg 2.135d; Brock §107lβ
46.31	Gib 62		47.20ff.	Sch §48.4.4.2
46.32	J-M §125i n 2, 154f, 155od; Gib 63 □ Berg 2.28g; Brock §96		47.20	J-M §147d, 147d n 1 □ Berg 2.27d, 2.57k; Brock §110b
46.33–34	Berg 2.43i		47.21	Dav §106c; GKC §139e n 3; J-M §156c, 176j; Gib 91, 182 □ Brock §123e
46.33	Dav §130c; GKC §112y, 112bb; Gib 154			
46.34	Dav §130c; GKC §127e; Gib 63 □ B-L 588l; Berg 2.28g; Brock §72b, 111e, 145bδ		47.22	GKC §112l; J-M §119v, 125i n 2; IBHS 535; Gib 38, 176 □ B-M 3.54; Berg 2.40c; Brock §96
47.1	Gib 66			
47.2	Gib 47		47.23	J-M §164a; IBHS 664 n 79, 684 □ Berg 2.43i; Brock §5b, 51
47.3	Dav §17, 116R3, 136; GKC §145r; IBHS 115; Gib 19, 37, 54 □ B-L 588l; Brock §17, 72b		47.23a	Brock §4
			47.23b	Brock §4
47.4	GKC §109b, 114g, 129h; J-M §114h, 130e, 155r; IBHS 158; Gib 36 □ GAHG 3.170 n 526, 3.174 n 576, 3.216 n 815; Berg 2.47e, 2.57k		47.24	Dav §38R6, 116; GKC §112bb, 134r n 3, 145u; J-M §150l; Gib 23, 171 □ Berg 1.71e, 1.127cc
			47.25	GKC §159c; J-M §114b n 1; IBHS 140 n 9 □ Berg 2.114l
47.5–6	Gib 179		47.26	Dav §1R2, 38R6; GKC §135p; IBHS 287; Gib 3 □ B-L 629a'
			47.29–30	Brock §135d

B-L: Bauer and Leander, *Historische Grammatik*   **B-M**: Beer, *Grammatik*   **Berg**: Bergsträsser, *Grammatik*
Brock: Brockelmann, *Syntax*   **Dav**: Davidson, *Syntax*   **GAHG**: Richter, *Grammatik*
Gib: Gibson, *Davidson's Syntax, 4th ed.*   **GKC**: *Gesenius' Grammar*   **IBHS**: Waltke and O'Connor, *Syntax*
Jen: Jenni, *Lehrbuch*   **J-M**: Joüon and Muraoka, *Grammar*   **Ros**: Rosenthal, *Grammar*
Sch: Schneider, *Grammatik*   **Wms**: Williams, *Syntax*

47.29	GKC §131h; IBHS 608 □ GAHG 3.170 n 526; Brock §164bβ	48.22	Dav §35R2, 101Rd; GKC §96 (p. 282), 106m, 130g; J-M §129o □ B-L 622b; Berg 2.27e; Brock §110f
47.30	Dav §107R1; GKC §112kk, 135a; J-M §146a; Gib 2	49	Gib 116
47.31	Dav §21d; GKC §51o; J-M §137f; IBHS 243 n 8; Gib 27 □ B-L 132c	49.1	GKC §75rr, 138e; J-M §116b; IBHS 331, 389 □ B-M 2.129, 3.100; Brock §135c
48.1	Dav §108; GKC §144d, 144d n 2; J-M §155e; IBHS 675; Gib 13 □ B-M 3.22; Brock §36d	49.3	GKC §29u; J-M §32c, 129a n 4 □ Berg 1.161e
48.2	GKC §144d n 2	49.4	Dav §17R2, 117, 145; GKC §53n, 107c, 124b, 144p, 147c; Gib 20, 72 □ B-L 333a'; Berg 2.34g, 2.119e
48.4	Dav §100e; J-M §79k; IBHS 536; Gib 137 □ B-M 3.34; Berg 2.72h		
48.5	J-M §154i, 154i n 4; Gib 14	49.6	IBHS 165; Gib 19 □ Berg 2.125b; Brock §16g, 17
48.6	GKC §145e; J-M §154i n 4; IBHS 109; Gib 67 □ B-M 3.20	49.7	Dav §59; Wms §180
48.7	Dav §101 n 1 (p. 143), 106b; J-M §89n, 93f, 133f; Wms §288; IBHS 217; Gib 149, 179, 182	49.8	Dav §106c; GKC §135e; Gib 181 □ B-L 443k; Brock §123b
		49.9	IBHS 132; Gib 12, 52, 55 □ Brock §27c, 133a
48.8–9	Gib 54	49.10–11	Berg 2.29i
48.9	GKC §58g, 60d, 66g; Gib 62 □ B-L 357; B-M 2.169; Berg 1.161e, 2.25b, 2.124f	49.10	GKC §20h, 119d, 164f; J-M §155m; Gib 158 □ B-L 600j'; Berg 1.68v; Brock §119a, 163b
48.10	Dav §101Rc, 113; GKC §44m, 107b; J-M §112a n 6, 113ga, 159f; IBHS 492; Gib 21, 148, 167, 178 □ Berg 2.27d, 2.30b	49.11	GKC §7c, 52l, 90l, 90m, 91e, 93v, 96 (p. 285), 106k, 116x, 118p; J-M §93m, 93n, 93r; IBHS 127, 128; Gib 24, 170 □ B-L 252k, 329h', 525j, 526l, 548a', 583v', 618j; B-M 1.95, 2.51, 2.70, 2.80; GAHG 1.126 n 403; Jen §25.3.2.3; Berg 1.99h, 2.95d; Brock §70f
48.11	GKC §75n, 115b □ B-L 426; B-M 3.75; Berg 2.55d*, 2.161c		
48.12	Brock §107a		
48.13	Dav §29a; Gib 40, 175		
48.14	Dav §41R3; GKC §141e, 156d; J-M §171f; Gib 65 □ Jen §8.3.4.1	49.12	Dav §101Rc; GKC §93dd; J-M §96Bb □ B-L 525j, 556e'; Brock §77f, 111h
48.15	Dav §3R1; Gib 4, 58, 135 □ B-M 3.111; Berg 2.69c; Brock §99a	49.13	GKC §95i □ B-L 603f; Berg 1.3l
		49.15	Dav §116R3, 146; GKC §117b n 1, 117h; J-M §157d; IBHS 646; Gib 44, 111, 116
48.16	GKC §116o; J-M §155ne; Gib 135 □ Brock §107iα		
48.17	J-M §113ga □ Berg 2.39b	49.17	Dav §49a, 65R6; GKC §20h, 109k; J-M §18k; IBHS 409; Gib 73, 101 □ B-L 274l, 557f'; B-M 2.65; Berg 1.68v, 2.38 n e, 2.49h
48.18	J-M §154ea n 3		
48.19	Dav §107; J-M §155nb, 172b; Wms §553; IBHS 265, 672 n 105; Gib 45 □ Jen §24.3.3.2; Berg 2.28g; Brock §134e		
		49.18	GKC §106g; Gib 63 □ Berg 2.28g, 2.167o; Brock §107c
		49.19	B-L 435p'; Berg 2.140q(bis)
48.20	J-M §48b n 1 □ Berg 2.84q	49.20	Gib 53
48.21	GKC §116p, 147b □ Berg 2.72h	49.21	GKC §126b □ B-L 581

B-L: Bauer and Leander, *Historische Grammatik*   **B-M**: Beer, *Grammatik*   **Berg**: Bergsträsser, *Grammatik*
Brock: Brockelmann, *Syntax*   **Dav**: Davidson, *Syntax*   **GAHG**: Richter, *Grammatik*
Gib: Gibson, *Davidson's Syntax, 4th ed.*   **GKC**: *Gesenius' Grammar*   **IBHS**: Waltke and O'Connor, *Syntax*
Jen: Jenni, *Lehrbuch*   **J-M**: Joüon and Muraoka, *Grammar*   **Ros**: Rosenthal, *Grammar*
Sch: Schneider, *Grammatik*   **Wms**: Williams, *Syntax*

49.22	Dav §116; GKC §44m, 80g, 96 (p. 285), 132 n 2, 145k; J-M §42f, 89n, 150g, 150h; IBHS 101 n 29; Gib 23 □ B-L 357, 511v, 618j; B-M 2.80, 2.160; Berg 2.15b; Brock §50a	50.8	J-M §125i n 2 □ GAHG 3.192 n 693; Brock §96
49.23	GKC §67m, 112rr, 128u; J-M §82l □ B-L 437, 438; Berg 2.133 n a, 2.174 n h; Brock §74b	50.10	Dav §67b, 144R3; Gib 115
		50.11	J-M §131n □ Brock §134d
		50.12	Berg 2.27d
49.24	J-M §91c □ B-L 533f; Berg 2.135d	50.13	GKC §138b n 1; J-M §158h n 1 □ Brock §152c
49.25	Dav §78R1; GKC §63m, 117ff., 119c; Wms §285, 348 □ Berg 2.113f	50.14	Gib 22
		50.15ff.	GKC §117ff
		50.15	Dav §131R1; GKC §159m, 159y, 159dd; J-M §167k; Wms §597; Gib 79 □ GAHG 3.179 n 618; Berg 2.63d; Brock §170a
49.26	Berg 2.19a		
49.27	Dav §44R3, 142; GKC §29l, 29u, 107g, 155f; J-M §32c, 158a; Gib 76 □ B-L 303g', 487qε; B-M 3.96; Berg 1.161e	50.16	Brock §107lα
		50.17	GKC §105a, 105b n 1 (p. 308); J-M §125k n 1; IBHS 684 □ GAHG 3.170 n 521, 3.215 n 815; Berg 1.132e
49.28	J-M §143a □ B-M 3.38		
49.29	GKC §164b; IBHS 628; Gib 137 □ Berg 2.72h	50.18	GKC §58k
		50.19	Wms §541 □ Sch §54.1.1.4
49.30	GKC §138b n 1; J-M §158h n 1	50.20	Dav §101Rd; GKC §75n, 120g; J-M §152h, 155nb, 174d n 3; Gib 178 □ B-L 425; B-M 2.160; Berg 2.161c
49.31	Dav §108; GKC §144f; J-M §155b; Gib 13 □ B-M 3.22; Sch §44.5		
49.33	J-M §47b	50.22	Gib 22
50.2	GKC §120f; J-M §177j	50.23	GKC §128v; J-M §130g □ B-L 156k'; GAHG 3.122 n 332
50.3	Dav §44a; Gib 74		
50.4	GKC §135m, 159o; J-M §176k	50.24	J-M §154fa □ B-M 2.112, 3.69; Berg 2.72h
50.5	Dav §62; GKC §116p; J-M §114d; Gib 82 □ GAHG 3.216 n 815; Berg 2.72h; Brock §4, 89	50.25	GKC §116v □ Berg 2.112c
		50.26	GKC §69q, 73f, 126r, 144d n 2 □ B-L 286m', 405; B-M 1.80; Berg 2.88c
50.6	J-M §114n; IBHS 572		

B-L: Bauer and Leander, *Historische Grammatik*   **B-M**: Beer, *Grammatik*   **Berg**: Bergsträsser, *Grammatik*
Brock: Brockelmann, *Syntax*   **Dav**: Davidson, *Syntax*   **GAHG**: Richter, *Grammatik*
Gib: Gibson, *Davidson's Syntax, 4th ed.*   **GKC**: *Gesenius' Grammar*   **IBHS**: Waltke and O'Connor, *Syntax*
Jen: Jenni, *Lehrbuch*   **J-M**: Joüon and Muraoka, *Grammar*   **Ros**: Rosenthal, *Grammar*
Sch: Schneider, *Grammatik*   **Wms**: Williams, *Syntax*

EXODUS

1.1	Dav §136R1; GKC §49b n 1	1.22	GKC §127b n 1; J-M §134c,
1.5	Dav §98R1; Gib 134 □ Jen		135c, 139s, 155s; IBHS 115,
	§6.3.1.6		375, 613 n 3; Gib 172 □ B-M
1.7	Dav §80; GKC §117z, 121d,		2.117; Berg 2.87c, 2.166m;
	133k; J-M §125d, 128c; IBHS		Brock §17, 89, 122k, 123b
	79, 168; Gib 113, 118 □ Jen	2.1	GKC §117d □ B-M 3.44; Brock
	§11.4.13; Brock §98b		§96
1.8	J-M §158f; IBHS 80 □ Brock	2.2	Dav §1R3; GKC §107k, 117h;
	§150c		J-M §157d; Gib 111
1.9	Gib 59, 91	2.3	GKC §20h, 58g, 114m, 126m;
1.10	Dav §53c, 57; GKC §47k, 75rr,		J-M §61i; IBHS 245; Gib 58,
	112y; J-M §61f, 105e; IBHS		128 □ B-L 212k, 346x″, 352;
	683; Gib 93, 188 □ Berg		GAHG 3.171 n 534; Berg 1.68v,
	2.20 n a, 2.47e, 2.128g; Brock		2.74a; Brock §137
	§110g	2.4	GKC §69m, 71h, 107k; J-M
1.12	Dav §151; GKC §107e; J-M		§53f; Gib 8, 79, 129 □ B-L 386t,
	§174a, 174b; Wms §264; IBHS		382; GAHG 1.72 n 135; Jen
	641; Gib 161 □ Berg 2.32d		§28.3.3; Berg 1.132f, 2.30a,
1.13	IBHS 79		2.126c, 2.129 n l; Brock §111d
1.14	GKC §119o; J-M §125j; IBHS	2.5	Gib 168 □ GAHG 3.100, 3.115;
	183; Gib 117, 177 □ B-L 156k′,		Berg 1.132f(tris); Brock §110i
	437; GAHG 3.53 n 156	2.6–7	Dav §146; GKC §2b, 131m; J-M
1.15	J-M §158b n 2, 176b n 2		§146e; Wms §71; IBHS 132,
1.16	Dav §1R2, 55b, 130a; GKC		233; Gib 5, 42, 54, 59, 98, 181 □
	§67k, 72w, 76i; J-M §176b n 2;		Berg 1.153c; Brock §68b
	IBHS 447; Gib 3, 94, 153 □ B-L	2.7	Dav §29R7; GKC §107q, 112p;
	13c, 423; Berg 2.17e,		J-M §103d; Gib 92, 106 □ B-L
	2.43i*(3ce), 2.139p, 2.148k;		13c, 632i, 635d; B-M 1.78; Berg
	Brock §41f		2.47d; Brock §6c
1.17	Gib 32, 173 □ B-L 303c′; Berg	2.9	Dav §53a, 65d; GKC §69x, 70e,
	2.19a(bis), 2.157c		135m; J-M §129h; IBHS 303;
1.18–19	GKC §47l		Gib 3 □ B-L 339y, 378j, 385g′;
1.18	Dav §47; Gib 96 □ B-L 303c′;		Berg 2.173 n g; Brock §4, 80d
	Berg 2.19a; Brock §133d	2.10	GKC §111d; J-M §118j; IBHS
1.19	Dav §53b, 54a; GKC §47l,		551; Gib 148 □ Berg 2.173 n g
	112oo; IBHS 402; Gib 72, 87 □	2.11ff.	GKC §2b
	B-L 13c, 303c′; Berg 2.19a;	2.11	J-M §126c □ GAHG
	Brock §42a, 163c, 176a		3.102 n 288; Brock §113a
1.20	GKC §145g; Gib 22 □ B-M	2.12	J-M §104d, 160g; IBHS 366;
	3.20; Berg 2.163f		Gib 36, 57 □ B-L 649l; Berg
1.21	Dav §115; GKC §135o; Gib 3 □		2.163f, 2.165k
	Brock §124b	2.13	Dav §45R1; Gib 76

B-L: Bauer and Leander, *Historische Grammatik*   **B-M**: Beer, *Grammatik*   **Berg**: Bergsträsser, *Grammatik*
Brock: Brockelmann, *Syntax*   **Dav**: Davidson, *Syntax*   **GAHG**: Richter, *Grammatik*
Gib: Gibson, *Davidson's Syntax, 4th ed.*   **GKC**: *Gesenius' Grammar*   **IBHS**: Waltke and O'Connor, *Syntax*
Jen: Jenni, *Lehrbuch*   **J-M**: Joüon and Muraoka, *Grammar*   **Ros**: Rosenthal, *Grammatik*
Sch: Schneider, *Grammatik*   **Wms**: Williams, *Syntax*

2.14	Dav §118; GKC §115a; J-M §131b; Gib 129 □ GAHG 2.33 n 133, 3.176 n 599; Sch §49.3.4.4; Berg 2.54c; Brock §63a	3.8	GKC §128x; J-M §121m; IBHS 616 n 23; Gib 31, 33
		3.9–10	Gib 91
		3.9	GKC §117r □ GAHG 3.204 n 772; Brock §93e
2.15	Dav §21d; GKC §126r; J-M §137n; Gib 27 □ Jen §28.3.3; Brock §21bβ, 111i	3.10	Dav §65d; GKC §110i; Gib 106 □ B-M 2.133; Berg 2.118d
2.16	GKC §75w; J-M §80b n 3; IBHS 408 □ Berg 2.157c, 2.167o	3.11	Dav §43b, 150; GKC §107u; J-M §169e; IBHS 319; Gib 7, 79, 160
2.17	GKC §60d, 60h, 135o; J-M §149b □ B-L 132d, 337j, 337n, 384c'; Berg 2.23g; Brock §124b	3.12	J-M §143a, 157e, 166l; Wms §452; IBHS 93, 110 □ B-L 418f''; Berg 2.20b; Brock §16e, 161a
2.18	GKC §114m; Wms §226; IBHS 602 □ B-M 1.76; Berg 2.55d*	3.13	GKC §112t, 116p, 147b; Wms §513, 581; IBHS 320 n 11; Gib 113 □ Berg 2.72h; Brock §164a
2.19	Berg 2.19a	
2.20	Dav §136R1; GKC §46f, 154b; J-M §44d n 2, 177m; IBHS 327; Gib 4, 185 □ B-L 376r; Berg 2.20a, 2.157 n c; Brock §80e, 135c	3.14	IBHS 93; Gib 3, 79, 141 □ Brock §156b
		3.15	GKC §133l; Gib 58 □ Brock §107b
2.21	J-M §140a	3.16	J-M §119l; Gib 35 □ Berg 2.53q; Brock §5b, 41f
2.22	J-M §118j	
2.23	Wms §74, 319 □ B-M 3.12	3.18	GKC §2b, 49l, 87a; J-M §90b, 114f □ B-L 13c, 217g; GAHG 3.216 n 815; Berg 1.124w, 2.17d
2.24	IBHS 366	
3.1	Dav §100R2; GKC §116r; J-M §21f; Wms §359; IBHS 193, 226; Gib 138, 167 □ Berg 2.73i*	3.19	GKC §69x, 157b n 2 □ B-M 2.142; Berg 2.131o
		3.20	GKC §63m □ Berg 2.117a
3.2	GKC §52s, 119i, 126r; J-M §16f n 1, 58b, 133b n 4, 137o, 160i; IBHS 375, 375 n 36, 420; Gib 136 □ B-L 287o'; B-M 2.117; Berg 2.70e, 2.88c; Brock §32d	3.21	GKC §135m, 164d; J-M §129h □ Berg 2.20b; Brock §80d
		3.22	GKC §95k, 139b □ Berg 1.148g
		4.1	GKC §107i; Wms §167; Gib 77 □ B-L 274g; Berg 1.67t
3.3	Dav §45R1, 62; GKC §108b, 126v; J-M §45b, 79o, 105c, 114d, 116b, 143h; IBHS 579; Gib 76, 82 □ B-L 274m; B-M 3.48; GAHG 3.173 n 547, 3.187 n 670; Sch §47.1.4; Berg 2.47d, 2.53q	4.2	GKC §37c; J-M §37c □ Berg 1.66s
		4.4	GKC §29g, 63i, 64c; J-M §31d, 69b; IBHS 225 □ B-L 354c; Berg 1.130c, 1.157p, 2.105i*; Brock §106a
3.4	B-L 159p'	
3.5	J-M §131c n 2, 150ia, 154i; Wms §463, 538; IBHS 626 □ Berg 2.71g, 2.122c	4.5	Dav §43c; GKC §165b; IBHS 639; Gib 35, 79, 110, 159 □ Jen §19.3.4
3.6	Wms §578; IBHS 234 n 16; Gib 35, 52	4.6	J-M §105c n 2 □ B-L 445p; Berg 2.23g
		4.7	IBHS 449 □ Berg 2.23g
3.7	Dav §111R3; J-M §149a, 158e; Wms §376; Gib 171 □ Berg 2.160a	4.8	Dav §57

B-L: Bauer and Leander, *Historische Grammatik*   **B-M**: Beer, *Grammatik*   **Berg**: Bergsträsser, *Grammatik*
Brock: Brockelmann, *Syntax*   **Dav**: Davidson, *Syntax*   **GAHG**: Richter, *Grammatik*
Gib: Gibson, *Davidson's Syntax, 4th ed.*   **GKC**: *Gesenius' Grammar*   **IBHS**: Waltke and O'Connor, *Syntax*
Jen: Jenni, *Lehrbuch*   **J-M**: Joüon and Muraoka, *Grammar*   **Ros**: Rosenthal, *Grammar*
Sch: Schneider, *Grammatik*   **Wms**: Williams, *Syntax*

4.9	Dav §57; GKC §118f; J-M §176b n 2; Wms §379; Gib 144, 153, 182 □ B-L 300q; Berg 2.20b, 2.44i; Brock §83b	5.1	Dav §114; Gib 22 □ B-L 436; Brock §135c
4.10	Dav §24d, 24R3, 145; GKC §61e, 128t, 152d; J-M §105c, 129j, 129p, 160c; Wms §399; IBHS 149; Gib 33, 55, 157, 174 □ GAHG 3.175 n 582; Jen §10.3.3; Sch §51.2.4.1; Berg 1.148g, 1.149h, 2.95d; Brock §77f, 111e, 158	5.2	GKC §107u; J-M §169f n 1; IBHS 322; Gib 7, 150 □ Berg 2.28g, 2.118b; Brock §138
		5.3	Dav §22R1, 152; J-M §114e, 114f; Wms §243; Gib 29, 39, 160 □ B-L 13c
		5.4	J-M §113d
4.11–12	IBHS 552	5.5	GKC §112cc; J-M §148b
4.11	GKC §73b; IBHS 89; Gib 177 □ B-L 399h″; B-M 2.149; Berg 2.152t	5.7	Dav §11b, 55a; GKC §68h; J-M §146a, 147a; IBHS 305; Gib 13, 94 □ Berg 2.53q, 2.123d, 2.171 n d
4.12	GKC §75ee; IBHS 442; Gib 92 □ Berg 2.167o	5.8	GKC §154a n 1; J-M §114e □ GAHG 2.13 n 36; Brock §128
4.13	Dav §25, 144; GKC §130d, 155n; J-M §105c, 129q, 158o; IBHS 156; Gib 11 □ GAHG 2.52 n 246, 3.215 n 815	5.10	Dav §100d, 127b; GKC §152m; Wms §407; IBHS 662; Gib 4, 57, 136 □ B-L 634w; Brock §32d, 159c
4.14	Dav §44a, 132a; GKC §159g; Gib 156 □ B-M 3.113; GAHG 3.204 n 771; Berg 2.35i, 2.44k, 2.72h	5.11	Dav §10R3, 11b; GKC §138e; J-M §158m; Gib 10 □ Berg 2.72h*
		5.14	Gib 62 □ B-M 2.67
		5.15	GKC §107h; J-M §113d
4.15	J-M §113m; IBHS 502 n 17, 508; Gib 78 □ Berg 2.166m	5.16	Dav §100d; GKC §74g, 116t, 152o; J-M §155f, 160i; Wms §587; IBHS 626, 678; Gib 136 □ B-L 375; Berg 2.69d, 2.71g, 2.158 n e; Brock §32d, 175
4.16	Gib 172		
4.17	Dav §9c; Gib 9		
4.18–19	IBHS 552	5.17	J-M §114e
4.18	J-M §114d, 114n; Gib 58 □ Jen §9.3.4.1; Berg 1.131e	5.18	GKC §163a; Gib 173
4.19	J-M §18m; Gib 96 □ B-L 220m; B-M 1.116; Brock §99a	5.19	GKC §57 n 1, 57 n 4, 135k; J-M §146k; Wms §195; IBHS 305; Gib 13
4.20	GKC §90e, 126r; J-M §93d, 137m	5.20	J-M §126b □ GAHG 3.34 n 101; Brock §103a
4.21	GKC §112mm, 143d	5.21	GKC §66i, 102f; J-M §124s, 155ne; Gib 82 □ B-L 638t; Berg 2.49h, 2.53q, 2.71g, 2.123d, 2.163f(bis); Brock §106l, 161a
4.22	Gib 52		
4.23	IBHS 227; Gib 59, 91 □ B-L 362a′; B-M 3.35; GAHG 2.12 n 27; Brock §65a		
4.24	IBHS 602 □ Berg 2.54d*	5.22	IBHS 449; Gib 184 □ Berg 1.162g
4.25	J-M §157c	5.23	GKC §113v; Gib 157 □ Berg 2.62c, 2.137k; Brock §111e
4.26	Gib 72 □ Berg 2.162f		
4.28	Dav §75, 80	6.1	GKC §107i; Wms §167; Gib 77
4.29	Berg 2.111c	6.2	IBHS 131; Gib 1
4.30	Brock §1071β		
4.31	J-M §157c; Gib 22 □ Brock §160a		

B-L: Bauer and Leander, *Historische Grammatik*   **B-M**: Beer, *Grammatik*   **Berg**: Bergsträsser, *Grammatik*
Brock: Brockelmann, *Syntax*   **Dav**: Davidson, *Syntax*   **GAHG**: Richter, *Grammatik*
Gib: Gibson, *Davidson's Syntax, 4th ed.*   **GKC**: *Gesenius' Grammar*   **IBHS**: Waltke and O'Connor, *Syntax*
Jen: Jenni, *Lehrbuch*   **J-M**: Joüon and Muraoka, *Grammar*   **Ros**: Rosenthal, *Grammar*
Sch: Schneider, *Grammatik*   **Wms**: Williams, *Syntax*

6.3	Dav §101Ra; GKC §119i, 144l n 3; J-M §126g, 133c; Wms §249; IBHS 198, 391; Gib 150 □ Berg 2.164h; Brock §106g
6.5	Gib 9
6.6ff.	GKC §112x
6.6-7	GKC §112c
6.6	Dav §57R1; GKC §112x; J-M §119e; IBHS 520, 534; Gib 88 □ GAHG 3.177 n 602; Berg 2.42g
6.7	GKC §112p; Gib 52
6.8	GAHG 3.106
6.9	Dav §101Rc
6.10	GKC §20c n 2; Gib 146 □ Berg 1.67u
6.11	Gib 179
6.12	Dav §24d; Gib 33, 59 □ GAHG 3.204 n 768
6.14	GKC §124r; J-M §136n □ B-M 3.30
6.16	J-M §177o
6.24	Berg 1.93h
6.25	B-L 618j; B-M 2.80
6.27	IBHS 131
6.28	Dav §25; GKC §52o, 117z, 130d; J-M §129p; Gib 12 □ GAHG 2.52 n 246; Berg 2.96 n f
6.29	GKC §20c n 2, 103g □ Berg 1.67u
6.30	Gib 59
7.1	J-M §105d
7.3	GKC §112p
7.5	Gib 94
7.7	Gib 167
7.9	Dav §65R4; GKC §109h, 159d; J-M §116i; Gib 107
7.11	Dav §29R7; GKC §131l; J-M §146e; IBHS 233; Gib 42, 175 □ Sch §46.1.3
7.12	Gib 172
7.14	Gib 63
7.15	J-M §146h, 154c; Wms §278; IBHS 627 □ Berg 2.72h, 2.113e; Brock §29a
7.16	B-L 13c; GAHG 1.182 n 604, 3.173 n 550; Brock §135c
7.17	Dav §55c; Gib 91, 94 □ Berg 1.155i, 2.113e
7.18	Gib 78 □ Berg 2.59n; Brock §17
7.19	Wms §42; IBHS 153 □ B-L 563x; Berg 2.122c
7.20	Dav §73R6, 114; GKC §119q; J-M §125m; Wms §244; Gib 22, 110
7.25	Brock §50a
7.26	J-M §119l n 2 □ Jen §9.5.4.10; Berg 2.46c; Brock §5b, 41f
7.27	Dav §130a; GKC §52s; J-M §52c; Gib 94, 153 □ B-L 217d, 356v; B-M 1.114; Berg 1.112 n e, 2.118b; Brock §165bα
7.28	GKC §117z; J-M §125d; IBHS 168; Gib 94 □ B-L 133d, 573x; Brock §90d
7.29	GKC §103g; J-M §18m □ B-L 133d, 640f'
8.1	GKC §20m, 66c, 75gg □ Berg 2.165k
8.2	Brock §50c
8.3	Berg 1.107c
8.4-5	GKC §63o
8.4	GKC §109f; J-M §177k; IBHS 577
8.5	J-M §9c, 161g; Gib 142
8.6	Brock §32d
8.7	IBHS 669 □ Berg 2.17e
8.9	J-M §150j
8.10	Dav §29R8; GKC §123e; J-M §135e; IBHS 119; Gib 42 □ B-M 2.131; Brock §92b
8.11	Dav §88R1; GKC §113z; J-M §123x; IBHS 438, 595 n 57, 597 □ Berg 2.67m
8.12	Dav §65R2; J-M §119m; Gib 107 □ Berg 2.165k
8.13	B-L 504kι; Berg 1.107e
8.14	B-L 504kι; Berg 1.107e
8.16	J-M §146h, 154c; IBHS 627 n 48 □ Berg 2.72h; Brock §29a
8.17	Dav §55c, 130a; GKC §117z; 152m, 159v; J-M §154l; IBHS 181, 314; Gib 94, 117, 153, 154 □ Brock §164bα
8.18	IBHS 314
8.19	IBHS 201
8.20	Dav §44R2; GKC §107b; Gib 74 □ B-L 133d; Brock §111i

B-L: Bauer and Leander, *Historische Grammatik*   **B-M**: Beer, *Grammatik*   **Berg**: Bergsträsser, *Grammatik*
Brock: Brockelmann, *Syntax*   **Dav**: Davidson, *Syntax*   **GAHG**: Richter, *Grammatik*
Gib: Gibson, *Davidson's Syntax, 4th ed.*   **GKC**: *Gesenius' Grammar*   **IBHS**: Waltke and O'Connor, *Syntax*
Jen: Jenni, *Lehrbuch*   **J-M**: Joüon and Muraoka, *Grammar*   **Ros**: Rosenthal, *Grammar*
Sch: Schneider, *Grammatik*   **Wms**: Williams, *Syntax*

8.22	Dav §132R2; GKC §150a, 159w; J-M §125i n 2; Gib 154 ☐ B-M 3.93; Brock §96, 141, 164d	9.21	GKC §111h; J-M §176o ☐ Brock §157
8.23	IBHS 528	9.22	J-M §119m
8.24	Dav §82, 86b; GKC §135a; J-M §123o; Gib 120, 124, 148 ☐ Berg 2.59n*; Brock §97c, 116b	9.23	GKC §63n, 69x; J-M §9c(5), 75g, 118e; Gib 99, 171 ☐ B-L 385g'; Berg 1.154e, 2.131o
8.25	GKC §63o, 116p; Gib 81, 110, 132, 176 ☐ Berg 1.160a, 2.48g, 2.72h, 2.105 n k	9.24	Dav §145; Gib 136, 157 ☐ GAHG 3.79 n 215
		9.25	Wms §313, 327 ☐ Berg 2.119e
8.27	Gib 178 ☐ Berg 2.144c	9.26	Brock §152b
8.28	J-M §137f n 4; IBHS 247	9.27	GKC §126k, 141b; J-M §105c n 6, 137f, 137l; Wms §33; IBHS 128, 246, 248, 297 n 29; Gib 55, 170, 178 ☐ GAHG 3.78 n 206; Brock §25a
9.1	GKC §165a; Gib 105 ☐ B-L 13c; Berg 2.46c		
9.2	Dav §100f; GKC §52s; J-M §52c; Gib 137, 187 ☐ Berg 1.112 n e	9.28	GKC §133c; ☐ B-L 643u'; GAHG 3.79 n 210; Brock §97c, 135c
9.3	GKC §116p; J-M §132g ☐ Berg 2.72h; Brock §62f, 63b	9.29	GKC §118u; J-M §125n; IBHS 170 n 17, 406; Gib 170 ☐ B-L 358v; Berg 2.20b; Brock §133c
9.4	GKC §130d, 155n; J-M §129q(3) ☐ Brock §24f	9.30	GKC §107c, 152r; J-M §160n ☐ Berg 2.20b, 2.31c; Brock §145bα
9.5	GKC §107i; B-M 3.42		
9.6	Gib 173 ☐ Berg 1.72g; Brock §111e	9.31	GKC §141d; IBHS 228 ☐ Brock §14bε
9.7	Dav §101Rb; IBHS 364	9.32	Dav §17R1; J-M §136b; Gib 20
9.8	J-M §119m; Gib 41, 105	9.33	J-M §125n; IBHS 170 n 17 ☐ Berg 2.111c
9.9	GKC §117z; J-M §125o ☐ Berg 1.136e	9.34	Berg 2.157b
9.10	Berg 1.136e	9.35	J-M §155m
9.13	J-M §116d; GKC §64d, 109f; Gib 105 ☐ B-L 13c	10.1	Dav §6, 32; GKC §126y; J-M §138g; IBHS 310; Gib 6 ☐ Brock §23d, 60b
9.14	GKC §107q, 165b ☐ B-L 651z; Berg 1.147d	10.2	IBHS 528
9.15	Dav §131R2; GKC §106p; Gib 101, 156 ☐ Berg 2.165k	10.3	Dav §41R2; GKC §51l, 106h; J-M §112e; IBHS 486, 490 ☐ B-L 13c, 228z; Berg 2.92 n i; Brock §41e
9.16	GKC §115e n 1; J-M §124s, 168e, 172b; Wms §522, 553; IBHS 603, 610 n 37, 672 n 105; Gib 174 ☐ Berg 2.56f, 2.112c; Brock §116m	10.4	GKC §65e; J-M §52c, 70e; Gib 154 ☐ Berg 1.112 n e, 2.72h, 2.118b
9.17–18	IBHS 627 ☐ Berg 2.72h	10.5	Dav §108; GKC §166a; IBHS 71; Gib 13 ☐ Brock §34a
9.17	GKC §116n; IBHS 425; Gib 137	10.6	GKC §161b; J-M §147f ☐ B-M 3.101; Berg 2.115l
9.18	Dav §96R3; GKC §91e, 127f; Wms §82 ☐ B-L 383; Jen §6.3.2.2; Berg 2.72h, 2.128g; Brock §73c, 109b	10.7	GKC §107c, 152r; J-M §112e n 2, 122i, 160n; Gib 185 ☐ B-M 3.20; Berg 2.31c; Brock §50b
9.19	GKC §112mm; Gib 181 ☐ Berg 2.40b		
9.20	J-M §176o		

B-L: Bauer and Leander, *Historische Grammatik*   **B-M**: Beer, *Grammatik*   **Berg**: Bergsträsser, *Grammatik*
Brock: Brockelmann, *Syntax*   **Dav**: Davidson, *Syntax*   **GAHG**: Richter, *Grammatik*
Gib: Gibson, *Davidson's Syntax, 4th ed.*   **GKC**: *Gesenius' Grammar*   **IBHS**: Waltke and O'Connor, *Syntax*
Jen: Jenni, *Lehrbuch*   **J-M**: Joüon and Muraoka, *Grammar*   **Ros**: Rosenthal, *Grammar*
Sch: Schneider, *Grammatik*   **Wms**: Williams, *Syntax*

10.8	Dav §7a, 79; GKC §121b, 137a; J-M §144a; IBHS 319, 384 n 18, 449; Gib 7, 36 □ Brock §129d	12.4	GKC §133c, 139c; J-M §119y n 1, 147d; IBHS 266; Gib 148, 178 □ Berg 2.134d; Brock §122o
10.9	GKC §91k, 127e; J-M §139c; Wms §248 □ B-L 534; Brock §106b	12.5	GKC §128v; J-M §129j, 135b n 3; IBHS 150 □ B-M 3.34
10.10	Dav §151; GKC §154a n 1; Gib 161 □ Berg 2.49h	12.6	GKC §88c; IBHS 200, 285
10.11	Dav §1R2; GKC §64g, 122q, 135p; J-M §152b; IBHS 110, 624; Gib 3 □ Brock §16e, 44d	12.8	Dav §101Rd; GKC §154a n 1; Wms §293; IBHS 382; Gib 149, 178
10.12	J-M §119m	12.9–11	Berg 2.52n
10.13	J-M §118e, 166j; Gib 99 □ Jen §18.3.4.1; Brock §16g	12.9	J-M §172c n 2; IBHS 419 □ Jen §26.3.2
10.14	GKC §106c	12.10	IBHS 510; Gib 173 □ Brock §122t
10.15	GKC §152b; J-M §160k	12.11	Dav §98R1, 140; Wms §494; Gib 134, 141, 179
10.17	GKC §109f; Wms §390 □ GAHG 3.215 n 815	12.12	GKC §124g; IBHS 122; Gib 171
10.19	Brock §16g, 89	12.13	GKC §159g; IBHS 134 n 19
10.21	Berg 2.137k	12.14	GKC §67n; J-M §82g; Gib 178 □ Berg 2.135d
10.22	GKC §133i; IBHS 267	12.15	Dav §32R2; GKC §20g, 112mm, 116w, 126w; J-M §138b, 156f, 156j, 156l; IBHS 260 n 16, 535; Gib 39, 44, 142 □ Berg 1.66t, 2.44i, 2.68c; Brock §123c
10.23	Gib 173		
10.24	GKC §145f; Gib 81 □ B-M 2.142		
10.26	Gib 8, 178		
10.27	Gib 120		
10.28	GKC §69v □ B-L 383; Berg 2.127e; Brock §107f	12.16	Dav §81, 106a; GKC §146c, 152b; J-M §132f, 150o, 160k; Wms §280; IBHS 285, 385; Gib 38, 119, 176, 182
10.29	Berg 2.79h		
11.2	J-M §105c n 2 □ B-L 101u; B-M 2.120	12.17	IBHS 310 n 13
11.4	Berg 2.72h*; Brock §106i	12.18	Dav §38R3; GKC §134o; J-M §142o; IBHS 285; Gib 51
11.5	Dav §99; GKC §116d; J-M §121i, 139a; Gib 135, 147 □ Sch §49.1.1; Brock §116c	12.19	Wms §250
11.6	Dav §116R1; GKC §135o □ Berg 2.79h, 2.165l	12.21	GKC §46d □ B-L 306l; B-M 2.114; Berg 2.80i(bis)
11.7	Dav §146; J-M §157c; Gib 110 □ Berg 2.20b; Brock §112, 119b	12.23	GKC §126m n 1
		12.24	J-M §13d
11.8	Dav §32R3; GKC §9v; Gib 6 □ Brock §23d, 117d	12.25	Berg 2.44i, 2.95d
		12.27	GKC §61a □ B-L 344e″, 367; Berg 2.82n
11.10	Gib 167		
12.1	Gib 100	12.29	Dav §51R1; GKC §111f, J-M §126h; Gib 99
12.2	GKC §141f		
12.3	Dav §38R2; J-M §119y n 1, 142o, 176k; Wms §131; IBHS 285, 510	12.30	GKC §152o
		12.31	GKC §20g □ B-M 1.68; Berg 1.66t
		12.32	J-M §119l; Gib 142 □ Brock §163b

B-L: Bauer and Leander, *Historische Grammatik*   **B-M**: Beer, *Grammatik*   **Berg**: Bergsträsser, *Grammatik*
Brock: Brockelmann, *Syntax*   **Dav**: Davidson, *Syntax*   **GAHG**: Richter, *Grammatik*
Gib: Gibson, *Davidson's Syntax, 4th ed.*   **GKC**: *Gesenius' Grammar*   **IBHS**: Waltke and O'Connor, *Syntax*
Jen: Jenni, *Lehrbuch*   **J-M**: Joüon and Muraoka, *Grammar*   **Ros**: Rosenthal, *Grammar*
Sch: Schneider, *Grammatik*   **Wms**: Williams, *Syntax*

12.33	GKC §122i; J-M §112g, 134g; IBHS 104		13.16	GKC §91d
			13.17–18	Brock §89
12.34	Dav §44R3, 145; GKC §107c; J-M §113j; IBHS 514; Gib 72, 73		13.17	GKC §111f, 152w □ B-L 398f″; Brock §133e
12.35	Gib 167		13.18	GKC §67y; J-M §82i □ GAHG 3.146 n 382, 3.152 n 417
12.37	Wms §257; Gib 39 □ Jen §18.4.8; Brock §116i		13.21–22	Berg 2.32d
			13.21	GKC §53q, 115e n 1 □ B-L 228a′, 649l; Berg 2.105 n k
12.39	GKC §117ii; J-M §125w; Gib 114 □ Berg 2.109c, 2.118b, 2.120a		13.22	GKC §107b; J-M §113f □ B-L 528s
12.41	GKC §111f; J-M §176b n 2		14.1	Berg 1.67u
12.42	J-M §136i; IBHS 212		14.2	Dav §101Rd; GKC §93q, 109f □ B-L 215k; Brock §116e
12.43	GKC §119m, 152b; J-M §133c			
12.44	GKC §112mm, 143d □ Berg 2.43i*		14.3	GKC §72v; J-M §80l; Gib 177 □ B-L 538i; B-M 2.152; Berg 2.147i
12.48	Dav §11Rb, 88R2, 107c n 3; GKC §113gg; J-M §119w, 123v, 130g; Wms §209; IBHS 204 n 54, 594; Gib 127 □ Berg 2.35i, 2.66k		14.5	GKC §136c; J-M §143g, 169h; IBHS 383, 640 □ Jen §19.3.4
			14.6	Gib 171 □ B-L 120m; Berg 1.154e, 2.112d; Brock §138
12.49	Dav §113, 116; GKC §145u; J-M §150k; Gib 21 □ Berg 1.124w, 2.144b		14.8	Wms §75
			14.9	GAHG 3.102 n 287
12.51	Wms §290		14.10	GKC §145f; IBHS 441; Gib 167
13.1	Berg 1.67u		14.11	Dav §91R4, 128; GKC §61c, 152y; J-M §143g, 160p; Wms §394 □ Berg 2.54c; Brock §145a
13.2	GKC §52n; Wms §250; IBHS 401 □ B-L 328y			
13.3	Dav §88R2; GKC §113bb; J-M §137s; Gib 6, 127 □ B-M 3.63; Berg 2.66k; Brock §2		14.12	Dav §65a, 90, 123; GKC §133a; J-M §141g; Gib 55, 106 128, 148, 183 □ Berg 2.54d, 2.145d; Brock §135c
13.5	B-L 638t			
13.7	Dav §72R3, 80; GKC §118k, 121b; J-M §126i, 128b; Wms §56, 227, 475; IBHS 181; Gib 117 □ B-M 3.77; GAHG 3.121 n 330; Sch §50.2.3; Brock §100b		14.13	GKC §138e, 161b; J-M §112a; IBHS 529; Gib 31, 94 □ Brock §115a
			14.14	Gib 172
			14.15	J-M §144e; Wms §126; IBHS 323; Gib 7, 107
13.8	GKC §138h; J-M §166l; Gib 7		14.16	GKC §110i; J-M §116f n 2; Gib 107, 172
13.9	Gib 148			
13.10	Wms §63; IBHS 186 □ GAHG 2.31 n 127		14.17	J-M §156m; Gib 172 □ Berg 1.106c
13.11	Berg 1.107e, 1.132f		14.18	GKC §61e; Gib 167 □ Berg 1.106c
13.12	J-M §96Ac □ B-L 134h; Berg 1.107e		14.19	Wms §375; IBHS 221
			14.20	Dav §5, 50b; GKC §139e n 3; IBHS 482; Gib 6 □ GAHG 3.119 n 326; Brock §98c
13.13	Gib 154, 172 □ Berg 1.107e			
13.14	B-L 135h; Berg 1.107e		14.21	IBHS 383
13.15	Dav §44a, 97R1; J-M §121d; IBHS 626, 630; Gib 75 □ Berg 2.58n, 2.71g		14.22	Gib 53
			14.24	Berg 2.135d

B-L: Bauer and Leander, *Historische Grammatik*   **B-M**: Beer, *Grammatik*   **Berg**: Bergsträsser, *Grammatik*
Brock: Brockelmann, *Syntax*   **Dav**: Davidson, *Syntax*   **GAHG**: Richter, *Grammatik*
Gib: Gibson, *Davidson's Syntax, 4th ed.*   **GKC**: *Gesenius' Grammar*   **IBHS**: Waltke and O'Connor, *Syntax*
Jen: Jenni, *Lehrbuch*   **J-M**: Joüon and Muraoka, *Grammar*   **Ros**: Rosenthal, *Grammar*
Sch: Schneider, *Grammatik*   **Wms**: Williams, *Syntax*

16.6	Dav §57R1; GKC §112oo; J-M §176g; Gib 85, 87 □ B-M 3.9; Brock §13a, 123f	16.34	J-M §174b
		16.35	IBHS 387, 480
		16.36	GKC §126n; IBHS 246
16.7	Dav §104c; GKC §32d, 72ee, 107u, 141l n 3; J-M §37e, 170j; IBHS 73 □ B-L 248h; Jen §8.4.2; Berg 2.151q; Brock §13a	17.1	GKC §115f; Gib 128 □ B-L 547
		17.2	GKC §47m; Gib 179 □ Berg 2.166m
		17.3	GKC §72ee, 117e; IBHS 517 n 61 □ Berg 2.112c; Brock §107c
16.8	Dav §104c, 127a; GKC §72ee, 141l n 3; Gib 178, 185 □ B-L 248h; B-M 2.14; Jen §8.4.2; Berg 2.123d, 2.151q	·17.4	Dav §56; GKC §112x, 112oo; Gib 58, 87 □ Brock §13a
		17.5	Dav §11Ra; J-M §119l; Gib 14 □ B-M 2.17, 3.33; Jen §28.3.3; Brock §111a
16.12	GKC §88c; J-M §125d; Gib 172 □ Brock §90d	17.6	GKC §49k; Gib 94
16.13	Gib 172 □ Brock §116h	17.7	Dav §122, 124; GKC §152k; J-M §160h, 160j, 170h; Wms §291, 409, 593; Gib 183, 184 □ B-M 3.88; GAHG 3.174 n 576; Brock §32d
16.14	GKC §55k □ Berg 2.107 n a, 1.112 n e		
16.15	GKC §37b; IBHS 317 n 5; Gib 14		
16.16	Dav §69R3; GKC §118h; J-M §125v; Gib 145 □ B-L 636h	17.8	B-L 321k; GAHG 3.121; Berg 2.91g
16.18	Wms §491, 576; Gib 171 □ Berg 2.103d*; Brock §122o	17.9	J-M §177e; Gib 168 □ Brock §133a
16.19	Gib 14 □ Berg 2.48f, 2.119e	17.10	GKC §118f; J-M §150p; Gib 144
16.20	GKC §27o, 67n, 121d n 2, 139h n 1 □ B-L 438, 615d'; B-M 2.144; Berg 1.150m, 2.135d; Brock §24e	17.11–12	IBHS 133
		17.11	Dav §54b, 116R5; GKC §112ee; J-M §141g n 3, 150e; Gib 23, 94 □ B-L 312t; B-M 3.110; Berg 2.42g*
16.21	Dav §132a; GKC §123c, 159g; J-M §135d; IBHS 6; Gib 156 □ Berg 2.32e, 2.44k, 2.136h; Brock §109f	17.12	GKC §141d, 145n; J-M §148b; IBHS 242, 257; Gib 14, 43, 51, 53 □ GAHG 3.151 n 414; Brock §115a, 137
16.22	Dav §36R3, 38R4; GKC §111f, 126n, 134e; J-M §142c n 1, 142q, 176f; IBHS 276; Gib 50, 51		
		17.13	GKC §47i □ Berg 2.110b
		17.14	GKC §126s; J-M §137m; IBHS 245 n 13; Gib 27
16.23	GKC §63i, 76d; J-M §152b □ B-L 442g; Berg 1.156m, 2.120a	17.16	GKC §133l
		18.2	Brock §19b
16.26	GKC §121d n 2	18.3	Gib 12
16.27	J-M §155a, 176f; Wms §324; IBHS 70 n 11, 214; Gib 99 □ Jen §28.3.3; Brock §34a, 105b, 111a	18.4	Dav §101Ra; GKC §119i, 157b; J-M §133c; Wms §249, 564; Gib 150
16.28	Dav §41R2; GKC §106h, J-M §112e; IBHS 329	18.5	GKC §118g; J-M §146c; IBHS 295; Gib 137
16.29	GKC §29e, 9l, 69p, 139d □ Berg 1.130c, 2.46c; Brock §114b	18.6	Berg 1.148g
		18.8	Brock §110m
16.31	Gib 170 □ B-L 512e'	18.9	GKC §75r; Gib 113 □ B-L 423; Berg 1.108 n e, 2.163g
16.32	GKC §117cc; J-M §137m		
16.33	GKC §125b; IBHS 251; Gib 25, 41 □ Berg 2.151q	18.10	Berg 2.74 n l

B-L: Bauer and Leander, *Historische Grammatik*   **B-M**: Beer, *Grammatik*   **Berg**: Bergsträsser, *Grammatik*
Brock: Brockelmann, *Syntax*   **Dav**: Davidson, *Syntax*   **GAHG**: Richter, *Grammatik*
Gib: Gibson, *Davidson's Syntax, 4th ed.*   **GKC**: *Gesenius' Grammar*   **IBHS**: Waltke and O'Connor, *Syntax*
Jen: Jenni, *Lehrbuch*   **J-M**: Joüon and Muraoka, *Grammar*   **Ros**: Rosenthal, *Grammar*
Sch: Schneider, *Grammatik*   **Wms**: Williams, *Syntax*

18.11	J-M §33 □ Jen §8.3.3.2; Berg 2.144b, 2.145e		19.9	IBHS 199, 219 □ B-L 534; Berg 1.144c
18.13	GKC §47i		19.11	GKC §134o, 134o n 1; Wms §268; IBHS 628 □ GAHG 2.45 n 195; Berg 2.74l
18.14	GKC §102b; J-M §137p; Gib 137, 168 □ B-L 642p'; B-M 2.178, 3.16			
18.15-16	Gib 75		19.12	Dav §132R2; GKC §66b; J-M §123p, 139i; IBHS 582; Gib 157, 178 □ B-L 363h; B-M 3.63; Berg 2.63d, 2.64f, 2.123c
18.15	Dav §44a			
18.16	GKC §112hh, 159bb; IBHS 526, 527; Gib 94 □ B-L 189s, 564			
18.17	Wms §399, 563		19.13	Dav §96R5, 152; GKC §69t, 113w; J-M §123p; IBHS 393, 582; Gib 39 □ B-L 444k; B-M 2.140; Berg 2.56f, 2.63d, 2.63f, 2.128g; Brock §169b
18.18	Dav §34R2; GKC §75n, 133c; J-M §141i; Gib 45, 177 □ B-L 425; Jen §8.3.3.2; Berg 2.161c			
18.19-22	Dav §55a			
18.19	Dav §107; GKC §135a; IBHS 569; Gib 2 □ Berg 2.46c, 2.49h, 2.115l, 2.126d; Brock §116f		19.14	Gib 148
			19.15-16	GKC §134o n 1
			19.15	J-M §121e n 2 □ GAHG 2.45 n 195; Berg 2.74l, 2.115l
18.20	Dav §142, 143; GKC §103b, 155d, 155i; Wms §540; IBHS 442; Gib 11 □ Jen §22.3.3; Brock §146		19.16	GKC §134o n 1
			19.18	GKC §93dd; J-M §96Bb, 159f, 170i; Wms §376, 534 □ B-L 557e'; B-M 2.63
18.21	GKC §97h; J-M §121l, 121m; IBHS 617 n 26			
18.22	GKC §110i, 127b; Wms §338; Gib 2 □ Berg 2.137k		19.19	Dav §86R4; GKC §113u; J-M §123s; Wms §221; Gib 126 □ Berg 2.31b, 2.73i*; Brock §93g
18.23	GKC §44e, 49i, 114m, 142f □ B-L 312u; B-M 2.115; Berg 1.150m, 2.78c			
			19.21	J-M §177e □ Berg 2.125b
			19.23	GKC §72i, 72w, 72x; J-M §119l □ B-L 404; Berg 2.148k, 2.150n
18.25-26	IBHS 533 □ Jen §9.5.4.12			
18.25	GKC §97h; J-M §119v		19.24	J-M §177e n 1, 177f; Gib 173 □ B-M 3.82; Berg 2.53p
18.26	GKC §47g, 112g; J-M §44c, 119v □ B-L 301s; Berg 2.42g*(bis), 2.79g		20.2ff.	B-M 1.74; Berg 1.77i
			20.2-14	Gib 179
18.27	GKC §119s		20.2	GKC §15p, 138d; J-M §158n; IBHS 239 □ B-L 58d; Brock §153a
19.1	GKC §102f; GKC §115f; J-M §124g, 176h □ B-L 638u; B-M 2.176; Berg 2.125c			
			20.3	GKC §107o, 132h; J-M §148a; IBHS 122, 218; Gib 81 □ B-M 3.30; Berg 2.51m; Brock §110k
19.2	Brock §116d			
19.3	GKC §53n □ B-L 367; Berg 2.39i, 2.51l			
			20.4	Wms §348 □ Jen §28.3.3; Berg 2.51m; Brock §5a, 111d
19.4	Dav §47; J-M §54c n 1; Gib 96 □ Berg 2.21d			
			20.5	Dav §98c; GKC §60b, 63p, 129e; J-M §63b, 130b; Gib 134 □ B-L 352; B-M 1.102, 3.32; Berg 2.79 n g; Brock §110b
19.5	GKC §113o, 119w; J-M §123g; IBHS 526, 527; Gib 92 □ GAHG 3.206 n 786; Berg 2.63d; Brock §106d, 164bγ			
			20.6	Dav §98c; J-M §121l; Gib 134 □ Brock §99a
19.6	Gib 178		20.7	B-L 442e
19.8	GKC §135r		20.8-10	Gib 178

B-L: Bauer and Leander, *Historische Grammatik*   **B-M**: Beer, *Grammatik*   **Berg**: Bergsträsser, *Grammatik*
Brock: Brockelmann, *Syntax*   **Dav**: Davidson, *Syntax*   **GAHG**: Richter, *Grammatik*
Gib: Gibson, *Davidson's Syntax, 4th ed.*   **GKC**: *Gesenius' Grammar*   **IBHS**: Waltke and O'Connor, *Syntax*
Jen: Jenni, *Lehrbuch*   **J-M**: Joüon and Muraoka, *Grammar*   **Ros**: Rosenthal, *Grammar*
Sch: Schneider, *Grammatik*   **Wms**: Williams, *Syntax*

20.8	GKC §113f, 113bb; J-M §123v; IBHS 593, 593 n 51, 593 n 52; Gib 127 □ GAHG 3.53 n 156; Berg 2.35i, 2.66k	21.3	Dav §130a; J-M §176d, 176n □ Brock §164bα
20.9	GKC §118k; J-M §126i; IBHS 171, 528; Gib 93 □ B-L 278h'	21.4	GKC §72t, 145h, 146e; J-M §150f, 150p, 176d; Wms §232; Gib 172, 177 □ B-M 3.21
20.10	Dav §32R2; GKC §126w, 152b; Wms §433; IBHS 108, 260; Gib 44, 149, 173	21.5	Dav §86a, 130R3; GKC §113o; J-M §123g; IBHS 489 n 17; Gib 124, 154, 155 □ Jen §10.3.1.1; Berg 2.63d; Brock §128
20.11	GKC §91i n 1; J-M §126i	21.6	J-M §137m, 176d; Gib 154
20.12	Dav §60; J-M §123v n 3; Wms §286; IBHS 517 n 61; Gib 80 □ B-M 2.101; Berg 2.72h*; Brock §145bγ	21.7–11	Gib 155
		21.7	J-M §176d, 176n; Gib 154
20.13–17	Wms §173	21.8	GKC §61b, 75ee, 103g; J-M §65b □ B-L 208o, 343b'', 425, 640f'; B-M 2.167; Berg 1.157o, 2.82n(bis), 2.106l; Brock §106h
20.13–15	Sch §51.4.6.3		
20.13	J-M §113m; IBHS 510		
20.15	GKC §107o; IBHS 9 □ B-M 3.48	21.9	Berg 2.126d
20.17	B-L 58d; Berg 2.112c	21.11	Dav §36R4, 140; Gib 48, 154 □ B-L 623e; GAHG 3.102 n 289; Berg 1.134a
20.18	GKC §116o; J-M §121f; Gib 171 □ Berg 2.71f		
20.19	IGKC §135a; BHS 295; Gib 2 □ Berg 2.47d, 2.49h; Brock §8a	21.12	Dav §55c, 86R2, 99; GKC §104g, 112n, 116w, 159i; J-M §104d, 119r, 121m, 125q, 128a, 156g, 156j, 176m; Wms §173, 205; IBHS 536; Gib 95, 125, 135, 157 □ B-M 3.69, 3.103; GAHG 3.169 n 513; Berg 2.69c; Brock §93c, 140
20.20	Dav §43c, 149R2; GKC §107q, 135m, 152x, 165b; J-M §133j, 160l, 168e; Wms §175, 424, 522, 524; IBHS 511, 640; Gib 148 □ B-M 3.103; GAHG 2.36; Jen §19.3.4; Brock §52bγ, 145a		
20.21	Gib 10	21.13	Dav §9a; GKC §112ii, 138c; J-M §176i; IBHS 529; Gib 10 □ Berg 2.42g, 2.172d
20.22	B-L 217c		
20.23	IBHS 195	21.14	Berg 2.51m, 2.153t
20.24	Dav §24b, 53b; GKC §127e; J-M §129f; IBHS 151; Gib 32, 93 □ B-M 3.48; Berg 2.51m	21.15	Gib 135
		21.16	GKC §112n, 162b; J-M §119r, 167b n 1, 175b; Wms §433; IBHS 536, 654 n 21; Gib 95, 157 □ Berg 2.41e
20.25	Dav §48d, 76, 132R2; GKC §72k, 117kk, 159r; J-M §80i; Gib 144, 154, 156 □ Berg 2.97h, 2.148k		
		21.17	J-M §175a; IBHS 654 n 20
20.26	Dav §149; J-M §168f; Wms §287, 466; IBHS 217; Gib 160 □ Brock §161bα	21.18	Dav §152; GKC §47m; IBHS 516; Gib 39 □ GAHG 2.68 n 298; Berg 2.21b
21	Gib 155	21.19	GKC §52o □ B-L 327p; Berg 2.96f
21.2ff.	B-M 1.12, 3.116		
21.2–5	Gib 155	21.20	GKC §104g, 113u, 126r; J-M §104d, 123p, 137m, 176m; IBHS 582; Gib 27, 125, 154 □ Jen §25.3.3; Berg 2.63d, 2.63f
21.2	GKC §2b, 159bb; Wms §278; IBHS 209; Gib 154 □ Sch §53.3.3.3; Brock §107iγ, 164cγ		
		21.21	IBHS 375 n 33 □ B-L 286m', 353v; GAHG 2.68 n 298; Berg 2.88c

B-L: Bauer and Leander, *Historische Grammatik* **B-M:** Beer, *Grammatik* **Berg:** Bergsträsser, *Grammatik*
Brock: Brockelmann, *Syntax* **Dav:** Davidson, *Syntax* **GAHG:** Richter, *Grammatik*
Gib: Gibson, *Davidson's Syntax, 4th ed.* **GKC:** *Gesenius' Grammar* **IBHS:** Waltke and O'Connor, *Syntax*
Jen: Jenni, *Lehrbuch* **J-M:** Joüon and Muraoka, *Grammar* **Ros:** Rosenthal, *Grammar*
Sch: Schneider, *Grammatik* **Wms:** Williams, *Syntax*

21.22	Dav §17R3; GKC §124o; J-M §136j, 167i, 176m; IBHS 389, 582; Gib 154 □ Berg 2.63d, 2.63f; Brock §93c
21.23	Wms §352; IBHS 220; Gib 149
21.25	Gib 174
21.26	Gib 154 □ Brock §107iγ, 137
21.27	GAHG 2.67 n 286
21.28–29	GKC §117d; IBHS 637 n 20
21.28	Dav §72R4, 79, 86a; GKC §121b; J-M §113m, 123h, 125h, 128b; IBHS 382, 582, 588, 655; Gib 116, 124, 154, 167 □ B-M 3.74; GAHG 3.120 n 330, 3.169 n 513; Brock §35d, 96
21.29	Dav §116R4; GKC §124i, 145h; J-M §150f; Wms §232; IBHS 498 n 8, 518; Gib 19 □ B-L 518z; Brock §19c, 50f
21.30	IBHS 275 n 32 □ B-L 286m'; Berg 2.88c
21.31	Dav §152; GKC §29i n 1; J-M §155oc, 167q, 175d n 1; Wms §443; IBHS 655; Gib 39 □ GAHG 3.192 n 694; Berg 1.66q; Brock §136a
21.32	J-M §155o; Wms §443; IBHS 655 n 24; Gib 39, 49 □ Brock §122h
21.33	IBHS 371; Gib 177
21.35	GKC §135m; Gib 171 □ B-L 263i; Berg 2.166m; Brock §164cγ
21.36	Dav §44b, 130b; GKC §159cc, 162a; J-M §167q; IBHS 509; Gib 74, 154, 177
21.37–22.3	Jen §16.3.4
21.37	Dav §36R3; GKC §47f, 122d, 123a; IBHS 278, 637 n 20; Gib 39 □ B-L 299k; B-M 3.114; Berg 2.44m, 2.84q
22.1	GKC §124n; IBHS 637 n 20; Gib 153 □ Brock §122k
22.2–5	Dav §130R5
22.2	Dav §130b; GKC §152o; IBHS 384, 637 n 20; Gib 153, 154 □ GAHG 3.174 n 576; Jen §16.3.4; Brock §164bβ
22.3	Dav §86a, 101Rb, 130R3; GKC §51k, 113o, 113w; J-M §101b, 123g, 123p, 142q; IBHS 286, 582; Gib 51, 56, 124, 125, 155 □ B-L 323b'; Berg 2.92i; Brock §93b
22.4	Dav §65R6; GKC §53n; Gib 154, 155 □ B-L 333z; B-M 2.124; GAHG 3.216 n 817; Berg 2.105i*, 2.115a
22.5	Dav §67b; GKC §117q; Gib 115, 155
22.6	J-M §101b; Gib 51, 154, 155 □ Sch §52.6.3
22.7–11	Dav §130R5
22.7	J-M §161f
22.8	Dav §116R4; GKC §138e; J-M §101b, 158m; Wms §289; IBHS 439; Gib 23, 51 □ Berg 2.21b; Brock §50f
22.9	Dav §140; J-M §159b; Wms §494; Gib 154, 155 □ Berg 2.44m
22.10	J-M §161f
22.11	Dav §130R3; GKC §113o; J-M §123p; IBHS 582; Gib 124, 155 □ Berg 2.63f
22.12	Dav §130R3; IBHS 375 n 31, 582; Gib 124, 155 □ Berg 2.63f
22.13	Dav §140; J-M §159b, 160i; Gib 155 □ Berg 2.44m
22.15	Berg 2.74a
22.16	Gib 124, 155 □ B-M 2.131 Anm 2; Berg 2.58n
22.17	GKC §94d
22.19	J-M §137d n 1; Wms §422; Gib 39 □ B-M 2.130
22.20	Berg 2.122 n a
22.21	GKC §152b □ Berg 2.166m
22.22	GKC §113m, 163c n 1; J-M §123d n 3, 123g; Gib 124, 155 □ Berg 2.160a
22.24–26	Gib 90
22.24	B-L 441c; Berg 2.69 n c, 2.159g
22.25	GKC §135o □ Berg 1.154e, 2.113g; Brock §115a
22.26	GKC §91e, 112y; IBHS 325; Gib 177 □ B-L 266i
22.28	B-L 371s; Berg 2.115a

B-L: Bauer and Leander, *Historische Grammatik* **B-M**: Beer, *Grammatik* **Berg**: Bergsträsser, *Grammatik*
Brock: Brockelmann, *Syntax* **Dav**: Davidson, *Syntax* **GAHG**: Richter, *Grammatik*
Gib: Gibson, *Davidson's Syntax, 4th ed.* **GKC**: *Gesenius' Grammar* **IBHS**: Waltke and O'Connor, *Syntax*
Jen: Jenni, *Lehrbuch* **J-M**: Joüon and Muraoka, *Grammar* **Ros**: Rosenthal, *Grammar*
Sch: Schneider, *Grammatik* **Wms**: Williams, *Syntax*

22.29	GKC §60d; J-M §176h □ B-L 337n; Berg 2.23g	23.31	Dav §98b; GKC §58g □ B-L 346v"; GAHG 3.106
22.30	GKC §131k □ B-L 333x; Berg 2.166m	23.32	Brock §122d
		24.2	IBHS 392; Gib 173
23.1	GKC §53e; J-M §47a n 2, 81e □ Berg 2.52n, 2.149m	24.3	GKC §118q; J-M §125s, 126d
23.2	GKC §114o; IBHS 218	24.4	Dav §37e; GKC §134f; Wms §349; IBHS 114, 279; Gib 48, 50 □ Brock §84c
23.4	Dav §86a; GKC §21h; J-M §148c n 1; Gib 124 □ GAHG 2.67		
		24.5	Dav §29b; GKC §131b; IBHS 230; Gib 40 □ B-L 74f; Brock §91(91?)
23.5	Gib 132 □ GAHG 3.102 n 289		
23.7–8	Berg 2.52n	24.6	IBHS 14; Gib 171 □ Brock §137
23.7	IBHS 439	24.7	IBHS 653; Gib 33 □ Berg 2.52o
23.8	Dav §44a; GKC §107g; J-M §113c; IBHS 413, 506, 563; Gib 74, 104, 170	24.8	Wms §290; IBHS 218; Gib 59 □ Brock §137
		24.10	Dav §11c; GKC §139g; J-M §147a; IBHS 451; Gib 13 □ Brock §107iα
23.9	Dav §105, 147; GKC §158a; J-M §170c; IBHS 651; Gib 158		
23.11	Brock §128	24.12	GKC §154a n 1b □ GAHG 3.79 n 211
23.12	Dav §53R1; Gib 93		
23.13	IBHS 388	24.13	B-M 3.35; Brock §64a
23.14	Dav §38R5; GKC §134r; J-M §125t, 142q; IBHS 287 □ Berg 2.134d; Brock §88, 93h	24.14	J-M §144g n 1; IBHS 149 n 28, 320; Gib 8 □ Brock §154, 163b
		24.17	Gib 168
23.15	GKC §118k; Gib 178	24.18	J-M §133c; Gib 149 □ Sch §47.3.5
23.16	GKC §61a □ Berg 2.82n		
23.17	Dav §38R5; Gib 51	25.3	GKC §104g; J-M §104d; IBHS 277 □ B-L 649l
23.18	Berg 2.152t		
23.19	IBHS 271 n 30 □ B-L 556e'	25.5	GKC §52q; J-M §56a □ Berg 2.96g
23.20	GKC §155n □ Berg 2.83n, 2.148k, 2.149l		
		25.7	Gib 32
23.21	GKC §51n, 67y □ B-L 322u; Berg 1.124w, 2.92g, 2.139o, 2.173 n g	25.9	IBHS 277, 451
		25.10	IBHS 134 □ B-L 148 n 5, 583x'
		25.11	Dav §78R2; GKC §49l; J-M §125u
23.22	GKC §113o; J-M §81a n 1, 123g; IBHS 181 □ B-M 2.148; Berg 2.63d, 2.140 n q	25.12	GKC §154a n 1b; Gib 47 □ B-L 557g'; Berg 1.133g, 2.16c
23.23	IBHS 394 □ Berg 2.148l	25.14	B-L 533f
23.24	GKC §60b; J-M §63b, 94g □ B-L 352; Berg 2.79 n g	25.15	GKC §135o n 3
		25.16	J-M §112i n 2
23.25	Berg 2.148k	25.18	Dav §76; GKC §117hh; IBHS 227, 276; Gib 144
23.26	GKC §94d		
23.27	Dav §78R7; GKC §117ii n 1 □ Brock §94c	25.19	GKC §135o
		25.20	J-M §121m; Gib 168 □ B-L 636l; Berg 2.73k
23.28	GKC §126t		
23.29	B-L 357; Brock §110b	25.21	J-M §112i n 2; Gib 171 □ B-L 133d
23.30	Dav §29R8, 145; GKC §113f, 123e, 133k; J-M §112i n 5; Wms §16; IBHS 116; Gib 42, 158 □ B-L 357; Brock §129a	25.24	GKC §49k
		25.27	Brock §116g

B-L: Bauer and Leander, *Historische Grammatik*   **B-M**: Beer, *Grammatik*   **Berg**: Bergsträsser, *Grammatik*
Brock: Brockelmann, *Syntax*   **Dav**: Davidson, *Syntax*   **GAHG**: Richter, *Grammatik*
Gib: Gibson, *Davidson's Syntax, 4th ed.*   **GKC**: Gesenius' *Grammar*   **IBHS**: Waltke and O'Connor, *Syntax*
Jen: Jenni, *Lehrbuch*   **J-M**: Joüon and Muraoka, *Grammar*   **Ros**: Rosenthal, *Grammar*
Sch: Schneider, *Grammatik*   **Wms**: Williams, *Syntax*

25.28	Dav §76, 81R3; GKC §117hh; J-M §128b; Gib 144	27.3	GKC §143e; IBHS 412 □ Brock §31a
25.29	GKC §20f, 117hh □ B-L 600j', 604g; Berg 1.101m, 1.119o, 2.139o	27.7	Dav §81R3, 91R1; GKC §121b; J-M §128b; Gib 130 □ B-L 441c; GAHG 3.121 n 330; Berg 2.123c
25.31	Dav §80; GKC §63h □ B-L 131, 425; Berg 2.110b	27.8	IBHS 442
25.33	GKC §123d	27.11	GKC §134n; J-M §142n
25.35	GKC §123d	27.12	IBHS 134; Gib 54
25.37	J-M §125v □ Berg 2.19a	27.13	GKC §130a; J-M §129l
25.38	Berg 1.148g	27.14	GKC §154a n 1, 154a n 1b; IBHS 134
25.40	GKC §121c; J-M §128c; IBHS 451	27.15	Dav §37a; GKC §134n, J-M §142n; IBHS 134; Gib 49
26	Gib 89	27.16	Dav §29d; IBHS 134; Gib 41 □ B-M 3.12; Brock §62d
26.1	GKC §117hh, 117ii		
26.2	Dav §37R4; GKC §134n; J-M §137o, 142n □ Brock §21cδ	27.17	IBHS 421; Gib 53
26.3	Dav §11Rc; GKC §123d, 139e; J-M §147c; Gib 14 □ Berg 2.17e, 2.19a	27.19	GKC §143e; Berg 1.147d; Brock §31a
		27.20	IBHS 256 □ Berg 1.160a
26.4	GKC §49k	27.21	Dav §22R3; J-M §137h; Gib 29
26.5	Dav §11Rc; J-M §154fc; Gib 14	28.3	Dav §116R1; GKC §117e; Gib 23
26.6-7	GKC §49k		
26.6	Brock §81c	28.7	GKC §145u; J-M §150l; IBHS 421
26.8	Brock §106e		
26.10ff.	GKC §49k	28.8	B-M 2.106; Berg 2.83p
26.12	GKC §124b, 146a; J-M §136c, 150n	28.9	GKC §117d; J-M §125h
		28.10	Dav §37R5; GKC §134c n 4
26.14-15	GKC §117hh	28.11	GKC §116l; J-M §121p □ B-M 2.147; Berg 2.138n
26.15-23	Jen §9.1		
26.16	Dav §38R6	28.14	J-M §90e
26.18	GKC §90d	28.17	Dav §29c; GKC §80f, 131d; IBHS 231; Gib 41 □ B-L 603f; Berg 1.134c, 2.17d, 2.157c
26.19	Dav §37e, 37f; GKC §123d; Gib 50		
26.23	B-L 600i', 603f; Berg 1.134c	28.19	B-L 511y
26.24	B-L 224h; Berg 2.39i	28.20	GKC §117y
26.25	GKC §112ss, 131d	28.21	GKC §139c; J-M §147d □ B-L 626p; Berg 2.19a
26.26	Dav §36R3; J-M §131d; Gib 48		
26.27	B-L 603f	28.22	B-L 482eδ; Berg 1.112 n e
26.29	GKC §117ee, 117hh	28.23	GKC §145a n, 154a n 1b
26.30	GKC §72i, 121c; J-M §80m, 128c □ Berg 2.150n	28.26	GAHG 2.31 n 127
		28.28	Berg 2.39i
26.32	IBHS 421 □ B-L 192i	28.32	GKC §165a; J-M §150k □ Berg 1.66s, 2.117a
26.33	Dav §34R4; GKC §53r, 130a n 3, 133i; J-M §33, 141l; IBHS 270; Gib 32, 46 □ B-L 333b'; Berg 2.17d; Brock §79b	28.34	GKC §123d
		28.35	GKC §109g
		28.38	Berg 1.126bb
27.1	GKC §117hh □ Brock §94dα	28.39	GKC §95r □ B-L 619p
27.2	Berg 2.19a	28.40	Berg 1.126bb

B-L: Bauer and Leander, *Historische Grammatik*   **B-M**: Beer, *Grammatik*   **Berg**: Bergsträsser, *Grammatik*
Brock: Brockelmann, *Syntax*   **Dav**: Davidson, *Syntax*   **GAHG**: Richter, *Grammatik*
Gib: Gibson, *Davidson's Syntax, 4th ed.*   **GKC**: *Gesenius' Grammar*   **IBHS**: Waltke and O'Connor, *Syntax*
Jen: Jenni, *Lehrbuch*   **J-M**: Joüon and Muraoka, *Grammar*   **Ros**: Rosenthal, *Grammar*
Sch: Schneider, *Grammatik*   **Wms**: Williams, *Syntax*

28.43	GKC §109g, 152z, 165a; J-M §160q □ B-L 441c	30.20	GKC §109g, 117y n 1, 165a □ Brock §90d
29.1	GKC §66g; IBHS 276 □ B-M 2.135; Berg 2.124 n f	30.21	Dav §109R2
29.2	GKC §117h, 126m	30.23	GKC §131d; J-M §131c; IBHS 230
29.5	Berg 2.16c	30.25	GKC §117ii; Gib 114 □ Berg 1.148g
29.7	IBHS 451		
29.9	Dav §78R2; GKC §117ee □ Berg 2.17d	30.26	Berg 2.16c
		30.27	GKC §143b
29.12	GKC §119w n 2	30.32	GKC §69q, 73f; IBHS 375 n 32 □ B-L 286m', 404; B-M 1.99; Berg 2.88c, 2.152t
29.13	GKC §118g; J-M §93e		
29.17	Berg 2.117a		
29.21	IBHS 401 □ Berg 2.17d, 2.77c, 2.112c	30.33	IBHS 536; Gib 182
		30.35	IBHS 422
29.24	GKC §72w □ Brock §78	30.36	GKC §113h; J-M §123r, 123r n 1 □ B-M 2.147; Berg 2.66h*, 2.137k; Brock §93d
29.27	GKC §122n		
29.28	Jen §11.3.4		
29.29	Dav §24c; GKC §45d, 128p; J-M §49d, 129f, 130e; IBHS 149; Gib 33, 128 □ Berg 2.56f, 2.83p; Brock §76d	30.38	Brock §123f; Gib 182
		31.2	J-M §105d
		31.4	GKC §63i, 126n □ B-L 348h; B-M 2.129; Berg 2.114i
29.30	GKC §60d; J-M §63a □ B-L 337n; Berg 2.23g	31.5	GKC §45e, 74h □ B-L 352, 375; Berg 2.83p, 2.158e
29.31	GKC §128p; J-M §129f n 1	31.6	Sch §45.4.5; Brock §21cγ
29.33	B-L 375	31.10	J-M §131k
29.34	Berg 2.35i; Brock §34a	31.13	GKC §60f; J-M §61d n 3 □ Berg 2.95d
29.35	GKC §103b □ B-L 642n'; Berg 2.167o		
29.36	Berg 2.157c; Brock §19b	31.14	Dav §116R1; GKC §145l; Wms §104; IBHS 289; Gib 23 □ B-M 3.21; Berg 2.44i, 2.97h
29.37	Wms §47; IBHS 154 □ B-L 582u'; Berg 1.126bb		
29.38	J-M §143a; Wms §386; IBHS 276	31.15	GKC §133i
		31.16	J-M §124o; Wms §195
29.40	Dav §29d; IBHS 288; Gib 41 □ B-L 629a'; B-M 2.90	31.17	GKC §29q, 51m, 118k; J-M §51b □ B-L 320g; Berg 2.91g
29.42	Berg 2.128g; Brock §71c	31.18	GKC §124g □ Brock §109b
29.43	Berg 2.16c	32.1	Dav §6R1; GKC §126aa, 136d n 2, 137c, 143b; J-M §143e, 143i; Wms §191; IBHS 309; Gib 6 □ Brock §23a, 123f, 133a
29.46	Berg 2.82n		
30.2	GAHG 3.77 n 203		
30.4	GKC §103g; J-M §150l □ B-L 640f'; Brock §137		
		32.2	Brock §128
30.7	Wms §100	32.3	GKC §54f, 117w; J-M §53i, 125c; IBHS 430 □ Brock §98a
30.9	Berg 2.122b		
30.10	B-L 329h'	32.4	Dav §76; GKC §117ii, 141a, 145i □ Berg 2.140 n q, 2.173 n h
30.12	Dav §91R1; GKC §109g; Gib 130 □ Berg 2.44i		
30.14	GKC §96 (p. 283, 285)	32.5	Wms §551 □ Berg 1.162g
30.18	GKC §45d; B-L 354g, 564; Berg 2.83p		

B-L: Bauer and Leander, *Historische Grammatik*   **B-M**: Beer, *Grammatik*   **Berg**: Bergsträsser, *Grammatik*   **Brock**: Brockelmann, *Syntax*   **Dav**: Davidson, *Syntax*   **GAHG**: Richter, *Grammatik*   **Gib**: Gibson, *Davidson's Syntax, 4th ed.*   **GKC**: *Gesenius' Grammar*   **IBHS**: Waltke and O'Connor, *Syntax*   **Jen**: Jenni, *Lehrbuch*   **J-M**: Joüon and Muraoka, *Grammar*   **Ros**: Rosenthal, *Grammar*   **Sch**: Schneider, *Grammatik*   **Wms**: Williams, *Syntax*

32.6	GKC §52n, 113e; J-M §124r; IBHS 597 □ B-L 427t″; Berg 1.161e, 2.62b, 2.95d; Brock §107h, 111e		32.33	Dav §8; GKC §137c; J-M §144g, 144g n 1; IBHS 321; Gib 8 □ B-L 267c; B-M 2.16; Brock §154
32.7	B-M 2.162; Sch §48.5.4; Berg 2.160a, 2.167o		32.34	Dav §10R3; GKC §66c, 112oo; J-M §155m; IBHS 537; Gib 10, 59, 87 □ Berg 2.42g; Brock §123f
32.8	IBHS 593; Gib 126 □ Berg 2.65h*; Brock §93d			
32.9	Dav §24d; J-M §129ia; Wms §46; IBHS 151; Gib 33		33.1	J-M §158k □ Berg 2.167o; Brock §152c
32.10	Dav §65a		33.3	GKC §27q, 75bb □ B-L 424; Berg 1.148g, 2.97h, 2.162d; Brock §77f, 106i
32.11	Gib 184 □ Berg 2.164i			
32.12	GKC §150e; J-M §155l, 161a n 1, 161h; Wms §252		33.5	GKC §159c; Wms §108
32.13	Dav §11b; J-M §125k; Wms §130; IBHS 184; Gib 13, 117 □ Brock §95		33.6	GKC §54f, 117w; J-M §125c □ Brock §98a
			33.7–11	Dav §54b; Gib 89 □ Berg 2.32d
32.16	J-M §154i; IBHS 298		33.7–9	Dav §57
32.18	B-L 118 n 3		33.7–8	Gib 89
32.19	Brock §122d		33.7	GKC §107e, 112e, 113h; J-M §113e, 123r; Gib 90 □ Jen §9.3.3.2; Berg 2.65h*; Brock §107c, 120a
32.20	GKC §67bb; IBHS 405 □ B-L 95f, 95 n 6; Berg 2.132a*, 2.162f; Brock §163b			
32.22	GKC §117h; J-M §157d		33.8	J-M §111i, 118n, 166m; IBHS 539; Gib 90
32.24	B-L 119 n 2; Brock §154			
32.25	GKC §5n, 58g, 116i; J-M §61i □ B-L 345q″, 362a′; Berg 1.5l		33.9	J-M §166m; Gib 89, 90
			33.10	GKC §112kk; Gib 86, 143, 156 □ GAHG 3.102 n 289
32.26	Dav §8; GKC §137c; J-M §144g n 1; Wms §121; IBHS 320; Gib 8 □ B-L 268g; B-M 2.16; Brock §154		33.11	Dav §44a; GKC §156c; J-M §113c n 3; Gib 74 □ B-L 618j; GAHG 3.151 n 413
32.27	Gib 14		33.12	Dav §138c; GKC §75gg; J-M §105d, 154fd; IBHS 442
32.28	Dav §37d; Gib 49			
32.29	Dav §48R2, 96R4; GKC §114p; Gib 132 □ B-L 119 n 2; Berg 2.60 n p		33.13	GKC §69b n 1, 91k; J-M §94j □ B-L 252r; B-M 2.55; GAHG 3.170 n 526; Berg 2.125c
32.30	Dav §65b; GKC §108h; J-M §114c; Wms §356; IBHS 574; Gib 83, 106 □ B-L 95 n 6; GAHG 3.215 n 812		33.14	Dav §11c; GKC §150a; Gib 13 □ Berg 2.16c, 2.148k
			33.15	J-M §154l; Gib 137, 154 □ GAHG 3.174 n 576
32.31	GKC §105a, 117q; J-M §105c n 4 □ Berg 1.72g		33.16	Dav §126R8; GKC §150l; J-M §79h; Wms §535; Gib 185 □ B-L 119 n 2; Brock §140
32.32	Dav §127b, 135R1; GKC §159v, 159dd, 167a; J-M §129t, 146g, 160j, 167o, 167r; Wms §597; Gib 186 □ B-M 3.115; Brock §169a			
			33.17	GKC §69b n 1
			33.18	GKC §117cc; IBHS 442 n 23
			33.19	GKC §67ee; J-M §158o □ Berg 2.133b; Brock §156a
			33.20	Dav §65R2; GKC §60d, 159gg; J-M §63a, 167t; Gib 107 □ B-L 337n, 423; Berg 2.23g

B-L: Bauer and Leander, *Historische Grammatik*   **B-M**: Beer, *Grammatik*   **Berg**: Bergsträsser, *Grammatik*
Brock: Brockelmann, *Syntax*   **Dav**: Davidson, *Syntax*   **GAHG**: Richter, *Grammatik*
Gib: Gibson, *Davidson's Syntax, 4th ed.*   **GKC**: *Gesenius' Grammar*   **IBHS**: Waltke and O'Connor, *Syntax*
Jen: Jenni, *Lehrbuch*   **J-M**: Joüon and Muraoka, *Grammar*   **Ros**: Rosenthal, *Grammar*
Sch: Schneider, *Grammatik*   **Wms**: Williams, *Syntax*

33.21	Berg 2.43i		34.29	Gib 168 □ Jen §25.3.3; Berg 2.125b
33.22	GKC §67ee □ B-L 437; Berg 2.172d		34.30	IBHS 213 □ Jen §6.3.1.2
33.23	GKC §124b; IBHS 120		34.32	GKC §117gg; IBHS 174
34.1	GKC §124q; J-M §119m □ B-L 232j; B-M 3.30; Berg 2.119e		34.33	Dav §51R1; Gib 132
			34.34–35	GKC §112e □ Berg 2.32d
34.2	GKC §57 n 4; J-M §121e n 2; Wms §268; IBHS 206; Gib 150 □ GAHG 2.45 n 195		34.34	GKC §159k; J-M §119u
			35.5	Dav §29R7; J-M §146e; Gib 42, 181
34.3	GKC §109c; J-M §114i, 147b, 160f; Gib 174 □ B-L 274j; B-M 3.48; Berg 2.52n, 2.164h		35.22	Wms §293; IBHS 217, 218 n 112 □ Berg 1.139b
			35.26	GKC §103b □ B-L 564, 642n'
34.5	Dav §73R6; Gib 110		35.32	GKC §126n □ B-L 348h
34.6	GKC §128x; J-M §129i, 141k; Wms §72; IBHS 151, 152; Gib 55 □ Brock §77f		35.33	GKC §45e □ B-L 352; Berg 2.83p
			35.34	GKC §135h □ Berg 1.107e
34.7	Dav §86b; J-M §123o; IBHS 583; Gib 124 □ Berg 2.160a		35.35	Berg 2.156b
			36	B-L 73d
34.8	GKC §57 n 4 □ Berg 2.164i		36.1	GKC §103g □ B-L 640f'
34.9	J-M §114h; IBHS 140, 569 □ B-M 2.142; GAHG 3.170 n 526; Berg 2.53q, 2.131o; Brock §164bβ		36.2	GKC §45d □ B-M 2.106; Berg 2.83p
			36.3	IBHS 482 □ Brock §129c
			36.4	GKC §123c □ J-M §135d, 147d □ Brock §129a
34.10	GKC §116p, 122q, 147b; J-M §147f; Wms §25 □ Berg 2.72h		36.5	GKC §114n n 2; J-M §141h □ Berg 2.59n*
34.12–13	J-M §134c			
34.12	J-M §168g n 3; IBHS 224 □ Brock §17, 107f		36.6	GKC §120f □ GAHG 3.171 n 536; Berg 2.48f
34.13	GKC §47m; J-M §94g; IBHS 516; Gib 170 □ B-L 300q, 328w; B-M 2.100; Jen §8.4.8		36.7	GKC §113z □ IBHS 596 n 60 □ Berg 2.66h*
			36.8	GKC §117hh
34.14	Gib 52		36.10	IBHS 277
34.15	Dav §127c; J-M §133c, 168g n 3; Gib 160		36.12	Berg 1.160a
			36.16	IBHS 277
34.18	GKC §161b		36.20–28	Jen §9.1
34.19	GKC §51g □ B-L 321n; Berg 2.92 n gh		36.24	Dav §37e, 37f; Gib 50
			36.28	B-L 600i', 603f
34.20	Gib 150		36.29–30	GKC §112tt
34.22	B-L 539i		36.29	GKC §112ss □ B-L 224h; Berg 2.45n
34.23	Dav §69R1; IBHS 115 □ Brock §117b			
			36.30	Dav §38R4; Gib 51 □ Berg 2.45n
34.24	GKC §51l □ B-L 228z; Berg 2.92 n i		36.31	J-M §131d
34.25	Brock §107b		36.34	Berg 2.164i
34.26	IBHS 271 n 30		36.35	Gib 178
34.27	J-M §42e □ B-L 315l'; Brock §110l		36.38	GKC §112rr □ Berg 2.45n
			37.8	GKC §95n □ Berg 1.102m
34.28	GKC §156f; J-M §142d; IBHS 277; Gib 33		37.10	Wms §43
			37.16	B-L 600j'; Berg 1.119o
			37.24	J-M §137u n 1

B-L: Bauer and Leander, *Historische Grammatik* **B-M**: Beer, *Grammatik* **Berg**: Bergsträsser, *Grammatik*
Brock: Brockelmann, *Syntax* **Dav**: Davidson, *Syntax* **GAHG**: Richter, *Grammatik*
Gib: Gibson, *Davidson's Syntax, 4th ed.* **GKC**: *Gesenius' Grammar* **IBHS**: Waltke and O'Connor, *Syntax*
Jen: Jenni, *Lehrbuch* **J-M**: Joüon and Muraoka, *Grammar* **Ros**: Rosenthal, *Grammar*
Sch: Schneider, *Grammatik* **Wms**: Williams, *Syntax*

38.3	Dav §76; GKC §117hh; IBHS 174; Gib 144
38.5	GKC §95n □ Berg 1.102 n o
38.10	IBHS 134
38.11	IBHS 134
38.12	IBHS 134 □ B-M 3.8
38.14	J-M §101a n 1
38.15	J-M §101a n 1
38.18	Brock §116g
38.21	J-M §137h
38.23	IBHS 135
38.24	Dav §37c; Gib 49 □ B-L 108g'
38.25	B-M 3.39
38.26	B-L 624h
38.27	GKC §69f, 115a, 134g □ J-M §142q; Gib 129 □ B-M 2.139, 3.39; Berg 2.127e
38.28	GKC §112rr □ B-M 1.98; Berg 2.45n
39.1	IBHS 210
39.3	GKC §112f, 112rr □ Berg 2.45n, 2.95d
39.4	GKC §95n □ Berg 1.102m
39.10	Dav §29c; GKC §131d, IBHS 274; Gib 41 □ B-L 375
39.12	B-L 511y
39.14	Gib 34
39.17	Dav §29c; GKC §127h, 131d; J-M §129f n 3, 131d; Wms §68; IBHS 226; Gib 40
39.18	GKC §60h □ B-L 337j
39.20	GKC §60h; B-L 337j
39.23	GKC §165a
39.27	GKC §127f n 1
39.32	Berg 2.163f
39.40	B-L 552r
39.41	J-M §130e
40	B-L 73d
40.2	J-M §125h
40.4	GKC §49k; J-M §43b □ Berg 2.17d
40.13	IBHS 413
40.18	B-M 1.102
40.20	Berg 2.138l
40.21	GKC §67p □ B-L 428e; Berg 2.80 n h
40.24	GKC §93i
40.30	J-M §119v
40.31	J-M §119v □ Berg 2.42g*
40.34	IBHS 366; Gib 171
40.35	Jen §10.3.1.3
40.36–38	Berg 2.31d
40.36–37	GKC §107e ⊔ Brock §42d
40.36	J-M §113e □ B-L 367
40.37	Dav §130b; GKC §159r; J-M §167h; Wms §515; Gib 154 □ Berg 2.54d; Brock §164bγ

B-L: Bauer and Leander, *Historische Grammatik* **B-M**: Beer, *Grammatik* **Berg**: Bergsträsser, *Grammatik*
Brock: Brockelmann, *Syntax* **Dav**: Davidson, *Syntax* **GAHG**: Richter, *Grammatik*
Gib: Gibson, *Davidson's Syntax, 4th ed.* **GKC**: *Gesenius' Grammar* **IBHS**: Waltke and O'Connor, *Syntax*
Jen: Jenni, *Lehrbuch* **J-M**: Joüon and Muraoka, *Grammar* **Ros**: Rosenthal, *Grammar*
Sch: Schneider, *Grammatik* **Wms**: Williams, *Syntax*

LEVITICUS

1.1	GKC §49b n 1; J-M §118c n 2; IBHS 554 □ Berg 2.37a
1.2	GKC §139d; J-M §119l, 147b n 1, 167i; IBHS 510, 637; Gib 183 □ Jen §16.3.4
1.3–4	IBHS 528
1.9	Brock §78
1.12	GKC §154a n 1, 154a n 1b
1.14	GKC §102b □ B-L 642p'; GAHG 3.77 n 203; Berg 2.43i*
1.17	Dav §141R3; GKC §156f; J-M §159c
2.1–2	Sch §48.3.4.2
2.1	GKC §139d, 145t; Gib 183
2.2	GKC §85b □ B-L 568i, 599i'
2.6	GKC §112u, 113bb; J-M §119p, 123v; Gib 52 □ Berg 2.62b; Brock §2
2.8	GKC §121b, 144b n 1, 144p n 1
2.12	GKC §154a □ B-M 3.91
2.13	IBHS 452; Gib 178 □ Berg 2.74a
3.1	IBHS 109 □ Brock §169b
3.3	J-M §14c(6), 35c, 102m
3.12	Gib 52
4.2	Dav §35R2, 101Rc, 130R5; GKC §119w n 2, 139d; J-M §133e, 147b n 1, 167e; Wms §325; Gib 14, 155, 183 □ B-M 2.16; Berg 2.35i; Brock §24d
4.3	GKC §159cc; J-M §167e □ Berg 2.83p
4.7	Gib 171
4.13	Wms §172 □ Berg 2.77c, 2.113f
4.14	J-M §117d
4.20	J-M §152fa
4.21	Gib 26, 53
4.22	GKC §159cc; J-M §167j; Gib 154 □ Brock §164d
4.23	Dav §130b; GKC §69w, 159cc; J-M §117d, 167q; IBHS 109; Gib 154 □ B-L 382; B-M 2.142; Berg 2.67m, 2.129 n i
4.24	GKC §130c; J-M §129q

4.26	Wms §273
4.27–28	GKC §159cc
4.28	GKC §69w; J-M §167q; IBHS 109 □ B-L 382; Berg 2.67m, 2.129 n i
4.31	IBHS 462
4.33	GKC §130c; J-M §129q
4.35	IBHS 462
5.1–4	Gib 177
5.1	Dav §130b, 130R5; GKC §139d, 145t, 159cc; J-M §175d; IBHS 655 n 24; Gib 154, 155, 168, 183 □ B-M 3.90
5.2	Dav §152; GKC §139d; Gib 39
5.3	GKC §162b; J-M §125l; IBHS 211
5.4	GKC §114o; IBHS 211 n 90; Gib 150, 155, 183 □ B-L 422t"; Berg 2.58n, 2.60p, 2.117a, 2.158e
5.5	Berg 2.44i, 2.112d
5.6	B-L 603g
5.7	Berg 2.43i*
5.8	GKC §119d
5.9	Dav §101Rc; GKC §75hh; IBHS 214; Gib 171 □ B-L 424; B-M 3.33; Berg 2.161b
5.11	Dav §38R6; GKC §131d □ Berg 2.43i*
5.12	B-L 568i
5.13	Dav §35R2; GKC §119w n 2, 139d□ Brock §24d
5.15	GKC §64c, 128d; J-M §127d; Gib 155, 183 □ B-L 353b; B-M 2.131; Berg 2.116e
5.16	B-L 629x
5.19	Berg 2.77c
5.21–22	Berg 2.44m
5.21	J-M §167q; Gib 183
5.22	GKC §29g, 114o; J-M §167q; IBHS 198, 218 n 111 □ B-L 640f'; Berg 1.130c, 2.60p, 2.116b

B-L: Bauer and Leander, *Historische Grammatik*   **B-M**: Beer, *Grammatik*   **Berg**: Bergsträsser, *Grammatik*
Brock: Brockelmann, *Syntax*   **Dav**: Davidson, *Syntax*   **GAHG**: Richter, *Grammatik*
Gib: Gibson, *Davidson's Syntax, 4th ed.*   **GKC**: *Gesenius' Grammar*   **IBHS**: Waltke and O'Connor, *Syntax*
Jen: Jenni, *Lehrbuch*   **J-M**: Joüon and Muraoka, *Grammar*   **Ros**: Rosenthal, *Grammar*
Sch: Schneider, *Grammatik*   **Wms**: Williams, *Syntax*

5.24	Dav §10R2; Gib 10 □ B-L 253b', 629x; Berg 2.83p	8.16	GKC §91c; J-M §94h □ B-L 252p, 581
5.26	GKC §45d, 114o; Berg 2.60p, 2.83p	8.23	Berg 1.160a
		8.25	GKC §91c; J-M §94h □ B-L 252p, 581
6.2	GKC §91e; J-M §94h □ B-L 548a'; Berg 2.126d, 2.164i	8.30	GKC §76c
6.3	Dav §29c, 29R4; GKC §128d, 131d; IBHS 304, 385 n 20; Gib 4, 41 □ B-L 564; Berg 2.77c	8.31	Berg 2.167o
		8.33	GKC §74h □ B-L 375; Berg 2.54d, 2.158e
6.4	Dav §73; IBHS 222; Gib 108 □ B-M 3.74	8.34	J-M §143j
		8.35	B-M 2.161; Berg 2.167o
6.7	Dav §88R5; GKC §113cc, 113gg; J-M §123v, 123y; Wms §212; Gib 127 □ Berg 2.62b	9.1	J-M §176f
		9.2	Brock §137
		9.6	Dav §83R1; GKC §107q, 120c; J-M §116e, 157b; Wms §518
6.8	GKC §118g, 135o n 3; J-M §146e □ Brock §68b	9.7	GKC §48i □ B-L 306n
6.9	GKC §118q; J-M §126c	9.22	B-M 2.56
6.11	Berg 1.124w	9.24	J-M §146a n 4 □ Berg 2.135d
6.13	Dav §29d; GKC §121b, 131c; J-M §128b; Gib 41 □ Jen §11.4.13	10.2	J-M §146a n 4
		10.3	J-M §129d; IBHS 148; Gib 3 □ Berg 2.92h, 2.138o
6.18	J-M §129q	10.5	Berg 1.126bb
6.19	IBHS 412	10.6	GKC §109g; J-M §116j □ Berg 1.160a, 2.52n
6.21	IBHS 374 n 30, 475 n 31, 462 □ B-L 287n'; Berg 2.87c, 2.88c	10.8	GKC §107n
		10.9	GKC §109g; J-M §116j □ B-M 2.157; Berg 2.51m, 2.162f
7.2	J-M §129q	10.10	Dav §96R4; GKC §114p; Gib 132
7.7	GKC §161c; J-M §147f, 174i; IBHS 642 □ Brock §109d	10.11	Dav §96R4
7.8	GKC §117d; J-M §125h	10.12	J-M §119l
7.9	Berg 2.111b*	10.13	J-M §119l □ B-M 2.67
7.16	GKC §112o	10.14	Dav §26
7.17	Brock §122t	10.16	IBHS 375 n 31 □ B-L 287n'; Berg 2.64 n g, 2.88c
7.18	GKC §51k, 135o n 3 □ B-L 323z; B-M 2.129; Berg 2.92i	10.17	J-M §129f
7.19	GAHG 3.120 n 330	10.18	GKC §107n, 121b □ B-L 588l; GAHG 3.120 n 330, 3.204 n 768; Berg 2.36k, 2.62c, 2.167o
7.20	Gib 182 □ Berg 2.44i		
7.21	Dav §130R5; Gib 155		
7.23	GKC §104g, 152b		
7.25	Berg 2.44i	10.19	GKC §75rr, 100k, 159g; J-M §167b □ B-L 631g; Berg 1.68v, 2.16c, 2.126d
7.27	Gib 182		
7.30	GKC §72i, 72k; J-M §19d, 80i n 1 □ B-L 403; B-M 2.152; Berg 1.106b, 2.149m	11.4–5	IBHS 244
		11.4	J-M §121m, 137i, 154p □ B-L 156k'
7.35	GKC §53l, 155l; Wms §489 □ Berg 2.106 n l; Brock §144	11.5	J-M §154p
7.38	GKC §93pp □ Berg 1.120 n o	11.7	GKC §65d, 67g □ Berg 2.138o
8.3	B-L 330c	11.10–11	GKC §152o
8.7	Berg 2.112d		
8.11	GKC §76c □ Berg 2.165k		
8.15	GKC §114o		

B-L: Bauer and Leander, *Historische Grammatik*   **B-M**: Beer, *Grammatik*   **Berg**: Bergsträsser, *Grammatik*
Brock: Brockelmann, *Syntax*   **Dav**: Davidson, *Syntax*   **Gib**: Gibson, *Davidson's Syntax, 4th ed.*   **GKC**: *Gesenius' Grammar*   **IBHS**: Waltke and O'Connor, *Syntax*
Jen: Jenni, *Lehrbuch*   **J-M**: Joüon and Muraoka, *Grammar*   **Ros**: Rosenthal, *Grammar*
Sch: Schneider, *Grammatik*   **Wms**: Williams, *Syntax*

11.10	J-M §154p □ GAHG 3.175 n 576
11.12	GAHG 3.175 n 576
11.13	Berg 1.110 n b
11.18	GKC §80k □ B-L 511v
11.20	GKC §29l □ Berg 1.160c
11.21	B-L 156k'
11.23	GKC §88f; J-M §91e; Wms §4 □ B-L 516s; Brock §18a
11.26	Dav §9R2
11.27–28	J-M §39a n 9
11.31	B-L 583w'
11.32	J-M §133e; Wms §326; IBHS 372 □ B-L 368t
11.34	GKC §145u n 2
11.35	GKC §53u; IBHS 375 n 32 □ B-L 286m'; Berg 2.88c
11.37	IBHS 375 n 35 □ Berg 2.88c, 2.117a
11.38	B-L 286m'; Berg 2.87c
11.39	Dav §9R2
11.41	IBHS 133
11.42	GKC §5n; Wms §313 □ Berg 1.5l
11.43	GKC §74k, 109g □ B-L 375; Berg 2.52n, 2.158d
11.44	GKC §27s, 54k □ B-L 328c'; B-M 2.122; Jen §15.4; Berg 2.99e
11.47	Dav §45R1, 97R1; GKC §116e; J-M §121i; IBHS 201, 387, 620 □ B-M 3.67; Berg 2.69d
12.2	IBHS 443 n 27; Gib 155, 183
12.4ff.	GKC §74h
12.4–5	GKC §45d, 91e
12.4	J-M §94h; IBHS 281; Gib 49 □ Berg 2.83p
12.5	J-M §94h, 96Db; Gib 49 □ Berg 2.83p
12.6	J-M §129j
12.7	B-L 95 n 6
12.8	B-L 108g'
13.2	Dav §35R2; Gib 46, 155 □ B-L 93c; Berg 2.44i
13.3–59	IBHS 403 n 25
13.3–5	IBHS 678 n 15
13.3	Dav §71R4; J-M §176b n 2 □ Berg 2.44k, 2.162d
13.4	Dav §71R4; GKC §91d, 91e □ B-L 557g'; Berg 2.43i*

13.5–9	J-M §167l n 2
13.5	Berg 2.44k
13.6	B-L 329h'; Berg 2.44k
13.7	Berg 2.43i*, 2.83p
13.9	Dav §116R2; GKC §146a; J-M §150n; Gib 23 □ Berg 2.44i
13.10	Dav §71R4
13.11	Berg 2.43i*
13.12	Dav §22R1; IBHS 246 n 14; Gib 29
13.16	B-L 119 n 2; Berg 2.44i
13.17	B-L 119 n 2; B-M 2.129
13.19	GKC §131i
13.20	B-L 557g'
13.21	GAHG 3.175 n 578; Berg 2.43i*
13.23	Berg 2.43i*, 2.165l
13.25	Berg 2.43i*
13.26	GAHG 3.204 n 777
13.29	IBHS 108; Gib 183 □ B-L 108g'
13.31	J-M §160i □ GAHG 3.204 n 777
13.32	J-M §160i
13.33	Berg 2.117a
13.34	J-M §160i; IBHS 403
13.35	Berg 2.83p
13.36	IBHS 132 □ GAHG 3.85 n 227
13.38	Gib 183
13.40	IBHS 375 n 31; Gib 183
13.41	IBHS 375 n 31
13.42	Dav §130R5; GKC §84b, 84n; Gib 155
13.45–46	IBHS 134 n 20
13.45	Dav §100R2; Gib 138, 182 □ Berg 2.74l, 2.113f
13.46	Dav §25; GKC §130c; J-M §129q; Wms §489; IBHS 645; Gib 12 □ Brock §162
13.47	B-L 108g'
13.48	B-L 108g', 119 n 2
13.49	Dav §81R1; GKC §84b, 84n, 121c; J-M §128c □ B-M 3.83; GAHG 3.123 n 336
13.52	B-L 95 n 6
13.53	Dav §130b; Gib 153 □ GAHG 3.204 n 777
13.55–56	GKC §121b; IBHS 432
13.55	GKC §54h, 94g; J-M §53h □ B-L 285j'; GAHG 3.204 n 777; Berg 2.99 n g

B-L: Bauer and Leander, *Historische Grammatik* **B-M**: Beer, *Grammatik* **Berg**: Bergsträsser, *Grammatik*
Brock: Brockelmann, *Syntax* **Dav**: Davidson, *Syntax* **GAHG**: Richter, *Grammatik*
Gib: Gibson, *Davidson's Syntax, 4th ed.* **GKC**: *Gesenius' Grammar* **IBHS**: Waltke and O'Connor, *Syntax*
Jen: Jenni, *Lehrbuch* **J-M**: Jöuon and Muraoka, *Grammar* **Ros**: Rosenthal, *Grammar*
Sch: Schneider, *Grammatik* **Wms**: Williams, *Syntax*

13.56	Dav §130b; GKC §54h; J-M §53h; Gib 153 □ B-L 285j"; Berg 2.99 n g
13.57	Dav §29R7, 130b; GKC §131m; J-M §146e; IBHS 233; Gib 42 □ GAHG 3.171 n 539
14.2	Berg 2.43i*
14.4	Berg 1.126bb
14.8	B-L 636k
14.9	GKC §112y; J-M §176f
14.10	B-L 603g
14.12	J-M §129f, 142m; IBHS 152 □ Brock §60b
14.13	J-M §129q
14.20	J-M §93e
14.21	GKC §53o
14.26	B-M 2.139; Berg 2.127e
14.30	GKC §102b
14.34	GKC §127e; J-M §140a; Gib 26
14.35	GKC §118x
14.36	GKC §101a □ B-L 188p; Brock §116c
14.37	B-L 483wδ, 613d'
14.41	Berg 2.174 n h
14.42	Berg 2.150p
14.43-44	IBHS 644
14.43	GKC §53l, 164d; J-M §56c n 1 □ B-L 351, 425; Berg 2.96 n f, 2.106 n l, 2.174 n h; Brock §145bζ
14.44	Brock §144
14.46	Dav §25; GKC §53l, 130d; J-M §129p; Gib 12 □ B-L 333i'; Berg 2.106 n l
14.48	GAHG 3.204 n 777
14.56	Berg 1.152a
14.57	J-M §124s
15.2	IBHS 298; Gib 53
15.5	Berg 2.53q
15.8	Berg 2.44i, 2.174 n h
15.12	IBHS 375 n 31
15.16	GKC §129e
15.18	GKC §118q; Gib 183 □ Berg 2.44i
15.20	Gib 53
15.23	GKC §66b □ B-L 363h; Berg 2.123c
15.24	Dav §65R6; J-M §167e; Gib 104
15.25	Brock §106m, 125a
15.28	IBHS 481
15.29	GKC §53r; J-M §33 □ B-L 445p; Berg 2.17e
15.32	GKC §45d □ Berg 2.83p
15.33	Berg 2.168p
16.1	J-M §116j; IBHS 562 □ Berg 2.38g
16.2	GKC §109g; J-M §139h, 160k, 177j n 2
16.4	GKC §119q, 131c; J-M §117d; Gib 52 □ Berg 2.77c, 2.114i
16.8	GKC §30n
16.9	Berg 2.162d
16.12	Brock §62c
16.17	GKC §152b
16.22	Wms §253 □ Brock §106a
16.23	IBHS 367
16.27	Dav §81R3; GKC §121b □ GAHG 3.120 n 330
16.29	IBHS 423 n 14
16.31	IBHS 423 n 14
16.33	Brock §79b
16.34	J-M §102f □ Berg 2.76 n b
17.3-4	Gib 182
17.4	Dav §130b
17.5	Dav §149; J-M §62h, 176b n 2; Gib 159 □ Berg 2.148l
17.8	Gib 183 □ B-M 1.77
17.9	Dav §130b
17.10	Wms §151; Gib 183
17.11	Dav §101Ra
17.13	Gib 183 □ Berg 2.35i, 2.44i, 2.162d
17.14	Dav §116R1; GKC §145l, 146c; Wms §104; Gib 23
17.15	Berg 2.44i
18.4	Wms §173
18.6	J-M §154fa
18.7-8	GKC §75hh
18.7	B-L 422t"; Berg 2.161b
18.8	IBHS 157 □ Berg 2.161b
18.9	GAHG 2.67 n 286; Berg 2.161b
18.10	GAHG 2.67 n 284; Berg 2.161b
18.11	Berg 2.161b
18.12-17	GKC §75hh
18.12	J-M §79n □ Berg 2.161b
18.13	J-M §79n □ Berg 2.161b
18.14	J-M §79n □ Berg 1.160a, 2.161b
18.15	J-M §79n; IBHS 132; Gib 4 □ B-L 147 n 2; Berg 2.161b

B-L: Bauer and Leander, *Historische Grammatik*   **B-M**: Beer, *Grammatik*   **Berg**: Bergsträsser, *Grammatik*
Brock: Brockelmann, *Syntax*   **Dav**: Davidson, *Syntax*   **GAHG**: Richter, *Grammatik*
Gib: Gibson, *Davidson's Syntax, 4th ed.*   **GKC**: *Gesenius' Grammar*   **IBHS**: Waltke and O'Connor, *Syntax*
Jen: Jenni, *Lehrbuch*   **J-M**: Joüon and Muraoka, *Grammar*   **Ros**: Rosenthal, *Grammar*
Sch: Schneider, *Grammatik*   **Wms**: Williams, *Syntax*

18.16	J-M §79n □ Berg 2.161b		19.34	GKC §117n; J-M §125k; IBHS
18.17	J-M §79n □ Berg 2.161b			204 n 54
18.18	Dav §101Rb; Gib 147 □ Berg		19.36	Dav §24c; GKC §128p; J-M
	2.133b; Brock §108b			§129f; Wms §41; IBHS 149; Gib
18.19	Berg 1.160a			32 □ Brock §76d
18.20	GKC §129e		19.38	B-M 2.176
18.21	GKC §95q n 1		20.3	J-M §169g; Wms §198, 526;
18.23	GKC §65a; J-M §155nf □ B-L			IBHS 639 n 25
	361x; Berg 2.82n		20.6	GKC §145t □ B-M 3.53; Berg
18.24–26	Berg 2.52n, 2.53q			2.40b
18.24	IBHS 395		20.7	GKC §54k □ B-L 328c'; Jen
18.25	GKC §76h □ B-L 445p; Berg			§15.4; Berg 2.99e
	2.157b		20.8	B-L 156k'
18.27	GKC §34b n 4		20.10	GKC §117d
18.28	GKC §116s □ B-L 373d; Berg		20.14	Dav §72R4; GKC §117d; Gib
	2.146e, 2.153t, 2.156a			116
18.30	Berg 2.59n		20.16	GKC §45d □ B-L 361x; Berg
19.1ff.	Sch §51.4.6.2			2.83p
19.2–3	GKC §107n		20.18	GKC §112m; Gib 94
19.3	Sch §52.6.3		20.19	GKC §75hh; J-M §79n □ Berg
19.4	Berg 2.52n			2.161b
19.6	Dav §32R2; Gib 44		20.20	GKC §118n □ GAHG
19.8	Dav §116R1; GKC §145l; J-M			3.146 n 382
	§155oc; Gib 23		20.21	B-L 156k'
19.9	GKC §61d, 142f n 2 □ B-L		20.23	Berg 2.21d
	343c"; B-M 2.167; Berg 2.82n;		20.24	Berg 2.127e
	Brock §122i		20.25	IBHS 200, 403 n 25
19.12	GKC §152z; J-M §154fa		21.1	GKC §74b; J-M §119l; IBHS
19.14	GKC §49k □ Berg 2.17d			425 □ B-M 1.108; Berg 2.35i,
19.15	Wms §252			2.156b
19.16	Dav §71R2; GKC §118q; J-M		21.3	GKC §107s; J-M §98d □ Berg
	§125q; Gib 145			2.35i
19.17	IBHS 588 □ Berg 2.63d		21.4	GKC §67t, 74b □ B-L 436; Berg
19.18	GKC §117n; J-M §125k; IBHS			2.35i, 2.137i
	211, 388 □ B-M 3.85; Jen		21.5	B-L 362a'
	§26.3.3 □ Berg 2.121a		21.7	J-M §132d; Wms §320; IBHS
19.19	GKC §95h, 95k			213; Gib 119
19.20	GKC §113w, 121b; J-M §123p;		21.9	GKC §67t, 164d; J-M §82m,
	IBHS 374 n 30 □ B-L 287n',			131b; Wms §65; IBHS 230, 394
	480wγ; B-M 3.15; Berg 2.63d,			□ B-L 436; B-M 2.146; Berg
	2.64f, 2.87c, 2.106n, 2.150o,			2.136i; Brock §63a
	2.160a, 2.165l		21.10	IBHS 451; Gib 118
19.27	Gib 150		21.13	IBHS 121 □ Berg 1.106c
19.28	GKC §102i; J-M §103c, 155oc □		21.18	GAHG 2.68 n 293
	B-L 638y		21.20	B-L 497zη
19.29	Berg 2.51m		21.21	GKC §142f n 2
19.31	B-L 328a'; Berg 2.51m		21.22	GKC §107s □ Berg 2.35i
19.32	GKC §49k; J-M §113m, 119h;		21.23	Gib 176 □ Berg 2.35i
	IBHS 510 □ Berg 2.17d		22.3	Gib 183

B-L: Bauer and Leander, *Historische Grammatik*   **B-M**: Beer, *Grammatik*   **Berg**: Bergsträsser, *Grammatik*
Brock: Brockelmann, *Syntax*   **Dav**: Davidson, *Syntax*   **GAHG**: Richter, *Grammatik*
Gib: Gibson, *Davidson's Syntax, 4th ed.*   **GKC**: *Gesenius' Grammar*   **IBHS**: Waltke and O'Connor, *Syntax*
Jen: Jenni, *Lehrbuch*   **J-M**: Joüon and Muraoka, *Grammar*   **Ros**: Rosenthal, *Grammar*
Sch: Schneider, *Grammatik*   **Wms**: Williams, *Syntax*

22.4	J-M §112i n 5, 129i; IBHS 144 □ B-L 208r		24.19	B-M 3.101
22.6	Dav §154; GKC §163c □ J-M §173b; Wms §556; IBHS 643; Gib 176		24.22	Dav §35R2; GKC §134d, 161c; IBHS 275; Gib 46
22.8–9	Berg 2.53q		24.23	Dav §77; Gib 145
22.8	Berg 2.51m		25.5	GKC §20h; J-M §18k □ B-L 212k, 302a', 557g'; B-M 1.68; Berg 1.68v, 2.84q
22.9	GKC §152z; J-M §160q □ Berg 2.51m		25.10	Dav §38R3; GKC §134k n 2, 134o n 2; J-M §142o; Gib 51
22.13	GKC §118u □ B-L 398f'', 405		25.11	Gib 51
22.15–16	Dav §9R3; GKC §152z; J-M §160q		25.14–15	Berg 2.52n
22.16	B-M 2.106		25.14	GKC §113z; J-M §123x; IBHS 596; Gib 127 □ Berg 2.67m, 2.160a
22.18	Gib 183		25.17	Berg 2.17d
22.22	J-M §88Ec □ B-L 477zβ		25.19	Brock §107a
22.27	Dav §32R2; Gib 44 □ B-M 1.90		25.20–21	IBHS 637
22.28	GKC §117e; J-M §147a		25.20	GKC §159w; J-M §167l □ GAHG 3.204 n 768; Jen §16.3.4
22.30	J-M §176h		25.21	GKC §49l, 75m □ B-L 411u; B-M 2.159; GAHG 3.171 n 539; Berg 1.99i, 2.17d, 2.165l
23.2	Dav §106R2 □ Berg 1.90c; Brock §30a			
23.5	IBHS 134 n 20, 158			
23.6	IBHS 158			
23.10	Berg 2.149l			
23.16	Brock §119c		25.22	Dav §72R3; J-M §126i; Gib 117
23.17	GKC §14d; J-M §20a n 1 □ B-L 126z, 445p; Berg 1.64n, 1.93h		25.25	B-L 315k'
23.18	B-L 581		25.28	Berg 2.43i*
23.22	GKC §61d □ B-L 343c''; Berg 2.82n(bis)		25.29	Berg 2.136f
			25.30	GKC §74h □ Brock §70f
23.29	IBHS 423		25.31	GAHG 3.175 n 576
23.30	J-M §68f; IBHS 435 □ Berg 2.112c		25.32	J-M §150m
23.32	Dav §38; GKC §134p; Gib 50 □ B-L 629z; B-M 2.93		25.33	Dav §116R2; GKC §145u n 3; J-M §149c; Gib 23
23.35	IBHS 649 n 5		25.34	GKC §10g □ B-L 208r; Berg 1.124w
23.39	GKC §61a; IBHS 135 □ B-L 344e''; B-M 2.167; Berg 2.82n		25.35–36	GKC §76i
			25.35	B-L 351; Berg 2.16c, 2.44i, 2.112c
23.42	GKC §126r		25.36	GKC §76i □ B-L 423; Berg 2.17d, 2.51m, 2.53q
23.43	J-M §166l			
24.2	J-M §177j		25.41	J-M §155pa
24.5	GKC §49l, 117ii □ B-L 416w'; Berg 2.17d		25.42	J-M §125r □ Brock §93l
			25.43	J-M §172a □ Berg 2.17d
24.8	GKC §123c, 123d		25.44	Gib 182
24.10	GKC §126r; J-M §88Mg		25.47	IBHS 649 n 5
24.11	GKC §67g; Anm 2, J-M §88Mg □ B-L 199l; B-M 2.134 Anm 2, 2.144; Berg 2.138o, 2.174 n h		25.48	Dav §145R1; GKC §130d, 164d; J-M §129p; IBHS 156; Gib 157 □ Brock §145bζ
24.15	Berg 2.44i		25.49	GKC §159cc; J-M §167q
24.16	J-M §174i; IBHS 204, 642 n 29; Gib 150 □ Berg 2.174 n h		25.51	GAHG 3.175 n 589
			25.52	Brock §109f

B-L: Bauer and Leander, *Historische Grammatik*   **B-M**: Beer, *Grammatik*   **Berg**: Bergsträsser, *Grammatik*
Brock: Brockelmann, *Syntax*   **Dav**: Davidson, *Syntax*   **GAHG**: Richter, *Grammatik*
Gib: Gibson, *Davidson's Syntax, 4th ed.*   **GKC**: *Gesenius' Grammar*   **IBHS**: Waltke and O'Connor, *Syntax*
Jen: Jenni, *Lehrbuch*   **J-M**: Joüon and Muraoka, *Grammar*   **Ros**: Rosenthal, *Grammar*
Sch: Schneider, *Grammatik*   **Wms**: Williams, *Syntax*

26.4	J-M §129h
26.5	GKC §117c; J-M §125h; IBHS 180
26.6	Dav §139; GKC §152l; IBHS 661; Gib 168 □ GAHG 3.106 n 301
26.9	Berg 1.45e
26.12	B-M 2.122
26.13	GKC §69x, 86k, 119y; J-M §159d; Wms §60, 321 □ B-L 385g'; B-M 2.113; Berg 2.21d
26.15	GKC §67dd □ B-L 438; Berg 2.137 n k
26.16	J-M §126d, 169h □ Berg 2.172 n e
26.18	GKC §52p; J-M §52c; IBHS 611 □ B-L 383; B-M 2.109; Berg 2.96f; Brock §88
26.21	Dav §71R2; GKC §134r; J-M §142q; IBHS 287; Gib 51, 145 □ B-L 629c'; Brock §89
26.22	IBHS 449 □ Berg 2.136h
26.23	Dav §71R2; GKC §121f; Gib 145 □ B-M 3.84; Berg 2.128g; Brock §89
26.24	Dav §71R2; GKC §134r; J-M §142q; IBHS 287; Gib 51, 145
26.25	GKC §49l, 66h □ Berg 2.16c
26.26	J-M §65b; IBHS 537; Gib 87 □ B-L 343b"; Berg 2.42g, 2.82n
26.27	Brock §23e
26.32	IBHS 450 □ Berg 2.132a, 2.138l
26.33	GKC §52n, 145p; J-M §52c, 150c; IBHS 110 □ B-L 423; Berg 2.95e, 2.148k
26.34	GKC §67y, 75m, 91e; IBHS 448 n 2 □ B-L 439p'; B-M 2.111; Berg 2.106n, 2.139o, 2.165l
26.35	Wms §492; IBHS 448 n 2, 450; Gib 91

26.36	Dav §67b; Gib 115, 182 □ B-L 374 n 1; Berg 2.17d, 2.17e, 2.42g
26.37	Dav §127b; GKC §118s n 2, 152k
26.39	Gib 38 □ Berg 2.136i
26.40–41	Berg 2.32e
26.41	Berg 2.32d
26.42	Dav §29R4; GKC §128d, 131r; J-M §129a n 4; Gib 41
26.43	Dav §65R6, 147R2; GKC §67y, 158b; J-M §116e, 132d, 170f n 2, 170n; IBHS 448 n 2; Gib 104 □ B-L 439p'; Berg 2.50l, 2.139 n o, 2.162f; Brock §145bβ
26.44–45	Berg 2.28e
26.44	GKC §154a n 1, 154a n 1a □ GAHG 2.65 n 278; Berg 2.28e, 2.137k
26.45	J-M §137i
26.46	J-M §103n
27.2	GKC §127i
27.3	GKC §96 (p. 285), 128d
27.5	GKC §128d
27.6	GKC §128d
27.8	B-L 95 n 5
27.9	GKC §135o n 3
27.12	IBHS 201, 250
27.16	IBHS 438
27.17–18	IBHS 213
27.18	Brock §110l
27.23	GKC §127i, 135r; Wms §82; IBHS 250; Gib 26 □ Brock §73d, 80b
27.24	Dav §10, 10R2; Gib 10 □ Berg 2.162d
27.32	B-L 119 n 2
27.33	J-M §103c n 4

B-L: Bauer and Leander, *Historische Grammatik*   **B-M**: Beer, *Grammatik*   **Berg**: Bergsträsser, *Grammatik*
Brock: Brockelmann, *Syntax*   **Dav**: Davidson, *Syntax*   **GAHG**: Richter, *Grammatik*
Gib: Gibson, *Davidson's Syntax, 4th ed.*   **GKC**: *Gesenius' Grammar*   **IBHS**: Waltke and O'Connor, *Syntax*
Jen: Jenni, *Lehrbuch*   **J-M**: Joüon and Muraoka, *Grammar*   **Ros**: Rosenthal, *Grammar*
Sch: Schneider, *Grammatik*   **Wms**: Williams, *Syntax*

NUMBERS

B-L: Bauer and Leander, *Historische Grammatik*   B-M: Beer, *Grammatik*   Berg: Bergsträsser, *Grammatik*
Brock: Brockelmann, *Syntax*   Dav: Davidson, *Syntax*   GAHG: Richter, *Grammatik*
Gib: Gibson, *Davidson's Syntax, 4th ed.*   GKC: *Gesenius' Grammar*   IBHS: Waltke and O'Connor, *Syntax*
Jen: Jenni, *Lehrbuch*   J-M: Joüon and Muraoka, *Grammar*   Ros: Rosenthal, *Grammar*
Sch: Schneider, *Grammatik*   Wms: Williams, *Syntax*

5.2	GKC §102i; J-M §103c, 177j □ B-L 638y	6.19	J-M §125c, 126a; IBHS 172, 262 □ Brock §116c
5.3	GKC §119e	6.23–24	IBHS 667
5.6	B-L 354e	6.23	Dav §87; GKC §113h; J-M
5.7	Dav §10R1		§123v; IBHS 569; Gib 126 □
5.8	B-L 405; GAHG 3.174 n 576		Sch §50.4.1
5.10	Dav §72R4; GKC §117m, 139c;	6.24–26	IBHS 566; Gib 179
	J-M §147d; Wms §58; IBHS	6.24	J-M §114g n 1, 114h, 155l □
	182; Gib 117 □ B-L 582u'; B-M		Sch §50.4.1
	3.72; GAHG 3.162 n 482; Brock	6.25–26	GKC §109b □ Berg 2.49h
	§51, 96	6.25	J-M §114g n 1; IBHS 569; Gib
5.13–14	GKC §32l		82 □ B-M 2.170; Berg 1.150n,
5.14	J-M §125bc, 167q		2.53q, 2.135d
5.15	GKC §53o; J-M §136g n 1 □	6.26	GKC §109b; J-M §114g n 1 □
	Brock §62c, 81d		B-L 274j; Berg 2.53q
5.17	GKC §128o, 128p; IBHS 151	6.27	Berg 2.17e
5.18	Dav §32R5; J-M §136g n 1;	7.1	B-L 424
	IBHS 262; Gib 44	7.2	GKC §5n, 116q □ Berg 1.51
5.19	Dav §130b; GKC §110i; Wms	7.3	J-M §137o □ B-L 624h
	§350; IBHS 572; Gib 149, 154 □	7.10	Dav §81R3; GKC §121b; J-M
	Berg 2.49h; Brock §114a		§128b; Wms §59
5.20–21	Brock §164cβ	7.11	GKC §123d
5.20	GKC §167a; J-M §167i, 167r;	7.12	IBHS 285
	Wms §515, 597; Gib 154 □	7.13	J-M §158b
	Berg 2.157c	7.17	GKC §134c; J-M §142d n 1
5.21	GAHG 3.102 n 287	7.19	Brock §90d
5.22	GKC §53q, 66f; J-M §54b □	7.48	IBHS 285
	B-L 228a', 368t; Berg 1.78m,	7.66	J-M §142o; IBHS 285
	2.105 n k(bis), 2.122 n a	7.68	Wms §590
5.23	GKC §126s, 142f; J-M §137m	7.72	J-M §142o; IBHS 285
5.25	J-M §136g n 1 □ Brock §21b	7.78	IBHS 285
5.27	Dav §48d, 57R3, 64c, 112gg,	7.84	Berg 1.119o
	130c; GKC §112y; IBHS 557;	7.85	Berg 1.126aa
	Gib 91, 101, 154 □ B-L 353b;	7.87–88	GKC §134f □ Brock §84b
	Berg 2.44k, 2.116e	7.88	Dav §37c; IBHS 280; Gib 49
5.28	GKC §117z □ Berg 1.126aa	7.89	IBHS 431 □ GAHG 3.102 n 289
5.29	J-M §136g n 1 □ Brock §164d	8.4	Dav §101Rb; Wms §313
5.30	Gib 177	8.6	J-M §119l
6.2	GKC §66b	8.7	GKC §27q, 29v, 64d □ B-L
6.5	GKC §113h, 113cc □ Berg		216n; Berg 1.152a, 2.115a
	2.66k	8.13	GKC §63o
6.7	GKC §74b, 96 (p. 283); J-M	8.16	GKC §123e; IBHS 119 n 12
	§98d □ Berg 2.156b	8.19	GKC §49e □ Berg 2.23f, 2.123c
6.8	Jen §8.3.4.2	8.23	Berg 1.67u
6.9	Dav §108R1; GKC §133k n 1,	8.24	GKC §45g; IBHS 667 □ B-L
	144e; J-M §155d, 176h; Gib 13		210f; Berg 1.122t
	□ B-L 113p'; Brock §37, 49a	8.26	IBHS 667; Gib 141
6.13	Dav §26	9.2	J-M §177l
6.14	J-M §142ba □ B-L 603g	9.6	Dav §113; GKC §145s; IBHS 314; Gib 21

B-L: Bauer and Leander, *Historische Grammatik*   **B-M**: Beer, *Grammatik*   **Berg**: Bergsträsser, *Grammatik*
Brock: Brockelmann, *Syntax*   **Dav**: Davidson, *Syntax*   **GAHG**: Richter, *Grammatik*
Gib: Gibson, *Davidson's Syntax, 4th ed.*   **GKC**: *Gesenius' Grammar*   **IBHS**: Waltke and O'Connor, *Syntax*
Jen: Jenni, *Lehrbuch*   **J-M**: Joüon and Muraoka, *Grammar*   **Ros**: Rosenthal, *Grammar*
Sch: Schneider, *Grammatik*   **Wms**: Williams, *Syntax*

9.10	Dav §130R5; GKC §5n, 102i; J-M §103c; Gib 155 □ B-L 79s, 638y; Berg 1.5l	10.34	B-L 135h, 363h
		10.35–36	Berg 2.32e
9.11	Dav §101Rd	10.35	GKC §5n; J-M §33, 118b, 118n □ B-L 79s; Berg 1.5l, 2.145e
9.13	Dav §9R2; J-M §158e, 158g9, 58 ; Gib 9, 58 □ B-L 636g; Brock §152a	10.36	GKC §91e, 118f; J-M §9c n 1 □ B-L 79s, 403; Berg 1.5l, 1.124w, 2.145d, 2.146e
9.14	Dav §136; GKC §145u, 162b; J-M §150k, 167b n 1; Gib 37	11.1	GKC §118x; Wms §261; J-M §146a n 4 □ Berg 2.172 n e
9.15–23	Berg 2.32d	11.2	Gib 175
9.15–16	GKC §115a	11.3	Berg 1.107e
9.15	Dav §91R1; GKC §107b; J-M §137h; IBHS 462; Gib 130 □ Berg 2.56f; Brock §31a	11.4	Dav §135; GKC §35d, 151a n 3; J-M §88Jb, 125q, 163d; IBHS 91, 167; Gib 175, 186 □ B-L 263f, 563x; B-M 3.90; Berg 1.91d; Brock §9
9.16	J-M §111i, 113a, 113f		
9.17–18	GKC §107e		
9.17	J-M §113f, 129q		
9.18	Dav §25; GKC §130c; J-M §129q; Wms §489; IBHS 503; Gib 12, 73 □ Brock §162	11.5	GKC §106g, 107e; J-M §112a, 123l; Wms §163; IBHS 464; Gib 73 □ Jen §24.3.3.2; Berg 1.136e, 2.28g, 2.31d; Brock §17, 42d
9.19ff.	GKC §112e	11.6	Wms §557; IBHS 672 n 103 □ B-L 135h
9.20–21	GKC §107b, 107e		
9.20	Dav §29d; GKC §131e; J-M §131f; Wms §69, 477; Gib 41 □ Brock §62e	11.7	GKC §93h □ B-L 573x; B-M 1.117;
9.21	J-M §119u; Wms §477	11.8	Dav §54R1; GKC §112h; J-M §125w; IBHS 175; Gib 177 □ Berg 2.44l, 2.44m, 2.172 n e
10.2	Dav §91R3; GKC §45e, 115d; J-M §49e; Gib 128 □ B-L 367, 376r; Berg 2.83p(bis)		
		11.9	GKC §107e; Gib 73
10.3	GKC §145c	11.10	GKC §117h; J-M §126b, 126h; Wms §57; IBHS 170 n 14, 172; Gib 144 □ GAHG 3.102 n 285, 3.102 n 289; Brock §107a, 107iα
10.4	Dav §38R5; GKC §134r n 1; Gib 51		
10.7	Dav §91R1; Gib 130		
10.9	Berg 2.132a*, 2.148k, 2.150n	11.11	GKC §23f, 74k; Wms §198 □ B-L 375; Berg 1.45e, 2.138l, 2.158d
10.11	GKC §111f		
10.17	GKC §112e, 112kk □ Berg 2.44k		
		11.12	Dav §22e, 124; GKC §44d, 69s, 107u, 122f n 1, 126o; J-M §113c n 3; Gib 28, 184 □ Berg 2.78e, 2.122c
10.21–22	Berg 2.42g*		
10.25	Dav §100R5; GKC §117n; J-M §126b; IBHS 171 n 18; Gib 138□ Berg 2.42g*		
		11.13	Dav §101 n 1(p. 143); Wms §288; Gib 185 □ Brock §135c
10.28	B-L 547		
10.29	GKC §138b; J-M §154fd, 158i; Wms §463 □ B-M 3.99; Brock §152c	11.14	GKC §133c; J-M §141i; Wms §318
10.30	Gib 174	11.15	Dav §65R3, 86c; GKC §32g, 113r; J-M §39a n 4, 39a n 5, 116j, 123ja; Wms §205; Gib 125 □ B-L 77l, 248e; B-M 2.8, 3.63; GAHG 2.34 n 143, 2.65 n 276, 3.168 n 506; Berg 2.64g
10.31	GKC §141d, 158b n 1; J-M §170h n 1		
10.32	Berg 2.42g*		
10.33	Gib 33		

B-L: Bauer and Leander, *Historische Grammatik*   **B-M**: Beer, *Grammatik*   **Berg**: Bergsträsser, *Grammatik*
Brock: Brockelmann, *Syntax*   **Dav**: Davidson, *Syntax*   **GAHG**: Richter, *Grammatik*
Gib: Gibson, *Davidson's Syntax, 4th ed.*   **GKC**: *Gesenius' Grammar*   **IBHS**: Waltke and O'Connor, *Syntax*
Jen: Jenni, *Lehrbuch*   **J-M**: Joüon and Muraoka, *Grammar*   **Ros**: Rosenthal, *Grammar*
Sch: Schneider, *Grammatik*   **Wms**: Williams, *Syntax*

11.16	GKC §48k, 63l; J-M §48d, 133d; Gib 52 □ B-L 347g; B-M 2.129; ; Berg 2.81i, 2.114k; Brock §152c
11.17	Dav §101Ra; GKC §119m; Wms §251 □ Berg 2.173 n h
11.18	J-M §152d □ Berg 2.144b
11.19	IBHS 517 n 61 □ Berg 2.20b
11.20–21	GKC §131d
11.20	Dav §29d, 147; GKC §80h, 111q; J-M §112i n 5, 170f, 170n; Wms §363; IBHS 640; Gib 41, 158 □ B-L 511x; B-M 3.106; Jen §20.3.3
11.22	Dav §81R3; J-M §128b, 152f, 161k; Wms §58 □ GAHG 3.121 n 330; Brock §98a
11.25	Dav §32R2; GKC §23d, 68f, 68i, 72q, 120d n 2, 126x; J-M §80k; IBHS 262; Gib 44 □ B-L 371t, 399h″; Berg 2.80 n h, 2.120 n d, 2.145d, 2.173 n h; Brock §85d
11.26	Dav §38R1; J-M §142m
11.27	GKC §126r; J-M §137n, 154fc; IBHS 243; Gib 137 □ Brock §21bβ
11.28	J-M §136h; IBHS 121 □ B-M 2.58; Berg 2.159g
11.29	Dav §100b, 135R3; GKC §151b, 154b; J-M §163d; Wms §547; Gib 136, 186 □ Brock §9
11.30	J-M §47b □ Berg 2.91g
11.31	Berg 2.135d; Brock §109a
11.32	Dav §86c; GKC §113r; J-M §123l, 139g n 1; Wms §206; IBHS 588; Gib 125 □ Berg 2.64g
11.33	Dav §44R3; J-M §125r □ Brock §93k
11.35	Brock §50e; Gib 73
12.1–2	Wms §230
12.1	Dav §114; GKC §146g; J-M §150q; Gib 22 □ B-M 3.22
12.2	Dav §153; GKC §133k n 1, 153; Wms §390; IBHS 669 n 91; Gib 39 □ Berg 2.95d; Brock §106a
12.4	Dav §36R4; GKC §97i; Gib 48 □ GAHG 2.26 n 103; Brock §130a
12.6	Dav §3R2; GKC §128d, 147e □ B-M 2.140; Brock §80d
12.7	GAHG 3.175 n 582
12.8	Dav §22R3, 140; J-M §126f, 177m; Gib 29 □ B-L 443i; GAHG 2.49 n 228, 3.151 n 413; Berg 1.106c; Brock §103b
12.11	B-M 3.48; GAHG 3.216 n 815; Berg 2.48g, 2.128g
12.12	Dav §51R4; GKC §143d □ B-L 77l; Berg 2.48g
12.13	GKC §105b n 1 (p. 308); J-M §125k n 1; IBHS 184; Gib 118 □ B-L 376r; Brock §107c
12.14	Dav §132R2, 136R1; GKC §154b, 159h; J-M §123g, 167b; IBHS 587; Gib 156□ Berg 2.63d, 2.174 n h
13.2	Dav §38R4; GKC §123d, 134q; J-M §142p; IBHS 288; Gib 51
13.3	Sch §45.3.2
13.4–15	Brock §128
13.13	Dav §117
13.16	IBHS 131
13.17–18	IBHS 529
13.17	Wms §118 □ Sch §13.3.2, 51.3.2
13.18	Dav §126R1; GKC §150i; J-M §161f, 161g; Wms §544 □ B-M 3.95; Sch §13.3.2, 51.3.2; Brock §169c
13.19	GKC §100l; Gib 52 □ B-L 640f′; Berg 1.68v
13.20	Dav §124; GKC §152k; J-M §160h, 160j □ GAHG 3.174 n 576; Jen §10.4.9; Berg 1.68v
13.21	GKC §102f □ B-L 510v, 638u; Berg 2.57 n k
13.22	IBHS 135
13.23	J-M §133c
13.27–28	IBHS 672 □ B-M 3.91;
13.27	GKC §20d, 118f, 138c; J-M §154fb, 158j; Gib 10 □ Berg 1.66s; Brock §152d
13.28	Dav §154; J-M §121m, 173a; Wms §558; IBHS 261; Gib 43, 176 □ B-M 3.18;
13.29	IBHS 134
13.30	IBHS 683 □ Berg 2.165k; Brock §107c

B-L: Bauer and Leander, *Historische Grammatik* **B-M**: Beer, *Grammatik* **Berg**: Bergsträsser, *Grammatik*
Brock: Brockelmann, *Syntax* **Dav**: Davidson, *Syntax* **GAHG**: Richter, *Grammatik*
Gib: Gibson, *Davidson's Syntax, 4th ed.* **GKC**: *Gesenius' Grammar* **IBHS**: Waltke and O'Connor, *Syntax*
Jen: Jenni, *Lehrbuch* **J-M**: Joüon and Muraoka, *Grammar* **Ros**: Rosenthal, *Grammar*
Sch: Schneider, *Grammatik* **Wms**: Williams, *Syntax*

13.32	GKC §72l, 124q; J-M §136o, 154i; IBHS 299 □ B-L 398e"; Berg 2.145e; Brock §106i	14.24	Dav §56; GKC §112nn, 119gg, 158b; J-M §170g; Wms §534; IBHS 219; Gib 10, 88, 159 □ B-M 3.106; Brock §145bε
13.33	Berg 2.164g		
14.1	Gib 3	14.25	Berg 2.122c; Brock §107f
14.2	Dav §39d, 134; GKC §106p, 151e; J-M §163c; Wms §166, 460, 548; IBHS 494, 680; Gib 69, 186 □ B-M 3.117; GAHG 3.179 n 618; Sch §51.4.3; Berg 2.146f(bis); Brock §8b	14.27	Dav §9R2; GKC §72ee; J-M §149a
		14.28	Brock §170c; Gib 77, 186, 187
		14.29	Berg 2.148k
		14.31	Dav §56; GKC §76h; IBHS 529; Gib 77, 88, 91, 182 □ B-L 445p; Berg 2.147 n k, 2.151q
14.3	Dav §141R3; GKC §28a; IBHS 133; Gib 168 □ B-L 559k; Berg 2.54d, 2.123c	14.32	Dav §1; GKC §135f; J-M §112a n 5, 146d; IBHS 299; Gib 2, 77
14.4	Berg 2.53q		
14.6	GKC §45e	14.33	GKC §91l, 141i; J-M §94j, 121f n 1 □ B-L 253b', 606k
14.7	Dav §34; GKC §133k; Gib 45, 53 □ Brock §129b	14.34	GKC §123d; Wms §15 □ B-L 441c
14.8	Dav §9R2; J-M §158e; IBHS 531 □ Berg 2.40d	14.35	Dav §115; GKC §67g; J-M §148a; Gib 22 □ B-M 2.144
14.9	GKC §153; IBHS 135, 195, 366, 373; Gib 176	14.36–37	GKC §111h, 111q; Gib 97
14.10	Berg 2.84q	14.36	GKC §114o; Gib 101 □ Berg 2.27d, 2.151q
14.11	Wms §242; IBHS 197 n 28, 329; Gib 150, 185 □ Berg 2.115a	14.37	Dav §32R2; GKC §126z; J-M §126a; IBHS 262; Gib 44 □ Brock §103a
14.12	IBHS 654		
14.13	Berg 2.167o	14.40	Dav §56; GKC §58k, 138b; J-M §158i; Gib 59, 88
14.14	Brock §152a		
14.15	Dav §132a; Gib 156 □ Berg 2.148k	14.41	Dav §1R2; GKC §135p; J-M §152b, 152c; IBHS 110
14.16	Dav §96R1; GKC §69n, 111h, 114ε; J-M §124h, 160l n 1, 170i; Gib 97, 132 □ B-L 382; B-M 2.140; Berg 2.56h, 2.83p, 2.128e; Brock §176a	14.42	J-M §113m; GKC §152l; IBHS 661; Gib 57, 107
		14.43	GKC §158b n 1; J-M §170h n 1 □ Brock §17
14.17	GKC §5n □ GAHG 3.170 n 522, 3.216 n 815	14.45	GKC §67y; J-M §82h n 3, 82i □ Berg 2.104 n h, 2.139p
14.18	Gib 55	15.4	Dav §29a, 38R6; IBHS 287, 288; Gib 41
14.20	Gib 61		
14.21	Dav §81R2, 119, 146R4; GKC §121e, 167b; J-M §128c n 1; Gib 118, 174, 186 □ B-L 204w; GAHG 3.120 n 330	15.5	IBHS 287
		15.6	B-L 629a'
		15.8	GKC §111g
		15.13	GKC §127b
14.22	J-M §143a; IBHS 311; Gib 51 □ Brock §23a	15.15	GKC §161c; IBHS 642 □ GAHG 3.77 n 202
		15.16	GKC §134d
14.23	GKC §64e; Gib 187 □ Berg 2.115a	15.18	GKC §111g
		15.21	Berg 1.72g
		15.23	Brock §106k

B-L: Bauer and Leander, *Historische Grammatik*   **B-M**: Beer, *Grammatik*   **Berg**: Bergsträsser, *Grammatik*
Brock: Brockelmann, *Syntax*   **Dav**: Davidson, *Syntax*   **GAHG**: Richter, *Grammatik*
Gib: Gibson, *Davidson's Syntax, 4th ed.*   **GKC**: Gesenius' *Grammar*   **IBHS**: Waltke and O'Connor, *Syntax*
Jen: Jenni, *Lehrbuch*   **J-M**: Joüon and Muraoka, *Grammar*   **Ros**: Rosenthal, *Grammar*
Sch: Schneider, *Grammatik*   **Wms**: Williams, *Syntax*

15.24	GKC §119w; Gib 154 □ B-L 613d'; Berg 2.44i, 2.111b*	16.29	Dav §81R2, 109, 127a, 130R4; GKC §47m, 121b, 152z, 159c n 2, 159q; J-M §125q, 125q n 2, 133i, 155m, 160e; IBHS 167; Gib 119 □ B-M 2.151; Berg 2.145d
15.28	GKC §91e; J-M §94h □ B-L 584z'		
15.29	GKC §143c, 145u; J-M §150k		
15.31	GKC §51k, 91e; J-M §51b, 94h □ B-L 323b', 538i; Berg 2.92i		
15.32	J-M §111i □ GAHG 3.102 n 288	16.30	J-M §126a
15.33	J-M §121i n 1 □ GAHG 3.102 n 289	16.31	IBHS 363 □ Berg 2.117a
		16.32	Dav §51R5; GKC §117e; J-M §125f □ B-M 3.74
15.34	IBHS 420	16.34	Gib 160
15.35	Dav §88R5; GKC §113h, 113gg; J-M §123r, 123y; Wms §209; IBHS 582, 589; Gib 127 □ Berg 2.62b, 2.66k, 2.139o; Brock §45	16.35	Dav §37R5; GKC §134k; J-M §146a n 4; IBHS 283 n 23; Gib 48
		17.2–3	Wms §59
15.40	Dav §53c; GKC §112p; Gib 93	17.2	B-M 1.90; Berg 2.77c
16.3	J-M §149a; GKC §135p; Gib 54□ GAHG 2.33 n 139	17.3	J-M §125w, 141d; Gib 182
		17.5	Dav §9R2, 149; GKC §107q; J-M §168d; Wms §367, 524; Gib 160 □ GAHG 3.77 n 203
16.5	Dav §57R1; Gib 87	·	
16.6	J-M §119l, 155o n 2		
16.7	J-M §119l, 158f, 158h; IBHS 131 n 16, 297; Gib 1	17.6	GKC §72w □ Berg 2.148k
		17.10	GKC §67t, 72dd □ B-L 404; Berg 2.140 n q
16.9	Dav §34R2; Gib 46		
16.10	GKC §112cc; J-M §119t □ Berg 2.41g	17.11	GKC §126r
		17.12	IBHS 678
16.11	Dav §150; GKC §166b; J-M §169e; Wms §527; IBHS 221; Gib 160, 182 □ B-M 3.104; GAHG 3.177 n 603; Berg 2.151q	17.13	GKC §65e □ B-L 207i, 353v; Berg 1.153c
		17.14	Gib 49
		17.15	J-M §166j □ Berg 2.113f
		17.17	GKC §139c; Gib 14
16.13	Dav §86c; GKC §54e, 113r, 115c; J-M §123l, 123p; IBHS 425, 582, 586; Gib 124, 125 □ Berg 2.64g	17.18	GKC §134q
		17.19	Berg 2.151q
		17.20	GKC §72ee; Gib 182 □ Berg 2.138l
16.14	GKC §152z; Wms §384 □ GAHG 3.173 n 548; Berg 2.148k	17.21	GKC §123d
		17.23	GKC §29f □ B-L 404, 443i; Berg 1.71e, 2.149m
16.15	Dav §72R4; GKC §96 (p. 283), 117d; J-M §125h; Gib 46, 116 □ B-M 2.157, 3.74; Berg 2.48g, 2.163f	17.25	GKC §128v; IBHS 149 n 27 □ Berg 2.45 n a, 2.164i
		17.27	Dav §41a; GKC §106n; J-M §112g; Wms §165; IBHS 490; Gib 59
16.17	J-M §119l		
16.22	GKC §100m, 129c, 150m	17.28	Dav §41a, 126R2; GKC §67e, 67dd, 106n, 150g n 1; J-M §82j, 112j □ B-L 215h, 439p'; B-M 2.145; Berg 2.29h, 2.59n*, 2.118b, 2.134c
16.26	J-M §105c, 114m; GKC §110d □ Berg 2.48f		
16.27	GKC §118p; J-M §126b, 159a □ Brock §130a		
		18.2	IBHS 195
16.28	J-M §155m □ Berg 2.20b	18.3	Dav §136; 109; GKC §109g; Gib 37

B-L: Bauer and Leander, *Historische Grammatik*   **B-M**: Beer, *Grammatik*   **Berg**: Bergsträsser, *Grammatik*
Brock: Brockelmann, *Syntax*   **Dav**: Davidson, *Syntax*   **GAHG**: Richter, *Grammatik*
Gib: Gibson, *Davidson's Syntax, 4th ed.*   **GKC**: *Gesenius' Grammar*   **IBHS**: Waltke and O'Connor, *Syntax*
Jen: Jenni, *Lehrbuch*   **J-M**: Joüon and Muraoka, *Grammar*   **Ros**: Rosenthal, *Grammar*
Sch: Schneider, *Grammatik*   **Wms**: Williams, *Syntax*

18.5	GKC §109g □ GAHG 3.175 n 584
18.6	IBHS 300 n 39 □ GAHG 3.203 n 766
18.8	GKC §143e □ GAHG 3.203 n 766
18.10	J-M §133c
18.12	IBHS 271 n 30
18.16	IBHS 134
18.17	J-M §135b n 3
18.20	Berg 1.160a
18.21	GAHG 3.203 n 766
18.23	Gib 2
18.24	IBHS 666
18.26	GKC §72i; J-M §133c □ Berg 2.44i, 2.150n
18.29	B-L 547; Jen §15.4; Berg 1.119o
18.30	Berg 2.43i, 2.43i*
19.6	Berg 1.147d
19.7	Dav §111
19.11	IBHS 535 □ Berg 2.41g
19.12	GKC §74b □ B-M 2.156; Berg 2.156b
19.13	IBHS 374 n 30 □ B-L 287n'; B-M 2.16; Berg 2.87c
19.14	IBHS 74 □ B-L 108g'
19.16	J-M §129i
19.18	Gib 63 □ Berg 2.28g
19.19	IBHS 412
19.20	GKC §74b, IBHS 374 n 30 □ B-L 287n'; Berg 2.87c
20.1	Jen §11.1
20.3–4	GKC §115f
20.3	Dav §134, 136R1; GKC §65a, 151e, 154b; J-M §70d, 163c, 177m; Gib 186 □ B-L 359j; GAHG 3.179 n 618; Berg 2.118b
20.4	IBHS 610; Gib 184 □ B-M 3.60; Brock §45
20.5	Dav §127b; GKC §59a, 114l, 114l n 5, 128a, 152a n 1, 152a n 1k; J-M §62a n 2 □ B-L 342t'; GAHG 3.173 n 562; Berg 2.18f, 2.57l
20.8	Dav §114; GKC §49k; J-M §43b; Gib 22 □ B-L 374m; Berg 2.17d
20.10	GKC §110d; J-M §105c, 114m, 161b; Gib 22 □ Berg 1.132e

20.11	Dav §115; J-M §124t; Gib 22
20.12	Dav §147; GKC §158b; J-M §170f, 170o; Wms §353, 489, 534; Gib 158 □ B-M 3.106; GAHG 3.173 n 549; Jen §13.4.3; Berg 2.54c, 2.112c; Brock §145bβ
20.13	GKC §138c; J-M §158j
20.14ff.	Sch §54.1.1.2
20.17	GKC §107l, 108c; J-M §105c, 112i n 5, 114f; Gib 77 □ B-L 274m, 535f; Berg 2.47e, 2.113f; Brock §6b, 89
20.18	GKC §152w; J-M §168g
20.19	J-M §114c; IBHS 574 □ B-L 637s; GAHG 3.215 n 812; Berg 2.113f
20.20	GKC §122i; J-M §134g; IBHS 104
20.21	GKC §66i, 114c, 157b n 2; J-M §72i, 124c; IBHS 602 □ B-M 2.136; Berg 2.54d*, 2.55d*, 2.115a, 2.123d
20.24	J-M §114o n 2 □ B-M 2.129
20.26	Dav §75; J-M §119l; IBHS 176 n 25; Gib 112
20.28	Dav §75; IBHS 176 n 25; Gib 112
20.29	B-M 2.148
21.1	GKC §51n, 75q □ B-L 321k; Berg 2.162f
21.2	Dav §130R3; GKC §113o; J-M §123g; Gib 154, 155 □ Brock §164bγ
21.3	GKC §157b n 2
21.4	GKC §45g, 67cc; J-M §82k □ B-L 210f; Berg 1.122t, 2.133b
21.5	GKC §59a; J-M §62a n 2; Gib 57 □ B-L 342t'; Berg 2.18f
21.6–9	IBHS 410 n 37
21.6	GKC §126r; J-M §137o □ Brock §106h
21.7	Gib 22, 107
21.8	Dav §56c; GKC §127b; Gib 95, 135, 157, 181 □ Berg 2.41e, 2.42g*, 2.69c

B-L: Bauer and Leander, *Historische Grammatik* **B-M**: Beer, *Grammatik* **Berg**: Bergsträsser, *Grammatik*
Brock: Brockelmann, *Syntax* **Dav**: Davidson, *Syntax* **GAHG**: Richter, *Grammatik*
Gib: Gibson, *Davidson's Syntax, 4th ed.* **GKC**: *Gesenius' Grammar* **IBHS**: Waltke and O'Connor, *Syntax*
Jen: Jenni, *Lehrbuch* **J-M**: Joüon and Muraoka, *Grammar* **Ros**: Rosenthal, *Grammar*
Sch: Schneider, *Grammatik* **Wms**: Williams, *Syntax*

21.9	Dav §54b, 57, 72R4, 130b; GKC §117d, 159o, 164d, 112ee, 112gg, 126r; J-M §125h, 137m, 167e, 167g; IBHS 181; Gib 116, 154 □ Berg 2.42g*; Brock §164bβ
21.14	GKC §127f; J-M §129u; IBHS 384
21.15	GKC §112pp □ Berg 2.125b
21.17	GKC §63l, 107c; J-M §68a n 1; Wms §177; Gib 72 □ Berg 1.156l, 2.33g, 2.114i
21.20	GKC §112ss
21.22	J-M §114c; Gib 82 □ Berg 2.47e, 2.113f; Brock §6d
21.23	GKC §157b n 2; J-M §125ba n 3 □ B-L 321k; B-M 2.118; Berg 2.91g; Brock §94b
21.24	B-L 442e; B-M 2.139; Berg 2.127e
21.26	Dav §48c; Gib 101
21.27	GKC §54c, 75hh; IBHS 360 n 30 □ B-L 198g, 403; B-M 1.108; Berg 1.109 n c, 2.99 n d
21.30	GKC §5n, 67g, 69r, 76f □ B-L 79s, 337n, 439p', 443k; B-M 2.140; Berg 2.23g, 2.127 n e, 2.139 n o
21.32	Berg 2.129h
21.34	Berg 2.53q
21.35	GKC §164d; J-M §54c, 54c n 3, 160l n 1 □ Berg 2.56h, 2.106 n l; Brock §52b*
22.1	GKC §125h
22.2	Gib 66
22.4	J-M §130q □ Brock §23d, 39bα
22.5	GAHG 3.106; Brock §119a
22.6	Dav §53R1, 83R1; GKC §20c, 53u, 67o, 120c, 138e; J-M §18i, 48d, 82l, 133d, 145a, 158m; Wms §271, 463; IBHS 75, 334, 375 n 32 □ B-L 286m', 357, 435 n 1; B-M 2.145; GAHG 3.185 n 656, 3.215 n 815; Berg 1.66s, 2.53p, 2.88c, 2.139 n p; Brock §106h, 143a, 152e
22.8	J-M §119m □ B-L 113p'; Brock §97c
22.9	GKC §137a □ B-L 113p'; B-M 3.116; Brock §82d
22.10	B-L 113p'
22.11	Dav §50b, 53b, 67o, 91b, 111u; J-M §82l; IBHS 561; Gib 91, 93, 97 □ B-L 438; Berg 2.53p, 2.139 n p; Brock §123f
22.12	GKC §103c □ B-L 644b"
22.13	Dav §91R4; GKC §69x, 115c; J-M §65a; Gib 63, 129
22.14	Berg 2.54d*
22.15	Wms §226 □ B-L 114q', 548z; Berg 1.139b
22.17	GKC §67o; J-M §82l □ B-L 113p', 438; Berg 2.139 n p
22.18	Dav §29d; J-M §167f, 171d; Gib 17, 41 □ B-M 3.105; Brock §164bγ
22.19	Dav §63R3; GKC §109d, 109i; J-M §65f; Gib 82 □ GAHG 3.170 n 522, 3.215 n 815; Berg 2.79h
22.20	GKC §114g; J-M §155r; Gib 154, 182 □ Berg 2.57k
22.21	Dav §50b
22.22	Dav §50b
22.23	Dav §91R4; IBHS 436 n 11 □ GAHG 3.102 n 289; Brock §89
22.24	Brock §23b
22.25	Dav §91R4; GKC §115c
22.26	Berg 2.57l, 2.84q
22.27	J-M §137m; Gib 27
22.28	Dav §38R5; GKC §134r; J-M §142q, 143a; IBHS 287 n 30; Gib 6 □ Brock §23a, 88
22.29	Dav §131; GKC §151e n 1, 159ee; J-M §167k, 167k n 1, 167s; Wms §548; IBHS 638; Gib 155 □ B-M 3.116; GAHG 3.173 n 556, 3.175 n 579, 3.178 n 618; Brock §165b
22.30	Dav §86a; GKC §138d; J-M §158n; Gib 4, 9, 124 □ Brock §153a
22.31	GAHG 3.102 n 289; Berg 2.164i
22.32	Dav §38R5; GKC §134r, 137b; IBHS 287 n 30, 325; Gib 184 □ Brock §88

B-L: Bauer and Leander, *Historische Grammatik*   **B-M**: Beer, *Grammatik*   **Berg**: Bergsträsser, *Grammatik*
Brock: Brockelmann, *Syntax*   **Dav**: Davidson, *Syntax*   **GAHG**: Richter, *Grammatik*
Gib: Gibson, *Davidson's Syntax, 4th ed.*   **GKC**: *Gesenius' Grammar*   **IBHS**: Waltke and O'Connor, *Syntax*
Jen: Jenni, *Lehrbuch*   **J-M**: Joüon and Muraoka, *Grammar*   **Ros**: Rosenthal, *Grammar*
Sch: Schneider, *Grammatik*   **Wms**: Williams, *Syntax*

B-L: Bauer and Leander, *Historische Grammatik*   **B-M**: Beer, *Grammatik*   **Berg**: Bergsträsser, *Grammatik*
Brock: Brockelmann, *Syntax*   **Dav**: Davidson, *Syntax*   **GAHG**: Richter, *Grammatik*
Gib: Gibson, *Davidson's Syntax, 4th ed.*   **GKC**: *Gesenius' Grammar*   **IBHS**: Waltke and O'Connor, *Syntax*
Jen: Jenni, *Lehrbuch*   **J-M**: Joüon and Muraoka, *Grammar*   **Ros**: Rosenthal, *Grammar*
Sch: Schneider, *Grammatik*   **Wms**: Williams, *Syntax*

24.9	Dav §116R1; J-M §137i; Wms §580; Gib 23 □ Berg 1.124w, 2.35i; Brock §28bγ, 133a	26.10	Dav §51R5; GKC §63i, J-M §125h □ B-L 197n', 348h; Berg 2.114i
24.10	GKC §113r; J-M §143a □ Berg 2.64g; Brock §23a	26.14	GKC §97f
		26.15–21	Jen §6.1
24.11	Brock §107f	26.22	Gib 49
24.13	Gib 17	26.23	Berg 1.93h
24.14	GAHG 3.100, 3.204 n 772; Jen §8.3.2.2; Berg 2.53p	26.35	Gib 39
		26.53ff.	GKC §121b
24.15	GKC §90o, 96 (p. 285); J-M §93r □ B-L 618j	26.53	J-M §133c; Gib 150
		26.54	GKC §139c; J-M §141g, 147d; IBHS 264 □ Berg 2.87c
24.16	Dav §97R1		
24.17	Dav §51R2; GKC §55f; IBHS 490, 518; Gib 68, 102, 140 □ Berg 2.44l, 2.108 n c	26.55	Dav §81R3; J-M §128b
		26.56	Brock §110l
		26.59	Dav §108R1; GKC §144d; J-M §155b n 1, 155e n 1; Gib 13 □ B-M 3.22
24.19	Dav §65R6 □ Berg 2.162f		
24.20	IBHS 271; Gib 46		
24.21	GKC §73f □ B-L 405; Berg 2.151s	26.60	GKC §121b; J-M §128b □ GAHG 3.122 n 332
24.22	GKC §29f, 114k n 2; IBHS 326 □ B-L 184k'; B-M 1.77; Berg 1.60d, 1.71e, 2.59o, 2.115a	26.62	GKC §54l; J-M §53g; IBHS 360 n 28 □ Berg 2.100i
		26.63	GKC §125h
24.23	Dav §91a; GKC §115k; Gib 129	27.3	J-M §155nd
24.24	GKC §2b, 93y □ B-L 13d; Berg 1.102n	27.4	GKC §65e □ Jen §10.3.4; Berg 1.66s, 2.117a
25.1	Berg 2.138l; Brock §108a	27.7	Dav §1R3; GKC §135o; Gib 3
25.2	GKC §47l □ B-L 303c'; Berg 2.19a, 2.157c	27.8	Gib 155 □ Jen §10.3.4; Berg 2.112c
25.3	GKC §51n; IBHS 391; Gib 34 □ B-L 321k; Berg 2.92g	27.9	Gib 57 □ B-M 3.114; Berg 2.43i*
25.4	J-M §168a n 1; Gib 107 □ Berg 2.174 n h; Brock §135c	27.10	Berg 2.43i*
		27.11	Berg 2.77c
25.6	GKC §126r	27.13	Berg 2.15a
25.8	J-M §166j □ B-L 208t, 600i'; Berg 1.126 n bb; Brock §116c	27.14	J-M §170k; Wms §260, 534 □ Berg 2.54c
25.11	GKC §117r □ B-L 376r; Berg 2.158e, 2.167o	27.16	Dav §10R2; GKC §129c; Gib 36
25.12	GKC §5n, 128d, 131r n 4 □ GAHG 3.177 n 602; Berg 1.5l	27.19	GKC §63o □ Berg 2.15a
		27.20	IBHS 216 n 105, 606 □ Jen §10.3.1.3
25.13	J-M §170g; Wms §353, 534; IBHS 220 n 118		
		27.24	Dav §28R5
25.14	Dav §28R5; Gib 35	28.4	GKC §126z, 134l; J-M §142m
25.17	GKC §113bb; J-M §123u □ Berg 2.132a*	28.5	IBHS 287
		28.6	GKC §128p
25.18	GKC §117n □ Berg 2.71 n f	28.7	GAHG 3.121 n 330
26.3	GKC §125h	28.10	Wms §292
26.9	IBHS 127 □ B-L 525h; Berg 1.132f	28.11	GKC §132g n 1
		28.14	IBHS 132 n 17
		28.19	GKC §134c; J-M §142d n 1
		28.26	J-M §14c n 3 □ B-L 240t', 539i; B-M 2.58; Berg 1.127cc

B-L: Bauer and Leander, *Historische Grammatik* **B-M**: Beer, *Grammatik* **Berg**: Bergsträsser, *Grammatik*
Brock: Brockelmann, *Syntax* **Dav**: Davidson, *Syntax* **GAHG**: Richter, *Grammatik*
Gib: Gibson, *Davidson's Syntax, 4th ed.* **GKC**: *Gesenius' Grammar* **IBHS**: Waltke and O'Connor, *Syntax*
Jen: Jenni, *Lehrbuch* **J-M**: Joüon and Muraoka, *Grammar* **Ros**: Rosenthal, *Grammar*
Sch: Schneider, *Grammatik* **Wms**: Williams, *Syntax*

28.31	Wms §42	31.47	B-M 1.76
29.6	Dav §24R4; Gib 34	31.49–50	IBHS 556
29.14	Gib 49	31.49	GKC §127a □ B-L 441c
29.15	GKC §5n; Gib 49 □ B-L 79s	31.50	J-M §118o □ Berg 1.136e
29.26	Gib 47	31.52	J-M §129b
29.33	GKC §91k	31.54	GKC §128a; J-M §129b □
29.39	GKC §93m □ B-L 581; Berg		GAHG 2.67 n 285
	1.122t	32.5	Dav §81R3; GKC §121b; J-M
30.2	Dav §28R5; IBHS 308; Gib 5,		§128b; Wms §159 □ GAHG
	36		3.120 n 330; Brock §35d
30.3	Dav §88R1; GKC §65e, 113z;	32.6	GKC §150m; IBHS 314
	J-M §82i, 123x; Wms §209;	32.7	B-L 79t
	IBHS 596; Gib 127, 155 □ B-L	32.8	J-M §70d □ Jen §15.7.5; Berg
	348h, 362a'; B-M 2.132, 2.143;		2.82n
	Berg 2.67m, 2.114i, 2.118b,	32.9	Berg 2.59n
	2.139o	32.10	IBHS 314 □ B-L 131
30.4	J-M §126h; GKC §93k; IBHS	32.11	B-L 375
	170 n 15; Gib 155	32.14	GKC §69h n 1, 118q; Wms
30.5	GKC §91k □ B-L 533f		§303; IBHS 194; Gib 145 □ B-L
30.6	Dav §130b □ B-L 533f		379q; Berg 2.127 n e, 2.171 n d
30.8	GKC §91k	32.15	GKC §117n; Gib 118 □ GAHG
30.9	Dav §130b □ B-L 445p; Berg		3.171 n 534; Brock §31a
	2.137k	32.17	Dav §145; GKC §106o; GKC
30.10	GKC §93k		§72p; J-M §112i; Wms §457;
30.11	B-L 217a		Gib 158 □ Berg 2.146 n g,
30.12	Dav §41R3; GKC §112kk		2.148k
30.13	B-M 3.147; Berg 2.137k, 2.138l	32.19	Wms §323 □ Brock §120b
30.14	Berg 2.138l	32.20	GKC §159c n 2, 167b
30.15	GKC §112ff; J-M §176d □	32.22	Wms §323
	Brock §108a	32.23	Dav §130R4; GKC §47m, 110i;
30.17	IBHS 200		159c n 2, 159q; Gib 111, 153 □
31.2	B-L 77m, Berg 1.3i		B-M 3.114; Berg 2.50k, 2.125c
31.3	IBHS 143	32.24	J-M §113m □ B-L 588l; Berg
31.4	GKC §123d; J-M §137o, 142p;		1.100 n k
	IBHS 288	32.25	Berg 2.71g
31.5	B-L 72b	32.29	IBHS 526
31.8	Wms §95, 292; IBHS 277	32.30	GKC §68i; J-M §73f □ B-L
31.13	Dav §114; Gib 22 □ B-M 3.22		371v, 583w'; B-M 2.137; Berg
31.15	Dav §73R7; J-M §161b		2.121d
31.16	B-L 72b	32.32	GKC §32d □ B-L 248h; Jen
31.19	B-L 578l'		§8.4.2
31.23–24	Berg 2.51m	32.33	GKC §131n; J-M §146e; Gib
31.23	GKC §74b		181 □ Brock §68b
31.28	Dav §35R1; GKC §72w, 134d;	32.38	B-M 2.147; Berg 2.138n
	J-M §80m, 134k □ Berg 2.150n	32.41	B-M 3.76
31.30	J-M §121m	32.42	GKC §91e; 103g; J-M §25a,
31.32	Gib 49		103f □ B-L 640f'; Berg 1.95e
31.36	J-M §101b	33.1	B-L 547
31.38	Gib 49	33.3	J-M §93f □ Berg 1.107e
31.43	J-M §101b	33.9	B-L 583v'

B-L: Bauer and Leander, *Historische Grammatik*   **B-M**: Beer, *Grammatik*   **Berg**: Bergsträsser, *Grammatik*
Brock: Brockelmann, *Syntax*   **Dav**: Davidson, *Syntax*   **GAHG**: Richter, *Grammatik*
Gib: Gibson, *Davidson's Syntax, 4th ed.*   **GKC**: *Gesenius' Grammar*   **IBHS**: Waltke and O'Connor, *Syntax*
Jen: Jenni, *Lehrbuch*   **J-M**: Joüon and Muraoka, *Grammar*   **Ros**: Rosenthal, *Grammar*
Sch: Schneider, *Grammatik*   **Wms**: Williams, *Syntax*

33.22–23	GKC §90g n 1
33.23	J-M §93f
33.33–34	GKC §90g n 1
33.33	Berg 1.134c
33.36	Berg 1.106c
33.38	Dav §38R3; GKC §115f, 134o; J-M §14c n 2, 124g, 142o; Gib 51 □ Berg 2.125c; Brock §86
33.39	B-L 583w'
33.52	Berg 2.121d
33.54	B-L 355m
33.55	B-M 2.143; Berg 2.132a*
33.56	Berg 2.167o
34.2	Dav §29a; GKC §131f; J-M §131h, 133c; Wms §70; Gib 40 □ GAHG 2.12 n 28; Sch §46.1.2
34.4	Berg 2.136h
34.5	GKC §90i □ B-L 132c; Berg 1.154e
34.6	Wms §441; IBHS 308 □ GAHG 3.161 n 480; Berg 2.42g
34.7–8	GKC §75bb n 1
34.7	Berg 2.115a
34.8	Berg 2.57 n k, 2.115a
34.11	Berg 2.158 n e
34.14	GKC §23c □ Berg 1.92e
34.18	Dav §38R4; 134q; Gib 51 □ B-L 363i; Berg 2.123c
35.2	J-M §177j; Gib 111 □ Berg 2.125b
35.4	IBHS 281
35.6	Dav §37c; GKC §115g, 117m; J-M §124g; IBHS 183, 280, 610; Gib 49, 50 □ Jen §10.3.1.3
35.7	IBHS 183; Gib 117
35.8	J-M §141g
35.16–23	Gib 177
35.16	IBHS 134
35.17	J-M §113l; IBHS 507
35.18	GKC §9l □ Berg 1.71e
35.19	GKC §65a, 114d; IBHS 75, 611; Gib 87 □ B-L 361x; Sch §49.3.4.2; Berg 2.82n
35.20	GKC §60a □ B-L 208r, 351; Berg 2.78g
35.21–22	GAHG 2.63
35.21	Berg 2.82n
35.22	Gib 14
35.23	Dav §100R3; GKC §114s, 152a n 1, 159c n 2; J-M §160b; Wms §400; IBHS 603; Gib 138 □ Berg 2.56h
35.24	Wms §290
35.25	IBHS 242
35.28	GKC §107n; J-M §113l, 113m
35.30	GKC §116w; J-M §121l, 156f, 156h, 156j □ Berg 1.152a, 2.68c
35.31	J-M §158g □ Berg 1.107e; Brock §152a
35.32	Berg 2.57k
35.33	IBHS 374 n 30 □ B-L 287n'; Berg 2.88c
36.2	GKC §121f; J-M §132e, 133c; Wms §245
36.3	GKC §65e □ B-L 95 n 4, 132d; Berg 2.117a
36.4	GKC §164d
36.6	GKC §135o
36.7	J-M §82h, 130b □ B-L 437
36.9	B-L 437

B-L: Bauer and Leander, *Historische Grammatik* **B-M**: Beer, *Grammatik* **Berg**: Bergsträsser, *Grammatik*
Brock: Brockelmann, *Syntax* **Dav**: Davidson, *Syntax* **GAHG**: Richter, *Grammatik*
Gib: Gibson, *Davidson's Syntax, 4th ed.* **GKC**: *Gesenius' Grammar* **IBHS**: Waltke and O'Connor, *Syntax*
Jen: Jenni, *Lehrbuch* **J-M**: Joüon and Muraoka, *Grammar* **Ros**: Rosenthal, *Grammar*
Sch: Schneider, *Grammatik* **Wms**: Williams, *Syntax*

DEUTERONOMY

B-L: Bauer and Leander, *Historische Grammatik*   B-M: Beer, *Grammatik*   Berg: Bergsträsser, *Grammatik*
Brock: Brockelmann, *Syntax*   Dav: Davidson, *Syntax*   GAHG: Richter, *Grammatik*
Gib: Gibson, *Davidson's Syntax, 4th ed.*   GKC: *Gesenius' Grammar*   IBHS: Waltke and O'Connor, *Syntax*
Jen: Jenni, *Lehrbuch*   J-M: Joüon and Muraoka, *Grammar*   Ros: Rosenthal, *Grammar*
Sch: Schneider, *Grammatik*   Wms: Williams, *Syntax*

2.5–6	Berg 2.51m
2.5	Berg 2.35i
2.6	J-M §119e, 119h □ Berg 2.35i
2.7	Dav §11Rb, 73, 73R1; IBHS 181; Gib 14, 113
2.8	B-L 510v; Berg 2.163f
2.9	GKC §67x, 75bb, 118q; J-M §126d □ B-L 404; Berg 2.140 n q, 2.164i; Brock §102
2.10	GKC §106f
2.11	Dav §44a; Gib 73, 74, 173
2.12	J-M §103n n 4; Gib 100
2.13	GKC §119s
2.14	GKC §134h
2.15	Berg 2.136f(bis)
2.16	Berg 2.59n*
2.18	J-M §154fd
2.19	IBHS 150 □ Berg 2.140 n q; Brock §116f
2.20	Dav §44a; J-M §128c; Gib 38, 73, 74 □ Berg 1.132f
2.21	GKC §104g □ Berg 1.107e
2.22	Berg 1.107e
2.23	GKC §126w; Wms §310 □ Berg 1.107e, 1.132f
2.24	Dav §83; GKC §20g, 69f, 75cc, 110h, 120g, 120h; Gib 120 □ Sch §50.6; Berg 1.66t, 2.53p, 2.127e, 2.137k, 2.164i; Brock §133a
2.25	GKC §112p, 114m; J-M §124c; IBHS 528, 602; Gib 93, 128 □ Sch §50.5.2; Berg 2.17e, 2.20b, 2.54d*, 2.137k; Brock §123f
2.26	GKC §131k □ Brock §63b
2.27	Dav §29R8, 62; GKC §108c, 123e, 133k, 156d; J-M §114c, 135e; IBHS 116; Gib 42 □ B-L 133d, 274m; B-M 3.47; Berg 2.47e
2.28	GKC §49m; J-M §114c, 119e; Gib 170, 176 □ B-L 133d; Berg 2.16c, 2.47e, 2.51m
2.29	B-L 133d
2.30	Dav §58a; J-M §124c; IBHS 540, 602, 605; Gib 103, 120, 131, 170□ B-L 133d; B-M 3.58; Berg 2.43 n b-k, 2.54d*

2.31	GKC §67w, 69f, 114m; J-M §82n, 124c □ B-L 436; Berg 2.54d*, 2.127e, 2.137k, 2.139 n o
2.33	GKC §76c; Berg 2.165k
2.34	Dav §72R4; Gib 116
2.35	GKC §67aa; J-M §82k □ B-L 430m; Sch §45.4.2; Berg 2.133b
2.37	J-M §160k n 1
3.1	Berg 2.163f, 2.163g
3.2	GKC §116o; J-M §158e □ Berg 2.71g
3.3	GKC §53l, 164d; J-M §54c n 3; Gib 175 □ Berg 2.56h, 2.106 n l; Brock §52b*
3.5	Dav §28R4; GKC §128c; J-M §131m; IBHS 132 n 17 □ B-M 3.62; Berg 2.65h*
3.6–7	Gib 171
3.6	J-M §123r n 1 □ Berg 2.65h*
3.7	GKC §67aa; J-M §82k □ Berg 2.133b
3.9	Gib 172 □ B-L 471tα
3.11	Dav §123R2; GKC §100i; J-M §142n; IBHS 134; Gib 47, 184 □ Brock §126a
3.12–13	Gib 172
3.12	B-M 3.68
3.13	GKC §125d n 1
3.17	Berg 1.122t
3.18	Dav §70a; IBHS 171 n 18; Gib 56 □ Berg 2.164i
3.20	J-M §133h; Gib 158, 175 □ Berg 2.72h*
3.21	Dav §99R3; GKC §116q, 126k; J-M §137l; IBHS 248, 621 □ Berg 2.69c, 2.167o
3.22	Dav §99R3
3.23	Gib 120
3.24	Dav §8R2; GKC §67w, 126u; J-M §82n □ B-L 436; B-M 2.147; GAHG 2.10 n 15, 3.80 n 219, 3.180 n 628; Brock §151
3.25	J-M §114d, 163a
3.26	Dav §63; GKC §69v; Wms §366 □ B-L 383; GAHG 3.171 n 536; Berg 2.127e
3.28	IBHS 176; Gib 2, 116, 117
3.29	Dav §75; Gib 112

B-L: Bauer and Leander, *Historische Grammatik*   **B-M**: Beer, *Grammatik*   **Berg**: Bergsträsser, *Grammatik*
Brock: Brockelmann, *Syntax*   **Dav**: Davidson, *Syntax*   **GAHG**: Richter, *Grammatik*
Gib: Gibson, *Davidson's Syntax, 4th ed.*   **GKC**: *Gesenius' Grammar*   **IBHS**: Waltke and O'Connor, *Syntax*
Jen: Jenni, *Lehrbuch*   **J-M**: Joüon and Muraoka, *Grammar*   **Ros**: Rosenthal, *Grammar*
Sch: Schneider, *Grammatik*   **Wms**: Williams, *Syntax*

4.1–2	IBHS 669	4.25	GKC §44o, J-M §124l, 169g;
4.1	GKC §44d, 69s; J-M §41b, 42d;		Wms §198 □ B-L 315l'; Berg
	Gib 93, 137, 159 □ B-L 384c';		2.128g
	B-M 2.115; Berg 2.58n, 2.78e	4.26	Dav §40b; GKC §51k; J-M
4.3–4	Gib 181		§51b, 80m; Gib 61, 77 □ B-L
4.3	GKC §116q; J-M §137l □		321h, 323b', 404; Berg 2.20b,
	GAHG 3.69 n 177; Berg 2.69c		2.28e, 2.65h*, 2.92i, 2.148k
4.4	IBHS 669	4.27	Dav §71R1; GKC §118q; J-M
4.5	Dav §75; J-M §125u; IBHS		§133c; Gib 56
	675 n 4; Gib 112, 116 □ B-L	4.28	GKC §68c □ Berg 2.20b(bis),
	653e		2.166m
4.6	Dav §1R2; IBHS 309, 670; Gib	4.29–30	J-M §166n
	3, 52 □ Berg 2.20b	4.30	IBHS 538; Gib 132 □ Berg
4.7	Dav §8R2; J-M §144b; IBHS		2.42g; Brock §145a
	320; Gib 8 □ GAHG	4.31	J-M §129a n 4, 129e
	3.180 n 628; Berg 2.157b	4.32	Wms §256; IBHS 204; Gib 150
4.8	GKC §128p		□ GAHG 3.170 n 521,
4.9	IBHS 388, 669 □ GAHG		3.215 n 815
	3.192 n 693	4.33	Dav §48b; IBHS 555; Gib 101 □
4.10	Dav §9c, 149; GKC §115d,		GAHG 3.102 n 289; Berg
	165b; J-M §44e, 168f; IBHS		2.164g
	442 n 23, 611, 639; Gib 159 □	4.34	Dav §99; IBHS 619; Gib 120,
	B-L 328w, 637p; B-M 2.106,		135 □ Berg 2.59n
	3.102; Jen §19.3.4; Berg 2.58n,	4.35	IBHS 297; Gib 1 □ B-M 2.162;
	2.83p, 2.114i		Brock §30a
4.11	GKC §49d n 1, 118q; J-M §44e;	4.36	GKC §61d; J-M §61f n 3, 65d;
	IBHS 516 □ Berg 2.21b		IBHS 600 □ B-L 383, 426; Jen
4.12	J-M §160g; Gib 136, 137, 173		§13.3.3; Berg 2.54c, 2.106l
4.13	Gib 47	4.37–49	Gib 87
4.15–16	IBHS 108	4.37	Dav §11c, 116R1; GKC §111q,
4.15	GKC §52o, 53l, 130d □ Berg		158b, Wms §353; IBHS 164;
	2.96 n f; Brock §144		Gib 13, 23, 159 □ Berg 2.77c
4.16	Dav §53c; Gib 93	4.38	B-L 638t
4.17	Dav §22R3	4.39	GKC §2i, 72w; J-M §80m, 154j;
4.19	Dav §53c; J-M §168h; Gib 93		Gib 58, 142 □ GAHG
4.20	GKC §74l; J-M §54c n 2, 78i;		3.175 n 593; Berg 2.43i, 2.150n
	Gib 173□ B-L 443i; Berg	4.40	Dav §43c; J-M §168f; Wms
	2.157b		§175, 466, 523; Gib 79, 159 □
4.21	Dav §91R1, 95, 96R1; GKC		Sch §53.4.4.2; Brock §161bα
	§54k; Wms §109; Gib 52, 130,	4.41	Dav §45, 145; GKC §90c, 90i,
	132, 167, 172 □ B-L 132c		107c; J-M §93c; Wms §177; Gib
4.22	Dav §55c, 100d, 100e; GKC		72 □ B-L 182y, 527q, 547;
	§116d; J-M §154fa n 2; Gib 94,		GAHG 2.31 n 130; Berg 2.33g
	136, 137, 174 □ B-L 278l'; Berg	4.42	Dav §100R5; GKC §34b; J-M
	2.72h*		§160b, 176b n 2; Wms §420;
4.23	Dav §127c; J-M §160k n 1; Gib		IBHS 366; Gib 129, 138 □ B-M
	160 □ Jen §10.4.8		3.59; GAHG 3.175 n 582; Brock
4.24	Dav §99; GKC §141h; J-M		§45
	§154i; Wms §215; IBHS 74,	4.46	Berg 2.71f
	619; Gib 53, 135	4.47	Dav §22R3; Gib 29

B-L: Bauer and Leander, *Historische Grammatik*   **B-M**: Beer, *Grammatik*   **Berg**: Bergsträsser, *Grammatik*
Brock: Brockelmann, *Syntax*   **Dav**: Davidson, *Syntax*   **GAHG**: Richter, *Grammatik*
Gib: Gibson, *Davidson's Syntax, 4th ed.*   **GKC**: *Gesenius' Grammar*   **IBHS**: Waltke and O'Connor, *Syntax*
Jen: Jenni, *Lehrbuch*   **J-M**: Joüon and Muraoka, *Grammar*   **Ros**: Rosenthal, *Grammar*
Sch: Schneider, *Grammatik*   **Wms**: Williams, *Syntax*

5.1	Wms §300		5.33	Berg 2.112c, 2.144b, 2.166m
5.2–5	Gib 179		6.2	IBHS 174; Gib 159 □ B-L 588l
5.3	GKC §135g; J-M §146d; Wms		6.3	GKC §118g, 165b; J-M §168f;
	§107; IBHS 299; Gib 2, 174			Wms §38; IBHS 147; Gib 159 □
5.4	Dav §140			B-L 409i; B-M 3.94; Berg
5.6ff.	B-M 1.74; Berg 1.77i			2.166m
5.6	GKC §15p, 138d; J-M §158n		6.4ff.	Sch §48.3.4.3
5.7–18	Gib 79		6.4–15	Gib 90
5.7	Berg 2.51m		6.4–9	Gib 89
5.8	Wms §273, 323 □ B-L 79t; Berg		6.4–5	Gib 88
	2.51m		6.4	IBHS 135, 274; Gib 47, 55 □
5.9	GKC §60b; J-M §63b; Wms			B-L 58d, 119l, 158 n 2; Berg
	§270 □ B-L 352; Berg 2.79 n g			1.4i
5.12	GKC §113f, 113bb; J-M §123v;		6.5	Dav §57R1; IBHS 659 n 49 □
	IBHS 593 n 52, 608; Gib 127 □			Jen §9.4.10; Berg 1.4i
	B-M 3.63; Berg 2.66k; Brock §2		6.7	GKC §119l; J-M §65b; IBHS
5.13	Gib 47, 79 □ Berg 2.35i			199 □ B-L 344d"; B-M 2.167;
5.14	Wms §98; IBHS 285 n 26; Gib			Berg 2.82m
	39, 44		6.10	Brock §65a; Gib 90
5.16	IBHS 593 n 52 □ Berg 2.72h*		6.11	Dav §98a; GKC §49m, 96
5.17–21	IBHS 593 n 52			(p. 285); Gib 133 □ Berg 1.72g,
5.19	Dav §28R4, 67R3; GKC §117t,			2.16c
	120d n 2; J-M §125s; Gib 115		6.13	Gib 55, 170 □ Berg 2.117a
5.20	GKC §49d n 1; J-M §44e □		6.14	Berg 2.20b
	Berg 2.21b		6.15	Dav §53c; Gib 93 □ Berg 2.16c
5.21	Dav §54a; J-M §125u, 128c;		6.16	IBHS 225
	IBHS 176, 487 □ B-L 426		6.17	GKC §58g, 113bb; J-M §123h;
5.22	GKC §159v; Gib 136, 153 □			IBHS 588 □ B-L 300q; B-M
	GAHG 3.171 n 539,			2.100; Jen §8.4.8, 10.3.1.1; Berg
	3.175 n 589, 3.206 n 786			2.63d, 2.162d; Brock §93a
5.23	Dav §31, 116R4; GKC §132h;		6.18	Dav §53c; Gib 93
	J-M §127a, 139h, 146a, 148a;		6.19	Berg 2.114i
	Wms §494; IBHS 497 n 2,		6.20ff.	Sch §48.4.5
	516 n 48; Gib 43 □ GAHG		6.21	Berg 2.44i
	3.102 n 289, 3.180 n 628; Berg		6.22–23	Gib 171
	2.21b, 2.83n		6.24	Berg 2.144b
5.24	GKC §32h; J-M §39a n 4; IBHS		6.25	Berg 2.59n
	497 n 2 □ B-L 248e; Berg 2.106l		7.1	Jen §6.1
5.26	Dav §32R3, 135R3; GKC		7.2	Berg 1.150n, 2.135d
	§115d, 151c; J-M §163d, 177h;		7.3	IBHS 671; Gib 23, 174
	IBHS 319; Gib 186 □ GAHG		7.5	Dav §45R4; GKC §52n; J-M
	3.102 n 289, 3.180 n 628			§94g; Wms §555; IBHS 671;
5.27–28	IBHS 208 n 78			Gib 29, 78, 174, 178 □ B-L
5.27	GKC §119s; J-M §39a n 5 □			600j'; Berg 2.20b
	Brock §34b		7.6	Wms §491; Gib 178
5.28	Gib 107		7.7	Dav §28R1, 33, 101Rc; Wms
5.29	Wms §74, 547; Gib 6 □ Berg			§93, 319, 535; Gib 45 □ B-L
	2.83p; Brock §9, 41f			147 n 2
5.30	J-M §139e n 1; Wms §272		7.8–9	IBHS 532 n 31
5.31	Wms §106			

B-L: Bauer and Leander, *Historische Grammatik*   **B-M**: Beer, *Grammatik*   **Berg**: Bergsträsser, *Grammatik*
Brock: Brockelmann, *Syntax*   **Dav**: Davidson, *Syntax*   **GAHG**: Richter, *Grammatik*
Gib: Gibson, *Davidson's Syntax, 4th ed.*   **GKC**: *Gesenius' Grammar*   **IBHS**: Waltke and O'Connor, *Syntax*
Jen: Jenni, *Lehrbuch*   **J-M**: Joüon and Muraoka, *Grammar*   **Ros**: Rosenthal, *Grammar*
Sch: Schneider, *Grammatik*   **Wms**: Williams, *Syntax*

7.8	J-M §137s, 170i; IBHS 605; Gib 129, 132 □ Jen §28.3.3; Berg 2.83p	8.10	J-M §112i; Wms §162; IBHS 484
7.9	GKC §134g; Wms §72, 266; IBHS 206; Gib 50, 150	8.11	Wms §195; Gib 132 □ Jen §10.4.6
7.10	Gib 78 □ Berg 2.121d	8.12ff.	GKC §150m n 2
7.12	GKC §158b, 158d; J-M §113b, 170g; Wms §72, 489; IBHS 520 □ Berg 2.20b; Brock §145bα	8.12	J-M §119d, 119f, 168h
		8.13	Dav §114; GKC §75u; J-M §150p; Gib 21 □ B-L 409k; Berg 2.166m
7.13	J-M §140c n 3 □ Berg 1.160a, 2.95d	8.14–16	GKC §116f
7.14	Dav §17R5	8.14	Berg 2.68a
7.15	GKC §60d □ B-L 337n, 405; Berg 2.23g	8.15	Dav §28R4; GKC §127i □ Berg 1.78m, 2.68a; Brock §73b
7.16	GKC §62r, 109d; J-M §80k □ B-L 399h"; B-M 2.149; Berg 2.52 n n, 2.145d	8.16	GKC §44l, 72o; J-M §42f; Wms §82; IBHS 516 n 49; Gib 134 □ B-L 382; Berg 2.15a, 2.68a; Brock §73b
7.17	IBHS 388; Gib 13	8.18	Dav §19R3; GKC §126k; J-M §137l; IBHS 606 □ GAHG 3.69 n 177; Berg 2.57l
7.18	GKC §113bb; J-M §123h n 1 □ Berg 2.63d		
7.19	J-M §158k	8.19	GKC §72x, 106i; J-M §80m, 112f, 123d n 3; Wms §73, 164; IBHS 73; Gib 147, 155 □ Berg 2.20b, 2.28e
7.20	GKC §63i; Gib 78 □ Berg 2.114i		
7.21	Gib 78 □ GAHG 2.60		
7.22	IBHS 116		
7.23	Dav §67b; GKC §61e; Gib 115 □ Berg 2.173 n f	8.20	GKC §158b, 158d; J-M §170g □ GAHG 3.173 n 549; Berg 2.20b(bis)
7.24	GKC §53l; J-M §54c; Wms §491, Gib 116 □ B-L 346x"; Berg 2.106 n l	9.1	J-M §154fd; Gib 43 □ B-M 3.30
		9.2	J-M §136o; Gib 7
7.25	Dav §65R2; GKC §127e; J-M §139c; IBHS 208; Gib 26, 78	9.3	Dav §19R3; J-M §137l; IBHS 619 n 33 □ Berg 2.112c
7.26	Dav §65R2; Wms §298; IBHS 414; Gib 107, 124 □ Berg 1.78m, 2.115a	9.6	Dav §24d; Gib 33
		9.7	Dav §60, 100R2, 146; GKC §138c; J-M §121f n 1, 123v n 2, 158k; Wms §186, 464; IBHS 180, 628 n 51; Gib 81, 110, 138, 178 □ B-M 3.94; Jen §10.3.1.1; Berg 2.73i*
8.1	GKC §69s; Wms §108		
8.2	Dav §6R2; J-M §161f; Gib 6 □ B-L 119 n 2		
8.3	Dav §75; GKC §44l, 72o; J-M §42f, 125u; IBHS 176, 401 n 22, 516 n 49; Gib 112 □ B-L 382; B-M 2.115; Berg 2.15a	9.8	GKC §54k; Wms §275 □ Berg 2.99e
		9.9	J-M §136o; IBHS 562 □ B-M 3.46; Berg 2.38g
8.5	GKC §61h; J-M §61f n 3, 66b; IBHS 219; Gib 134, 148 □ B-L 118 n 3, 345m", 548a'; Berg 2.68a	9.10	Berg 2.27d
		9.11	Wms §484; Gib 99 □ B-M 3.93
		9.13	Dav §24d; Gib 33, 59
8.7	Dav §28R4; IBHS 623 □ Berg 2.119e	9.14	GKC §75gg □ Berg 2.165k
		9.15	Gib 168 □ Berg 2.163f
8.8	J-M §136b; Gib 35	9.16	Wms §491; Gib 178
8.9	Dav §9R1; GKC §93aa, 152b, 152e □ B-L 564		

B-L: Bauer and Leander, *Historische Grammatik*   **B-M**: Beer, *Grammatik*   **Berg**: Bergsträsser, *Grammatik*
Brock: Brockelmann, *Syntax*   **Dav**: Davidson, *Syntax*   **GAHG**: Richter, *Grammatik*
Gib: Gibson, *Davidson's Syntax, 4th ed.*   **GKC**: *Gesenius' Grammar*   **IBHS**: Waltke and O'Connor, *Syntax*
Jen: Jenni, *Lehrbuch*   **J-M**: Joüon and Muraoka, *Grammar*   **Ros**: Rosenthal, *Grammar*
Sch: Schneider, *Grammatik*   **Wms**: Williams, *Syntax*

9.18   GKC §54k; J-M §133h; Wms
        §291; IBHS 607; Gib 131 □
        Berg 2.99e
9.19   IBHS 373
9.20   Wms §199, 275 □ B-L 346x"
9.21   Dav §87; GKC §67g, 67bb,
        113k; J-M §54c n 1, 123r n 2;
        Wms §274; IBHS 207, 592; Gib
        126 □ Berg 2.21d, 2.65h*(bis),
        2.132a*, 2.138o; Brock §159d
9.22   J-M §121f n 1; IBHS 628 n 51;
        Gib 138 □ Berg 2.73i*
9.24   J-M §116r, 121f n 1; Wms §316;
        IBHS 628 n 51; Gib 138 □ Berg
        2.73i*
9.25   Dav §37f, 72R3; GKC §118k;
        J-M §126i; Wms §56; IBHS 181;
        Gib 117
9.26–27 Berg 2.48g
9.26   J-M §114i, 163a
9.27   J-M §125k; Wms §273 □ Berg
        1.124w; Brock §95
9.28   GKC §145e; J-M §49d, 124h,
        170l n 1, 170i; Wms §420; Gib
        130 □ B-L 382; Berg 2.56h,
        2.83p(bis), 2.128e
10.1   Wms §40
10.3   B-M 2.158; Berg 2.163g(bis)
10.4   Dav §36b; Gib 47
10.5   GKC §29g □ B-L 188q; Berg
        1.130c, 2.21d, 2.163f
10.6   Gib 167 □ Jen §11.1
10.7   GKC §90g n 1; J-M §93f
10.8   GKC §125d n 1
10.9   J-M §154j; Gib 52
10.10   Wms §193; IBHS 602; Gib 120,
        128 □ Berg 2.54d*
10.11   GKC §45e; J-M §49e □ B-L
        367; Berg 2.83p
10.12   GKC §115d; J-M §125e □ B-L
        354g; Berg 2.83p
10.13   J-M §168d
10.15–16 IBHS 532; Gib 88
10.15   Dav §91b; GKC §115d; J-M
        §124f; Gib 129, 176 □ B-M
        2.106
10.16   J-M §129ia; Gib 171 □ Berg
        2.43i*; Brock §5b
10.17–19 IBHS 536

10.17   Dav §34R4, 44a, 106d; GKC
        §102m, 126v, 133i; J-M §138a,
        141l; Wms §47; IBHS 123, 154;
        Gib 19, 46, 52, 74
10.18   Wms §29
10.19   GKC §112aa; J-M §119e; Wms
        §33 □ B-L 276y; B-M 3.54;
        Berg 2.43i*; Brock §5b
10.20ff. Sch §48.3.3
10.21   J-M §143f; Wms §341; Gib 170
10.22   GKC §119i; J-M §133c
11.2   GKC §117l
11.6   GKC §117e; J-M §125e □ Brock
        §152c
11.7   GKC §126k, 126u; J-M §137l,
        138a □ GAHG 2.58 n 256,
        3.69 n 177; Sch §47.1.3; Berg
        2.69c
11.8   Brock §44a
11.10   Dav §54a; J-M §43b, 125p;
        Wms §35, 463; IBHS 166; Gib
        94 □ Berg 2.31d, 2.32d
11.12   Dav §22R3; Gib 29 □ B-L 606k
11.13   J-M §123g □ Berg 1.135d
11.14   Gib 153
11.15   GKC §49m
11.16–17 Brock §41f
11.17   IBHS 435 □ B-M 3.78; Brock
        §104
11.18–22 Dav §56
11.18   Dav §32R3; Gib 6
11.19   J-M §65b □ B-L 344d"; Berg
        2.82m
11.22   GKC §45d; Gib 130 □ B-L
        316d; Berg 2.83p
11.23   Dav §33; IBHS 264; Gib 45
11.24   Dav §44R2
11.26–28 IBHS 637
11.26   B-L 653e
11.27–28 GKC §159cc; Jen §16.3.4
11.27   J-M §167j; Wms §469, 515 □
        Brock §164d
11.28   Wms §358, 469 □ Brock §164d
11.30   GKC §150e; J-M §161c; Wms
        §54, 359; IBHS 684 n 48
12.1   Gib 5
12.2   Dav §86a; J-M §113m, 123h;
        Gib 124
12.3   GKC §52n; J-M §94g □ B-L
        600j'; GAHG 3.106 n 301

B-L: Bauer and Leander, *Historische Grammatik*   **B-M**: Beer, *Grammatik*   **Berg**: Bergsträsser, *Grammatik*
Brock: Brockelmann, *Syntax*   **Dav**: Davidson, *Syntax*   **GAHG**: Richter, *Grammatik*
Gib: Gibson, *Davidson's Syntax, 4th ed.*   **GKC**: *Gesenius' Grammar*   **IBHS**: Waltke and O'Connor, *Syntax*
Jen: Jenni, *Lehrbuch*   **J-M**: Joüon and Muraoka, *Grammar*   **Ros**: Rosenthal, *Grammar*
Sch: Schneider, *Grammatik*   **Wms**: Williams, *Syntax*

12.5	Berg 2.82n	13.10	J-M §123e; Gib 124
12.7	Wms §492	13.11	Dav §77, 116f; Gib 134, 145 □
12.8	Gib 137		Berg 2.68a
12.11	Dav §34R5; Wms §35; Gib 46 □	13.12	Wms §180 □ Berg 2.20b
	B-L 126z; Berg 2.122b	13.13–15	Jen §9.3.3.2
12.13	IBHS 670	13.13	Gib 154
12.14	GKC §61h; J-M §61f n 3, 66b □	13.14	GKC §130e; J-M §114e, 131b
	B-L 588l; GAHG 2.11 n 23;	13.15	GKC §113k; J-M §123r,
	Berg 2.68a		167l n 2; Wms §204, 485, 562;
12.15	Wms §560; IBHS 196, 670		IBHS 592, 644 □ Berg 2.65h*
12.16	Gib 38	13.16	B-L 442e; Berg 2.160a
12.17	B-L 367	13.17	Gib 58
12.18	Gib 36	13.18	B-L 133d, 355n; Berg 2.116e
12.20	Dav §62; J-M §114c; Wms	13.19	J-M §124o; IBHS 609 □ Jen
	§184; IBHS 574; Gib 82 □ Berg		§10.3.1.3; Berg 1.50g
	2.35i; Brock §35b	14.1	GKC §141b □ Jen §8.3.4.2
12.22	Dav §79; Wms §59, 491; IBHS	14.2	GKC §133b; J-M §141h
	385; Gib 118 □ GAHG	14.4	J-M §137i
	3.120 n 330	14.5	Gib 36 □ Berg 1.92e
12.23	GKC §63i; Wms §328 □ Jen	14.7	Dav §116R3; J-M §137i
	§8.3.1.2; Berg 2.59n*, 2.114i	14.12	J-M §143a; IBHS 183 □ Berg
12.26	B-L 582u'; Berg 2.17d		1.110 n b
12.28	GKC §61h; J-M §61f n 3, 66b □	14.14	IBHS 183
	B-L 588l; Berg 2.68a	14.17	GKC §80k; J-M §93k □ B-L
12.29	Gib 77		511y, 557e'
12.30	J-M §176k; Gib 150 □ Berg	14.18	B-L 133d
	2.171c	14.21	Dav §88R1; J-M §123x; Gib 127
12.31	Gib 175		□ GAHG 3.53 n 156; Berg
13.1–3	Gib 154		2.67m
13.1	Dav §63R2, 106c; GKC §109d;	14.22	GKC §123c; Dav §29R8; J-M
	J-M §75f □ B-L 383; Berg		§125n, 135d; IBHS 116,
	2.79h		170 n 17, 233; Gib 42
13.2	Dav §130c, 152; IBHS 194;	14.23	Berg 2.58n
	Gib 39	14.24	Wms §318 □ B-L 441c; Berg
13.3	GKC §60b; J-M §63b, 114e;		2.123c
	IBHS 574; Gib 82 □ B-L 352;	14.25	Berg 2.140 n q
	Berg 2.79 n g	14.26	GKC §117gg
13.4	Dav §125; J-M §102k, 121m,	14.27	Gib 182
	154l; Wms §479, 543 □ B-M	14.29	Berg 2.117a
	2.174; Brock §79a	15.2	Dav §88, 88R5, 108; GKC
13.5	Dav §45R4; J-M §44e □ B-L		§113gg; J-M §123v, 123y; Wms
	300q		§209; Gib 127 □ B-M 2.134;
13.6	GKC §116f, 127i; J-M		Berg 2.35i, 2.66k, 2.159g(bis)
	§155o n 2; Gib 134 □ GAHG	15.3	J-M §113l; IBHS 508 □ Berg
	2.10 n 15; Berg 2.68a		2.35i, 2.51 n l
13.7	Dav §9b, 62; J-M §114e, 146i,	15.4	Dav §154; J-M §173a; Gib 176
	158f, 158h; Wms §185; IBHS	15.5	J-M §123g; Wms §393 □
	333; Gib 9 □ Berg 2.151q		GAHG 3.191 n 681
13.9	GKC §72r, 109d; J-M §80k □	15.6	Dav §51R2 □ Berg 2.113f
	B-L 442g; Berg 2.52 n n		

B-L: Bauer and Leander, *Historische Grammatik*   **B-M**: Beer, *Grammatik*   **Berg**: Bergsträsser, *Grammatik*
Brock: Brockelmann, *Syntax*   **Dav**: Davidson, *Syntax*   **GAHG**: Richter, *Grammatik*
Gib: Gibson, *Davidson's Syntax, 4th ed.*   **GKC**: *Gesenius' Grammar*   **IBHS**: Waltke and O'Connor, *Syntax*
Jen: Jenni, *Lehrbuch*   **J-M**: Joüon and Muraoka, *Grammar*   **Ros**: Rosenthal, *Grammar*
Sch: Schneider, *Grammatik*   **Wms**: Williams, *Syntax*

15.7	Dav §35R2, 101Rc; GKC §119w n 2, 139d □ Brock §24d, 111b
15.8	J-M §123k n 1 □ Berg 2.111c, 2.113f
15.9	Dav §38R3; GKC §134o, 134p; J-M §142o; Gib 51 □ Brock §86
15.11	Berg 2.111c
15.14	GKC §53k, 93k; IBHS 207 □ B-L 581; Berg 2.105i
15.16	GKC §59i, 117e; J-M §112a, 125e; Gib 154
15.17	GKC §153; J-M §137m; Gib 27, 38, 175
15.18	GKC §118n, 128c □ B-L 360v; Berg 2.118d; Brock §79c
15.19	Berg 2.134d
15.20	GKC §123c; IBHS 116; Gib 42 □ Brock §129c
16.3	Berg 2.54d
16.4	Dav §36a; IBHS 206, 214; Gib 47, 148, 150 □ Jen §27.3.3; Brock §34a
16.6	GKC §119g; J-M §166m; IBHS 604
16.8	Dav §36a; Gib 47
16.9	IBHS 605; Gib 47 □ B-M 2.147; Berg 2.137k
16.11	Berg 1.160a
16.12	Wms §490 □ B-M 3.94
16.13	Dav §36a; GKC §93k; Gib 47 □ B-L 581
16.15	Gib 39
16.16	Gib 47
16.18	Dav §67b; IBHS 614; Gib 115
16.19	Dav §44a; Gib 74, 104
16.20	GKC §133k; Wms §16; Gib 42 □ Brock §129f
16.21	Dav §11Rb, 29c; IBHS 231; Gib 14, 40
17.2	Dav §130b; GKC §167b; Gib 154
17.3	Dav §130b; J-M §160k; IBHS 242; Gib 154
17.4–5	IBHS 678 n 14
17.4	J-M §167l n 2; Wms §485
17.5	GKC §124o; J-M §148c n 1; IBHS 122 n 15; Gib 20 □ Berg 2.44i
17.6	GKC §144e; J-M §155d; IBHS 276; Gib 47 □ Brock §83b
17.7	GAHG 3.106 n 301
17.8	Dav §34R2; GKC §102h, 133c; Wms §273; IBHS 200, 266 n 24; Gib 45 □ B-L 93c, 638w; Brock §111g
17.9	Gib 6 □ Berg 2.17d
17.12	GKC §64g; Gib 132 □ B-L 356s; Berg 2.116b
17.13	IBHS 517 n 61, 654
17.14–20	Gib 90
17.14–15	IBHS 526 n 24
17.14	Dav §62; GKC §44d, 49m, 69s; J-M §41b, 114c; Wms §184, 546; Gib 82 □ B-L 384c'; Berg 2.78e
17.15	Dav §9R2; J-M §113l, 123h, 158g; Wms §562; Gib 9 □ Berg 2.151s; Brock §93a
17.17	Dav §65R2; GKC §109g; J-M §116j; Gib 107
17.18	Dav §5; Gib 90 7 □ B-M 3.108
17.20	Dav §65R2; Gib 107
18.1	GKC §68c, 131h □ Berg 2.20b
18.2	Dav §106d; J-M §150k; Wms §578
18.3	Dav §152; IBHS 535 n 35; Gib 39 □ B-L 208t; Brock §169b
18.6–8	IBHS 526 n 24
18.6	J-M §113n
18.10	Gib 36 □ B-M 2.129; Berg 1.113 n e
18.11	Gib 36
18.12	IBHS 618 n 27 □ GAHG 3.106 n 301
18.13	Gib 148
18.14	Gib 181 □ Berg 1.113 n e
18.15	J-M §155o □ B-L 651z
18.16	Dav §63R3; GKC §109d; J-M §114g, 139e n 1 □ B-L 279 n 1, 301 n 4; Berg 2.52o, 2.79h
18.17–20	Gib 89
18.19–20	Gib 180, 181
18.20	Gib 176
18.21	Gib 185
19.1	GKC §44d, 69s; B-L 384c'; Berg 2.78e
19.2	Dav §36a; IBHS 278; Gib 47
19.3	GKC §115g; IBHS 414

B-L: Bauer and Leander, *Historische Grammatik* **B-M**: Beer, *Grammatik* **Berg**: Bergsträsser, *Grammatik*
Brock: Brockelmann, *Syntax* **Dav**: Davidson, *Syntax* **GAHG**: Richter, *Grammatik*
Gib: Gibson, *Davidson's Syntax, 4th ed.* **GKC**: *Gesenius' Grammar* **IBHS**: Waltke and O'Connor, *Syntax*
Jen: Jenni, *Lehrbuch* **J-M**: Joüon and Muraoka, *Grammar* **Ros**: Rosenthal, *Grammar*
Sch: Schneider, *Grammatik* **Wms**: Williams, *Syntax*

19.4–5	Sch §51.2.4.2
19.4	J-M §160b; Gib 52, 138
19.5	GKC §126r □ B-L 348h; Berg 2.114i
19.6	Dav §71; 67p; Gib 145 □ B-L 353v; B-M 2.144; GAHG 3.175 n 577; Berg 2.125 n a-e, 2.135d
19.8–9	Gib 86
19.8	J-M §166p
19.9	Dav §36R4, 37R5; J-M §142l; Gib 48 □ GAHG 3.171 n 534; Brock §85b
19.10	Dav §53c, 65R2; Gib 93, 107
19.11	Gib 145
19.13	Dav §32R5; 72r; J-M §80k; Gib 44 □ Berg 2.52 n n
19.14	J-M §113m, 137i □ Berg 1.160a, 2.151q
19.16	J-M §15e; Gib 154
19.18	J-M §167l n 2 □ Brock §126a
19.20	IBHS 654
19.21	GKC §72r; J-M §80k; Gib 150 □ Jen §25.3.3; Berg 2.52 n n
20.1	GKC §93rr, 116f; Wms §82 □ B-L 587j; Berg 2.68a; Brock §73b
20.2	GKC §61d; J-M §65c; IBHS 519; Gib 87 □ B-L 358v; Berg 1.135d, 2.83n
20.3	Berg 2.135d
20.4	J-M §137l; Gib 130 □ GAHG 3.69 n 177
20.5	GKC §137c; J-M §114g n 1; IBHS 321, 569; Gib 8, 82 □ B-L 267c; Berg 2.49i; Brock §154, 155a
20.6	Berg 2.49i; Brock §154
20.7	B-L 197b; B-M 1.107; Berg 2.49i
20.8	GKC §121b; J-M §145fa □ Berg 2.49i, 2.136 n i; Brock §154
20.9	B-L 424
20.10	Wms §288; Gib 149
20.11	Gib 153 □ Berg 2.162d
20.12	IBHS 451
20.13	GKC §49k
20.14	GKC §128h □ Berg 2.134d
20.15	Dav §9R2; GKC §138b; J-M §158g □ GAHG 3.77 n 203
20.16	Gib 176
20.18	Dav §149; Gib 160 □ GAHG 3.173 n 549
20.19	GKC §100m □ B-L 235u, 363h; Berg 2.123c
20.20	Dav §9R2 □ GAHG 3.175 n 582; Brock §152c
21.1	Dav §41R3; Gib 8, 56
21.3	Dav §109; GKC §121a, 121f, 145q; J-M §128ba, 132e, 152fa; IBHS 269, 374 n 30; Gib 45 □ B-L 287n'; Berg 2.88c; Brock §35c
21.4	Dav §109; GKC §121a; J-M §152fa
21.7	Dav §116; GKC §44m, 145k; J-M §42f, 150h; Gib 23 □ B-L 315o'; Berg 2.15b; Brock §50c
21.8	GKC §55k; J-M §59f; Gib 40 □ B-L 283s; B-M 2.123; Berg 2.108 n b
21.9	Berg 2.115a
21.10	Dav §116R1; GKC §135p, 145m; Gib 23
21.11	Dav §28R6; GKC §49m, 96 (p. 285), 130e; J-M §122r; Gib 36 □ GAHG 2.60 n 261; Berg 2.16c; Brock §70d
21.12	Gib 5, 110 □ B-L 582u'; Berg 2.149l
21.13	GKC §101a, 131d; Gib 41, 109
21.14	Dav §86j; J-M §18j, 123o, 141a; IBHS 583, 637; Gib 124, 149, 150 □ Berg :65q, 2.44i; Brock §80c
21.15	J-M §142m
21.16	GKC §115a
21.17	J-M §101b; IBHS 276
21.18	B-L 424
21.20	IBHS 132 □ B-L 424
21.21	IBHS 654
21.23	J-M §123e, 143j; IBHS 314 □ Berg :124w
22.1	GKC §96 (p. 286), 159gg; J-M §98e, 148c n 1, 167t □ B-L 620u; B-M 2.83; GAHG 3.102 n 289
22.2	GKC §72w; Gib 55, 116 □ Berg 2.150n

B-L: Bauer and Leander, *Historische Grammatik*   **B-M**: Beer, *Grammatik*   **Berg**: Bergsträsser, *Grammatik*
Brock: Brockelmann, *Syntax*   **Dav**: Davidson, *Syntax*   **GAHG**: Richter, *Grammatik*
Gib: Gibson, *Davidson's Syntax, 4th ed.*   **GKC**: *Gesenius' Grammar*   **IBHS**: Waltke and O'Connor, *Syntax*
Jen: Jenni, *Lehrbuch*   **J-M**: Joüon and Muraoka, *Grammar*   **Ros**: Rosenthal, *Grammar*
Sch: Schneider, *Grammatik*   **Wms**: Williams, *Syntax*

22.3	Dav §132a; Gib 156 □ B-M 2.123; Berg 2.99e, 2.119a
22.4	J-M §148c n 1, 167t □ GAHG 3.102 n 289; Berg 2.105i, 2.149m
22.5	Dav §73; Gib 108 □ Berg 2.51m
22.6	GKC §119aa n 1, 119aa n 2 □ B-L 565x
22.7	GKC §65e
22.8	Dav §108R1; GKC §144e; J-M §155d; Wms §222, 315; Gib 13 □ Berg 2.44i
22.9	J-M §125p
22.10	Brock §106c
22.12	Brock §127b
22.13	J-M §117d
22.14	J-M §129f, 130g; IBHS 153
22.15	Berg 1.154e
22.17	Gib 27
22.19	GKC §17c, 127e; J-M §139c; IBHS 241; Gib 26 □ Berg 1.3h; Brock §73a
22.20	Dav §130b; Gib 154 □ Brock §27c
22.21	Gib 154 □ B-L 217a
22.22	Gib 56
22.23	GKC §131b, 145q; J-M §131b; Gib 40
22.24	J-M §170h □ GAHG 3.173 n 549; Brock §162
22.26	GKC §117ll; J-M §126g; Gib 14 □ Brock §24f
22.27	Gib 57, 136
23.2	B-L 603f; Berg 1.134c
23.3	J-M §130g
23.5	Dav §91R4; GKC §61d, 119n, 130c n 1; J-M §61f n 3, 65d, 166l, 170h; IBHS 413, 600 n 10; Gib 130, 159 □ B-L 438; B-M 3.107; Berg 2.54c; Brock §71b, 162
23.6	J-M §112a
23.8	Gib 53
23.9	GAHG 3.122 n 332
23.11	GKC §20h □ Berg 1.113 n e; Brock §120a
23.12	GKC §114f n 1 □ Berg 2.57k
23.14	GKC §49m □ Berg 1.147 n d, 2.16c, 2.17d

23.15	Dav §53c; GKC §93ss, 128p; J-M §96Ce, 129f; Wms §358; IBHS 154; Gib 93
23.16–17	GAHG 2.11 n 23
23.20	J-M §32c □ Berg 2.75 n a, 2.76 n b
23.22	J-M §113m
23.23	J-M §119h
23.25	GKC §96 (p. 286) □ Berg 1.149g
24.1	GKC §167b
24.4	Dav §145; GKC §54h; J-M §53h, 124s; IBHS 155, 432; Gib 157 □ B-L 285j′; B-M 2.156; Berg 2.59n*, 2.99 n g
24.6	Berg 1.154e, 2.113g
24.7	GKC §162b; J-M §175b; IBHS 654 n 21; Gib 56 □ Berg 2.119e
24.8	GKC §51n
24.10	GKC §23d; J-M §42e □ Berg 2.159g
24.13	GKC §10g, 58i; J-M §61f n 3; IBHS 517 n 64 □ B-L 357
24.18	J-M §155p □ GAHG 3.106 n 301
24.19	GKC §49m □ Berg 1.160a, 2.16c
24.21	J-M §152f
25.1	IBHS 402 n 24
25.2	Dav §90R2; GKC §96 (p. 285), 128v; J-M §54d; IBHS 601 □ B-L 618j; B-M 2.80; Berg 2.54d, 2.56f
25.3	GKC §150m n 2; J-M §168h
25.4	Berg 2.152t
25.7	GKC §115c; J-M §65a; IBHS 606; Gib 63 □ Berg 1.154e, 2.54d*, 2.58n, 2.77c
25.8	J-M §167b; Gib 63 □ Berg 2.58n
25.9	J-M §167b; IBHS 392 n 33 □ Berg 2.174 n h
25.10	GKC §116k; J-M §121o
25.12	GKC §67aa, 72r, 67ee; J-M §80k □ Berg 2.52 n n
25.13	Dav §29R8; GKC §115g, 123f; J-M §135d; IBHS 116, 233; Gib 37, 42
25.14	Dav §29R8; Gib 42
25.15	Dav §24c; Gib 33

B-L: Bauer and Leander, *Historische Grammatik* **B-M**: Beer, *Grammatik* **Berg**: Bergsträsser, *Grammatik*
Brock: Brockelmann, *Syntax* **Dav**: Davidson, *Syntax* **GAHG**: Richter, *Grammatik*
Gib: Gibson, *Davidson's Syntax, 4th ed.* **GKC**: *Gesenius' Grammar* **IBHS**: Waltke and O'Connor, *Syntax*
Jen: Jenni, *Lehrbuch* **J-M**: Joüon and Muraoka, *Grammar* **Ros**: Rosenthal, *Grammar*
Sch: Schneider, *Grammatik* **Wms**: Williams, *Syntax*

25.16	Gib 5		28.11	J-M §140c n 3
25.17	Brock §151		28.14	Gib 14
25.18	IBHS 412		28.15	Gib 114
25.19	J-M §124g; IBHS 26		28.20	GKC §61e; J-M §158i □ Berg
26.1	GKC §69s □ Berg 2.44i			2.82n, 2.91g, 2.114i
26.3	Dav §40b; J-M §112f; IBHS		28.21	Dav §22R1, 65R6; GKC §109k;
	488; Gib 61 □ Berg 2.16d, 2.28e			J-M §114l; IBHS 246; Gib 29,
26.5	Dav §24R4; GKC §119i, 128n;			73 □ B-L 274l; Berg 2.51l
	Wms §249; Gib 34 □ B-L 23n;		28.22	Dav §22R1; Gib 29 □ B-L
	B-M 1.29; Brock §42c, 71c,			345q″; Berg 2.108c
	106b		28.23	Wms §286
26.9	B-M 3.34		28.24	GKC §61e □ B-L 345p″
26.10	GAHG 3.59 n 163, 3.204 n 772		28.25	Dav §76 □ Berg 2.123d
26.11	IBHS 198		28.27	Dav §150; Gib 161 □ B-L 376r
26.12	GKC §53k, 53q □ B-L 228a′,		28.29	J-M §113c n 3, 121e; IBHS 629;
	322t, 353v; B-M 2.26; Berg			Gib 74, 138 □ Berg 2.73k, 2.74l
	2.82 n m		28.31–32	Berg 2.72h*
26.14	J-M §133c □ Jen §25.3.3		28.31	J-M §51c n 3, 121e, 121q; IBHS
26.15	Gib 40 □ B-M 2.10			627 □ Brock §28bβ
26.16	J-M §121h n 2; Gib 136		28.32	GKC §146d; J-M §51c n 3,
26.17	Dav §40b			139g, 148d □ Berg 1.101m,
26.19	Dav §91R4; J-M §124f; Gib 130			2.168p
	□ Berg 2.95d		28.33	IBHS 669
27.2	GKC §72w; J-M §80m □ Berg		28.35	GKC §166b □ B-L 345q″; Berg
	2.44i, 2.150n			1.126bb
27.3	Jen §19.3.4		28.36	Dav §65R6; GKC §109k, 131d;
27.4	Berg 2.83n			J-M §114l; Gib 73 □ Berg
27.6	Dav §76; GKC §117hh; J-M			2.16c, 2.51l
	§43b, 125v, 125w, 128c; Wms		28.38	Berg 2.120b
	§53; IBHS 174; Gib 144 □		28.43	Dav §29R8; GKC §133k; Gib 42
	GAHG 3.100 n 278; Berg 2.17d,		28.45	GKC §58g □ B-L 345p″; Berg
	2.112c; Brock §94dα			2.162d
27.8	GKC §113k □ B-M 2.131; Berg		28.47	Brock §163b; Gib 159
	2.65h*, 2.66h*, 2.115a		28.48	Dav §32R5, 116R1; GKC §53l,
27.9	GKC §16b □ Berg 1.70b			145m; J-M §54c; IBHS 263; Gib
27.12	Berg 1.135d			44□ B-L 346x″; Berg 2.106 n l
27.14	J-M §125s □ Brock §93n		28.49	GKC §155d; J-M §158f, 158h;
27.15–26	IBHS 681 n 30			IBHS 333; Gib 9 □ B-M 3.99
27.15	IBHS 134 □ Berg 2.74 n l		28.50	J-M §130a □ B-L 437
27.16	Sch §44.3		28.51	Dav §150; Gib 161 □ B-L
27.19	J-M §13d			345p″
27.24	Berg 2.153t		28.52	GKC §67v □ Berg 2.137k
27.25	Dav §32R5; Gib 44		28.53	J-M §140c n 3
28	Gib 73		28.54	J-M §141j; IBHS 270
28.1	J-M §123g		28.55	GKC §158b; J-M §169h; Wms
28.3	Gib 54			§418; IBHS 605 □ B-M 3.106;
28.4	J-M §140c n 3			Berg 2.106 n l
28.5	IBHS 134			
28.8	Dav §65R6; GKC §109k; J-M			
	§114l; Gib 73 □ Berg 2.50l			

B-L: Bauer and Leander, *Historische Grammatik*   **B-M**: Beer, *Grammatik*   **Berg**: Bergsträsser, *Grammatik*
Brock: Brockelmann, *Syntax*   **Dav**: Davidson, *Syntax*   **GAHG**: Richter, *Grammatik*
Gib: Gibson, *Davidson's Syntax, 4th ed.*   **GKC**: *Gesenius' Grammar*   **IBHS**: Waltke and O'Connor, *Syntax*
Jen: Jenni, *Lehrbuch*   **J-M**: Joüon and Muraoka, *Grammar*   **Ros**: Rosenthal, *Grammar*
Sch: Schneider, *Grammatik*   **Wms**: Williams, *Syntax*

28.56	GKC §113d, 113f, 142f n 2, 157b n 2; J-M §123b n 1; Wms §203; IBHS 597 □ B-L 383; B-M 2.141; Berg 2.61b	29.28	GKC §5n; IBHS 135 □ B-L 79s; Berg 1.4i
28.57	GKC §74i □ B-L 613d'; Berg 1.89b, 2.158d	30.1	GKC §72w; J-M §80m □ Berg 2.150n
28.59	GKC §91n; J-M §78g, 94g, 129h □ B-L 253s, 376r, 591l; Berg 2.158e	30.3	Wms §315; Gib 10 □ Berg 2.95d
		30.4	GKC §92b n 1, 60f □ B-L 548z; Berg 2.95d, 2.118d
28.61	Dav §100R3; J-M §139a, 160c; Wms §399; Gib 138 □ B-L 345p"	30.6	Wms §376
		30.9	GKC §114n n 2 □ B-L 399h"; Berg 2.59n*, 2.152t
28.62	GKC §119i; J-M §133c; Wms §249, 352 □ Brock §106b	30.10	J-M §139a
28.63	GKC §75ff □ IBHS 393 □ Berg 2.152t	30.11	GKC §74i, 133c □ GAHG 3.175 n 583; Berg 1.90b
28.64	Berg 2.16c	30.12	IBHS 518 □ GAHG 3.175 n 582, 3.175 n 583
28.66	GKC §75rr □ B-L 427t"; Berg 2.168q	30.15	Gib 6, 61
28.67	Dav §135R3; GKC §151b; J-M §137p, 163d; Wms §547; IBHS 321; Gib 186 □ Sch §51.4.4; Brock §9	30.18	Dav §40b; Gib 61□ Berg 2.28e
		30.19	Dav §40b; J-M §80m; IBHS 533; Gib 61 □ Berg 2.20b, 2.28e, 2.43i
28.68	J-M §158i □ B-M 2.170; Berg 2.148l	31.2	Berg 2.125c
29.2	J-M §143k; IBHS 532	31.3	GKC §69s; IBHS 132 □ B-L 384c'; Berg 2.78e
29.4	IBHS 532 □ B-L 385g'; Berg 2.21d	31.6	Gib 81
29.7	GKC §125d n 1 □ Berg 2.23g	31.7	Dav §72R1, 75; J-M §125u; Gib 112, 116
29.8	IBHS 502 n 17, 532 □ Berg 2.43i*	31.8	IBHS 297 □ GAHG 3.69 n 177
29.9	J-M §134c, 135c; IBHS 115	31.9ff.	IBHS 16
29.10	J-M §135c; IBHS 114	31.9	Berg 2.23g
29.14	GKC §100o n 2; J-M §102k, 156m; Gib 137	31.10	Gib 47
		31.11–12	Berg 2.52n
29.15	GKC §157c	31.11	Dav §36a; GKC §51l
29.16	GKC §103c □ B-L 644b"; GAHG 3.100, 3.115	31.12	GKC §120e; J-M §177h
		31.13	J-M §177h
29.17	Dav §128R4; Wms §461 □ GAHG 3.175 n 580; Brock §133e	31.16	GKC §93gg; J-M §96Bc □ B-L 554z; B-M 2.64
		31.17	GKC §158b; J-M §170h; Gib 6, 91, 159, 183 □ Berg 2.59o
29.18	GKC §69h n 1 □ B-L 379q; Jen §10.3.1.3	31.18	IBHS 314
29.19	Berg 2.54d*, 2.113f	31.19	Berg 2.23g
29.20	J-M §139a	31.20	Gib 92 □ Berg 2.117a
29.21	GKC §167b; IBHS 401	31.21	GKC §164d; Gib 72 □ Berg 2.19a, 2.117a, 2.157c
29.22	Dav §91R3 □ Berg 2.117a	31.24	J-M §166m □ B-M 2.116
29.23	J-M §37c □ B-L 266g	31.26	Dav §55a; Gib 94, 127 □ Berg 2.66k
29.24	Gib 159	31.27	J-M §121f n 1, 129ia; IBHS 628 n 51 □ GAHG 3.177 n 605, 3.204 n 768; Berg 1.149g, 2.73i*

B-L: Bauer and Leander, *Historische Grammatik*   **B-M**: Beer, *Grammatik*   **Berg**: Bergsträsser, *Grammatik*
Brock: Brockelmann, *Syntax*   **Dav**: Davidson, *Syntax*   **GAHG**: Richter, *Grammatik*
Gib: Gibson, *Davidson's Syntax, 4th ed.*   **GKC**: *Gesenius' Grammar*   **IBHS**: Waltke and O'Connor, *Syntax*
Jen: Jenni, *Lehrbuch*   **J-M**: Joüon and Muraoka, *Grammar*   **Ros**: Rosenthal, *Grammar*
Sch: Schneider, *Grammatik*   **Wms**: Williams, *Syntax*

31.29	GKC §74g; J-M §157d n 2 □ Berg 2.168q		32.19	Dav §28R4; Gib 35 □ B-L 274l
32	Dav §72; IBHS 14; Gib 116		32.20	GKC §108a, 108a n 2; J-M §79o
32.1	GKC §2r, 91l, 108d, 117b; J-M §115c n 3, 116b, 137g		32.21	Dav §128R1; GKC §152a n 1; J-M §160d, 160k; IBHS 661 n 59; Gib 142 □ B-L 376r; GAHG 2.63; Jen §10.3.3; Berg 2.25b; Brock §13b, 125a
32.2	B-L 114b			
32.3	GKC §69o □ Berg 2.125c			
32.4	GKC §126c; Gib 52, 53 □ B-L 582u'; B-M 1.77		32.22	GKC §69f □ Berg 2.126d
32.5	GKC §13c, 152e □ Berg 1.67u		32.23	GKC §69h n 1, 103p n 2; J-M §103m □ Berg 2.171 n d
32.6	GKC §20g, 75ll, 100i, 100i n 1, 152a n 1; J-M §160d; IBHS 661 n 59; Gib 138 □ Berg 1.67t; Brock §146		32.24	Dav §98b; GKC §116h, 116l; J-M §121p; Gib 134 □ B-L 562v
			32.26	GKC §58a n 1, 75mm □ B-L 425; Berg 2.162d
32.7	GKC §60f, 60g, 87n, 96 (p. 286), 123c; J-M §98f, 135d; Wms §101, 442; IBHS 116; Gib 37 □ B-L 367, 618n; B-M 2.83; Berg 1.70b, 2.104h, 2.153t; Brock §97a, 135c, 176c		32.27	Dav §127c, 131R1; GKC §139y; J-M §167k; Gib 160 □ B-M 3.116; Brock §165b
			32.28	GKC §50e, 93qq, 124e; J-M §96Cc; IBHS 653 □ Berg 2.85r
32.8–20	Gib 71		32.29	Dav §131; GKC §159x; J-M §167k n 1; IBHS 434, 638; Gib 155 □ B-M 3.116; GAHG 3.178 n 618; Jen §16.3.4; Brock §165b
32.8	Dav §65R6; GKC §53k, 109k; J-M §54c; IBHS 498, 598; Gib 18, 71 □ B-L 367; Berg 2.34h, 2.104h			
32.10–17	Berg 2.35h		32.30	GKC §134s; Gib 48
32.10	Dav §45R2; GKC §58i, 58k; J-M §61h, 113h; Wms §177; IBHS 518 □ B-L 197d, 338q, 339s; B-M 1.107, 1.112; Berg 2.122b, 2.151s		32.31	GKC §156b n 1
			32.32	GKC §20h; J-M §18k □ B-L 557g'; Berg 1.68v
			32.33	B-L 533f
32.11	Dav §44R3; GKC §52n, 155g; Gib 76 □ Berg 1.161e, 2.35h, 2.95d		32.35	Dav §25, 45R2, 113; GKC §52o, 145o, 155l; IBHS 110, 134 n 20; Gib 12, 21 □ B-M 3.20; Berg 2.96 n f
32.13	J-M §97Eb, 125u; IBHS 558; Gib 100 □ B-L 203q, 516q, 588k, 597h'; Berg 1.131d		32.36	Dav §17R5; GKC §29v, 44f, 152s; J-M §42f; Gib 142 □ B-L 216n, 355m, 371s; B-M 2.104; GAHG 3.78 n 207; Berg 2.14a, 2.115a; Brock §17
32.14	J-M §113o n 2; IBHS 498 □ GAHG 3.152 n 417; Berg 2.35h			
32.15	Dav §41R4, 143; GKC §20g, 144p, 154a n 1, 154a n 1a; Gib 10 □ Berg 1.67t		32.37	Dav §143; GKC §29t, 75u; IBHS 327; Gib 11, 185 □ B-L 253z; B-M 2.57; Berg 2.166m
32.16	Brock §138		32.38	B-L 411v
32.17	Dav §128R1, 143; GKC §144p, 152a n 1, 155e, 155f, 155h; J-M §158a; Wms §540; Gib 11 □ B-M 3.97; Brock §13b, 148		32.39	GKC §141h n 2; J-M §167k n 1; IBHS 618 n 28; Gib 148 □ B-L 376r
32.18–19	IBHS 558		32.40	Dav §119, 120R5; GKC §93aa n 1; IBHS 458, 500; Gib 186 □ Berg 2.16c
32.18	Dav §65R6; GKC §75s, 109k; Gib 71 □ Berg 2.163 n g			

B-L: Bauer and Leander, *Historische Grammatik* **B-M:** Beer, *Grammatik* **Berg:** Bergsträsser, *Grammatik*
Brock: Brockelmann, *Syntax* **Dav:** Davidson, *Syntax* **GAHG:** Richter, *Grammatik*
Gib: Gibson, *Davidson's Syntax, 4th ed.* **GKC:** *Gesenius' Grammar* **IBHS:** Waltke and O'Connor, *Syntax*
Jen: Jenni, *Lehrbuch* **J-M:** Joüon and Muraoka, *Grammar* **Ros:** Rosenthal, *Grammar*
Sch: Schneider, *Grammatik* **Wms:** Williams, *Syntax*

32.41	Dav §130b; GKC §159n; Gib 104, 153 □ B-L 430m; B-M 2.137; Berg 2.97h, 2.120b, 2.134c
32.43	B-L 368t; Berg 2.133b
32.46	GKC §117gg, 165b; J-M §168f; Gib 159
32.50	GKC §110c; J-M §47b, 114o □ Berg 2.50k
32.51	Jen §13.4.3
33	Gib 116
33.2–3	Brock §41i
33.2	GKC §103f n 3, 112pp; J-M §103f □ Berg 2.43 n b-k, 2.129h; Brock §147
33.3	GKC §116s; J-M §154c; Gib 175
33.4	GKC §131s
33.6	Dav §65R3; J-M §131f; IBHS 569; Gib 107 □ Berg 2.49h(bis), 2.164g
33.7	Berg 2.52n
33.8	IBHS 134 n 20 □ Berg 2.34h
33.9	GKC §19c, 117b n 1; J-M §113o n 2; IBHS 360 n 27, 467 n 67; Gib 116 □ B-L 199l, 368t; B-M 2.134; Berg 2.69c
33.10	B-M 2.61
33.11	Dav §71, 98R1, 149R4; GKC §116i, 117ll, 165b; J-M §126g; Wms §321; IBHS 160; Gib 134, 145 □ B-M 3.26, 3.31
33.12	GKC §44c □ Berg 2.172d
33.14ff.	GKC §48d
33.15	Berg 1.123v

33.16	Dav §63R1; GKC §48d, 90l, 90m; J-M §93n; IBHS 128; Gib 83 □ B-L 444p, 525j, 549a'; B-M 2.51; GAHG 1.72 n 136, 1.116 n 348; Jen §25.3.2.3; Berg 2.20 n a
33.17	J-M §9c n 1; IBHS 282 □ Berg 2.117a
33.19	Dav §28R6; GKC §130f, 133h □ Berg 2.126d; Brock §70d
33.21	GKC §68h, 76d □ B-L 442g; B-M 2.164; GAHG 3.79 n 215; Berg 1.91d, 2.120 n c, 2.163g
33.22	IBHS 132 n 18; Gib 55
33.23	GKC §48i, 69f; IBHS 653 □ B-M 2.139; Berg 2.81k, 2.127e
33.24	GKC §119w, 126m □ Berg 2.49h
33.25	B-M 2.35
33.27	GKC §131s; IBHS 132 □ B-L 74f
33.28	J-M §113o n 2; Gib 175
33.29	GKC §91l; J-M §132e; IBHS 385, 681 □ B-L 253z
34.1–3	IBHS 309
34.3	Berg 2.106l
34.4	IBHS 309; Gib 5 □ B-L 426
34.6	B-L 582v'; B-M 2.71; Brock §116f
34.7	GKC §91e
34.8	GKC §67g □ B-M 2.144; Berg 2.139p
34.9	GKC §116f; IBHS 366 □ GAHG 2.24 n 93
34.10	GKC §156c □ GAHG 3.171 n 534

B-L: Bauer and Leander, *Historische Grammatik*   **B-M**: Beer, *Grammatik*   **Berg**: Bergsträsser, *Grammatik*
Brock: Brockelmann, *Syntax*   **Dav**: Davidson, *Syntax*   **GAHG**: Richter, *Grammatik*
Gib: Gibson, *Davidson's Syntax, 4th ed.*   **GKC**: *Gesenius' Grammar*   **IBHS**: Waltke and O'Connor, *Syntax*
Jen: Jenni, *Lehrbuch*   **J-M**: Joüon and Muraoka, *Grammar*   **Ros**: Rosenthal, *Grammar*
Sch: Schneider, *Grammatik*   **Wms**: Williams, *Syntax*

JOSHUA

1–12	Brock §84a, 85a	2.5	Dav § 94; GKC §114k; J-M §123r, 124l, 166d; Wms §196, 204; IBHS 603; Gib 131, 133 □ B-M 3.58; Berg 2.28g, 2.56f, 2.60o, 2.84q; Brock §93d
1.1	GKC §49b n 1; J-M §118c n 2; IBHS 554 □ B-M [R] 1.66, 1.110; Berg 2.37a		
1.2	GKC §131n; J-M §146e; IBHS 233 □ Sch §46.1.3–4; Brock §68b, 133a	2.6	GKC §59g □ B-L 563x; Berg 2.18f, 2.165l; Brock §89
1.3	IBHS 508; Gib 182	2.7	Dav §145R1 □ B-L 599i'; Brock §163b
1.4	J-M §126h; Gib 143 □ Brock §100a	2.8	Dav §127d; GKC §152r, 164c; Gib 73, 169 □ Berg 2.20b
1.5	GKC §106c □ Berg 2.26b		
1.6	IBHS 441	2.9	IBHS 393
1.7–8	Berg 2.52n	2.10	GKC §117c, 157c; J-M §125g, 157c, 166l; IBHS 180; Gib 111 □ B-M 3.94; Berg 2.112c; Brock §160b
1.7	GKC §107p, 135o n 3; Wms §491 □ Berg 2.52 n n		
1.8	GKC §91k; J-M §94j		
1.9	Dav §123R2; Gib 184	2.11	GAHG 3.171 n 534
1.10	B-M [R] 1.58	2.12	GAHG 3.215 n 815
1.11	Gib 47	2.13	GKC §63q, 96; J-M §98d □ B-L 616c; B-M 2.80; Berg 2.114l
1.12	GKC §125d n 1; J-M §135c; 137b n 1; IBHS 115		
1.13	GKC §113bb; J-M §123u; Gib 94, 127 □ Jen §10.3.1.1; Berg 2.66k	2.14	Dav § 32R3; Wms §72; IBHS 539; Gib 6, 87 □ Berg 2.42g*
		2.15	GKC §126r; J-M §137m; Wms §84, 355; IBHS 202; Gib 27, 148 □ Brock §21bβ
1.14	J-M §125b; IBHS 171 n 18; Gib 20, 56		
1.15	GKC §103l; J-M §126h, 133h; Wms §263; Gib 143 □ Brock §21b, 100a	2.16	GKC §63c, 72q, 74k; J-M §80k, 155s □ B-L 375, 399h''; Berg 2.35i, 2.36k, 2.111b*, 2.145d, 2.158d; Brock §46c, 107a, 122k
1.16ff.	Sch §48.3.2		
1.16	J-M §158i n 1; Gib 10 □ B-M 3.99; Brock §152d	2.17	Dav §32R3, 55c; GKC §34a n 2, 59h; J-M §62f; Wms §33, 74, 579; Gib 6 □ B-L 362a'; Berg 2.18f
1.17	GKC §106c		
2.1	Sch §53.1.2.2; Brock §103a		
2.2	GKC §63i; IBHS 675 □ B-L 320g, 348h; B-M [R] 1.58; Berg 2.114i	2.18	GKC §59h, 116p; J-M §177a □ B-L 383; B-M 3.114; Berg 2.18f, 2.72h; Brock §164a
2.3	GKC §114g; J-M §155r □ B-L 348h; Berg 2.57k, 2.114i	2.20	Dav § 32R3, 55c; GKC §126y; J-M §62f, 138g; Wms §74, 117; IBHS 310 □ B-L 362a'; Berg 2.18f; Brock §60b
2.4	Dav §116R1, 126; GKC §60d, 135p; J-M §161g, 161l n 1; Gib 23, 184, 185 □ B-L 337n; B-M 1.79; Berg 2.24 n g, 2.28g; Brock §143c		
		2.22	GKC §107c, 164d; Gib 158 □ B-L 328a'; B-M 3.109; Brock §145bζ
		2.23	Gib 17

B-L: Bauer and Leander, *Historische Grammatik*   **B-M:** Beer, *Grammatik*   **Berg:** Bergsträsser, *Grammatik*
Brock: Brockelmann, *Syntax*   **Dav:** Davidson, *Syntax*   **GAHG:** Richter, *Grammatik*
Gib: Gibson, *Davidson's Syntax, 4th ed.*   **GKC:** *Gesenius' Grammar*   **IBHS:** Waltke and O'Connor, *Syntax*
Jen: Jenni, *Lehrbuch*   **J-M:** Joüon and Muraoka, *Grammar*   **Ros:** Rosenthal, *Grammar*
Sch: Schneider, *Grammatik*   **Wms:** Williams, *Syntax*

2.24	GKC §157b; J-M §6d n 3; Gib 111	4.8	Dav § 37a; GKC §97d; Wms §96; IBHS 279; Gib 48 □ B-L 626p
3.1	GKC §107c; J-M §113j; IBHS 514, 643; Gib 73 □ Jen §18.3.4.2; Brock §145bα	4.9	Dav § 48b; GKC §111d; IBHS 556 □ Berg 1.130c; Brock §114b
3.3	B-L 367; Brock §163c	4.10	J-M §159f
3.4	Dav § 32R5; J-M §103n; IBHS 263; Gib 44, 176 □ B-L 645h''	4.11–12	J-M §118k
		4.11	Berg 2.59n*, 2.84q
3.5	GKC §54k; Gib 17	4.14	GKC §52l; J-M §176h; IBHS 437 □ Berg 2.95d, 2.126d
3.7	GKC §114m, 115c, 165b; J-M §124c, 168f; Wms §466, 523; IBHS 310, 403, 599; Gib 6 □ Berg 2.20b, 2.54d*; Brock §161bα	4.16	GKC §109f; J-M §116b n 1, 177j □ Berg 2.164i; Brock §135b
		4.20	Wms §96; Gib 50
		4.21	Wms §469, 515; Gib 154 □ B-L 300q; Sch §53.4.5; Berg 2.20b; Brock §164d
3.8	Brock §163c		
3.9	GKC §66c □ B-L 367; B-M 2.135; Berg 2.122c	4.22	Wms §575 □ Sch §53.4.5; Brock §122l
3.10	B-M [R] 1.69; Berg 2.20b, 2.105i	4.23	Wms §468
3.11	Dav § 20R4; GKC §127g, 128c; IBHS 123	4.24	Dav §149R1; GKC §74g, 107q n 1, 165c □ B-L 443i; Berg 2.157 n c; Brock §145bγ*
3.12	Dav § 29R8, 38R4; GKC §134q; IBHS 116 n 6; Gib 42, 51 □ B-L 629b'; Sch §47.3.5; Brock §87	5.1	GAHG 3.171 n 534, 175 n 584; Brock §25cβ
3.13	J-M §80k; IBHS 123 □ B-L 321h; Berg 2.20b, 2.145d	5.2	Dav §83; GKC §120g, 124q; Wms §572; Gib 120 □ B-L 403; Berg 2.150p; Brock §72a
3.14	Dav §29R5; GKC §127g; Wms §29 □ B-L 533f	5.3	J-M §97Ac □ B-L 604g
3.15	B-L 603g; Berg 1.101m	5.4	J-M §148a, 158i
3.16	Dav §87; GKC §113h, 120g, 120h; J-M §123r, 177g; IBHS 592; Gib 126 □ Berg 2.65h*; Brock §133b	5.5	J-M §116r, 121f n 1, 148a; IBHS 628 □ B-M 2.117, 2.151; Berg 2.69c, 2.74l, 2.87c, 2.147g
		5.6	Gib 132 □ Berg 2.58n; Brock §125b
3.17	Dav §87; GKC §113h, 127g; J-M §80n, 123r; Gib 126 □ Berg 2.59n*, 2.66h*, 2.84q, 2.149 n m; Brock §50e	5.8	Dav §101Rd; GKC §63q; Gib 149 □ Berg 2.59n*, 2.115l; Brock §114b
4.1	Berg 2.59n*, 2.84q	5.9	GKC §67aa; J-M §129g; IBHS 551; Gib 96
4.2	GKC §134f □ Brock §84b, 129a		
4.3	Dav §86R3; GKC §72z; J-M §62a n 2, 80n □ B-L 403; B-M 3.38; Berg 2.65 n h, 2.149 n m	5.11	GKC §80g n 1
		5.12	GAHG 3.171 n 534; Brock §47
		5.13–14	Dav §124 □ B-M 3.88
4.4	Dav §37R5; GKC §133l n 1, 134k; Wms §96; Gib 48 □ B-M [R] 1.56; Brock §85b	5.13	J-M §161e, 161l; Wms §282, 455; IBHS 685; Gib 163, 184 □ Sch §53.5.2.2; Brock §169c
4.5	Dav §26	5.14	GKC §152c; J-M §172c □ Berg 1.67u
4.6	GKC §47m; Wms §469 □ B-L 300q; Berg 2.20b	5.15	J-M §131c n 2, 150ia
4.7	GKC §9v □ B-L 212k, 352	6.1	IBHS 623; Gib 136 □ B-M 3.67

B-L: Bauer and Leander, *Historische Grammatik* **B-M**: Beer, *Grammatik* **Berg**: Bergsträsser, *Grammatik*
Brock: Brockelmann, *Syntax* **Dav**: Davidson, *Syntax* **GAHG**: Richter, *Grammatik*
Gib: Gibson, *Davidson's Syntax, 4th ed.* **GKC**: *Gesenius' Grammar* **IBHS**: Waltke and O'Connor, *Syntax*
Jen: Jenni, *Lehrbuch* **J-M**: Joüon and Muraoka, *Grammar* **Ros**: Rosenthal, *Grammar*
Sch: Schneider, *Grammatik* **Wms**: Williams, *Syntax*

6.3	Dav §38R5, 87; J-M §123r n 1; IBHS 287, 589; Gib 47, 51, 126 □ Berg 2.65h*, 2.105i	7.10	Brock §107f
		7.12	J-M §126g; IBHS 173 □ GAHG 3.107 n 301; Jen §23.3.3
6.4	GKC §124q; Gib 47	7.13	Brock §47, 133a
6.5	Gib 149 □ B-M [R] 1.58; Brock §114b	7.14	B-L 93c; Brock §107iα
6.7	Berg 2.135e	7.15	Dav §81R3; GKC §121b; J-M §128b; IBHS 375 n 31
6.8	GKC §134l; Gib 47 □ B-L 650s; Berg 2.43 n b-k, 2.120a	7.19	IBHS 393, 451 □ GAHG 3.215 n 815
6.9	Dav §86R4; GKC §113u; Gib 125 □ Berg 2.65h; Brock §17	7.20	J-M §93h, 152a; IBHS 662; Gib 14
6.10	Berg 2.148k, 2.150n	7.21	Dav §20R2, 20R4; GKC §127i, 134g; J-M §129f, 140c, 158b; Wms §82; IBHS 152, 241, 249, 282; Gib 26, 49 □ GAHG 2.10 n 17; Brock §62a, 76c, 84c
6.11	J-M §123r n 1, 125u n 1; Gib 126 □ Berg 2.65h*, 2.105i		
6.13	Dav §86R4; GKC §112i, 113t; J-M §119v, 123m, 123n; Gib 125 □ Berg 2.65h, 2.65 n h; Brock §93g		
		7.22	Sch §50.2.2; Brock §89
		7.23	Berg 2.129 n m
6.16	GKC §134r; J-M §104f, 142q □ Brock §88, 122a	7.24	GKC §154a n 1(a) □ B-M 1.69; Berg 1.127cc
6.17	GKC §75oo □ B-L 375; Berg 2.15 n a, 2.158e	7.25	[R] 2.166; Dav §77; GKC §117ee; J-M §126l, 137f n 4; Wms §53; IBHS 247; Gib 144, 145 □ B-M 1.56; Brock §93m
6.19	J-M §125n, 154i; IBHS 170; Gib 144		
6.20	Berg 1.75g, 2.149m	7.26	Brock §36d
6.22	GKC §35b, 134l □ Berg 1.127cc, 1.142f; Brock §83b	8.2	Wms §359
		8.3	GKC §60c; Wms §56
6.23	Gib 47 □ Berg 1.127cc, 1.142f	8.4	GKC §104f □ Berg 2.53q, 2.74l
6.24	GKC §118f; Gib 144	8.5	Gib 154
6.25	B-L 375; Berg 1.127cc	8.6	Dav §100R6; Wms §587; IBHS 624; Gib 138
6.26	IBHS 232 □ Berg 2.114l; Brock §65a	8.8	Berg 2.83n; Brock §47
7.1	Dav §67b; GKC §75t; Gib 115	8.10	GKC §130a n 3; Wms §224
7.3	J-M §114j; IBHS 282; Gib 47 □ Berg 2.48f	8.11	Dav §20R4, 29R5; GKC §127g □ B-L 645h"; Brock §71d, 120a
7.5	Brock §107lα	8.12	IBHS 278; Gib 47
7.6	Dav §17R4	8.13	Wms §323; IBHS 212
7.7	Dav §48d, 83, 134; GKC §63p, 113x, 120e, 151e, 154b; J-M §68f, 163c, 177d, 177m; Wms §548; IBHS 638; Gib 101, 120, 186 □ B-L 352; GAHG 3.179 n 618; Berg 1.154e, 2.64 n f, 2.111 n c	8.14	Wms §224
		8.15	Berg 1.128dd
		8.17	GAHG 3.102 n 287, 3.102 n 289, 3.115
		8.18	GKC §119q □ J-M §125m
		8.19	Dav §22b, 73R1; J-M §137i □ Brock §104
7.8	Dav §145R1; J-M §105c, 126g; Gib 158 □ B-M [R] 1.56; Brock §163b	8.20	J-M §96Bb □ B-L 557e'
		8.21	B-L 557e'
7.9	GKC §75hh; J-M §79n, 82h; IBHS 178 n 32 □ B-L 636k; Berg 2.17e, 2.39i, 2.161b		

B-L: Bauer and Leander, *Historische Grammatik*   **B-M**: Beer, *Grammatik*   **Berg**: Bergsträsser, *Grammatik*
Brock: Brockelmann, *Syntax*   **Dav**: Davidson, *Syntax*   **GAHG**: Richter, *Grammatik*
Gib: Gibson, *Davidson's Syntax, 4th ed.*   **GKC**: *Gesenius' Grammar*   **IBHS**: Waltke and O'Connor, *Syntax*
Jen: Jenni, *Lehrbuch*   **J-M**: Joüon and Muraoka, *Grammar*   **Ros**: Rosenthal, *Grammar*
Sch: Schneider, *Grammatik*   **Wms**: Williams, *Syntax*

8.22	Dav §5; GKC §164d; J-M §54c n 3; Wms §116; Gib 6 □ B-M 3.111 Anm 1; GAHG 3.151 n 415; Berg 2.56h, 2.106 n l	9.25	GAHG 3.204 n 772
		9.27	Dav §78R3
		10.1	Dav §48c; Gib 101 □ B-M 3.73; Berg 1.75g, 2.23g
8.24	Berg 1.106c	10.5	IBHS 389 □ Brock §110b
8.25	GKC §146c	10.6	Berg 2.165k
8.28	GKC §20g, 117ii □ B-M 3.76; Brock §94dβ	10.7	Wms §315
		10.9	J-M §111e; Wms §491; IBHS 646
8.29	Dav §21e; J-M §137m; Gib 27		
8.30–31	IBHS 558	10.10	Berg 2.135d; Brock §89, 93k
8.30	Dav §51R2; J-M §113i; Wms §177; IBHS 514; Gib 72, 102 □ B-M [R] 2.34; Berg 2.33g; Brock §42a	10.11	J-M §141h n 2, 157a, 158l; IBHS 331 □ B-M 3.100; Brock §106c, 151
		10.12–13	IBHS 251
		10.12	Dav §51R2; GKC §107c; J-M §137h n 1; Wms §177; IBHS 558; Gib 72, 102 □ B-L 436; B-M 3.27; Berg 2.33g, 2.135e; Brock §10
8.31	Dav §51R2; Gib 102 □ Brock §36d		
8.32	GKC §29h, 47m □ B-L 299j		
8.33	Dav §20R4; GKC §127f, 127i; J-M §140c; Wms §82; Gib 26 □ GAHG 2.10 n 17; Brock §73d	10.13	Dav §1R2; GKC §107c, 135p, 150e; J-M §113k, 137h n 1, 161c, 164d; IBHS 301; Gib 3 □ B-L 368t; B-M 3.87; Berg 2.26c; Brock §42g, 138
9.2	Dav §71R2; GKC §118q; J-M §126d; Gib 145 □ B-M 3.78; Brock §104		
		10.16	Dav §36b; Gib 47
9.3	IBHS 148	10.17	GKC §93oo □ B-L 234p, 541j; Berg 2.111b*; Brock §103a
9.5	J-M §90e		
9.6	J-M §135c □ Brock §17	10.19	J-M §119l n 2; IBHS 412
9.7	Gib 185 □ B-L 357; Berg 2.84q	10.20	J-M §137f n 1, 124f □ Berg 1.129b
9.8	GKC §137a; IBHS 505; Gib 76		
9.9	Dav §67b; Gib 115 □ B-L 636k	10.23	Brock §128
9.11	Gib 4 □ Brock §5b	10.24	Dav §22R4; GKC §23i, 44l, 138i; J-M §145d n 1; Wms §91; IBHS 248, 339; Gib 29 □ B-L 265e, 385g'; B-M 2.16; GAHG 2.52 n 249; Berg 1.44c, 2.15 n a; Brock §150a
9.12–13	GKC §126aa		
9.12	Dav §6R1; GKC §54f, 72m, 112ss, 126aa; J-M §125c, 126a, 143i n 1; IBHS 172, 425, 430; Gib 6 □ B-L 395l'; GAHG 3.204 n 772; Berg 2.43 n b-k, 2.153u; Brock §98a		
		10.25	Brock §152a
		10.26	B-L 427t''; Berg 2.168q
		10.27	GKC §139g; J-M §143k; Gib 99 □ Brock §107b
9.13	Dav §6R1; J-M §143i n 1; Gib 6, 142		
9.14	Berg 2.77c	10.29	B-L 321k
9.16	Wms §360, 501; Gib 157 □ B-M 3.110; Brock §108b, 163b	10.32	Berg 2.23g
		10.33	J-M §54c n 3, 113i; Wms §177; Gib 72 □ B-L 348h; B-M 2.175; Berg 2.33g, 2.56h, 2.106 n l, 2.114i
9.20	GKC §113z □ B-M 3.64; Berg 2.62b, 2.67l; Brock §46c		
9.24	Dav §79; GKC §53t, 75hh; J-M §57b, 79n; Wms §59; IBHS 451; Gib 150 □ B-L 425; B-M 3.83; Berg 2.63e, 2.106n, 2.161b; Brock §35d		
		10.36	GKC §90e
		10.38	B-L 321k

B-L: Bauer and Leander, *Historische Grammatik*   **B-M**: Beer, *Grammatik*   **Berg**: Bergsträsser, *Grammatik*
Brock: Brockelmann, *Syntax*   **Dav**: Davidson, *Syntax*   **GAHG**: Richter, *Grammatik*
Gib: Gibson, *Davidson's Syntax, 4th ed.*   **GKC**: *Gesenius' Grammar*   **IBHS**: Waltke and O'Connor, *Syntax*
Jen: Jenni, *Lehrbuch*   **J-M**: Joüon and Muraoka, *Grammar*   **Ros**: Rosenthal, *Grammar*
Sch: Schneider, *Grammatik*   **Wms**: Williams, *Syntax*

10.39	J-M §63d □ Jen §6.3.1.5; Berg 2.23g		14.8	GKC §75ii □ B-L 424; Berg 2.166 n m, 2.171 n d
10.40	J-M §118i □ Berg 2.161b		14.9	Dav §120; Gib 187 □ B-L 132c
11.2	GKC §10g; J-M §9c(5) □ Berg 1.124w		14.10	J-M §129p, 143a; IBHS 311; Gib 6, 91, 157 □ GAHG 3.204 n 772; Brock §23a, 158
11.3	Gib 182			
11.4	Berg 1.127cc; Brock §107iα		14.11	Dav §151R2; GKC §115k, 161c; J-M §174i; Wms §256; Gib 129
11.6	Gib 114 □ Brock §109b			
11.7	Brock §106h		14.12	J-M §103j
11.8	GKC §126y, 164d; J-M §54c n 3, 63d □ Berg 2.56h, 2.106 n l; Brock §20b, 52b*, 60b		14.14	Dav §73R5 □ Brock §163a
			14.15	GKC §133g
			15.1	Brock §20b
11.9	GKC §126n; IBHS 245 □ B-M 3.28		15.3–11	Berg 2.43 n b-k
			15.3	Dav §44R2; GKC §112ss; Gib 75 □ Brock §119b
11.10	Brock §138			
11.11	Dav §113		15.4	GKC §44m □ B-L 423; Berg 2.15b, 2.43 n b-k
11.12	Berg 1.129b			
11.13	Gib 176		15.5	GKC §90d
11.14	GKC §53l; J-M §54c □ B-L 346x"; Berg 1.127cc, 2.106 n l		15.7	IBHS 240 □ Brock §20b
			15.8	B-L 582v'
11.20	Dav §109R2; J-M §54c; IBHS 605, 644; Gib 159 □ B-L 346x"; Berg 2.58m		15.9	B-L 547; Brock §116e??
			15.10	GKC §90e; J-M §93f; Wms §64 □ Jen §25.3.2.7
11.21	Wms §333; IBHS 219 □ GAHG 3.107 n 301		15.12	GKC §90f
			15.13	Wms §307; IBHS 194
11.22	Brock §138		15.14	GKC §134l; Gib 47 □ B-M 3.39; Brock §85c
11.23	Berg 2.23g; Brock §107iβ			
12.1	Dav §69a; Gib 143 □ B-M 3.31		15.16	J-M §156k, 156l, 176i □ Brock §157
12.6	IBHS 145			
12.9	GKC §2r(end)		15.18	GKC §16f □ Berg 2.84q
12.24	Gib 49		15.19	Dav §135R3; GKC §117x, 117ff., 126y; J-M §125ba; IBHS 174; Gib 112
13–24	Brock §84a, 85a			
13	B-L 627u			
13.1	Dav §58a □ Berg 2.15a, 2.27d; Brock §142		15.21	Dav §69R2; GKC §90e, 130a n 3; J-M §93f; Gib 145 □ Jen §25.3.2.7
13.4	Dav §69R2			
13.5	Dav §29R5; GKC §127f; IBHS 608 □ Berg 2.57 n k		15.29	GKC §19k n 2
			15.31	IBHS 280
13.6	J-M §133c		15.33	B-L 281f
13.7	GKC §125d n 1; J-M §133c		15.34	J-M §88o, 91h □ B-L 519d'
13.8	IBHS 484		15.36	J-M §91b, 95o □ B-L 516q
13.9	Dav §20R4		15.38	GKC §21e n 1 □ Berg 1.135d
13.14	Dav §116R1; GKC §145u n 3; J-M §149c		15.39	B-L 510v
			15.41	Gib 49
14.1	GKC §64d		15.45ff.	GKC §122h n 5
14.5	IBHS 406		15.46	GKC §112ss
14.6	J-M §146a; Gib 2		15.55	GKC §104g
14.7	GKC §72aa, 115i; J-M §80n □ B-L 360p; Berg 2.21d; Brock §47		15.56	GKC §21e n 1 □ Berg 1.136d
			15.59	B-L 281f
			15.60	B-M [R] 1.80

B-L: Bauer and Leander, *Historische Grammatik* **B-M**: Beer, *Grammatik* **Berg**: Bergsträsser, *Grammatik*
Brock: Brockelmann, *Syntax* **Dav**: Davidson, *Syntax* **GAHG**: Richter, *Grammatik*
Gib: Gibson, *Davidson's Syntax, 4th ed.* **GKC**: *Gesenius' Grammar* **IBHS**: Waltke and O'Connor, *Syntax*
Jen: Jenni, *Lehrbuch* **J-M**: Joüon and Muraoka, *Grammar* **Ros**: Rosenthal, *Grammar*
Sch: Schneider, *Grammatik* **Wms**: Williams, *Syntax*

16.1	GKC §126z	19.13	GKC §90i; J-M §93c □ B-L
16.2	GKC §112ss □ Berg 2.43 n b-k		527q, 563x, 564; Berg
16.3ff.	GKC §126y		2.43 n b-k
16.3	GKC §126y □ Berg 2.43 n b-k	19.22	Berg 2.43 n b-k
16.5	GKC §126y	19.25	GKC §104g □ B-L 510v
16.6–8	Berg 2.43 n b-k	19.26–29	Berg 2.43 n b-k
16.6	B-L 510v	19.28	GKC §126y
16.8	Dav §44R2; J-M §137q; Gib 75	19.29	B-L 574y
17.1	GKC §127a; IBHS 157 □ B-M	19.30	Gib 49
	3.9, 3.12	19.34	Berg 2.43 n b-k
17.2	GKC §114l	19.35	B-L 511v
17.3	GKC §113n	19.43	GKC §90i n 1
17.4	B-L 638t; B-M 2.176	19.44	B-L 281f, 510v
17.5	J-M §150j n 3 □ Berg 2.157c	19.49	B-L 316c, 363i; Berg 2.83o n 1
17.7–9	Berg 2.43 n b-k	19.50	J-M §79m □ Berg 2.161b
17.7	B-L 510v	19.51	Dav §28R5; GKC §129d; J-M
17.9	GKC §112ss		§130c; IBHS 406; Gib 36 □
17.11	Dav §72R4; GKC §97c, 117l;		Berg 1.78m
	J-M §125j; Gib 117	20.4	Berg 1.129b
17.13	J-M §123i; Gib 157 □ GAHG	20.5	Dav §130R2
	2.64 n 272; Berg 2.62c	21	Gib 47
17.14	Dav §138a; Gib 168	21.1	Brock §74a
17.15	GKC §90i; Gib 153 □ Berg	21.10	B-L 628w
	1.154e; Brock §107f	21.11	GKC §91k □ B-L 252r; Berg
17.16	Dav §81; GKC §143e; IBHS		1.144c
	385 n 19	21.14	B-L 281f
18.1	Berg 2.27d; Brock §139b	21.23	B-L 281f
18.2	IBHS 406 □ Berg 2.26d	21.31	B-L 510v
18.3	Berg 2.25b	21.32	GKC §88c □ B-L 519d'
18.4	GKC §119s	21.39	Gib 49
18.5	Dav §73R4	21.41	IBHS 281
18.10	IBHS 406	21.42	J-M §6d n 3 □ Berg 2.30b
18.12ff.	GKC §44m	21.45	B-M 3.51
18.12–21	Berg 2.43 n b-k	22.1	Gib 72, 102 □ Berg 2.33g
18.12	GKC §90i, 112ss □ Berg 2.15b	22.3	GKC §112ss; J-M §143a; Gib
18.13	GKC §126y		103 □ Brock §23a
18.14	Berg 2.15b	22.4	IBHS 208
18.18	Brock §116f	22.5	Jen §7.1
18.19	GKC §44m □ Berg 2.15b	22.8	Wms §335 □ Berg 2.65h*
18.20	GKC §47f □ B-L 299k; Berg	22.9	GKC §68i; J-M §73f; IBHS 391
	2.84q(bis), 1.129b		□ B-L 371v; Berg 2.121d
18.28	B-L 510v	22.14	Brock §129a
19.3	GKC §19k n 2	22.16	Berg 2.82n; Brock §106h
19.6	B-L 470nα	22.17	Dav §72R4; GKC §117aa; J-M
19.7	GKC §104g		§125j; Wms §59; IBHS 183, 425;
19.11–14	Berg 2.43 n b-k		Gib 117 □ B-M 3.75; Brock
19.11	GKC §112ss		§102
19.12	B-L 510v; GAHG 3.152 n 417	22.18	Gib 156
		22.19	Brock §116k

B-L: Bauer and Leander, *Historische Grammatik*   **B-M**: Beer, *Grammatik*   **Berg**: Bergsträsser, *Grammatik*
Brock: Brockelmann, *Syntax*   **Dav**: Davidson, *Syntax*   **GAHG**: Richter, *Grammatik*
Gib: Gibson, *Davidson's Syntax, 4th ed.*   **GKC**: Gesenius' *Grammar*   **IBHS**: Waltke and O'Connor, *Syntax*
Jen: Jenni, *Lehrbuch*   **J-M**: Joüon and Muraoka, *Grammar*   **Ros**: Rosenthal, *Grammar*
Sch: Schneider, *Grammatik*   **Wms**: Williams, *Syntax*

22.20	Dav §67b; GKC §150m; Gib 115 □ B-M 3.75	24.4	Brock §99b
22.21	Gib 111	24.6	Brock §50e
22.22	B-L 135h, 158; Berg 1.132f	24.7	GKC §145m □ Brock §151??
22.24	Berg 1.65p	24.8	Berg 2.21d; Brock §117b
22.25	GKC §69n, 103p n 1; IBHS 201 □ B-L 645h″; Berg 1.52k, 2.83p, 2.157b	24.10	Dav §86R1; GKC §113r; J-M §123l □ Berg 2.21d, 2.64f, 2.64g; Brock §107
22.26	Dav §93 □ B-L 135h; Berg 1.65p	24.12	J-M §47a, 69d
22.27	Gib 148	24.13	B-M 3.81; Berg 2.71g
22.28	Dav §57R1, 136R1	24.14–15	GKC §117c
22.29	Dav §117R1 □ Berg 1.65p, 2.58m	24.14	Dav §32R5; GKC §75oo; J-M §119l; Gib 44 □ B-L 443i; B-M 3.74; Berg 1.93g, 2.127d, 2.158e; Brock §96, 137
22.31	Dav §67b, 107c; IBHS 667; Gib 72, 115 □ Berg 2.34g	24.15	GKC §47m; J-M §124b; Wms §192, 591; IBHS 69, 321, 605; Gib 8 □ Sch §51.4.6, 50.1.5.1; Berg 2.20b; Brock §15g, 136b, 169b
22.32	Dav §114; Gib 22 □ B-M 3.76		
22.33	Berg 2.71f		
23.1	Wms §489; IBHS 645; Gib 148 □ Brock §163b		
23.3	J-M §137l	24.17	J-M §137l □ Jen §22.3.3; Brock §99a
23.4	J-M §126h, 133c; Gib 143	24.18	J-M §121m
23.5	GKC §60a □ B-L 351; Berg 2.79g	24.19	GKC §124h, 132h, 145i; J-M §148a; IBHS 122 n 16, 257 n 5; Gib 19 □ B-M 1.102; Brock §19c, 59c
23.6	Berg 2.59n*		
23.9	GKC §135f; J-M §156b		
23.11	Berg 2.59n; Brock §99b	24.20	Brock §163b
23.13	Berg 2.82n	24.24	Brock §106d
23.14	Berg 2.43i; Brock §41f	24.25	IBHS 16
23.15	GKC §103b; J-M §54c □ B-L 346x″, 642n′	24.26	IBHS 16
23.16	IBHS 537 □ Berg 2.41f	24.27	Brock §106h
24	B-L 627u	24.28	B-M 2.17
24.2	Gib 35, 148	24.32	GKC §127e
24.3	GKC §69v □ B-L 385g′; Berg 2.21d, 2.165k	24.33	J-M §150n

B-L: Bauer and Leander, *Historische Grammatik*   **B-M**: Beer, *Grammatik*   **Berg**: Bergsträsser, *Grammatik*
Brock: Brockelmann, *Syntax*   **Dav**: Davidson, *Syntax*   **GAHG**: Richter, *Grammatik*
Gib: Gibson, *Davidson's Syntax, 4th ed.*   **GKC**: *Gesenius' Grammar*   **IBHS**: Waltke and O'Connor, *Syntax*
Jen: Jenni, *Lehrbuch*   **J-M**: Joüon and Muraoka, *Grammar*   **Ros**: Rosenthal, *Grammar*
Sch: Schneider, *Grammatik*   **Wms**: Williams, *Syntax*

JUDGES

B-L: Bauer and Leander, *Historische Grammatik*   **B-M**: Beer, *Grammatik*   **Berg**: Bergsträsser, *Grammatik*
Brock: Brockelmann, *Syntax*   **Dav**: Davidson, *Syntax*   **GAHG**: Richter, *Grammatik*
Gib: Gibson, *Davidson's Syntax, 4th ed.*   **GKC**: *Gesenius' Grammar*   **IBHS**: Waltke and O'Connor, *Syntax*
Jen: Jenni, *Lehrbuch*   **J-M**: Joüon and Muraoka, *Grammar*   **Ros**: Rosenthal, *Grammar*
Sch: Schneider, *Grammatik*   **Wms**: Williams, *Syntax*

3.14	IBHS 280; Gib 49		4.11	Dav §48c, 105R1; Wms §310;
3.15	GKC §127d; J-M §125f, 127d,			IBHS 195; Gib 101, 148
	140b; IBHS 173, 304; Gib 33 □		4.13	Gib 47
	Brock §93a, 81e		4.14	Dav §4, 9c; GKC §125i; Wms
3.16	Dav §139, 139R1; GKC §135i;			§114; IBHS 310; Gib 5, 9
	J-M §98e, 146k, 155t, 159d;		4.15	J-M §137f, 146g
	IBHS 221 n 120, 305; Gib 13,		4.16	IBHS 216; Gib 183
	47, 168 □ B-M 2.81; Jen		4.18	GKC §72s, 72t, 126r; J-M §33;
	§12.3.3; Brock §80c, 120a			Gib 27 □ B-L 398c″; Berg
3.17	IBHS 268, 440; Gib 45			1.153c, 2.145e
3.18	J-M §166b n 1, 166n; IBHS 643		4.19	Dav §75; GKC §74k; J-M
	□ Jen §18.3.4.2			§125u; IBHS 176; Gib 27 □ B-L
3.19	GKC §147d; Wms §339; Gib 27,			387r; B-M 1.51; Berg 2.158d;
	188 □ B-L 652b; B-M 2.145;			Brock §21bβ
	Berg 2.135e; Brock §108a		4.20	Dav §116R6, 126; GKC §58g,
3.20	J-M §137f; IBHS 243 n 8; Gib			64f, 110k, 112bb, 112ff, 147c,
	27, 149, 167, 168			150n, 152k, 159s; J-M §160j,
3.22	Berg 2.27d			161l, 176d; Gib 90, 154, 183 □
3.23	Dav §58R1; GKC §112tt; J-M			B-M 3.87, 3.114; Jen §9.3.3.2;
	§119z □ Berg 2.43 n b-k; Brock			Berg 2.20 n a, 2.43i
	§116b		4.21	GKC §72p, 72t; J-M §80k,
3.24	Dav §100b; GKC §67v, 93h,			137m; Gib 27 □ B-L 403, 534;
	164b; Gib 169, 176 □ B-L 437;			Sch §52.5.7.3; Berg 1.44c,
	B-M 3.108; Berg 2.70e,			1.149h, 2.147g, 2.173 n g
	2.80 n h, 2.140q		4.22	Dav §75, 97R1; IBHS 176, 616,
3.25	GKC §116d; J-M §112a n 5;			630; Gib 112, 137 □ Jen §8.3.2.2
	IBHS 626, 676 n 9; Gib 27, 57,		4.24	Dav §86R4; GKC §113h n 2,
	136 □ Berg 2.69 n c, 2.70e,			113u; J-M §123s; Gib 125, 158
	2.173 n f; Brock §19c			□ GAHG 3.168 n 503; Berg
3.26	Wms §311 □ Berg 2.109c			2.65 n h; Brock §93g
3.28	GKC §129e; J-M §155o □ B-M		5	Dav §72; J-M §137f n 1; IBHS
	3.32			4, 14; Gib 116 □ B-L 3d
3.29	Gib 47		5.1	Dav §114; GKC §2r, 73e, 117b,
3.30	Dav §47; Gib 96			146g; J-M §81e; Gib 22 □ Berg
3.31	Gib 27			2.149m
4.1	Gib 168		5.2	J-M §137f n 1
4.3	Gib 65, 167		5.3	Dav §107R1; J-M §137f n 1;
4.4	Dav §19R1; GKC §131b; Gib			IBHS 296; Gib 2 □ Brock §34b
	25, 182 □ B-M 3.35; Brock §63a		5.4	Dav §73R2; GKC §117z; J-M
4.6	Dav §60R4; GKC §150e; J-M			§69b, 125d, 137f n 1; IBHS 438
	§161c; Gib 47 □ Berg 2.53q			□ B-L 354e; Berg 2.116d; Brock
4.8	Dav §130a; GKC §49m; J-M			§20b, 135a
	§113n, 176d; Wms §171; Gib		5.5	Dav §6R1; GKC §67dd,
	86, 153 □ Jen §16.3.4; Berg			136 n 2; J-M §137f n 1, 143i;
	2.16c			IBHS 337; Gib 6 □ B-L 431t;
4.9	Dav §3R2,154; GKC §135m;			B-M 2.146, 3.32; Berg 2.139p;
	J-M §123i, 129h, 173a; Wms			Brock §75
	§427, 558; IBHS 147, 303, 586,		5.6	Gib 134
	672; Gib 3, 176 □ Brock §80d			
4.10	Brock §117d			

B-L: Bauer and Leander, *Historische Grammatik*   **B-M**: Beer, *Grammatik*   **Berg**: Bergsträsser, *Grammatik*
Brock: Brockelmann, *Syntax*   **Dav**: Davidson, *Syntax*   **GAHG**: Richter, *Grammatik*
Gib: Gibson, *Davidson's Syntax, 4th ed.*   **GKC**: *Gesenius' Grammar*   **IBHS**: Waltke and O'Connor, *Syntax*
Jen: Jenni, *Lehrbuch*   **J-M**: Joüon and Muraoka, *Grammar*   **Ros**: Rosenthal, *Grammar*
Sch: Schneider, *Grammatik*   **Wms**: Williams, *Syntax*

5.7	GKC §20i, 36, 44h n 1; J-M §18g n 1, 38, 38 n 6; Wms §472; IBHS 332, 335 n 14 □ B-L 218c, 264b, 351, 404, 517v; B-M 1.68, 2.15, 2.150, 3.110; Berg 1.69y, 2.15 n a, 2.77c; Brock §150c, 163b
5.8	Dav §44R1, 122; GKC §107b, 149e; Gib 74, 183 □ Berg 2.30b; Brock §54f
5.9	J-M §129f(8), 137f n 1, 155nd
5.10	Dav §28R1; GKC §87e, 130a; J-M §90c, 129m; Wms §30; IBHS 118, 155 n 34; Gib 34 □ B-L 517t, 564; Berg 2.152t; Brock §71d
5.11	GKC §167c; Gib 31, 72 □ Berg 2.34g
5.12	GKC §10g, 72s; J-M §9c(4) □ B-L 208r, 426; B-M 1.65; Berg 1.70b, 1.124w, 1.148g, 2.144b, 2.145e
5.13	GKC §69g, 75bb □ B-L 383 n 2; Berg 2.50l, 2.164i
5.14	GKC §93aa, 147c; J-M §103d □ B-L 564; B-M 2.65
5.15	Dav §151; GKC §10g, 87g, 93bb; J-M §96Ap; Gib 161 □ B-L 564
5.16	B-L 98l; Berg 1.157o
5.17	GKC §117bb; J-M §113o n 2 □ B-L 302a'; B-M 3.75; Berg 2.84q; Brock §107a
5.19	J-M §155k; Gib 72 □ Berg 2.34g
5.20	J-M §137f n 1 □ Sch §45.5
5.21	Dav §71R2; GKC §118q; Gib 145
5.22	Dav §28R6, 29R8; GKC §20h, 123e; Gib 36, 42 □ Berg 1.68v, 2.34g
5.23	J-M §123ja; Gib 125 □ B-L 435p'; B-M 2.145; Berg 2.132a*, 2.135e
5.24	GKC §119w
5.25	Gib 110
5.26	GKC §47k; J-M §61f, 113h; IBHS 517 n 63 □ B-M 3.46; Berg 2.20 n a, 2.33f, 2.43 n b-k(bis)
5.27	Dav §10R3, 32R5, 41R4; GKC §154a n 1a; J-M §177a; IBHS 248 n 19, 332 n 4; Gib 10, 29 □ Brock §133a, 152e
5.28	GKC §64h; Wms §355; Gib 148 □ B-L 371s; Berg 1.152a, 2.115a
5.29	GKC §75w, 128i, 133h; IBHS 101 n 29; Gib 38, 44 □ B-L 425; Berg 2.167o; Brock §76b
5.30	GKC §93g; J-M §96Ai □ B-L 213o, 568l
5.31–6.2	Sch §48.6.1.4
5.31	IBHS 666; Gib 141
6.2–6	Dav §54b
6.2–3	Gib 90
6.2	Gib 90
6.3–5	Berg 2.33 n e
6.3	Dav §57, 130b; GKC §112ee, 112gg, 164d; J-M §166p; IBHS 539, 643; Gib 90, 154 □ Jen §18.3.4.2; Berg 2.42g*
6.4	Dav §29R5, 44R1, 54R1, 152; GKC §107e; J-M §155h; Gib 39, 73, 90 □ Brock §36e
6.5	Dav §44R1; Gib 73 □ Berg 2.31b
6.6	Berg 2.138o
6.8	Dav §19R1; IBHS 252; Gib 25 □ Brock §34b, 63a
6.9–10	IBHS 577
6.9	GKC §49c, 49e □ B-L 357; Berg 2.21d, 2.22e, 2.23f
6.10	GKC §49e; J-M §154fa □ Brock §41f
6.11	GKC §127d; J-M §139a n 1; IBHS 245; Gib 26, 168
6.12	J-M §137g, 154f, 163b; Gib 27
6.13	Dav §132R2, 136R1; GKC §150dd, 159i; J-M §105c, 115c n 3, 167b, 167o, 177m; Gib 156 □ Jen §16.3.4
6.14	Dav §32R3, 123R2; GKC §126y; J-M §138g; Wms §74; Gib 6, 184 □ Sch §47.1.6; Brock §60b
6.15	J-M §105c; IBHS 269 n 29; Gib 45 □ GAHG 3.78 n 206; Brock §25a
6.16	Dav §53a, 146R2; GKC §49l, 112p; J-M §119e, 157c; IBHS 528; Gib 92, 111

B-L: Bauer and Leander, *Historische Grammatik*   **B-M**: Beer, *Grammatik*   **Berg**: Bergsträsser, *Grammatik*
Brock: Brockelmann, *Syntax*   **Dav**: Davidson, *Syntax*   **GAHG**: Richter, *Grammatik*
Gib: Gibson, *Davidson's Syntax, 4th ed.*   **GKC**: *Gesenius' Grammar*   **IBHS**: Waltke and O'Connor, *Syntax*
Jen: Jenni, *Lehrbuch*   **J-M**: Joüon and Muraoka, *Grammar*   **Ros**: Rosenthal, *Grammar*
Sch: Schneider, *Grammatik*   **Wms**: Williams, *Syntax*

6.17	GKC §36; J-M §38, 38 n 6; Wms §472; IBHS 335 n 14 ☐ B-L 264b, 264c; GAHG 3.170 n 526; Sch §13.2.2; Berg 2.41d; Brock §150c, 170c	7.2	Dav §34R2; J-M §154fa, 155nb; IBHS 267; Gib 45
6.18	Dav §96R2, 107R1; GKC §72t, 112v, 114q, 114r, 135a; J-M §80k, 119o, 124q, 146a; Gib 2, 94, 131 ☐ Berg 2.17d, 2.41f, 2.52 n n; Brock §137	7.3	Dav §8, 37c; GKC §137c; J-M §118f, 144f n 1; Wms §121; IBHS 280, 320; Gib 8, 49 ☐ B-L 265f; B-M 2.16, 2.102; GAHG 3.180 n 625, 3.215 n 815; Berg 2.49i; Brock §154
6.19	Dav §24b, 41R3; GKC §53n, 156d; Gib 32, 167 ☐ B-L 232j, 333a'; Berg 2.104i; Brock §119b	7.4	Dav §4; GKC §136b; J-M §103j n 1, 146a, 154fa; Wms §113; IBHS 195 n 21, 308 ☐ B-M 3.16; Sch §52.4.3.1; Brock §23c
6.20	GKC §34f; Gib 26 ☐ B-L 261f, 306j; Berg 2.84q; Brock §137	7.5	Dav §44a; Wms §92; IBHS 244, 506; Gib 28, 74 ☐ Berg 2.134d
6.22	J-M §139a n 1; Gib 26 ☐ GAHG 2.49 n 228, 3.151 n 413; Brock §103b	7.6	GKC §93n; J-M §52d ☐ B-L 567 n 1
6.23	J-M §163b; Gib 188	7.7	Dav §11Rd, 37f; IBHS 283; Gib 14, 49 ☐ Brock §84c
6.24	GKC §128c; IBHS 245; Gib 26	7.8	GKC §131s; Gib 14, 165 ☐ B-L 581
6.25	Dav §28R5, 111R2; GKC §126w, 128c; J-M §119l; Gib 36	7.9	J-M §133i ☐ Brock §133a
6.26	GKC §49k, 126w; J-M §43b, 113b ☐ Berg 2.17d, 2.112c	7.10	J-M §119l n 2, 133i; Gib 2, 137
6.27	J-M §170k; Wms §260	7.11	J-M §119l n 2, 150d; Wms §231; Gib 2
6.28	Dav §81R3, 99; GKC §63p; J-M §68f, 121q, 155ng; Wms §58, 218; IBHS 374 n 30, 420 n 6, 621; Gib 135 ☐ B-L 287n', 355p, 425; Berg 1.154e, 2.27d, 2.87c; Brock §138	7.12	GKC §36; J-M §112a n 5; Wms §129, 471, 537; IBHS 335; Gib 12 ☐ B-L 264b; Jen §27.3.3; Brock §150c
6.29	J-M §147c, 155nh	7.13	Dav §58R1; GKC §112qq, 128o; Gib 32, 103 ☐ Berg 2.43 n b-k
6.30	GKC §109f; Dav §65a; IBHS 578; Gib 106	7.14	Wms §422
6.31	GKC §73e, 100m; Wms §311; Gib 153, 156 ☐ Berg 2.48f, 2.149m	7.15	Berg 1.75g
		7.16	Dav §17R4
6.32	Berg 2.48f, 2.149m	7.17	GKC §116p; J-M §155p; IBHS 677 ☐ Berg 2.72h; Brock §123g
6.33	Gib 167	7.18	GKC §147c
6.36	GKC §116q, 159v; J-M §154l; IBHS 624; Gib 57, 137, 153 ☐ B-L 232j; Berg 2.72h*; Brock §30b, 80e	7.19	Dav §17R4, 86a, 88, 141R2; GKC §113z; J-M §123k, 123x, 136l; Wms §210; IBHS 588; Gib 124, 126, 176 ☐ Berg 2.62c, 2.67m
6.37	B-L 232j	7.20	GKC §147c; IBHS 381 ☐ Berg 2.84q; Brock §7a
6.38	J-M §137m; Gib 27 ☐ B-L 95f; Berg 2.144c, 2.162f	7.21	Dav §101Rd ☐ Brock §116h
6.39	GKC §108d, 109a n 2; IBHS 575 n 24 ☐ Berg 2.47e(bis), 2.49h	7.22	Dav §37d, 37f, 136R1; IBHS 283; Gib 49, 50 ☐ B-L 510v
6.40	J-M §118f	7.23	GKC §102b ☐ B-L 642p'

B-L: Bauer and Leander, *Historische Grammatik* B-M: Beer, *Grammatik* Berg: Bergsträsser, *Grammatik*
Brock: Brockelmann, *Syntax* Dav: Davidson, *Syntax* GAHG: Richter, *Grammatik*
Gib: Gibson, *Davidson's Syntax, 4th ed.* GKC: *Gesenius' Grammar* IBHS: Waltke and O'Connor, *Syntax*
Jen: Jenni, *Lehrbuch* J-M: Joüon and Muraoka, *Grammar* Ros: Rosenthal, *Grammar*
Sch: Schneider, *Grammatik* Wms: Williams, *Syntax*

7.25	Dav §17R4; GKC §124r; J-M §136l, 155od; Gib 171 □ Brock §138	8.30	Dav §98R1; Gib 49, 134
8.1	Dav §95, 144R1; GKC §49d n 1, 74h, 155d, 155h; J-M §44e, 158c; Gib 8, 11 □ B-L 376r; Berg 2.21b, 2.158e	8.32	Dav §29R5; GKC §125h, 128c
		8.33	J-M §166n; Gib 157 □ Brock §107iβ
		8.34	IBHS 492; Gib 135
8.2	Dav §116R3; GKC §20m, 103h; J-M §154h n 1; Gib 8, 37, 44 □ Berg 1.141f	9.2	Dav §90, 91a, 115g, 124; J-M §124b, 141g; IBHS 264, 601, 611; Gib 46, 128, 129, 184 □ Jen §10.3.1.3; Berg 2.54d
8.3	J-M §155p; Gib 72	9.3	Gib 4, 53 □ B-M 3.51; Berg 2.27d; Brock §110e
8.4	GKC §118n □ GAHG 3.146 n 382	9.5	IBHS 251, 394 □ Sch §45.3.1; Berg 2.111b*
8.5	Brock §117d	9.6	Dav §101Rd
8.6	Wms §228, 450; IBHS 508; Gib 68, 79	9.7	IBHS 563
8.7	Dav §55b; Wms §345 □ GAHG 3.176 n 603	9.8	Dav §60R1, 86a; GKC §48i, 48i n 2, 113o; J-M §123k; IBHS 571; Gib 81, 124 □ B-L 30, 306o; B-M 2.114; Sch §52.5.7.1, 54.2.2.5; Berg 2.63e, 2.81k
8.8	IBHS 222; Gib 132 □ B-M 3.79		
8.10	GKC §97e; J-M §100e, 121i, 139i □ B-L 625n	9.9	Dav §41R2, 51R2; GKC §63k, 100n, 106n, 112s; J-M §112j; Gib 67, 93, 102 □ B-L 208t, 239k', 351, 623j; B-M 2.173; Berg 2.44l, 2.110 n b, 2.145d
8.11	Dav §28R1, 71R2, 138c; GKC §130a n 2; Wms §29, 82; IBHS 87 n 13; Gib 168 □ Berg 1.156m; Brock §21d, 73b, 99b, 120a		
		9.10ff.	GKC §46e
8.12	B-M 2.113; Brock §83b	9.10	GKC §46d; J-M §48c □ B-L 306l; Berg 2.80i
8.14	Dav §27; J-M §129a □ B-M 2.113; GAHG 2.67 n 288	9.11	Gib 68 □ B-L 208t, 239k, 351, 632j; B-M 3.52; Berg 2.44l, 2.110 n b; Brock §41e
8.15	GKC §138b; J-M §158k □ B-L 221p; Brock §122d		
8.16	Berg 2.129h	9.12	B-L 30, 306l, 306o; B-M 2.114; Berg 2.80i, 2.81k
8.18	Dav §11Rd, 151R2; GKC §126o, 161c; J-M §174i; Gib 14, 26 □ Brock §126a	9.13	Gib 68 □ B-L 208t, 239k', 351, 632j; Berg 2.44l, 2.110 n b
8.19	Dav §39d, 119, 131; GKC §63q, 159x; J-M §167k; Wms §166, 516; IBHS 494; Gib 155, 186 □ GAHG 3.178 n 618; Berg 2.114l; Brock §165b	9.14	Dav §60R1, 86a; IBHS 571; Gib 81
		9.15	Dav §127b, 130a; GKC §152k, 159v; J-M §154fe, 160j; Gib 153, 154 □ GAHG 3.174 n 576; Brock §164bα, 169a
8.20	Gib 58		
8.21	GKC §135a; Gib 2, 22 □ B-M 3.11; Brock §34b	9.16	Dav §32R5, 47; GKC §167a; IBHS 263; Gib 44, 96
8.23	Dav §107; J-M §146a, 155nb; Gib 2	9.17	Dav §101Rd; GKC §119bb; Wms §295; Gib 149
8.24	Dav §136R1	9.18	Jen §29.3.3
8.25	GKC §126r; J-M §137m; Gib 27	9.19	Dav §130b, 167a; Gib 153
8.26	GKC §36; IBHS 335 n 16 □ B-L 264b; Brock §150c	9.20	GAHG 3.174 n 576; Brock §169a
8.28	Dav §17R4, 47; Gib 96	9.22	GKC §116u □ Berg 2.138 n l

B-L: Bauer and Leander, *Historische Grammatik* **B-M**: Beer, *Grammatik* **Berg**: Bergsträsser, *Grammatik*
Brock: Brockelmann, *Syntax* **Dav**: Davidson, *Syntax* **GAHG**: Richter, *Grammatik*
Gib: Gibson, *Davidson's Syntax, 4th ed.* **GKC**: *Gesenius' Grammar* **IBHS**: Waltke and O'Connor, *Syntax*
Jen: Jenni, *Lehrbuch* **J-M**: Joüon and Muraoka, *Grammar* **Ros**: Rosenthal, *Grammar*
Sch: Schneider, *Grammatik* **Wms**: Williams, *Syntax*

9.24	J-M §124l		9.55	Dav §11Rd, 115; GKC §145d;
9.25	IBHS 416			J-M §150e; Gib 14, 22
9.27	Dav §135R3 □ B-L 438		10.1	J-M §154h n 1; Gib 26
9.28	Dav §43b, 102; GKC §107u,		10.2	Dav §37c; Gib 49
	137a; J-M §144b, 154d; Gib 68,		10.3	Dav §37c; Gib 49
	79		10.4	Dav §37b; GKC §96 (p. 286);
9.29	Dav §65b; GKC §48l, 75cc, 76e,			Gib 49 □ B-L 620r
	108f, 151b, 154b; J-M §116c,		10.9	Dav §109; GKC §144b; J-M
	163d; Gib 106, 186 □ B-L 426;			§152d; IBHS 377 n 45 □ B-L
	Berg 2.125c, 2.161b; Brock §9			428f; Brock §35b
9.30	Berg 2.115a		10.10	Dav §146R2; Gib 62
9.31	Berg 2.140 n q		10.11	GKC §167b □ B-L 642p′
9.32	[R] 1.100; IBHS 416 □ B-M		10.12	GKC §49e □ Berg 2.23f
	1.100,		10.13	J-M §146a n 2, 155p; IBHS 297
9.33	GKC §116p; IBHS 677 ⨆ Berg			□ B-M 3.11; Brock §34b
	2.72h; Brock §109b		10.14	GKC §110a
9.34	J-M §126c; Gib 47 □ Brock		10.15	GAHG 3.170 n 521, 3.215 n 815
	§103a		10.18	GKC §137c; J-M §144g n 1;
9.35	Berg 1.148f			IBHS 321; Gib 8 □ B-M 2.16;
9.36–37	J-M §150e			Brock §154
9.36	Dav §100R1, 111R1, 115; J-M		11	Gib 99
	§121d; Gib 22, 137		11.1	Dav §24c; J-M §129f; IBHS 149,
9.37	Dav §115; Gib 22 ⨆ Berg			293; Gib 32, 97, 99
	1.113 n e		11.2–3	Gib 100
9.38	GKC §150l; Gib 185 □ Brock		11.2	Gib 100
	§55b		11.3	Gib 100
9.39	GKC §9l, 69p □ B-L 442h		11.4	Gib 99, 100 □ Jen §28.3.3
9.40	J-M §150j n 3		11.5	GKC §21b; J-M §19c; Gib 100,
9.41	GKC §23d, 35d; J-M §103b □			157
	B-L 224h; Berg 1.91d		11.6	Gib 100
9.43	Gib 59 □ Berg 1.154f, 1.155f,		11.7	J-M §146a n 2, 166n; IBHS 294;
	2.70e			Gib 62, 101 □ Brock §34b, 35b
9.45	Dav §77; GKC §117ee, 120g;		11.8	IBHS 294, 533; Gib 88
	J-M §125u, 139g n 1; IBHS 176;		11.9	GKC §159v; J-M §154fd, 154fe;
	Gib 144 □ Brock §94b, 138			IBHS 296; Gib 2, 136, 137, 153
9.48	Dav §1R1, 41R3, 146R1; GKC			□ Berg 2.150n*; Brock §34b
	§157a; J-M §137m, 144g n 1;		11.10	GKC §159n n 1
	Wms §125, 490; IBHS 645; Gib		11.12	Dav §8R3; IBHS 324; Gib 8
	22, 27, 111 □ B-L 265f; GAHG		11.13	Dav §146R2 □ Brock §115a
	3.102 n 285, 3.180 n 625		11.15	Gib 66
9.49	Brock §109a		11.14	B-M 2.133
9.51	J-M §99c; Wms §355; IBHS 202		11.16	GKC §111b □ Berg 2.38g
9.53	Dav §19R1; GKC §27o, 67p,		11.17	J-M §114d
	125b; J-M §137u; IBHS 251;		11.18	GKC §47m, 49d n 1, 67u □
	Gib 25 □ B-L 264n, 428e, 438;			B-M 2.102; Berg 2.21b, 2.166m
	B-M 2.19; Jen §17.3.3; Berg		11.19	J-M §114f, 129d; IBHS
	2.80 n h, 2.138 n l, 2.140 n q;			148 n 24
	Brock §20a		11.20	GKC §157b n 2
9.54	J-M §168g; IBHS 640 □ Jen		11.23	GKC §150a; J-M §161a □ B-M
	§19.3.4			3.86

B-L: Bauer and Leander, *Historische Grammatik* **B-M**: Beer, *Grammatik* **Berg**: Bergsträsser, *Grammatik*
Brock: Brockelmann, *Syntax* **Dav**: Davidson, *Syntax* **GAHG**: Richter, *Grammatik*
Gib: Gibson, *Davidson's Syntax, 4th ed.* **GKC**: *Gesenius' Grammar* **IBHS**: Waltke and O'Connor, *Syntax*
Jen: Jenni, *Lehrbuch* **J-M**: Joüon and Muraoka, *Grammar* **Ros**: Rosenthal, *Grammar*
Sch: Schneider, *Grammatik* **Wms**: Williams, *Syntax*

11.24	Berg 1.128dd	13.3	Dav §57R1; GKC §112x; J-M §119c; IBHS 534; Gib 88 □ GAHG 3.170 n 524; Berg 2.41g
11.25	Dav §86c, 124; GKC §51i, 73d, 113q, 133a n 2, 133a n 3; J-M §80q, 81e; Gib 124, 184 □ B-L 322y; GAHG 3.206 n 786; Berg 2.63d, 2.92i, 2.144b, 2.151s	13.4	Gib 14 □ GAHG 3.215 n 815; Berg 2.48f
		13.5ff.	GKC §80d, 94f
11.27	J-M §154fa; Wms §342; IBHS 195 n 21, 488	13.5	GKC §80d; J-M §89j □ B-L 198i
11.29	Dav §24R6; GKC §118f; Gib 34	13.6	GKC §44d, 64f, 127e; J-M §139c; Gib 185 □ B-L 357; Berg 1.157o, 2.78e; Brock §73a
11.30	J-M §118j; Gib 124, 155		
11.31	Berg 2.112c		
11.33	GKC §134e		
11.34	Dav §116R1; GKC §135o, 135o n 3; Gib 98 □ Brock §111f	13.7	GKC §112hh; J-M §89j; Gib 33 □ B-L 198i
11.35	Dav §101Ra; GKC §59h, 119i; J-M §133c, 136f; IBHS 123, 445, 683; Gib 19 □ B-L 341i'; Berg 1.75g, 2.18f	13.8	Dav §22R4; GKC §52s, 116e; J-M §58b, 105c; Wms §573; IBHS 375 n 34; Gib 29 □ B-L 287o'; GAHG 3.171 n 538, 3.216 n 815; Berg 2.69d, 2.87c
11.36	Dav §92, 145R1; GKC §124e; J-M §136j; Gib 20, 131, 157, 158	13.9	J-M §121f, 160i, 166h; GKC §116o, 141e; Gib 168
11.37	J-M §136h □ Berg 2.165k	13.10	Gib 28
11.38	Dav §114; J-M §146c; IBHS 294; Gib 2	13.11	GKC §150n; J-M §154fa, 154g, 158n, 161l; Gib 163
11.39	Dav §1R2, 109; GKC §144b; J-M §129t; IBHS 301 n 42; Gib 3, 9	13.12	Dav §132R2; GKC §135m, 159c; Gib 156 □ B-M 3.112
11.40	GKC §107g; J-M §113c; Wms §63; IBHS 186 n 47	13.14	Dav §65R3; Gib 107 □ Berg 2.52n
12	IBHS 59	13.16	GKC §119m
12.3	Dav §126R6a; GKC §49e; Gib 184 □ Berg 2.23f	13.17	Dav §8R1; GKC §37a, 137a, 145o; J-M §144b; IBHS 320; Gib 8 □ B-L 265a; B-M 2.13
12.4	J-M §155p		
12.5–6	Gib 90 □ Berg 2.33 n e	13.18	Berg 1.92 n g
12.5	Dav §54R1, 126; GKC §100m, 112ee; J-M §114c, 118n; Wms §271, 398, 445; Gib 52, 54, 82 □ B-M 3.86; Sch §13.3.2, 51.3.4; Berg 1.67u, 2.42g*	13.19	GKC §126r; Dav §108R2
		13.20	Gib 168
		13.21	GKC §74y; J-M §123c; Wms §207 □ B-L 426; Berg 2.161c; Brock §46c
12.6	Dav §54R1; GKC §2w; J-M §3c n 1; Wms §308 □ B-L 19 n 2, 28v, 70 n 1; B-M 2.29, 1.47; Berg 1.2g	13.23	Dav §39d, 131; GKC §106p, 115c; J-M §167k; Wms §459, 516; IBHS 494, 638; Gib 69, 130, 155 □ B-L 426; GAHG 3.178 n 618; Berg 2.58n
12.7	Dav §17R3; GKC §124o; Gib 20	13.25	GKC §61c; J-M §69b □ B-L 281f; Berg 2.116d
12.8	Wms §322; IBHS 212	14.1	Gib 165
12.9	J-M §155od	14.2	GKC §90e; J-M §93f
12.14	Dav §37b; Wms §96; Gib 49	14.3	Dav §122; GKC §135a, 142f; J-M §146a; IBHS 295; Gib 116, 183
13.2	Dav §19R1; GKC §125b; J-M §137u; IBHS 251, 274; Gib 25		

B-L: Bauer and Leander, *Historische Grammatik*   **B-M**: Beer, *Grammatik*   **Berg**: Bergsträsser, *Grammatik*
Brock: Brockelmann, *Syntax*   **Dav**: Davidson, *Syntax*   **GAHG**: Richter, *Grammatik*
Gib: Gibson, *Davidson's Syntax, 4th ed.*   **GKC**: *Gesenius' Grammar*   **IBHS**: Waltke and O'Connor, *Syntax*
Jen: Jenni, *Lehrbuch*   **J-M**: Joüon and Muraoka, *Grammar*   **Ros**: Rosenthal, *Grammar*
Sch: Schneider, *Grammatik*   **Wms**: Williams, *Syntax*

14.4	Dav §1R2, 81, 111R1; GKC §122q, 135p; J-M §152b; IBHS 301; Gib 3, 119, 137 □ Berg 1.154e	15.10	GKC §114g; J-M §155r □ B-L 348h; Berg 1.156k, 2.57k, 2.84q, 2.114i
14.5	GKC §119gg; J-M §93f	15.11	GKC §136c; Gib 47, 54 □ Berg 2.71g
14.6	Dav §91R3; GKC §152p; J-M §124s, 133g, 137i; Wms §256; IBHS 244; Gib 28, 129, 130, 150 □ Berg 2.118b; Brock §151??	15.12	GKC §135o, 152w □ Berg 2.82n, 2.114i
		15.13	Dav §86a, 118; GKC §113p, 113v; J-M §123i, 123o; Wms §205; IBHS 586; Gib 124 □ B-M 3.63; GAHG 3.168 n 508; Berg 2.62c(bis), 2.111c
14.8	Dav §91R4; Gib 130		
14.9	Dav §86c; GKC §113u; J-M §123m; Wms §206; IBHS 590; Gib 125 □ Jen §10.3.1.1; Berg 2.65h		
		15.14	GKC §119gg, 164b; J-M §91c; Wms §235, 573; Gib 169 □ B-L 473dβ; Berg 2.136i, 2.150n
14.10	GKC §107e	15.18	GKC §135a; Gib 92
14.11–13	Gib 49	15.19	IBHS 381
14.12	Dav §47; Gib 47, 124, 154	16.1	GKC §90e; GAHG 3.102 n 284
14.13	J-M §155na; Gib 154	16.2	Dav §53b, 57R1; GKC §112oo; IBHS 538; Gib 88, 150 □ Berg 1.128dd, 2.42h, 2.144b; Brock §163c
14.14	Dav §32R5; Gib 44		
14.15	Dav §123R2, 126R2; GKC §9v, 69m, 69n, 150g n 1 □ B-L 212k, 384c'; Berg 1.71e, 2.174 n h		
		16.3	GKC §135o; J-M §149b □ B-L 353b, 371u; B-M 2.137; Berg 2.116e, 2.120b
14.16	Dav §40a, p. 143 n , 131; J-M §112a, 161a; Wms §391, 439; Gib 51, 183 □ Jen §24.3.3.2	16.4	J-M §118b; IBHS 196; Gib 98
		16.5	GKC §66h; IBHS 317 n 4, 326, 528 □ Berg 2.123d
14.17	GKC §118k, 134m □ Berg 2.148l	16.6	IBHS 317 n 4, 375 n 31 □ Berg 2.35i
14.18	GKC §37d, 90f, 93x, 106p, 133a, 159x; Wms §317, 459; IBHS 264, 638 n 22; Gib 45, 73, 148, 155 □ B-L 566d, 577j'; B-M 3.36; Berg 1.103q	16.8	Gib 47
		16.9	GKC §126o; Gib 28 □ Brock §176a
		16.10	Dav §47; GKC §67dd; IBHS 317 n 4, 375 n 31; Gib 96 □ B-L 439p'; GAHG 3.215 n 815; Berg 2.105 n k, 2.134 n c; Brock §106h
14.19	B-M 3.38		
14.20	Berg 2.115a		
15.1	GKC §90f, 119n; Gib 97		
15.2	Dav §63, 86a; J-M §114h; Wms §185; IBHS 269, 569, 579; Gib 45, 81, 124 □ Berg 2.48g	16.11	GKC §113o
		16.12	Berg 1.161d
		16.13–14	Brock §73c
15.3	Gib 63, 68, 137 □ Berg 2.28g	16.13	GKC §28c n 1; IBHS 317 n 4, 375 n 31 □ Berg 2.35i, 2.105 n k, 2.111c
15.4	GKC §134g; IBHS 282; Gib 49 □ Berg 2.165k		
15.5	Berg 2.105i*	16.14	GKC §127g □ Berg 1.149h
15.7	Dav §120R5, 130R4; GKC §136c n 1, 163c n 1, 163d; Gib 153 □ Berg 2.112c	16.15	Dav §6R2; GKC §141e; J-M §160i; Wms §528; IBHS 317 n 4; Gib 6, 79 □ Berg 2.105 n k
15.8	GKC §117q; J-M §61a; Gib 145 □ Brock §103b		

B-L: Bauer and Leander, *Historische Grammatik*   **B-M**: Beer, *Grammatik*   **Berg**: Bergsträsser, *Grammatik*
Brock: Brockelmann, *Syntax*   **Dav**: Davidson, *Syntax*   **GAHG**: Richter, *Grammatik*
Gib: Gibson, *Davidson's Syntax, 4th ed.*   **GKC**: *Gesenius' Grammar*   **IBHS**: Waltke and O'Connor, *Syntax*
Jen: Jenni, *Lehrbuch*   **J-M**: Joüon and Muraoka, *Grammar*   **Ros**: Rosenthal, *Grammar*
Sch: Schneider, *Grammatik*   **Wms**: Williams, *Syntax*

16.16	GKC §10g, 52d, 60d, 164d; J-M §9c2; IBHS 269; Gib 98 □ B-L 351; Berg 1.124w, 1.161d, 2.97h
16.17	Dav §130b; GKC §159o; IBHS 450, 531; Gib 86, 153 □ Berg 2.40d; Brock §166, 176a
16.18	GKC §112tt; Gib 104 □ Berg 2.43 n b-k
16.19	GKC §126r; J-M §54d n 3
16.20	Dav §29R8; GKC §123c; IBHS 360 n 27; Gib 10, 42 □ Berg 2.92h; Brock §128c
16.21	Dav §100R2; GKC §116r; J-M §121f, 125bc, 126h; Wms §213; IBHS 166, 420; Gib 27 □ B-L 538i; B-M 3.69; Berg 1.91d, 2.74l
16.22	Berg 2.118b
16.23	J-M §118k; IBHS 551 □ Berg 2.83p
16.24	Gib 135 □ B-L 436
16.25	GKC §52n, 111g; Gib 98 □ Berg 2.55 n e
16.26	GKC §67v; J-M §82o □ B-L 437; Berg 2.140q
16.27	Dav §99R1; GKC §126x; J-M §145d n 1; Gib 135 □ Berg 2.55 n e; Brock §21cβ
16.28	GKC §34a n 2, 88f, 97b n 1; J-M §91ea n 2 □ B-L 622c; GAHG 3.215 n 815
16.29	GAHG 3.151 n 414
16.30	GKC §72r; Gib 9 □ B-L 403; Berg 2.47d, 2.144c
16.31	Dav §138c; Gib 167
17.1–5	Sch §52.2, 52.3.1, 52.7, 54.2.2.4
17.1–2	IBHS 553
17.1	B-M 3.45
17.2	GKC §32h, 121f; J-M §121p; Wms §96, 340, 551 □ B-L 248f, 422t″; B-M 2.8
17.3	Dav §37f; GKC §154a n 1b; IBHS 283; Gib 49
17.4	J-M §125w, 126h; IBHS 175, 305
17.5	Dav §96 (p. 283), 106b; Gib 180, 182 □ Jen §6.3.2
17.6	Dav §111; J-M §155nf; Wms §576; Gib 73 □ B-M 3.43; GAHG 3.174 n 565, 3.174 n 568, 3.174 n 573; Berg 1.50g; Brock §122o
17.7	Brock §71b
17.8	Dav §43b, 45R1; GKC §138e; Gib 79
17.9	Dav §43b, 45R1; Gib 76, 185
17.10	Dav §36R3; J-M §135d n 1; IBHS 206, 578; Gib 50 □ Berg 1.127cc; Brock §107iβ
17.11	J-M §129o; IBHS 155 n 35
17.12	J-M §126h
17.13	IBHS 209 □ Berg 2.28g
17.14	GAHG 1.182 n 604
18.1	Dav §73R5; GKC §125d n 1; Gib 110 □ GAHG 3.174 n 565, 3.174 n 568, 3.174 n 573; Berg 2.27d, 2.71f
18.2	Dav §91R4; Gib 130
18.3	Dav §141; GKC §142e; J-M §166g; Wms §120, 329; Gib 137, 167 □ B-M 3.16
18.4	Berg 2.163g; Brock §24b
18.6	Brock §116e
18.7	J-M §154fa; Gib 47 □ GAHG 3.174 n 566, 3.174 n 568, 3.174 n 569, 3.174 n 574
18.9	IBHS 676 n 10 □ B-L 653d; Jen §8.3.3.2; Berg 2.59n, 2.47e
18.10	GKC §152o; J-M §154f
18.11	Dav §98R1, 100R7; GKC §116k, 121d; J-M §121o; IBHS 616; Gib 133
18.12	Wms §359; IBHS 193 n 18
18.14	GAHG 3.173 n 557, 3.175 n 580
18.16	Dav §37R1; J-M §121o, 126h; IBHS 616 n 21; Gib 50
18.17	J-M §121o; IBHS 616 n 21; Gib 50
18.18	Dav §8R1
18.19	GKC §20g, 150g; J-M §154h n 1, 161e; Wms §94, 544; IBHS 274; Gib 128 □ Berg 1.67t, 2.54d; Brock §136b, 169c
18.22	GKC §53n; J-M §53e; Gib 169 □ B-L 333c′
18.23	GKC §67g, 67y, 107v; Gib 68 □ Berg 2.139o

B-L: Bauer and Leander, *Historische Grammatik*   **B-M**: Beer, *Grammatik*   **Berg**: Bergsträsser, *Grammatik*
Brock: Brockelmann, *Syntax*   **Dav**: Davidson, *Syntax*   **GAHG**: Richter, *Grammatik*
Gib: Gibson, *Davidson's Syntax, 4th ed.*   **GKC**: *Gesenius' Grammar*   **IBHS**: Waltke and O'Connor, *Syntax*
Jen: Jenni, *Lehrbuch*   **J-M**: Joüon and Muraoka, *Grammar*   **Ros**: Rosenthal, *Grammar*
Sch: Schneider, *Grammatik*   **Wms**: Williams, *Syntax*

18.24	GKC §136c; J-M §143g; Gib 8, 184 □ B-M 3.89; GAHG 3.171 n 538
18.25	Dav §22R3; Gib 29, 33, 160
18.26	Sch §47.2.3
18.27	Jen §6.3.2
18.28	Dav §144R3; J-M §154fa □ GAHG 3.174 n 565, 3.174 n 566, 3.174 n 568, 3.174 n 574
18.29	GKC §52q
18.30	GKC §5n □ B-L 80u; Berg 1.5l
19.1	GKC §131b; IBHS 70 □ GAHG 3.174 n 566, 3.174 n 569, 3.174 n 574; Berg 1.134c; Brock §63a
19.2	GKC §75t □ B-L 423; Berg 2.161b
19.3	GKC §119gg
19.4	Dav §36a; GKC §53n; Gib 47 □ B-L 333z; Berg 2.105i*; Brock §117b
19.5	GKC §9u, 64c n 2, 117ff.; J-M §48a n 1, 125u n 2; IBHS 284; Gib 50, 113 □ B-L 354c; Berg 2.116e; Brock §94b
19.6	GKC §110h, 120d; J-M §177d; Gib 120 □ B-M 2.141; Berg 2.129h
19.8	GKC §64c; J-M §48a n 1, 69b □ B-L 354c; Jen §28.3.2.1; Berg 2.109c, 2.116e
19.9	GKC §91k; IBHS 444 □ B-L 580u′; GAHG 3.170 n 524; Berg 2.84q
19.11	Dav §86R2; GKC §19i, 69g, 107n; J-M §119j; IBHS 574; Gib 82, 169 □ B-L 383; GAHG 1.55 n 56; Berg 2.47e, 2.52o, 2.126 n c; Brock §113
19.12	Dav §9R2; J-M §131b □ Berg 2.52o, 2.53q; Brock §22d
19.13	GKC §48i, 69x, 73d; J-M §119j, 134m; IBHS 530, 574; Gib 82, 94 □ Berg 2.47e, 2.53q, 2.131o, 2.146f; Brock §6a
19.14	J-M §130c □ Brock §117c
19.15	GAHG 3.174 n 565, 3.174 n 568, 3.174 n 572; Sch §54.2.3.1
19.16	GKC §102b □ B-L 642p′
19.17	Dav §45R1; Gib 76 □ Brock §63a
19.18	Dav §72R3; GKC §118e n 3; J-M §125bb, 154fe; Gib 144 □ GAHG 3.174 n 565, 3.174 n 572, 3.174 n 568
19.19	GKC §127b; GAHG 3.173 n 558, 173 n 559, 3.174 n 572, 3.174 n 568; Brock §12
19.20	Dav §101Rd; GKC §29q, 73e; Gib 149 □ B-L 233j; B-M 2.150; Berg 2.50k, 2.149m
19.21	B-L 435p′; Berg 2.135d
19.22	Dav §28R6, 73R4; GKC §54c, 116u, 117w, 130e; J-M §82h, 125c; Wms §42; IBHS 165; Gib 109, 169 □ B-L 198f, 328v; Berg 1.109b, 2.70e*, 2.140 n q; Brock §70d, 98a
19.23	GAHG 3.170 n 523; Berg 2.137k
19.24	GKC §91d, 135o □ B-L 251g
19.25	B-M 1.77
19.26	GKC §114f n 1; J-M §103m n 1; IBHS 608 □ Berg 2.57k; Brock §107b
19.27	Gib 137, 168 □ B-L 559k
19.28	IBHS 574; Gib 82 □ GAHG 3.174 n 565, 3.174 n 568; Berg 2.47e
19.29	GKC §126r; J-M §137m
19.30	Dav §101Rb, 132R3; GKC §112ee, 112oo, 116w; J-M §112d, 156e; IBHS 487; Gib 14, 62, 90, 157 □ B-L 383; Berg 2.42g*, 2.126 n d, 2.173 n g
20.2	GKC §29f □ Berg 1.71e
20.3	Gib 185
20.4	Dav §99; J-M §155s; Gib 135
20.5	J-M §82h
20.6	GKC §49c, 68e; J-M §52d □ Berg 2.22e, 2.120b; Brock §39bα
20.7	GKC §119s
20.8	Dav §29R6 □ B-L 636k
20.9	IBHS 312
20.11	J-M §47b □ Berg 2.91g
20.13	GKC §130e □ B-L 77m; B-M 1.81

B-L: Bauer and Leander, *Historische Grammatik*　**B-M**: Beer, *Grammatik*　**Berg**: Bergsträsser, *Grammatik*
Brock: Brockelmann, *Syntax*　**Dav**: Davidson, *Syntax*　**GAHG**: Richter, *Grammatik*
Gib: Gibson, *Davidson's Syntax, 4th ed.*　**GKC**: *Gesenius' Grammar*　**IBHS**: Waltke and O'Connor, *Syntax*
Jen: Jenni, *Lehrbuch*　**J-M**: Joüon and Muraoka, *Grammar*　**Ros**: Rosenthal, *Grammar*
Sch: Schneider, *Grammatik*　**Wms**: Williams, *Syntax*

20.14–15	GKC §102b
20.14	B-L 642p'
20.15ff.	GKC §54l
20.15	GKC §155d; J-M §53g; IBHS 427; Gib 49 □ B-L 281f, 642p'; B-M 2.126; GAHG 1.72 n 136; Berg 2.100i(bis)
20.16	Dav §14, 45R1; GKC §90e, 90l, 90l n 3, 122t, 126r; J-M §137m; IBHS 313; Gib 18 □ Berg 2.103d*
20.17	J-M §53g □ B-L 281f; B-M 2.123; GAHG 1.72 n 134; Berg 2.100i
20.20	Wms §277
20.21	Gib 49
20.23	Berg 2.123c
20.24	Gib 117
20.25	GKC §97e; J-M §100e □ B-L 625n; B-M 2.87
20.28	Gib 184 □ B-M 3.88; GAHG 3.171 n 536, 3.171 n 538; Brock §136b
20.30	GKC §123c
20.31	Dav §41R3, 114; GKC §66f, GKC §75v □ B-L 199l, 368t; Berg 2.122 n a, 2.137k
20.32	GKC §20h; J-M §133h, 154fd; Wms §263 □ B-L 368t; Berg 1.68v
20.33	GKC §73a □ Berg 2.153t
20.34	Berg 2.77c
20.35	Gib 49
20.37	GKC §73a □ Berg 2.152 n t; Brock §17
20.38	GKC §75gg □ Berg 2.165k
20.39–40	GKC §164b
20.39	GKC §118u; J-M §41a, 123e; IBHS 586 □ Berg 2.62c
20.40	Berg 2.137k
20.43	GKC §20h, 22s □ B-L 127a', 212k, 222s, 353v; Berg 1.68v, 2.106m
20.44ff.	GKC §117m
20.44	Dav §72R4; GKC §117m; J-M §125j; IBHS 182 □ B-M 3.7; GAHG 3.162 n 482, 3.177 n 606; Brock §31b
20.45	B-L 333c'
20.46	GKC §145o; J-M §125j; Gib 49 □ B-M 3.72
20.48	IBHS 387; Gib 175
21.1	J-M §155fn; Gib 186 □ Brock §82c
21.2	Gib 115 □ B-M 3.75
21.3	J-M §37d
21.4	Brock §111c
21.5	J-M §155nf; Gib 8 □ Brock §93c
21.7	GKC §131n; J-M §146e □ B-M 3.36; Berg 1.155f; Brock §68b
21.8	Dav §8R2; J-M §144a; IBHS 319; Gib 7 □ GAHG 3.204 n 777
21.9	GKC §54l; J-M §53g; IBHS 426 □ B-L 281f; B-M 2.126; GAHG 1.72 n 136, 3.174 n 570, 3.174 n 571, 3.204 n 777; Berg 2.100i
21.12	GKC §131b, 134g; IBHS 114, 282; Gib 19, 50
21.16	GKC §123b; J-M §135c; IBHS 114
21.18	Berg 1.129b
21.19	Dav §32R2; GKC §90e, 126w; J-M §93f, 138c, 58t; Gib 44 □ Brock §60a
21.21	GKC §145p; J-M §150c, 166p; Wms §234; IBHS 110; Gib 154 □ Berg 2.152t
21.22	GKC §135o; Gib 39 □ B-L 399h''; Berg 2.112d, 2.135e, 2.152 n t; Brock §90c
21.25	GKC §107e; Wms §569; Gib 6, 57 □ GAHG 3.174 n 565; Berg 2.30b

B-L: Bauer and Leander, *Historische Grammatik*   **B-M**: Beer, *Grammatik*   **Berg**: Bergsträsser, *Grammatik*
Brock: Brockelmann, *Syntax*   **Dav**: Davidson, *Syntax*   **GAHG**: Richter, *Grammatik*
Gib: Gibson, *Davidson's Syntax, 4th ed.*   **GKC**: *Gesenius' Grammar*   **IBHS**: Waltke and O'Connor, *Syntax*
Jen: Jenni, *Lehrbuch*   **J-M**: Joüon and Muraoka, *Grammar*   **Ros**: Rosenthal, *Grammar*
Sch: Schneider, *Grammatik*   **Wms**: Williams, *Syntax*

1 SAMUEL

1.1–2	Gib 55
1.1	Dav §19R1, 144R3; GKC §49b n 1, 125b, 125h, 156b; J-M §118c n 2, 137u; IBHS 251, 550, 554; Gib 11, 25, 148 □ Berg 2.37a; Brock §20a
1.2	Dav §104c, 113; GKC §114n n 2, 134l, 145o; J-M §142m, 150j, 154f, 154ff.; IBHS 560; Gib 12, 47 □ GAHG 3.77 n 205; Berg 2.38d; Brock §21cε
1.3	GKC §112dd, 123c; J-M §119v, 137f □ B-M 3.52; Berg 2.42g*; Brock §41a
1.4–7	Dav §54b
1.4–5	IBHS 550
1.4	GKC §112g, 126s; J-M §137n, 137n n 2; IBHS 244; Gib 28, 90
1.5	IBHS 474; Gib 73 □ Berg 2.27d
1.6	Dav §67b; GKC §20h, 22s, 59g, 117p; J-M §18k; Gib 114 □ B-L 127a', 222s, 357; GAHG 2.33 n 139; Berg 1.68v, 2.18f, 2.106m; Brock §93d
1.7–8	IBHS 550 □ B-L 639a'
1.7	Dav §29R8, 44R1, 145; GKC §68c, 107e, 123c; J-M §79m; Wms §102, 254; IBHS 503; Gib 42, 73, 131, 158 □ Berg 2.31d, 2.33 n e, 2.119a, 2.161b
1.8	Dav §45R1; GKC §37e, 102l, 107f; J-M §37d, 113d; Wms §167; IBHS 316, 324; Gib 47, 76
1.9	Dav §84R1; GKC §91e, 113e n 3, 141e; J-M §123c, 137f; Wms §207; IBHS 591, 651 n 14; Gib 123 □ B-L 871', 427t''; Berg 2.84 n p, 2.160 n a; Brock §46c
1.10	GKC §128y; J-M §154fa; IBHS 504; Gib 74, 147 □ Berg 2.31b, 2.160a
1.11	Dav §86a, 130c, 130R3; GKC §112p, 112ff, 113o; J-M §119f, 123g, 176d; Gib 92, 124, 154, 155 □ B-L 637p; Berg 1.157p
1.12	Dav §58c, 82, 100c; GKC §112uu, 114n n 2, 164d; J-M §119z; Gib 103, 120, 136 □ Berg 2.43 n b-k, 2.59n*
1.13	Dav §44b, 113; GKC §20g, 145n; J-M §121f; Gib 13, 21, 74 □ Berg 2.31b; Brock §107iα
1.14	GKC §47o; IBHS 425, 516; Gib 185 □ B-L 328w; Berg 2.19a
1.15	J-M §129ia; Gib 163 □ Brock §71a
1.16	Dav §24R3, 101Rc; GKC §128v; Wms §373; IBHS 149 n 27, 221; Gib 33 □ Brock §107iα, 107lα
1.17	GKC §23f, 95h □ B-L 600j'; Berg 1.91d
1.18	Berg 2.119a
1.20	Dav §83R4, 127c; GKC §44d, 64f, 90k n 2; J-M §41b, 42d □ B-L 357; B-M 2.131; Berg 2.78e, 1.157o; Brock §72b
1.22	Dav §69R1, 105, 145; GKC §112oo, 164d; J-M §112i n b; Wms §573; Gib 158 □ Berg 2.42h
1.23	Dav §63, 72R1, 133; Wms §184, 546; Gib 82, 116, 176, 185 □ B-M 2.102
1.24	Dav §36c, 69b; GKC §135i; J-M §146k; Gib 144 □ B-L 197b
1.25	Gib 13
1.26	Dav §99; GKC §103c; J-M §105c; Gib 135, 147 □ B-L 204w, 644b''; B-M 3.15
1.27	Dav §101Rb; GKC §95h; Gib 147 □ Brock §108a
1.28	GKC §64f, 145u; Wms §381; Gib 67 □ B-L 357; Berg 2.105i*
2	Dav §72; GKC §117b; Gib 116

B-L: Bauer and Leander, *Historische Grammatik*   **B-M**: Beer, *Grammatik*   **Berg**: Bergsträsser, *Grammatik*
Brock: Brockelmann, *Syntax*   **Dav**: Davidson, *Syntax*   **GAHG**: Richter, *Grammatik*
Gib: Gibson, *Davidson's Syntax, 4th ed.*   **GKC**: *Gesenius' Grammar*   **IBHS**: Waltke and O'Connor, *Syntax*
Jen: Jenni, *Lehrbuch*   **J-M**: Joüon and Muraoka, *Grammar*   **Ros**: Rosenthal, *Grammar*
Sch: Schneider, *Grammatik*   **Wms**: Williams, *Syntax*

2.1	GKC §2r, 106g; Gib 63 □ Berg 2.28g(4 times); Brock §41c
2.2	Wms §422; IBHS 653; Gib 39 □ B-M 2.180
2.3	Dav §17R2, 29R8, 83, 128R6; GKC §103g, 120g, 124e, 133k, 152z; J-M §136g, 142k, 177g; Wms §225; IBHS 121, 233; Gib 20, 42, 120 □ B-L 494 n 2; Brock §133b, 143a
2.4	Dav §73R3, 116R2; GKC §146a; J-M §82b, 150n n 2; IBHS 168, 408 n 34; Gib 23, 108 □ B-M 3.21; Sch §44.6.2; Brock §124a
2.5	Dav §101Rb; Gib 8, 33 □ B-L 218c, 351; Berg 1.69y, 2.77c, 2.107a
2.6–8	J-M §121h n 1; IBHS 618 n 28
2.6	GKC §111u, 116x; J-M §118r, 121j; Gib 101, 137 □ Berg 2.38 n d; Brock §42c
2.7	Wms §384; Gib 175 □ Berg 2.174 n h
2.8	GKC §107g, 114r, 116x, 135p; J-M §113c, 121j, 124q; Gib 137, 148 □ Berg 2.37a
2.9	GKC §67g; Gib 141 □ B-M 2.146; Berg 2.136i, 2.139p, 2.171 n d
2.10	Dav §65R6; J-M §177l; Gib 73 □ B-L 641i'; Berg 2.153t
2.11	Dav §69R1, 100R2; GKC §116r; J-M §121f; Wms §213; IBHS 629; Gib 138 □ Berg 2.73i*
2.13–16	Dav §54b □ Berg 2.42g*
2.13	Dav §55c, 132R2; GKC §112oo, 116w, 131c, 159i, 164a; J-M §91e, 121l, 131c; IBHS 104, 230; Gib 40, 130, 137, 157 □ B-M 3.108; Berg 2.42g*, 2.69c; Brock §18a, 62f, 123g, 144
2.14	Dav §55c; GKC §131h, 132g; Gib 39
2.15	Dav §45, 53b; GKC §112oo; J-M §44e n 1; Gib 73 □ B-L 333x
2.16	Dav §50b, 54R1, 86R2, 118, 130R4; GKC §103g, 106m, 112ll, 113w, 159f, 159dd; J-M §112g, 118n, 123p, 160j, 167o; IBHS 205 n 59, 582; Gib 90, 125, 153, 163 □ B-L 333x, 631c; Berg 1.44c, 1.67u, 2.33 n e, 2.49i, 2.51m, 2.63e, 2.64 n f; Brock §93c
2.18	Dav §98R1, 100R7; GKC §116k, 118q, 121d; J-M §121o; Gib 133
2.19–20	Berg 2.32d
2.19	Dav §44b, 54b, 111; GKC §112e, 112e n 1, 112h n 3; J-M §119u; Gib 73, 94, 113 □ Berg 2.112c, 2.165l; Brock §41f
2.20	Dav §54b, 116R6; GKC §145u; J-M §143d; Gib 94 □ Berg 2.49h
2.22–25	Berg 2.42g*
2.22	GKC §107e, 112k; J-M §119v; Gib 111 □ Berg 2.20b, 2.21b
2.23	Dav §32R2, 32R3; GKC §126y; J-M §149d, 154fe; Gib 44 □ Berg 2.33 n e
2.24	GKC §116s; Gib 55 □ GAHG 3.175 n 582
2.25	Dav §91R4; GKC §117x; Gib 130 □ B-L 437; GAHG 3.119 n 326; Berg 2.97h; Brock §98c
2.26	Dav §86R4, 136; GKC §113u; J-M §80q, 123s, 177q; Gib 37, 126 □ Berg 2.71f, 2.85r, 2.144b; Brock §93a
2.27–28	IBHS 596 □ B-M 3.64; Brock §46c
2.27	Dav §88R1, 126R3; GKC §113q, 114e, 150e; J-M §139c, 161b; Gib 124, 127 □ B-L 322y, 422i''; B-M 2.161, 3.58; Berg 2.65h, 2.92i, 2.160a; Brock §54b, 73a
2.28	Dav §72R1; GKC §49e, 113z, 119w; J-M §123x; Wms §210; Gib 116, 127 □ Berg 2.23f, 2.62b
2.29	GKC §111t, 118g, 133b; J-M §118q; IBHS 404, 559

B-L: Bauer and Leander, *Historische Grammatik*   **B-M**: Beer, *Grammatik*   **Berg**: Bergsträsser, *Grammatik*
Brock: Brockelmann, *Syntax*   **Dav**: Davidson, *Syntax*   **GAHG**: Richter, *Grammatik*
Gib: Gibson, *Davidson's Syntax, 4th ed.*   **GKC**: *Gesenius' Grammar*   **IBHS**: Waltke and O'Connor, *Syntax*
Jen: Jenni, *Lehrbuch*   **J-M**: Joüon and Muraoka, *Grammar*   **Ros**: Rosenthal, *Grammar*
Sch: Schneider, *Grammatik*   **Wms**: Williams, *Syntax*

2.30	Dav §86a, 98c; GKC §113p, 116g, 149a; IBHS 402, 586; Gib 124, 134 □ Berg 2.63d, 2.135d	3.13	GKC §112qq, 130c n 1, 119p; IBHS 615; Gib 54 □ B-L 77l
2.31	GKC §112x, 116d; IBHS 677; Gib 88, 137 □ B-M 3.67; Berg 2.72h	3.14	GKC §149c; J-M §165d; Gib 187
2.32	J-M §158i	3.17	Dav §120R4; GKC §149d; J-M §139g, 165a n 1; Gib 187 □ B-M 3.49; Sch §53.5.3.1; Berg 2.51m; Brock §80d, 170c
2.33	Dav §71R1, 115; GKC §53q, 118q, 145e; J-M §54b, 130g; IBHS 74; Gib 22 □ B-L 228a'; GAHG 3.146 n 381; Berg 2.105 n k	3.18	Brock §67b
		3.19	Jen §7.3.1.1; Brock §111a
2.34	IBHS 274; Gib 46	3.21	GKC §75y; J-M §123c; Wms §207 □ B-L 426; Berg 2.161c; Brock §46c
2.35	B-M [R]1.70, 1.98; Berg 2.16c	4.1	GKC §131c, 145c
2.36	J-M §124s, 137v; IBHS 252; Gib 90 □ Berg 1.145d	4.2	Berg 2.92g
		4.3	GKC §127g
3.1	J-M §160i; Gib 40, 136 □ Berg 2.70e*	4.4	J-M §155p
		4.5	GKC §72h, 145c □ Berg 2.172 n f
3.2	Dav §83R2; GKC §107b, 120b; J-M §143j n 2, 155nc, 157g; Gib 43, 121 □ B-M 2.147; Berg 2.27d, 2.30b; Brock §103a	4.6	GKC §37f □ B-L 13c, 266i; B-M 2.15
		4.7	GKC §125e □ Berg 2.126d; Brock §11c
3.3	Dav §127a; GKC §107c, 152r; Gib 73, 181 □ Berg 2.31c	4.8	GKC §132h, 136d, 147d; Gib 7, 135 □ Brock §59c
3.4	Gib 59	4.9	J-M §168g □ B-L 13c; Berg 2.114l
3.5–6	GKC §46c; Wms §225		
3.5	Dav §83; GKC §120g, 120h; J-M §177b; Gib 120	4.10	Dav §29R6; GKC §124b, 145o; J-M §150j; Gib 42
3.6	Wms §226 □ GAHG 3.170 n 532; Jen §5.3.1.4	4.11	Berg 2.124f
3.7	GKC §107c; J-M §113j ; Gib 181 □ Berg 2.31c	4.12	Dav §138b; GKC §127e; J-M §139c, 143j; IBHS 314; Gib 26, 98, 168
3.8	Dav §38R5, 146; GKC §114m, 134r; J-M §142q; Wms §226; Gib 51, 110 □ Jen §23.3.3; Brock §88	4.14	J-M §37e
		4.15	Dav §24R3, 116; GKC §44m, 145k, 145n; J-M §150d, 150h; Gib 21, 23, 33 □ B-L 404; Berg 2.15b; Brock §50a, 50c
3.9	GKC §46c, 120g, 120h; Gib 90, 121, 136 □ Jen §9.5.4.9		
3.10	GKC §54k, 118u, 123c; J-M §53c □ Berg 2.99e	4.16	Dav §99R3; GKC §116q, 126k; J-M §137l; IBHS 248 □ B-L 266g
3.11	GKC §67g, 67p, 116p, 116w, 155d; J-M §158f; IBHS 627; Gib 91, 137 □ B-M 2.144; Berg 2.68c, 2.72h, 2.80h, 2.134c, 2.135d	4.18	B-L 345o"; B-M 2.168; Berg 2.77d
		4.19	Dav §96R2; GKC §69m, 111b, 112tt, 114i; Wms §306; IBHS 608 □ B-L 198h, 382; B-M 1.108; Jen §10.4.11; Berg 1.109c, 2.43 n b-k, 2.57k, 2.125b
3.12	Dav §87; GKC §113h; J-M §123r, 176h; Wms §204; IBHS 589; Gib 6, 126 □ B-L 424; B-M 2.161; Berg 2.66h*, 2.160a; Brock §93d	4.20	J-M §121i n 1; IBHS 553

B-L: Bauer and Leander, *Historische Grammatik*   **B-M**: Beer, *Grammatik*   **Berg**: Bergsträsser, *Grammatik*
Brock: Brockelmann, *Syntax*   **Dav**: Davidson, *Syntax*   **GAHG**: Richter, *Grammatik*
Gib: Gibson, *Davidson's Syntax, 4th ed.*   **GKC**: *Gesenius' Grammar*   **IBHS**: Waltke and O'Connor, *Syntax*
Jen: Jenni, *Lehrbuch*   **J-M**: Joüon and Muraoka, *Grammar*   **Ros**: Rosenthal, *Grammar*
Sch: Schneider, *Grammatik*   **Wms**: Williams, *Syntax*

4.21	Dav §128R3; GKC §152q; J-M §102j n 2, 118j; Gib 142 □ Jen §10.4.11
4.22	B-M 2.134
5.1	GKC §131c; Gib 26
5.3	GKC §116d □ Jen §8.3.2.2; Berg 1.145d, 2.69 n c
5.4	Berg 2.69 n c
5.5	GKC §107g; Gib 74 □ Berg 1.50g
5.6	J-M §61a □ Berg 2.138l
5.7	GKC §112f, 112rr; J-M §119z; Gib 103 □ Berg 2.43 n b-k
5.8	GKC §67g, 67y, 118f; J-M §125n, 155s □ B-L 437; B-M 2.147; Berg 2.139o; Brock §122k
5.9–10	GKC §67v
5.9	Dav §145R1; GKC §130d, 164d; Wms §313, 327, 360, 501; Gib 157 □ B-M 2.147, 3.109; Berg 2.137k; Brock §145bζ
5.10	GKC §115c, 117e, 145m; J-M §125e; Gib 129 □ Berg 2.54c, 2.137k; Brock §17, 50b
5.11	Dav §65a; GKC §109f, 117e; J-M §125e; Gib 106
6.3	Dav §100a; GKC §116s; IBHS 585 n 28; Gib 124, 153
6.4	GKC §118h, 135r; J-M §125v, 146j
6.5	GKC §112aa; Gib 79 □ B-M 3.54; Berg 2.43i, 2.137k
6.6	J-M §52d n 3; IBHS 438
6.7	Dav §1R3; GKC §72i n 2, 135o; J-M §119l, 149b; Gib 3 □ B-M 2.153; Berg 2.150n
6.8	GKC §72i, 126s □ Berg 2.150n; Brock §97c
6.9	Dav §130R4; GKC §155d, 155f, 159q, 159dd; J-M §158a, 158a n 3, 167o
6.10	Dav §1R3; GKC §60h, 75qq, 135o; J-M §78g, 149b; Gib 3 □ B-L 337j, 375; Berg 2.159g; Brock §124b
6.11	GKC §154a n 1, 154a n 1b; Wms §436 □ Brock §130a
6.12–13	J-M §155pa
6.12	Dav §86c; GKC §47k, 71, 75n, 113s; J-M §44d, 77a n 2, 123m, 123s; Wms §206; IBHS 590; Gib 125 □ B-L 384c'; Berg 2.20a, 2.65h, 2.130m, 2.160a; Brock §93a
6.13	GKC §145c □ Brock §22d
6.14	GKC §127d □ Brock §73a
6.18	Dav §32R2; GKC §126x; J-M §138c, 154e; Gib 44 □ Brock §62e, 81d
6.19	GKC §119k; IBHS 199; Gib 66 □ Berg 2.27d; Brock §93k
7.1	IBHS 438
7.2	Gib 148
7.3	GKC §109f; J-M §116d; Gib 136, 153 □ Jen §21.3.4; Brock §176c
7.5	Wms §356
7.7	Berg 2.126d
7.8	Dav §101; Gib 147
7.9	Dav §19R1; GKC §125b, 131k; J-M §137u; Wms §356; IBHS 169, 251 n 26; Gib 25
7.10	Dav §141R1; GKC §111g, 116u; J-M §166f; Gib 169 □ Berg 2.70e*
7.11	GKC §119c □ Brock §119c
7.12	Dav §19R1; GKC §111d, 125b, 131c; J-M §137u; IBHS 251 n 26, 274; Gib 25
7.13	IBHS 394
7.14	GKC §72k; IBHS 201; Gib 9 □ B-L 405; Berg 2.146f
7.15–16	IBHS 534
7.15	J-M §119v
7.16	Dav §54R1; GKC §112f; J-M §119v □ Berg 2.42g*, 2.132a*
7.17	GKC §29i n 1 □ Berg 1.160a; Brock §89
7.28	GKC §136d
8.1	J-M §125w; Wms §52; IBHS 175
8.5	IBHS 300
8.6	Wms §262
8.7	Dav §72R1, 101Rc; GKC §117e, Wms §574; Gib 116, 141 □ Brock §97bα
8.8	GKC §111q; J-M §118j; IBHS 552; Gib 96

B-L: Bauer and Leander, *Historische Grammatik*   **B-M**: Beer, *Grammatik*   **Berg**: Bergsträsser, *Grammatik*
Brock: Brockelmann, *Syntax*   **Dav**: Davidson, *Syntax*   **GAHG**: Richter, *Grammatik*
Gib: Gibson, *Davidson's Syntax, 4th ed.*   **GKC**: *Gesenius' Grammar*   **IBHS**: Waltke and O'Connor, *Syntax*
Jen: Jenni, *Lehrbuch*   **J-M**: Joüon and Muraoka, *Grammar*   **Ros**: Rosenthal, *Grammar*
Sch: Schneider, *Grammatik*   **Wms**: Williams, *Syntax*

8.9	IBHS 242; Gib 141 □ GAHG 3.177 n 605; Brock §159a	9.10	GKC §120g, 141f; J-M §114e, 177f □ Berg 2.47e
8.11	GKC §721 □ Berg 2.17e	9.11	Dav §100a; GKC §116u, 150d;
8.12	Dav §96R4; GKC §114p; Gib 132 □ Berg 2.60 n p		J-M §166f; Wms §57, 237; IBHS 624; Gib 135, 137, 169, 183 □
8.14	J-M §141j; IBHS 269 □ B-L 637p		GAHG 3.102 n 289; Berg 2.70e*
8.15ff.	GKC §53k	9.12	Wms §266, 481; IBHS 205; Gib 163 □ B-L 425; GAHG
8.15	IBHS 414 □ Berg 2.82 n m, 2.113f		3.204 n 769; Brock §97c
8.17	IBHS 414 □ Berg 2.82 n m, 2.113f	9.13	GKC §35n, 47m; J-M §35e, 166m; Gib 72, 161 □ B-M 2.19
8.18	IBHS 314	9.14	GKC §116u; J-M §111d, 166e;
8.19	GKC §20g, 163a; Wms §555; IBHS 671 □ Berg 1.67t; Brock §168		Wms §236; Gib 137, 169 □ Berg 2.70e, 2.70e*
8.20	Brock §98a	9.15	GKC §106f, 142b; Wms §162; Gib 65, 131, 157 □ Berg 2.27d
8.22	Dav §55a; Gib 14, 94	9.16	GKC §118e n 2; Wms §262;
9.1	Dav §144R3; Wms §41; IBHS 553; Gib 11 □ B-L 510v		IBHS 205 □ Brock §107iγ
9.2	Dav §33; GKC §133a; J-M §141g; Wms §76; Gib 11, 45 □ GAHG 2.50	9.17	GKC §138b; J-M §158i, 166c □ Jen §6.3.1.6; Berg 2.113f, 2.162d
		9.18	J-M §125bb, 161g
9.3	Dav §35R2, 72R4; GKC §96 (p. 283), 117d, 130g; J-M §125h, 130g, 142m; Wms §30; IBHS 155, 180, 553; Gib 46, 116 □ Berg 2.119a; Brock §21cε, 71d, 96, 133a	9.20	GKC §73e, 134m 135o, 143c; J-M §81e, 130g, 156d; Wms §271, 273 □ B-M 2.150; Berg 2.149m
		9.21	GKC §133g; J-M §113d n 2; Wms §33; IBHS 270; Gib 45 □ Brock §21cα, 25a
9.4	GKC §90g n 1, 104g, 152k; Wms §409 □ B-L 649k	9.22	Wms §257
9.5	GKC §164b; J-M §111d, 166c, 168h; Wms §179, 235; Gib 93, 169 □ Jen §18.3.4.1; Berg 2.47e	9.23	Dav §60R1; GKC §138b; J-M §158i; Gib 81, 148
9.6	Dav §44a; GKC §113n; J-M §114e, 123e; IBHS 586; Gib 75 □ GAHG 3.170 n 524; Jen §10.3.1.1; Berg 2.62c	9.24	Dav §22R4; GKC §138i, 138k; J-M §145d n 1; IBHS 87 n 13, 339 n 30; Gib 29 □ B-M 3.98; Berg 1.129b; Brock §150a
		9.26	B-L 563x
9.7	Dav §132R2; GKC §159w n 1; J-M §167l n 2; Wms §340; IBHS 195, 678 n 15; Gib 148, 156 □ Berg 2.571	9.27	Dav §141; GKC §116u; Wms §237; Gib 107, 137, 167, 169 □ B-L 132d; Berg 2.70e*
		10.1	J-M §125b, 125i, 161j; Wms §451
9.8	Dav §38R6; GKC §112x; IBHS 288 □ B-L 629a'	10.2	Dav §58b, 101Rd; IBHS 541; GKC §49k; Gib 9, 103 □ Berg 2.16d, 2.42g
9.9	GKC §107e, 144d n 1; J-M §105e, 127c; Wms §84, 92, 309; IBHS 574; Gib 27, 82 □ B-M 3.22; Berg 2.32e, 2.47e; Brock §36b, 81b	10.3	Dav §37R4; GKC §97c; J-M §100d n 1; Wms §05 □ B-L 623d; Berg 2.17d
		10.4–5	Brock §134d
		10.4	Dav §36R3, 37R4; GKC §134n; J-M §119w, 142n; IBHS 276

B-L: Bauer and Leander, *Historische Grammatik*   **B-M**: Beer, *Grammatik*   **Berg**: Bergsträsser, *Grammatik*
Brock: Brockelmann, *Syntax*   **Dav**: Davidson, *Syntax*   **GAHG**: Richter, *Grammatik*
Gib: Gibson, *Davidson's Syntax, 4th ed.*   **GKC**: *Gesenius' Grammar*   **IBHS**: Waltke and O'Connor, *Syntax*
Jen: Jenni, *Lehrbuch*   **J-M**: Joüon and Muraoka, *Grammar*   **Ros**: Rosenthal, *Grammar*
Sch: Schneider, *Grammatik*   **Wms**: Williams, *Syntax*

10.5–6	IBHS 312
10.5	Dav §65R6, 138b; GKC §29g, 101a, 109k, 112z; J-M §31d, 119z, 126b; Gib 168 □ B-L 188p; Berg 2.50l
10.6	GKC §75qq; IBHS 426 □ B-L 440c; Berg 2.17d, 2.158e
10.7	Dav §60R2; GKC §76g; IBHS 312 □ Berg 2.146f
10.8	Dav §63, 63R2; GKC §112v, 114r; J-M §114g; IBHS 537; Gib 81, 94 □ Berg 2.41f, 2.51l, 2.128h
10.9	GKC §112uu; J-M §119z, 143k; Gib 104 □ Berg 2.43 n b-k
10.11	Dav §7c, 144R1; GKC §20h, 111g, 116s, 116w, 136c; J-M §143g, 154c; Wms §118; IBHS 313, 324, 391; Gib 8, 11, 99 □ Berg 1.68v, 1.142 n f, 2.69c, 2.70e
10.12	Dav §109R2, 136R1; GKC §154b; J-M §177m; Wms §439
10.13	GKC §75qq □ B-L 440c; Berg 2.158e
10.14	GKC §152k; IBHS 329
10.16	Dav §86a; GKC §113o; J-M §123k; Gib 124 □ Berg 2.63e
10.18	GKC §135a □ Berg 2.21d; Brock §59c
10.19	Dav §9R2, 146R1; J-M §158e; IBHS 207, 661 n 59; Gib 111 □ Berg 1.131d; Brock §107iα, 152a
10.21	B-L 346x″; Berg 2.97h
10.22	IBHS 300; Gib 137 □ GAHG 3.171 n 538; Brock §108a
10.23	GKC §133b; J-M §141h; IBHS 271 □ B-M 3.36; Brock §120b
10.24	GKC §22s, 100l; J-M §23a, 102m, 161b; Wms §184; IBHS 569; Gib 82 □ B-L 127a′, 222s, 426, 632h; B-M 2.172; Berg 1.68v, 2.49h
10.25	GKC §126s; J-M §137m; Wms §84; IBHS 16, 245 n 13; Gib 14, 27 □ Jen §26.3.2; Sch §52.5.7.2; Brock §21bβ
10.27	GKC §136b; J-M §143d
11.1–2	Sch §52.6.3
11.1	GKC §125h
11.2	Dav §1R2, 109R2; GKC §135p; J-M §130g; Gib 5 □ Berg 2.84q(bis)
11.3	IBHS 534; Gib 107, 133 □ Berg 2.40c
11.4	Gib 34
11.5	GKC §107f, 107v; J-M §113d, 137f, 161i; IBHS 323; Gib 8
11.6	IBHS 611 □ Jen §10.3.1.3
11.7	Wms §81
11.8	J-M §135c □ Brock §17
11.11	Dav §51; GKC §111g, 116w; J-M §125w, 126c; IBHS 392 n 33; Gib 99 □ Berg 2.69c
11.12	GKC §107t, 150a; Wms §542; IBHS 621 □ Jen §8.3.2.2; Brock §54a, 154
11.14	Berg 2.47e, 2.52o
11.15	GKC §131b; Wms §312; Gib 22
12.2–3	Gib 91
12.2	Dav §58a; Wms §161; IBHS 540; Gib 103, 137 □ GAHG 3.203 n 766, 3.204 n 772; Jen §28.3.3; Berg 2.153t
12.3	Dav §7a; GKC §63l, 137b; J-M §68a n 1; Wms §574; IBHS 487; Gib 7, 62 □ Berg 1.107e, 1.156l, 2.113f, 2.114i
12.4	Dav §11Rb; Gib 14
12.5	Wms §598; Gib 62, 163
12.7	GKC §51p; Wms §137, 341, 344; IBHS 389
12.11	Dav §70b; Wms §60; Gib 144
12.12	J-M §171f
12.13	GKC §44d, 64f; J-M §41b, 42d □ B-L 357; GAHG 3.204 n 772; Berg 1.157o, 2.78e
12.14–15	Brock §116c, 170b
12.14	GKC §167a; J-M §111h; Wms §597; Gib 63, 154, 176
12.15	Gib 154
12.16	J-M §143f, 143h □ GAHG 2.61; Brock §44b
12.17	GKC §110i, 114o; J-M §7c, 114b n 1, 124o, 154f; Wms §195, 563; Gib 106, 131 □ Berg 2.50k, 2.84q
12.18	J-M §7c

B-L: Bauer and Leander, *Historische Grammatik* **B-M**: Beer, *Grammatik* **Berg**: Bergsträsser, *Grammatik* **Brock**: Brockelmann, *Syntax* **Dav**: Davidson, *Syntax* **GAHG**: Richter, *Grammatik* **Gib**: Gibson, *Davidson's Syntax, 4th ed.* **GKC**: *Gesenius' Grammar* **IBHS**: Waltke and O'Connor, *Syntax* **Jen**: Jenni, *Lehrbuch* **J-M**: Joüon and Muraoka, *Grammar* **Ros**: Rosenthal, *Grammar* **Sch**: Schneider, *Grammatik* **Wms**: Williams, *Syntax*

12.19	Dav §65R3; GKC §107p; J-M §116j; Wms §292; IBHS 217; Gib 107, 131 □ Berg 2.52 n n, 2.52o	13.20	GKC §118f □ B-L 563x; Berg 2.33 n e, 2.84q
12.20	GKC §135a	13.21	GKC §35n, 96 (p. 286), 112dd; J-M §98e n 1 □ B-L 563x, 620s; Berg 1.144c
12.22	Dav §30; J-M §138a; IBHS 259; Gib 43 □ B-L 367	13.22	GKC §112ee; J-M §119z
12.23	Dav §32R2; GKC §126x, 135g; J-M §124q, 138c, 156d; Wms §73, 107; IBHS 260, 301; Gib 44, 182 □ Brock §60a	13.23	GKC §92g □ Berg 1.120 n o
		14.1	GKC §34f, 126s; J-M §137n; Gib 28 □ B-M 3.28; Jen §26.3.2; Sch §52.5.7.4
12.24	GKC §75oo; J-M §119l; Gib 94 □ Berg 1.93g; Brock §151	14.2	Gib 112
12.25	GKC §29o, 113o; J-M §123g; Gib 86, 154 □ Berg 2.137k	14.3	J-M §102j n 2
		14.4	J-M §134a n 2; IBHS 104 □ B-L 562v, 599i'
13.1	J-M §91ea n 1, 124g, 166l	14.5	J-M §134a n 2; IBHS 104 □ Brock §60b
13.2	Dav §11Ra; IBHS 148, 157; Gib 14	14.6	Berg 2.57l
13.3	GKC §2b □ Brock §20b	14.8ff.	GKC §112t
13.5	Wms §335; IBHS 282; Gib 49 □ Brock §116a	14.8	GKC §75x; J-M §79h, 154fe; Gib 94
13.6	GKC §93w; IBHS 393; Gib 22 □ Brock §21bγ	14.9	Dav §86R4, 101Rd; Wms §351; IBHS 220; Gib 149 □ Brock §114b
13.7–8	Berg 2.30b	14.11	GKC §93w; Gib 137 □ B-L 13c
13.7	Dav §101, 145R3; GKC §119gg; Gib 58	14.12	Dav §75; J-M §125u; IBHS 176; Gib 116 □ Berg 2.46c, 2.47d
13.8	GKC §69t □ B-L 382c'	14.13	GKC §72m; Wms §358
13.10	IBHS 678	14.14	GKC §118s n 2; IBHS 284
13.11	Dav §146R2; GKC §67dd; Gib 111	14.15	Dav §34R6; GKC §95g; J-M §141n, 155ng; Wms §81; IBHS 268; Gib 46 □ B-L 600j'; Berg 1.122t
13.12	GKC §54k □ Berg 2.167o		
13.13	GKC §106p, 159dd; Gib 155 □ Berg 2.162d; Brock §108c	14.16	GKC §129b; J-M §130a; Wms §270; IBHS 157; Gib 35 □ B-M 3.31; GAHG 2.52 n 247
13.14	Wms §259 □ Brock §107iβ	14.18	J-M §48d, 94i □ GAHG 3.161 n 480
13.15	Dav §31; GKC §93oo, 132g; J-M §148a; Wms §73; IBHS 257; Gib 22, 43 □ B-L 541j; Berg 2.69d; Brock §59b	14.19	GKC §111h, 113u, 164d; J-M §82b, 123s; Wms §206, 311; IBHS 384 n 14; Gib 125 □ Berg 2.65 n h; Brock §145bζ
13.16	J-M §148a; IBHS 257 n 4; Gib 22	14.21	Dav §94; GKC §2b, 114i □ B-M 1.12; GAHG 3.161 n 480; Berg 2.59 n mop
13.17–18	GKC §107b, Wms §60; Gib 74 □ B-M 3.29		
13.17	GKC §118q, 126m, 126z, 134l, 134n; J-M §125w, 126c; Wms §94; IBHS 259, 274; Gib 44 □ Brock §17	14.22	GKC §53n; J-M §54c □ B-L 333c'; Berg 2.104 n h
13.18	J-M §142m □ Brock §21cε, 60b	14.24	Dav §48R2; GKC §76d, 112w; Gib 96 □ B-L 422t''; Berg 2.41f, 2.172 n e; Brock §145bζ
13.19	Dav §44b; GKC §107e, 152w; J-M §113ga; IBHS 507; Gib 74 □ B-L 13c; Berg 2.30b	14.25	Gib 22

B-L: Bauer and Leander, *Historische Grammatik*   **B-M**: Beer, *Grammatik*   **Berg**: Bergsträsser, *Grammatik*
Brock: Brockelmann, *Syntax*   **Dav**: Davidson, *Syntax*   **GAHG**: Richter, *Grammatik*
Gib: Gibson, *Davidson's Syntax, 4th ed.*   **GKC**: *Gesenius' Grammar*   **IBHS**: Waltke and O'Connor, *Syntax*
Jen: Jenni, *Lehrbuch*   **J-M**: Joüon and Muraoka, *Grammar*   **Ros**: Rosenthal, *Grammar*
Sch: Schneider, *Grammatik*   **Wms**: Williams, *Syntax*

14.27	GKC §72h, 72k, 142b; J-M §80q; IBHS 372 □ B-M 2.149; Jen §28.4.3; Berg 2.144b; Brock §16c	14.45	Dav §101Rc; GKC §119w n 2, 149c; J-M §133e; Wms §325, 336; IBHS 214, 219; Gib 187 □ Brock §34a, 111b
14.28	GKC §72t; GKC §113o; J-M §80k; Wms §580; Gib 124 □ Berg 2.63e, 2.173 n g	14.47	J-M §113e n 2; Gib 10, 74 □ Berg 2.31d
14.29	GKC §126x; Gib 62 □ Berg 2.144b	14.49	GKC §47b n 1; Gib 12 □ Berg 1.95e, 1.105, 1.105t
14.30	Dav §130R3, 131; GKC §106p, 113o, 159l, 159x, 159ee; J-M §123g, 167s; Wms §387; IBHS 587; Gib 124, 155, 175 □ B-M 2.173; GAHG 2.33 n 136, 3.168 n 508, 3.177 n 605, 3.179 n 618, 3.191 n 682; Berg 1.44c, 2.63d	14.52	GKC §112ll; J-M §118n; Gib 33, 156 □ Berg 2.33 n e, 2.42g*, 2.44k
		15.1	GKC §9v, 142f; J-M §155o; Wms §278 □ B-L 360s; Berg 1.71e, 2.82n
		15.2	GKC §106g; Wms §492 □ Berg 2.28e
14.31	GKC §72t; J-M §80k	15.3	GKC §44g, 49k, 112r □ B-L 315n'; B-M 2.130; Berg 2.17d, 2.53q, 2.112c
14.32	GKC §72ff □ B-L 404; Berg 2.149m		
14.33	Dav §93; GKC §23c, 74i, 75oo, 114o; J-M §78g, 124o; Wms §195; Gib 91, 131 □ B-L 548a'; Berg 1.92e, 2.156a	15.4	GKC §93x
		15.5	GKC §68i □ B-L 351; Berg 2.120 n d
		15.6	GKC §20g, 22s, 60f, 61h, 68h, 154a n 1a; J-M §61d n 3 □ B-L 127a', 222s, 371u; Berg 1.66t, 2.15a, 2.120 n b, 2.171 n d
14.34	Dav §101Rb; GKC §96 (p. 286); J-M §98e; Wms §304; IBHS 194 □ B-L 620u; B-M 2.83		
14.35	Gib 121 □ B-M 3.76; Brock §34b	15.9	Dav §32R2, 32R4, 34R5101R; GKC §67t, 75y, 132d, 135c n 1; J-M §148a n 1; Gib 44, 46 □ B-L 422t''; Berg 2.54d*, 2.92 n gh; Brock §59c*
14.36	Dav §63R1, 63R2; GKC §48g n 1, 67dd, 109d; J-M §82j, 114l; Gib 82 □ B-L 435p'; GAHG 3.215 n 814; Berg 2.21 n c, 2.51l, 2.139p; Brock §5a		
		15.10	Gib 30
		15.12	GKC §116s; J-M §154c; Wms §226 □ B-L 564
14.37	Dav §126R2; IBHS 316	15.13	GKC §121f; J-M §132f; Gib 119 □ Jen §5.3.1.5, 6.3.1.3, 18.3.4.1
14.38	GKC §66c □ B-L 367; Berg 2.122c		
14.39	Dav §120R5; GKC §100o n 2, 149c; J-M §102k, 165i; Gib 4, 187 □ B-L 204w	15.14	GKC §37f, 154b
		15.15	GKC §158b; J-M §170e; Wms §468, 533; IBHS 639; Gib 46 □ B-L 233j; Jen §19.3.4; Brock §161a
14.40	Wms §267; Gib 22		
14.42	Dav §73R5; Wms §589; Gib 110		
14.43	GKC §113p; Gib 124 □ Berg 2.15a, 2.63d	15.16	GKC §165a; Gib 107
		15.17	IBHS 551; Gib 96, 149
14.44	Dav §120R4; GKC §149d; J-M §165a, 165a n 1; Wms §449; Gib 187, 188 □ Berg 2.51m	15.18	GKC §112r; Gib 94 □ Berg 2.53q
		15.19	Dav §48b; GKC §72ff.; Gib 101 □ B-L 404; Berg 2.149m

B-L: Bauer and Leander, *Historische Grammatik*   **B-M**: Beer, *Grammatik*   **Berg**: Bergsträsser, *Grammatik*
Brock: Brockelmann, *Syntax*   **Dav**: Davidson, *Syntax*   **GAHG**: Richter, *Grammatik*
Gib: Gibson, *Davidson's Syntax, 4th ed.*   **GKC**: *Gesenius' Grammar*   **IBHS**: Waltke and O'Connor, *Syntax*
Jen: Jenni, *Lehrbuch*   **J-M**: Joüon and Muraoka, *Grammar*   **Ros**: Rosenthal, *Grammar*
Sch: Schneider, *Grammatik*   **Wms**: Williams, *Syntax*

15.20	Dav §146R2; GKC §157c; J-M §157ca; Wms §178, 467 □ B-L 233j; Sch §53.4.5; Berg 1.161d, 2.21d	16.9	J-M §103c n 1; Gib 39
15.22	J-M §124m, 133i; Wms §238; IBHS 223; Gib 128 □ Berg 2.54d; Brock §15g	16.10	Dav §36b; IBHS 277; Gib 47 □ Sch §47.3.2
		16.11	GKC §133g; J-M §64a; IBHS 517 n 64, 678; Gib 58 □ B-L 340c'; Berg 2.124f, 2.134 n d; Brock §21cα, 25a
15.23	Dav §50b, 101; GKC §29q, 53l, 111h, 119x, 165c; J-M §123b, 133e, 176e; Wms §321, 440; IBHS 548, 591, 640; Gib 97, 123, 147 □ B-L 333h'; Jen §20.3.3; Berg 1.161e, 2.62 n b, 2.79g; Brock §111f, 176c	16.12	Dav §101Rd; GKC §128x; Gib 52 □ B-L 577j'; GAHG 2.60 n 261; Berg 1.126bb; Brock §113
		16.13	Brock §120b
		16.14	GKC §112h; J-M §119v; IBHS 393 □ Berg 2.27d, 2.42g*; Brock §82d
15.24	Gib 101		
15.25	Dav §65R2; J-M §119m; Gib 107 □ GAHG 3.215 n 815	16.15	GKC §116n □ B-L 614; GAHG 3.170 n 524; Berg 2.71g
15.26	GKC §119x; J-M §133e, 169h; Wms §321; Gib 147 □ Berg 2.15a, 2.79g	16.16	GKC §120b n 1, 124i; J-M §124c, 136d n 6, 139c; Gib 90, 121, 129 □ B-L 328a'; Berg 2.120a; Brock §103a
15.27	Berg 2.117a		
15.28	J-M §140a; IBHS 532; Gib 88 □ Berg 2.41g	16.17	GKC §114n; J-M §124n n 1; Gib 120 □ Berg 2.59n*
15.29	GKC §152d; J-M §160c; Wms §579; Gib 106 □ Berg 2.57k	16.18	Dav §27, 28R5; GKC §128t, 129c; J-M §130b; Wms §270; IBHS 157, 207; Gib 35, 46 □ GAHG 2.50 n 231, 3.102 n 284, 3.102 n 288; Jen §7.3.1.1; Brock §74a
15.30	J-M §119i n 2, 119m; Gib 107 □ GAHG 3.215 n 815; Berg 2.17d	
15.32	Dav §71R2, 70b; GKC §118q; Gib 144 □ GAHG 2.33 n 133	
15.33	Dav §111; GKC §119w, 142f	16.20	GKC §128q; IBHS 152; Gib 32 □ Berg 1.92f
15.34	J-M §118f	16.21	IBHS 628 □ Berg 2.74l
15.35	Wms §306; Gib 147	16.23	Dav §32R2, 54R1; GKC §112ee, 112oo, 126x; J-M §138c, 152d; Wms §86; IBHS 243, 260, 377; Gib 44, 90 □ Berg 2.42g*; Brock §60a
16.1	GKC §65h, 127d □ Berg 2.72h*; Brock §122d	
16.2	GKC §114g, 159g; J-M §155r; IBHS 531; Gib 156 □ Berg 2.51m, 2.57k	
		17.1	Dav §144R3
16.3	GKC §117c, 138e; J-M §125g; IBHS 180; Gib 116	17.3	GAHG 3.151 n 415; Jen §28.3.3; Brock §111a
16.4–5	J-M §154g	17.4	Dav §144R3; GKC §80g; J-M §158b; IBHS 199; Gib 11 □ B-L 510v, 635b
16.4	GKC §141n, 144d, 144e, 145u, 150a; J-M §161a; Wms §542; Gib 183 □ Brock §36d	
		17.5	GKC §121d, 131q, 134g; J-M §121o; Gib 41, 49 □ B-L 547; B-M 1.102
16.6	Wms §389; IBHS 671	
16.7	GKC §35g, 114n, 132c; Gib 45, 74 □ B-L 263g, 557f'; Berg 1.67u; Brock §15a	17.7	Gib 49
		17.8	Dav §28R5, 45R1; GKC §129c; J-M §137l; Gib 35, 76
16.8	GKC §125i; J-M §103c n 1; Gib 39, 120	17.9	Gib 154 □ Berg 1.161d

B-L: Bauer and Leander, *Historische Grammatik*   **B-M**: Beer, *Grammatik*   **Berg**: Bergsträsser, *Grammatik*
Brock: Brockelmann, *Syntax*   **Dav**: Davidson, *Syntax*   **GAHG**: Richter, *Grammatik*
Gib: Gibson, *Davidson's Syntax, 4th ed.*   **GKC**: *Gesenius' Grammar*   **IBHS**: Waltke and O'Connor, *Syntax*
Jen: Jenni, *Lehrbuch*   **J-M**: Joüon and Muraoka, *Grammar*   **Ros**: Rosenthal, *Grammar*
Sch: Schneider, *Grammatik*   **Wms**: Williams, *Syntax*

17.10	J-M §143j; IBHS 389, 489 n 17; Gib 61, 107	17.34	Dav §72R4; GKC §112kk, 126r, 154a n 1b; J-M §137o; Wms §92; IBHS 182; Gib 28, 117 □ Berg 2.44k; Brock §21bγ
17.12	GKC §126x; J-M §118j; Gib 11, 47	17.35	GKC §72w, 112ll; J-M §118n n 1; Wms §588; IBHS 520 □ B-L 403; Jen §28.3.3; Berg 2.16c, 2.33 n e, 2.112c, 2.148k
17.13	IBHS 259; Gib 47		
17.14	Dav §34, 36b, 106d; GKC §133g, 134l; J-M §137l; IBHS 248; Gib 45, 47 □ Sch §47.3.3, 53.1.1; Brock §25a		
17.15	GKC §113u, 118g; J-M §126h □ Berg 2.71f	17.36	IBHS 531 □ Berg 2.41g
		17.37	IBHS 578
17.16	GKC §113k; J-M §102e, 123r; Wms §204; IBHS 444, 592 n 47; Gib 126 □ B-L 333g'; Berg 2.66h*, 2.104g, 2.105i; Brock §93i	17.38	Dav §75; GKC §112tt; IBHS 177; Gib 103, 112, 116 □ B-L 535f, 547; Berg 1.144c, 2.43 n b-k
		17.39	Dav §82 □ Berg 2.167o; Brock §120a
17.17	Dav §32R4, 36R3, 37R4; GKC §126x, 134n; J-M §102g; Gib 32, 50, 144 □ B-L 564	17.40	GKC §132c; J-M §141d; Wms §434; IBHS 261, 649; Gib 45 □ GAHG 2.24 n 92; Brock §76b
17.19	IBHS 616; Gib 133		
17.20	GKC §112rr; Gib 103, 144 □ B-L 405; Berg 2.150n	17.41	GKC §113u; J-M §123s; Wms §221, 494; Gib 125 □ Berg 2.65 n h
17.21	GKC §122i; J-M §134g; IBHS 104 □ Brock §50b	17.42	Dav §101Rd □ Berg 2.161b; Brock §113
17.23	GKC §80g, 116u; IBHS 199; Gib 11, 169 □ B-L 635b; Berg 2.70e, 2.70e*	17.43	Dav §17R3, 104c; GKC §124o; J-M §136j
		17.45	IBHS 237; Gib 34 □ B-L 233j
17.24	GKC §111h; Gib 98, 182 □ Brock §163c	17.46	Dav §17R4; GKC §145e; J-M §150e; Wms §229, 478; Gib 22, 57 □ B-M 3.17, 3.21; Sch §44.6.2
17.25	GKC §22s, 53n, 60g, 100l, 114g, 116s; J-M §23a, 63c, 102m, 155r, 161b; Gib 90, 115 □ B-L 127a', 222s, 353v, 632h; Berg 1.68v, 2.57k, 2.71g, 2.104 n h; Brock §93k	17.47	GKC §53q, 145c; J-M §54b □ B-L 229f', 384c'; Berg 2.42g, 2.105 n k
		17.48	GKC §112uu; J-M §119z; Gib 129 □ Berg 2.43 n b-k
17.26	Dav §39c, 116R4; GKC §34f, 112p, 132h; J-M §148a; Wms §8; IBHS 322; Gib 7, 43, 68, 93 □ Brock §19c	17.49	B-M 3.13
		17.50	GKC §111k; J-M §118i □ Berg 2.23g
		17.52	J-M §150j n 3 □ Berg 2.23g
17.28	GKC §128r, 136c; J-M §35d; Wms §118 □ B-M 3.30; Brock §59b	17.53	Berg 2.174 n k; Brock §97a
		17.54	Jen §6.3.1.1
17.31	Dav §73R5; Gib 4	17.55–56	GKC §137b
17.32	Dav §53b; GKC §112p; IBHS 528; Gib 93, 140	17.55	GKC §111b, 136c, 137b; J-M §137g; Wms §456; IBHS 240 n 6, 247, 318; Gib 26, 187 □ GAHG 3.102 n 289
17.33	J-M §154fa; Gib 53		
17.34ff.	GKC §117k		
17.34–36	Dav §54b; Gib 90	17.56	GKC §135a; IBHS 319; Gib 8 □ Brock §34b
17.34–35	Berg 2.42g*	17.57	GKC §111b

B-L: Bauer and Leander, *Historische Grammatik*   **B-M**: Beer, *Grammatik*   **Berg**: Bergsträsser, *Grammatik*
Brock: Brockelmann, *Syntax*   **Dav**: Davidson, *Syntax*   **GAHG**: Richter, *Grammatik*
Gib: Gibson, *Davidson's Syntax, 4th ed.*   **GKC**: *Gesenius' Grammar*   **IBHS**: Waltke and O'Connor, *Syntax*
Jen: Jenni, *Lehrbuch*   **J-M**: Joüon and Muraoka, *Grammar*   **Ros**: Rosenthal, *Grammar*
Sch: Schneider, *Grammatik*   **Wms**: Williams, *Syntax*

17.58	GKC §126e, 126f, 137b; J-M §137g; IBHS 130, 245, 247; Gib 26, 27, 184	18.25	GKC §134g; Gib 49 □ B-L 368t
		18.27	B-L 375
18.1	Dav §11c; GKC §60d, 142a; Gib 13, 99 □ B-L 337n; Berg 2.23g, 2.26c	18.28	GKC §59g, 59i □ B-L 197d, 342q'; B-M 1.107; Berg 2.18f
		18.29	GKC §68h, 69n, 116f; Gib 138 □ B-L 443i; B-M 3.66; Berg 1.44c, 2.73i*, 2.83p, 2.126 n d, 2.157b, 2.171 n d
18.2	Dav §82; Gib 120		
18.3	Dav §11c; Gib 13, 22, 116 □ Brock §132		
18.4	Dav §75; Wms §313; IBHS 176 n 25, 430; Gib 13, 109, 112 □ Brock §115b	18.30	GKC §69f, 111f, IBHS 271, 486; Gib 45, 99, 158 □ Berg 2.126d
		19.1	Dav §91b; GKC §115a; J-M §124i; IBHS 611; Gib 129, 130 □ Jen §10.3.1.3; Brock §99b
18.5	Dav §141R3; 107e; Gib 74 □ Berg 2.32d, 2.32 n d		
18.6	B-L 399h"; Berg 1.143a, 2.152t	19.2	GKC §51n, 63c □ B-L 375; B-M 2.118, 3.60; GAHG 3.215 n 815; Berg 2.111b*
18.7	B-L 425; GAHG 3.178 n 614; Berg 1.121r, 2.19a		
18.8	Wms §388; Gib 142	19.3	Dav §8, 132a; GKC §119l, 137c, 159g; J-M §144f, 167b; Wms §125, 512; IBHS 134 n 19; Gib 8, 54, 156 □ Brock §21bβ, 24a, 143d
18.9	GKC §55c; J-M §121f; Wms §316 □ Berg 2.153u, 2.108 n b		
18.10	GKC §54e, 118u; J-M §137f; Wms §254; IBHS 204 n 56, 241 □ Brock §21bβ, 129c		
		19.4	Dav §116R3; Gib 44
18.11	J-M §118k	19.5	GKC §114o; J-M §124o; Gib 102, 131
18.13	GKC §106d; J-M §125w		
18.15	Dav §146; GKC §157c; J-M §157c; Wms §464, 490; IBHS 645; Gib 110 □ B-M 3.94; Sch §53.4.5	19.6	Dav §120; IBHS 325; Gib 187 □ B-L 132c
		19.8	B-M [R]1.71
		19.10	Dav §32R3; GKC §116q, 126y; J-M §138h; Wms §74; Gib 6
18.16	IBHS 366		
18.17	Dav §34; GKC §142f; J-M §114j; Wms §73, 242, 388, 559; IBHS 269, 670 n 94; Gib 45 □ Berg 2.47d	19.11	Dav §91R4; GKC §159v; J-M §154l; IBHS 624; Gib 130, 135, 153, 154 □ Sch §49.3.4.2; Berg 2.72h*(bis), 2.150o
		19.12	GAHG 3.203 n 766
18.18	Dav §8R1, 43b; GKC §107u, 137a; IBHS 322; Gib 7, 79	19.13	Dav §31, 73R5; GKC §124h, 126r; 132h n 1; J-M §136d; Wms §588; IBHS 122 n 14; Gib 5, 27, 43, 110
18.19	Dav §91R1, 91R3, 96R5; GKC §114q, 115e n 1; J-M §124s; Gib 130, 133 □ Berg 2.54d, 2.56f		
		19.16	GKC §124h, 132h n 2; J-M §126h; Gib 43
18.20	Berg 1.155f	19.17	Dav §126R5; GKC §59h, 150e; J-M §161h; IBHS 324; Gib 101, 184 □ B-L 341i'; Berg 2.18f; Brock §173
18.21	Dav §38R5; GKC §134r; Gib 51, 107 □ Berg 2.35i		
18.22	GKC §59c, 59i □ B-L 534; Berg 2.147g; Brock §138		
		19.18	Wms §230
18.23	Dav §90R1, 138a; GKC §114a; J-M §124b, 154b; Wms §117, 192; IBHS 105; Gib 128, 168 □ B-L 405; Berg 2.55 n d, 2.147g; Brock §16e	19.20	IBHS 171 n 18; Gib 56 □ GAHG 3.102 n 289
		19.22	Dav §32R2; GKC §126x; J-M §138c; IBHS 328 □ Berg 1.103q

B-L: Bauer and Leander, *Historische Grammatik*   **B-M**: Beer, *Grammatik*   **Berg**: Bergsträsser, *Grammatik*
Brock: Brockelmann, *Syntax*   **Dav**: Davidson, *Syntax*   **GAHG**: Richter, *Grammatik*
Gib: Gibson, *Davidson's Syntax, 4th ed.*   **GKC**: *Gesenius' Grammar*   **IBHS**: Waltke and O'Connor, *Syntax*
Jen: Jenni, *Lehrbuch*   **J-M**: Joüon and Muraoka, *Grammar*   **Ros**: Rosenthal, *Grammar*
Sch: Schneider, *Grammatik*   **Wms**: Williams, *Syntax*

19.23 Dav §86R4; GKC §113t, 135g; J-M §123n, 146d; IBHS 301; Gib 2, 125 □ GAHG 1.186 n 640; Berg 2.65 n h; Brock §67b, 93g

19.24 Dav §73; J-M §112a n 5; IBHS 168; Gib 74, 108 □ Berg 2.76 n b

20.1–2 Sch §52.6.3

20.1 GKC §37d, 116s; J-M §154c; Wms §372 □ Berg 2.71g

20.2 Dav §43b; GKC §107g; 103g, 156f; Gib 79 □ Berg 1.44c

20.3 Dav §119; GKC §113o, 118x, 149a n 1; Wms §261; IBHS 202; Gib 124, 186, 187 □ B-L 132c; Berg 2.63e, 2.125c

20.4 GKC §137c; IBHS 325 □ B-L 265f; B-M 2.16

20.5 Dav §43b; Gib 79 □ B-L 384c'; Berg 1.129b, 2.84q

20.6 GKC §51e, 51i, 112ff, 113n, 113o, 159s; J-M §51b, 123g, 123j, 125q, 176d; Wms §136, 566; IBHS 73, 388, 588 n 33; Gib 124, 154, 155 □ B-L 277d', 322y; Berg 2.43i, 2.43 n b-k, 2.63e, 2.92i; Brock §93a

20.7 J-M §123g; IBHS 492; Gib 154, 155

20.8 Dav §110; GKC §135a, 142g, 159v; Gib 2, 57

20.9 Dav §121; GKC §142f, 150a; J-M §123g; Gib 124, 155, 183 □ Berg 2.58m; Brock §7a

20.10 GKC §150i, 151a; J-M §144d; IBHS 318 n 6; Gib 8, 112, 116 □ B-M 3.76, 3.95

20.11 GKC §118f; J-M §114b n 1

20.12 J-M §167l n 1

20.13 Dav §72R4, 120R4; GKC §117l n 2, 149d; J-M §165a n 1; Wms §59; IBHS 569 n 13; Gib 117, 154, 156, 188 □ GAHG 3.92 n 244; Berg 2.49h, 2.51m; Brock §35b, 102

20.14 GKC §109g; J-M §129g

20.16 Dav §73R5; GKC §117g; J-M §125bd; Wms §589; Gib 110 □ Brock §127b

20.17 Dav §67b; J-M §125q, 125q n 2, 125r, 174g; IBHS 388; Gib 115 □ B-M 3.85; Brock §93l

20.18 GKC §112oo, IBHS 535 □ B-M 2.119, 3.54; Berg 2.16c, 2.40c

20.19 Dav §83; GKC §34f, 120c; IBHS 414 □ Berg 2.16d

20.20 GKC §91e, 127e; Gib 131

20.21–22 GKC §159s

20.21 J-M §123g; IBHS 517 n 64, 587; Gib 124, 154, 155 □ B-L 340c'; Brock §120b

20.22 B-L 359i; Berg 2.118d; Brock §120b

20.23 GKC §143a; Gib 22, 91 □ B-M 3.14

20.25 Brock §108c, 129c

20.26 GKC §152d, 152t; J-M §160m; Wms §421; Gib 141 □ B-M 2.180; Brock §32a, 125b

20.27 GKC §80g n 1; Wms §378; Gib 37

20.28 J-M §123j; IBHS 388; Gib 124 □ B-L 322y; Berg 2.92i

20.29 Dav §106R2 □ Berg 1.132e, 2.97h

20.31 GKC §128v, 138c; J-M §129j, 158k; IBHS 150 □ Brock §152d

20.33 GKC §115c; J-M §65a, 137f; IBHS 600 □ Berg 2.58m

20.34 IBHS 386 □ Berg 1.154e, 2.113f; Brock §122d

20.36 GKC §114o, 116u, Gib 137, 169 □ Berg 2.60p, 2.70e*

20.37 GKC §150e; J-M §161c

20.38 Berg 2.152 n t

20.40 Dav §28R5; GKC §72y; J-M §130e □ B-L 445p; Berg 2.149m

20.41 Gib 169 □ Berg 2.122b

20.42 Dav §36R4; GKC §134d, 135f, 158b; J-M §146d; IBHS 299; Gib 2, 48 □ Brock §161a

21.2 GKC §90i, 119gg, 152o; J-M §93c □ B-L 529v, 534

21.3 Dav §9b, 11R3, 75; GKC §55b, 137c; J-M §93h, 129f, 147f; IBHS 153; Gib 14, 112 □ Berg 2.125c, 2.108 n b; Brock §24c

B-L: Bauer and Leander, *Historische Grammatik*   **B-M**: Beer, *Grammatik*   **Berg**: Bergsträsser, *Grammatik*
Brock: Brockelmann, *Syntax*   **Dav**: Davidson, *Syntax*   **GAHG**: Richter, *Grammatik*
Gib: Gibson, *Davidson's Syntax, 4th ed.*   **GKC**: *Gesenius' Grammar*   **IBHS**: Waltke and O'Connor, *Syntax*
Jen: Jenni, *Lehrbuch*   **J-M**: Joüon and Muraoka, *Grammar*   **Ros**: Rosenthal, *Grammar*
Sch: Schneider, *Grammatik*   **Wms**: Williams, *Syntax*

21.4	J-M §142n; Gib 50 □ GAHG 3.206 n 786	22.17	B-L 361x, 535f; Berg 1.122t
21.5	GKC §119e n 1; Gib 57, 154, 174 □ GAHG 3.173 n 559, 175 n 580	22.18	GKC §135a; J-M §82h; IBHS 297; Gib 50 □ B-M 3.38; Berg 1.93h; Brock §34b
21.6	GKC §111b, 123b; J-M §135c	22.20	Berg 1.71e
21.7	Wms §567	22.22	Berg 1.93h, 2.30a
21.8	GKC §84b, 84f, 129h; J-M §130e; Gib 36 □ B-L 533f	23.1	GKC §93r, 116n; J-M §96Ag; Wms §213; IBHS 627 □ B-L 581; Berg 1.126bb, 2.71g
21.9	Dav §128R3; GKC §150c n 3; Wms §569; Gib 37 □ Berg 1.99 n h	23.2	Dav §53a; J-M §170c; Gib 92
		23.3	Wms §387
21.10	GKC §80g, 102g, 126r, 142f, 159s; J-M §113n, 137m, 176k; Wms §171; IBHS 237, 509, ‡517 n 64; Gib 27, 116, 154 □ B-L 340c′, 399h″; Berg 2.124f, 2.147g	23.4	Berg 2.84q; Brock §44b
		23.5	B-L 252r; B-M 2.55f, 2.141; Sch §17.2.1
		23.7	GKC §128a; J-M §129b
		23.9	IBHS 227
21.12	J-M §143i	23.10	Dav §73R7; GKC §113o, 117n; Wms §273; IBHS 184, 211; Gib 117 □ Berg 2.63e; Brock §95
21.14	GKC §60d, 131m n 3, 75bb, 131m n 3 □ B-L 204z, 337n, 426, 427t″; Berg 2.24 n g, 2.164 n , 2.167 n p	23.11	Dav §126R2; GKC §150g n 1, 150n; J-M §161l; Gib 184 □ GAHG 3.215 n 815
21.15–16	Sch §51.3.3	23.12	J-M §161l; Gib 184
21.15	Dav §45R1; IBHS 425 □ GAHG 3.102 n 288, 3.102 n 289	23.13	J-M §158o; Wms §484; IBHS 70, 429 n 18, 644; Gib 10, 56, 79 □ B-M 3.22; Berg 2.30b
21.16	Dav §4, 121; GKC §136b, Wms §288; IBHS 425, 684; Gib 5, 183 □ Brock §54a	23.14	B-L 346x″
		23.15	GKC §90e; Wms §64; IBHS 186
22.2	GKC §75oo; Gib 33 □ B-L 441c; Berg 2.159g; Brock §107iβ	23.17	Berg 2.156a
		23.18–19	Wms §64
		23.18	Jen §6.3.1.6
22.3	Gib 158	23.19	GKC §90e, 150e; J-M §161c; IBHS 425, 430
22.4	Brock §162		
22.5	GKC §119s; J-M§131k □ GAHG 3.148 n 394	23.20	GKC §114a, 114b, 114l n 4; J-M §124b; Wms §284; IBHS 601; Gib 128 □ Berg 2.17d, 2.54d
22.6	Gib 168		
22.7	GKC §117n, 124p, 150a, 153; J-M §125w, 136m; Wms §12; Gib 142, 183 □ Brock §54a, 95	23.21	GKC §121f; J-M §132f
		23.22	Dav §60R4; GKC §63n, 135b, 144d n 2; J-M §123p; IBHS 582; Gib 13, 74, 124, 125 □ B-L 353v; B-M 2.128; Berg 2.63e, 2.64 n f, 2.80 n h
22.8	Gib 136 □ Brock §107iβ		
22.9	GKC §90i; J-M §93c, 126b n 1 □ B-L 529v, 534		
22.13	Dav §88R1; GKC §113e; J-M §124r, 124x; IBHS 597; Gib 127 □ B-M 2.62; Berg 2.62b; Brock §46c	23.23	Dav §60R4; GKC §100o n 2, 159v; J-M §102k, 119l; Wms §307
		23.26–27	Gib 169
		23.26	Dav §141 □ Berg 2.72h*, 2.73i*
22.14	GKC §154b; IBHS 319; Gib 7	23.28	GKC §22s, 102b; Gib 13 □ B-L 127a′, 222s
22.15	Dav §83R2; GKC §67w; J-M §82n; Gib 121, 183 □ B-L 436; Berg 2.48g, 2.84q	24.1	J-M §96Dd; IBHS 240

B-L: Bauer and Leander, *Historische Grammatik* **B-M**: Beer, *Grammatik* **Berg**: Bergsträsser, *Grammatik*
Brock: Brockelmann, *Syntax* **Dav**: Davidson, *Syntax* **GAHG**: Richter, *Grammatik*
Gib: Gibson, *Davidson's Syntax, 4th ed.* **GKC**: *Gesenius' Grammar* **IBHS**: Waltke and O'Connor, *Syntax*
Jen: Jenni, *Lehrbuch* **J-M**: Joüon and Muraoka, *Grammar* **Ros**: Rosenthal, *Grammar*
Sch: Schneider, *Grammatik* **Wms**: Williams, *Syntax*

24.4	Berg 2.80 n h	25.8	GKC §72o, 74k, 76g; J-M
24.5	GKC §138b; J-M §158i; Gib 116		§116d ☐ B-L 444p; Berg 2.48g,
	☐ Berg 2.147g; Brock §152d		2.158d
24.6	Dav §72R4; GKC §117d	25.10–11	IBHS 535
24.7	Dav §117R1; J-M §165k; IBHS	25.10	GKC §67ee, 126w; J-M §138c;
	680		IBHS 322; Gib 7, 63, 103, 135 ☐
24.9	GKC §126e; J-M §137g; IBHS		Berg 2.28g
	247	25.11	GKC §112cc, 150a; Gib 183,
24.10	B-L 351; Berg 1.124w		185 ☐ Berg 2.28g, 2.42h
24.11–12	Gib 87	25.13	J-M §147d; Gib 108
24.11	Dav §73R5; GKC §9v, 112rr,	25.14	GKC §72ff., 73e ☐ B-L 404;
	144o, 157e; J-M §143j; Wms		Berg 2.149m
	§490; IBHS 645 n 38 ☐ Berg	25.15	Dav §25, 28R1; GKC §130d;
	2.82n		J-M §129p; Wms §30, 489;
24.12	GKC §114r, 154a n 1c; J-M		IBHS 156, 645; Gib 12 ☐
	§124q; Wms §379; Gib 131 ☐		GAHG 2.52 n 246; Brock §144
	GAHG 2.33 n 139, 3.178 n 614;	25.16	IBHS 216 ☐ Berg 2.74 n l;
	Sch §49.3.5; Berg 2.172d		Brock §162
24.14	Dav §44a; GKC §137b; J-M	25.17	Dav §101Rc; J-M §129j,
	§114b n 1; Wms §322		133b n 1
24.15	J-M §112k; IBHS 274; Gib 7	25.18	GKC §24b, 75v, 132g, 134g;
24.16	Dav §65R2, 101; GKC §112aa;		J-M §79p, 121q; IBHS 282; Gib
	J-M §154ea n 3; Gib 82 ☐ Berg		49 ☐ B-L 599h'; Berg 1.97c
	2.43i, 2.49h; Brock §8a, 139b	25.19	Dav §29R2; Wms §70; IBHS
24.18	Dav §104a; GKC §117ff.; J-M		232 n 12; Gib 40
	§125u; Gib 45 ☐ B-L 248e; B-M	25.20	Dav §58c, 141R1; GKC §47k,
	3.76; Brock §21cγ, 90c, 94b		112uu; J-M §119z; Wms §220,
24.19	GKC §112hh n 2; GKC		236; Gib 169 ☐ B-L 303e'; Berg
	§112hh n 2; J-M §127b; Wms		1.134a, 2.43 n b-k, 2.168p
	§87, 475 ☐ Brock §160b	25.21	GKC §106f, 142b; Gib 65, 145
24.20	GKC §150a ☐ B-L 302a'; Jen		☐ Berg 2.27d; Brock §21cγ
	§13.3.3	25.22	Dav §120R4; GKC §149b, 149d;
24.21	Dav §43a; GKC §113n; J-M		J-M §165a, 165a n 1; Wms
	§123e ☐ GAHG 3.204 n 772;		§311; IBHS 424 n 1; Gib 188 ☐
	Sch §50.4.2		B-L 405; B-M 2.151; Berg
24.22	J-M §165d; Gib 187 ☐ B-L 132c		2.51m
25.1	GKC §21d ☐ B-M 1.113; Sch	25.24	Dav §1, 133; GKC §135g; J-M
	§50.1.4.1		§146d, 177l; IBHS 299; Gib 2,
25.2	Dav §36a; GKC §67cc, 134g;		185
	J-M §82k; IBHS 281; Gib 47	25.25	GKC §107p, 126u; J-M
25.3	Dav §24d; J-M §129ia; IBHS		§114g n 1, 129j; IBHS 566 ☐
	151; Gib 33 ☐ B-L 501xθ;		GAHG 3.215 n 814; Berg
	GAHG 2.24 n 91		2.52 n n; Brock §8a
25.5	GKC §44d, 64f, 90i; J-M §42d,	25.26	Dav §88R5, 119; GKC §65f,
	93c, 118k ☐ B-L 564; Berg		113e, 113gg, 144l n 3,
	2.78e		149a n 1; J-M §123x, 124r;
25.6	Brock §7b		IBHS 597 n 62; Gib 127 ☐ Berg
25.7	GKC §53p, 63q; J-M §54c,		2.62b(bis)
	130e; IBHS 385 ☐ B-L 346x'';	25.27	Dav §116R6; GKC §143d, 150o,
	Berg 2.106l; Brock §162		150o n 1; Gib 88 ☐ Berg 2.43i

B-L: Bauer and Leander, *Historische Grammatik*   **B-M**: Beer, *Grammatik*   **Berg**: Bergsträsser, *Grammatik*
Brock: Brockelmann, *Syntax*   **Dav**: Davidson, *Syntax*   **GAHG**: Richter, *Grammatik*
Gib: Gibson, *Davidson's Syntax, 4th ed.*   **GKC**: *Gesenius' Grammar*   **IBHS**: Waltke and O'Connor, *Syntax*
Jen: Jenni, *Lehrbuch*   **J-M**: Joüon and Muraoka, *Grammar*   **Ros**: Rosenthal, *Grammar*
Sch: Schneider, *Grammatik*   **Wms**: Williams, *Syntax*

25.28	GKC §119w n 2; Gib 3, 148 □ B-M 1.71; Brock §111e	26.17	Dav §126, 150n; J-M §146h, 154ea n 3; Gib 184 □ Brock §29a
25.29	GKC §143c; J-M §156c, 176j; Gib 181 □ Berg 1.122t, 2.38 n a-f, 2.83n; Brock §123e	26.18	J-M §127b, 144d; IBHS 318, 323; Gib 8
25.31	GKC §114p; Gib 156 □ Berg 2.60 n p	26.19	Dav §130b; GKC §72aa; IBHS 425; Gib 153, 163 □ GAHG 3.216 n 815; Berg 2.48g, 2.118b, 2.148l, 2.149m, 2.151q
25.32	Gib 129		
25.33	GKC §65f, 114p, 75qq, 144l n 3; J-M §78g □ B-L 375; Berg 2.159g	26.20	Dav §72R4; GKC §117d, 126o; J-M §137i; IBHS 244; Gib 13, 28, 116 □ Berg 2.48g
25.34	Dav §48d, 131; GKC §48d, 76h, 106p, 149d, 159x; J-M §130g; IBHS 424 n 1, 557; Gib 101, 155, 187 □ B-L 444p; GAIIG 1.72 n 136, 1.116 n 348; Berg 2.20 n a	26.21	GKC §158b; IBHS 592; Gib 126, 140, 159 □ B-M 3.107; GAHG 3.171 n 539; Berg 2.48g, 2.65h*, 2.103e
		26.22	GKC §127f; Gib 26, 46
25.36	J-M §154f; IBHS 375 n 35; Gib 26	26.23	GKC §150m n 2; J-M §147d, 170e, 170m □ Brock §161a
25.38	GKC §134m	26.25	Gib 174 □ Berg 2.160a
25.41	GAHG 3.148 n 391	27.1	GKC §115c; J-M §51b; IBHS 171; Gib 13, 129 □ B-L 323b', 346x"; Berg 2.54c, 2.92h(bis), 2.92i, 2.97h, 2.128g
25.42	Dav §101Rb; J-M §137m; Wms §95, 436 □ Brock §117d		
25.43	Gib 48 □ B-L 622c		
26.5	B-M 3.19	27.4	Wms §484 □ B-L 346x"; Berg 2.97h
26.2	Gib 47		
26.6	J-M §103j n 1, 113n; IBHS 296	27.5	GKC §108d; J-M §116b; Gib 13 □ GAHG 3.170 n 526; Brock §164bβ
26.7	Dav §69a; Gib 143 □ B-L 253s, 600i'; B-M 2.117; Berg 2.85r		
26.8	GAIIG 3.216 n 815	27.8	Gib 22
26.9	Dav §41R2, 51R2; GKC §112h, 151a; J-M §112j; Gib 68, 102	27.9–11	Berg 2.33 n e, 2.42g*
		27.9	Dav §54R1; GKC §107e, 112e, 112dd
26.10	J-M §63a; IBHS 528, 680 □ B-L 367; Berg 2.79g	27.10	Dav §128R2; GKC §150a n 2; Gib 163 □ GAHG 3.172 n 542; Brock §52a, 108c
26.11–12	IBHS 208 n 78		
26.11	Dav §117R1; IBHS 579; Gib 188 □ GAHG 3.215 n 815; Berg 2.46c	27.11	GKC §152w
		27.12	IBHS 634 □ Berg 2.42g; Brock §106d
26.12	Dav §34R6; GKC §87s, 152l; J-M §141n; Gib 136 □ B-L 516q, 600i'; Berg 1.113 n e, 1.147d	28.1	Dav §43b
		28.2	Gib 114 □ GAHG 3.177 n 602
		28.3	GKC §106f, 111q, 142d, 154a n 1b; J-M §118d; IBHS 484, 490; Gib 97 □ Berg 2.27d (bis)
26.13	GKC §156c		
26.14	GKC §155m; IBHS 319, 684 n 48; Gib 11		
26.15	J-M §170da; Gib 184 □ Sch §51.3.5; Brock §24d	28.7	Dav §28R6; GKC §52d, 96, 128u, 130e; J-M §129j, 129r; Wms §42; IBHS 150; Gib 34, 36, 107 □ B-L 328a'; B-M 2.120; GAHG 2.57 n 253; Berg 2.97h; Brock §70d, 74b
26.16	Dav §24R3, 72R4; GKC §117l, 117m n 3, 158b; J-M §165e, 170e; Gib 33, 117, 158, 185		

B-L: Bauer and Leander, *Historische Grammatik* **B-M**: Beer, *Grammatik* **Berg**: Bergsträsser, *Grammatik*
Brock: Brockelmann, *Syntax* **Dav**: Davidson, *Syntax* **Gib**: Gibson, *Davidson's Syntax, 4th ed.* **GKC**: *Gesenius' Grammar* **IBHS**: Waltke and O'Connor, *Syntax*
Jen: Jenni, *Lehrbuch* **J-M**: Joüon and Muraoka, *Grammar* **Ros**: Rosenthal, *Grammar*
Sch: Schneider, *Grammatik* **Wms**: Williams, *Syntax*

28.8	GKC §10h, 46d, 46e; Gib 13, 108 ☐ B-L 3, 212j, 306l, 306o; B-M 2.113; Berg 1.126bb, 2.80i, 2.81k	30.2	Dav §41R3, 48c; GKC §156f; Gib 101 ☐ Brock §139a
28.9	Dav §107R1; GKC §115c; Gib 2, 129 ☐ Berg 2.171c	30.3	J-M §118i; IBHS 676; Gib 136
		30.4	GAHG 3.175 n 576; Gib 158 ☐ Berg 2.571; Brock §163b
28.10	GKC §20h; Gib 187 ☐ B-L 132c, 425; Berg 1.68v	30.6	Dav §109; GKC §144b; J-M §152d; IBHS 377 n 45 ☐ B-L 428f; B-M 2.144, 3.22f; Jen §14.3.3
28.11	GKC §137b; Gib 7 ☐ B-M 2.13		
28.13	GKC §132h n 1 ☐ GAHG 3.102 n 289	30.7	Gib 40
		30.8	GKC §150a n 1c, 154a n 1
28.14	Dav §73; GKC §93q; J-M §96Aj, 125d; IBHS 168 ☐ B-L 582u′	30.11	Berg 1.162g
		30.12	J-M §89a n 2 ☐ Berg 2.27d
		30.13	GKC §132o1, 134o n 1; IBHS 328, 392, 401
28.15	GKC §27u, 48d, 50f, 75ll, 102l ☐ B-L 376r, 639a′; Berg 2.23 n f, 2.54c, 2.162d	30.15	GKC §51o; J-M §113n, 165d; Gib 187
28.16	Dav §45R1; GKC §154b; Gib 76	30.16	Gib 136
28.18	J-M §170k, 170o; Wms §260, 534	30.17	Dav §3R3; GKC §131b ☐ Berg 1.129b
28.20	GKC §153; J-M §102g, 126j, 139g n 1; IBHS 171; Gib 66 ☐ B-M 3.77; Brock §101	30.19	J-M §141j
		30.21	Dav §37f; J-M §125bb; IBHS 283; Gib 49
28.21	Berg 2.21d	30.22	Dav §24c, 147; J-M §170f, 170l; Gib 33, 158 ☐ Brock §17
28.22	J-M §116h; Gib 82 ☐ GAHG 3.215 n 815; Jen §21.3.4; Berg 2.84q	30.24	Dav §151R2; GKC §161c; J-M §174i
28.23	J-M §114c n 3	30.26	GKC §91k, 91l; J-M §94i ☐ B-L 253v, 535f
28.24	GKC §68h ☐ B-L 399h″, 442g; Berg 2.121e, 2.144c; Brock §92b	30.28	GKC §10g
29.1	Gib 149 ☐ Brock §106a	31.1	J-M §150j n 3
29.2	Wms §103, 281 ☐ Jen §27.3.3; Brock §107iα	31.2	GKC §53n ☐ B-L 333c′ ☐ Berg 2.104 n h
29.3	Dav §6R2; GKC §61b; J-M §65b, 144c; IBHS 320; Gib 6, 8 ☐ B-L 13c, 368t; Berg 2.82n, 2.123c; Brock §111e	31.3	B-M 2.141 ☐ Berg 2.127 n e, 2.149m, 2.152t
		31.6	GKC §111k; J-M §118i
29.4	J-M §143e, 143k	31.7	GKC §103g; J-M §150q ☐ B-L 640f′
29.6	GKC §149c; Gib 128, 176, 187		
29.7	Jen §25.3.3	31.8	J-M §121e n 2 ☐ GAHG 3.102 n 289 ☐ Berg 2.69 n c
29.8	GKC §49m, 130c ☐ Berg 2.16c	31.9	GKC §124r; J-M §136n; Gib 20 ☐ Brock §90b
29.9	Gib 119		
29.10	Dav §132a; GKC §144c, 164b; J-M §146c, 152e; IBHS 376; Gib 156 ☐ Berg 2.144b; Brock §35a	31.11ff.	Sch §48.2.2
		31.12	Sch §50.1.4
30.1–2	Gib 100	31.13	GKC §90e; Wms §64 ☐ Sch §50.1.4; Brock §137
30.1	Gib 101 ☐ Berg 2.26c		

B-L: Bauer and Leander, *Historische Grammatik* **B-M**: Beer, *Grammatik* **Berg**: Bergsträsser, *Grammatik*
Brock: Brockelmann, *Syntax* **Dav**: Davidson, *Syntax* **GAHG**: Richter, *Grammatik*
Gib: Gibson, *Davidson's Syntax, 4th ed.* **GKC**: *Gesenius' Grammar* **IBHS**: Waltke and O'Connor, *Syntax*
Jen: Jenni, *Lehrbuch* **J-M**: Joüon and Muraoka, *Grammar* **Ros**: Rosenthal, *Grammar*
Sch: Schneider, *Grammatik* **Wms**: Williams, *Syntax*

2 SAMUEL

1.1	J-M §91ea n 1, 118c n 2, 142c; IBHS 554 □ B-M 3.37; Berg 2.37a	1.24	Dav §98a, 99; GKC §116f; IBHS 619; Gib 133, 135 □ Berg 2.68a
1.2	J-M §166l	1.25	Dav §117; GKC §148b; J-M §162b; Gib 185
1.3	Gib 76	1.26	GKC §75oo; J-M §78g; Gib 150
1.4	Dav §146R2; GKC §157c; Wms §467; IBHS 70, 591 □ GAHG 3.92 n 246; Berg 2.65h*; Brock §34a		□ B-L 375; B-M 2.155; Berg 1.70b, 2.158e; Brock §35b
1.5	IBHS 328; Gib 185	1.27	GKC §148b; Gib 185
1.6	Dav §24R3, 86a; GKC §75rr, 113o; J-M §79l; Gib 124 □ B-L 322y; Berg 2.63e	2.1	Gib 46, 185
		2.5	GKC §121f; J-M §132f, 170e; Wms §533 □ Brock §65a
1.8	Jen §8.3.4.2	2.6	J-M §170e; Wms §72 □ Berg 2.49h
1.9	Dav §22R1, 28R3; GKC §72m, 128e; Wms §30; IBHS 246 n 15 □ B-M 2.129; GAHG 3.171 n 539; Brock §70f, 78	2.7	J-M §150d
		2.8	GKC §129h; J-M §130e, 137r; IBHS 240; Gib 26, 36
1.10	GKC §49c, 61b, 107b n 2; J-M §65b □ B-L 368t, 403; Berg 1.136e, 2.22e, 2.82n, 2.123c	2.9	Dav §29R6; GKC §91e, 127c; IBHS 231; Gib 42, 147 □ GAHG 2.12 n 29; Brock §62f, 108c
1.13	Gib 185	2.10	J-M §166l; Wms §56; Gib 176
1.14	Gib 185	2.13	Gib 6 □ GAHG 3.151 n 415; Brock §23b
1.15	Gib 179 □ B-L 367; Berg 2.122c; Brock §133a	2.16	GKC §144d; J-M §119v, 155e
		2.17	IBHS 268; Gib 4b
1.18	GKC §150e; J-M §124s, 161c; IBHS 16 □ B-M 3.87	2.18	J-M §137v, 146g; IBHS 252 □ B-L 215li, 579p'; Berg 1.101m
1.19	IBHS 329; Gib 185 □ GAHG 2.11 n 23	2.19	J-M §175a; IBHS 654 n 20
1.20	Gib 160	2.20	GKC §136d; J-M §143a; Gib 184
1.21	Dav §100R3, 128R5; GKC §126m, 126n, 130a, 152g; J-M §129n, 160m; Wms §30, 419, 595; IBHS 26 n 73; Gib 138, 142 □ GAHG 3.171 n 542; Brock §7b, 125b	2.21	GKC §64c, 119s; J-M §69b, 133d, 175a; IBHS 655; Gib 46 □ B-L 354c, 535f; Berg 1.157p
		2.22	GKC §102l, 150e; J-M §161h; IBHS 208 n 78; Gib 79, 184 □ B-L 345q", 639a'; Brock §173
1.22	Dav §44R1; GKC §107e; J-M §112d; IBHS 487; Gib 74 □ Berg 2.32e; Brock §122s	2.23	Dav §71R3, 101Rd; GKC §111g, 111q, 116w; J-M §134c, 135c, 139i, 156e; Wms §351, 357; IBHS 87 n 13, 220; Gib 66, 99, 157 □ B-L 645d"; Berg 2.69c; Brock §114b
1.23	Dav §33, 136R1; GKC §44c, 154a n 1b; IBHS 265, 387; Gib 45 □ B-L 583w'; Berg 2.69d, 2.119e	2.24	GKC §164b; J-M §111d; Gib 169

B-L: Bauer and Leander, *Historische Grammatik*   **B-M**: Beer, *Grammatik*   **Berg**: Bergsträsser, *Grammatik*
Brock: Brockelmann, *Syntax*   **Dav**: Davidson, *Syntax*   **GAHG**: Richter, *Grammatik*
Gib: Gibson, *Davidson's Syntax, 4th ed.*   **GKC**: *Gesenius' Grammar*   **IBHS**: Waltke and O'Connor, *Syntax*
Jen: Jenni, *Lehrbuch*   **J-M**: Joüon and Muraoka, *Grammar*   **Ros**: Rosenthal, *Grammar*
Sch: Schneider, *Grammatik*   **Wms**: Williams, *Syntax*

2.26	GKC §44g; J-M §42f; Gib 17 □ B-L 315n'	3.27	GKC §117ll; J-M §126g; Gib 150 □ B-M 3.77; Berg 1.104r
2.27	Dav §119, 120R5, 131R2; GKC §159x, 159ee; J-M §167s; Gib 155, 186 □ B-L 204w; Berg 2.34g; Brock §176b	3.30	GKC §117n, 158b; J-M §170h; Wms §273, 534; IBHS 441; Gib 118, 131, 159 □ B-M 3.106; Jen §20.3.3; Brock §95
2.28	GKC §107b; Gib 74	3.31	IBHS 232; Gib 40
2.30	IBHS 280; Gib 49	3.32	Brock §108b
2.32	Dav §69a; GKC §72r, 118g; J-M §80b n 2, 126h, 152e; Gib 143 □ B-L 393a'; Berg 2.144b; Brock §35a	3.33	Dav §43b; GKC §107t; J-M §113m, 125q n 2; Gib 79 □ Berg 1.68v, 2.36k
3.1	Dav §86R4; GKC §113u, 145c; J-M §123s; IBHS 626; Gib 126 □ Berg 2.71f; Brock §28bβ, 93g	3.34	Dav §91R1, 100R3; GKC §45g, 152d, 152e; J-M §49f, 160c; Wms §256, 399; IBHS 149 n 27; Gib 130, 138 □ B-M 3.8; Berg 1.122t, 2.84q; Brock §32a
3.2	GKC §107c, 129g □ GAHG 3.122 n 332	3.35	Dav §120R5; J-M §149d; Wms §507; Gib 157, 187 □ B-L 132c;
3.5	GAHG 3.122 n 332		B-M 3.118; GAHG
3.6	GKC §116r; J-M §121f; IBHS 628; Gib 99, 138 □ Berg 2.73i		3.170 n 529; Berg 2.51m; Brock §170c
3.7	Gib 11, 138		
3.8	GKC §75qq, 111e □ B-L 375; Berg 2.158e	3.37	IBHS 213, 606 □ Berg 2.58m
		3.39	Dav §136R1; GKC §141e □ Brock §111g
3.9	Dav §120R4, 120R5; J-M §165a n 1; Gib 187, 188 □ Berg 2.51m, 2.53p	4.1	Dav §113; GKC §145p; J-M §150d; Wms §234
3.10	GKC §114o	4.2	GKC §128c; J-M §142m; Wms §95, 98 □ Berg 1.129b
3.11	GKC §115d; J-M §125b, 170i; Wms §319, 535; IBHS 179; Gib 131 □ B-M 3.80	4.4	GKC §122f n 1, 128h; J-M §158b n 2, 166l; Gib 33 □ Berg 2.117a
3.12	B-L 645d"; Berg 2.137k	4.5	J-M §125r; IBHS 181 □ Brock §93d, 93l
3.13	Dav §107R1, 146R1; GKC §135a; J-M §146a, 154fe; Gib 2, 111, 176 □ Jen §8.3.1.2; Berg 2.106l	4.6	Gib 134
		4.7	GKC §141e
		4.8	Dav §17R2; J-M §136j
3.14	Gib 49	4.10	Dav §94; GKC §111h, 114l n 3; J-M §156i □ Berg 2.23f, 2.112c, 2.120b
3.16	Dav §86R4; GKC §113u; Gib 125 □ Berg 2.65h		
3.17	Wms §565; IBHS 629 □ GAHG 2.45 n 195, 3.80 n 219; Brock §44e	4.11	Dav §72R4, 154 n 1; GKC §117d; J-M §125h; Wms §387, 475; Gib 116 □ GAHG 3.206 n 786; Brock §96
3.18	GKC §113dd n 4 □ Berg 2.66 n k		
3.20	Gib 49	4.12	Gib 111
3.21	J-M §119e	4.13	Berg 2.145c
3.22	J-M §156m; Gib 21	5.2	Dav §19R3; GKC §72z, 74k; J-M §137l, 154m □ B-L 443i; Berg 2.158d
3.23	J-M §118g, 155nd; Gib 100		
3.24	Dav §86c; Gib 124		
3.25	GKC §117h; J-M §155r; Wms §58	5.4	IBHS 604 □ Jen §10.3.1.3

B-L: Bauer and Leander, *Historische Grammatik* **B-M**: Beer, *Grammatik* **Berg**: Bergsträsser, *Grammatik* **Brock**: Brockelmann, *Syntax* **Dav**: Davidson, *Syntax* **GAHG**: Richter, *Grammatik* **Gib**: Gibson, *Davidson's Syntax, 4th ed.* **GKC**: *Gesenius' Grammar* **IBHS**: Waltke and O'Connor, *Syntax* **Jen**: Jenni, *Lehrbuch* **J-M**: Joüon and Muraoka, *Grammar* **Ros**: Rosenthal, *Grammar* **Sch**: Schneider, *Grammatik* **Wms**: Williams, *Syntax*

5.6	GKC §35g, 106m □ B-L 263g; Berg 2.148 n 1	6.16	Dav §58c, 141; GKC §117g; J-M §119z; Gib 169 □ GAHG 3.102 n 289; Berg 2.43 n b-k, 2.162f
5.8	Dav §98b; GKC §35g, 116w, 197a; Gib 74, 134 □ B-L 263g; Berg 2.68c		
		6.18	B-L 156k'
5.9	GAHG 2.31 n 128; Brock §120b	6.19	J-M §137u n 1, 147d, 150e; Gib 14 □ Brock §119b
5.10	Dav §24R6, 86R4; GKC §113u, 125h; J-M §123s; IBHS 590; Gib 34, 126 □ GAHG 2.69 n 306, 3.168 n 503; Jen §10.3.1.1; Berg 2.65h*; Brock §93g	6.20	Dav §86c; GKC §75y, 148b; Gib 124 □ B-L 422t''; Berg 2.161 n c; Brock §12
		6.22	Wms §337; IBHS 392 n 31; Gib 45, 181 □ Berg 2.134c
5.11	J-M §129g; IBHS 138, 152 □ B-L 521c; B-M 2.45	6.23	Dav §106b; GKC §24a n 1, 143c; J-M §156d; Gib 181, 182 □ B-L 96 n 5, 192i
5.12	Berg 2.148l, 2.156b		
5.13	GAHG 3.122 n 332	7.2	GAHG 3.170 n 527
5.14	J-M §177o n 1	7.3	Dav §60R4
5.19	Dav §86a, 126R2; J-M §170c; IBHS 635; Gib 124 □ GAHG 1.116 n 351; Jen §20.3.3	7.5	3.87; Dav §60R4; GKC §112r, 150d; J-M §119l n 2; IBHS 530; Gib 183 □ B-L 276y; B-M 1.78; Berg 2.53q
5.21	GKC §146f		
5.23	Brock §119b	7.6	IBHS 74; Gib 138 □ Brock §119b
5.24	Dav §41c, 72R4; GKC §109k, 112z, 117d; J-M §119z, 166l n 2; IBHS 569; Gib 67 □ Berg 2.34 n g, 2.48f		
		7.7	Dav §29a; IBHS 181
		7.8	Dav §29a; J-M §131i; IBHS 227 □ B-M 3.35; Brock §65a
5.25	Dav §151; Gib 161	7.9–13	Wms §182
6.1	Dav §63R3, 72R4; GKC §68h; Gib 116 □ B-L 371u; B-M 2.137; Berg 2.120b	7.9	Dav §10R3, 57R1; J-M §141j; IBHS 270, 544; Gib 10 □ Berg 2.23f(bis), 2.42g
6.2	GKC §125c; IBHS 223 □ Jen §5.3.1.4	7.10–11	GAHG 2.33 n 141
		7.10	J-M §62g, 131i n 2 □ GAHG 3.161 n 480; Brock §114b
6.3	GKC §126z; IBHS 224; Gib 44 □ B-L 511x		
		7.11	Berg 2.16c, 2.148k
6.5	J-M §132g; IBHS 224 □ Berg 1.149g, 2.108c	7.12	IBHS 395; Gib 154 □ Berg 2.148k
6.6	Dav §73R5; IBHS 198 n 35; Gib 110 □ B-M 2.137; Berg 2.120b; Brock §127b	7.13	IBHS 395, 448
		7.14ff.	GKC §159k
		7.14	GKC §112mm □ B-M 3.113; Brock §123g, 163c
6.8	B-L 156k'		
6.9	Gib 79	7.16	IBHS 395 □ B-L 548a'
6.10	Berg 1.129b	7.17	J-M §139e n 1
6.11	J-M §177k; Gib 109, 134	7.18	GKC §107v; J-M §144b; IBHS 320
6.12	Gib 66		
6.13	Gib 134	7.19	B-M 2.112; GAHG 2.18 n 58
6.14	J-M §121o □ B-M 2.127; Berg 2.109c	7.20	GAHG 3.171 n 538
		7.22	IBHS 437 □ Brock §116l
		7.23	Dav §8R2; GKC §145i; J-M §131i n 2, 150f □ Brock §50f
		7.24	Berg 2.109d

B-L: Bauer and Leander, *Historische Grammatik*   **B-M**: Beer, *Grammatik*   **Berg**: Bergsträsser, *Grammatik*
Brock: Brockelmann, *Syntax*   **Dav**: Davidson, *Syntax*   **GAHG**: Richter, *Grammatik*
Gib: Gibson, *Davidson's Syntax, 4th ed.*   **GKC**: *Gesenius' Grammar*   **IBHS**: Waltke and O'Connor, *Syntax*
Jen: Jenni, *Lehrbuch*   **J-M**: Joüon and Muraoka, *Grammar*   **Ros**: Rosenthal, *Grammar*
Sch: Schneider, *Grammatik*   **Wms**: Williams, *Syntax*

7.28	Dav §106R2; GKC §141h, J-M §154j; Wms §115; IBHS 298; Gib 2	9.10	Dav §101d; Wms §96; Gib 48, 49, 149 □ Berg 2.17d
7.29	Dav §83, 91R1; GKC §120d; J-M §112k, 177d; IBHS 422; Gib 120, 130	9.11	J-M §129e; IBHS 157 □ GAHG 2.52, 3.109 n 310, 3.158 n 464
8.1	IBHS 394	9.13	Dav §24d; J-M §146g; Gib 33 □ GAHG 2.61, 3.157 n 463, 3.158 n 464
8.2	Dav §87, 116R5; GKC §113h, 122i, 126n; J-M §121l, 123r, 134g, 150e, 150e n 1; Wms §23; IBHS 104, 589; Gib 24, 126 □ Berg 2.62b, 2.65h*; Brock §93i	10.1	Gib 186
		10.2	GAHG 3.150 n 407, 3.185 n 657
		10.3	Wms §522; Gib 160 □ GAHG 3.150 n 409, 3.157 n 458, 3.158 n 464, 3.179 n 624
8.3	GKC §17b □ B-L 77m	10.4	B-L 549a'; GAHG 3.109, 3.124
8.4	GKC §69v, 134g; IBHS 282; Gib 49 □ B-L 384c'; Berg 2.129h; Brock §84c	10.5	GKC §164d; GAHG 3.109, 3.124, 3.229 n 883
8.5	J-M §134g, 150e n 1; Wms §23; Gib 24 □ B-L 348h; Brock §84c	10.6	J-M §131m, 131n; IBHS 391 □ B-L 511x
8.6	J-M §150e n 1; Gib 10, 24	10.7	GKC §131b; IBHS 230; Gib 40 □ Sch §46.2
8.8	Dav §29d; GKC §131e; Gib 41	10.8	B-L 511x
8.10	Dav §23; J-M §129b n 3; IBHS 147; Gib 31 □ Brock §70f	10.9	Dav §116R4; GKC §145k, 146a; J-M §150i; Gib 23 □ GAHG 2.51, 2.62; Brock §124a
8.13	J-M §100n; Wms §590 □ B-L 582v'	10.11	Dav §116R5; J-M §150e; Gib 24 □ GAHG 3.150 n 410, 3.157 n 460
8.15	GAHG 3.228 n 874; Berg 2.73i*		
8.16	IBHS 217	10.12	GKC §54k, 107n □ GAHG 3.157 n 457; Berg 2.52o, 2.99e
8.17	GAHG 3.81		
8.18	GAHG 2.68	10.14	J-M §118e; Wms §23
9.1	Dav §126R3; GKC §150d, 165a; J-M §161j; Wms §181, 426, 451, 487; Gib 57 □ B-M 3.86; GAHG 3.157 n 457, 3.171 n 538, 3.175 n 592, 3.175 n 597, 3.180 n 631, 3.201 n 757; Brock §135b, 159a	10.16	GAHG 2.55, 3.128 n 353
		10.17	Dav §116R5; J-M §150e; Gib 23 □ GAHG 3.111
		10.18	GAHG 3.154 n 428
		10.19	GAHG 3.150 n 407
		11.1	GKC §23g □ GAHG 3.83, 3.127; Brock §107b
9.2	Dav §126; Gib 184	11.2	GAHG 3.83, 3.102 n 288, 3.102 n 289, 3.110, 3.115, 3.126, 3.144 n 376, 3.154 n 424; Berg 2.127 n e
9.3	Dav §126, 127d; GKC §128y, 152s, 165a; J-M §160n; Wms §426, 569 □ GAHG 3.175 n 586		
9.4	Dav §69a; J-M §126h; Gib 143, 185		
		11.3	GAHG 2.55; Brock §107c
9.5	GAHG 3.103, 3.116	11.4	GKC §141e □ GAHG 3.108
9.6	Gib 183	11.5	GAHG 3.140
9.7	GAHG 3.154 n 426, 3.155 n 437, 3.157 n 457, 3.158 n 473, 3.168 n 508, 3.169 n 510; Berg 2.148k	11.8	GAHG 3.103, 3.121
		11.9	GAHG 2.56
		11.11	Dav §120R2, 121; GKC §149a n 1, 149c, 150a; J-M §161a, 165f; Wms §456, 542; Gib 183, 187 □ B-M 3.117; GAHG 3.179 n 620, 3.182 n 643
9.8	J-M §151b, 158f; Wms §261; Gib 14		

B-L: Bauer and Leander, *Historische Grammatik*   **B-M**: Beer, *Grammatik*   **Berg**: Bergsträsser, *Grammatik*
Brock: Brockelmann, *Syntax*   **Dav**: Davidson, *Syntax*   **GAHG**: Richter, *Grammatik*
Gib: Gibson, *Davidson's Syntax, 4th ed.*   **GKC**: *Gesenius' Grammar*   **IBHS**: Waltke and O'Connor, *Syntax*
Jen: Jenni, *Lehrbuch*   **J-M**: Joüon and Muraoka, *Grammar*   **Ros**: Rosenthal, *Grammar*
Sch: Schneider, *Grammatik*   **Wms**: Williams, *Syntax*

11.12–13 Gib 97
11.12   Dav §50b □ GAHG 3.96,
         3.102 n 288, 3.147 n 388; Brock
         §111e
11.13   GAHG 3.125 n 346,
         3.150 n 410, 3.157 n 460
11.14   GAHG 3.153 n 421, 3.153 n 422
11.15   GAHG 2.39 n 166, 3.103, 3.129
11.17   Dav §29a, 102; IBHS 70 n 11
11.19   GKC §142f n 2 □ Brock §122i
11.20   Dav §146; GKC §157c; Gib 110
         □ Berg 2.127c; Brock §160b
11.21   GAHG 3.111, 3.126 n 349,
         3.128, 3.154 n 426, 3.179 n 624
11.22   J-M §158i n 1
11.24   GKC §69r, 75rr □ B-L 444k,
         588l; Berg 2.127e, 2.168q
11.25   Dav §44a, 72R4; GKC §117l;
         J-M §125j, 152d; Wms §59, 256;
         Gib 74, 117, 119 □ B-M 3.72f;
         GAHG 3.92 n 244, 3.124,
         3.162 n 482; Berg 2.23g; Brock
         §35v, 102
11.27   GKC §60d □ GAHG 3.95; Berg
         2.23g
12.1   GKC §9a, 72p; J-M §80k, 147a
         □ B-L 405; GAHG 3.78 n 207,
         3.83; Berg 2.147g
12.2   GKC §126d, 146f; J-M §138c,
         150q; IBHS 592 n 46 □ GAHG
         2.66, 3.229 n 875
12.3   GKC §29l, 107e, 152p; J-M
         §160k; Gib 73 □ GAHG 3.124,
         3.149 n 401; Berg 2.31d
12.4   Dav §32R2; GKC §91a, 126x;
         J-M §80k, 91a, 126x, 133b n 3,
         138c; Gib 44 □ GAHG
         2.21 n 77, 2.22 n 81,
         3.150 n 407; Berg 2.58n, 2.147g;
         Brock §60a
12.5   GKC §128v, J-M §165e; IBHS
         679 □ GAHG 2.61, 3.182 n 641;
         Sch §53.3.1.3
12.6   GKC §97h, 158b; J-M §100o,
         170g; IBHS 286; Gib 51, 159 □
         B-L 629c'; B-M 3.107; GAHG
         3.150 n 407, 3.156 n 450; Brock
         §163a
12.7   B-M 3.15; J-M §146a; Gib 1

12.8   GKC §69h n 1, 159v □ GAHG
         1.116 n 350, 2.67, 3.116; Berg
         2.23f
12.9   GKC §144n □ GAHG
         3.150 n 406, 3.150 n 411,
         3.153 n 421, 3.164 n 501
12.10   GKC §114g, 158b; J-M §170g;
         Wms §534; Gib 159 □ B-M
         3.107; GAHG 3.98 n 265,
         3.150 n 406, 3.155 n 437,
         3.164 n 501, 3.172 n 545; Berg
         2.57k; Brock §163a
12.11   GAHG 3.154 n 427
12.13–14 IBHS 672
12.13   J-M §177a; Wms §381 □
         GAHG 3.127, 3.172 n 544
12.14   Dav §154; GKC §52o; J-M §52c;
         Wms §558 □ B-L 366t; GAHG
         3.168 n 504, 3.168 n 508,
         3.169 n 511; Berg 2.62c, 2.96 n f
12.15   GKC §51m, 29q□ B-L 320g;
         Berg 2.91g
12.16   Dav §54R1; GKC §112f, 117q □
         GAHG 3.147 n 389,
         3.157 n 457; Berg 2.44k
12.17   GKC §75rr □ B-L 422t'';
         GAHG 3.150 n 407,
         3.157 n 460, 3.185 n 656; Berg
         2.168q; Brock §110a
12.18   Dav §53b, 126R4, 112p □
         GAHG 3.96, 3.150 n 407,
         3.180 n 629
12.19   Gib 137, 184 □ GAHG
         3.153 n 422
12.20   GAHG 3.96, 3.121,
         3.126 n 348; Berg 2.80 n h,
         2.152t
12.21   Dav §70a; J-M §143g n 2 □
         GAHG 2.13 n 34; Brock §81f,
         144
12.22   Dav §43R1; J-M §129p; IBHS
         321; Gib 7, 80 □ B-L 423;
         GAHG 3.170 n 529; Berg
         2.132a*
12.23   GKC §136c; IBHS 324; Gib 8,
         137 □ GAHG 3.150 n 407,
         3.170 n 532, 3.171 n 538,
         3.172 n 544, 3.185 n 656
12.24   J-M §112b □ GAHG 3.100,
         3.115

B-L: Bauer and Leander, *Historische Grammatik* **B-M**: Beer, *Grammatik* **Berg**: Bergsträsser, *Grammatik*
Brock: Brockelmann, *Syntax* **Dav**: Davidson, *Syntax* **GAHG**: Richter, *Grammatik*
Gib: Gibson, *Davidson's Syntax, 4th ed.* **GKC**: *Gesenius' Grammar* **IBHS**: Waltke and O'Connor, *Syntax*
Jen: Jenni, *Lehrbuch* **J-M**: Joüon and Muraoka, *Grammar* **Ros**: Rosenthal, *Grammar*
Sch: Schneider, *Grammatik* **Wms**: Williams, *Syntax*

12.25	GAHG 3.153 n 421, 3.157 n 457	13.17	Dav §4; GKC §64c; J-M §69b,
12.26	B-L 321k		137e, 125g, 143b, 143d; IBHS
12.27	Gib 66 □ GAHG 3.103		239, 308; Gib 5 □ B-L 354c;
12.28	GKC §61f, 135a, 150m n 2; Gib		GAHG 3.154 n 427; Berg
	2 □ Sch §51.4.5; Berg 2.23g		2.116e
12.29–30	Brock §22d	13.18	Dav §58R1; GKC §47l, 107e,
12.30	GKC §127e; J-M §158b n 1;		112tt n 1, 156b; J-M §113a,
	Wms §436 □ GAHG		119z; Wms §182 □ B-L 303c';
	3.156 n 448		B-M 3.43; GAHG 3.128 n 353,
12.31	GKC §112f; Gib 73 □ GAHG		3.155 n 437, 3.180 n 631,
	2.40 n 167; Berg 2.31d,		3.205 n 783; Berg 2.19a, 2.31d;
	2.32 n d, 2.43 n b-k, 2.174 n k		Brock §42d
13.2	J-M §152d; Wms §199, 275 □	13.19	GKC §112h, 112i, 113t, 113u;
	GAHG 3.95, 3.128		J-M §123n; IBHS 538; Gib 125
13.3	GAHG 2.55, 2.61, 3.82,		□ GAHG 2.56, 2.69; Berg
	3.171 n 540; Jen §7.3.1.2/3		2.65 n h; Brock §93g
13.4	GKC §142f(d) n 1 (p. 457) □	13.20	Dav §136R1; GKC §84a, 84s,
	GAHG 3.150 n 407; Sch §44.4		86g n 1, 118p, 154a n 1b; Wms
13.5	Gib 159 □ GKC §75cc; J-M		§435; Gib 37 □ GAHG
	§53i, 119k; Wms §367; IBHS		2.33 n 141, 2.57, 3.110, 3.126,
	216, 431 □ B-M 2.161; GAHG		3.161 n 480, 3.229 n 882
	3.127; Berg 2.164i	13.21	GAHG 3.156 n 453; Jen §6.3.1.6
13.6	J-M §53i, 142c; IBHS 412 □	13.22	J-M §170h □ Brock §119b, 162
	B-M 2.161; GAHG 3.110,	13.23	GKC §131d; IBHS 206; Gib 41
	3.124 n 342, 3.126; Berg 2.140r,		□ Jen §27.3.3
	2.164i; Brock §91	13.24	J-M §114h □ GAHG
13.8	GKC §72t; IBHS 412 □ B-L		3.148 n 399, 3.149 n 401,
	399h", 403; GAHG 3.124 n 342,		3.170 n 524
	3.126 n 348; Berg 2.140r, 2.144c	13.25	Dav §65a; GKC §109g, 152g,
13.9	GAHG 3.128 n 353,		165a; J-M §114b n 1, 114f; Gib
	3.150 n 407, 3.185 n 657; Berg		106 □ GAHG 3.150 n 407,
	2.84q		3.158 n 464, 3.172 n 542,
13.11	J-M §124s		3.185 n 656; Jen §10.4.7
13.12	Dav §117; GKC §75hh, 107g;	13.26	Dav §132R2; GKC §104g, 147c,
	J-M §79n; Wms §172; Gib 188		159dd; J-M §104d n 1,
	□ B-M 3.43; GAHG		161a n 1, 161h, 167o; Gib 156
	3.171 n 540, 3.171 n 541,		□ GAHG 3.148 n 399,
	3.172 n 545; Berg 2.35i, 2.161b		3.148 n 400, 3.149 n 401,
13.13	J-M §137v; IBHS 252 □ GAHG		3.202 n 758; Brock §134c, 168
	3.170 n 522, 3.215 n 815	13.27	GAHG 3.148 n 400, 3.149 n 402
13.14	GKC §117u □ GAHG 3.107,	13.28	GKC §72w, 159g; J-M §161j;
	3.108, 3.185 n 656		Wms §451; IBHS 537 □ GAHG
13.15	Dav §67b; GKC §117q; Gib 115		3.179 n 624; Berg 2.144b,
	□ GAHG 3.147 n 389; Brock		2.148k
	§93k	13.30	Dav §141R1; GKC §111g
13.16	GAHG 3.150 n 407,	13.31	Dav §98R1; GKC §116k; J-M
	3.185 n 656; Berg 2.54c		§121o; IBHS 617; Gib 134 □
			GAHG 3.157 n 461
		13.32	GKC §73f; J-M §81b, 129q □
			B-M 2.151; Berg 2.147g, 2.151s

B-L: Bauer and Leander, *Historische Grammatik*   **B-M**: Beer, *Grammatik*   **Berg**: Bergsträsser, *Grammatik*
Brock: Brockelmann, *Syntax*   **Dav**: Davidson, *Syntax*   **GAHG**: Richter, *Grammatik*
Gib: Gibson, *Davidson's Syntax, 4th ed.*   **GKC**: *Gesenius' Grammar*   **IBHS**: Waltke and O'Connor, *Syntax*
Jen: Jenni, *Lehrbuch*   **J-M**: Joüon and Muraoka, *Grammar*   **Ros**: Rosenthal, *Grammar*
Sch: Schneider, *Grammatik*   **Wms**: Williams, *Syntax*

13.33	Berg 2.48g; Brock §168
13.34	Berg 2.70e
13.36	GKC §117g; Gib 115 □ GAHG 3.147 n 389
13.39	Dav §29R1; GKC §131g, 144o □ B-M 3.35; GAHG 2.12 n 25, 3.150 n 407, 3.157 n 457, 3.185 n 657
14.1	IBHS 224
14.2	GKC §75m, 136d; J-M §143a; IBHS 311; Gib 6 □ GAHG 3.121; Berg 2.167o; Brock §111e
14.3	GKC §76g
14.4	GKC §126e; Wms §34; IBHS 77, 129; Gib 27 □ B-M 3.27; GAHG 2.58; Jen §26.3.2; Brock §10
14.5	Dav §47, 118; J-M §131b; IBHS 252, 551, 653; Gib 25, 96 □ B-M 3.35; GAHG 3.176 n 598
14.6–7	IBHS 678
14.6	GKC §60d, 139e n 3 □ B-L 337n, 442e; GAHG 3.110, 3.129; Berg 2.24 n g, 2.167 n p
14.7	GKC §73b; J-M §58c; Gib 88, 107 □ B-L 399h″; GAHG 3.127; Berg 2.46c, 2.47d, 2.60p, 2.152t
14.9	J-M §148d, 150p; Gib 165 □ GAHG 3.82
14.10	Dav §55c, 56, 99; GKC §GKC §112mm, 116w, 143d; J-M §156h; IBHS 166, 536, 621; Gib 135, 157 □ B-L 445p; GAHG 3.170 n 531, 3.172 n 545, 3.185 n 657; Berg 2.43i, 2.69c, 2.123c; Brock §123f
14.11	Dav §101Rc; GKC §75ff., 119w n 2; Wms §325; Gib 187 □ B-L 426; GAHG 3.198 n 739; Berg 2.160 n a; Brock §34a
14.12	GAHG 3.109 n 310; Brock §122d
14.13	GKC §92b n 1, 115i; IBHS 425 □ B-L 548z; GAHG 3.180 n 629; Berg 1.120 n o, 2.58n

14.14	Dav §43c, 149R2; GKC §107q, 152x, 165b; J-M §160l; Wms §424, 524; IBHS 449, 621; Gib 79 □ B-L 423; GAHG 2.33 n 141, 2.36. 3.147 n 389, 3.161 n 480, 3.168 n 504, 3.168 n 508, 3.169 n 511; Berg 2.35i, 2.36i, 2.164 n ; Brock §145a
14.15	GAHG 3.150 n 410, 3.206 n 786
14.16	B-M 3.59; GAHG 2.63, 3.150 n 411; Jen §12.4.4; Brock §47
14.17	GKC §117e; GAHG 2.34 n 143, 3.169 n 515, 3.215 n 813; Berg 2.49h, 2.160b
14.18	Gib 133
14.19	Dav §94; GKC §47b n 1, 70c, 114l n 6; IBHS 93, 443; Gib 132 □ B-L 357, 634u; GAHG 2.18 n 58, 3.109 n 310, 3.198 n 738; Berg 1.104 n t, 2.58m, 2.110e
14.20	Dav §149R1; J-M §139c, 154d; Wms §522; IBHS 434, 607; Gib 131 □ B-M 1.113; GAHG 3.150 n 409; Berg 2.57k, 2.141r
14.21	GKC §106m □ GAHG 2.62 n 266, 3.170 n 524; Berg 2.28e; Brock §64a
14.22	GAHG 2.18 n 58
14.23	GAHG 3.110, 3.127
14.24	GAHG 3.172 n 545
14.25	Dav §93; GKC §114o; J-M §124l; Gib 90, 131 □ B-L 208r; GAHG 3.229 n 881
14.26	GKC §112ee, 112oo, 118h, 134g; J-M §125v; Gib 18, 49 □ GAHG 3.147 n 388, 3.156 n 444, 3.156 n 449, 3.156 n 451, 3.162 n 482; Berg 2.31d, 2.40d, 2.42g*(bis), 2.117a; Brock §84c
14.27	GAHG 2.60, 3.121, 3.122 n 332, 3.129
14.28	GKC §131d; GAHG 3.147 n 388, 3.155 n 437
14.29	GAHG 3.150 n 407, 3.156 n 448, 3.170 n 531, 3.185 n 656, 3.185 n 657

B-L: Bauer and Leander, *Historische Grammatik* **B-M**: Beer, *Grammatik* **Berg**: Bergsträsser, *Grammatik*
Brock: Brockmann, *Syntax* **Dav**: Davidson, *Syntax* **GAHG**: Richter, *Grammatik*
Gib: Gibson, *Davidson's Syntax, 4th ed.* **GKC**: *Gesenius' Grammar* **IBHS**: Waltke and O'Connor, *Syntax*
Jen: Jenni, *Lehrbuch* **J-M**: Joüon and Muraoka, *Grammar* **Ros**: Rosenthal, *Grammar*
Sch: Schneider, *Grammatik* **Wms**: Williams, *Syntax*

14.30	GKC §71 □ GAHG 3.153 n 421, 3.153 n 422; Berg 2.130m
14.31	GKC §102l; J-M §130e □ B-L 639a'; GAHG 3.153 n 421
14.32	Dav §90R1; J-M §119w, 141g, 157a □ GAHG 3.175 n 580, 3.175 n 586; Berg 2.42g*, 2.148l
15.1	GKC §112g; J-M §119v; Wms §96 □ Brock §85d
15.2–5	Berg 2.32e
15.2	GKC §111g, 112f, 112ll, 127b n 1; J-M §118n, 119v, 124l, 127b, 143h □ B-L 267l; GAHG 3.110; Brock §55a
15.3	J-M §105d □ GAHG 3.203 n 761
15.4	Dav §135; GKC §112p, 151a; J-M §163d; Wms §122, 547; IBHS 321; Gib 186 □ B-M 3.90; GAHG 3.126, 3.181 n 639; Brock §9, 110a
15.5	GKC §10g n 3, 112f, 112ee, 112oo; J-M §118n; Gib 90 □ Berg 2.42g*
15.6	Gib 25, 116 □ GAHG 3.124 n 344, 3.126
15.7	GKC §10g; J-M §114d; Gib 9 □ GAHG 3.169 n 517
15.8	B-L 399h''; GAHG 3.128 n 353, 3.147 n 389, 3.150 n 408, 3.154 n 433, 3.168 n 504, 3.168 n 508; Berg 2.145 n d
15.9	J-M §114n □ GAHG 3.149 n 404, 3.155 n 438, 3.156 n 441, 3.156 n 442
15.10	Dav §51R1; GKC §112oo
15.11	GAHG 3.146 n 382, 3.147 n 387, 3.148 n 399, 3.149 n 401
15.12	Dav §86R4; GKC §104g, 113u; J-M §82b, 123s □ GAHG 2.66, 3.150 n 408, 3.154 n 433, 3.158 n 465, 3.228 n 874; Berg 2.71f
15.13	GKC §126r; J-M §137n; IBHS 244
15.14	IBHS 574; Gib 82 □ GAHG 3.150 n 407, 3.169 n 517, 3.198 n 739; Berg 2.47e
15.16	GKC §117d, 131b; J-M §131b □ B-M 3.74; Brock §96
15.18	Gib 137
15.19	GAHG 3.148 n 399, 3.149 n 401
15.20	GKC §150a; J-M §158o; Wms §72; IBHS 601 n 12; Gib 10 □ GAHG 3.82, 3.149 n 402, 3.155 n 438, 3.179 n 620, 3.198 n 738; Berg 2.54d, 2.151r; Brock §156a
15.21	Dav §25, 120R5, 152; GKC §93aa n 1, 130c, 163d; J-M §129q, 175c; Gib 12, 39, 186 □ GAHG 3.229 n 883
15.23	Dav §67R3, 115; GKC §117t, 145e; J-M §125s; IBHS 167; Gib 22, 115, 137 □ GAHG 3.157 n 462; Brock §28bβ, 93n
15.24	Berg 2.59n*, 2.84q, 2.129 n m
15.25	GKC §117e; J-M §125e; Gib 116 □ B-M 3.74; Brock §97bβ
15.26	Gib 59 □ GAHG 3.205 n 783
15.27	GKC §72s □ GAHG 3.149 n 404, 3.156 n 441, 3.156 n 442; Berg 2.146e
15.28	Jen §28.3.2.1; Berg 2.109c
15.29	GAHG 3.128 n 353
15.30	Dav §100f; Wms §221; Gib 137 □ GAHG 2.40 n 167, 2.69, 3.157 n 461
15.31	Dav §78R8; GKC §116o; Gib 13, 149 □ GAHG 3.82, 3.125 n 346; Berg 2.69c
15.32	Dav §98R1; GKC §116k, 121d; J-M §113c, 121o, 127b; Wms §57; IBHS 616, 678 n 17 □ B-M 3.68; GAHG 2.49 n 226, 3.82; Berg 2.31d; Brock §81e
15.33	Dav §130b; GKC §49l, 75w, 159o; IBHS 531; Gib 67, 86, 153 □ GAHG 3.148 n 399; Berg 2.17d, 2.40d
15.34	Dav §130c, 136R1; GKC §67dd, 143d; Wms §323, 435; Gib 154 □ B-L 438; B-M 3.14; GAHG 2.33 n 141, 3.81, 3.161 n 480, 3.178 n 609, 3.228 n 874; Berg 2.134c, 2.137k
15.35	Gib 90

B-L: Bauer and Leander, *Historische Grammatik*   **B-M**: Beer, *Grammatik*   **Berg**: Bergsträsser, *Grammatik*
Brock: Brockelmann, *Syntax*   **Dav**: Davidson, *Syntax*   **GAHG**: Richter, *Grammatik*
Gib: Gibson, *Davidson's Syntax, 4th ed.*   **GKC**: *Gesenius' Grammar*   **IBHS**: Waltke and O'Connor, *Syntax*
Jen: Jenni, *Lehrbuch*   **J-M**: Joüon and Muraoka, *Grammar*   **Ros**: Rosenthal, *Grammar*
Sch: Schneider, *Grammatik*   **Wms**: Williams, *Syntax*

15.36	GAHG 2.50, 3.153 n 421; Berg 2.43i	16.19	J-M §114d; Gib 82 □ B-L 352
15.37	Dav §45R2; GKC §93ll; J-M §96Ce, 113ga; IBHS 504; Gib 74 □ B-L 588l; B-M 3.43; Berg 1.101l, 2.30b	16.20	GKC §119s; Gib 41
		16.21	IBHS 391 n 27 □ GAHG 3.128; Berg 2.84q
		16.22	GAHG 3.154 n 426
16.1	Dav §139; GKC §134g, 134n, 156b; IBHS 678 n 17; Gib 49, 168 □ GAHG 2.58	16.23	J-M §174d n 2; Gib 13, 31 □ B-L 77m
		17.1–3	Gib 78
16.2	Berg 2.84q	17.1	J-M §119j; Gib 105 □ GAHG 3.147 n 388, 3.169 n 517
16.4	Dav §40b; J-M §112f; IBHS 488; Gib 61 □ B-M 3.50; GAHG 2.18 n 58; Berg 2.28e, 2.52o; Brock §41d	17.2	J-M §119j □ GAHG 2.63; Brock §77f
		17.3	Dav §29e; J-M §119j; Gib 28, 42 □ Brock §14bε
16.5	Dav §58R1, 86R4; GKC §112tt, 113t; J-M §123n; Gib 104, 125 □ GAHG 2.40 n 167, 2.69; Sch §50.4.3.3; Berg 2.43 n b-k, 2.65 n h; Brock §93g	17.5	Dav §1; GKC §106i, 135f; J-M §146d; Wms §107; Gib 2 □ GAHG 1.186 n 640
		17.6	Brock §136b, 169a
		17.7–13	Gib 78
16.6	GAHG 3.124 n 344, 3.153 n 421; Jen §28.3.3; Brock §111d	17.8	Dav §107R1, 146; GKC §117h; J-M §137i, 157d; Gib 2, 111
16.7	GKC §128t; J-M §124i n 2, 129j; IBHS 149; Gib 33 □ B-L 438; GAHG 2.67, 3.150 n 408; Berg 2.97h	17.9	GKC §144e; J-M §155d; Wms §222; Gib 13
		17.10	GKC §67t; IBHS 244; Gib 28, 38 □ B-L 323b', 431u; B-M 2.146; Berg 2.92i, 2.136i, 2.137i
16.8	J-M §129d □ Sch §45.4.4		
16.9	GKC §107h, 108c; J-M §113d, 116b □ GAHG 3.125 n 346, 3.169 n 517; Berg 2.35i, 2.47e	17.11	Dav §11c, 40b; GKC §106i; J-M §112f, 131fa; IBHS 464, 488; Gib 13, 61 □ B-M 2.129; GAHG 2.68, 3.169 n 510; Berg 2.27e; Brock §41d
16.10	Dav §8R3; Gib 8 ⊔ B-M 3.43; GAHG 3.125 n 346, 3.180 n 629; Berg 2.35i	17.12	Dav §63R1, 63R2; GKC §109d, 122l; J-M §114l, 134m, 137v; IBHS 252; Gib 82 □ GAHG 3.171 n 542, 3.215 n 814; Berg 2.21 n c, 2.52 n n
16.11	GKC §165a; Gib 175 □ GAHG 3.125 n 346, 3.177 n 605		
16.12	Gib 93 □ B-L 77l	17.13	GKC §106o □ GAHG 3.154 n 424
16.13	Dav §57R1, 86R4; GKC §93gg, 112f, 113t; J-M §123n; IBHS 412; Gib 125 □ GAHG 2.40 n 167, 2.69, 3.153 n 421, 3.168 n 503; Berg 2.65 n h; Brock §93g, 116g, 126b	17.14	Gib 130 □ GAHG 2.57, 2.58, 3.150 n 407, 3.157 n 458, 3.185 n 657; Berg 2.27d
		17.15	Dav §11R3; GKC §106i, 135a; J-M §147f; IBHS 295, 312; Gib 14 □ B-M 3.15; Brock §23e
16.14	GAHG 3.146 n 382		
16.15	Gib 21 □ GAHG 2.55		
16.16	GKC §93ll; J-M §96Ce □ Berg 1.101l, 2.49h		
16.17	GKC §150a; Gib 183, 184 □ GAHG 3.148 n 399, 3.149 n 401, 3.179 n 620		
16.18	Dav §118 □ GAHG 3.191 n 685		

B-L: Bauer and Leander, *Historische Grammatik*   **B-M**: Beer, *Grammatik*   **Berg**: Bergsträsser, *Grammatik*
Brock: Brockelmann, *Syntax*   **Dav**: Davidson, *Syntax*   **GAHG**: Richter, *Grammatik*
Gib: Gibson, *Davidson's Syntax, 4th ed.*   **GKC**: *Gesenius' Grammar*   **IBHS**: Waltke and O'Connor, *Syntax*
Jen: Jenni, *Lehrbuch*   **J-M**: Joüon and Muraoka, *Grammar*   **Ros**: Rosenthal, *Grammar*
Sch: Schneider, *Grammatik*   **Wms**: Williams, *Syntax*

17.16	Dav §109; GKC §121a; J-M §123i, 132f n 1, 152fa; Wms §273; IBHS 184, 207 n 71, 211, 420; Gib 118 □ B-L 403; GAHG 2.65 n 275, 3.146 n 382, 3.156 n 440, 3.168 n 509, 3.169 n 510; Berg 2.84q, 2.149m; Brock §93d	18.11	Dav §101Rd, 132R2, 136R1; GKC §114l, 119aa, 154b, 159w n 1; J-M §124b, 133f, 167l n 2; Wms §294, 439; IBHS 217, 609; Gib 128, 149, 156 □ B-M 3.115; GAHG 3.76 n 201, 3.83, 3.180 n 629, 3.198 n 738; Berg 2.58m; Brock §15g, 110b, 164a
17.17	Dav §55c; GKC §112k, 112k n 4, 126r; J-M §113ga, 119v, 137n; IBHS 536, 625; Gib 27, 73, 95 □ GAHG 3.150 n 407, 3.185 n 656; Berg 2.30b, 2.42g*, 2.71f	18.12	Dav §8, 131; GKC §137c, 154b, 159z; J-M §144f n 1, 167f, 167k; Wms §459, 516, 590; IBHS 321; Gib 8, 155 □ B-M 2.16; GAHG 2.33 n 136, 3.148 n 395, 3.156 n 451, 3.178 n 618, 3.191 n 682, 193 n 705; Brock §24a, 165b
17.18	GKC §112k n 4 □ GAHG 3.146 n 382, 3.156 n 440		
17.19	Gib 14 □ GAHG 3.129		
17.20	GAHG 2.66	18.13	GKC §159cc; J-M §167q; Gib 14 □ GAHG 3.110
17.21	GAHG 3.156 n 440, 3.205 n 783		
17.22	GKC §96 (p. 282), 130g; J-M §129o; Wms §311, 314 □ B-L 622b; GAHG 3.155 n 436	18.14	Dav §63R2, 140; GKC §108c, 156c; J-M §159b; Gib 82 □ B-M 3.92; GAHG 3.172 n 543, 3.205 n 783, 3.213 n 803, 3.215 n 812, 3.215 n 814; Brock §117e
17.23	GKC §51m; J-M §137m □ B-L 320g; GAHG 3.121, 3.129; Berg 2.91g		
17.24	Gib 169	18.15	GAHG 2.56, 3.127
17.25	J-M §88Mg □ Brock §114c	18.16	GKC §22s, 102b □ B-L 127a', 222s
17.26	GKC §118g; J-M §126h		
17.27–29	GAHG 3.222 n 849	18.17	J-M §137o; Gib 65, 98 □ GAHG 2.58, 2.62, 3.126 n 349, 3.127
17.28	GKC §93aa; J-M §96An; Gib 20		
17.29	GAHG 2.66		
18.1	GAHG 3.150 n 406	18.18	Dav §72R4; GKC §106f, 117d; J-M §118d; IBHS 442 n 26; Gib 100, 101 □ B-L 492tζ, 631b'; Brock §106f, 137
18.2	J-M §123k; IBHS 287 □ GAHG 2.68, 3.124 n 343, 3.169 n 510		
18.3	Dav §86a, 146; GKC §63i, 97g; J-M §141g, 142d n 2; Gib 56, 124 □ B-L 348h, 468w'', 627s; B-M 2.26, 2.88; GAHG 3.168 n 504, 3.168 n 508; Berg 2.82 n m	18.19	GKC §119ff. □ GAHG 3.109, 3.169 n 517
		18.20	GKC §158b n 1; J-M §170h n 1; IBHS 149 n 27 □ B-L 77m; GAHG 3.155 n 437
18.4	GAHG 3.156 n 449		
18.5	GAHG 2.62 n 266	18.21	GAHG 3.110
18.6	GAHG 3.228 n 874	18.22	GKC §GKC §37d, 74i, 103g, 137c; J-M §144f; Gib 184 □ B-L 640f'; GAHG 3.169 n 517, 3.170 n 520, 3.170 n 531; Berg 1.89b, 2.47e
18.8	J-M §102g, 141h; Gib 45 □ GAHG 3.155 n 437, 3.198 n 739; Berg 2.165k		
18.9	J-M §137o □ GAHG 2.68, 3.107, 3.111, 3.128	18.23	Dav §8, 60; GKC §110b, 137c; J-M §112f n 2, 114n; IBHS 571; Gib 8, 81 □ Berg 2.49i; Brock §3
18.10	J-M §137u □ GAHG 3.102 n 289, 3.205 n 778		

B-L: Bauer and Leander, *Historische Grammatik*   **B-M**: Beer, *Grammatik*   **Berg**: Bergsträsser, *Grammatik*
Brock: Brockelmann, *Syntax*   **Dav**: Davidson, *Syntax*   **GAHG**: Richter, *Grammatik*
Gib: Gibson, *Davidson's Syntax, 4th ed.*   **GKC**: *Gesenius' Grammar*   **IBHS**: Waltke and O'Connor, *Syntax*
Jen: Jenni, *Lehrbuch*   **J-M**: Joüon and Muraoka, *Grammar*   **Ros**: Rosenthal, *Grammar*
Sch: Schneider, *Grammatik*   **Wms**: Williams, *Syntax*

18.24	Wms §85; Gib 27 □ Berg 2.70e		19.9	J-M §155b □ Brock §36c
18.25	Dav §86R4; GKC §113u; J-M §123s; Wms §206; IBHS 589 n 39; Gib 125 □ GAHG 2.69; Berg 2.65 n h; Brock §93g		19.10	GAHG 3.109; Berg 2.151s
			19.11	J-M §33, 37d □ B-M 1.66, [R] 1.66; GAHG 3.158 n 466, 3.185 n 657, 3.206 n 786
18.26	GAHG 3.102, 3.102 n 289, 3.115		19.12	GKC §142a; GAHG 3.229 n 882
18.28	Jen §6.3.5; Brock §106h		19.13	GAHG 3.229 n 882
18.29	Dav §91a, 121; GKC §114f n 1, 115k, 150a, 150a n 1; J-M §137o, 144f, 161a; IBHS 685; Gib 129, 183 □ B-M 3.86; GAHG 2.57, 2.62 n 266, 3.179 n 620; Berg 2.28g		19.14	GKC §68h; J-M §137r, 165a, 165a n 1; IBHS 240; Gib 187 □ B-L 370p; Berg 2.51m, 2.121e
			19.15	Berg 2.165k
			19.16	GAHG 3.150 n 410; Brock §96
			19.17-18	IBHS 542
18.30	Berg 2.32e		19.17	GAHG 3.148 n 399, 3.148 n 400, 3.149 n 401, 3.150 n 410
18.32	Dav §133; GKC §150a, 150a n 1; J-M §161a; IBHS 685; Gib 185 □ GAHG 2.62 n 266			
			19.18	GKC §97e, 112tt; J-M §100e; IBHS 280; Gib 49 □ B-L 625n; GAHG 3.154 n 427; Berg 2.43 n b-k
18.33	GKC §133l n 2			
19.1	Dav §1, 135; GKC §135f, 151b; J-M §146d, 163d; Wms §107, 547; IBHS 299; Gib 2, 186 □ GAHG 2.13 n 35, 3.150 n 408, 3.154 n 433, 3.181 n 640; Brock §9		19.19	GKC §53q; J-M §54b, 129j □ B-L 228a', 352; B-M 2.129; Berg 2.43 n b-k, 2.105k
			19.20	Dav §91R2; GKC §5n, 115g; J-M §124g; Gib 130 □ B-L 79s; Berg 2.113h
19.2	Dav §51R4, 111u; J-M §118r; IBHS 562 □ GAHG 3.110; Berg 2.38 n a-f		19.21	Dav §71R1; GKC §129c; J-M §126a, 130b; IBHS 172, 677 n 13 □ GAHG 3.147 n 388, 3.150 n 410
19.3	Berg 1.154e, 2.113f			
19.4	GKC §114n n 2; J-M §53i; Gib 120 □ GAHG 3.126; Berg 2.59n*		19.22	IBHS 403 □ GAHG 3.125 n 346, 3.179 n 621
			19.23	Gib 8, 183 □ GAHG 3.179 n 619
19.5	J-M §125s □ B-L 403; GAHG 3.147 n 389; Sch §50.2.1; Berg 2.146 n g; Brock §93n(bis)		19.24	B-L 132c; GAHG 3.172 n 544
			19.25-26	Sch §48.2.3, 54.2.2.4
19.6-7	GAHG 3.150 n 411		19.25	Dav §9c, 96R3; GKC §521, 127f; J-M §52c, 158k; IBHS 334; Gib 9 □ B-L 329h'; GAHG 3.155 n 437; Berg 2.95d; Brock §73c
19.6	GKC §70c, 128a; IBHS 139 □ Berg 2.171 n d			
19.7	Dav §131; GKC §159ee; J-M §49d, 167s; Wms §511, 516; Gib 61, 155 □ B-M 2.173; GAHG 2.33 n 136, 3.157 n 463, 3.178 n 618, 3.191 n 682, 193 n 705; Brock §176b		19.26	J-M §166o; Gib 184 □ GAHG 3.148 n 399, 3.149 n 401; Jen §18.3.4.2
			19.27	GKC §122f; J-M §137m; Gib 27 □ GAHG 3.148 n 399, 3.149 n 401; Berg 2.52o, 2.113g
19.8	Dav §40b, 109, 132R2; GKC §159bb; J-M §126i, 165d, 167i; Wms §446, 515; Gib 45, 156 □ B-M 3.114; GAHG 3.147 n 388, 3.155 n 437; Brock §164cα		19.28	GAHG 2.49

B-L: Bauer and Leander, *Historische Grammatik*   **B-M**: Beer, *Grammatik*   **Berg**: Bergsträsser, *Grammatik*
Brock: Brockelmann, *Syntax*   **Dav**: Davidson, *Syntax*   **GAHG**: Richter, *Grammatik*
Gib: Gibson, *Davidson's Syntax, 4th ed.*   **GKC**: *Gesenius' Grammar*   **IBHS**: Waltke and O'Connor, *Syntax*
Jen: Jenni, *Lehrbuch*   **J-M**: Joüon and Muraoka, *Grammar*   **Ros**: Rosenthal, *Grammar*
Sch: Schneider, *Grammatik*   **Wms**: Williams, *Syntax*

19.29	J-M §144d; IBHS 318; Gib 8 □ GAHG 3.175 n 592, 3.175 n 597, 3.175 n 581	20.6	Dav §128R4; 107q n 3, 152w; Gib 45 □ B-M 2.144; GAHG 3.213 n 803; Berg 2.135d
19.30	GKC §106i; J-M §111d, 112f; Wms §164; IBHS 488; Gib 61 □ GAHG 3.171 n 538; Berg 2.27e	20.7	GAHG 3.150 n 410, 3.157 n 460; Brock §32b
19.31	Gib 131, 157, 158 □ GAHG 3.149 n 404, 3.156 n 441, 3.156 n 442	20.8	Dav §139; GKC §142e; J-M §121o □ B-L 564, 641i'; GAHG 2.60, 3.83; Brock §113
19.33	B-L 282o; B-M 2.126; GAHG 2.59; Berg 2.108c	20.9	GKC §23f, 66b, 68h, 141c n 3 □ B-L 363h, 371u; Berg 1.45e, 2.121e, 2.123c
19.34	Gib 94 □ GAHG 3.148 n 399, 3.158 n 473, 3.213 n 803	20.10	Dav §71R3, 114; IBHS 381; Gib 21 □ Jen §11.3.1.2
19.35	Gib 185 □ B-L 651w; GAHG 3.148 n 399, 3.149 n 401	20.11	GKC §137c; J-M §144g; Gib 8 □ B-L 267c; Brock §155a
19.36	J-M §137p, 151b; Wms §273; IBHS 200 n 43; Gib 148, 184 □ GAHG 2.59, 3.171 n 538, 3.229 n 882; Brock §112, 129e	20.12	Dav §100R4; GKC §112oo; Gib 137 □ GAHG 3.126 n 349; Berg 2.42g*
19.37	GAHG 3.149 n 402, 3.156 n 448, 3.180 n 629	20.13	GKC §69w □ Berg 2.87 n c, 2.128 n h
19.38	J-M §114h; IBHS 650; Gib 82 □ B-M 2.102; GAHG 3.154 n 426, 3.169 n 515; Berg 2.47e, 2.52o, 2.144c; Brock §113	20.14	GKC §125h
		20.15	GKC §90e; Wms §64 □ GAHG 3.158 n 466
		20.17	J-M §154fe □ B-M 3.86; Jen §10.3.4
19.39	J-M §114h; IBHS 569 □ GAHG · 3.148 n 399	20.18	GKC §113o, 113w; J-M §52d, 123p; IBHS 582; Gib 73, 125 □ GAHG 3.169 n 510, 3.169 n 511; Berg 2.31d, 2.63e(bis), 2.115a, 2.137k
19.41	GKC §111h; GAHG 3.148 n 399		
19.43	GKC §76b, 113q; J-M §123f; IBHS 587; Gib 184 □ GAHG 3.168 n 507; Berg 2.63d		
19.44	Dav §34R2; GKC §67w; IBHS 284, 439 n 15 □ B-L 438; B-M 2.91; GAHG 3.95, 3.180 n 629, 3.229 n 881; Berg 2.138l, 2.162f	20.19	Dav §28R6, 126R5; GKC §122h n 5, 130f n 4; Gib 36, 184 □ GAHG 3.124 n 344, 3.185 n 657
20.1	GKC §147c; J-M §144h, 158b n 2, 159d; Wms §128; IBHS 326 n 22 □ B-L 77l; GAHG 3.129; Brock §7a	20.20	Dav §117R1; GKC §149a, 149e; J-M §165k □ GAHG 3.124 n 344, 3.182 n 643; Berg 2.117a
20.2	GAHG 3.154 n 424	20.21	GKC §53s, 116e, 116p, 155e; J-M §121e, 131i n 2, 158b, 158b n 2, 172c; IBHS 202 n 47, 452; Gib 11 □ GAHG 3.158 n 464; Berg 2.72h*
20.3	Gib 44, 144 □ GAHG 3.103; Berg 2.84q; Brock §85d, 96, 124b		
20.4	B-M 2.130; GAHG 3.147 n 388, 3.213 n 803; Berg 2.105i*	20.22	IBHS 452 □ GAHG 2.59, 3.126 n 349, 3.156 n 441, 3.156 n 442; Brock §89
20.5	GKC §68i; Gib 45□ B-L 371r; GAHG 3.150 n 410; Berg 2.121d	20.23	GKC §16b, 127f □ Berg 1.70b
		20.26	GAHG 3.229 n 875
		21.1	GKC §91e

B-L: Bauer and Leander, *Historische Grammatik*   **B-M**: Beer, *Grammatik*   **Berg**: Bergsträsser, *Grammatik*
Brock: Brockelmann, *Syntax*   **Dav**: Davidson, *Syntax*   **GAHG**: Richter, *Grammatik*
Gib: Gibson, *Davidson's Syntax, 4th ed.*   **GKC**: *Gesenius' Grammar*   **IBHS**: Waltke and O'Connor, *Syntax*
Jen: Jenni, *Lehrbuch*   **J-M**: Joüon and Muraoka, *Grammar*   **Ros**: Rosenthal, *Grammar*
Sch: Schneider, *Grammatik*   **Wms**: Williams, *Syntax*

21.2	GKC §74h, 115c, 152d; J-M §160b □ B-L 376r; Berg 2.158e(bis)	22.6	Berg 2.132a*; Brock §138
		22.7–23	Berg 2.34h
21.3	Dav §65d; GKC §110i; J-M §116g, 161m; Wms §189, 519; Gib 106 □ Jen §21.3.4	22.7	IBHS 498; Gib 71 □ Brock §35b, 145a
		22.8	Berg 2.108 n b; Brock §138
		22.10	B-L 233j, 383; Berg 2.125c
21.4	Dav §1R1, 41R3; GKC §120c; J-M §144g n 1; Wms §410; IBHS 609; Gib 148 □ Berg 2.57l	22.12	IBHS 498, 546; Gib 71 □ Berg 2.34h
		22.14	Dav §65R6; IBHS 225 n 132, 498; Gib 71 □ Berg 2.34h
21.6	Dav §65R2, 79; GKC §135a; Gib 47, 107, 118 □ Berg 2.118c, 2.129h, 2.174 n h	22.15	GAHG 2.68 n 293; Berg 2.135d, 2.174 n h
21.7	IBHS 201	22.16	J-M §129u; IBHS 159; Gib 25
21.9	Dav §36R4, 68; GKC §118i; J-M §126i n 2; Gib 48, 144 □ B-L 624i; B-M 2.86; Berg 2.150o, 2.174 n h	22.17	Berg 2.173 n g; Brock §138
		22.19	B-L 215l
		22.20	Gib 116
		22.23	Gib 41
21.10	J-M §80k □ Berg 2.145d	22.24	Dav §51R7; GKC §49e; IBHS 425; Gib 102 □ B-L 328x; Berg 2.23f
21.11	GKC §121a; J-M §128b; Wms §493 □ Brock §35d		
21.12	GKC §75rr; Gib 28 □ B-L 427t"; Berg 2.168q	22.26	IBHS 425
		22.27	GKC §671 □ GAHG 1.72 n 135; Berg 2.136 n h, 2.136 n i
21.13	Berg 2.129i		
21.14	GKC §51n	22.28	Gib 116
21.15	GKC §72t; J-M §80k □ Berg 2.173 n g	22.30	GKC §103g □ B-L 640f'; Berg 2.140 n q
21.16	J-M §121o; Gib 182	22.33	Dav §29R4; GKC §131r
21.17	GKC §109g; Gib 186 □ Berg 2.33g, 2.113h	22.34	Wms §583
		22.36–46	Berg 2.32e
21.18	J-M §113i □ Berg 2.33g	22.36	Dav §90R1 □ Berg 1.149g
21.20	GKC §35n, 118h, 134q; J-M §127b; Wms §101; IBHS 116 n 6; Gib 42, 145 □ B-L 629b'; Brock §87, 129d	22.37	GKC §103d, J-M §103e n 1 □ B-L 645d"
		22.38	GKC §108e; IBHS 576 n 28 □ Berg 2.50l
21.21	Berg 2.116b	22.39	IBHS 498, 507
21.22	GKC §121b; J-M §128b; Wms §58; Gib 47, 48, 117, 118, 119 □ GAHG 3.120 n 330, 3.122 n 332; Brock §35e	22.40	GKC §23f, 68k, 103d; J-M §103e n 1 □ B-L 350v; Berg 1.91e, 2.121d
		22.41	GKC §19i, 66k, 116w, 117ii n 1 □ B-L 368t; GAHG 1.55 n 56; Berg 1.133 n g, 2.123 n d
22	GKC §2r, 3g; IBHS 14, 17, 498 □ B-L 73d; GAHG 2.39 n 164, 3.218 n 827	22.42	IBHS 394
22.1	GKC §53l, 130d; 54c n 3 □ GAHG 3.199 n 745; Berg 2.106 n l; Brock §144	22.43	Berg 2.138l
		22.44	GKC §87f; J-M §158c; IBHS 498 □ Brock §148
22.2	GKC §135m n 3; J-M §146f	22.45	Berg 2.84q
22.3	B-L 538i; Berg 1.145d	22.46	GKC §91n □ B-L 591l
22.4	IBHS 394 □ Berg 2.69d, 2.117a, 2.128g	22.48	GKC §103d; J-M §103e n 1
22.5	Brock §138	22.50	GKC §107n

B-L: Bauer and Leander, *Historische Grammatik* B-M: Beer, *Grammatik* Berg: Bergsträsser, *Grammatik*
Brock: Brockelmann, *Syntax* Dav: Davidson, *Syntax* GAHG: Richter, *Grammatik*
Gib: Gibson, *Davidson's Syntax, 4th ed.* GKC: *Gesenius' Grammar* IBHS: Waltke and O'Connor, *Syntax*
Jen: Jenni, *Lehrbuch* J-M: Joüon and Muraoka, *Grammar* Ros: Rosenthal, *Grammar*
Sch: Schneider, *Grammatik* Wms: Williams, *Syntax*

23.1	GKC §2r, 29g; J-M §103a; Wms §285; IBHS 216 □ Berg 2.150o	24.4	Gib 150
23.2	Brock §16g	24.6	GKC §90i
23.3	Dav §71R2; GKC §116w, 118q; Gib 133, 145 □ Berg 2.69c	24.8	J-M §118i
		24.9	GKC §122i; J-M §139g, 150e; IBHS 104; Gib 24
23.4	Dav §128R3; GKC §152u; J-M §90e, 160o □ Brock §125a	24.10	GAHG 3.215 n 815; Brock §145bζ
23.5	Dav §2; GKC §135m, 150a n 2; Gib 183 □ B-M 2.129; Berg 2.129h	24.11–12	Jen §10.3.1.1
		24.11	GKC §93rr; J-M §96Ce □ Berg 1.101l
23.6	Dav §22R3; GKC §91f, 128v, 143a; J-M §94h □ B-L 252o, 268j; B-M 2.54; Berg 2.150o, 2.151q	24.12	J-M §123u, 152g; IBHS 594; Gib 127 □ Berg 2.66k(bis)
		24.13	Dav §29d, 90R1, 116R1; GKC §115c, 145h, 145k, 145o; J-M §142d, 144d, 150g; Wms §455; IBHS 227, 231, 278, 318 n 6; Gib 8, 23, 41, 112, 184 □ B-M 3.88; Berg 2.54d; Brock §136a
23.7	GKC §113w; J-M §123p; IBHS 582 □ Berg 2.63d, 2.63f		
23.8	GKC §47b n 1, 87f; IBHS 114; Gib 19 □ Berg 1.105t		
23.9–10	IBHS 504		
23.10	Gib 74, 158 □ Berg 2.30b		
23.11	Dav §28R5; GKC §127e; J-M §139b, 150e □ Brock §73a	24.14	Dav §62; GKC §108c; J-M §94d n 2, 114b n 1, 114c, 160f; IBHS 574; Gib 82, 140, 185 □ Berg 2.49h(bis); Brock §6d, 8a
23.13	GKC §134k		
23.15	Dav §135; GKC §151a; J-M §163d; Wms §547; IBHS 321; Gib 186 □ B-M 2.161	24.15	GKC §135a; J-M §150j
		24.16	GKC §142f; Wms §306; IBHS 194 □ Berg 2.91g; Brock §11a
23.16	Gib 47	24.17	GKC §135a; J-M §146a; IBHS 295 □ Berg 2.25b
23.17	Dav §117R1; GKC §167a; Wms §246; IBHS 197; Gib 150 □ B-M 3.29; Brock §106e	24.20	GAHG 3.102 n 289
		24.21	GKC §165a □ B-L 353v; Berg 2.119e
23.19	GKC §150d; Wms §312; IBHS 216	24.22–23	IBHS 488
23.20	Berg 2.43 n b-k	24.22	GKC §93pp □ B-L 131; B-M 2.162
23.21	GKC §126r; J-M §125h, 137f n 2, 137m	24.23	GKC §106m; J-M §112f; Gib 61
23.23	Gib 48	24.24	Dav §29d, 86a; GKC §75n, 113p, 134e; J-M §123e, 123i; IBHS 586; Gib 34, 41, 124 □ GAHG 3.168 n 508, 3.169 n 510; Berg 2.62c, 2.160a
23.28	B-L 127a′		
23.33	GKC §35d □ B-L 263f, 563x; Berg 1.91d		
23.37	GKC §23f		
24.1	Berg 2.151q		
24.2	J-M §119i n 2, 119m		
24.3	Dav §38R5, 113, 136R1; GKC §134r, 145n, 154b; J-M §103c, 177l; IBHS 287; Gib 21, 51 □ Berg 2.49h		

B-L: Bauer and Leander, *Historische Grammatik* **B-M**: Beer, *Grammatik* **Berg**: Bergsträsser, *Grammatik*
Brock: Brockelmann, *Syntax* **Dav**: Davidson, *Syntax* **GAHG**: Richter, *Grammatik*
Gib: Gibson, *Davidson's Syntax, 4th ed.* **GKC**: *Gesenius' Grammar* **IBHS**: Waltke and O'Connor, *Syntax*
Jen: Jenni, *Lehrbuch* **J-M**: Joüon and Muraoka, *Grammar* **Ros**: Rosenthal, *Grammar*
Sch: Schneider, *Grammatik* **Wms**: Williams, *Syntax*

1 KINGS

B-L: Bauer and Leander, *Historische Grammatik*   B-M: Beer, *Grammatik*   Berg: Bergsträsser, *Grammatik*
Brock: Brockelmann, *Syntax*   Dav: Davidson, *Syntax*   GAHG: Richter, *Grammatik*
Gib: Gibson, *Davidson's Syntax, 4th ed.*   GKC: *Gesenius' Grammar*   IBHS: Waltke and O'Connor, *Syntax*
Jen: Jenni, *Lehrbuch*   J-M: Joüon and Muraoka, *Grammar*   Ros: Rosenthal, *Grammar*
Sch: Schneider, *Grammatik*   Wms: Williams, *Syntax*

1.39	Berg 2.49h
1.40	Dav §98a; GKC §117q, 145c; J-M §132e; IBHS 197, 381, 616; Gib 115, 134 □ GAHG 3.129; Berg 2.97h, 2.140 n r; Brock §99a
1.41	Dav §138c; GKC §146a; J-M §127a; Gib 22, 168 □ B-L 590h; GAHG 3.150 n 407; Berg 2.27d; Brock §82e, 124a
1.42	GKC §116u; Gib 137 □ Berg 2.70e*
1.43	IBHS 123; Gib 19, 141 □ GAHG 3.176 n 598; Brock §56b
1.44	GKC §111d; GAHG 2.68, 3.149 n 402; Brock §122f
1.45	J-M §127b □ GAHG 3.100, 3.111 n 313, 3.115, 3.146 n 382; Berg 2.172 n f
1.46	IBHS 255
1.47	GKC §70e; J-M §137f □ GAHG 3.109, 3.110, 3.126; Berg 2.49h, 2.105i; Brock §111g
1.48	Gib 168 □ GAHG 3.205 n 783
1.49	Brock §82e
1.50	GAHG 3.97
1.51	Dav §120; Gib 187 □ GAHG 3.97, 3.121, 3.153 n 421, 3.153 n 422
1.52	GKC §119w n 2; J-M §129j, 176n; IBHS 150; Gib 18, 154 □ Brock §34a, 105b
1.53	GAHG 3.128 n 353
2.1	Berg 2.57k
2.2	Dav §55c; GKC §112aa, 116p; J-M §103b; IBHS 628; Gib 94 □ GAHG 3.95; Berg 2.72h*
2.3	GKC §95u, 114o; J-M §124o; Gib 176
2.4	J-M §130g
2.5	Dav §26, 47, 107R1; GKC §111q; J-M §118j; IBHS 552; Gib 2, 96 □ GAHG 3.156 n 441, III156 n 442
2.6	Dav §63R2; GKC §109d, 112aa; J-M §114l; IBHS 567; Gib 82 □ B-M 3.55; GAHG 2.63 n 151, 3.128 n 353, 3.156 n 441, III156 n 442, 3.171 n 542, 3.172 n 545, 3.215 n 814; Berg 2.43i, 2.52 n n
2.7	GKC §116h; J-M §129e; Gib 134
2.8	Dav §78, 146R1; J-M §118e; Gib 111 □ B-L 438; B-M 2.118; GAHG 3.147 n 389, 3.150 n 408, 3.154 n 433, 3.153 n 421; Berg 2.92h, 2.97h
2.9	J-M §125n; IBHS 171 □ GAHG 3.97, 3.124, 3.125 n 346, 3.128 n 353, 3.156 n 441, III156 n 444
2.10	J-M §155b n 2
2.11	IBHS 481 □ GAHG 3.147 n 388
2.12	GAHG 3.111
2.13	J-M §141a, 154g, 161a; Wms §562; IBHS 256
2.14	J-M §154d; Gib 142 □ GAHG 3.83
2.15	Dav §107R1; J-M §18j, 124s; Wms §322; Gib 2 □ GAHG 3.97, 3.229 n 883
2.17	GKC §131g; J-M §131k; Wms §70 □ GAHG 3.106, 3.116, 3.121, 3.172 n 545
2.18	Dav §107R1; GKC §135a; J-M §146a; Wms §295; IBHS 217; Gib 2, 149
2.19	J-M §131k; IBHS 205 □ B-M 2.102; GAHG 2.49, 3.96, 3.157 n 460; Brock §110e
2.20	GKC §72aa, 109c; J-M §47a n 2, 80n, 114i, 142ba □ B-L 405; GAHG 3.171 n 540, 3.172 n 545; Berg 2.149m
2.21	Dav §79; GKC §121b; J-M §128b; Wms §59; IBHS 375 n 32 □ GAHG 2.68, 3.120 n 330, 3.121
2.22	Dav §60, 126R6a, 136R1; GKC §110a, 154b; J-M §113d n 2, 114m, 177m; Wms §441; IBHS 572; Gib 81, 184

B-L: Bauer and Leander, *Historische Grammatik*   **B-M**: Beer, *Grammatik*   **Berg**: Bergsträsser, *Grammatik*   **Brock**: Brockelmann, *Syntax*   **Dav**: Davidson, *Syntax*   **GAHG**: Richter, *Grammatik*   **Gib**: Gibson, *Davidson's Syntax, 4th ed.*   **GKC**: *Gesenius' Grammar*   **IBHS**: Waltke and O'Connor, *Syntax*   **Jen**: Jenni, *Lehrbuch*   **J-M**: Joüon and Muraoka, *Grammar*   **Ros**: Rosenthal, *Grammar*   **Sch**: Schneider, *Grammatik*   **Wms**: Williams, *Syntax*

2.23	GKC §149d; J-M §146k, 165a, 165a n 1; Wms §246; Gib 187 □ B-L 132c; GAHG 3.205 n 783; Jen §17.3.4; Berg 2.51m	2.42	Dav §40b, 55b; GKC §72aa, 112v; J-M §93c, 119o, 124q; IBHS 329 n 30; Gib 61, 94 □ B-L 216o, 529v, 631f; GAHG 3.127, 3.150 n 408, 3.154 n 433, 3.168 n 504, 3.168 n 508, 3.169 n 510, 3.169 n 511; Berg 2.21d, 2.41f
2.24	GKC §60d □ B-L 337n, 384c'; GAHG 3.121; Berg 2.23g		
2.25	GAHG 3.153 n 421; Brock §127b		
2.26	Dav §24R3, 110; GKC §75z, 93ss, 118f, 128t; J-M §96Ce, 125n, 129j, 155s, 158i; Wms §432; IBHS 150 □ B-M 2.161; GAHG 3.213 n 803; Brock §122k	2.43	GKC §128h; J-M §129g; IBHS 147
		2.44	Dav §57R1
		2.45	J-M §121e □ B-M 3.69; GAHG 3.158 n 467, 3.229 n 875
		3.2	J-M §121f; IBHS 625; Gib 137 □ GAHG 3.192 n 693
2.27	J-M §124l; Wms §198 □ GAHG 2.50, 3.124	3.3	Wms §213, 390, 560; IBHS 626 n 46, 670 □ B-M 3.68; Brock §44c
2.28	Dav §105 □ Berg 2.27d		
2.29	IBHS 675		
2.30	GKC §75ll; J-M §165a n 1 □ GAHG 3.110, 3.154 n 428, 3.205 n 783; Berg 1.67u	3.4	Dav §37d, 44R2; GKC §107b, 134g; Gib 49 □ Berg 2.31d; Brock §60c
2.31	Dav §24R4, 55a; GKC §128w; J-M §119c, 119l, 129l, 132c; Gib 34, 94 □ B-L 404; B-M 3.30; GAHG 2.51, 2.51 n 238; Berg 2.16c; Brock §71c	3.5	J-M §133b; IBHS 514 n 38
		3.6	Dav §32, 107R1; Gib 2, 6
		3.7	Dav §90; GKC §114c; J-M §124c; Wms §193; IBHS 75, 602; Gib 128 □ Berg 2.54d*
2.32	J-M §155m; Gib 117 □ GAHG 2.55, 3.153 n 421	3.8	GKC §166b □ B-M 3.104
2.34	GAHG 2.62	3.9	J-M §103c n 4; IBHS 613; Gib 6 □ Jen §8.3.2.2, 9.3.3.2
2.36	GKC §80i, 90i; J-M §31c n 1, 93c, 119l; IBHS 329 n 30; Gib 94 □ B-L 216o, 529v, 631f; GAHG 3.106; Berg 2.16c, 2.53q		
		3.11	Dav §58b, 147; GKC §112tt; J-M §15e, 124c, 172a; Wms §552; IBHS 541; Gib 103, 158 □ Berg 2.44n, 2.55d*
2.37	GKC §112v, 159g; J-M §119o, 124q; IBHS 537; Gib 90 □ B-M 3.54, 3.60; GAHG 3.168 n 504, 3.168 n 508, 3.169 n 510, 3.169 n 511, 3.229 n 875; Berg 2.41f, 2.43i	3.12–13	Wms §465
		3.12	GKC §166b; Wms §527; Gib 161 □ B-M 3.104; Sch §53.4.4.2; Berg 2.27e, 2.28e
		3.13	Gib 61, 161 □ Berg 2.27e
2.38	GKC §106c; IBHS 256; Gib 43 □ GAHG 3.147 n 388, 3.155 n 437; Berg 2.26b	3.14	GKC §112ff; J-M §176d
		3.15	GKC §71
		3.16–17	Sch §54.1.4
2.39	Dav §27, 28R5; Gib 35	3.16	Dav §36a, 51R2; GKC §107c, 131b; J-M §113i, 131b, 142c; IBHS 230, 252, 513; Gib 25, 47, 72, 102 □ Sch §48.4.3.4; Berg 2.33g; Brock §83b
2.40–41	IBHS 171 □ Jen §11.3.3		
2.40	GKC §90i; J-M §93c □ B-L 173g, 563x; GAHG 3.158 n 460		
2.41	Gib 101	3.17	J-M §105c, 132a, 147a

B-L: Bauer and Leander, *Historische Grammatik*   **B-M**: Beer, *Grammatik*   **Berg**: Bergsträsser, *Grammatik*
Brock: Brockelmann, *Syntax*   **Dav**: Davidson, *Syntax*   **GAHG**: Richter, *Grammatik*
Gib: Gibson, *Davidson's Syntax, 4th ed.*   **GKC**: *Gesenius' Grammar*   **IBHS**: Waltke and O'Connor, *Syntax*
Jen: Jenni, *Lehrbuch*   **J-M**: Joüon and Muraoka, *Grammar*   **Ros**: Rosenthal, *Grammar*
Sch: Schneider, *Grammatik*   **Wms**: Williams, *Syntax*

B-L: Bauer and Leander, *Historische Grammatik*   **B-M**: Beer, *Grammatik*   **Berg**: Bergsträsser, *Grammatik*
Brock: Brockelmann, *Syntax*   **Dav**: Davidson, *Syntax*   **GAHG**: Richter, *Grammatik*
Gib: Gibson, *Davidson's Syntax, 4th ed.*   **GKC**: *Gesenius' Grammar*   **IBHS**: Waltke and O'Connor, *Syntax*
Jen: Jenni, *Lehrbuch*   **J-M**: Joüon and Muraoka, *Grammar*   **Ros**: Rosenthal, *Grammar*
Sch: Schneider, *Grammatik*   **Wms**: Williams, *Syntax*

8.27	Dav §34R4, 44b, 118; GKC §133i; J-M §141l; Wms §387; IBHS 270; Gib 46, 141, 175 □ GAHG 3.177 n 605	8.54	J-M §166b n 1, 166m □ Brock §89
8.28	GKC §128a; J-M §129a; IBHS 139 □ B-M 3.31; GAHG 2.67, 2.67 n 288; Berg 2.43i; Brock §70e	8.55	Dav §67R3, 78; GKC §117t; J-M §125s; Gib 115
8.29-30	Wms §299	8.56	J-M §139e n 1
8.29	GKC §91k, 138b; J-M §157c n 3, 158i; IBHS 194	8.57	Berg 2.49h
		8.59-61	Berg 2.53q
8.30	GKC §119g, 159g; Gib 86, 156 □ B-L 437; Jen §16.3.4; Berg 2.100h; Brock §164d	8.59	Dav §32R3; J-M §124s, 158i; Gib 6
		8.60-61	IBHS 537 n 38
8.31	GKC §145o; Wms §469; Gib 154 □ B-M 2.61; Berg 2.159g	8.60	J-M §154j □ GAHG 3.175 n 593
8.32	Dav §93; GKC §118g; J-M §126h; IBHS 170, 439; Gib 131 □ B-L 650p; Jen §11.3.3	8.62	Berg 2.71f
		8.63	Dav §111; Wms §572
		8.64	Dav §34R2; GKC §133c; J-M §176h; Wms §76, 318; Gib 45
8.33	GKC §158b, 158d; IBHS 430 □ B-L 438; Berg 1.142f(bis), 2.100h	8.65	Berg 2.57 n k
		8.66	J-M §176h □ GAHG 3.146 n 382, 3.152 n 417
8.34	GKC §72i; IBHS 170 n 16 □ Berg 2.150n	9.3	GKC §75w
8.35	J-M §44e n 1	9.4	Berg 2.60 n p
8.36	IBHS 170 n 16 □ Jen §22.3.3	9.6	Dav §130c; GKC §47m; J-M §44e n 1; Gib 154
8.37	Gib 155 □ B-L 438; Berg 2.138l	9.8	GKC §67g; IBHS 184 n 42 □ Berg 2.136i, 2.138o
8.38	GKC §47m n 1 (p. 129); J-M §44e n 1, 150k □ Berg 2.20b, 2.21b	9.9	Gib 159
		9.10	Wms §39; IBHS 145
8.39	J-M §147d; IBHS 112 n 3, 170 n 16	9.11	GKC §75oo; Gib 72 □ Berg 2.33g, 2.156b
8.41	Dav §9R2; IBHS 263	9.12	GAHG 3.156 n 453
8.42	GKC §47m n 1; IBHS 255 □ Berg 2.20b	9.13	J-M §155nd □ B-L 265c
		9.14	Dav §37e
8.43	Dav §69R1; J-M §44e n 1; IBHS 170 n 16, 516 □ Berg 2.21b; Brock §99b	9.16	Berg 2.23g
		9.17	GKC §126y
		9.20-21	GKC §111h □ Brock §123f
8.44	GKC §75w □ B-L 438	9.20	GKC §111h, 138b; J-M §177o
8.45	IBHS 170 n 16	9.21	IBHS 444
8.46-49	Brock §176a	9.23	GKC §116f
8.46	Dav §44a; GKC §49m; Gib 74, 154 □ GAHG 2.68 n 293	9.24	GKC §164b n 1; J-M §113i; IBHS 514 □ B-M 3.43, 3.51; Jen §24.3.3.6; Berg 2.33g; Brock §42a
8.47	Dav §58a; J-M §112i; IBHS 540; Gib 103 □ Berg 2.43 n b-k, 2.100h	9.25	Dav §54R1, 88; GKC §112dd, 113z; J-M §123x; Gib 90, 126 □ Berg 2.42g*, 2.105i
8.48	GKC §44i □ B-L 422t'', 438; Berg 2.15a	9.26	Dav §14; GKC §122t; Wms §339; IBHS 195 n 22; Gib 18 □ Brock §117b
8.49	J-M §99f n 2; IBHS 170 n 16	10.1	IBHS 625 □ Brock §44c
8.52	Gib 128	10.2	Wms §248, 337; IBHS 197 □ Brock §17, 113

B-L: Bauer and Leander, *Historische Grammatik*   **B-M**: Beer, *Grammatik*   **Berg**: Bergsträsser, *Grammatik*
Brock: Brockelmann, *Syntax*   **Dav**: Davidson, *Syntax*   **GAHG**: Richter, *Grammatik*
Gib: Gibson, *Davidson's Syntax, 4th ed.*   **GKC**: *Gesenius' Grammar*   **IBHS**: Waltke and O'Connor, *Syntax*
Jen: Jenni, *Lehrbuch*   **J-M**: Joüon and Muraoka, *Grammar*   **Ros**: Rosenthal, *Grammar*
Sch: Schneider, *Grammatik*   **Wms**: Williams, *Syntax*

10.3	IBHS 613 □ B-M 2.129; Berg 2.74l, 2.112c	10.29	Dav §101Ra; GKC §75t; J-M §79m; Wms §246; IBHS 197 □ Berg 2.33 n e
10.5	Dav §44R2; GKC §107e; Gib 73 □ GAHG 3.175 n 548, 3.175 n 587; Berg 2.31d	11.1	GKC §10h; Wms §438 □ Berg 1.126bb, 2.77c
10.6	Dav §29e; J-M §154m; Wms §67, 562; Gib 42	11.2	Wms §253; IBHS 670 n 97 □ B-M 3.80; Brock §152c
10.7	Dav §101Rb; Wms §305, 311; IBHS 194, 643, 676; Gib 147 □ B-L 583x'; Jen §18.3.4.2; Brock §108b	11.3	Dav §113; GKC §145o, 145p; J-M §150c, 150j; Wms §234; Gib 18, 21, 47, 49
10.8	Dav §32R3; GKC §126y; IBHS 681; Gib 6	11.4	Gib 99
		11.5	Dav §12; GKC §122f; J-M §134d; IBHS 108; Gib 16
10.9	Dav §50b, 91a; GKC §114o; 115d; J-M §129d; Wms §37; IBHS 143; Gib 31, 97, 129 □ Berg 2.49h	11.6	J-M §132a □ Sch §47.2.1; Brock §82a
10.10	Gib 142	11.7	Dav §51R2; J-M §113i; Gib 72 □ Jen §24.3.3.6; Berg 2.33g
10.11–12	GKC §35m	11.8	GKC §131h n 1; J-M §127a; IBHS 172 n 19
10.11	GKC §35m □ Berg 1.112d	11.9–10	IBHS 542
10.12	GKC §117ii □ Berg 1.112d	11.9	Dav §22R4; GKC §54k, 138k; J-M §145e; Wms §91, 539; Gib 29, 66
10.13	Berg 2.163f; Brock §119a		
10.14	Dav §37R3	11.10	Dav §58R1, 95; Gib 132 □ Berg 2.45n, 2.58n
10.15	Gib 32 □ Berg 1.113 n e		
10.16	Dav §37e, 37R4, 44R2; GKC §134n; IBHS 227; Gib 50, 75 □ Berg 2.30b; Brock §42b	11.11	J-M §140a □ Brock §73a
		11.12	GKC §135p; Gib 3 □ Brock §107lγ
10.17	GKC §134g; Gib 49, 50 □ Brock §42b	11.14	Dav §29a
10.18	Berg 2.138 n n	11.15	GKC §52f; J-M §52d
10.19	GKC §93kk, J-M §75m, 91d; Gib 47 □ B-L 548a'; Berg 1.44c, 2.55e	11.16	Dav §36R1; GKC §53l; IBHS 26; Gib 47 □ Berg 2.106 n l
		11.17	B-M 3.8; Sch §53.1.2.1
10.20	Berg 1.102o; Brock §111d	11.19ff.	Sch §48.2.2
10.21	Dav §100R3, 128; GKC §152y n 1 □ B-M 3.8; Brock §32e	11.19	GKC §54k
		11.20	B-L 510v
		11.21	GKC §165a
10.22	Dav §38R4, 38R5; GKC §74i; J-M §142p; Wms §281; IBHS 288; Gib 51 □ B-L 612y; Berg 1.92f; Brock §107b	11.22	Dav §146R2; GKC §65e; J-M §157c; Gib 111, 124 □ Berg 1.67u, 2.85r
		11.24	Gib 129 □ Jen §13.4.3
10.23	GKC §119u; Gib 45	11.25	GKC §117m n 3 □ Sch §53.4.2
10.24	GKC §145e □ Berg 2.71f, 2.97h; Brock §28bβ	11.26	J-M §131b; Gib 182 □ Brock §106h
10.25	Wms §40; IBHS 151 □ Brock §24e	11.27	J-M §158i
10.26	IBHS 282 n 22	11.30	Dav §78R3; GKC §117ii; J-M §125w; Gib 114
10.27	GKC §126p; Gib 28 □ Brock §107iα	11.31–39	Gib 90
10.28	Berg 2.31d	11.31	GKC §134l; J-M §100d; IBHS 277

B-L: Bauer and Leander, *Historische Grammatik* **B-M**: Beer, *Grammatik* **Berg**: Bergsträsser, *Grammatik*
Brock: Brockelmann, *Syntax* **Dav**: Davidson, *Syntax* **GAHG**: Richter, *Grammatik*
Gib: Gibson, *Davidson's Syntax, 4th ed.* **GKC**: *Gesenius' Grammar* **IBHS**: Waltke and O'Connor, *Syntax*
Jen: Jenni, *Lehrbuch* **J-M**: Joüon and Muraoka, *Grammar* **Ros**: Rosenthal, *Grammar*
Sch: Schneider, *Grammatik* **Wms**: Williams, *Syntax*

11.32	Brock §106d	12.26	J-M §113l; Gib 13
11.33	GKC §87e, 111q; J-M §90c;	12.27	J-M §113b
	IBHS 118 □ B-L 517t	12.28	GKC §133c; J-M §141i, 150f □
11.34	GKC §117ii; J-M §125w □		Brock §111g
	Brock §106d	12.31	Dav §15, 72R4; GKC §117d;
11.35	J-M §142d; IBHS 277		J-M §136n; Wms §14, 475
11.36	Berg 1.129b	12.32	GKC §21d, 65e, 112pp; J-M
11.37	Berg 1.160a		§119z; Gib 104 □ Jen §6.3.1.5;
11.38	Dav §130c; Gib 90, 154		Berg 1.105a, 2.45n, 2.118b
11.39	GKC §23d; J-M §24e; Wms	13.2	Dav §55c, 100R4, 144R3; GKC
	§366 □ B-L 425; Berg 2.96e		§116e; J-M §158b; Gib 94, 137
11.41	GKC §150e; J-M §161c		□ B-M 3.69; Berg 2.72h*
11.42	GKC §138c; J-M §158k	13.3	Dav §55c, 100R4; GKC §112tt;
11.43	J-M §155b n 2; Wms §352		Gib 94, 104, 137 □ Berg
12.1	J-M §125n, 155s □ Berg 2.27d		2.45n
12.2	GKC §131g; 138d	13.4	GKC §115i; J-M §132a □ Berg
12.5	GAHG 3.171 n 535		1.75g, 2.126d
12.6	Dav §65R2, 75, 100f; GKC	13.5	J-M §118f
	§64b, 117gg; IBHS 328, 389;	13.6	J-M §133h; Gib 107 □ B-M
	Gib 106, 107, 112, 137, 185 □		2.161; Berg 2.49h, 2.164i; Brock
	B-M 2.130; Berg 1.157o,		§8a
	2.116e	13.7	GKC §10h, 46d; J-M §41a,
12.7	Gib 154		116b, 116f, 169i □ B-L 357;
12.8	Dav §99R2; GKC §116q; J-M		B-M 3.39; Berg 1.126aa, 2.81k
	§129t, 158ea n 2; Gib 135 □	13.8	J-M §167f
	B-M [R] 1.78	13.9	J-M §114i
12.9	GKC §117n; Dav §65d; Gib	13.11	GKC §125b; J-M §137u, 142ba;
	106, 107		IBHS 251; Gib 25
12.10	GKC §93q; J-M §52d n 3 □ B-L	13.12	Dav §48R2, 144R1; GKC
	582u'; Berg 1.135d		§155d; IBHS 327, 553; Gib 11,
12.11	Wms §591		96
12.12	Dav §8R4; GKC §74k □ B-L	13.13	Dav §21d; J-M §137m; Gib 27
	444p; Berg 2.158d		□ Berg 2.113g
12.13	Dav §75; IBHS 174; Gib 112	13.14	GKC §126r; J-M §158n, 161l □
12.14	Wms §591		GAHG 3.102 n 289; Brock
12.15	GKC §115a; Gib 129		§153a
12.16	Dav §8R2, 8R3; GKC §147c;	13.17	GKC §114n n 2; J-M §114i □
	J-M §144d, 144h, 159oa; Wms		Berg 1.79m, 2.59n*
	§128; IBHS 318 n 6, 327,	13.18	Dav §41R3; GKC §156d; IBHS
	680 n 28; Gib 8 □ B-L 771;		578; Gib 107 □ Brock §135c,
	GAHG 3.181 n 636; Brock §32b		139a
12.17	Dav §50b, 106b; GKC §111h;	13.20	Dav §141R2; GKC §107e, 119g;
	IBHS 553; Gib 97, 182 □ Brock		J-M §80m; Wms §308; Gib 147,
	§123f		169 □ Sch §53.2.1
12.18	Brock §64b, 106h	13.21	Dav §147; GKC §112oo, 115h;
12.21	J-M §121i; Gib 134		Gib 158 □ Jen §7.1
12.24	J-M §44e n 1; GKC §47m n 1	13.22	J-M §114i, 160f; Wms §186
	(p. 129); IBHS 517 n 61 □ B-L	13.23	J-M §80m; Wms §360
	320h; Berg 2.21b	13.26	J-M §80m
12.25	J-M §158j n 1	13.27	Dav §21d; Gib 27

B-L: Bauer and Leander, *Historische Grammatik* **B-M**: Beer, *Grammatik* **Berg**: Bergsträsser, *Grammatik*
Brock: Brockelmann, *Syntax* **Dav**: Davidson, *Syntax* **GAHG**: Richter, *Grammatik*
Gib: Gibson, *Davidson's Syntax, 4th ed.* **GKC**: *Gesenius' Grammar* **IBHS**: Waltke and O'Connor, *Syntax*
Jen: Jenni, *Lehrbuch* **J-M**: Joüon and Muraoka, *Grammar* **Ros**: Rosenthal, *Grammar*
Sch: Schneider, *Grammatik* **Wms**: Williams, *Syntax*

13.28	J-M §177a		14.21	GKC §10g; J-M §111e □ B-L
13.30	Dav §117; GKC §147d; J-M			208r, 624i; Berg 1.124w
	§162d; Gib 188 □ Brock §11a		14.24	Dav §20R4; GKC §127g; Wms
13.31	Dav §56, 57R1; J-M §176g; Gib			§29 □ Brock §17, 73c
	88, 129 □ B-M 3.14; Berg 2.43i;		14.25	Dav §28R5, 51R1; Gib 36, 99 □
	Brock §117c, 123f			Jen §25.3.3
13.32	J-M §130f, 132a, 136n; Gib 20		14.27	GKC §112g; J-M §119za; Gib
	□ Berg 2.160a			104 □ Berg 2.45n
13.33	GKC §107e, 109f; J-M §116e;		14.28	Dav §145; GKC §107e, 112e,
	Gib 107 □ Berg 2.31b			112g; J-M §111i, 117d, 118b,
14.2	GKC §32h; GKC §109g; J-M			119u; Wms §510; Gib 158 □
	§116j; IBHS 425; Gib 13 □ B-L			Berg 2.32d, 2.32e, 2.149l
	248f; Jen §10.4.8		14.29	J-M §116c
14.3	GKC §65g; J-M §142n □ Berg		14.31	J-M §155b n 2
	2.118c		15.4	GKC §115a; Gib 129
14.4	Dav §101Rc □ B-L 458v′		15.8	J-M §155b n 2; Gib 13
14.5	Dav §11R3, 65R6; GKC §94d,		15.13	Dav §50b, 101; GKC §111h,
	112z; J-M §119z, 152a,			119x; J-M §125j, 156c, 156l,
	165a n 1; IBHS 110; Gib 105 □			176a; Wms §574; IBHS 183,
	Berg 2.51m; Brock §16e, 23e			553; Gib 97, 117, 147, 182 □
14.6	Dav §75, 80; GKC §118p,			Brock §111f, 123f
	121d n 1; J-M §127a; Gib 118 □		15.15	Jen §15.4
	GAHG 3.102 n 289; Brock §81f,		15.19	IBHS 201, 489; Gib 61 □ B-M
	103a			2.147; Berg 2.137k
14.7	Dav §76, 78R3, 147; Gib 114,		15.20	J-M §131n, 136o; Wms §13,
	158			293
14.8	Dav §93; GKC §114o; J-M		15.23	Dav §28R5, 71, 71R3, 72R3,
	§124o; Gib 131			123R2; GKC §118q, 128x, 129d;
14.9	J-M §124n; Gib 45, 120 □ Berg			J-M §126g, 146g; Wms §57,
	2.59n*, 2.138l, 2.161b			475; IBHS 181; Gib 36, 117,
14.10	Dav §17R5; GKC §64d; J-M			145, 184 □ B-M 3.77; GAHG
	§130g, 170o; Wms §361 □			3.147 n 490, 3.148 n 391; Jen
	Brock §17			§11.3.3; Brock §82b, 102
14.11	Dav §111; IBHS 207 □ Brock		15.24	J-M §155b n 2
	§50e		15.25	Dav §38; GKC §134p; IBHS
14.12	GKC §72r n 1 □ Berg 2.42g,			286; Gib 51 □ B-L 629z; B-M
	2.143 n b; Brock §163c			2.94; GAHG 3.102 n 289
14.13	Dav §28R5, 147; GKC §129g;		15.28	Dav §38; J-M §130d; IBHS 286;
	J-M §130g; Gib 158			Gib 51 □ B-M 2.90; GAHG
14.14	Dav §6R1; GKC §136d n 2; J-M			3.102 n 289
	§143i		15.29	J-M §166l; IBHS 604; Gib 99 □
14.15	GKC §91n, 126o; J-M §94g,			Jen §10.3.1.3; Berg 2.106 n l
	126b, 129h; IBHS 171 n 18,		15.31	IBHS 210 n 82
	420 n 7; Gib 28, 158 □ B-L 591l		16.2	GKC §74l; J-M §78i □ B-L
14.16	GKC §23c			374n; Berg 2.157b
14.17	GKC §90c; 116u; IBHS 625 □		16.7	Berg 2.58n
	GAHG 2.31 n 127; Berg 2.70e*		16.8	Dav §38; Gib 51 □ Brock §86
14.19	GKC §129d, 150e; J-M §130c,		16.9	Jen §29.3.3
	149a, 161c; IBHS 158 □ B-M			
	3.32; Sch §45.3.3			

16.10	Dav §38; GKC §134o; J-M §142o; Wms §99; Gib 51 □ B-L 629y; Brock §86		17.16	Dav §116R2; GKC §146a; J-M §150n; Gib 23 □ Berg 2.165l; Brock §124a
16.11	Dav §17; J-M §166l; Gib 19		17.17	Wms §502; Gib 99, 158
16.13	J-M §124l		17.21	Dav §63; Gib 82 □ GAHG
16.15	Dav §38; Gib 51			3.216 n 815; Berg 2.49h; Brock
16.16	Dav §22R3; J-M §137r; IBHS 240; Gib 29		17.24	§8a Dav §6R2; GKC §136d; Wms
16.17	J-M §79m □ Berg 2.161b			§118; Gib 6 □ Berg 2.28g;
16.18	Dav §22R3, 72R4; Gib 29			Brock §23a
16.19	Gib 131 □ B-L 375		18.1	B-M 1.78, 2.161; Berg 2.164h
16.21	IBHS 287, 514; Gib 40, 51, 72 □ B-L 510v, 583x'; Berg 2.33g		18.2	Wms §494
			18.3	J-M §121f; Gib 133 □ Berg
16.22	Dav §73R4; J-M §158e, 158g □ B-L 510v		18.4	2.73i Dav §37d; GKC §112g, 134g;
16.24	Dav §20R4, 29a, 29d; GKC §29f, 88b, 131d; J-M §91b, 130h, 131e; Gib 40, 41 □ B-L 234p, 547			J-M §125u; IBHS 281; Gib 49 □ B-M 3.39; Brock §84c, 94b
			18.5	GKC §119w n 2; Wms §324; IBHS 214; Gib 79 □ B-L 547,
16.25	GKC §67x; J-M §79m □ Berg 2.161b			642p'; Brock §17
16.29	Gib 51		18.6	J-M §177a
16.31	Dav §90R1, 126R5; GKC §150d □ Berg 2.54d, 2.136h; Brock §20b		18.7	Dav §141, 141R1; J-M §166g; Wms §118; IBHS 678 n 17; Gib 167
16.34	GKC §127d		18.9	GKC §116d; J-M §37c, 124s □
17.1	Dav §152; GKC §93pp; J-M §96Cb n 2, 112a, 126i, 175a □ Jen §27.3.3; Brock §100b, 107lð, 168		18.10	B-M 2.14; Berg 2.71g Dav §54b, 132; GKC §107e, 112kk, 152k; J-M §165f; Gib 73, 94, 156, 163, 186 □ Berg
17.3	GKC §119s □ GAHG 3.148 n 394		18.12	2.44k Dav §141; GKC §112y, 138e;
17.4	Berg 2.109c			J-M §151b, 158m, 166i; Gib 10,
17.6	J-M §121f, 166c n 1			32, 167 □ Berg 2.42g*, 2.156a;
17.7	Berg 2.126d			Brock §16g
17.9	GKC §90i; J-M §93c, 131b; Gib 25		18.13	Dav §38R4, 47, 75; GKC §110a, 111q; J-M §118j, 125u, 128b;
17.10	Gib 113 □ Brock §63a			Wms §475, 493; IBHS 176; Gib
17.11	GKC §66g □ B-M 2.135; Berg 2.124 n f			96, 113 □ Berg 2.21d; Brock §35d
17.12	J-M §142c; Gib 47, 137 □ Brock §19a, 168		18.14	J-M §119c; Gib 32 □ Berg 2.42g
17.13	GKC §75m; J-M §119l; Wms §388, 559; IBHS 670; Gib 94,		18.15	Dav §120; J-M §112a, 165e; Gib 186, 187
	176		18.16	J-M §102d n 2
17.14	Dav §22R4; GKC §66i, 75rr; J-M §79l, 150n □ B-L 424; Berg 2.123d, 2.168q		18.17	J-M §161b; Wms §118 □ Brock §47
17.15	GKC §32l □ Berg 2.161b		18.18	GKC §114r; J-M §124q; Wms §247, 535; Gib 102 □ Berg 2.38g

B-L: Bauer and Leander, *Historische Grammatik*   B-M: Beer, *Grammatik*   Berg: Bergsträsser, *Grammatik*
Brock: Brockelmann, *Syntax*   Dav: Davidson, *Syntax*   GAHG: Richter, *Grammatik*
Gib: Gibson, *Davidson's Syntax, 4th ed.*   GKC: *Gesenius' Grammar*   IBHS: Waltke and O'Connor, *Syntax*
Jen: Jenni, *Lehrbuch*   J-M: Joüon and Muraoka, *Grammar*   Ros: Rosenthal, *Grammar*
Sch: Schneider, *Grammatik*   Wms: Williams, *Syntax*

18.19	GKC §116d; J-M §121n; IBHS 148, 616 n 23	18.45	GAHG 1.182 n 604; Berg 2.26c; Brock §24b
18.21	Dav §75, 130a; GKC §141f; J-M §137l, 154j; Gib 14, 153, 163, 185	18.46	Dav §108R3; Gib 14
		19.1	Dav §146
18.22	J-M §130b; Wms §270	19.2	Dav §35R2, 120R4; GKC §145i; J-M §165a n 1; Gib 46, 188
18.23	J-M §119i n 1, 177l; Wms §160, 185; Gib 46, 47 □ GAHG 3.115; Brock §137	19.3–4	Gib 99
		19.3	Wms §302; IBHS 194; Gib 147
18.24	Wms §229 □ Brock §30a	19.4	Dav §69c; GKC §157b n 2; J-M §118e, 125b, 137u, 137u n 1, 157b n 2, 160c; Wms §58; IBHS 171; Gib 25, 144 □ GAHG 2.11 n 22; Brock §11a
18.25	J-M §137l, 142j; Wms §33; IBHS 248 □ GAHG 3.78 n 206; Brock §25a		
18.26	Dav §21j; IBHS 247 n 17, 264; Gib 13, 27, 46	19.5	Dav §6R2; GKC §136c; J-M §143a; Wms §118; IBHS 313; Gib 6, 59 □ GAHG 2.31 n 130; Berg 2.84q, 2.127d, 1.160a
18.27	GKC §53q, 67y; J-M §102g, 141g; Wms §172, 180; IBHS 264; Gib 46, 107 □ B-L 229f′, 439p′; Berg 2.105 n k, 2.82n; Brock §106h		
		19.6	Dav §83; J-M §118k, 129g; Wms §224; IBHS 153; Gib 120 □ GAHG 3.204 n 775
18.28	Dav §91R3; Gib 129	19.7	J-M §177e; Gib 45 □ Jen §28.3.3; Brock §111g
18.29	Dav §101Rb; Wms §311; IBHS 608 □ B-M 3.59; Berg 2.52 n n, 2.57k		
		19.8	Berg 2.161b
		19.9	GKC §126r; J-M §137n
18.30	Dav §99; Gib 135	19.10	Dav §111; GKC §52o; J-M §155m; Wms §58 □ B-L 327p; Berg 2.63e, 2.96f, 2.128g, 2.157c
18.31–32	Sch §50.1.5.2		
18.31	Gib 49		
18.32	GKC §117ii, 117kk; J-M §79m, 125w; Wms §52; IBHS 175, 222; Gib 41, 114 □ B-M 3.75; GAHG 3.100; Brock §94dα	19.11	Dav §32R2, 32R4; GKC §132d; J-M §148a n 1; Wms §399, 565; IBHS 73, 258 n 6, 678; Gib 44 □ B-M 3.29; Brock §59cᵏ
18.33	Berg 2.117a; Brock §137		
18.34	GKC §69f; IBHS 414; Gib 113 □ Berg 2.127e	19.12	Wms §399
		19.13	Dav §69a; Gib 143
18.36	J-M §166m; Gib 35	19.14	Berg 2.63e, 2.128g
18.37	B-M 2.147; Berg 2.138l	19.15	GKC §26h, 90c, 90i; J-M §93c; Wms §62 □ B-L 174l; B-M 2.61
18.38	J-M §130f □ Brock §138		
18.39	Dav §106d, 115; J-M §150e, 154j; Wms §88, 115; IBHS 297; Gib 1, 22 □ GAHG 3.80 n 219	19.17	Gib 90
		19.18	Brock §18a
		19.19	Dav §38R3; GKC §134o; J-M §142o, 166h; Wms §99, 248; Gib 51
18.41	J-M §105c n 2, 162e, 177e; IBHS 653 □ B-L 427t″		
18.42	J-M §79m, 168c; Wms §520 □ Berg 2.161b	19.20	J-M §9b n 2, 9d, 114d, 116b; Gib 82 □ B-L 208t, 368t; Berg 1.126aa, 2.47e
18.43	GKC §152p; J-M §105c n 2		
18.44	GKC §58g, 109g, 134r; J-M §102f, 116j, 177e; Gib 51 □ B-L 345q″; Brock §88	19.21	Dav §29R7, 71; GKC §20m, 131m

B-L: Bauer and Leander, *Historische Grammatik*   **B-M**: Beer, *Grammatik*   **Berg**: Bergsträsser, *Grammatik*
Brock: Brockelmann, *Syntax*   **Dav**: Davidson, *Syntax*   **GAHG**: Richter, *Grammatik*
Gib: Gibson, *Davidson's Syntax, 4th ed.*   **GKC**: *Gesenius' Grammar*   **IBHS**: Waltke and O'Connor, *Syntax*
Jen: Jenni, *Lehrbuch*   **J-M**: Joüon and Muraoka, *Grammar*   **Ros**: Rosenthal, *Grammar*
Sch: Schneider, *Grammatik*   **Wms**: Williams, *Syntax*

20.1	Dav §17, 37e; J-M §142e n 1; IBHS 114, 280; Gib 19, 50, 165, 167 □ B-M 2.150; Berg 2.144c
20.3	IBHS 207
20.6	Dav §120R5; J-M §173c
20.7	Dav §60R4
20.8	Dav §63; J-M §119i n 1 □ B-L 442g
20.9	J-M §158i n 1
20.10	GKC §145i; J-M §165a, 165a n 1
20.12	Dav §91R1; Wms §586; Gib 130
20.13	GKC §125b; J-M §112a, 121e, 137u, 161b; Wms §214
20.14	Dav §28R6; GKC §137b □ Berg 2.112d
20.16	Dav §37R1; J-M §142e n 1; Gib 50
20.18	Dav §70a, 111R3; Gib 114
20.19	J-M §118g
20.20	Dav §58R1, 116R5; GKC §145c; J-M §150e; Wms §229; Gib 23 □ B-M 3.20
20.21	GKC §112tt; Wms §182; Gib 103 □ Berg 2.43 n b-k
20.22	GKC §54k; IBHS 627 □ B-M 2.122, 3.69, 3.84; Berg 2.99e; Brock §44b
20.23–24	Berg 42.48g
20.23	J-M §114b n 1, 165j; Gib 167, 174, 187
20.24–25	Berg 52.52n
20.25	GKC §103b; J-M §114b n 1 □ B-L 642o'
20.27	GKC §54l; J-M §53g, 142c; IBHS 360 n 28 □ B-L 285h', 403; B-M 2.126, 2.152; Jen §28.3.2.1; Berg 2.100i, 2.109c
20.28	Dav §56; GKC §112nn; Gib 87 □ Jen §8.3.4.2
20.29	IBHS 281; Gib 6
20.30	Wms §102 □ GAHG 3.151 n 413
20.31	Dav §24c, 106d, 146; J-M §114b n 1, 129f; IBHS 149, 565 n 3, 677; Gib 32, 91 □ GAHG 3.170 n 524
20.32	Berg 2.47e
20.33	Dav §50a; GKC §53n; Gib 100 □ B-L 351; Berg 2.104 n h
20.35	Dav §91R4; GKC §75mm, 115c, 128v; J-M §79k; Gib 32, 130, 167 □ B-L 442e; GAHG 3.216 n 815; Berg 2.162d
20.36	GKC §112t, 126r; J-M §119n, 137o, 166b; Gib 95, 157 □ Berg 2.72h
20.37	Dav §86c; J-M §79k, 123m; IBHS 590; Gib 125 □ B-L 442e; Berg 2.162d
20.38	Gib 13
20.39	Dav §141; GKC §51k; J-M §51b, 123g, 143d; IBHS 587; Gib 167, 169 □ B-L 302a', 323b'; Berg 2.92i
20.40	Dav §4, 5, 141R1; GKC §75v; 116g n 1; Gib 57, 161, 169 □ Berg 2.161b
20.41	J-M §102g, 157d
20.42	J-M §129g; IBHS 144; Gib 87
20.43	Berg 2.85r
21.2	Dav §4; GKC §34c, 125i; J-M §116d, 116i, 143b; Wms §187, 352 □ B-L 261c; Jen §21.3.4
21.3	Dav §117R1; J-M §124s n 1
21.4	J-M §118j □ Berg 2.85r
21.5	J-M §143g, 154l; Wms §219; IBHS 312, 323; Gib 8, 184
21.6	Dav §45R2, 130a, 146R2; GKC §107b; J-M §113g; Wms §246, 452; IBHS 498 n 5; Gib 111, 153 □ B-M 3.44; Jen §24.4.8; Berg 2.21d, 2.33f, 2.85r; Brock §42b
21.7	Dav §45R1, 121; GKC §135a; J-M §146a n 2; IBHS 296; Gib 183
21.8	GKC §124b n 1 □ Brock §126b
21.10	Dav §22R3; GKC §104g, 109f, 130e, 150n; J-M §125b; Gib 29 □ B-L 649l; B-M 3.37
21.11	Dav §99R2; GKC §116q; J-M §140b, 158ae n 2, 158i n 1; Gib 135
21.12	Dav §58b; GKC §112qq; Gib 103 □ Berg 2.43 n b-k

B-L: Bauer and Leander, *Historische Grammatik*   **B-M**: Beer, *Grammatik*   **Berg**: Bergsträsser, *Grammatik*
Brock: Brockelmann, *Syntax*   **Dav**: Davidson, *Syntax*   **GAHG**: Richter, *Grammatik*
Gib: Gibson, *Davidson's Syntax, 4th ed.*   **GKC**: *Gesenius' Grammar*   **IBHS**: Waltke and O'Connor, *Syntax*
Jen: Jenni, *Lehrbuch*   **J-M**: Joüon and Muraoka, *Grammar*   **Ros**: Rosenthal, *Grammar*
Sch: Schneider, *Grammatik*   **Wms**: Williams, *Syntax*

B-L: Bauer and Leander, *Historische Grammatik* **B-M**: Beer, *Grammatik* **Berg**: Bergsträsser, *Grammatik*
Brock: Brockelmann, *Syntax* **Dav**: Davidson, *Syntax* **GAHG**: Richter, *Grammatik*
Gib: Gibson, *Davidson's Syntax, 4th ed.* **GKC**: Gesenius' *Grammar* **IBHS**: Waltke and O'Connor, *Syntax*
Jen: Jenni, *Lehrbuch* **J-M**: Joüon and Muraoka, *Grammar* **Ros**: Rosenthal, *Grammar*
Sch: Schneider, *Grammatik* **Wms**: Williams, *Syntax*

22.35	Dav §100R2; GKC §71; J-M §77b, 79m, 137f; Gib 138 □ B-L 380x; B-M 2.130; Berg 2.127 n e, 2.161b	22.44	J-M §121f □ GAHG 3.175 n 586
		22.46	Gib 58
		22.47	Dav §17; Gib 19
22.36	Dav §117R3, 145o, 147c; IBHS 110; Gib 188 □ B-M 3.20	22.49	GKC §44m □ B-L 322x; Berg 2.15 n b
22.38	GKC §142d; J-M §155e	22.50	Berg 2.33g
22.41	Dav §38; J-M §118f; Gib 51	22.54	Berg 2.161b

B-L: Bauer and Leander, *Historische Grammatik*   **B-M**: Beer, *Grammatik*   **Berg**: Bergsträsser, *Grammatik*
Brock: Brockelmann, *Syntax*   **Dav**: Davidson, *Syntax*   **GAHG**: Richter, *Grammatik*
Gib: Gibson, *Davidson's Syntax, 4th ed.*   **GKC**: *Gesenius' Grammar*   **IBHS**: Waltke and O'Connor, *Syntax*
Jen: Jenni, *Lehrbuch*   **J-M**: Joüon and Muraoka, *Grammar*   **Ros**: Rosenthal, *Grammar*
Sch: Schneider, *Grammatik*   **Wms**: Williams, *Syntax*

2 KINGS

1.1	GKC §49b n 1; J-M §118c n 2; IBHS 554 □ Berg 2.37a	2.10	Dav §82; GKC §52s, 114n n 2; GKC §152k, 159v; J-M §58b, 124n n 2, 160j; Wms §226; IBHS 374, 375 n 34; Gib 120 □ B-L 287o'; GAHG 3.102 n 289; Berg 2.50l, 2.59n*, 2.84q, 2.87c; Brock §169a
1.2	Dav §32R3, 125; GKC §126y, 150i; J-M §118k, 138g, 161f; Wms §543; Gib 7 □ B-M 3.95; Sch §51.3.2, 53.5.2.1; Berg 2.114l, 2.163g; Brock §60b		
1.3	Dav §128; GKC §152y; J-M §160p; Wms §394 □ Brock §32e, 133a, 145a	2.11	Dav §86R4, 100f, 141; GKC §111g, 113u, 116u; J-M §52c, 123m, 166g; IBHS 560, 589 n 39; Gib 125, 137 □ B-L 637s; Sch §44.3; Berg 2.38d, 2.65h, 2.70e*
1.4	Dav §106b; Wms §575; IBHS 77; Gib 182		
1.5	J-M §143g; Gib 184		
1.6	GKC §152y; Wms §394	2.12	J-M §129a; Wms §220, 236; IBHS 282 n 22, 415; GAHG 2.67 n 291
1.7	GKC §37f □ B-L 266i		
1.8	Dav §24R3; GKC §128u; Gib 33		
1.9	GKC §97i; Gib 48 □ Berg 2.125b	2.14	Gib 185
		2.15	Berg 1.127cc
1.10	GKC §154b; Gib 153 □ Berg 2.125b	2.16	Dav §37e, 128R4; GKC §93v, 107q n 3; J-M §70g, 114h; IBHS 104 n 37, 117r, 162a; Gib 49, 50 □ B-L 582v'; B-M 2.71; GAHG 3.170 n 524, 3.175 n 578, 3.204 n 769; Berg 1.102o; Brock §84b, 133e
1.11	Dav §83; GKC §120d; Gib 120 □ Sch §50.6; Berg 2.125b		
1.13	Dav §37R5, 83; GKC §120d; Wms §74; Gib 48, 120		
1.14	Dav §37R5; Gib 48		
1.16	GKC §152y; Wms §394 □ Sch §48.3.2	2.17	Dav §36a, 37e; J-M §114n; IBHS 571; Gib 47, 50
1.17	Brock §109c	2.18–22	Sch §52.5.1 - 52.5.6
2.1	GKC §10h, 114n n 2, 114q □ B-L 637s; Berg 1.126aa	2.19	IBHS 579 □ GAHG 3.170 n 524
2.2	GKC §150i; Gib 187	2.20	GKC §72aa □ GAHG 3.120 n 330
2.3	Gib 143 □ B-L 424; Berg 2.106l	2.21	GKC §75oo; J-M §78g, 125k n 1 □ B-L 376r; GAHG 3.175 n 584, 3.175 n 587; Berg 2.159g
2.4	GAHG 3.215 n 815		
2.5	B-L 424; Berg 2.106l		
2.6	GKC §152y		
2.7	IBHS 216	2.22	GKC §75qq; J-M §78g □ B-L 376r; Berg 1.91e, 2.159g
2.8	GKC §128u		
2.9	Dav §136R1; GKC §107c; J-M §101b; Wms §181, 185; Gib 99 □ Berg 2.48g, 2.92h	2.23	GKC §116u; J-M §166f □ Berg 2.70e*
		2.24	GKC §122e; J-M §134c; Gib 16, 47, 49 □ B-L 438
		3	B-L 33b'
		3.1	Dav §38; Gib 51

B-L: Bauer and Leander, *Historische Grammatik* **B-M**: Beer, *Grammatik* **Berg**: Bergsträsser, *Grammatik*
Brock: Brockelmann, *Syntax* **Dav**: Davidson, *Syntax* **GAHG**: Richter, *Grammatik*
Gib: Gibson, *Davidson's Syntax, 4th ed.* **GKC**: *Gesenius' Grammar* **IBHS**: Waltke and O'Connor, *Syntax*
Jen: Jenni, *Lehrbuch* **J-M**: Joüon and Muraoka, *Grammar* **Ros**: Rosenthal, *Grammar*
Sch: Schneider, *Grammatik* **Wms**: Williams, *Syntax*

3.2	J-M §79m □ B-L 613b′; Berg 2.161b	3.26	Dav §113; GKC §145o; Wms §228; Gib 21 □ Sch §44.6.2
3.3	Dav §116; GKC §135p; J-M §139a, 149a, 158i, 177a □ Berg 2.77c	3.27	Dav §43a; GKC §107k; J-M §113b, 121i □ Berg 2.36k
3.4ff.	Berg 1.2d	4.1	Dav §19R1, 107R1; GKC §125b; J-M §121f, 121l, 137u; Wms
3.4–27	B-M 1.25		§94; IBHS 274; Gib 2, 25, 167 □
3.4	Dav §29d, 37d, 54R1; GKC §2d, 112h, 131k, 134g; J-M §100n, 111e, 119v; Wms §68; IBHS 534; Gib 41, 49 □ B-M 3.35; Brock §62b		Berg 2.69 n c, 2.73i
		4.2	GKC §91e, 103g; J-M §94h, 94i; Wms §478 □ GAHG 3.175 n 581
3.7	Gib 66	4.3	GKC §91l, 133c n 3; J-M §94i, 133d, 141h n 3 □ B-L 557f′
3.8	Dav §8R4, 144R1; GKC §155d; J-M §102i; IBHS 313, 327 n 26; Gib 11 □ B-L 267l; B-M 2.15	4.4	J-M §143k
		4.5	GKC §116u; J-M §166e; Wms §220, 588; IBHS 451 □ B-L 383;
3.9	Wms §230		B-M 2.141; Berg 2.71f, 2.129h
3.10	J-M §143e; IBHS 311	4.6	J-M §140a; Gib 58 □ GAHG
3.11	Dav §65c, 65d, 122; Gib 106, 183		3.175 n 593
		4.7	GKC §91l; J-M §94i □ B-L 203q, 253u, 583x′, 618j; Brock §132
3.13	Dav §118, 128R2; J-M §129b; Wms §403 □ B-L 631c		
3.14	Dav §120R5, 131; GKC §159z; J-M §112a, 167k; Wms §456, 459, 516; Gib 155, 187 □ Brock §165b	4.8	Dav §21R2, 145; GKC §107e, 126s; J-M §118b, 137n; Wms §84; Gib 28, 73, 158 □ Berg 2.32e; Brock §21bβ, 42d
3.15	GKC §112uu; J-M §119z; Gib 103 □ Berg 2.43 n b-k	4.9	Dav §30; J-M §138a; IBHS 259 □ GAHG 3.170 n 524; Sch §47.1.2
3.16	Dav §29R8, 88R2; GKC §113bb, 123e; J-M §123u; Wms §16; IBHS 119, 594; Gib 42, 127 □ Berg 2.66k	4.10	J-M §114b n 1, 114f; Gib 90 □ B-M 2.159
		4.11	Dav §21R2, 145; GKC §126s; J-M §137n; Gib 28
3.17	J-M §143k	4.12	J-M §143e
3.18	Wms §25, 228; Gib 21 □ Berg 2.136h; Brock §50a	4.13	Dav §67b, 94, 122; GKC §114k, 117r; Wms §51, 196, 480; IBHS 609; Gib 131, 183 □ Berg 2.58m(bis)
3.19	J-M §141j; IBHS 437 □ B-L 547		
3.20	J-M §166m; Wms §475; IBHS 386 □ B-M 3.84; Berg 2.70e	4.14	GKC §154b; J-M §160h, 177m □ GAHG 3.175 n 577, 3.176 n 598; Brock §56b
3.21	J-M §121i; Wms §327		
3.22	Wms §92, 495 □ GAHG 3.100	4.16	GKC §32h, 116p; J-M §121e; Wms §268; Gib 137 □ B-L 248f;
3.23	GKC §113w; J-M §123p; Wms §598; IBHS 582; Gib 125 □ Berg 2.64f, 2.106n		Berg 2.72h*
		4.18	Dav §21R2, 145; GKC §126s; J-M §137n; Gib 28
3.24	Dav §86R3; GKC §75ff., 113x; J-M §123q □ B-L 442e; Berg 2.161 n c	4.19	Dav §117; J-M §162c; IBHS 681; Gib 188
3.25	GKC §112e; J-M §119u; Gib 74 □ B-L 375; Berg 2.32d, 2.106 n l, 2.112c	4.21	IBHS 449

B-L: Bauer and Leander, *Historische Grammatik* **B-M**: Beer, *Grammatik* **Berg**: Bergsträsser, *Grammatik*
Brock: Brockelmann, *Syntax* **Dav**: Davidson, *Syntax* **GAHG**: Richter, *Grammatik*
Gib: Gibson, *Davidson's Syntax, 4th ed.* **GKC**: *Gesenius' Grammar* **IBHS**: Waltke and O'Connor, *Syntax*
Jen: Jenni, *Lehrbuch* **J-M**: Joüon and Muraoka, *Grammar* **Ros**: Rosenthal, *Grammar*
Sch: Schneider, *Grammatik* **Wms**: Williams, *Syntax*

4.23	GKC §32h, 90n; J-M §93o; Wms §562, 598 □ B-L 248f; Berg 2.15a
4.24	GKC §66c □ B-L 363i; B-M 2.135; Berg 2.113h, 2.122c
4.25	GKC §34f; J-M §36b n 2, 143e; IBHS 311 □ B-L 261f
4.26	Wms §598; IBHS 63 □ GAHG 3.170 n 522, 3.215 n 815
4.27	GKC §63e □ Berg 2.113f
4.28	Berg 1.104r
4.29	Dav §130a; Wms §446, 511; IBHS 637; Gib 153
4.31	GKC §29k; J-M §118d
4.32	J-M §48a; IBHS 449
4.34	IBHS 449; Gib 149, 151 □ B-M 2.144; Berg 2.134 n d
4.36	J-M §143e
4.38	Gib 167
4.39	J-M §150n; IBHS 104 n 37 □ B-M 2.69; Brock §16g
4.40	Berg 2.127e
4.41	Dav §136R1; GKC §69f □ B-M 2.139; Berg 2.127e
4.42	GKC §90g n 1; Gib 167 □ Berg 2.123d
4.43	Dav §4R1, 7b, 88; GKC §113ee; J-M §123w, 155i; Wms §126, 209; IBHS 326, 594; Gib 5, 8, 127 □ B-M 3.63; Berg 2.66k, 2.671; Brock §46a
5.1	J-M §121o; Wms §372 □ B-L 441c; Berg 2.158e
5.2	Dav §71R1; GKC §118q; J-M §126c □ GAHG 3.146 n 382; Brock §103a
5.3	Dav §135R2; GKC §151e; J-M §105b n 2, 130f, 130fa, 163c; Wms §549; Gib 186 □ B-M 3.117; GAHG 3.178 n 617; Brock §7b
5.4	Dav §11R3; J-M §130fa; Gib 14
5.5	Dav §29R3
5.6	Dav §136R1; IBHS 532; Gib 61 □ Berg 2.28e
5.7	GKC §150d; Wms §271; IBHS 639; Gib 160 □ GAHG 3.170 n 521, 3.177 n 602, 3.178 n 611, 3.178 n 614, 3.215 n 815
5.8	Wms §477; Gib 107 □ GAHG 3.175 n 580
5.9	GKC §129d; J-M §130c; Wms §54, 270; Gib 36
5.10	Dav §60R4, 65d; GKC §110i, 113bb, 159d; J-M §116d, 116f, 116h, 119p, 123u; Wms §189, 211; Gib 127 □ B-M 2.131, 3.54; Berg 2.50k, 2.66k; Brock §3
5.11	Dav §21R2, 86c; GKC §112p, 113r; J-M §123l, 146k; Wms §205; Gib 92, 124 □ Berg 2.65 n h
5.12	Dav §116R3, 126R4; GKC §107t; J-M §113l, 154g, 161m; IBHS 104; Gib 17, 44 □ Berg 1.111 n c
5.13	Dav §64, 111R1; GKC §110f, 142f, 159cc; J-M §105f, 116f, 155o; Wms §287; Gib 105 □ GAHG 3.177 n 605, 3.192 n 699; Berg 2.50k; Brock §122r, 165d
5.15	GAHG 3.170 n 524, 3.215 n 815
5.16	J-M §112a
5.17	Dav §79, 132R2; GKC §104g, 131d, 147c, 159dd; J-M §104d n 1, 167o; Wms §68; Gib 41, 156 □ GAHG 3.202 n 758; Brock §62c, 81d, 134c, 168
5.18	GKC §75kk; J-M §79t □ B-L 77m, 426; Berg 2.17d, 2.160 n a
5.20	Dav §51R2, 120R3; GKC §112gg, 151e, 163d; J-M §112f, 164c, 165e, 173c; Wms §449; IBHS 532; Gib 59, 187 □ B-M 3.54; Berg 2.41d
5.21	Dav §21a; Gib 27 □ GAHG 3.102 n 289
5.22	Dav §6R2, 36a; GKC §136d; J-M §114m, 163a; IBHS 572; Gib 6, 47 □ B-L 277c'; Brock §3
5.23	Dav §29d, 83; GKC §72t, 88b, 131d; J-M §91b, 177d; Gib 41, 120 □ B-L 234p, 547; Berg 2.140 n q
5.24–25	Gib 99
5.25	Dav §152; J-M §93c, 118e, 155m; IBHS 329 n 29, 329 n 30

B-L: Bauer and Leander, *Historische Grammatik* **B-M**: Beer, *Grammatik* **Berg**: Bergsträsser, *Grammatik* **Brock**: Brockelmann, *Syntax* **Dav**: Davidson, *Syntax* **GAHG**: Richter, *Grammatik* **Gib**: Gibson, *Davidson's Syntax, 4th ed.* **GKC**: *Gesenius' Grammar* **IBHS**: Waltke and O'Connor, *Syntax* **Jen**: Jenni, *Lehrbuch* **J-M**: Joüon and Muraoka, *Grammar* **Ros**: Rosenthal, *Grammar* **Sch**: Schneider, *Grammatik* **Wms**: Williams, *Syntax*

5.26	Dav §121; GKC §150a n 1; Gib 183	6.29	GKC §74l; J-M §61f, 78i □ B-L 374n; Berg 2.157b
5.27	Wms §92, 266	6.30	Berg 2.70e
6.1	Gib 130 □ GAHG 3.170 n 524	6.31	Dav §120R4; J-M §165a,
6.2	J-M §114f, 114n		165a n 1; IBHS 679 n 18; Gib
6.3	Dav §83, 107R1; J-M §146a,		187 □ Jen §17.3.4
	177d; Gib 120 □ Berg 2.129h	6.32	Dav §45; GKC §22s, 100l; J-M
6.5	Dav §72R4; GKC §111g;		§23a, 102m, 161b; IBHS 643 □
	117m n 3; J-M §166f; Wms §58;		B-L 127a', 222s, 632h; Jen
	IBHS 182; Gib 117 □ GAHG		§18.3.4.2; Berg 1.68v
	3.177 n 606	6.33	Dav §6R1, 100f; J-M §143i;
6.6	Dav §75; Gib 112		Wms §126; IBHS 313; Gib 137
6.7	Berg 2.149m		□ GAHG 3.171 n 538
6.8	Dav §11Re; GKC §91n; J-M	7.1	Dav §29d; GKC §131d; Wms
	§129f; IBHS 629; Gib 14 □ B-L		§68; IBHS 231; Gib 41
	591l; GAHG 1.72 n 136; Berg	7.2	GKC §116p, 154b, 159i; Wms
	2.73i*; Brock §24c		§513; IBHS 627, 628; Gib 157 □
6.9	Dav §96R1; GKC §51n; Gib 23,		B-L 653g; Berg 2.72h(bis)
	132 □ B-M 2.118; Berg 2.92g	7.3	Dav §41c, 145; GKC §72c n 1;
6.10	Dav §38R5; GKC §112f,134r;		J-M §112i, 126c; Wms §126;
	J-M §119v; IBHS 275; Gib 51 □		IBHS 323; Gib 7, 67, 158 □
	B-L 629c'; Berg 2.44k		Brock §62a
6.11	GKC §36, 117m n 3; Wms §129,	7.4	Dav §130b; GKC §72c n 1,
	300, 301, 537; IBHS 194, 319,		106p, 112ff., 112gg, 159o, 159r;
	333 n 15 □ B-L 264b		J-M §104d, 112i, 167h n 1,
6.12	Dav §35R2, 44a; J-M §130f,		167o, 176o; IBHS 637; Gib 69,
	140b; Gib 46, 75		153 □ B-L 649k; B-M 2.181;
6.13	GKC §88c; J-M §91h; IBHS		Berg 2.40d, 2.47e
	328 n 28 □ B-L 519d'; GAHG	7.5	GAHG 3.204 n 777
	3.180 n 128	7.6	J-M §125u; Gib 112 □ Sch
6.14	Sch §50.1.1		§49.3.1
6.15	B-M 3.59; Berg 2.59n*	7.7	Dav §1R1; Wms §302
6.16	Dav §10; J-M §103j; IBHS 335;	7.8	Dav §19R1; GKC §10g, 47i; Gib
	Gib 10		25 □ B-L 297b; B-M 2.112;
6.17	J-M §114g n 1, 116d; IBHS 566		Berg 2.80 n h
	□ GAHG 3.215 n 815	7.9	Dav §78R8, 128R1, 132a,
6.18	J-M §136h; Gib 29		132R2; GKC §116n, 152a n 1;
6.19	Dav §97R1; GKC §34b n 3, 52n;		Wms §213; IBHS 310 n 13; Gib
	IBHS 630 □ B-L 261b, 328w;		156 □ Berg 1.45e, 2.47e, 2.72h*
	Berg 2.20b	7.10	GKC §135p n 1 □ GAHG
6.20	Dav §4		3.204 n 777
6.22	Dav §111R1; GKC §142f(d) n 1;	7.11	Gib 142
	J-M §121h n 1; Gib 107	7.12	GKC §35n □ B-L 375; Berg
6.25	Dav §38R6 □ B-L 583x', 629a'		2.158e
6.26	GKC §111g; J-M §166f; Wms	7.13	Dav §20R4, 136R1; GKC §127f,
	§89		154b; J-M §177l; Gib 26 □ B-M
6.27	GKC §109h, 150g, 152f; J-M		2.145
	§161e □ Brock §169c	7.16	Dav §29d; GKC §131d; Gib 41
6.28	J-M §61f, 143d	7.17	Wms §162 □ Berg 2.27d

B-L: Bauer and Leander, *Historische Grammatik*   **B-M**: Beer, *Grammatik*   **Berg**: Bergsträsser, *Grammatik*
Brock: Brockelmann, *Syntax*   **Dav**: Davidson, *Syntax*   **GAHG**: Richter, *Grammatik*
Gib: Gibson, *Davidson's Syntax, 4th ed.*   **GKC**: *Gesenius' Grammar*   **IBHS**: Waltke and O'Connor, *Syntax*
Jen: Jenni, *Lehrbuch*   **J-M**: Joüon and Muraoka, *Grammar*   **Ros**: Rosenthal, *Grammar*
Sch: Schneider, *Grammatik*   **Wms**: Williams, *Syntax*

7.18	Dav §29d; GKC §10h, 131d; Gib 41 □ Berg 1.126aa	9.4	Dav §29b; GKC §127g; J-M §131b; Gib 40
7.19	Dav §136R1; GKC §154b, 159i; Wms §439; IBHS 677 □ Berg 2.72h	9.5	Dav §21f; GKC §126e; J-M §137g; IBHS 247; Gib 27
7.20	B-M 1.78	9.7	GKC §44g; J-M §42f □ B-L 315n'; Berg 2.17d
8.1	GKC §32h; J-M §158o; Gib 10 □ B-L 248f; Brock §156a	9.8	Dav §17R5
8.4	IBHS 230; Gib 17	9.10	Dav §139
8.5	Dav §141; Wms §236, 475, 490; IBHS 646; Gib 167 □ Berg 2.70e, 2.70e*	9.11	J-M §118e, 161a
		9.12	Dav §11R3, 117; Gib 14
		9.13	J-M §111h, 155k
8.6	GKC §53m, 72y, 91e, 125b; J-M §54c, 94h, 137u, 155i; Wms §489; IBHS 251; Gib 25 □ B-L 405; Berg 2.105i, 2.149m	9.14	Berg 2.73i*
		9.15	Dav §29R1; GKC §159v; Gib 75 □ GAHG 3.175 n 580; Berg 2.33 n b-h, 2.105k
		9.16	Berg 2.27d
8.7	J-M §155nd; Wms §494	9.17	GKC §10g, 80f; J-M §126b n 1 □ B-L 208r, 362a', 511v; Berg 1.124w
8.8–9	GKC §126y		
8.8	Dav §32R3; GKC §126y; J-M §103j; Gib 7	9.18	Dav §1R1, 7b, 8R3; GKC §32n, 103o, 119b; J-M §103m n 2; IBHS 221, 291 n 9, 324; Gib 3, 7, 8 □ B-L 641i'; Brock §119b
8.9	Dav §32R3; Gib 7		
8.10	Dav §58b; J-M §172a; Wms §182; Gib 103 □ Berg 2.160a		
8.12	J-M §127b; Wms §190; IBHS 408; Gib 77 □ Berg 2.117a	9.19	GKC §150a n 1; Gib 8
		9.20	Dav §44a; Gib 74
8.13	Dav §22c, 43b, 72R1, 75, 146R2; GKC §37d, 107u; J-M §126c, 157c; Wms §452; IBHS 172, 326; Gib 8, 28, 111, 112, 116 □ B-L 266e; Berg 2.106l	9.21	Berg 2.112d
		9.22	Wms §311; IBHS 215; Gib 149
		9.24	J-M §91c, 146g
		9.25	Dav §28R5, 146R3; Gib 36, 111
		9.26	Dav §57R1, 120; Wms §456; Gib 187 □ Berg 2.42g
8.17	Dav §36R3; GKC §134e; J-M §124d n 3; IBHS 278; Gib 50	9.27	GKC §147c
8.21	GKC §50e, 111f	9.30	Berg 2.27d; Brock §116b
8.22	Dav §45R2; Gib 72 □ Berg 2.33g	9.31	GKC §144p; Gib 28 □ Brock §153c
8.25	Dav §38; IBHS 286, 480, 481; Gib 51, 63	9.32	Dav §36R5; GKC §134s; Wms §346, 433; IBHS 195; Gib 48 □ Brock §131
8.28	GKC §35d		
8.29	Dav §29R1, 44R2; GKC §107e, 131g; IBHS 231, 498 n 5; Gib 40, 75 □ Berg 2.33 n b-h	9.33	Dav §102; GKC §76c; IBHS 70 □ Berg 2.163g
		9.35	Dav §91R4; GKC §119m; Gib 130
9.1	Dav §35R2; J-M §125i; Gib 40, 46, 65, 98	9.37	GKC §75m, 116b; J-M §113l, 169f; Wms §169, 465; IBHS 639; Gib 160 □ B-L 411u; Jen §19.3.4; Berg 2.165l
9.2	GKC §72w, 76h □ B-L 445p; GAHG 3.151 n 413; Berg 2.147 n k, 2.150n	10.1	GKC §124b n 1, 127f; Gib 49
		10.2	Dav §55b, 136R1
9.3	Dav §40b; GKC §44g; J-M §42f; Gib 61 □ B-L 315n', 403; Berg 2.16c	10.3	Dav §55b; J-M §141j; Wms §93, 295; IBHS 214 □ B-M 3.37

B-L: Bauer and Leander, *Historische Grammatik*   **B-M**: Beer, *Grammatik*   **Berg**: Bergsträsser, *Grammatik*
Brock: Brockelmann, *Syntax*   **Dav**: Davidson, *Syntax*   **GAHG**: Richter, *Grammatik*
Gib: Gibson, *Davidson's Syntax, 4th ed.*   **GKC**: *Gesenius' Grammar*   **IBHS**: Waltke and O'Connor, *Syntax*
Jen: Jenni, *Lehrbuch*   **J-M**: Joüon and Muraoka, *Grammar*   **Ros**: Rosenthal, *Grammar*
Sch: Schneider, *Grammatik*   **Wms**: Williams, *Syntax*

10.4	Dav §107; Gib 2 □ GAHG 3.204 n 770	11.5	GKC §47m n 1 (p. 129), 116h; J-M §141a; Wms §578; IBHS 256 □ GAHG 3.161 n 480; Berg 2.21b
10.5	GKC §150n		
10.6	Dav §28R6, 34; GKC §118p, 130e, 131h n 1; IBHS 270; Gib 36, 45, 136, 153 □ Brock §39bδ	11.7	GKC §134r n 3; J-M §139i
		11.9–10	GKC §97g
10.7	J-M §96Al, 137m	11.9	J-M §100k n 1
10.10	Dav §102; IBHS 70 n 11 □ Brock §34a	11.10	Dav §17; J-M §100k n 1; Gib 19
		11.12	Dav §17R4; GKC §74l; J-M §78i □ Berg 2.49h, 2.157b
10.11	J-M §54c n 3 □ Berg 2.56h, 2.106 n l		
		11.13	GKC §87e; IBHS 118 □ B-L 517t, 535f; B-M 2.44
10.13	Dav §73R5, 104c; J-M §129b □ B-M 3.89		
		11.14	Dav §117; GKC §29k; Wms §259; IBHS 203; Gib 188 □ Berg 2.70e
10.14	Dav §37c; Gib 49		
10.15	Dav §32R5, 126, 132R2; GKC §159cc; J-M §104d n 1, 137f, 167o; Wms §481; IBHS 182; Gib 44, 117, 148, 156, 183 □ B-M 3.112; GAHG 3.202 n 758; Brock §134c		
		11.15	GKC §97g, 113cc, 119e; J-M §100k n 1 □ Brock §120a
		11.19	GKC §118f; IBHS 256 n 2
		12.3	J-M §158t □ Berg 2.162d
		12.9	GKC §66g, 72h, 93h; Gib 132 □ B-L 366t; Berg 2.124f, 2.144b
10.17	Berg 2.106 n l		
10.18	Berg 2.65h*	12.10–17	Berg 2.32e
10.19	J-M §114i; Wms §367 □ Berg 1.134c	12.10	Dav §35R2, 108R1; GKC §35o, 112g, 125b; J-M §119v, 137u; IBHS 275; Gib 46 □ B-L 199l; B-M 2.134 Anm 2
10.21	GKC §102h; J-M §103c □ B-L 638w; B-M 2.176; GAHG 3.151 n 413		
		12.11	GKC §112f; J-M §119v, 166q □ Berg 2.140 n q
10.22	GKC §138e □ B-M 3.100; Berg 1.148g		
		12.12–17	Dav §44R2; Gib 75
10.23	Dav §128R4; GKC §152w □ GAHG 3.175 n 580	12.12–13	GKC §112f, 112pp n 3
		12.12	GKC §112pp n 3; J-M §119v
10.25	Dav §11Rb; Gib 14	12.13	Berg 2.84 n p
10.26	GKC §135p □ Berg 1.147d	12.14	J-M §129b n 3
10.27	B-L 613b'; Berg 2.122b	12.15	GKC §112e; J-M §119u
10.29	GKC §93o, 143b; J-M §126h, 130f	12.16–17	Dav §71R2; GKC §112e; Gib 145 □ Berg 2.32d
10.30	GKC §78b; J-M §130g □ B-L 402r''; Berg 2.59n*	12.18	Dav §51R2; J-M §113i; Gib 102 □ Berg 2.33g(bis)
10.32	Berg 2.174 n h	12.19	B-L 582u'
11.1	GKC §112pp; J-M §141a; IBHS 435	12.21	Dav §67b; Gib 115
		12.22	B-L 510v
11.2	GKC §116e □ B-M 3.67; Berg 2.69d	13.2	GKC §135p; J-M §149a; Wms §358; IBHS 193; Gib 147
11.3	J-M §126h □ Berg 2.74 n l	13.6	GKC §74k, 135p; J-M §78f; Gib 176 □ B-L 375; Berg 2.158d, 2.158e
11.4	Dav §28R5, 75; GKC §75gg, 75q, 97g; J-M §79i, 100k n 1, 130c; Gib 36, 112 □ B-L 426, 627t; Jen §25.4.3; Berg 2.165k		
		13.7	Gib 49 □ Berg 2.152t
		13.9	GKC §152a n 1
		13.10	GKC §134o □ Brock §86

B-L: Bauer and Leander, *Historische Grammatik*   **B-M:** Beer, *Grammatik*   **Berg:** Bergsträsser, *Grammatik*
Brock: Brockelmann, *Syntax*   **Dav:** Davidson, *Syntax*   **GAHG:** Richter, *Grammatik*
Gib: Gibson, *Davidson's Syntax, 4th ed.*   **GKC:** *Gesenius' Grammar*   **IBHS:** Waltke and O'Connor, *Syntax*
Jen: Jenni, *Lehrbuch*   **J-M:** Joüon and Muraoka, *Grammar*   **Ros:** Rosenthal, *Grammar*
Sch: Schneider, *Grammatik*   **Wms:** Williams, *Syntax*

B-L: Bauer and Leander, *Historische Grammatik*   **B-M:** Beer, *Grammatik*   **Berg**: Bergsträsser, *Grammatik*
Brock: Brockelmann, *Syntax*   **Dav:** Davidson, *Syntax*   **GAHG**: Richter, *Grammatik*
Gib: Gibson, *Davidson's Syntax, 4th ed.*   **GKC**: *Gesenius' Grammar*   **IBHS**: Waltke and O'Connor, *Syntax*
Jen: Jenni, *Lehrbuch*   **J-M**: Joüon and Muraoka, *Grammar*   **Ros**: Rosenthal, *Grammar*
Sch: Schneider, *Grammatik*   **Wms**: Williams, *Syntax*

17.11	GKC §53p; J-M §111e □ B-L 423; Berg 2.106l		18.23	Dav §20R4, 37d; GKC §127f; J-M §116b n 1, 142g n 1; IBHS 249, 282; Gib 49 □ B-L 356s; B-M 2.132; GAHG 3.215 n 815; Berg 2.116b
17.13	Dav §28R6; GKC §72aa □ Berg 2.149m			
17.15	GKC §103l; J-M §103c n 3 □ B-L 651z		18.24	IBHS 282 n 22
17.16	B-L 600j'		18.26–32	Dav §60
17.18	Wms §392		18.26	GKC §2a, 2q n 1; Ros §3; IBHS 4, 8 n 16; Gib 81 □ B-L 13a; B-M 1.11, 1.31; Berg 1.2d
17.21	Dav §78 □ Berg 2.172 n e			
17.22	J-M §129t, 149a			
17.23	B-M 2.158; Berg 2.162f		18.27	B-L 77n, 583x'
17.25–41	Gib 138		18.28	GKC §2a □ B-L 13a; B-M 1.11
17.25	J-M §121g; Wms §213, 251 □ Berg 2.73i*		18.29	GKC §74l; J-M §78i □ Berg 2.157b
17.26	Dav §127b; J-M §160b, 160i, 170k; Wms §260, 534; Gib 57, 137 □ Berg 2.106l		18.30	GKC §121b n 1; J-M §128b; Wms §59 □ GAHG 3.120 n 330; Brock §35d
17.27	B-L 93c; Berg 2.106l		18.31–32	Gib 81
17.28–41	Dav §100R2		18.31	Dav §64; GKC §127f; J-M §116f; IBHS 249; Gib 105 □ Jen §21.3.4
17.28	GKC §116r; J-M §121g; Gib 185 □ B-M 3.69; Berg 2.36k, 2.106l			
17.29	Dav §29R8; GKC §124r; J-M §121g, 136n; Gib 42		18.32	Dav §55b, 65d, 96; GKC §114r; IBHS 599; Gib 94, 131 □ Berg 2.41f, 2.151q
17.32–33	Berg 2.73i		18.33	Gib 124
17.32	J-M §121g, 136n □ Berg 2.73i		18.34	Wms §450
17.33	J-M §121g □ Berg 2.73i, 2.106l		18.35	GKC § 37a
17.36	Gib 182		18.36	Dav §58b; GKC §112tt; Gib 103
17.41	J-M §121g □ Berg 2.73i(bis)		18.37	Dav §70a; J-M §121o; Gib 56
18.1	GKC §134p □ B-L 629z		19.1	Dav §78R5; J-M §128c □ Berg 2.164i
18.4	Dav §58b; GKC §112tt; Wms §182; IBHS 629; Gib 103, 138 □ Berg 2.45n, 2.73i*, 2.119e		19.2	GKC §118p; 131h n 1; J-M §127a □ GAHG 3.146 n 382
18.7	Berg 2.32d, 2.42g*		19.3	Dav §127b; GKC §69m, 152k; Wms §408, 569; Gib 57 □ B-L 382; GAHG 3.173 n 562; Berg 2.57l, 2.126c
18.9	Dav §38; IBHS 284; Gib 50			
18.10	Dav §38; Wms §98; Gib 51			
18.11	GKC §75gg			
18.13–20.19	GKC §3g; IBHS 17		19.4	Dav §9b, 31, 53b; GKC §132h; J-M §148a; Wms §8; Gib 9, 43, 79, 93 □ Brock §60b
18.13	B-L 73d; Gib 79			
18.14	Wms §294			
18.16	GKC §52l □ Berg 2.95d		19.8	GAHG 3.108 n 307
18.17	Dav §32R5; GKC §128w n 1; J-M §137s; IBHS 261; Gib 44		19.10	Berg 2.156a
			19.11	Dav §107R1, 121; Gib 183
18.19ff.	Berg 2.28g		19.13	IBHS 327 □ B-M 3.36
18.19	Gib 63 □ Brock §93d		19.14	Dav §116R1; GKC §124b n 1
18.20	GKC §44i; Gib 63 □ B-L 370q; Brock §110e		19.15	J-M §154j; Gib 55
			19.16	GKC §132h; J-M §148a □ Berg 2.165k; Gib 43
18.21	Dav §132a; Gib 156		19.17	Dav §118; IBHS 663 n 68
18.22	Wms §446; Gib 154		19.18	J-M §123x; IBHS 595 n 57

B-L: Bauer and Leander, *Historische Grammatik*   **B-M**: Beer, *Grammatik*   **Berg**: Bergsträsser, *Grammatik*
Brock: Brockelmann, *Syntax*   **Dav**: Davidson, *Syntax*   **GAHG**: Richter, *Grammatik*
Gib: Gibson, *Davidson's Syntax, 4th ed.*   **GKC**: *Gesenius' Grammar*   **IBHS**: Waltke and O'Connor, *Syntax*
Jen: Jenni, *Lehrbuch*   **J-M**: Joüon and Muraoka, *Grammar*   **Ros**: Rosenthal, *Grammar*
Sch: Schneider, *Grammatik*   **Wms**: Williams, *Syntax*

19.19	GAHG 3.215 n 815
19.21	GKC §72l; Wms §42, 361; IBHS 193 □ B-L 398e"; B-M 2.151; Berg 2.146e; Brock §70d
19.22	Dav §7a, 58a; Gib 7, 103
19.23–25	Berg 52.33 n b-h
19.23	GKC §91e; J-M §129k □ Berg 1.149i
19.25	Dav §65R1, 109R2; GKC §23f, 75qq, 76h; J-M §24e; Gib 107 □ B-L 445p; Berg 1.92 n g, 1.101m, 2.60o, 2.147 n k
19.26	B-L 573x; Berg 2.134c, 2.144b
19.27	Dav §90; Wms §193; Gib 128 □ Berg 2.55d*
19.28	Dav §56; Wms §535
19.29	GKC §66c, 113ee; J-M §114p, 123u, 123x, 137f; IBHS 246, 572; Gib 81 □ B-L 363h; Berg 1.112d, 2.122c
19.31	B-L 77m
19.32	Dav §77; Gib 144 □ Berg 2.127e
19.34	GKC §67ee
19.35	B-M 3.45
19.37	Dav §141R1; GKC §111g, 116u; J-M §166f; Wms §54 □ B-L 77m; Berg 2.70e*
20	GKC §3g
20.1	GKC §49a; J-M §154fa; Wms §199, 572 □ B-M 3.44
20.3	Dav §146; GKC §105a; Gib 110, 116 □ B-M 2.114; GAHG 3.215 n 815; Brock §160b
20.4	Dav §32R2, 73R1, 141R1; Wms §235; IBHS 260 n 14; Gib 44, 169 □ Berg 2.26c, 2.26d
20.5	GKC §116f; J-M §123u n 2, 176h
20.9	Dav §41R2, 124; Gib 68, 184
20.10	GKC §67t □ Berg 2.28g, 2.58m
20.12	Dav §16; Gib 18
20.13	GKC §126x; Dav §32R2; Gib 44 □ B-L 426
20.14	Dav §45R1; Gib 76
20.17	J-M §119n
20.19	GKC §141n □ B-L 73d
20.20	B-L 33c'; Berg 1.2d
21.3–4	IBHS 541
21.4	Berg 2.45n; Gib 104

21.6	Dav §82; GKC §114n n 2; Wms §182; IBHS 413; Gib 120 □ Berg 2.45n, 2.59n*
21.8	GKC §115b; GAHG 3.185 n 681; Berg 2.140 n q
21.11	GKC §74l; J-M §78i □ B-L 374n; B-M 2.156; Berg 2.157b
21.12	Dav §113, 132R2; GKC §67g; Gib 157 □ B-M 2.144; Berg 2.68c, 2.72h, 2.80h, 2.134c, 2.139o
21.13	Dav §86c; GKC §29u, 113h n 2
21.15	GKC §112tt; IBHS 629 □ Berg 2.73i*
21.16	J-M §103c □ GAHG 3.151 n 413
21.19	Berg 1.134c
21.21	J-M §139e n 1
21.22	Gib 21
21.26	GKC §144d n 2
22.1	Dav §36R3; GKC §134e; J-M §142d n 3; IBHS 330; Gib 47, 50 □ B-L 510v
22.2	IBHS 330
22.4	IBHS 330
22.6	B-L 547
22.7	Gib 176
22.8	Dav §111; GKC §142f; Wms §574
22.12	B-M [R] 1.69
22.13	Dav §9a; GKC §138b; J-M §158g □ Berg 2.130m
22.14	B-M [R] 1.56, 1.69
22.17	J-M §124l n 5, 169g, 170g; Wms §198, 353, 368, 534; IBHS 639 n 25; Gib 159
22.18	Dav §99; GKC §135c n 1; Wms §90, 539; IBHS 248; Gib 135, 181
22.19	Berg 2.161b; Gib 158
22.20	Dav §17R3, 113; GKC §61h, 124c; Wms §8; Gib 20, 21
22.29	GKC §93qq
23	GAHG 3.219 n 832
23.3	Dav §22R3; GKC §127c; Gib 29
23.4–5	GKC §112pp; Wms §182
23.4	GKC §75v, 112pp, 112pp n 3; J-M §119z; IBHS 541; Gib 104 □ Berg 1.97c, 2.45n, 2.168p

B-L: Bauer and Leander, *Historische Grammatik*   **B-M**: Beer, *Grammatik*   **Berg**: Bergsträsser, *Grammatik*
Brock: Brockelmann, *Syntax*   **Dav**: Davidson, *Syntax*   **GAHG**: Richter, *Grammatik*
Gib: Gibson, *Davidson's Syntax, 4th ed.*   **GKC**: *Gesenius' Grammar*   **IBHS**: Waltke and O'Connor, *Syntax*
Jen: Jenni, *Lehrbuch*   **J-M**: Joüon and Muraoka, *Grammar*   **Ros**: Rosenthal, *Grammar*
Sch: Schneider, *Grammatik*   **Wms**: Williams, *Syntax*

23.5	GKC §112pp n 3; J-M §119z □ Berg 2.27d, 2.45n	24.17	B-L 73d
23.6	Berg 2.138l	24.18–25.30	GKC §3g; IBHS 17
23.8	Dav §108R1; GKC §90d, 112pp, 112pp n 3; J-M §93e; Wms §61 □ Berg 1.129b, 2.45n	24.18	IBHS 127 □ B-L 524h
		24.20	Wms §312 □ B-L 346x″
23.9	Dav §44b, 155; Gib 74, 174 □ Berg 2.36k	25.1	Dav §17, 38R2; GKC §134p; Wms §590; IBHS 284; Gib 19, 51
23.10–11	B-M 3.46	25.4	IBHS 448 □ B-L 516q, 598
23.10	Dav §96R1; GKC §112pp, 114s; J-M §119z, 168c; Wms §524; Gib 104 □ Berg 2.45n, 2.56h	25.5	Dav §115; GKC §145c; J-M §118d; Gib 22
		25.8	Dav §38; GKC §134p; J-M §137r; IBHS 240; Gib 50, 51 □ Brock §20b
23.12	GKC §112pp, 112rr, 127f; J-M §119z; Gib 103 □ Berg 2.45n	25.9	Dav §32R5; GKC §117c, 117d; IBHS 262; Gib 44 □ B-M 3.91
23.13	GKC §130a n 3		
23.14	GKC §112pp, 112pp n 3; J-M §136l □ Berg 2.45n	25.10	Dav §144R5
		25.11	J-M §131d n 1 □ Berg 2.106l
23.15	GKC §67v, 112pp; J-M §119z □ B-M 2.147; Berg 2.45n, 2.137k	25.14	GKC §107e □ Berg 2.31d
		25.15	Dav §29R8; GKC §123e; J-M §135e; Wms §16; IBHS 116, 233
23.17	Dav §20R4, 29c; GKC §34f, 127f, 127g; Wms §29, 82 □ Brock §62a*, 73b*	25.16	Dav §32R2; GKC §126z, 134l; IBHS 259, 283; Gib 44, 47
23.18	J-M §47a n 2, 80k n 3	25.17	Dav §36R3; GKC §134e; J-M §142d n 3; Gib 50
23.19	GKC §124r, 142f; J-M §136n; Wms §574	25.18	GKC §131b; Gib 47
23.20	GKC §117d	25.19	Dav §9R2; GKC §127f; Wms §29, 95; IBHS 278 □ Brock §61
23.22	J-M §129b n 4		
23.25	Jen §9.4.10; Sch §48.6.1.4	25.21	J-M §61a
23.31	IBHS 127 □ B-L 524h	25.22	GKC §111h □ Gib 98
23.35	J-M §147d	25.23	GKC §124g
23.36	GKC §102b □ B-L 642p′	25.24	J-M §116d □ B-L 132c
24.3	Dav §101Rd, 109R2 □ Berg 2.58m	25.25	J-M §141a; IBHS 255
		25.27	Dav §38; GKC §134o; IBHS 284, 285; Gib 50
24.4	Gib 44		
24.7	GKC §139c	25.28	GKC §122q; J-M §134n, 136l; Gib 17
24.12	Dav §38; Gib 51		
24.14	Dav §17, 37e; GKC §75ee, 97g, 112tt; J-M §79q, 93q, 134o, 142d n 2; Gib 18, 19 □ B-L 423, 627s; B-M 2.162; Berg 1.149g, 2.45n, 2.106l; Brock §116l	25.29	GKC §75rr □ B-L 426; Berg 2.45n, 2.168q
		25.30	J-M §140b n 1 □ Berg 1.66s

B-L: Bauer and Leander, *Historische Grammatik*   **B-M**: Beer, *Grammatik*   **Berg**: Bergsträsser, *Grammatik*
Brock: Brockelmann, *Syntax*   **Dav**: Davidson, *Syntax*   **GAHG**: Richter, *Grammatik*
Gib: Gibson, *Davidson's Syntax, 4th ed.*   **GKC**: *Gesenius' Grammar*   **IBHS**: Waltke and O'Connor, *Syntax*
Jen: Jenni, *Lehrbuch*   **J-M**: Joüon and Muraoka, *Grammar*   **Ros**: Rosenthal, *Grammar*
Sch: Schneider, *Grammatik*   **Wms**: Williams, *Syntax*

ISAIAH

1–66	Brock §84a, 85a
1.1	J-M §129b; Gib 149
1.2–3	Sch §44.2.2
1.2	Dav §58a, 105; GKC §126e; J-M §137g, 155m; IBHS 136, 137, 161, 540; Gib 81, 103, 173, 179 □ Berg 2.45n
1.3	Dav §105; GKC §124i; IBHS 123, 137, 165; Gib 19 □ B-L 110i'; Berg 1.156m, 2.28g(bis), 2.99e
1.4	Dav §24a, 39b, 117; GKC §128l, 128x, 147d; J-M §112e; Wms §162; IBHS 137, 145, 153, 161; Gib 32, 33, 62, 188 □ B-L 375; Berg 2.158e
1.5	Dav §22R3, 101Rb; GKC §37e, 127c, 137b, 156d; J-M §139e, 139e n 1; IBHS 325; Gib 29, 53, 184 □ B-L 637p; B-M 2.162; GAHG 3.171 n 538
1.6	Dav §22R3, 101Rb; GKC §67m, 126m, 126n, 144b, 152o; J-M §82l; IBHS 374 n 30, 661 □ B-L 287n'; B-M 2.117, 2.145; Berg 2.87c, 2.150p
1.7	Dav §98b, 106c; GKC §116l, 116n, 118x, 143a; J-M §121p, 156aa; Wms §45; IBHS 144, 617; Gib 31, 134, 137, 180, 181, □ B-M 3.14; GAHG 2.24 n 92, 2.61 n 263; Jen §8.3.2.2; Berg 2.71g
1.8	Dav §58b; IBHS 137; Gib 17, 103 □ Berg 2.43 n b-k; Brock §77a
1.9	Dav §39d, 131; GKC §106p, 118x, 159x; Gib 155 □ B-M 3.116; Berg 2.28g
1.10	B-M 1.89; Sch §54.1.3
1.11	Dav §28R4, 40b, 73; GKC §106g, 107f, 117z; J-M §112a; IBHS 137, 168; Gib 35, 63, 109, 113 □ B-L 562v; Berg 2.28g(bis); Brock §175
1.12	GKC §51l, 106g, 164d; J-M §51b □ B-L 228z; Berg 2.54dˣ, 2.55 n d
1.13	Dav §96 Obs., 106a; GKC §107f □ B-M 2.112
1.14	Dav §90, 101Rd; GKC §66b, 76b, 102h, 114c, 119aa; J-M §103c, 124c, 133f; Gib 128 □ B-L 101u, 441c, 638y; Berg 2.55d*, 2.123c
1.15	Dav §73, 111, 113; GKC §54f, 60f, 61e, 117z, 124n, 145n, 159bb, 160b; J-M §61d n 3, 125d, 160g, 171c; Wms §382, 530; IBHS 168, 407, 491, 493; Gib 61, 63, 113, 154 □ B-L 358v; B-M 2.129, 3.105; GAHG 3.177 n 605; Berg 2.28g, 2.95d; Brock §167
1.16	GKC §54d, 128r; J-M §124c; IBHS 424 n 2, 597; Gib 120 □ B-L 197a; B-M 1.107, 1.115; Jen §14.4.5; Berg 1.109b, 2.61b
1.17	Dav §84; GKC §113d, 117u; J-M §123b; Wms §203; IBHS 75, 592; Gib 123 □ B-L 277g'; B-M 3.62; Jen §10.3.1.1; Sch §50.4.1; Berg 2.61b, 2.153t
1.18–20	Gib 154
1.18	Dav §22e, 40b; GKC §126o, 159r, 160a; J-M §171d; IBHS 245, 444, 574, 684; Gib 28, 82, 86 □ B-M 3.28; Jen §26.3.2; Berg 2.47e, 2.112d; Brock §21cβ, 138, 175
1.19	Dav §34R5, 83; GKC §120e; J-M §177h; Gib 46, 63, 120 □ GAHG 3.184 n 655; Brock §52bζ, 165c

B-L: Bauer and Leander, *Historische Grammatik*   **B-M**: Beer, *Grammatik*   **Berg**: Bergsträsser, *Grammatik*
Brock: Brockelmann, *Syntax*   **Dav**: Davidson, *Syntax*   **GAHG**: Richter, *Grammatik*
Gib: Gibson, *Davidson's Syntax, 4th ed.*   **GKC**: *Gesenius' Grammar*   **IBHS**: Waltke and O'Connor, *Syntax*
Jen: Jenni, *Lehrbuch*   **J-M**: Joüon and Muraoka, *Grammar*   **Ros**: Rosenthal, *Grammar*
Sch: Schneider, *Grammatik*   **Wms**: Williams, *Syntax*

1.20	GKC §52e, 121c; J-M §128c; IBHS 375 n 36 □ B-L 286n'; B-M 3.83; Berg 2.87 n c	2.7	Dav §80; GKC §117z; IBHS 661 n 61; Gib 118 □ B-L 579q'; Berg 1.103q
1.21	Dav §117; GKC §90l, 95h, 107b, 148b; J-M §93m, 113f, 162b; IBHS 128, 329; Gib 185 □ B-L 274g, 526k, 600j'; B-M 3.89; Jen §25.3.2.3	2.8	Dav §80, 116R1; GKC §145m; Gib 23, 118
		2.9	Dav §41R1, 49b, 73R5, 128R2; GKC §67g, 109e, 117g; J-M §135c; IBHS 114, 661; Gib 102, 110 □ Berg 2.139o
1.22	GKC §77f, 126m; IBHS 26 n 73; Gib 30	2.10	J-M §141m; IBHS 267
1.23	Dav §44a, 116R1; GKC §107g, 124f; J-M §146j; Gib 53, 75	2.11	Dav §51R2, 116R2; GKC §111w, 112s, 146a; IBHS 151 n 31; Gib 6, 23, 68, 93, 102, 172 □ Berg 2.132a*
1.24–26	Berg 2.52o		
1.24	Dav §62; GKC §51p; IBHS 388; Gib 82 □ Berg 2.92h	2.12	IBHS 208; Gib 150
1.25	Dav §101Rd; GKC §118w, 124l; J-M §136b	2.13ff.	GKC §162b
		2.17	GKC §111w, 145o; J-M §150j; Gib 6, 30 □ B-M 3.20; Berg 2.132a*
1.26	Dav §81R2; GKC §118s n 2, 135m; J-M §133h		
1.27–28	Gib 172	2.18	GKC §15f □ B-M 1.73
1.27	GKC §116i; IBHS 665	2.20	Dav §3, 24R2, 116R1; GKC §63i, 84^b n, 135n, 145m; J-M §140b; IBHS 304; Gib 4, 6, 23, 32, 33 □ B-L 348h, 483lδ; B-M 2.123; Berg 2.114i
1.28	GKC §147c; Gib 35		
1.29–30	IBHS 665		
1.29	GKC §144p □ Berg 2.111c		
1.30	Dav §24d, 98R1; GKC §91d, 116i, 118g, 152o; IBHS 617; Gib 33, 134, 159 □ B-M 3.96	2.22	Dav §97R1, 101Rb; GKC §102k, 116e, 119s; IBHS 208 n 78; Gib 133 □ B-L 242d"; B-M 2.114; Berg 2.69d; Brock §107f
1.31	GKC §93q; J-M §96Aj □ B-L 475tβ, 582u'; Berg 1.154e		
2.1–2	IBHS 539	3.1	Dav §17R5, 100R1; GKC §116p, 122v; IBHS 106, 675; Gib 17, 91 □ GAHG 3.294 n 771; Sch §44.2.2; Berg 1.146b, 2.72h
2.1	GKC §3g, 154a n 1, 154a n 1b		
2.2ff.	GKC §3g		
2.2–4	IBHS 17; Gib 89		
2.2–3	IBHS 528	3.3	Dav §24d, 98R1; GKC §116k; Gib 33, 134
2.2	Dav §57R1, 100R2, 136R1; GKC §112y, 116r; J-M §119c, 121e; Gib 90, 138 □ B-L 73d; Berg 2.42g*, 2.74l; Brock §78	3.4	J-M §125w □ Jen §13.3.3
		3.5	Gib 14, 78
		3.6	Dav §69a; GKC §103g, 118g; J-M §126h; Gib 143 □ B-L 640f'
2.3	IBHS 654; Gib 107 □ Berg 2.47d, 2.47e		
2.4	GKC §91n; IBHS 661; Gib 147, 148 □ B-L 563x	3.7	Dav §73R5, 75, 76; GKC §117g, 117ii, 156b; Wms §589; IBHS 175, 314; Gib 110, 114, 137 □ B-M 3.92
2.5	Jen §9.3.4.1; Berg 2.47e; Brock §6c		
2.6–7	IBHS 556	3.8	Dav §41R1; GKC §9i, 53q, 122i; J-M §134g; IBHS 104; Gib 159 □ B-L 228a', 583v'; Berg 2.105 n k; Brock §138
2.6	GKC §44g; J-M §113o n 2; Gib 63, 159 □ B-L 315n'; Berg 1.113 n e		

B-L: Bauer and Leander, *Historische Grammatik*   **B-M**: Beer, *Grammatik*   **Berg**: Bergsträsser, *Grammatik*
Brock: Brockelmann, *Syntax*   **Dav**: Davidson, *Syntax*   **GAHG**: Richter, *Grammatik*
Gib: Gibson, *Davidson's Syntax, 4th ed.*   **GKC**: *Gesenius' Grammar*   **IBHS**: Waltke and O'Connor, *Syntax*
Jen: Jenni, *Lehrbuch*   **J-M**: Joüon and Muraoka, *Grammar*   **Ros**: Rosenthal, *Grammar*
Sch: Schneider, *Grammatik*   **Wms**: Williams, *Syntax*

3.9	Dav §11b, 41R3; GKC §85c, 135i, 156g; J-M §88Lb, 146k; IBHS 305; Gib 13, 188 □ B-L 486jɛ; Brock §11c	5.2	Dav §77; GKC §114m, 117ee; Wms §146; IBHS 175, 412 n 47, 415, 422 n 11; Gib 144 □ Berg 2.26c, 2.76 n b, 2.164i; Brock §94b
3.11	Gib 188		
3.12	Dav §106b; GKC §124k, 145l; Gib 181 □ B-M 2.137	5.3	GKC §110a; IBHS 572; Gib 140 □ GAHG 3.215 n 815
3.13	GKC §115b; J-M §124i; IBHS 581 n 10; Gib 129	5.4	Dav §94, 126R4; GKC §75z, 114k, 150m; J-M §161k; IBHS 610; Gib 129, 132 □ B-M 2.161, 3.44, 3.60; GAHG 3.171 n 538; Berg 2.58m, 2.59n(bis), 2.167o; Brock §47
3.14	GKC §128h, 154b		
3.15	Dav §41R3; GKC §37c; J-M §37c; IBHS 317 n 5 □ B-L 265c; B-M 2.14; Berg 1.66s; Brock §133d, 138		
3.16–17	Gib 87		
3.16	Dav §1R3, 51R2, 56, 86c, 147, 158b; GKC §52n, 75v, 111r, 112nn, 113u, 135o; J-M §52c, 118p, 123m, 176e; Wms §534; IBHS 302, 556, 590; Gib 3, 63, 102, 125, 158 □ B-L 328b', 441e, 599h'; B-M 2.119; Berg 1.97c, 2.65h, 2.95d, 2.167p; Brock §124b	5.5	Dav §55b, 88; GKC §9o, 112u, 113d, 113f, 114k n 2, 116d, 116p; J-M §114d, 119p, 123w; IBHS 538, 595 n 55, 684; Gib 91, 94, 123, 127, 140, 179 □ B-M 3.63; GAHG 3.170 n 522, 3.216 n 815; Berg 1.45e, 2.59o, 2.67l, 2.72h*
		5.6	Dav §73R2, 78R3, 96R1; GKC §108b, 117z, 117ii, 119y; J-M §123w, 125o, 125w; IBHS 661 n 60; Gib 114, 132 □ B-L 649l; Brock §35a, 111f
3.17	Dav §56; GKC §91c, 91f, 142f; J-M §176e □ B-L 252p, 451l; B-M 2.54; Berg 2.42g		
3.18	GKC §86g n 1; IBHS 314	5.7	B-L 583x; Brock §138; Gib 53, 159, 172
3.20	Berg 1.136e		
3.22	GKC §35f □ B-M 2.19	5.8	Dav §100e, 100R4, 127d; GKC §112w, 116x, 144p, 147d; J-M §160n; Wms §426; IBHS 630; Gib 88, 134, 137, 142 □ B-L 140r; Berg 2.129i
3.24	Dav §29e; GKC §24b, 112y, 131b; IBHS 230; Gib 41 □ B-L 485gɛ; Berg 1.97f		
3.26	Dav §141R3 □ Berg 2.165l, 2.172 n e	5.9	Dav §30, 120R3, 128; GKC §149e, 152y; J-M §160p, 165j; Gib 43, 187 □ Jen §28.3.3; Brock §111f, 145a
4.1	Dav §111; IBHS 314; Gib 176		
4.2	Dav §4, 6		
4.3	Dav §106b; GKC §112y; Gib 182	5.10	GKC §93m; J-M §96Ad □ B-L 99o, 115c, 582u'; Berg 1.122t
4.4–5	GKC §112gg	5.11–12	Gib 75
4.4	Dav §41c, 51R2, 130b; GKC §106o, 107l, 113e, 159n n 1, 164d; Gib 67, 77, 102, 153 □ B-M 3.109; Berg 2.61b	5.11	Dav §28R1, 141R3; GKC §112m, 120c, 130a, 147d, 156d; J-M §129m, 129n, 159c; Wms §30; IBHS 155 n 34; Gib 34 □ Brock §99a, 139a
4.6	Brock §111f		
5.1–5	IBHS 667	5.12–14	IBHS 666
5.1	Dav §14, 24R3, 62, 101Rb; GKC §108b, 128v; J-M §114d; Gib 18, 82 □ B-L 637o; B-M 3.34	5.12	Dav §29e, 45R3; GKC §93ss, 106l, 141d; Wms §177; IBHS 228; Gib 42, 173 □ B-L 140r

B-L: Bauer and Leander, *Historische Grammatik*   **B-M**: Beer, *Grammatik*   **Berg**: Bergsträsser, *Grammatik*
Brock: Brockelmann, *Syntax*   **Dav**: Davidson, *Syntax*   **GAHG**: Richter, *Grammatik*
Gib: Gibson, *Davidson's Syntax, 4th ed.*   **GKC**: *Gesenius' Grammar*   **IBHS**: Waltke and O'Connor, *Syntax*
Jen: Jenni, *Lehrbuch*   **J-M**: Joüon and Muraoka, *Grammar*   **Ros**: Rosenthal, *Grammar*
Sch: Schneider, *Grammatik*   **Wms**: Williams, *Syntax*

5.13	Dav §41b, 41R1, 115; GKC §106n, 128t; Wms §165; Gib 22, 68 □ B-M 3.52; Jen §24.3.3.5; Berg 2.29h	6.1–4	Sch §48.4.3.2
		6.1	Dav §50b, 138b; GKC §111b; IBHS 553; Gib 97, 98, 114, 168 □ B-M 3.45; Brock §123f
5.14	Dav §41b, 41R1, 115; GKC §20f, 112s; Wms §420; Gib 68, 93 □ B-L 121p, 140r; Berg 2.29h, 2.44l	6.2	Dav §11Rd, 29R8, 38R4, 100f, 101Rd, 127c; GKC §88f, 112k, 119cc, 134q; J-M §91e, 119v; Wms §4; IBHS 117, 119 n 12, 222, 288; Gib 14, 42, 51, 137, 149 □ B-L 158, 516s; GAHG 3.102 n 289; Berg 2.31b(bis); Brock §18a
5.15–16	GKC §111w		
5.15	Gib 68, 102 □ B-L 140r; B-M 2.112		
5.16	B-L 121p, 140r		
5.17	Dav §41R1, 101Rd, 111R1; GKC §118t, 142f; IBHS 204 □ B-L 115c, 140r; Brock §122r, 138	6.3	Dav §5, 29R8, 54R1, 102; GKC §112k, 133k, 139e n 3, 141l; J-M §119v, 154e; Wms §116, 132; IBHS 43 n 54, 233 n 15, 311; Gib 5, 42, 91 □ B-L 159o'; Brock §14bγ
5.18	GKC §147d; IBHS 146; Gib 31, 134		
5.19	Dav §63R1, 148; GKC §48d, 108d; J-M §45a n 1, 116b, 168a n 2; Gib 83, 107, 159 □ B-L 107e', 122r, 140r, 159o', 402u", 444p; B-M 2.101, 3.48; GAHG 1.116 n 351; Berg 2.23f	6.4	Dav §80; GKC §107b, 107d, 117z; J-M §113f, 128c; IBHS 504; Gib 74, 113, 118, 148 □ Berg 2.30b
5.20	GKC §147d; IBHS 209, 622; Gib 135 □ B-L 107e', 115c; Brock §107iγ	6.5	Dav §24d, 41a, 110, 117; GKC §106n, 128y, 147d; J-M §112g, 129i, 162d; IBHS 151, 682 n 36; Gib 33, 52, 188 □ B-M 2.161; Berg 2.29h; Brock §11c
5.21	Berg 2.147i		
5.22	GKC §147d □ Berg 2.60p	6.6	Dav §139, 143; GKC §72t, 94b, 119b n 1, 155h, 156b; J-M §159d; Gib 11, 168 □ Berg 2.26d
5.23	Dav §100e, 116R1; GKC §116x, 145m; J-M §121j; IBHS 146; Gib 23, 31, 137 □ Brock §79a		
5.24	Dav §91a, 96; GKC §111w, 114r, 115k; Gib 131 □ B-L 99o; Jen §26.3.3; Berg 1.157p	6.7	Dav §56, 105R2; GKC §112x; J-M §119e; IBHS 532; Gib 88 □ B-L 236 n 2; Berg 2.42g
		6.8–9	Sch §48.5.1
5.25	Dav §4R1, 17R4, 49b; GKC §111w, 136b; J-M §152; Gib 5, 58, 102, 146, 150 a □ Brock §23e	6.8	Dav §7a, 101Rb; GKC §61g, 117c, 124g n 2, 137b; J-M §64a, 114a, 125g, 127a; IBHS 179, 317, 675; Gib 7, 59, 81, 116, 150 □ GAHG 3.102 n 289; Sch §49.1.1; Berg 2.81k
5.26	Dav §71R2; GKC §133k n 1, 145m; Gib 145 □ B-L 140r		
5.27	Dav §127a; IBHS 386, 662; Gib 136 □ B-L 140r	6.9	Dav §60R4, 67a, 86c; GKC §75n, 113r; J-M §123l; IBHS 586; Gib 81, 125 □ Jen §10.3.1.1; Berg 2.64g
5.28	Dav §100f; GKC §20h; Gib 53, 137 □ B-L 212k; Berg 1.68v		
5.29	Dav §59; GKC §152l; Wms §180 □ B-L 354b; Berg 2.116e	6.10	Dav §53c, 108, 127c; GKC §67v, 75gg, 112p, 136b, 144d; IBHS 661; Gib 13, 30, 93, 160 □ B-L 107e', 432b'; B-M 2.147; Berg 2.137k
5.30	GKC §136b; J-M §143j; IBHS 314 □ B-L 140r, 354b; GAHG 3.204 n 775; Berg 2.116e		

B-L: Bauer and Leander, *Historische Grammatik*   **B-M**: Beer, *Grammatik*   **Berg**: Bergsträsser, *Grammatik*
Brock: Brockelmann, *Syntax*   **Dav**: Davidson, *Syntax*   **GAHG**: Richter, *Grammatik*
Gib: Gibson, *Davidson's Syntax, 4th ed.*   **GKC**: *Gesenius' Grammar*   **IBHS**: Waltke and O'Connor, *Syntax*
Jen: Jenni, *Lehrbuch*   **J-M**: Joüon and Muraoka, *Grammar*   **Ros**: Rosenthal, *Grammar*
Sch: Schneider, *Grammatik*   **Wms**: Williams, *Syntax*

6.11	Dav §41c, 80, 128, 145; GKC §106o, 107l, 121d, 152y; J-M §112i, 128c; Gib 67, 77, 118, 158 □ Sch §51.2.5.1; Brock §98b, 163b	7.15	Dav §84; GKC §113d, 113f; J-M §123b; IBHS 597 n 63; Gib 123 □ B-M 3.62; Berg 2.57k, 2.61b
6.12	GKC §67k	7.16	J-M §123b; IBHS 597 n 63; Gib 72 □ B-L 107e'; Berg 2.61b, 2.62b
6.13	Dav §83, 132R2; GKC §112mm, 114k n 2, 120d; J-M §101b, 177b; Gib 120, 156 □ B-L 111k', 122q, 398f"; Berg 2.59o, 2.96f	7.17–18	GKC §49a
		7.17	GKC §138e; J-M §147f, 174f; Gib 128
7.1	Wms §484	7.18–19	Sch §48.3.4.5
7.2	Dav §116R5; GKC §72q, 122i; J-M §80k, 134g; Wms §9; Gib 24 □ B-L 399h"; Berg 2.144c, 2.145d	7.18	GKC §112y, 124e; J-M §143f; IBHS 104
		7.19	Berg 2.17e
		7.20	GKC §90i n 3; 126x; J-M §96Bc; IBHS 120; Gib 18 □ B-L 107e', 115c, 122q
7.3	GKC §95s; J-M §105c n 2, 137s; IBHS 240	7.21ff.	GKC §112y
7.4	GKC §67p, 113bb □ B-L 322u; Berg 2.92g	7.21	B-L 122q
		7.22	Gib 130
7.5	Dav §101Rd, 147; Gib 158	7.23	Dav §17; GKC §134n; IBHS 114; Gib 19 □ Jen §25.3.3; Brock §106e
7.6	Dav §29a; GKC §29q, 122i; J-M §134g; IBHS 104	7.24	Dav §29e, 108; Gib 13, 42
7.7	Dav §1R2, 109R2; GKC §122q, 144b; J-M §152c; Gib 3	7.25	Dav §71R4, 108R3; GKC §118l, 144h; J-M §126k; Gib 14 □ B-M 3.22, 3.78, 3.80; GAHG 3.157 n 456; Brock §100c, 104
7.8	Dav §101; GKC §67t, 119y □ B-M 3.104; Sch §50.3.2; Brock §111f	8.1	Dav §101Rb; GKC §29l, 52s, 119u; IBHS 206 n 65 □ B-L 122q; B-M 1.39; Berg 2.96 n f
7.9	Dav §130R3; GKC §148d, 159ee; J-M §167s; IBHS 661; Gib 52, 141, 154, 155 □ Jen §16.4.8	8.2	GKC §49e, 96 (p. 285); IBHS 232 □ Berg 1.152a
		8.3	GKC §52s □ Berg 2.96 n f
7.11	GKC §29u, 113h; J-M §32c, 123r □ B-L 122q, 535f; Berg 2.66h*	8.4	Dav §108; GKC §144d; J-M §155e, 157ca n 1; Gib 13, 72 □ Berg 2.54d*, 2.62b
7.12	B-L 111k'	8.5	Gib 62
7.13	Dav §34R2, 90; GKC §114a, 133c; J-M §124b, 141i; IBHS 601 n 12; Gib 45, 128 □ B-L 122r; B-M 3.58; Berg 2.54d	8.6	Dav §99, 147; GKC §2d n 1, 130a; J-M §129n; Wms §274, 539; Gib 135, 158 □ B-L 559k; B-M 1.56, 2.66; Berg 1.2f
7.14	Dav §11b, 21e; GKC §74g, 94f, 112t, 126r, 135a n 1, 135c; J-M §119n, 137n n 1, 146c, 147a; IBHS 536; Gib 2, 13, 27, 59, 137 □ B-L 122r, 376r; B-M 2.19; GAHG 2.12 n 30; Jen §8.3.1.2; Berg 2.158e; Brock §67b	8.7–8	GKC §112c, 112t
		8.7	GKC §154b; J-M §119n; Gib 43 □ B-L 111k'
		8.8	GKC §145b, 145o; IBHS 215
		8.9–10	GKC §110a, 110f
		8.9	Dav §64, 132b; IBHS 430; Gib 105, 156 □ B-M 3.48; Berg 1.148g, 2.50k, 2.135 n e(bis)

B-L: Bauer and Leander, *Historische Grammatik*   **B-M**: Beer, *Grammatik*   **Berg**: Bergsträsser, *Grammatik*
Brock: Brockelmann, *Syntax*   **Dav**: Davidson, *Syntax*   **GAHG**: Richter, *Grammatik*
Gib: Gibson, *Davidson's Syntax, 4th ed.*   **GKC**: *Gesenius' Grammar*   **IBHS**: Waltke and O'Connor, *Syntax*
Jen: Jenni, *Lehrbuch*   **J-M**: Joüon and Muraoka, *Grammar*   **Ros**: Rosenthal, *Grammar*
Sch: Schneider, *Grammatik*   **Wms**: Williams, *Syntax*

8.10	Dav §64, 132b; GKC §110g; J-M §116j □ B-L 383; Jen §21.4.11; Berg 2.126 n d, 2.138n, 2.173 n g	9.5	Dav §24a, 41R1, 49b; GKC §93k, 111w, 144d; J-M §112h, 118s, 155e; IBHS 338 n 25, 557; Gib 32, 68, 102, 179 □ B-M 2.117; Sch §44.5; Brock §38c
8.11	GKC §45d, 59h; J-M §77a n 2 □ B-L 122q, 348i; Berg 2.18 n f, 2.83p	9.6	Dav §23; GKC §5n, 64a, 152u; J-M §160o; IBHS 661 n 61; Gib 31 □ B-L 354e; Berg 1.5l, 2.116d
8.12–13	Gib 182		
8.12	Dav §10R2; GKC §47m, 117r; Gib 10	9.7	Berg 2.43 n b-k
8.13	Dav §106c; GKC §135c n 1 □ B-L 122q; B-M 3.14	9.8	Dav §29R6, 115; GKC §127c, 145c; Gib 22, 42 □ Berg 2.43 n b-k
8.15	GKC §29w □ B-L 107e'; Berg 2.128g	9.9–19	Berg 2.34h
8.16	GKC §67n □ B-L 111k', 438; Berg 2.132a*	9.9	IBHS 421; Gib 118
8.17	GKC §75z; Gib 135 □ Berg 2.17d	9.10	B-L 405; Berg 2.109c
8.18	Gib 135	9.11	Dav §4R1, 22R3; GKC §116q, 127c; Wms §242; Gib 5 □ Jen §25.3.3
8.19	GKC §164d □ B-L 122q; Berg 2.109c	9.12	GKC §116f, 127i; J-M §121k; Wms §82; Gib 134 □ B-M 2.168, 3.69; GAHG 2.10 n 15; Berg 2.68a; Brock §73b, 99a
8.20	Dav §116R1; GKC §145m		
8.21	GKC §54k, 118n		
8.23–9.1	IBHS 490	9.13	IBHS 131 n 16
8.23	Dav §10R2; GKC §67v, 90f, 128h; IBHS 439 n 15; Gib 10 □ B-L 528t; Berg 2.137k	9.14	Dav §106d; J-M §154j; IBHS 131 n 16
9.1–6	Berg 2.29h; Gib 68	9.16	GKC §116q; J-M §146j □ Berg 2.137k
9.1	Dav §22R1, 41b, 106b; GKC §106n, 130a, 132g, 143b; J-M §93n n 1, 112h, 129m, 148a, 153 n 2; IBHS 155, 155 n 34; Gib 29, 34, 68, 135, 181	9.17	Wms §177; Gib 75 □ Berg 2.130m
		9.18	GKC §145o; J-M §150j; IBHS 110; Gib 118, 179
		9.19	Berg 2.119e
9.2	Dav §28R1, 41b; GKC §103g, 130a; J-M §129n; IBHS 155; Gib 34, 63 □ B-M 3.31; GAHG 2.51 n 239; Sch §45.5; Brock §71a	10.1	GKC §10g, 93bb; J-M §96Ap; IBHS 416 □ B-L 564
		10.2	GKC §114r; J-M §124q, 125h; Gib 131
		10.3	IBHS 206 n 61; Gib 10, 185
9.3	GKC §10h, 20h, 67w, 93q, 118q, 135n; J-M §82n; IBHS 204; Gib 33 □ B-L 437, 581; Jen §26.3.3; Berg 1.68v, 1.135c, 2.133 n b, 2.139 n o	10.4	GKC §163c; Wms §557; IBHS 672 n 103; Gib 176
		10.5	IBHS 682 □ GAHG 2.18 n 61
		10.6	J-M §82k, 129g; IBHS 144; Gib 31 □ B-L 399h, 435p'; B-M 2.145, 2.170; Berg 2.133b, 2.136f, 2.152t
9.4	GKC §112mm, 124n, 143d, 146e; J-M §150p; Gib 88, 181 □ Berg 2.42g	10.7	Dav §29d, 90; Gib 41 □ B-M 2.128; Berg 2.58m, 2.113h
		10.9	GKC §21d
		10.10	Dav §34R3; GKC §133e; Wms §584; IBHS 265; Gib 46

B-L: Bauer and Leander, *Historische Grammatik* **B-M**: Beer, *Grammatik* **Berg**: Bergsträsser, *Grammatik*
Brock: Brockelmann, *Syntax* **Dav**: Davidson, *Syntax* **GAHG**: Richter, *Grammatik*
Gib: Gibson, *Davidson's Syntax, 4th ed.* **GKC**: *Gesenius' Grammar* **IBHS**: Waltke and O'Connor, *Syntax*
Jen: Jenni, *Lehrbuch* **J-M**: Joüon and Muraoka, *Grammar* **Ros**: Rosenthal, *Grammar*
Sch: Schneider, *Grammatik* **Wms**: Williams, *Syntax*

10.11	GKC §23d; Gib 34	11.1	J-M §119c
10.12	Dav §26; GKC §47b, 127a, 128a □ Berg 1.103 n t	11.2	GKC §128a n 1; J-M §129a n 5; IBHS 144 n 18, 146; Gib 31
10.13	Dav §51R6; GKC §23d, 55b, 75z, 107b n 2; Gib 105 □ B-L 115c, 381j, 426; B-M 2.152; Berg 1.91 n e, 2.33 n b-h, 2.108 n b, 2.147i, 2.151s	11.3	Dav §101Rb; Gib 77 □ B-L 302a'
		11.4	Gib 173
		11.5	Dav §22R1; IBHS 246; Gib 29
		11.6	Dav §52, 138b; Gib 77, 90, 168
10.14	Dav §22e, 91R1, 91R3; GKC §118w, 126o, 126p, 132e; J-M §124s, 137i; IBHS 258; Gib 28, 129, 130 □ B-L 158; Berg 1.99h, 2.109c, 2.140 n q	11.7	GKC §122e
		11.8	Dav §41b, 111, 111R3; GKC §142f; Gib 68 □ B-L 282o; Berg 1.144d, 2.29i; Brock §138
10.15	Dav §91c, 91R2, 128R1; GKC §115i, 124k, 150h, 152a n 1; J-M §136e, 161e; Wms §256, 400; IBHS 123, 203; Gib 19, 129, 130, 142 □ B-L 115c; B-M 3.89; Brock §45	11.9	Dav §73R7, 100R5; GKC §106u, 114c, 115d, 116f n 2, 117n, 126z; J-M §124j, 125k, 138f; IBHS 184, 222; Gib 68, 118, 128, 138, 174 □ B-M 3.79; Sch §50.1.2; Berg 2.55d*; Brock §99b
10.16	GKC §69f, 69p; Gib 77 □ B-L 383; Berg 2.126d, 2.126 n d	11.10	Dav §106b; GKC §119gg, 143b; IBHS 77; Sch §53.2.2
10.17	GKC §93v □ B-L 583v'; B-M 2.70; Berg 1.92e	11.11	B-L 158; Gib 51
10.18	GKC §67cc □ Berg 2.133 n b	11.12	GKC §20m □ B-M 1.116; Berg 1.142 n f, 2.171 n d
10.19	Berg 2.36k	11.13	Dav §105R2 □ Berg 2.134d
10.20	Dav §98c; Gib 134	11.14	Dav §29R5; GKC §93hh □ B-L 122r; Berg 2.17e; Brock §14b
10.22	Dav §73R2, 99; GKC §117z, 159r, 160a; Gib 154, 187	11.15	Berg 1.156k
10.24	Dav §101Ra, 143; GKC §58i, 119o, 156d; IBHS 518 □ B-L 345q''	12.1	Dav §65R6; GKC §109k, 150m n 2; J-M §170m; IBHS 567 □ Berg 2.34h
10.25	Dav §56; GKC §112x, 112oo; Gib 58, 87 □ GAHG 3.171 n 539; Brock §13a, 123f	12.2	GKC §80g; J-M §89n □ B-M [R] 1.106; Berg 2.38d
		12.3	IBHS 197 □ B-L 547
10.26	Dav §56, 101Rd; Gib 88	12.4	Gib 136
10.27	Dav §57; GKC §10h; Gib 90 □ Berg 1.68v, 1.135c	12.5	Dav §133; GKC §116e; J-M §54b; Gib 185 □ Berg 2.69d, 2.129i
10.28	Dav §41b; GKC §106n, J-M §112h □ B-L 510v; Berg 2.34h	12.6	Dav §14; GKC §122s; J-M §134o; IBHS 423; Gib 18 □ B-L 429j; B-M 2.145, 3.18; Berg 2.134c
10.30	Dav §32R1, 109R3; GKC §132b, 144m; J-M §125s, 151c n 1; IBHS 262 □ Brock §93n	13	J-M §112h n 2
10.31	Brock §127b	13.1	IBHS 152
10.32	Dav §69R2, 94; GKC §114k, 119o; Gib 131	13.2	Dav §60R3; IBHS 570, 572; Gib 81
10.33	GKC §23c; IBHS 413; Gib 91 □ Berg 1.89b, 1.144d, 2.115a	13.3	Dav §3, 24c; GKC §135n; Wms §380; Gib 4. 33, 175 □ B-L 110i'; Berg 2.167o
10.34	GKC §119o □ B-L 368t; Berg 2.122a		
11.1–9	Gib 90		

B-L: Bauer and Leander, *Historische Grammatik*   **B-M**: Beer, *Grammatik*   **Berg**: Bergsträsser, *Grammatik*
Brock: Brockelmann, *Syntax*   **Dav**: Davidson, *Syntax*   **GAHG**: Richter, *Grammatik*
Gib: Gibson, *Davidson's Syntax, 4th ed.*   **GKC**: *Gesenius' Grammar*   **IBHS**: Waltke and O'Connor, *Syntax*
Jen: Jenni, *Lehrbuch*   **J-M**: Joüon and Muraoka, *Grammar*   **Ros**: Rosenthal, *Grammar*
Sch: Schneider, *Grammatik*   **Wms**: Williams, *Syntax*

13.4	Dav §117R3; GKC §146b, 147c; J-M §162e; Gib 179, 188	14.4	GKC §49k, 49m, 148b; IBHS 458 □ Brock §12
13.5	Gib 138	14.5	Brock §128; Gib 62
13.6	GKC §118x	14.6	Dav §67b, 67R2; GKC §117q,
13.7–9	Gib 93		130a, 152t, 156g; J-M §160m;
13.7	J-M §150d; IBHS 117 □ B-L 516s; Gib 20		Wms §418, 421; Gib 115□ Brock §125b
13.8	Dav §24c, 29R6, 101; GKC §47m, 119gg, 128p; IBHS 516;	14.7–8	IBHS 664
		14.7	J-M §125o
	Gib 33, 42, 147 □ Berg 2.20b	14.8	Dav §44a, 99; IBHS 622; Gib
13.9	Dav §41R1, 96; GKC §114r;		75, 135, 157, 175 □ Brock §158
	J-M §124q; Gib 68, 131	14.9	GKC §145t; J-M §150j; Gib 17
13.10	B-L 109i', 113q', 533f; B-M	14.10	IBHS 419, 664; Gib 175
	1.66, [R] 1.66; Berg 2.29i; Gib	14.11	GKC §93ss, 145o; J-M §150j,
	68		152fa; IBHS 110; Gib 144 □
13.12	Berg 2.129h; Gib 78		B-L 109i'
13.14	Dav §22R2, 139; Gib 28, 42,	14.12	GKC §148b
	168 □ B-L 109i'	14.14	GKC §87s; J-M §97Eb; IBHS
13.15	GKC §111w		425 □ Berg 1.131d
13.16	IBHS 375 n 31; Gib 78 □ B-L	14.15	Gib 176
	232j; Berg 2.91g, 2.136i,	14.17	Dav §101; GKC §116x, 117o;
	2.174 n k		Gib 137 □ B-L 109i', 110i';
13.17ff.	GKC §111w		B-M 1.100, [R] 1.100
13.17	Dav §44a; Gib 59, 74, 91 □	14.18	Brock §62f
	Berg 2.113h	14.19	Dav §28R1, 98b; GKC §29f,
13.18	Dav §44a; GKC §52n, 72r, 142f;		53s, 126p, 130a; J-M §57a,
	J-M §52c, 80k; Gib 74 □ B-L		121n, 129m; IBHS 148 n 25,
	328b'; B-M 2.120; Berg 2.51l,		617; Gib 34, 134 □ Berg 1.130c,
	2.95d, 2.145d		1.150n, 2.106n
13.19	GKC §45e, 115d; Gib 129 □	14.20	GKC §44o □ B-L 109i', 315l';
	Berg 2.84p		Berg 2.125b
13.20	GKC §68k, 145o; IBHS 413 □	14.21	GKC §152t; IBHS 573 □ B-L
	B-L 109i'; Berg 1.92e, 2.172 n f		109i', 113q'
13.21	Berg 1.97f	14.22	Wms §72; IBHS 649
13.22	Dav §113; GKC §145o; Gib 21	14.23	Dav §78R5, 84; GKC §55f,
	□ B-L 565x; B-M 3.20; Berg		113e; J-M §123c; Wms §207;
	2.57k		IBHS 591; Gib 123 □ B-L 375,
14.1–3	Gib 90		563x; B-M 3.62; Berg 2.108c
14.1	GAHG 3.171 n 539	14.24	Dav §1R2, 41R1, 109R2; GKC
14.2	Dav §73R4, 73R7, 100R5; GKC		§144b, 149b; J-M §152c, 165c;
	§54f, 57 n 2, 117w; J-M §62h,		IBHS 679; Gib 3, 62, 68, 187 □
	125c, 125k; Gib 138 □ B-L		Jen §17.3.4; Berg 2.29i, 2.165l
	344h''; B-M 2.165	14.25	Dav §105R2; GKC §10h, 114r;
14.3–4	GKC §112y, IBHS 539		J-M §124q □ Berg 1.68v, 1.135c
14.3	Dav §91R2, 109; GKC §22s,	14.26	Brock §61; Gib 5
	102b, 115g, 121b, 121f; J-M	14.27	Dav §99R3; GKC §116q, 126k
	§132e, 152fa; IBHS 374 n 30;		□ B-L 432a'; B-M 2.147
	Gib 43, 90 □ B-L 101u, 113q',	14.29	J-M §94h, 147j; IBHS 127 n 5,
	287n'; Berg 1.152a, 2.88c		665; Gib 42 □ B-L 268j
14.4–21	J-M §112h n 2	14.30	GKC §72w, 133h □ B-L 101u

B-L: Bauer and Leander, *Historische Grammatik*   **B-M**: Beer, *Grammatik*   **Berg**: Bergsträsser, *Grammatik*
Brock: Brockelmann, *Syntax*   **Dav**: Davidson, *Syntax*   **GAHG**: Richter, *Grammatik*
Gib: Gibson, *Davidson's Syntax, 4th ed.*   **GKC**: *Gesenius' Grammar*   **IBHS**: Waltke and O'Connor, *Syntax*
Jen: Jenni, *Lehrbuch*   **J-M**: Joüon and Muraoka, *Grammar*   **Ros**: Rosenthal, *Grammar*
Sch: Schneider, *Grammatik*   **Wms**: Williams, *Syntax*

14.31	Dav §29R6, 88R2; GKC §72v, 113bb; J-M §94h, 123u; Wms §211; IBHS 594; Gib 42, 127 □ B-L 268j; Berg 2.66k; Brock §16g
14.32	Dav §108; Gib 13 □ B-L 110i'
15.1	IBHS 374 n 29 □ B-L 276x; Berg 2.87c
15.2	GKC §70d, 96 □ B-L 382, 620t; GAHG 3.161 n 480; Berg 2.128 n h
15.3	Dav §29R6, 73R3; J-M §146j; IBHS 127 n 5; Gib 42
15.4	Gib 22
15.5–7	IBHS 666
15.5	GKC §72cc, 88c; J-M §101b □ B-L 404; Berg 2.109c
15.7	Dav §115, 143; GKC §80g, 155h; J-M §89n; Gib 11
15.8	Dav §69R1; GKC §119hh; J-M §132g; IBHS 9
16.2	Dav §22R2, 69R1; GKC §118g, 126p □ B-M 3.28
16.3	GKC §90f
16.4	Dav §115; GKC §145d; Gib 22 □ B-L 423; Berg 2.132a*, 2.143 n h, 2.153u
16.5	IBHS 448
16.6	GKC §122v
16.7	GKC §70d; Gib 42
16.8	Dav §116; GKC §75m, 145u; J-M §150l; Gib 23 □ B-L 427t''; Berg 1.141 n a, 2.166n
16.9	Dav §20R4, 75; GKC §72gg, 75dd; IBHS 176, 198; Gib 113 □ B-L 426; Berg 2.167 n p
16.10	Dav §108R1, 109; GKC §72bb, 121a, 121b, 144e; J-M §152fa, 155d; IBHS 423; Gib 13 □ B-L 471qα
16.12	Dav §41c, 130b; Gib 67, 153 □ B-L 547
16.13	Gib 157
16.14	IBHS 538; Gib 87 □ Berg 2.42g
17.1	Dav §101; GKC §116p, 119x, 121b □ B-L 490cζ; Berg 2.72h*
17.2	Dav §100d, 139; IBHS 619; Gib 136, 168
17.4	GKC §67g, 128r □ B-M [R] 1.66
17.5	Dav §91R3; GKC §122n; Gib 129 □ B-L 302a'
17.6	Dav §32R2, 36R5, 113; GKC §118u, 131n n 1, 132 n 2, 134s; Gib 21, 48, 118 □ B-L 357, 547
17.8	GKC §35f, 154a n 1(b) □ B-M 2.19
17.10–11	GKC §107b □ Berg 2.36i
17.10	GKC §20m n 3, 47k □ B-L 303b'; B-M 2.104; Berg 2.20 n a, 2.118c
17.11	GKC §72n, 55f □ Berg 2.82n, 2.109c, 2.143 n b
17.12	GKC §47m, 75u □ Berg 2.166m(bis)
17.13	Dav §116R1 □ Berg 2.166m
17.14	Dav §145R2 □ B-L 113q'
18.1	Dav §116R5; GKC §124e
18.2	Dav §1R1, 99, 116R5; GKC §52s, 67l, 103m; IBHS 291 n 9, 375 n 34; Gib 135 □ B-L 110i', 287o', 644y'; Berg 1.112 n e, 1.113 n e, 2.88c
18.3	Dav §96R5; GKC §66b, 107n; J-M §113m; Gib 133 □ B-L ‡113q, 441c; B-M 1.66, [R] 1.66, 2.132; Berg 2.56f
18.4	GKC §10h; J-M §7b n 4 □ B-L 301u, 534; Berg 1.126bb, 2.79g
18.5	Dav §41R4, 56; GKC §29q, 112oo, 67v, 72dd, 142f, 145q; Gib 88 □ B-L 232j; Berg 2.136f, 2.137k
18.6	GKC §73h; Gib 78 □ Berg 2.74a, 2.153t
18.7	GKC §67l □ IBHS 375 n 34 □ B-L 110i', 287o', 644y'; Berg 1.113 n e, 2.88c
19.1	GKC §72l □ B-L 398f''; Jen §9.3.3.2; Berg 2.17e, 2.136i
19.2	IBHS 107 n 39 □ B-L 405; Berg 2.109c
19.3	GKC §67dd □ B-L 431t; Berg 2.117a, 2.139p

B-L: Bauer and Leander, *Historische Grammatik* **B-M**: Beer, *Grammatik* **Berg**: Bergsträsser, *Grammatik* **Brock**: Brockelmann, *Syntax* **Dav**: Davidson, *Syntax* **GAHG**: Richter, *Grammatik* **Gib**: Gibson, *Davidson's Syntax, 4th ed.* **GKC**: *Gesenius' Grammar* **IBHS**: Waltke and O'Connor, *Syntax* **Jen**: Jenni, *Lehrbuch* **J-M**: Joüon and Muraoka, *Grammar* **Ros**: Rosenthal, *Grammar* **Sch**: Schneider, *Grammatik* **Wms**: Williams, *Syntax*

19.4	Dav §31, 116R4; GKC §124i, 132h; J-M §148a; Wms §8; IBHS 257; Gib 43 □ B-M 3.18; Brock §19c	20.4	Dav §24d, 70a, 71R1; GKC §87g, 118o; J-M §126a; IBHS 172 n 19; Gib 77, 114 □ B-L 274i, 502eι; Berg 1.101 n l
19.6ff.	Berg 2.29i	20.5	Berg 1.148g
19.6	GKC §53g, 53p, 124e; J-M §82k; IBHS 445 □ B-L 361a'; B-M 2.145; Berg 1.161e, 2.77c, 2.105 n k, 2.132a*	20.6	Dav §107; Gib 2, 185
		21.1	Dav §93; GKC §114o; IBHS 387; Gib 131 □ Berg 2.60p
19.7	GKC §106n □ Berg 2.126d	21.2	GKC §44o, 72s, 91e, 121b, 122i; J-M §94h, 128b, 134g □ B-L 315l', 398e'', 600j'; Berg 2.145e; Brock §26
19.8	Dav §28R3; GKC §130a; Wms §30; Gib 134 □ B-L 493fη; Berg 2.107a, 2.172 n e; Brock §70f		
		21.3	Berg 2.108c
19.9	GKC §86i; Gib 134 □ B-L 512d'; Berg 1.144d, 2.144b	21.4	Berg 1.157o
		21.5	Dav §84, 88R2; GKC §113ff; Gib 123, 127 □ Berg 2.67l, 2.160a
19.10	GKC §128y; IBHS 148; Gib 33 □ B-L 549a'		
19.11	Dav §32R5; GKC §107t, 133h; IBHS 261, 391; Gib 39, 44, 53, 142	21.7	Dav §32R1, 67b, 132a; GKC §93dd, 117q; J-M §129c, 141b; IBHS 259; Gib 44, 115, 156 □ Brock §93d
19.12	Dav §65d, 126R8; GKC §109f, 150l; Gib 106, 185 □ B-M 3.36; Jen §27.3.2; Brock §55b		
		21.8	Dav §70a; GKC §118r; J-M §126e, 136b
19.13	Dav §111, 115; GKC §142f; J-M §155ne; IBHS 391; Gib 22 □ Berg 2.122b, 2.151q	21.9	GKC §136d; J-M §143a; IBHS 104
19.14	Dav §67R1; GKC §67l; Gib 31 □ Berg 1.101m; Brock §19b	21.11	Dav §108; GKC §90f, 93w, 116t; J-M §96Am, 155f; Gib 14 □ B-L 202k, 457o'; B-M 1.100; Brock §37
19.16	J-M §150e; Gib 23		
19.17	GKC §80h, 95d, 143b □ B-L 511x, 603g	21.12	Dav §83; GKC §29t, 75u, 75rr, 76d; Gib 120 □ B-L 409k, 410q, 442g; B-M 2.159; Berg 1.156m, 2.20b, 2.121d, 2.166m(tris), 2.168q
19.18	Dav §67R3; GKC §2a; IBHS 8 n 16; Gib 115 □ B-L 13a; B-M 1.11; Berg 1.2e		
19.19	Dav §113 □ Berg 1.101 n l	21.13	B-L 597h'
19.20	J-M §119y n 2; Gib 135	21.14	GKC §68i, 76d □ B-L 442g; Berg 1.91d, 2.121e, 2.121d, 2.166m
19.21	IBHS 390		
19.22	Dav §86c; GKC §113s; J-M §123m; IBHS 390, 590; Gib 125 □ Berg 2.65h	21.16	Berg 2.42g; Gib 87
		21.17	GKC §127a, 128a, 146a □ Brock §70b, 124a
19.24	J-M §101b	22.1	GKC §91e, 107v, 150l; J-M §94h; IBHS 222; Gib 185 □ B-L 251j, 268j; B-M 3.79
20.1	Dav §91a; GKC §115k; Gib 129 □ B-L 113q'		
20.2	Dav §88; GKC §113i, 118n □ B-M 3.64, 3.78; GAHG 3.152 n 417; Sch §50.4.1; Berg 2.65h*	22.2	Dav §24c, 98b, 98R1; GKC §75v, 91e, 117z, 126e, 128x, 152d; IBHS 144, 247 n 17; Gib 31, 33, 134 □ B-L 590h; B-M 3.27; Berg 2.144b; Brock §32a
20.3	Dav §70a; J-M §126a; IBHS 172		

B-L: Bauer and Leander, *Historische Grammatik*   **B-M**: Beer, *Grammatik*   **Berg**: Bergsträsser, *Grammatik*
Brock: Brockelmann, *Syntax*   **Dav**: Davidson, *Syntax*   **GAHG**: Richter, *Grammatik*
Gib: Gibson, *Davidson's Syntax, 4th ed.*   **GKC**: *Gesenius' Grammar*   **IBHS**: Waltke and O'Connor, *Syntax*
Jen: Jenni, *Lehrbuch*   **J-M**: Joüon and Muraoka, *Grammar*   **Ros**: Rosenthal, *Grammar*
Sch: Schneider, *Grammatik*   **Wms**: Williams, *Syntax*

22.3	Dav §98R1, 101Rc; GKC §119w; IBHS 375 n 31; Gib 134 □ B-L 286n'; Berg 1.92e, 2.88c	23.8–9	Gib 62
		23.8	GKC §93pp □ B-L 548z, 564; Berg 1.140c, 2.113f
22.5	GKC §55f, 85l, 128a, 133l; IBHS 144; Gib 33 □ B-L 438; Berg 2.109c	23.9	IBHS 439 n 15
		23.11	GKC §20o, 53q □ B-L 228a', 564; Berg 1.110 n b, 2.105k
22.6	IBHS 282 n 22	23.12	Dav §28R6, 32R1, 97R1; GKC §35b, 46e, 118f, 130e, 132b; J-M §152d, 155s; IBHS 262; Gib 36, 44 □ B-L 221p; Berg 2.81k; Brock §35b, 122k
22.7	GKC §73d, 111w, 128r □ Berg 2.151s		
22.9	Berg 2.134c		
22.10	GKC §20m □ B-L 368t; Berg 1.142f, 2.122b		

22.11   Dav §109R2; GKC §95o, 124k; J-M §136e n 1; IBHS 123; Gib 19

23.13   GKC §126e, 126aa, 136d n 2; J-M §143i; IBHS 309, 337 n 22; Gib 6 □ B-L 425; GAHG 3.294 n 768; Berg 2.172d

22.12–13 IBHS 678

22.12   Berg 2.114i

23.14   B-L 240t'

22.13   Dav §84, 88R2; GKC §75n, 113d, 113f, 113dd; J-M §79p; IBHS 594; Gib 123, 127 □ B-L 427t"; Berg 2.67 n 1, 2.161 n c

23.15   Dav §101Rd; GKC §44f, 116p, 118t; J-M §42f □ Berg 2.14a

23.16   Dav §82; J-M §137g; Gib 120 □ Berg 2.55d*

22.14   GKC §107c, 112ss, 149b, 149e; J-M §112i n 5, 165j; Gib 103, 187 □ Brock §175

23.17   GKC §72l, 91e; J-M §94h □ B-L 398f"', 405, 563x; Berg 2.17e

22.15   B-M 1.28

23.18   B-L 563x

24.1   Berg 2.29i; Gib 91

22.16   Dav §21f, 69R1; GKC §90m, 144p; J-M §93n; IBHS 128; Gib 24, 28 □ B-L 526l, 548a'; Brock §70f

24.2   Dav §20R4, 151R2; GKC §35g, 116s, 127i, 161c; J-M §131d n 1, 140c, 174i; IBHS 204, 204 n 53, 249 □ B-L 263g, 441c; Berg 2.69 n c, 2.159g

22.17   Dav §86c; GKC §113r; Gib 91, 125 □ Berg 1.148g, 2.64g, 2.108c

24.3   GKC §67t; J-M §82m □ B-L 323z, 435p'; B-M 2.146; Berg 2.136i, 2.137i

22.18   GKC §118r

22.19   GKC §144p □ Brock §138

24.4   Jen §28.3.2.1; Berg 2.107a

22.21   IBHS 176 n 25 □ B-M 2.61

24.5   GKC §67v; Wms §350

22.22   B-M [R] 2.34; Gib 136, 172

24.6   GKC §67ee; Berg 2.37b, 2.134c

22.24   Dav §32R5; GKC §128w, 133h; J-M §141f; Wms §30; IBHS 262; Gib 44 □ Brock §60a, 76e

24.7   Dav §22R3 □ Berg 1.147d, 2.107a

24.9   GKC §67p □ Berg 2.135d

22.25   Berg 2.127d

24.10   GKC §119x; Wms §105; IBHS 289 □ Brock §78

23.1–2   IBHS 570

23.1   GKC §110k, 119y □ Berg 2.20 n a, 2.87c; Brock §3

24.12   Dav §80, 113; GKC §67y, 121d; J-M §82i, 128c; IBHS 375 n 32; Gib 21, 118 □ B-L 286m'; B-M 3.84; Berg 2.88c

23.2   B-L 375

23.3   B-L 574x, 581

23.4   Dav §128R6; GKC §152z; J-M §160q; IBHS 570 □ Berg 2.144b

24.13   GKC §164d; Gib 141 □ B-M 3.109

23.5   Dav §23; GKC §118u, 128h; IBHS 152; Gib 33 □ Berg 2.152t

24.16   Dav §67b; GKC §117q; Gib 115

24.17   J-M §104d

23.7   GKC §126z n 1 □ Berg 2.128h

B-L: Bauer and Leander, *Historische Grammatik*   B-M: Beer, *Grammatik*   Berg: Bergsträsser, *Grammatik*
Brock: Brockelmann, *Syntax*   Dav: Davidson, *Syntax*   GAHG: Richter, *Grammatik*
Gib: Gibson, *Davidson's Syntax, 4th ed.*   GKC: *Gesenius' Grammar*   IBHS: Waltke and O'Connor, *Syntax*
Jen: Jenni, *Lehrbuch*   J-M: Joüon and Muraoka, *Grammar*   Ros: Rosenthal, *Grammar*
Sch: Schneider, *Grammatik*   Wms: Williams, *Syntax*

24.18	Dav §49b; IBHS 160; Gib 102 □ Berg 2.37b	26.16	GKC §44l, 72o; J-M §42f; IBHS 516 n 49 □ B-L 404; Berg 2.15 n a, 2.173 n h
24.19–20	GKC §67l, 67o		
24.19	GKC §80k, 113w; J-M §123p; IBHS 582; Gib 125 □ B-L 438; Berg 2.63e, 2.64f, 2.132a*, 2.133 n a, 2.136 n g	26.17	Berg 2.57k
		26.18	GKC §124e; J-M §136g; IBHS 121 □ Berg 1.130c; Brock §52bβ
		26.19	GKC §95h, 122s, 145c; IBHS 423 □ B-L 438
24.20	GKC §126o □ B-L 312t; Berg 2.63e, 2.77c	26.20	GKC §75qq □ B-L 352, 375, 613d′; Berg 1.124w, 2.158e
24.21	J-M §133i; IBHS 109 n 45; Gib 77	26.21	GAHG 3.294 n 771; Berg 1.129b
24.22	GKC §117q, 118r; J-M §125r □ Berg 2.97h; Brock §111e	27.1	Dav §30; J-M §141a; IBHS 259; Gib 43
24.23	Dav §32R6; IBHS 263; Gib 45	27.2	J-M §150n; IBHS 104 n 37; Gib 91, 182 □ Brock §16g
25.1	GKC §60f; J-M §61d n 3 □ B-L 405; Jen §25.3.2.6; Berg 2.95d	27.3	GKC §60a; J-M §137i □ B-L 368t; Berg 2.79g, 2.88 n d, 2.122b
25.4	Brock §145a		
25.5	GAHG 3.206 n 786	27.4	Dav §65R4; GKC §10h, 48c, 65b, 71, 108f, 117x, 151b; J-M §77b, 116i, 125ba; IBHS 169, 575; Gib 4, 107 □ B-L 208t, 362a′, 383; B-M 3.81; Berg 1.126aa, 2.173 n h
25.6	GKC §75dd, 93ss; IBHS 420 □ B-L 424, 588l; Berg 1.101m, 2.166m		
25.7	GKC §72p □ B-L 399h″; Berg 2.147g, 2.173 n g		
25.9	Dav §65b, 65R1; IBHS 337; Gib 44, 107	27.5	Dav §65R6; GKC §162a
		27.6	Dav §65R6; IBHS 443; Gib 73, 90 □ Berg 2.51l, 2.152t
25.10	GKC §72v □ B-L 402u″; Berg 2.147 n i	27.7	IBHS 375 n 31, 420; Gib 115 □ B-L 286n′; Berg 1.68v, 2.88c
25.12	Berg 2.137k		
26.1	J-M §125w; IBHS 375 n 32; Gib 18 □ B-L 286m′, 562v; Berg 2.88c	27.8	GKC §55f □ Berg 2.109c
		27.9	GKC §156f □ GAHG 2.18 n 61
		27.10	GKC §126o
26.3	Dav §100R7; GKC §50f, 116s; Wms §16; Gib 138 □ Berg 2.88 n d	27.11	Dav §17R2; GKC §47k, 70a n 2, 72n, 124e, 145c; J-M §124h, 136g; IBHS 121 □ B-L 382, 637a; Berg 1.150n, 2.20 n a, 2.126d; Brock §19b
26.4	GKC §119i n 3 □ B-L 548z		
26.5	J-M §61f, 113o □ Berg 2.23g		
26.7	Dav §76		
26.9	Dav §109R3; GKC §144m; J-M §151c, 151c n 1 □ Brock §93m*	27.12	Dav §35R2; GKC §96a, 130g; J-M §129o □ B-L 622b
26.10	Dav §132R2; GKC §122q, 159c; J-M §134n, 160m; IBHS 375 n 32; Gib 17, 156 □ B-L 286m′; Berg 2.88c; Brock §52bβ	27.13	Dav §109 □ Berg 2.69c, 2.117a
		28.1	Dav §28R3, 98b; GKC §124e, 128c, 128w; IBHS 682; Gib 35, 134 □ Brock §83e
26.11	GKC §47m, 75u; J-M §44e □ B-M 2.101, 3.12; Berg 2.166m; Brock §52bβ	28.2	Dav §22R3, 41b; GKC §125c; Gib 68
26.14	GKC §152t; J-M §130g; IBHS 666 □ Berg 1.72g; Brock §52bβ	28.3	GKC §47k □ Berg 2.20 n a; Brock §70b

B-L: Bauer and Leander, *Historische Grammatik*   **B-M**: Beer, *Grammatik*   **Berg**: Bergsträsser, *Grammatik*
Brock: Brockelmann, *Syntax*   **Dav**: Davidson, *Syntax*   **GAHG**: Richter, *Grammatik*
Gib: Gibson, *Davidson's Syntax, 4th ed.*   **GKC**: *Gesenius' Grammar*   **IBHS**: Waltke and O'Connor, *Syntax*
Jen: Jenni, *Lehrbuch*   **J-M**: Joüon and Muraoka, *Grammar*   **Ros**: Rosenthal, *Grammar*
Sch: Schneider, *Grammatik*   **Wms**: Williams, *Syntax*

28.4	Dav §28R3, 32R5, 108R1; GKC §91e, 128p, 128w, 135n, 144e; J-M §141f, 155d; Wms §30; IBHS 262; Gib 13, 33, 35, 44 □ B-L 597h'; B-M 3.34; Brock §37, 49a	28.27	Dav §44a, 128R6; GKC §152z; J-M §160q; IBHS 375 n 32 □ B-L 286m', 434 n 3; Berg 2.88c, 2.139o
28.5	Gib 90	28.28	Dav §44a, 86a, 86R2; GKC §112m, 113w n 3, 150a; Gib 124, 125 □ B-L 402u'', 481dδ; B-M 2.147; Berg 2.63e, 2.64 n f, 2.135d, 2.138n, 2.140q, 2.172 n e
28.6	Dav §101; GKC §90i, 119hh; IBHS 617; Gib 134		
28.7	Dav §22d, 101Rc; GKC §72l, 118g; J-M §80j; Gib 28 □ B-L 398e''; Berg 2.145e	28.29	Dav §19R4, 65R2
28.8	Dav §22R3; GKC §127c; J-M §139f	29.1	Dav §18, 25; GKC §19c, 66f, 69h n 1, 130d; J-M §129p; IBHS 139, 156; Gib 12 □ B-L 199l, 368t, 397q, 522j; B-M 2.134; GAHG 2.52 n 246; Berg 2.122a, 2.127e; Brock §144
28.9	Dav §28R1, 75; GKC §130a; J-M §125u, 129m; IBHS 155; Gib 34, 112		
28.10	GKC §86g n 1, 102h, 147c □ B-L 638w	29.2	Dav §73R7; Gib 118 □ Berg 2.148k
28.11	GKC §116b □ B-M 3.66	29.4	Dav §83; GKC §120g; Gib 91 □ Berg 2.109c
28.12	GKC §23i, 44l, 114m n 1 □ B-L 442g; Berg 1.44c, 2.15 n a, 2.54d*	29.5	GKC §126p, 133k n 1; J-M §137i; Gib 28, 91
28.13	Dav §53c; GKC §86g n 1, 112p; J-M §119f; Gib 93 □ B-L 638w	29.6	GKC §84[a]s, 144b; J-M §97Ca
28.15	Dav §69R4, 76, 78R3; J-M §125ba; Gib 114, 155	29.7	Dav §98R1; GKC §75qq, 116i, 118t; Gib 91 □ B-L 491iζ; Berg 2.156a
28.16	Dav §28R3, 99; GKC §71, 119i, 130f n 4, 155f; J-M §77a n 2; Wms §30; IBHS 622; Gib 35, 44, 135 □ B-L 379t; B-M 1.81, 2.142, 2.176 Anm 2; Berg 2.130m, 2.152 n t	29.8	Dav §54a, 100a; GKC §112y, 116s, 126o; J-M §137i, 154c; IBHS 245; Gib 94, 136 □ GAHG 3.204 n 775; Berg 2.71g
28.17	Dav §78R5, 111R1; GKC §29u, 142f □ B-M 2.143, 2.151; Brock §122r	29.9	Dav §88R4; GKC §55g, 72l; J-M §125d □ B-L 398e''; B-M 2.145; Berg 2.108 n c, 2.135e, 2.145e, 2.174 n k
28.18	GKC §145o; J-M §150j; Gib 41, 155	29.11	Dav §54a, 132a; J-M §119q, 143b; IBHS 308; Gib 5, 94, 156
28.19	Dav §145; Gib 128, 158 □ Berg 2.54d; Brock §106f	29.12	Dav §54a, 132a □ Berg 2.28g; Gib 94, 156
28.20	GKC §133c; J-M §124s □ Berg 2.118b	29.13	GKC §115d, 127a, 142d; J-M §52d n 3, 170o; Gib 158 □ Brock §163a
28.21	Dav §32R1, 101Rd; GKC §118t, 132b; J-M §133h; Wms §263; IBHS 202; Gib 44 □ Jen §26.3.3	29.14	Dav §86R3; GKC §50e, 113w, 155f; J-M §170o; Gib 91, 125 □ Berg 2.64g, 2.85 n r; Brock §99b
28.22	J-M §141g n 3; Gib 17		
28.24	Dav §108R1; GKC §144e; J-M §155d; Gib 13		
28.25	Berg 2.41g; Gib 154		
28.26	Dav §58b; GKC §112rr; Gib 103		

B-L: Bauer and Leander, *Historische Grammatik* **B-M**: Beer, *Grammatik* **Berg**: Bergsträsser, *Grammatik* **Brock**: Brockelmann, *Syntax* **Dav**: Davidson, *Syntax* **GAHG**: Richter, *Grammatik* **Gib**: Gibson, *Davidson's Syntax, 4th ed.* **GKC**: *Gesenius' Grammar* **IBHS**: Waltke and O'Connor, *Syntax* **Jen**: Jenni, *Lehrbuch* **J-M**: Joüon and Muraoka, *Grammar* **Ros**: Rosenthal, *Grammar* **Sch**: Schneider, *Grammatik* **Wms**: Williams, *Syntax*

29.15	Dav §82; GKC §53q, 112n, 116f, 144p; J-M §54b, 111i, 118r, 119r; Gib 95, 120 □ B-L 228a'; Berg 2.59n*, 2.105 n k; Brock §33	30.14	Dav §44R3, 67R1; GKC §63i, 113i, 156g, 158c; J-M §68e; Gib 76 □ B-L 348h, 352; Berg 2.114i(bis)
29.16	Dav §51R5, 117, 122; GKC §107u, 147c, 150f; J-M §161d, 162c; Gib 183, 188 □ B-M 3.87; Berg 2.82n(bis); Brock §11a, 54f, 136b	30.15	Dav §84R1; Gib 123 □ B-L 321h
		30.16	Dav §32R6, 118; GKC §132 n 2; IBHS 263; Gib 45, 141 □ Berg 2.136i
29.17	GKC §112x, 112oo; GAHG 3.171 n 538; Gib 87	30.17	J-M §112i; Gib 158
29.19	GKC §128l, 132c, 133h; J-M §141d; Gib 32 □ Berg 2.83p; Brock §76a	30.18	GKC §67cc, 130a; J-M §129m; IBHS 155 n 34, 416; Gib 34 □ B-L 437; B-M 1.116, [R] 1.116; Berg 2.133b
29.20	Dav §58a □ Berg 2.44l	30.19	Dav §41a, 86b; GKC §45d, 58g, 67n, 75ll; J-M §63b; Wms §205; IBHS 599; Gib 124 □ B-L 437; B-M 2.171; Berg 2.83p, 2.116d, 2.134 n d, 2.160a, 2.162d
29.21	J-M §54d n 1; Gib 134, 137 □ B-L 399h''; Berg 2.15 n a, 2.125 n a-e, 2.174 n h		
29.22	J-M §158t □ Berg 2.153u	30.20	Dav §113; GKC §131c, 145n; J-M §127b; Gib 21, 41 □ Brock §62g
29.23	GKC §131o		
29.24	J-M §125q; Gib 33		
30.1	Dav §101; GKC §69h n 1 □ B-L 379q; Berg 2.127 n e, 2.171 n d	30.21	GKC §56 □ B-L 382; Berg 2.110e, 2.173 n g
30.2	GKC §63i, 72q; J-M §68e, 80k; Gib 137 □ B-L 348h; Berg 2.114i, 2.145d	30.22	Dav §24R2, 116R1; GKC §135n, 145m; Gib 4, 23, 33
		30.23	GKC §93ss, 117ee; J-M §96Ce; Gib 4
30.3	Berg 2.42g		
30.5	GKC §70c, 78b, 103f n 3; Gib 10	30.24	GKC §52s, 116t; J-M §155f □ B-L 287o'; Berg 2.96 n f
30.6	Dav §14R2; GKC §135p □ B-L 583v', 600j'; B-M 2.71	30.25	GKC §74i □ B-M 2.116
		30.26	GKC §97h, 114r, 134m, 134r; J-M §100o; Gib 51, 131
30.7	Dav §71R2; Gib 145 □ B-M 2.128; Berg 2.113h		
30.8	Dav §109R2; GKC §61f, 135p; J-M §64b □ B-L 339u; B-M 2.166; Berg 2.23g, 2.135e, 2.139p	30.27	B-L 612y
		30.28	GKC §72z, 85c, 115d; J-M §80n □ B-L 403, 486jε; Berg 1.120 n o, 2.106m
		30.29	IBHS 432 □ B-L 328y; Brock §144
30.9	GKC §114m □ B-L 542l; Berg 1.152a, 2.54d*		
30.10	B-L 600j'; Berg 1.139b; Gib 17	30.30	J-M §97Ca
30.11	GKC §102b; J-M §103d □ B-L 643v'; B-M 2.178	30.31	GKC §156d
		30.32	Berg 2.29i
30.12–13	Gib 87	30.33	GKC §32l □ Berg 1.144d, 2.113f
30.12	Dav §96, 147; GKC §61d, 111v, 114d, 114r; J-M §65c; IBHS 556, 605; Gib 102, 130, 131, 158, □ B-L 354f; B-M 3.58; Berg 2.38g, 2.116d	31.1	Dav §105R2; IBHS 668; Gib 137
		31.2	GKC §141f
30.13	GKC §116d, 133k n 1	31.3	Dav §105R2; GKC §75u □ Berg 2.166m

B-L: Bauer and Leander, *Historische Grammatik*   **B-M**: Beer, *Grammatik*   **Berg**: Bergsträsser, *Grammatik*
Brock: Brockelmann, *Syntax*   **Dav**: Davidson, *Syntax*   **GAHG**: Richter, *Grammatik*
Gib: Gibson, *Davidson's Syntax, 4th ed.*   **GKC**: *Gesenius' Grammar*   **IBHS**: Waltke and O'Connor, *Syntax*
Jen: Jenni, *Lehrbuch*   **J-M**: Joüon and Muraoka, *Grammar*   **Ros**: Rosenthal, *Grammar*
Sch: Schneider, *Grammatik*   **Wms**: Williams, *Syntax*

31.4	Dav §151; IBHS 641 □ B-L 210f; Gib 161
31.5	Dav §55b, 86R4; GKC §67p, 113h n 2, 113t; J-M §54c n 3, 123n, 123p; IBHS 582; Gib 94, 125, 126 □ B-M 2.144; Berg 2.64f, 2.65 n h, 2.79h, 2.132a*, 2.135d; Brock §93a
31.6	Dav §10R2; GKC §138f n 2, 144p; J-M §158i; Gib 10, 62
31.7	GKC §135n □ Berg 2.20b; Gib 33
31.8	Dav §128R1; GKC §108b, 125c, 152a n 1; J-M §160k; Gib 142
31.9	Berg 2.134c
32.1	GKC §143e □ Berg 2.134d; Brock §38a, 49b
32.2	Dav §23, 24c; J-M §129e; Gib 31, 33
32.3	Brock §138
32.4	Dav §14; IBHS 104; Gib 17
32.5	B-L 502eε
32.6	GKC §107g; J-M §113c
32.7	GKC §115i, 154a n 1b □ B-L 502eε
32.8	Dav §14, 111; Gib 17
32.9	GKC §44o; IBHS 258 □ B-L 303d', 362a'; Berg 2.118c, 2.146f
32.10	Wms §418 □ B-M 3.12; Brock §52bβ
32.11	Dav §113; GKC §46f, 48i, 67o, 110k; Gib 18 □ B-L 305g, 351, 353v, 425; B-M 2.114; Berg 2.20a, 2.135e, 2.171 n d
32.12	Dav §108; GKC §116s, 144i; J-M §89n, 155f; Gib 13
32.13	Dav §28R3; GKC §128c; J-M §164b; Gib 141
32.14	IBHS 374 n 30 □ B-L 287n'; Berg 2.88c
32.15	GKC §112p; Gib 93
32.16	GKC §44c □ Brock §138
32.17	GKC §113c; J-M §123b; IBHS 591 □ B-M 3.62; GAHG 3.73 n 190; Berg 2.62 n b
32.18	GKC §124e; J-M §136g; IBHS 121, 257
32.20	IBHS 87 n 13
33.1	Dav §83R2; GKC §20h, 53q, 53u, 67v, 120b, 156f; J-M §157g; IBHS 374 n 29; Gib 121 □ B-L 228a', 386m', 439p', 442e; B-M 2.117, 3.82; Berg 1.68v, 2.87c, 2.105 n k, 2.122 n a, 2.140q
33.2	J-M §137i; IBHS 245
33.3	GKC §67dd
33.4	Dav §67R1; GKC §85h, 116t; J-M §155f □ B-L 491kζ; Brock §37
33.5	GKC §116s; J-M §154c □ Berg 2.71g
33.6	Dav §28R1, 106d; GKC §130b; J-M §129s
33.7	GKC §75u; J-M §102c □ B-M 2.157; Berg 2.166m; Brock §93g
33.9	Dav §116R6; GKC §29q, 44c, 145t; J-M §150j; Gib 24, 63 □ B-L 232j, 312t; B-M 2.115; Berg 1.161e, 2.77c
33.10	Dav §40b; GKC §54c, 133l □ B-L 405; Berg 1.109 n c, 2.52o, 2.92h, 2.99 n d
33.11	B-L 336f; B-M 2.166
33.12	GKC §20i □ B-L 218c, 383; Berg 1.69bN, 2.130m
33.14	Dav §73; GKC §84ᵃs, 107t, 117bb; J-M §97Ca, 130g; IBHS 170
33.15	GKC §117r n 4, 119z, 124e; IBHS 121
33.16	Dav §73; GKC §124b; J-M §96Dd
33.17	Berg 1.148g
33.18	IBHS 328
33.19	Berg 1.157o, 2.128 n g, 2.173 n g
33.20	GKC §152t
33.21	Berg 2.131o
33.22	GKC §140a; Gib 55
33.23	B-L 563v
33.24	Dav §98R1; GKC §116k; J-M §121o □ Brock §77f; Gib 134
34.3	Berg 1.121r, 2.106n; Gib 28
34.4	Dav §22e, 67R1; GKC §67t, 126o; J-M §82m, 137i; IBHS 245 □ B-L 366t, 431t; B-M 2.135; Berg 2.136h(bis)

B-L: Bauer and Leander, *Historische Grammatik*   **B-M**: Beer, *Grammatik*   **Berg**: Bergsträsser, *Grammatik*
Brock: Brockelmann, *Syntax*   **Dav**: Davidson, *Syntax*   **GAHG**: Richter, *Grammatik*
Gib: Gibson, *Davidson's Syntax, 4th ed.*   **GKC**: *Gesenius' Grammar*   **IBHS**: Waltke and O'Connor, *Syntax*
Jen: Jenni, *Lehrbuch*   **J-M**: Joüon and Muraoka, *Grammar*   **Ros**: Rosenthal, *Grammar*
Sch: Schneider, *Grammatik*   **Wms**: Williams, *Syntax*

34.5	GKC §52k		36.8	Dav §20R4; GKC §127f, 134g; IBHS 249; Gib 91 □ B-L 356s; GAHG 3.215 n 815
34.6	GKC §54h; J-M §53h; IBHS 432 □ B-L 285j′, 329d′; Berg 2.99 n g			
			36.9	Dav §27, 35R2; GKC §119s, 119u, 126u; Gib 35, 46 □ B-M 3.81
34.7	GKC §52k; IBHS 422 □ B-L 583y′			
34.8	J-M §136i; IBHS 121; Gib 33 □ Brock §19b		36.11	GKC §2a, 2q n 1 □ B-L 13a; B-M 1.11; Berg 1.2e
34.9	GKC §84ᵃs		36.12	B-L 77n, 583x′; Berg 1.92 n g
34.10	Dav §34R4; GKC §102i, 133i; J-M §103c; IBHS 267; Gib 46		36.13	B-L 13a, 156k′; B-M 1.11; Berg 1.2e
34.11	GKC §21c, 80g □ B-L 383; Berg 1.106b, 1.144d, 2.77c		36.14	GKC §74l; J-M §78i □ B-L 374n, 441c; B-M 2.156; Berg 2.52 n n, 2.157b
34.12	Wms §425			
34.13	Dav §73R2, 116; GKC §117z, 145k; J-M §125o, 150g; Gib 23 □ Brock §50c		36.15	GKC §121b n 1; Wms §59 □ Brock §35e
			36.16	Dav §20R4; GKC §110f, 127f; Wms §82, 190; IBHS 249 □ GAHG 2.17 n 51; Brock §62a, 73c
34.14–15	IBHS 670 n 93			
34.14	B-M [R] 2.34			
34.15	J-M §147c □ B-L 479jγ; Berg 2.97h		36.17	GKC §114r □ Brock §145bζ
			36.18	Dav §127c; J-M §168g n 3; Wms §461; Gib 160
34.16	Dav §11Rc; Gib 14 □ B-L 226r, 341m′; Brock §16g			
			36.20	IBHS 319; Gib 7
34.17	GKC §59g □ Berg 2.18f		36.22	J-M §121o □ Brock §71a, 77f
35.1–2	IBHS 570 □ Berg 2.53q		37.3	GKC §69m, 114l n 5, 152k; IBHS 661; Gib 33, 35 □ B-L 156k′; GAHG 3.173 n 562; Berg 2.57l, 2.126c
35.1	Dav §65R6; GKC §47n; Gib 78, 104 □ B-L 405; Berg 2.48f, 2.151 n r			
35.2	Dav §28R1, 41R1, 65R6, 86R3; GKC §117q, 130b; IBHS 167; Gib 68, 104, 125		37.4	GKC §132h □ Brock §152a
			37.8	GAHG 3.102 n 289
35.3	Dav §31; J-M §148a; IBHS 257; Gib 43 □ Brock §59a		37.11	GKC §150a; J-M §161a □ Brock §54a
35.4	GKC §65f, 69v □ B-L 384c′; Berg 2.118d		37.14	GKC §124b n 1
			37.16	Dav §106R2; GKC §141h; IBHS 298 n 30; Gib 2, 55
35.6	B-M 2.144; Gib 68			
35.7	GKC §135p		37.17	GKC §10g, 132h □ B-L 208r; Berg 1.124w
35.9	Dav §32R5; GKC §84ᵇf, 132c; J-M §141d □ B-M 2.30			
			37.18–19	Brock §46c
35.10	Berg 2.17e		37.18	IBHS 663
35.11	B-L 13a		37.19	GKC §113f, 113z; J-M §123x; IBHS 595 n 57 □ Berg 2.67m
35.13	B-L 13a			
36–39	IBHS 17		37.22	Dav §22R3, 24a, 28R6; GKC §130e; J-M §129f, 129r; IBHS 104; Gib 29, 32, 36 □ B-L 398e″; Berg 2.146e; Brock §70d
36	B-L 73d			
36.2	GKC §128w n 1; J-M §137s; IBHS 240			
36.4	Brock §93e		37.23	GKC §44g, 117c □ B-L 315n′
36.5	GKC §44i □ B-L 370q; Gib 39		37.24–26	Berg 2.33 n b-h
36.6	Dav §54a; IBHS 388; Gib 94		37.24	GKC §91e, 128r; J-M §129k
			37.25	GKC §124e

B-L: Bauer and Leander, *Historische Grammatik* **B-M**: Beer, *Grammatik* **Berg**: Bergsträsser, *Grammatik*
Brock: Brockelmann, *Syntax* **Dav**: Davidson, *Syntax* **GAHG**: Richter, *Grammatik*
Gib: Gibson, *Davidson's Syntax, 4th ed.* **GKC**: *Gesenius' Grammar* **IBHS**: Waltke and O'Connor, *Syntax*
Jen: Jenni, *Lehrbuch* **J-M**: Joüon and Muraoka, *Grammar* **Ros**: Rosenthal, *Grammar*
Sch: Schneider, *Grammatik* **Wms**: Williams, *Syntax*

37.26	GKC §23f, 75qq, 112oo, 114k, 117ii; J-M §24fa; Gib 114 □ B-L 445p, 643s'; Jen §28.3.3; Berg 1.92 n g, 2.60o
37.27	B-L 573x
37.28	GKC §114c; J-M §124c; Wms §193; Gib 128 □ Berg 2.55d*
37.29	Dav §56, 90R1, 147; GKC §112nn; Wms §535; Gib 87, 158
37.30	Dav §60R2, 88; GKC §66c, 91c, 110c, 113z, 113ee, 126b; J-M §114p, 123x; IBHS 246; Gib 127 □ B-L 278h'; Berg 1.112d, 2.50k, 2.671
37.32	Brock §123f
37.33	Berg 2.127e
37.38	GKC §111g, 116u □ Berg 2.70e*
38.3	GKC §16f n 1, 157c □ GAHG 3.215 n 815; Brock §93g, 160b
38.5	GKC §50e, 113bb, 155f; J-M §123u n 2 □ B-M 3.63; Berg 2.66k, 2.85 n r
38.7	Dav §146; J-M §157c, 157e □ Brock §161a
38.9	GKC §114r; J-M §124q; Gib 30 □ Berg 2.38g
38.10	Dav §80; GKC §108g, 121d; J-M §96As, 114c n 2, 128c; Gib 83, 118 □ B-L 577i'; B-M 3.11; Berg 2.50l; Brock §34b
38.12	B-L 93c; Berg 2.45n
38.13	J-M §137i □ Jen §26.3.2; Berg 2.167o
38.14	GKC §48i n 2, 61f n 1; J-M §82k, 137i □ Berg 2.81i, 2.109c, 2.133 n a, 2.134c
38.15	Dav §58R1, 101Rd; GKC §30m, 55g; IBHS 425; Gib 149 □ B-L 265c
38.16	GKC §75mm, 103g, 135p, 144f; J-M §155b □ B-L 971, 423, 640f'; Berg 2.162d
38.17	Dav §101; GKC §119ff. □ Brock §52bβ
38.18	Dav §98R1, 128R6; GKC §116h, 152z; J-M §121n, 160e, 160q; IBHS 148, 617; Gib 31, 134 □ B-L 436; GAHG 3.97
38.20	94; GKC §86i, 114i; IBHS 212, 610; Gib 131 □ B-L 203q Nachtr.; B-M 3.60; Berg 2.59 n mop; Brock §47
38.21	Berg 2.164g; Gib 96
38.22	Gib 96
39	B-L 73d
39.1	Dav §48c, 48R2; GKC §111q, 124b n 1; Gib 96, 101 □ Berg 1.44 n c
39.2	GKC §15f n 1, 126x; J-M §15j □ Berg 2.69d
39.3	Dav §29R1; IBHS 227; Gib 40, 185
39.6	GKC §112t, 112x; J-M §119n
40	Gib 3
40.1–11	Gib 179
40.1–2	Sch §48.5.3
40.1	Dav §40b; GKC §107f; J-M §123d n 1; IBHS 473, 506 □ Berg 1.5l; Brock §175
40.2	J-M §100o □ Brock §106c
40.3	GKC §146b; J-M §15k, 162e; IBHS 470; Gib 179
40.4	GKC §93v □ B-L 203p, 582v'; B-M 2.71
40.6	GKC §112qq, 127c; J-M §119z, 162e; Gib 13, 53, 91
40.7–8	Gib 62
40.7	Dav §40c; J-M §112d; IBHS 473, 488, 670 n 97; Gib 52, 53, 141, 179 □ GAHG 2.33 n 133; Brock §35a
40.8	Dav §40c; J-M §112d; Gib 31
40.9	GKC §119s; IBHS 208 n 78, 570; Gib 32, 180 □ B-L 113q'
40.10	Dav §101Ra; GKC §119i; J-M §133c; IBHS 652 □ Brock §106g
40.11	GKC §93x; Gib 180 □ B-L 588l; Berg 1.103o
40.12	GKC §73b □ B-M 2.90; Gib 7, 172
40.14	Dav §17R2; GKC §124e; Gib 20 □ Berg 2.128g; Brock §19b
40.15	B-L 367, 577i'; Gib 59
40.17	Dav §34R3, 80, 127d; J-M §132f; Wms §406; IBHS 265 n 22; Gib 46, 118

B-L: Bauer and Leander, *Historische Grammatik*   **B-M**: Beer, *Grammatik*   **Berg**: Bergsträsser, *Grammatik*
Brock: Brockelmann, *Syntax*   **Dav**: Davidson, *Syntax*   **GAHG**: Richter, *Grammatik*
Gib: Gibson, *Davidson's Syntax, 4th ed.*   **GKC**: *Gesenius' Grammar*   **IBHS**: Waltke and O'Connor, *Syntax*
Jen: Jenni, *Lehrbuch*   **J-M**: Joüon and Muraoka, *Grammar*   **Ros**: Rosenthal, *Grammar*
Sch: Schneider, *Grammatik*   **Wms**: Williams, *Syntax*

40.18	Dav §8R2; GKC §15c, 15c n 4, 75dd; Gib 7, 8 □ B-L 412a'; Berg 1.131d, 2.166m	41.7	Dav §72R4; GKC §29f, 117c; J-M §121n, 125h; IBHS 144; Gib 116 □ B-L 548a'; Berg 2.85r
40.19	GKC §119hh; J-M §113o n 2, 154c	41.8	GKC §138d; J-M §158n □ Brock §153a
40.20	Dav §24R5, 44R3, 143; GKC §52n, 121d, 155f, 156g; Wms §540; Gib 10, 34, 76 □ B-L 328y	41.9	Brock §138
		41.10	GKC §75bb; IBHS 664; Gib 38, 175 □ B-M 2.123; Berg 2.164i
40.21	IBHS 685; Gib 62, 184 □ Berg 2.148k	41.11	GKC §128t, 135n; IBHS 654; Gib 59 □ Berg 1.101m
40.22–23	IBHS 622	41.12	GKC §135n; Wms §425 □ B-L 346x''
40.22	Dav §99R2; GKC §126b; J-M §138e; Gib 135 □ B-L 93c; Brock §42c	41.14	Brock §77b; Gib 2, 32
40.23	Dav §99R2; Wms §406; Gib 135	41.15	Dav §24R3; GKC §96 (p. 286); J-M §96Cb, 98e; IBHS 149 n 27 □ B-L 620s; Berg 1.140c, 2.134d
40.24	Dav §49a; GKC §29w; Wms §386, 413; IBHS 375, 393, 555; Gib 101, 175 □ B-L 281j, 287n'; B-M 2.126; Berg 2.29i, 2.37b, 2.87c, 2.108 n b, 2.126d	41.16	Berg 2.152t; Brock §138; Gib 78
		41.17	GKC §20i □ B-L 368t; Berg 1.69y
40.25	Dav §40b, 65d; GKC §75dd, 108d, 150m; J-M §116c; Gib 7, 106 □ Berg 2.166m; Brock §175	41.20	Dav §14R2, 53R1; Wms §589; Gib 93, 159 □ Brock §127
40.26	Dav §69R2, 101Rc; GKC §124e; J-M §136g; IBHS 121	41.21	Berg 1.139 n b
		41.22	B-L 339z
40.27	Dav §45R1, 53R1; Gib 93	41.23	Dav §63R1; GKC §48g n 1, 75l, 75v, 109d; J-M §79o, 79p; IBHS 425; Gib 82 □ B-L 409l, 590h; B-M 2.123, 2.159; Berg 2.21 n c, 2.22f, 2.115a, 2.116b, 2.162 n f
40.28	Berg 2.126d(bis); Gib 52		
40.29	GKC §152v; J-M §136f, 136g, 160o		
40.30	Dav §59, 132R2; GKC §69q, 113w; J-M §123p; IBHS 582; Gib 104 □ Berg 2.63e, 2.63f, 2.126d	41.24	Dav §34R3, 144; GKC §155n; J-M §157a, 158d; IBHS 265 n 22; Gib 11, 46 □ B-L 487 n 4; B-M 3.13, 3.97; Brock §141, 147
40.31	GKC §8k; IBHS 415	41.25	Dav §60R4, 144; GKC §23d, 72x, 76d; J-M §24e, 80m; Gib 11 □ B-L 404, 442g; Berg 1.91 n bd, 2.120 n c, 2.148k, 2.163g
41.1	Dav §101; GKC §119gg, 135r; J-M §133b; IBHS 668 □ B-M 2.113		
41.2	Dav §22R2, 144; GKC §35n n 1, 75gg, 155n; Gib 11, 28 □ B-L 376r; B-M 2.162; Berg 2.165k, 2.174 n h	41.26	Dav §65d; GKC §48c, 108d; J-M §116b n 1, 116c; IBHS 575; Gib 106, 175 □ B-L 581; Berg 2.49k
41.3	GKC §118q	41.28	Dav §63R1, 65d, 132b; GKC §109h, cf. 159d; J-M §114g; Gib ‡82, 106, 156 □ Berg 2.21c, 2.33 n b-h, 2.163f
41.4	Dav §106R2; GKC §135a n 1; J-M §154j; IBHS 520; Gib 3 □ Berg 2.45n; Brock §67b		
41.5–7	Gib 75	41.29	J-M §96Ad
41.5	Dav §45R2; GKC §47m, 75u; J-M §44e, 113h; IBHS 516 □ B-L 442g; Berg 2.21b, 2.166m	42	B-L 101 n 4

B-L: Bauer and Leander, *Historische Grammatik*   **B-M**: Beer, *Grammatik*   **Berg**: Bergsträsser, *Grammatik*
Brock: Brockelmann, *Syntax*   **Dav**: Davidson, *Syntax*   **GAHG**: Richter, *Grammatik*
Gib: Gibson, *Davidson's Syntax, 4th ed.*   **GKC**: *Gesenius' Grammar*   **IBHS**: Waltke and O'Connor, *Syntax*
Jen: Jenni, *Lehrbuch*   **J-M**: Joüon and Muraoka, *Grammar*   **Ros**: Rosenthal, *Grammar*
Sch: Schneider, *Grammatik*   **Wms**: Williams, *Syntax*

42.1	GKC §155i □ B-L 101u; B-M 2.112; Brock §35b; Gib 61	42.24	Dav §6R3, 9R1, 84; GKC §113d, 114m n 1, 138g, 142f n 2; J-M §123b n 1; IBHS 337, 597; Gib 123 □ Berg 2.61b; Brock §150b
42.2	Dav §73R5; Wms §589; Gib 110 □ B-L 113q'; Brock §127b		
42.3	Wms §274; Gib 18 □ B-L 302a'	42.25	GKC §107b n 2, 110b n 2, 131k
42.4	GKC §67q; Gib 172 □ B-L 438; Berg 2.80 n h, 2.140 n q	43	B-L 101 n 4
42.5	GKC §65d, 93ss, 124k, 154a n 1b; J-M §136e n 1; IBHS 123; Gib 19 □ Jen §10.4.5	43.1	GKC §61h, 74e, 91d; IBHS 618 n 28; Gib 14 □ B-L 373d; B-M 2.154; Jen §23.5.4.10; Berg 1.148g, 2.156a
42.6	Dav §65R6; GKC §107b n 2, 109k; J-M §114g; IBHS 567; Gib 104 □ B-L 197l', 279 n 1, 301 n 4; B-M 3.91; Berg 2.21 n c, 2.33 n b-h	43.2	GKC §159dd, 159ff.; J-M §167p; Gib 154
		43.3–4	J-M §158m n 2
42.7	Dav §31; GKC §84b, 84n; IBHS 257; Gib 43 □ B-L 614; B-M 3.30	43.3	Gib 61 □ B-M 3.52, 3.106; Berg 2.27e
		43.4	Dav §92; J-M §170i; Wms §319, 534; IBHS 641; Gib 131, 159 □ Jen §20.3.3; Sch §53.4.3; Brock §163a, 176a
42.9	Gib 17, 59, 172		
42.11	GKC §122i; J-M §134g □ Berg 2.153u		
42.13	GKC §126p; Wms §386	43.6	GKC §122v; J-M §48b, 134l; Gib 17, 170 □ B-M 2.135; Berg 2.123d
42.14	IBHS 108 □ Brock §139a		
42.15	Gib 78	43.7	GKC §116x □ Brock §147
42.16	Dav §143; J-M §125ba n 2, 158c; Gib 11, 78 □ B-M 3.97; Brock §148	43.8	GKC §53m, 69v, 74l; J-M §78i □ B-L 443i; B-M [R] 2.48; GAHG 3.173 n 559; Berg 2.104i, 2.157b
42.17	Dav §67b; GKC §117q; Gib 115		
42.18	Dav §21j; GKC §35g, 126e, 126f; IBHS 130; Gib 27 □ B-L 263g	43.9	Dav §41R5; GKC §51o, 106n n 2, 106n n 3, 136b; Gib 7, 69 □ B-L 322v; Berg 2.92 n gh
42.19	GKC §126f □ Brock §168; Gib 39	43.10	Dav §106R2; GKC §70a, 135a n 1; J-M §154j; Gib 3 □ Berg 2.128g
42.20	GKC §75n, 144p; J-M §79p; IBHS 594 □ B-L 101u, 426; Berg 2.161 n c	43.11	Gib 1
		43.12	Dav §146R4; Gib 2 □ Berg 2.43 n b-k, 2.45n; Brock §67b
42.21	Dav §83R1; GKC §120c; J-M §157b; Gib 121 □ B-M 1.93; Berg 1.154e, 2.112d; Brock §143a	43.13	Dav §14R2, 32R2, 106R2; GKC §135a n 1; IBHS 110; Gib 3, 44, 175 □ Brock §16e
42.22	Dav §88R3, 88R5; GKC §29q, 63d, 72y, 119hh, 124q; J-M §124q n 4; Wms §13; IBHS 452; Gib 127 □ B-L 110i', 396r'; Berg 1.161e, 2.149m	43.14	GKC §93qq; IBHS 532; Gib 68, 93, 102 □ Berg 2.44l
		43.16	Berg 2.69c
		43.17	B-L 649l; Berg 2.69c; Gib 18, 75, 179
42.23	Gib 7	43.18	Gib 17
		43.19	Gib 59, 91
		43.20	IBHS 227 □ B-M 3.35; Brock §65a
		43.21	GKC §138g

B-L: Bauer and Leander, *Historische Grammatik* **B-M**: Beer, *Grammatik* **Berg**: Bergsträsser, *Grammatik*
Brock: Brockelmann, *Syntax* **Dav**: Davidson, *Syntax* **GAHG**: Richter, *Grammatik*
Gib: Gibson, *Davidson's Syntax, 4th ed.* **GKC**: *Gesenius' Grammar* **IBHS**: Waltke and O'Connor, *Syntax*
Jen: Jenni, *Lehrbuch* **J-M**: Joüon and Muraoka, *Grammar* **Ros**: Rosenthal, *Grammar*
Sch: Schneider, *Grammatik* **Wms**: Williams, *Syntax*

43.22	GKC §117e		44.24	GKC §65d; J-M §138e; IBHS
43.23	GKC §76h; J-M §68f, 125u □			618 n 28 □ Jen §10.4.5
	B-L 445p; Berg 2.128h,		44.25	B-M 2.147; Berg 2.137k; Gib
	2.147 n k; Brock §94b			137
43.24	Gib 176		44.26	Jen §27.4.9; Berg 2.151r; Gib
43.25	Dav §106R2; GKC §136d, 141h;			137
	J-M §154j; IBHS 298; Gib 1 □		44.27	GKC §46d, 63l, 126b □ B-L
	GAHG 3.80 n 219; Sch §44.4			11k', 208t, 352; Berg 2.81k,
43.28	Dav §24c, 51R6; GKC			2.114i
	§107b n 2, 107k n 2; Gib 32,		44.28	Dav §96R4; GKC §53n, 114p;
	105 □ GAHG 3.107 n 303			Gib 132 □ B-L 122r
44.1	IBHS 653; Gib 62		45.1	Dav §96; GKC §67p, 114r; J-M
44.2	IBHS 618 n 28			§82l, 124q; Gib 131 □ B-L
44.3	GKC §71			430o; Berg 2.117a, 2.135 n f,
44.5	Brock §106d			2.174 n h
44.7	IBHS 618 n 28 □ B-L 156k'		45.2	GKC §70b □ Berg 1.99h, 2.117a
44.8	Dav §145; IBHS 442, 660 n 58;		45.3	J-M §137l □ B-L 534; Berg
	Gib 57			1.145d
44.9	GKC §5n; IBHS 618 n 28 □ B-L		45.4	Dav §50b, 139; GKC §111b n 2,
	79s; Berg 1.5l			131g; Gib 97
44.10	Berg 2.60p		45.5	Dav §139; Gib 58 □ B-L 644c'';
44.11	IBHS 618 n 28			Berg 2.121d
44.12ff.	Berg 2.29i; Gib 38, 174		45.6	GKC §90e, 91e, 152s; J-M §94h
44.12	Dav §49b; GKC §71; IBHS 492,			□ B-L 252l, 557h'
	559 □ Berg 2.128e		45.7	GKC §29e n 1 □ GAHG
44.13	Dav §49b; GKC §64i; IBHS 170			1.87 n 233
	□ B-L 122r, 357; Berg 2.115a		45.9	Dav §45R1; GKC §152u; Gib
44.14	Dav §93 □ B-L 107e', 495jŋ;			148 □ B-L 100q, 115c; Berg
	Berg 2.59 n mop			2.153t
44.15	GKC §66e, 103f n 3 (p. 302),		45.10	Dav §45R1; GKC §47o; IBHS
	117ii; J-M §103f; IBHS 527 □			516 □ B-M 2.100; Berg 2.19a
	B-L 100q, 368u; B-M 3.59; Berg		45.11	Berg 2.77c
	2.59o, 2.124 n g, 2.134 n d		45.12	J-M §146a, 146e, 156b; IBHS
44.16	Dav §117; GKC §67ee; IBHS			300, 671 □ B-L 441e; Berg
	683; Gib 188 □ B-L 100q,			2.167o
	156k', 430m; B-M 2.144; Berg		45.13	GKC §72x; J-M §80m □ B-L
	2.134c, 2.134 n d			404; Berg 2.117a
44.18	GKC §145o; IBHS 618 n 28 □		45.14	Dav §127d; GKC §10g □ B-L
	B-M 3.21; Berg 2.150p			208r, 574x, 581; Berg 1.124w,
44.19	GKC §150a, 152d □ B-L 107e';			2.99e
	Berg 2.34h		45.15	IBHS 671 □ GAHG 2.33 n 133,
44.20	B-M 2.147; Berg 2.138n, 2.162d			3.176 n 599
44.21	Dav §73R4; GKC §20f, 57 n 2,		45.17	Dav §16, 67b; GKC §117q,
	117x; IBHS 169; Gib 4 □ B-L			117r; J-M §128a, 132e; IBHS
	344h''; GAHG 1.93 n 265			382 n 10; Gib 18, 115
44.22	Berg 2.146e		45.19	Dav §69R1 □ Berg 2.97h
44.23	GKC §67ff; J-M §125o; IBHS		45.20	GKC §135r □ B-L 122r; Berg
	77 n 15 □ B-M 2.145; Berg			2.100h
	2.134c		45.21	GKC §152k □ IBHS 443 □ B-L
				644c''; GAHG 3.121

B-L: Bauer and Leander, *Historische Grammatik* **B-M**: Beer, *Grammatik* **Berg**: Bergsträsser, *Grammatik* **Brock**: Brockelmann, *Syntax* **Dav**: Davidson, *Syntax* **GAHG**: Richter, *Grammatik* **Gib**: Gibson, *Davidson's Syntax, 4th ed.* **GKC**: *Gesenius' Grammar* **IBHS**: Waltke and O'Connor, *Syntax* **Jen**: Jenni, *Lehrbuch* **J-M**: Joüon and Muraoka, *Grammar* **Ros**: Rosenthal, *Grammar* **Sch**: Schneider, *Grammatik* **Wms**: Williams, *Syntax*

45.22	GKC §110c, 110f; J-M §116f; Wms §519; Gib 105 □ GAHG 3.175 n 593; Berg 2.50k
45.23	Dav §120; J-M §165b; Gib 187
45.25	B-L 436; B-M 2.122; Berg 2.99g
46.2	GKC §139f n 5
46.3	J-M §103d □ B-L 115c
46.4	Dav §106R2; GKC §106c, 135a n 1; J-M §154j; Gib 3 □ B-L 115c
46.5	GKC §75dd □ Berg 2.166m
46.6	GKC §116x, 126b; J-M §138e
46.7	J-M §155e □ Brock §114b
46.9	Dav §127d; GKC §152s □ GAHG 3.175 n 593
46.11	GKC §106c □ Berg 2.26b; Gib 175
46.12	B-L 122q, 642q'
46.13	IBHS 402; Gib 68
47.1	Dav §83R1, 140; GKC §120c, 122i, 152u; J-M §177c; IBHS 104; Gib 120 □ B-M 3.82; Brock §70d, 139a
47.2	GKC §46d, 63l; J-M §21e □ B-L 115c, 347g, 352; Berg 1.122t, 1.130c, 2.114k
47.3	GKC §109a n 2; J-M §114g n 1; IBHS 569; Gib 38 □ Berg 1.160a, 2.49h, 2.164h
47.5	GKC §100g n 2, 118o, 120c; J-M §126a, 177c
47.6	IBHS 668
47.7	GKC §94g, 135o; IBHS 305; Gib 3
47.8	Dav §127d; GKC §90l, 144p, 152s; J-M §160n; Gib 13, 28, 58
47.9	Dav §36R4, 41R1; J-M §152g; IBHS 276; Gib 48, 68 □ Berg 2.83p
47.10	Dav §127d; GKC §59g, 61h, 75v, 90l, 91f, 116f, 152s; J-M §66b, 121k, 160n; IBHS 618; Gib 134 □ B-L 344f", 588l; Berg 2.68a, 2.162d
47.11	Dav §139; GKC §145o; J-M §150j □ Brock §50a
47.12	Dav §9R3; GKC §110a, 110d, 138f; J-M §158m, 158m n 3; IBHS 663; Gib 141 □ B-L 353v; Berg 2.48f, 2.84q, 2.118c; Brock §152d
47.13	GKC §91l; J-M §94j, 158m n 2 □ B-L 253b', 600i'; B-M 2.57
47.14	GKC §28b, 59g, 67cc, 152z; J-M §160q □ B-L 436; Berg 2.18f, 2.139 n p
47.15	GKC §138f □ Berg 2.118c, 2.166n; Brock §152d*
48.1	GKC §144p □ Gib 137
48.3	Dav §51R6; GKC §107b n 2 □ Berg 2.33 n b-h; Brock §122q
48.4–5	Gib 97
48.4	GKC §111g; J-M §170i; Gib 53
48.5	Berg 1.134c; Gib 73
48.6	IBHS 127 n 5, 441 n 21; Gib 17 □ Berg 2.18f
48.7	B-M 3.51; Berg 2.18f, 2.25b
48.8	Dav §146R3; GKC §52k, 157a; J-M §123k; IBHS 374 n 30; Gib 111, 175 □ B-L 287n'; B-M 2.155; Berg 2.88c
48.9	Dav §101; GKC §119hh; J-M §132g
48.11	GKC §67t; J-M §82m □ Berg 2.136i
48.12	Dav §106R2; GKC §135a n 1; J-M §154j; IBHS 374 n 30; Gib 3 □ B-L 287n'; GAHG 2.12 n 30; Berg 2.88c; Brock §67b
48.13	Dav §132R2; Gib 156
48.14	GKC §119hh; IBHS 223 □ GAHG 3.179 n 618
48.17	GKC §61h, 93qq, 155h □ Berg 1.157o(bis), 2.58n, 2.95d
48.18	Dav §39d, 134; GKC §111x, 151e; J-M §163c; IBHS 146, 680 □ Jen §24.3.3.1
48.19	Berg 1.90c
48.20	Dav §49b; Gib 102
48.21	Dav §49b; Gib 102
48.22	Brock §175
49.1	B-L 94 n 2
49.2	IBHS 394, 452
49.3	B-L 355m

B-L: Bauer and Leander, *Historische Grammatik* **B-M**: Beer, *Grammatik* **Berg**: Bergsträsser, *Grammatik*
Brock: Brockelmann, *Syntax* **Dav**: Davidson, *Syntax* **GAHG**: Richter, *Grammatik*
Gib: Gibson, *Davidson's Syntax, 4th ed.* **GKC**: *Gesenius' Grammar* **IBHS**: Waltke and O'Connor, *Syntax*
Jen: Jenni, *Lehrbuch* **J-M**: Joüon and Muraoka, *Grammar* **Ros**: Rosenthal, *Grammar*
Sch: Schneider, *Grammatik* **Wms**: Williams, *Syntax*

49.4	Dav §71R2; IBHS 671; Gib 145, 148 □ GAHG 2.33 n 133; Brock §122g	50.5	J-M §80l □ B-L 193q; Berg 2.147i
49.5	GKC §114r; IBHS 436 □ B-M 2.67	50.6	Berg 2.69c
		50.7	IBHS 484, 556 □ Berg 2.113h
49.6	Dav §34R2, 111R2; GKC §67t, 115a, 142f n 2; IBHS 532; Gib 45, 63 □ Berg 2.40d; Brock §122i	50.8	GKC §15c, 20f; J-M §27d, 121k; IBHS 149 n 27; Gib 7, 8, 33, 134 □ Berg 1.130c; Brock §154
		50.9	Dav §144R1; GKC §136c; J-M §144a n 1; Gib 7, 11
49.7	GKC §111q; IBHS 422 n 12; Gib 92 □ Berg 2.37a, 2.161c	50.10	Dav §73R1; GKC §137c; J-M §121l □ Brock §89, 164d
49.8	GKC §71 □ B-L 367; Berg 2.127e	50.11	Dav §101Rb; GKC §20n, 93bb; Gib 7, 59 □ B-L 563x; Berg 1.140 n a, 2.20b
49.9	GKC §110c □ Berg 2.125b	51.1	Dav §143; GKC §155k; J-M §158c; IBHS 338, 375, 420; Gib 11 □ B-L 287n'; Jen §8.3.2.2; Berg 2.88c; Brock §148
49.11	GKC §145u		
49.13	GKC §126o; J-M §125o □ Berg 2.152t		
49.14	Berg 2.117a; Gib 62		
49.15	GKC §119y, 160b; IBHS 107; Gib 175 □ B-M 3.104f; Berg 1.68v; Brock §16a	51.2	Dav §44R3, 51R6; GKC §59g n 1, 60f, 107b, 107b n 2; J-M §158a* n 1; Gib 71, 105 □ Berg 2.33 n b-h
49.18	GKC §32c; IBHS 512 □ B-L 248d	51.3	GKC §146e; IBHS 268
49.19	GKC §67dd, 133c □ B-L 438; Brock §111g	51.5	J-M §91c
		51.6	Berg 1.107e
49.20	J-M §136h; IBHS 121; Gib 58, 77 □ B-M 2.143; GAHG 3.170 n 533	51.7	J-M §158b
		51.8	Gib 28
49.21	Dav §138b; GKC §52l, 72p; J-M §161k; IBHS 620; Gib 7, 168, 185 □ Berg 1.108e, 2.95d, 2.146 n g	51.9	Dav §101Rd, 106R2; GKC §72s, 118u, 124q; IBHS 298 n 30; Gib 2 □ B-L 398e''; Berg 1.127cc, 1.133h, 2.145e
49.22–23	GKC §122v	51.10	Dav §22R4, 106R2; GKC §93pp, 117ii, 138k; J-M §145e; IBHS 298 n 30; Gib 2, 29
49.22	Berg 2.157c		
49.23	GKC §122f n 1, 138d, 156c, 156c n 2; J-M §158n □ Berg 1.106d, 2.118c	51.11	Gib 33
		51.12	Dav §44R3, 51R3, 106R2; GKC §61h, 96i, 111m, 111v, 141h; J-M §118h n 1, 154j, 155f, 158a; IBHS 298 n 30, 561; Gib 1, 76, 97 □ B-M 3.9; Berg 1.157o(bis)
49.25	IBHS 663 n 73; Gib 174		
49.26	GKC §135l; J-M §125d; Gib 13		
50.1	GKC §122i, IBHS 327; Gib 59 □ Berg 1.106c, 2.159g	51.13	Dav §51R3; GKC §52k
		51.14	Berg 2.118b
50.2	Dav §65R6, 86a, 126R4, 128; GKC §109k, 117ii, 133c, 150m, 152y; J-M §114l, 123f, 161k, 170i; IBHS 266, 587; Gib 59, 124 □ Berg 2.51l, 2.57l	51.15	GKC §65d; J-M §118r, 177n □ Berg 1.155f, 2.38 n e
		51.16	GKC §66b, 69n; J-M §77a n 2 □ B-L 363h, 383; B-M 2.139; Berg 2.21d, 2.123c, 2.126d
50.4	Dav §72R4, 75; GKC §117c; J-M §125h; Gib 113, 116 □ Berg 1.144d	51.17	GKC §128q; IBHS 146 □ Brock §133b

B-L: Bauer and Leander, *Historische Grammatik*   **B-M**: Beer, *Grammatik*   **Berg**: Bergsträsser, *Grammatik*
Brock: Brockelmann, *Syntax*   **Dav**: Davidson, *Syntax*   **GAHG**: Richter, *Grammatik*
Gib: Gibson, *Davidson's Syntax, 4th ed.*   **GKC**: *Gesenius' Grammar*   **IBHS**: Waltke and O'Connor, *Syntax*
Jen: Jenni, *Lehrbuch*   **J-M**: Joüon and Muraoka, *Grammar*   **Ros**: Rosenthal, *Grammar*
Sch: Schneider, *Grammatik*   **Wms**: Williams, *Syntax*

51.19	Dav §8R1; GKC §47b, 122q, 75rr; J-M §152g □ Berg 1.102n; Brock §55c, 127b
51.20	B-L 535f; Berg 1.92e
51.21	Dav §28R1, 98R1; GKC §50f, 130b □ GAHG 3.215 n 815
51.23	IBHS 361 n 35 □ Berg 2.113f, 2.170 n c
52.1	GKC §120c, 120h □ B-L 398e"; Berg 2.145e
52.4	J-M §125n, 155s
52.5	GKC §53q, 55b, 70d; J-M §76d n 2; Gib 91 □ B-L 198g, 229f', 366t, 382; B-M 2.126; Berg 2.99 n d, 2.105 n k, 2.108 n b
52.6	Dav §106R2; Wms §115; IBHS 298 n 30 □ Brock §30a
52.7	GKC §75x, 106g; J-M §162a; Gib 63 □ B-L 422t"; Berg 1.90 n bd, 2.28g, 2.107 n a
52.8	GKC §5c n 1, 117a n 2, 146b
52.11	GKC §67t; J-M §125b □ B-M 2.146; Berg 2.136i
52.12	GKC §60f, 61h □ Berg 2.20b, 2.95d
52.13	IBHS 145, 668
52.14–15	GKC §161b
52.14	GKC §93q, 144p; J-M §96Λj; Gib 161 □ B-L 582u', Berg 1.154e
52.15	Dav §10, 41R1; Gib 68, 161
53.1	GKC §151a
53.2	Dav §65c; GKC §166a; J-M §116c, 159oa; Gib 106 □ B-L 352; Berg 2.112c
53.3–4	IBHS 671
53.3	Dav §28R4, 100R7; GKC §50f, 96, 128q; J-M §99b n 1; IBHS 620 n 37; Gib 138 □ B-L 616d; B-M 2.80; Berg 2.88d, 2.104h
53.4	Dav §28R4, 76, 98b, 118; GKC §116l, 117ii; J-M §121p; Wms §45; IBHS 143, 419 n 4, 617; Gib 31, 114, 134, 141 □ B-L 111k'; B-M 2.161; GAHG 2.33 n 133, 3.176 n 599

53.5	Dav §3, 39R1, 101Rc, 109; GKC §121a, 128q; J-M §128ba, 132f n 1, 152fa; Wms §44; IBHS 146, 210, 384; Gib 4, 31, 148 □ B-L 122r, 480sγ, 598; B-M 3.83; Jen §28.3.3; Berg 1.139 n b; Brock §35c
53.6	Dav §22e; GKC §126o; IBHS 205; Gib 28, 64, 101, 172
53.7	Dav §22e, 138b; GKC §155g; Gib 28, 119 □ B-L 122q; Berg 2.112d
53.8	GKC §103f n 3 (p. 30); J-M §103f □ B-L 115c; Berg 2.151s
53.9	Dav §101Rd; GKC §160c; J-M §171e; Wms §288, 531; Gib 149 □ B-L 583w'; B-M 3.105; Brock §145a
53.10	GKC §74k, 75ii; IBHS 497 n 2 □ B-L 424; Berg 2.55d*, 2.146f, 2.168 n q
53.11	Dav §32R1, 83R5; GKC §117n, 120h, 132b; IBHS 210, 223, 262; Gib 44
53.12	J-M §170g; Wms §344; Gib 159
54.1ff.	GKC §122i
54.1	GKC §67ff., 144p, 155f; J-M §125o, 134g, 158n; IBHS 77 n 15; Gib 28 □ B-L 429j; B-M 2.145; GAHG 3.78 n 207; Brock §93f
54.2	B-L 115c
54.4	GKC §91l; J-M §94j, 136h □ B-L 253b', 606k
54.5	GKC §124k, 124k n 4; J-M §136e, 158b; IBHS 123; Gib 19
54.6	GKC §58g; J-M §61i; IBHS 121; Gib 33 □ B-L 376r
54.8	Brock §175
54.9	GKC §119y; Gib 132
54.10	GKC §103b; J-M §80b n 3, 103j, 171b □ B-L 642o'; B-M 3.105; Brock §167, 175
54.11	Dav §100R3; GKC §144p, 152a n 1; Gib 28, 138 □ B-L 122q, 287o', 357; Berg 2.96 n f, 2.115a
54.12	GKC §21d; J-M §125w n 2 □ Berg 1.106a, 1.135c

B-L: Bauer and Leander, *Historische Grammatik* **B-M**: Beer, *Grammatik* **Berg**: Bergsträsser, *Grammatik*
Brock: Brockelmann, *Syntax* **Dav**: Davidson, *Syntax* **GAHG**: Richter, *Grammatik*
Gib: Gibson, *Davidson's Syntax, 4th ed.* **GKC**: *Gesenius' Grammar* **IBHS**: Waltke and O'Connor, *Syntax*
Jen: Jenni, *Lehrbuch* **J-M**: Joüon and Muraoka, *Grammar* **Ros**: Rosenthal, *Grammar*
Sch: Schneider, *Grammatik* **Wms**: Williams, *Syntax*

54.14	Dav §60R2; GKC §54c, 110c; IBHS 572; Gib 81 □ B-L 403; Berg 1.109 n c, 2.99 n d	56.9	Dav §22R3; GKC §29t, 76d, 90o; J-M §93r; Gib 29 □ B-L 410q; Berg 1.156m, 2.121d
54.15	Dav §130R3; GKC §137c, 159w; Gib 8, 155 □ Berg 2.147g	56.10	Dav §28R1, 90; GKC §130a; J-M §129m; IBHS 155 n 34; Gib 34, 128
54.17	IBHS 375 n 32 □ B-M 2.140; Berg 2.88c, 2.129i	56.12	GKC §29t, 76d □ B-L 410q; Berg 1.156m, 2.47e, 2.53q, 2.121d
55.1	IBHS 682	57.1	IBHS 384; Gib 62 □ B-L 111k'; Brock §145a
55.2	GKC §54k, 110g, 152a n 1; J-M §123l; IBHS 588 □ Berg 2.99e; Brock §125a	57.2	Dav §71R2; GKC §118q; Gib 145 □ Brock §89
55.3	GKC §93m; Gib 107 □ Berg 1.122t	57.3	Dav §144R4; Gib 12 □ B-L 423; Berg 1.113 n e, 2.115a
55.4	Dav §28R4; Gib 35	57.4	GKC §93m; IBHS 165 □ B-L 574y
55.5	Dav §143; J-M §61i, 133d; Gib 11 □ B-L 357; GAHG 3.294 n 768	57.5	GKC §67u □ B-L 434k'; Berg 2.125 n a-e
55.7	GKC §114n n 2; Gib 120 □ GAHG 1.78 n 169; Berg 2.48g, 2.59n*	57.6	GKC §20h; IBHS 664 □ B-L 212k, 556e'; Berg 1.68v, 2.167o
55.8	Gib 31, 53	57.8	Dav §116R6; GKC §47k, 75m, 145t; Gib 18 □ B-L 357; Berg 2.20 n a
55.9	Dav §151; GKC §106g, 161b; J-M §112a, 174e; Gib 63, 161 □ Berg 1.127cc, 2.28g; Brock §41b	57.9	IBHS 269 □ Brock §119c
55.10	Dav §51R2, 154; GKC §163c; J-M §173b; Gib 113, 176 □ Berg 2.41d	57.11	Dav §136R1; GKC §117e, 154a n 1b; Gib 37 □ B-L 122q; GAHG 3.161 n 480
55.11	Brock §151	57.14	IBHS 570 □ Berg 1.107e, 2.135e
55.12	J-M §125o □ B-L 332r, 333x	57.15	GKC §117k □ B-L 302a'; Berg 2.159f; Gib 11
55.13	Dav §44R3, 143; J-M §158a; Gib 10 □ B-L 107e'	57.16	B-L 302a', 353v
56.1	GKC §110a; IBHS 608 n 31; Gib 105, 170 □ Berg 2.57k	57.17	Dav §51R6, 87, 87R1; GKC §107b n 2, 113h; Gib 105, 126 □ B-L 277e'; Berg 2.33 n b-h, 2.65h*
56.2	GKC §155f; J-M §158a; Gib 10		
56.3	Dav §22R4; GKC §138k; J-M §145e; Gib 29 □ B-L 337n; Berg 2.23g	57.19	GKC §118p □ B-L 159o'; Brock §175
56.4	GKC §138f □ Brock §152d	57.20	Dav §32R2, 70a, 84; GKC §113d; J-M §123b, 123b n 1; IBHS 262, 597 n 63; Gib 44, 123 □ B-L 332t; Berg 2.61b
56.5	Dav §116R1; GKC §112mm, GKC §112mm; Gib 23 □ Jen §25.3.3		
56.6–7	GKC §143d	58.1	B-L 352
56.6	GKC §115d	58.2	IBHS 174; Gib 112 □ B-L 159o', 650p; Berg 2.55d*
56.7	GKC §135m, 135n; J-M §140b; IBHS 9 □ Berg 2.42g	58.3	GKC §19c, 20h, 150m; J-M §161k □ B-L 198l, 367; B-M 2.134; Berg 1.68v, 2.121a, 2.145d
56.8	GKC §20m □ GAHG 3.170 n 533; Berg 1.142 n f, 2.171 n d	58.4	B-L 228a'

B-L: Bauer and Leander, *Historische Grammatik*   **B-M**: Beer, *Grammatik*   **Berg**: Bergsträsser, *Grammatik*
Brock: Brockelmann, *Syntax*   **Dav**: Davidson, *Syntax*   **GAHG**: Richter, *Grammatik*
Gib: Gibson, *Davidson's Syntax, 4th ed.*   **GKC**: *Gesenius' Grammar*   **IBHS**: Waltke and O'Connor, *Syntax*
Jen: Jenni, *Lehrbuch*   **J-M**: Joüon and Muraoka, *Grammar*   **Ros**: Rosenthal, *Grammar*
Sch: Schneider, *Grammatik*   **Wms**: Williams, *Syntax*

58.5	GKC §113b □ B-M 2.141; Berg 2.130m, 2.136f; Gib 33
58.6–7	GKC §113f
58.6	Dav §88, 88R3; J-M §123b, 124q n 4; IBHS 592; Gib 123, 127 □ Berg 2.67l, 2.118b
58.7	GKC §112hh; J-M §123b, 124q n 4 □ B-L 122r
58.8	Brock §104
58.9	GKC §65a, 115b; J-M §70d, 119y n 2 □ B-L 233n, 359j; Berg 2.118 n b
58.10	Dav §65R6; Gib 104
58.11	Dav §78R5; Gib 17, 114 □ Berg 2.168p
58.12	Berg 2.88c
58.13	GKC §91k, 119hh; IBHS 419 n 4
58.14	GKC §54k; J-M §97Eb □ B-L 597h'; Berg 1.131d, 2.99e
59.1	GAHG 3.294 n 768
59.2	Dav §100R2; Gib 138 □ B-L 645h″; Berg 2.73i*; Brock §112
59.3	GKC §51h; IBHS 417 □ B-L 356v; Berg 2.92 n gh
59.4	Dav §84, 88R2; GKC §53k, 113ff; J-M §123w; IBHS 595; Gib 123, 127 □ B-M 3.64; Berg 2.67l, 2.105i, 2.160a; Brock §46b
59.5	GKC §73d, 80i; GKC §27u; J-M §125o □ B-L 512f', 512 n 3; Berg 2.111c
59.6	IBHS 426
59.8	Dav §116
59.9	GKC §93r; Gib 17
59.10	Dav §65R5; GKC §152v; J-M §160o; IBHS 404 n 28, 577; Gib 83 □ B-L 263g; Berg 1.142f, 2.50l, 2.97h; Brock §125a
59.11	J-M §123k
59.12–13	IBHS 592 □ Berg 2.67l
59.12	Dav §116; GKC §67k, 145k; J-M §149a, 150g; Wms §347; Gib 23 □ Berg 2.118c, 2.134c; Brock §106h
59.13	Dav §84, 88R2; GKC §52e, 72v, 75n, 113d; Gib 123, 127 □ B-L 288r', 423; B-M 2.152; Berg 1.139 n b, 2.92i, 2.128 n h, 2.147i, 2.161 n c
59.14	GKC §72ee □ Berg 2.151q
59.15	IBHS 425
59.16	GKC §59g □ Berg 2.18f
59.17	GKC §29u; J-M §125d; IBHS 168 □ B-L 496vη, 547; Berg 2.163g
59.18	GKC §118s n 2
59.19	Dav §140
59.20	GKC §116h; J-M §121n; IBHS 148; Gib 31
59.21	GKC §143a; J-M §156b □ B-M 3.14; Berg 1.106c; Brock §175
60.1	Berg 2.144b
60.2	GAHG 3.294 n 771
60.4	GKC §51m, 122v; Gib 68 □ B-L 351; Berg 2.20a
60.5	Berg 2.126 n d
60.6	Berg 1.135c
60.7	Dav §101Rd; GKC §60e; IBHS 218 n 111; Gib 149 □ B-L 338p, 582v'; Berg 2.24g
60.8	GKC §37a; IBHS 318 □ Berg 2.146f
60.9	GKC §58g; J-M §61i □ B-L 357
60.10	B-L 338p; Berg 1.148g, 2.24g
60.11	GKC §52k; Gib 168
60.14	Dav §24R6, 71R2; GKC §64e, 118q, 125h; J-M §126d, 131n; Gib 34, 145 □ Berg 2.65 n h, 2.115a, 2.133 n b; Brock §89
60.15	Berg 2.42g, 2.74l; Brock §114c, 176a
60.18	Berg 1.49d
60.20	Brock §138
61.1	GKC §84ᵇn, 117n; J-M §59d □ B-L 483oδ; Brock §145bβ
61.3	J-M §88Le
61.4	J-M §137i
61.6	B-L 403; Berg 2.129 n l
61.7	GKC §119hh, 144p
61.8	B-L 357
61.10–11	GKC §155g

B-L: Bauer and Leander, *Historische Grammatik*   **B-M**: Beer, *Grammatik*   **Berg**: Bergsträsser, *Grammatik*
Brock: Brockelmann, *Syntax*   **Dav**: Davidson, *Syntax*   **GAHG**: Richter, *Grammatik*
Gib: Gibson, *Davidson's Syntax, 4th ed.*   **GKC**: *Gesenius' Grammar*   **IBHS**: Waltke and O'Connor, *Syntax*
Jen: Jenni, *Lehrbuch*   **J-M**: Joüon and Muraoka, *Grammar*   **Ros**: Rosenthal, *Grammar*
Sch: Schneider, *Grammatik*   **Wms**: Williams, *Syntax*

61.10	Dav §22R2, 65R6, 73R3; J-M §125d; IBHS 596 n 60; Gib 73, 108, 150 □ B-L 135h, 424; Berg 1.65p, 2.47d, 2.52o, 2.151s, 2.173 n g	63.16	GKC §60d □ B-L 337n; Berg 2.23g
		63.17	Berg 2.162d
		63.19	Dav §39d, 134; GKC §67t, 151e, 155m; J-M §157a, 158d, 163c; Gib 69, 186 □ B-L 431t; GAHG 3.179 n 618; Berg 2.136h; Brock §8b, 149
61.11	Dav §22R2; GKC §155g; J-M §158a* n 2, 174d; IBHS 375 n 35 □ B-L 135h, 135i; Berg 1.107e, 2.88c		
		64.1	GKC §67t
62.1	Dav §44R3; GKC §155g; J-M §137i; Gib 76 □ B-L 135h, 135i, 302a'	64.2	GKC §155h □ B-L 431t; Gib 17
		64.3	GKC §75hh, 130a; J-M §29m; IBHS 155 n 34; Gib 34 □ B-L 425; Berg 2.161b, 2.165l
62.2	GKC §16f, 60a, 152g □ B-L 368t; Berg 1.133f, 2.79g		
		64.4	GKC §72cc; J-M §125h
62.3	B-L 135h	64.5–6	GKC §91k
62.4	Berg 1.107e	64.5	B-L 252r, 366t; Berg 2.172 n e
62.5	Dav §151; GKC §117r; J-M §125r, 174e n 1; Gib 161 □ Brock §93l	64.6	Berg 2.151 n r
		64.7	Gib 172
		64.8	J-M §160f; IBHS 567 □ B-L 333z; GAHG 3.170 n 522, 3.205 n 779, 3.215 n 815
62.6	J-M §139g n 1; Wms §595 □ B-L 577i'; Brock §7b		
62.8	B-L 135h; GAHG 3.171 n 539; Berg 1.107e, 1.138i	64.9	Dav §24R2; Gib 33
		64.10	Dav §24R2, 28R4, 116R2; GKC §146c; J-M §158j; Gib 23, 33, 35 □ B-L 436; Berg 2.97h
62.9	GKC §20m, 52p □ B-L 135h, 220m, 436; Berg 1.141 n a, 2.97h(bis)		
		64.11	GKC §54k
62.10	IBHS 570 □ Brock §22d	65.1	Dav §81, 144; GKC §51c, 155n; IBHS 338, 390; Gib 4, 11, 119 □ B-L 346x"; B-M 3.97; Berg 2.157c; Brock §147
62.11	IBHS 443		
62.12	Dav §100R3; GKC §152a n 1		
63.1	GKC §136c □ Berg 2.60p		
63.2	GKC §141d n 4; J-M §133h	65.2	Dav §99R1; GKC §126z, 152a n 1; J-M §138c, 138f, 148a; Wms §362; IBHS 407; Brock §60b; Gib 135
63.3–5	Dav §51R6		
63.3	Dav §65R6; GKC §53p, 76c, 107b n 2; Gib 105 □ B-L 356v; GAHG 1.116 n 348; Berg 2.33 n b-h, 2.105 n k, 2.163g		
		65.3	Gib 135
		65.4	Dav §29e; Gib 42
		65.5	Dav §73R4; GKC §117x; J-M §125ba n 2 □ Brock §97a
63.5–6	Gib 105		
63.5	Berg 2.33 n b-h		
63.6	Berg 2.33 n b-h	65.6	GKC §163c; J-M §173b
63.7	Dav §32R1; GKC §118s n 2; Gib 44	65.8	Gib 161
		65.11	GKC §35g □ B-L 263g; Berg 2.85r
63.8	Gib 141, 176		
63.9	B-L 348i	65.12	GKC §150m n 2; J-M §158m
63.10	IBHS 208; Gib 13, 103 □ Berg 2.45n	65.14	GKC §70d □ B-L 382
		65.16	IBHS 681 n 30 □ GAHG 3.177 n 600
63.11	Dav §28R3, 98c; GKC §116f, 128c; IBHS 618; Gib 134 □ Berg 2.68a; Brock §99a		
		65.17	GKC §29i n 1, 51m □ Berg 1.151a, 1.160a
63.13	GKC §116g, 125g		

B-L: Bauer and Leander, *Historische Grammatik*   **B-M**: Beer, *Grammatik*   **Berg**: Bergsträsser, *Grammatik*
Brock: Brockelmann, *Syntax*   **Dav**: Davidson, *Syntax*   **GAHG**: Richter, *Grammatik*
Gib: Gibson, *Davidson's Syntax, 4th ed.*   **GKC**: *Gesenius' Grammar*   **IBHS**: Waltke and O'Connor, *Syntax*
Jen: Jenni, *Lehrbuch*   **J-M**: Joüon and Muraoka, *Grammar*   **Ros**: Rosenthal, *Grammar*
Sch: Schneider, *Grammatik*   **Wms**: Williams, *Syntax*

65.18	Dav §60R2, 78R3; GKC §110a, 110c; Gib 81, 105, 114 □ Berg 2.152t	66.7	Brock §176a; Gib 73
65.20	Dav §71R1; GKC §75oo, 118q, 139h; IBHS 419 □ B-L 375; Berg 2.158e; Brock §134b	66.8	GKC §73a, 106b; J-M §112d; IBHS 375 n 32, 487; Gib 170 □ B-L 286m'; Jen §26.3.3; Berg 2.25b, 2.88c
65.23	GKC §69q □ Berg 2.126d; Gib 145	66.9	GKC §116q; J-M §137l □ Berg 2.16c, 2.41e, 2.69c
65.24	GKC §107c; Gib 72 □ Jen §27.3.2	66.10	Dav §67b; Gib 105, 115
65.25	IBHS 275	66.11	Berg 2.134d
66.1	J-M §143g, 158b □ Sch §52.4.3.3, 52.4.3.4	66.12	B-L 285h'; Berg 2.108c
		66.13	GKC §155d; J-M §158f
66.3	GKC §29f, 126i; IBHS 664 □ B-L 99o; Berg 1.71e	66.15	GKC §119i □ GAHG 3.294 n 771
66.4	B-L 598; Berg 1.145d	66.17	Berg 1.128dd
66.5	B-M 3.10; Berg 2.172 n e; Gib 138	66.18	GKC §167b
		66.20	Berg 2.109c
66.6	Dav §117R3; GKC §146b; J-M §162e	66.21	GKC §131h
		66.22	Berg 2.72h*

B-L: Bauer and Leander, *Historische Grammatik*   **B-M**: Beer, *Grammatik*   **Berg**: Bergsträsser, *Grammatik*
Brock: Brockelmann, *Syntax*   **Dav**: Davidson, *Syntax*   **GAHG**: Richter, *Grammatik*
Gib: Gibson, *Davidson's Syntax, 4th ed.*   **GKC**: *Gesenius' Grammar*   **IBHS**: Waltke and O'Connor, *Syntax*
Jen: Jenni, *Lehrbuch*   **J-M**: Joüon and Muraoka, *Grammatik*   **Ros**: Rosenthal, *Grammatik*
Sch: Schneider, *Grammatik*   **Wms**: Williams, *Syntax*

JEREMIAH

1–52	Brock §85a		2.9	GAHG 3.171 n 539
1.1	Gib 31		2.10	GKC §118f; J-M §125n, 155s □
1.2	Wms §37; IBHS 143			Brock §122k
1.5	Dav §45; GKC §71, 107c □		2.11	Dav §138a, 144; GKC §72e,
	B-M 2.139; Berg 2.127e,			155n; J-M §158d; Gib 11, 168 □
	2.173 n h			B-L 771, 403; Berg 2.173 n g;
1.6	Berg 2.28g, 2.54d*; Gib 120			Brock §147
1.7–8	Brock §22c		2.12	GKC §46d; Gib 52 □ B-L 352;
1.7	J-M §158i			Berg 2.80i, 2.135e
1.10	GKC §45g, 66b; IBHS 489 n 17		2.13	J-M §121q □ B-L 348h; Berg
	□ B-L 210f; B-M 2.116, [R]			2.114i
	1.63, 1.70, 2.116; Berg 1.122t,		2.14	Gib 184
	2.123c		2.15	GKC §44m, 145k, 152y; J-M
1.11	Dav §111R1 □ B-L 195a'			§150h, 160p □ B-L 383, 442e;
1.12	Dav §82; GKC §114n n 2; J-M			Berg 2.15b, 2.34h
	§102g, 124n; Gib 120 □ GAHG		2.16	Dav §71; GKC §117ll; J-M
	1.78 n 169, 3.111 n 312; Berg			§126g; Gib 145 □ Berg
	2.59n, 2.59n*			2.174 n h
1.13	GKC §90e		2.17	Dav §90R1, 100R6; GKC §114a,
1.14	Berg 2.117a			116g n 1; Gib 138 □ Berg
1.15	GKC §130a			2.55 n d
1.16	IBHS 181; Gib 117 □ Sch		2.18	Dav §8R3; Gib 8 □ GAHG
	§53.4.1			3.206 n 786
1.17	Berg 2.112d, 2.138l		2.19	Dav §90R1; GKC §60a, 110c;
1.18	J-M §125l, 133d; IBHS 211 □			J-M §63a; IBHS 105, 654; Gib
	GAHG 3.203 n 766; Berg			172 □ Berg 2.50k, 2.54d; Brock
	2.102d			§3, 16e
2.1–2	Sch §48.5.1		2.20	GKC §44h n 1; J-M §1 n 3 □
2.1	Dav §60R4			B-L 310k, 352, 368t; Berg
2.2	Dav §100R3, 101Rb; GKC			2.15 n a
	§49k, 113bb, 118p, 152a n 1;		2.21	Dav §32R2, 71R4, 101Rb; GKC
	J-M §136h, 160d; Wms §400;			§126z; J-M §146j; Gib 42
	IBHS 121, 619 n 34, 623; Gib		2.23	GKC §75m; Gib 185
	127, 138 □ Jen §10.3.3; Berg		2.24	GKC §60e, 122d; Gib 16 □ B-L
	2.17d, 2.66k; Brock §41c			338p; Berg 2.24g
2.5	Dav §8R2; J-M §144d; Wms		2.25	Dav §32R5; IBHS 583; Gib 44
	§450; IBHS 318 n 6, 323; Gib 8		2.26	GKC §154a n 1a
2.6	Dav §143; GKC §155i; J-M		2.27	Dav §22R3, 55c; GKC §44d,
	§158db; Gib 11, 175			59h, 69s; J-M §62f, 126g; IBHS
2.7	Berg 2.21d			660 n 56 □ B-L 382; Berg 2.18f,
2.8	Dav §144; GKC §155n; J-M			2.78e
	§129q, 158d; IBHS 156, 338;		2.28	Dav §60R3; GKC §141d; J-M
	Gib 11 □ B-M 3.97; Berg			§125v, 154e; Gib 145
	1.109 n c; Brock §147		2.30	GKC §126p

B-L: Bauer and Leander, *Historische Grammatik*   **B-M**: Beer, *Grammatik*   **Berg**: Bergsträsser, *Grammatik*
Brock: Brockelmann, *Syntax*   **Dav**: Davidson, *Syntax*   **GAHG**: Richter, *Grammatik*
Gib: Gibson, *Davidson's Syntax, 4th ed.*   **GKC**: *Gesenius' Grammar*   **IBHS**: Waltke and O'Connor, *Syntax*
Jen: Jenni, *Lehrbuch*   **J-M**: Joüon and Muraoka, *Grammar*   **Ros**: Rosenthal, *Grammar*
Sch: Schneider, *Grammatik*   **Wms**: Williams, *Syntax*

2.31	Dav §21f; GKC §85h; Gib 27 □ B-L 503iι	3.15	Dav §87; GKC §53k, 113h; IBHS 598; Gib 126 □ Berg 2.65h, 2.105i
2.32	Dav §140; IBHS 661 n 61	3.18	GKC §75n □ B-L 108g′
2.33	GKC §44h; IBHS 663 n 73; Gib 175 □ B-L 329g′; B-M 1.118, 2.104; Berg 2.15a	3.19	GKC §133i; J-M §141l; IBHS 267; Gib 46, 79 □ B-L 71a′, 579p′; Berg 1.102 n o
2.34	Dav §116R6 □ GAHG 1.87 n 233; Berg 2.18f; Brock §124a	3.20	Dav §151; GKC §161b; J-M §174e; IBHS 641 n 28; Gib 161 □ B-M 3.101
2.35	GKC §114d; J-M §170h; Wms §291; IBHS 605 □ B-L 278i′; B-M 3.58	3.22	GKC §75pp, 75rr; J-M §1, 78g, 79l; IBHS 675 □ B-L 376r, 442g; B-M 2.155; Berg 2.159g, 2.168q
2.36	GKC §68h □ B-L 371r; Berg 1.91d, 2.120c, 2.121e, 2.144b, 2.173 n f	3.23	IBHS 670 n 98 □ GAHG 2.33 n 133
2.37	Dav §138a; J-M §136g, 159d; IBHS 121, 446; Gib 168 □ B-L 219g; Berg 1.139b	3.25	Dav §65R5; GKC §108g; J-M §45a □ B-M 2.113; Berg 2.46c
3.1	Dav §88R2; GKC §112p, 113q, 113ee, 159w; J-M §123w; Gib 92, 127 □ Berg 2.63d	4.1	GKC §143d
		4.2	GKC §10g; IBHS 680 □ Berg 1.124w, 2.16c
3.2	IBHS 328, 375 n 31 □ B-L 253b′, 287n′, 606k; Berg 2.88c	4.3	Dav §60; Gib 81 □ Berg 2.152t
3.3	GKC §29i n 1 □ Berg 2.54d*	4.4	Dav §60
3.4–5	GKC §44h	4.5	Dav §83R5; GKC §120h; J-M §177g; Gib 172 □ B-L 375; Berg 2.46c, 2.52o
3.4	B-L 376r; Berg 1.49d, 2.15a		
3.5	Dav §73R5, 116R6; GKC §47k, 66f, 69r, 117g, 145t; Gib 18, 110 □ B-L 198l, 329g′, 367, 382; Berg 2.15a, 2.20 n a, 2.121a; Brock §127b	4.7	Dav §128; GKC §20h, 93t, 154a n 1a; J-M §18k □ B-L 580r′; Berg 1.68v
		4.9	Berg 2.136h
3.6	GKC §74ii, 132b; J-M §161b □ B-L 423; Berg 2.20 n a, 2.160 n a	4.10	Dav §58b; Gib 103 □ GAHG 2.33 n 133, 3.176 n 599; Berg 2.157c
3.7	Dav §32R1; GKC §84ᵃk; Gib 44 □ B-L 240t′; Berg 1.120 n o	4.11	Dav §28R3, 95; GKC §67v; Gib 35 □ B-L 433d′; B-M 2.147; Berg 1.129b, 2.137k
3.8	GKC §GKC §84ᵃs, 91l, 158b □ B-L 253b′, 606k; B-M 3.101 Anm 2, 3.107; Berg 1.120 n o, 2.115a, 2.162f; Brock §162	4.12	Gib 175
		4.13	Dav §41a; GKC §67ee; Gib 63 □ GAHG 3.170 n 525; Berg 2.28g
3.9	GKC §29i n 1, 112ss; Gib 103	4.14	Dav §116; GKC §145k; J-M §150g; Gib 23, 185 □ B-M 3.20
3.10	Dav §32R1; GKC §84ᵃk; Gib 44 □ B-L 240t′; Berg 1.120 n o	4.16	GKC §111w; IBHS 562 □ Berg 2.38d
3.11	IBHS 404 □ B-L 294f‴; Berg 1.120 n o	4.17	GKC §117e □ B-L 588k; Berg 2.165l
3.12	GKC §49k, 72s □ B-L 367; B-M 2.105; Berg 2.16d, 2.66k; Gib 127	4.18	GKC §75n □ Berg 2.132a*, 2.160a
3.13	Berg 1.154e, 2.118c; Gib 176		
3.14	GKC §134s; Gib 48		

B-L: Bauer and Leander, *Historische Grammatik*   **B-M**: Beer, *Grammatik*   **Berg**: Bergsträsser, *Grammatik*
Brock: Brockelmann, *Syntax*   **Dav**: Davidson, *Syntax*   **Gib**: Gibson, *Davidson's Syntax, 4th ed.*   **GKC**: *Gesenius' Grammar*   **IBHS**: Waltke and O'Connor, *Syntax*
Jen: Jenni, *Lehrbuch*   **J-M**: Joüon and Muraoka, *Grammar*   **Ros**: Rosenthal, *Grammar*
Sch: Schneider, *Grammatik*   **Wms**: Williams, *Syntax*

4.19	Dav §65R5, 65R6; GKC §44h, 108g, 133l n 2; J-M §114c n 2, 133d, 133f; Gib 83, 188 □ B-L 362a'; Berg 2.15a, 2.152t	5.16	Gib 53
		5.17	B-L 640f'; B-M 3.31
		5.18	Dav §78R7
		5.21–22	Gib 75
4.20	B-L 439p', 581; Berg 1.142f, 2.96g	5.22	Dav §132R2; GKC §58i, 58k, 60e; J-M §61h, 63e; IBHS 428; Gib 156 □ B-L 338p, 339s; Berg 2.24g, 2.39 n a-f, 2.108 n b
4.21	Dav §65R5, 65R6; J-M §114c n 2; IBHS 577; Gib 83 □ Berg 2.50l		
		5.23	B-L 424
4.22	Dav §100R3; GKC §117e, 152d; J-M §160b; Gib 138 □ B-M 3.85	5.24	Gib 13
		5.25	GAHG 1.87 n 233
4.23	B-L 649l	5.26	GKC §67p; J-M §82l □ B-L 430o, 538i; Berg 2.135 n f
4.24	Berg 2.109c		
4.26	GAHG 3.171 n 539	5.28	GKC §117z
4.28	Dav §109R2; GKC §67aa □ B-L 430m; B-M 2.14; Berg 2.133b; Brock §110e	5.29	GKC §150h; J-M §158f, 161e
		5.31	B-L 132d; Berg 1.107e
		6.2	B-L 422t'', 599h; Berg 2.107 n a
4.29	GKC §127b; J-M §139g; Gib 68	6.3	Berg 1.156m
4.30	Dav §97R1, 141R3; GKC §32h, 145t □ B-L 248f; B-M 2.164; Berg 2.113f, 2.129l	6.4	GKC §10g □ B-L 132d, 565x; GAHG 1.93 n 265
		6.5	B-L 132d; Berg 2.47e
4.31	GKC §65e; J-M §112a; IBHS 443; Gib 188 □ B-L 383, 399h''; GAHG 2.34 n 145; Berg 2.104g, 2.117a, 2.143 n b, 2.129l, 2.172d, 2.173 n g	6.6	GKC §91e
		6.7	Wms §72; IBHS 70 □ B-L 132d, 438; Berg 2.137k, 2.140q
		6.8	Dav §100R3; GKC §51c, 152a n 1 □ Berg 2.174 n h
5.1	Dav §60R4, 125; GKC §150i; J-M §161f □ B-L 328a'; B-M 2.120, 3.67, 3.95; GAHG 3.173 n 555; Berg 2.97h	6.9	Berg 2.63e
		6.10	Dav §65R5; GKC §108g; J-M § n 2; IBHS 574; Gib 83 □ Berg 2.46d
5.2	GKC §68c		
5.3–5	IBHS 671	6.11	B-L 71a', 375; Berg 2.55d*, 2.157c
5.3	Berg 2.54d*		
5.4	Gib 176	6.12	J-M §82h □ Berg 2.17e, 2.136h
5.5	GKC §135a; J-M §114c □ Berg 1.124w	6.13–14	IBHS 562
		6.13	Dav §34; GKC §133g; J-M §146j; IBHS 270; Gib 45
5.6	GKC §20b, 67cc, 67ee; IBHS 375 n 31; Gib 63 □ B-L 439p'; Berg 2.28g(bis), 2.29i, 2.133b	6.14	Dav §101Rd; GKC §122q, 133l; J-M §134n; IBHS 218 n 11; Gib 149 □ B-L 376r; B-M 2.146; Berg 2.136h
5.7	Dav §8R4; GKC §65b, 152a n 1; J-M §143h; IBHS 328, 445 □ B-L 361a'; B-M 2.132; Berg 2.34h, 2.117a		
		6.15	Dav §86b, 96R5; GKC §114c, 116g n 1, 130d; J-M §129p(2); Wms §380; Gib 124, 174 □ Berg 2.54d*, 2.144b
5.9	Dav §11Re; J-M §147f, 158f; Wms §256; IBHS 430; Gib 14		
5.10	B-L 599h'	6.16	Dav §8R4, 32R2; J-M §110f, 114c n 3, 116f, 161g; IBHS 260 n 15, 327; Gib 44 □ Berg 2.50k
5.13	Dav §19R2; GKC §52o, 138i □ B-L 329j'; Berg 2.96 n f		
5.14	Berg 1.148g; Gib 158	6.17	GKC §112dd; J-M §118n
5.15	Dav §9R2, 143; Gib 11		

B-L: Bauer and Leander, *Historische Grammatik*   **B-M**: Beer, *Grammatik*   **Berg**: Bergsträsser, *Grammatik*
Brock: Brockelmann, *Syntax*   **Dav**: Davidson, *Syntax*   **GAHG**: Richter, *Grammatik*
Gib: Gibson, *Davidson's Syntax, 4th ed.*   **GKC**: *Gesenius' Grammar*   **IBHS**: Waltke and O'Connor, *Syntax*
Jen: Jenni, *Lehrbuch*   **J-M**: Joüon and Muraoka, *Grammar*   **Ros**: Rosenthal, *Grammar*
Sch: Schneider, *Grammatik*   **Wms**: Williams, *Syntax*

6.19	GKC §111h, 143d; J-M §176o; Gib 97 □ Jen §27.3.2; Brock §123f		7.21	GKC §69h n 1, 110a □ B-L 379q; Berg 2.127e
6.20	Dav §32R2; GKC §126x; Wms §73; IBHS 260; Gib 44 □ Berg 1.161d; Brock §60a		7.23	GKC §117gg; J-M §139e n 1
			7.24	Wms §267
			7.25	J-M §123r n 1
6.21	J-M §94h □ B-L 535f; B-M 2.53; Jen §9.4.11		7.26	GKC §156d □ B-M 3.92; Berg 2.137k; Brock §139a; Gib 110
6.22	B-M 2.151		7.27	GKC §49l □ Berg 2.43i
6.23	Gib 75		7.28	Berg 2.43 n b-k
6.25	Gib 172		7.29	GKC §67ff; J-M §129g □ Berg 2.134c
6.26	Berg 2.81k		7.31	GKC §144b; J-M §152c, 158q □ Berg 2.43 n b-k
6.27	Berg 1.160b			
6.28	GKC §133i; IBHS 267; Gib 46		7.32	GAHG 3.204 n 771
6.29	Dav §86c; GKC §67u, 113r; Gib 125 □ B-L 434k'; B-M 3.63; Berg 2.64g, 2.136 n h		8.1	GKC §128a; J-M §129b
			8.3	Dav §41c, 80; J-M §112i, 132f, 132f n 1; Wms §74, 162; IBHS 210, 259, 385 n 19, 491; Gib 67, 119 □ Brock §111g
7.1–2	Sch §48.3.4.4			
7.3	Gib 63			
7.4	GKC §133l n 2; Wms §39; IBHS 208; Gib 30 □ GAHG 1.87 n 233; Berg 2.133b		8.4	GKC §150m; J-M §161k; Gib 13
7.5	B-M [R] 2.65; Berg 2.105i		8.5	Dav §29R5, 67b; GKC §128c; J-M §48b n 1; Gib 115 □ B-L 233n, 614
7.6	Dav §109 □ Berg 2.52n			
7.8	Berg 2.60p		8.6	J-M §146j; IBHS 556; Gib 42, 101
7.9	Dav §55b, 88R2; GKC §51k n 2, 112o, 113ee; J-M §119s, 123w, 161b; IBHS 595; Gib 94, 127 □ B-L 323b', 362a'; Berg 2.67l, 2.92i		8.7	Dav §40c; GKC §91f; J-M §94h, 112d; IBHS 485; Gib 62 □ B-L 252p, 444p; B-M 2.54
			8.8	J-M §129a n 4; GAHG 2.33 n 133, 3.176 n 599, 3.204 n 771
7.10	Dav §55b; J-M §119s; Gib 94 □ Berg 1.161d			
7.11	J-M §112a □ GAHG 3.204 n 771; Berg 1.50g		8.9	Dav §7b; GKC §137b; J-M §144c; IBHS 317; Gib 7 □ B-L 265c; B-M 2.14
7.12	GAHG 3.215 n 815		8.10	J-M §146j; Gib 42
7.13	Dav §87R1; GKC §114r; J-M §13; J-M §123r n 3; IBHS 590; Gib 87, 126, 158 □ Berg 1.128dd, 2.38g, 2.65h; Brock §93g		8.11	GKC §23f, 75qq, 133l □ B-L 376r; Berg 1.91e, 2.159g
			8.12	Berg 2.54d*
			8.13	Dav §86R2, 144; GKC §72aa, 113w n 3; Gib 11, 125 □ Berg 2.64 n f, 2.173 n g
7.16–20	Jen §10.3.4			
7.16	Jen §10.1; Brock §116b			
7.17	Dav §122, 123; Gib 183		8.14	GKC §67dd; Gib 20 □ Berg 2.46c, 2.52o, 2.138l, 2.139p, 2.171 n d
7.18	Dav §88R1; GKC §113e; J-M §123x; IBHS 597; Gib 127 □ B-L 367; B-M 3.18; Berg 2.62b			
			8.15	Dav §88R2; GKC §113ff; J-M §123w; Gib 127 □ Berg 2.67l, 2.160a
7.19	Dav §11b; GKC §57 n 4, 135k, 142f(d) n 1 (p. 457); J-M §146k; Wms §130; Gib 13 □ Jen §12.3.3			

B-L: Bauer and Leander, *Historische Grammatik* **B-M**: Beer, *Grammatik* **Berg**: Bergsträsser, *Grammatik*
Brock: Brockelmann, *Syntax* **Dav**: Davidson, *Syntax* **GAHG**: Richter, *Grammatik*
Gib: Gibson, *Davidson's Syntax, 4th ed.* **GKC**: *Gesenius' Grammar* **IBHS**: Waltke and O'Connor, *Syntax*
Jen: Jenni, *Lehrbuch* **J-M**: Joüon and Muraoka, *Grammar* **Ros**: Rosenthal, *Grammar*
Sch: Schneider, *Grammatik* **Wms**: Williams, *Syntax*

8.16	Dav §28R1, 32R6, 49b; GKC §130a, 132 n 2; Gib 34, 45, 102 □ GAHG 2.50 n 237	9.22	Gib 105, 140
		9.23	Dav §72R1, 88, 108R1; GKC §113d, 113g, 144e; J-M §123t, 155d; Wms §222; Gib 116, 123 □ B-M 3.61, [R] 1.198; Berg 2.55 n d, 2.62b, 2.671, 2.105i
8.17	IBHS 409; Gib 91		
8.18	Dav §101Rd, 101 n 1 (p. 143); J-M §133f; Gib 149		
8.19	GKC §100m, 102m; J-M §102n, 162e □ B-L 632i; GAHG 3.175 n 581; Berg 1.148g	9.24	B-M 2.151
		10.2	GKC §103m □ B-L 644y'
		10.3	Dav §1R2; GKC §145u n 3; J-M §149c; Gib 23, 53
8.21	GKC §59g □ B-L 233j; Berg 2.119e	10.4	Dav §78R5; GKC §109g; J-M §116j □ B-L 548a'
8.22	Gib 57	10.5	Dav §84; GKC §23i, 47n, 75oo, 113b, 113w; J-M §123b, 123p; IBHS 582; Gib 123 □ B-L 441c; B-M 3.62; Jen §10.3.1.1; Berg 2.20 n a, 2.61b, 2.62c, 2.63f, 2.105i
8.23	Dav §65b, 135R3; GKC §151b; J-M §163d; Gib 106, 186		
9.1	Dav §65b, 135R3; GKC §108f, 151b; J-M §97Bc, 116c, 125ba; IBHS 576; Gib 106, 186		
9.2	GKC §53n, 119u; J-M §129a n 4 □ B-L 357; Berg 2.104 n h	10.7	GKC §122q, 144b □ Berg 2.156a
9.3–4	Brock §122o	10.9	IBHS 421 □ Berg 2.138 n n
9.3	GKC §29o n 2, 63c □ B-M 2.142; Berg 1.69x, 2.92g, 2.113f, 2.131o	10.10	Dav §116R4; GKC §132h, 141c; J-M §102d, 131c □ Sch §44.3; Berg 1.148g
9.4	GKC §53q, 67y, 113d; J-M §123b n 1, 124c; IBHS 392 n 33 □ B-L 229f', 439p'; Berg 2.55d*, 2.62b, 2.105 n k, 2.161c	10.11	GKC §1c; Ros §1, 17, 20, 32, 108, 121; IBHS 5 n 6 □ B-L 4f; B-M 1.11; GAHG 1.87 n 233; Berg 1.1d
		10.12	J-M §112l, 138e
9.5	Dav §96R3, 117g □ Berg 2.54d, 2.54d*	10.13	GKC §111v; J-M §112l; IBHS 501, 562; Gib 101, 102 □ Berg 2.161b
9.7	GKC §135m		
9.8	J-M §158f	10.14	Dav §101Rc; J-M §159oa
9.9	B-L 588l; B-M 1.101; Berg 2.140 n q	10.15	J-M §133i □ Berg 2.109c
9.10	IBHS 209	10.17	GKC §46d, 90n; J-M §93o □ B-L 371v, 526l, 614; Berg 1.122t, 2.15a
9.11	GKC §109i; J-M §161m, 169b; Gib 184 □ Berg 2.23g		
9.12	GKC §49k, 114r; J-M §124q, 170h; IBHS 611; Gib 131 □ B-M [R] 1.56, 2.168	10.18	GKC §67ee □ Berg 2.16c, 2.138l
		10.19	GKC §63c, 126y □ Berg 2.111b*
		10.20	Dav §73R1; J-M §125ba n 2, 125n; Wms §55; IBHS 170 n 17; Gib 58
9.14	Dav §29R7, 98c; GKC §131m, 134s; J-M §121k, 146e; IBHS 619; Gib 134		
9.16	B-L 444p; Berg 1.142f, 2.146f(bis)	10.22	GKC §146b; J-M §162e □ GAHG 3.203 n 766
9.17	Dav §73R2; GKC §74k, 117z; J-M §125d □ B-L 441c; Berg 2.158d; Brock §90d	10.23	GKC §72z □ B-L 403; Jen §27.3.3; Berg 2.149 n m
		10.24	GKC §152h; IBHS 567, 661 n 59
9.19	B-L 362a'		
9.21	Dav §136R1, 139; Gib 62, 136, 168	11.4	Berg 1.70b, 1.129b
		11.5	Berg 2.163g

B-L: Bauer and Leander, *Historische Grammatik*   **B-M**: Beer, *Grammatik*   **Berg**: Bergsträsser, *Grammatik*
Brock: Brockelmann, *Syntax*   **Dav**: Davidson, *Syntax*   **GAHG**: Richter, *Grammatik*
Gib: Gibson, *Davidson's Syntax, 4th ed.*   **GKC**: *Gesenius' Grammar*   **IBHS**: Waltke and O'Connor, *Syntax*
Jen: Jenni, *Lehrbuch*   **J-M**: Joüon and Muraoka, *Grammar*   **Ros**: Rosenthal, *Grammar*
Sch: Schneider, *Grammatik*   **Wms**: Williams, *Syntax*

11.6	J-M §119l		13.10	Dav §32R3, 65R6; GKC §52s,
11.7	Dav §87R1; GKC §113k; J-M			116x; J-M §52c, 143h; Wms
	§80m, 123r n 3; Gib 126 □ Berg			§74; Gib 137 □ B-L 220n, 356v;
	2.65h			B-M 1.114; Berg 1.112 n e,
11.8	Berg 2.21d, 2.108c			2.38e
11.10	Berg 2.137k		13.12	Dav §86b; GKC §113q, 133v;
11.15	GKC §53n, 90g, 91e; J-M §94h;			J-M §123f; Gib 124 □ Berg
	IBHS 302, 302 n 45 □ B-L 251j,			2.63d
	352, 599h'; B-M 2.10; Berg		13.13	J-M §130g
	2.104 n h		13.14	B-L 352; B-M 2.128
11.16	GKC §84^{a}g □ B-L 606i; Berg		13.16	GKC §112p, 122o, 144c, 145p;
	2.130m, 2.134c			IBHS 110; Gib 93 □ Berg
11.17	GKC §84^{a}a			1.123v; Brock §35a
11.18	Berg 2.23 n f, 2.34g, 2.106l		13.17	GKC §69p, 117z; J-M §136g □
11.19	GKC §45g; J-M §124s; Gib 150			B-L 383; Berg 2.125c
	□ B-L 210f; Berg 1.122t		13.18	Dav §82, 83; GKC §120g, 145p;
11.20	Berg 2.167o			J-M §150j; Gib 120 □ Berg
11.21	GKC §109g			1.112d, 2.125b
11.22	Gib 59		13.19	Dav §29R6, 116R5; GKC §75m,
12.1	Dav §104; J-M §121m; IBHS			118q; J-M §150e; Gib 24, 42 □
	73, 77, 261; Gib 43 □ Berg			Berg 2.165l; Brock §50b
	1.104r, 2.168p		13.20	Dav §142, 143; GKC §145m;
12.2	B-L 285e'; B-M 2.126; Berg			J-M §158a* n 2; Wms §540; Gib
	2.108 n b			10 □ B-M 3.96; Brock §146
12.3	GKC §112m; Wms §44, 279;		13.21	GKC §64a, 69m; IBHS 601 □
	IBHS 145, 527; Gib 33			Berg 1.156l, 2.15a, 2.120b,
12.4	Dav §116; GKC §145k; J-M			2.126c
	§150g; Gib 23 □ Brock §50c		13.22	B-L 94 n 2
12.5	GKC §55h; J-M §59e □ B-L		13.23	J-M §121m, 167m; Gib 128
	424; B-M 2.127; GAHG		13.25	GKC §65f, 65g □ Berg 1.119o,
	1.72 n 135; Berg 2.110e			1.154e, 2.118c
12.6	Dav §83R5, 106a; Gib 182 □		13.26	Berg 2.28e
	Brock §93n		13.27	Dav §24R4; IBHS 682; Gib 181,
12.7	Gib 62			182
12.8	Dav §73R6; GKC §119q; J-M		14.1	GKC §138e n 2
	§125m; Gib 110		14.2–6	Gib 62
12.9	GKC §68i □ B-L 442g; Berg		14.2	Berg 2.107a
	1.91d, 2.114k, 2.121d		14.4	Berg 2.105i
12.12	Dav §28R5; Gib 35		14.5	GKC §113y; Gib 126 □ B-L
12.14	B-L 368t			569p; Berg 2.67m
12.15	GKC §139b		14.6	GKC §145n
12.16	B-L 360p; Berg 2.118b		14.7	GKC §91k
12.17	Dav §87; J-M §123m; IBHS		14.8	Dav §143; Gib 10
	590; Gib 126		14.9	Dav §143; Gib 11
13.1	Berg 2.66k		14.10	IBHS 666; Gib 141
13.2	Berg 2.21d; Brock §137		14.12	J-M §171b □ Brock §164cẏ; Gib
13.4	Dav §20R2; GKC §127e; J-M			57
	§139b; IBHS 241 □ Brock §73a		14.14	J-M §125c
13.7	Dav §44b; GKC §107b, 152b		14.15	Dav §138c; GKC §142d

B-L: Bauer and Leander, *Historische Grammatik* **B-M**: Beer, *Grammatik* **Berg**: Bergsträsser, *Grammatik*
Brock: Brockelmann, *Syntax* **Dav**: Davidson, *Syntax* **GAHG**: Richter, *Grammatik*
Gib: Gibson, *Davidson's Syntax, 4th ed.* **GKC**: *Gesenius' Grammar* **IBHS**: Waltke and O'Connor, *Syntax*
Jen: Jenni, *Lehrbuch* **J-M**: Joüon and Muraoka, *Grammar* **Ros**: Rosenthal, *Grammar*
Sch: Schneider, *Grammatik* **Wms**: Williams, *Syntax*

14.16	Dav §100R2; GKC §103g; Gib 138 □ B-L 640f'
14.17	GKC §117q, 131e; J-M §122r; IBHS 382 n 10; Gib 36, 115, 118 □ Berg 2.47d, 2.172d; Brock §70b
14.18	Dav §130b; GKC §155h, 159p; IBHS 91; Gib 153
14.19	Dav §88R2; GKC §113ff; Gib 127 □ Berg 2.63d, 2.67l, 2.160a
14.22	Dav §106R2; GKC §141h; IBHS 298 n 30, 443 n 27; Gib 2
15.1	GKC §117m n 3; Wms §301, 454; IBHS 194 □ Brock §108a
15.2	Berg 2.43i
15.4	Berg 1.127cc
15.6–7	GKC §111w n 1
15.6	IBHS 386 □ Berg 2.55d*, 2.165k
15.9	Dav §24R6 □ Berg 2.45n
15.10	Dav §29R6; GKC §44d, 59h, 61h, 91c n 1; J-M §146j □ B-L 341i', 382, 438, 548a'; Berg 2.18f, 2.68a, 2.78e, 2.97h, 2.159g(bis)
15.11	Gib 187
15.12	Berg 2.135d
15.13	Dav §136R1; Gib 37 □ Brock §122q
15.14	GKC §63o; J-M §21i, 158a □ Berg 1.157n, 2.126d
15.15	Dav §32R5, 90; GKC §139b, 152h; J-M §160f; IBHS 567; Gib 44, 45, 128 □ B-L 441c
15.17	Berg 2.113f
15.18	Dav §126R7; GKC §50f, 102l □ B-L 639a'; B-M 2.129
16.3	B-M 1.105
16.4	Berg 1.144d; Brock §93l
16.6	Dav §108, 109; GKC §65e; Gib 13 □ B-L 362a'; Berg 2.99e, 2.117a
16.7	GKC §145m n 4; IBHS 121; Gib 31
16.8	Gib 144
16.12	Dav §82, 95; IBHS 661; Gib 120, 132 □ Berg 1.50g, 2.59n*
16.13	Dav §72R4; J-M §80m, 125h; Gib 116 □ Berg 2.148k
16.14	Dav §155; Gib 174

16.15	Dav §155
16.16	GKC §73b, 132b; J-M §141b; IBHS 259; Gib 44 □ B-L 293w; Berg 2.151 n s; Brock §58
16.18	J-M §170h
16.19	Wms §388 □ B-L 538i; Berg 1.145d
16.21	B-L 346u"
17.1	J-M §133d
17.2	Dav §32R2; GKC §28a, 45g, 126x; J-M §138c; Gib 44 □ B-L 210f, 600j'; B-M 2.116; Berg 1.122t
17.3	GKC §93aa □ B-L 564
17.4	J-M §68f, 158a □ Berg 2.112c, 2.126d
17.5–8	Dav §54a; Gib 89, 94
17.6	Dav §73 □ B-L 465h'''
17.7	GKC §93oo; Gib 11 □ Berg 1.139b
17.8	GKC §84^{a}t □ B-L 582u'; Berg 1.145d
17.9	IBHS 271
17.10	Dav §96R4; GKC §154a n 1b; J-M §124p, 147d; Gib 132
17.11	GKC §29i n 1, 161a; J-M §174h □ B-M 3.100
17.13	B-L 488rε; Berg 2.146 n g
17.14	J-M §114b n 1; IBHS 565 n 3
17.16	GKC §75z, 119x □ B-M 2.161; Berg 2.28g
17.17	GKC §75hh □ B-L 423; Berg 2.161b
17.18	Dav §62, 107; GKC §53m, 72y, 74l, 108c, 131q; J-M §78i, 114c, 146a; Wms §184; IBHS 295; Gib 2, 82 □ B-L 445p; B-M 3.11; Berg 2.46c, 2.49h, 2.104i, 2.157b; Brock §34b
17.19	Berg 2.66k
17.23	Dav §95; Gib 132 □ Berg 2.58n
17.24	Dav §95; J-M §123g; Gib 132 □ Berg 2.59n
17.25	J-M §159a
17.26	J-M §121l
17.27	Dav §95; Gib 132 □ Berg 2.16c
18.2	GKC §65h, 90d; J-M §93e; Gib 144, 145
18.3	J-M §102k; Gib 4, 59 □ B-L 653g

B-L: Bauer and Leander, *Historische Grammatik*　**B-M**: Beer, *Grammatik*　**Berg**: Bergsträsser, *Grammatik*
Brock: Brockelmann, *Syntax*　**Dav**: Davidson, *Syntax*　**GAHG**: Richter, *Grammatik*
Gib: Gibson, *Davidson's Syntax, 4th ed.*　**GKC**: *Gesenius' Grammar*　**IBHS**: Waltke and O'Connor, *Syntax*
Jen: Jenni, *Lehrbuch*　**J-M**: Joüon and Muraoka, *Grammar*　**Ros**: Rosenthal, *Grammar*
Sch: Schneider, *Grammatik*　**Wms**: Williams, *Syntax*

18.4	Dav §132a; J-M §118n, 167b; Gib 156 □ Berg 2.33 n e, 2.44k	20.7	Dav §73R4; GKC §91e, 116b; J-M §146j; Gib 42, 62 □ B-M 3.66; GAHG 1.86 n 220; Berg 2.55e, 2.164h
18.5	J-M §48b n 1		
18.7	GKC §45g □ Berg 1.122t		
18.8	Dav §132a; Gib 156	20.8	Dav §145; Wms §72, 510; Gib 158 □ Berg 1.50g
18.11	B-L 132d; GAHG 3.215 n 815		
18.13	J-M §129f □ B-M 3.33	20.9	Dav §32R4, 132a; GKC §21d, 112kk, 132d, 159g; J-M §148a n 1; IBHS 258 n 6; Gib 44, 94, 156 □ Berg 1.106a, 1.135c, 2.17d, 2.42g*, 2.55d*, 2.108c
18.15	Dav §100R3; J-M §160d; Gib 138		
18.16	Dav §73R6; GKC §119q; J-M §125m, 139i; Gib 110		
18.17	GKC §117ii n 1; J-M §126g; IBHS 660, 661 n 59		
		20.10	Dav §53R1, 65b; GKC §108f; J-M §116c; IBHS 419 n 4, 576; Gib 106, 141 □ B-L 557g'
18.18	Dav §62; GKC §108b; J-M §61f, 114e; Gib 82 □ Berg 2.47d(tris), 2.47e; Brock §6a		
		20.11	Dav §67R2, 143 □ Berg 2.117a
18.19	B-M 2.124	20.12	Berg 2.167o
18.20	J-M §124c □ B-L 581	20.13	B-L 436; Berg 2.97h
18.21	GKC §75w; Gib 134 □ Brock §110i	20.14	J-M §113h; IBHS 447, 569; Gib 82 □ Berg 2.49h
18.23	GKC §75ii □ B-L 424; Berg 2.160 n a, 2.164 n	20.15	GKC §59f, 156d; J-M §62c
		20.17	Dav §45R2, 48a; GKC §91e, 111l, 111x, 122n n 2; J-M §94h, 118h; IBHS 548; Gib 33, 62, 101, 158 □ B-L 598; Berg 1.120 n o
19.1	Sch §49.2.2; Gib 14		
19.3	GKC §67g □ Jen §27.3.2; Berg 2.80h, 2.134c		
19.5	GKC §144b; J-M §152c		
19.6	GAHG 3.204 n 771	20.18	Dav §45R2, 48a
19.7	B-L 434l'	21.1	Dav §91a; GKC §115i; Gib 129
19.8	GKC §91k	21.2	IBHS 93
19.9	GAHG 1.78 n 169; Berg 2.112c	21.3	Berg 2.21b
19.10–11	IBHS 667	21.4	Berg 1.45e, 2.137k
19.11	Dav §11Ra; GKC §75pp, 75qq □ B-L 376r; GAHG 3.171 n 539; Berg 2.159g	21.7	GKC §72r; J-M §80k □ B-M 3.92
		21.8	Gib 31
19.12	Dav §96R4; J-M §124p; Gib 132	21.9	Dav §55c; GKC §112t; IBHS 536; Gib 95 □ B-L 423; Brock §140
19.13	Dav §88R1; GKC §113z; IBHS 595 n 57; Gib 127 □ B-M 3.64; Berg 2.67m		
		21.12	J-M §88Ea1
		21.13	GKC §66f; Wms §303 □ B-L 198k; B-M 1.109; Berg 2.173 n f
19.15	GKC §74k; J-M §78f □ B-L 445p; Sch §49.3.6; Berg 2.58n, 2.158d		
		22.3	GKC §76f; J-M §88Ea n 1 □ Berg 2.52n
20.1	GKC §131b; J-M §125c		
20.4	B-L 423; B-M 2.162; Berg 1.148g, 2.106l	22.4	Dav §28R5, 116R1; J-M §130g
		22.5	GKC §106i; J-M §165b; Wms §164; Gib 61, 187 □ Berg 2.27e
20.6	GKC §118f; J-M §125m, 155s □ Jen §11.1; Berg 2.157c; Brock §122k		
		22.6	GKC §44m, 149b, 149c □ B-L 384c'; B-M 3.117; Berg 2.15b

B-L: Bauer and Leander, *Historische Grammatik*   **B-M**: Beer, *Grammatik*   **Berg**: Bergsträsser, *Grammatik*
Brock: Brockelmann, *Syntax*   **Dav**: Davidson, *Syntax*   **GAHG**: Richter, *Grammatik*
Gib: Gibson, *Davidson's Syntax, 4th ed.*   **GKC**: *Gesenius' Grammar*   **IBHS**: Waltke and O'Connor, *Syntax*
Jen: Jenni, *Lehrbuch*   **J-M**: Joüon and Muraoka, *Grammar*   **Ros**: Rosenthal, *Grammar*
Sch: Schneider, *Grammatik*   **Wms**: Williams, *Syntax*

22.10	Dav §86c; GKC §113r; J-M §123k, 123l; IBHS 208, 588; Gib 93, 125 □ GAHG 3.171 n 539; Berg 2.64g
22.12	GKC §130c; J-M §129q; IBHS 660; Gib 12 □ Brock §151
22.13	GKC §144p, 152a n 1; J-M §96Aj, 121l; Wms §400 □ B-L 582u'; Berg 1.154e
22.14	Dav §88R1; GKC §29q, 87g, 88c; Gib 127 □ Berg 2.66k
22.15	GKC §10g, 55h, 100n, 142g; J-M §118k, 166a n 1; IBHS 520 □ B-L 303e', 424; GAHG 1.72 n 135; Berg 1.135c, 2.45n, 2.110e
22.16	Dav §19; GKC §115d, 117r, 144p; J-M §124d n 2 □ Berg 2.55 n d, 2.55e
22.17	Dav §32R5; GKC §128w; Gib 44
22.18	Dav §117; GKC §144p, 147d; IBHS 682; Gib 188
22.19	Dav §67b, 87; GKC §113h, 117q; J-M §123r, 125q, 125q n 2; IBHS 75, 167, 589, 596; Gib 115, 126 □ Berg 2.65h*; Brock §120a
22.20	GKC §10h, 46d □ B-L 357; Berg 1.126aa, 2.81k
22.22	Berg 1.66s
22.23	GKC §23f, 23f n 1, 80d, 90n, 148b; J-M §82i, 89j, 93o □ B-L 351, 612z, 614; Berg 1.137 n g, 2.15a, 2.139o
22.24	Dav §120R5, 130R3; GKC §58i, 58k; J-M §61h; IBHS 518; Gib 155, 187 □ B-L 198l, 339s
22.25	B-M 2.117; Berg 2.85r
22.26	GKC §72k, 126z; IBHS 452; Gib 44 □ Berg 2.18f
22.28	GKC §10g; J-M §57a; IBHS 452 □ B-L 208r; B-M 1.112; Berg 1.124w, 1.135d, 2.106n, 2.150o
22.29	GKC §133l n 2
22.30	Dav §76, 83R2; GKC §120b; J-M §157g □ B-M 3.82
23.2	IBHS 613
23.4	GKC §8l
23.5	Berg 2.77d
23.6	GKC §20d, 60c, 60d, 74e □ B-L 337n, 376r; Berg 2.23g, 2.79 n g
23.8	GKC §90d
23.9	GKC §126p, 155h; J-M §137i, 158db; Gib 11
23.12	B-L 423; Berg 2.164 n
23.13	IBHS 360 n 30 □ B-L 198g, 440c; B-M 1.108; Berg 1.109 n c, 2.99 n d
23.14	Dav §55b, 149R2; GKC §112i, 113d, 113h n 2, 152x; J-M §119s, 124q n 4, 160l, 168c; IBHS 538; Gib 94 □ B-M 3.54; Berg 2.67l
23.15	Gib 134
23.17	Dav §86c; GKC §64e, 113r; Gib 125, 128 □ Sch §50.4.2; Berg 2.115a
23.18	Dav §65d; Gib 107
23.20	GKC §115g
23.22	Gib 153
23.23	GKC §130a; J-M §129l, 129n; IBHS 155
23.24	J-M §136j
23.25	J-M §125c
23.27	J-M §125u
23.28	Dav §71R2; IBHS 324; Gib 145 □ B-M 3.89
23.29	Dav §44R3, 143; GKC §29f, 155g; J-M §137i; Gib 11, 76 □ Berg 1.71e
23.30	Gib 134
23.32	GKC §52s, 53k □ Berg 1.129b, 2.105i
23.33–35	Sch §52.6.1, 52.6.2
23.33	GKC §117m n 3; Gib 154
23.34	Berg 2.40b
23.36	Dav §31, 116R4; GKC §132h; J-M §148a; Gib 43
23.37	GKC §58g, 75ll, 144h □ B-M 2.171; Berg 2.162d
23.38	GKC §68c; IBHS 640; Gib 158 □ Jen §20.3.3; Berg 2.82n, ‡2.114i
23.39	Dav §56, 86c; GKC §23l Gib 88, 124 □ Berg 1.44c, 2.159g(bis)
24.2	Dav §29e, 32R2; GKC §128m, 134l; J-M §142m, 154e; IBHS 152, 228; Gib 32, 42, 44 □ B-L 480uγ, 597h'; B-M 3.34; Berg 2.36k, 2.91g; Brock §14bβ, 60b

B-L: Bauer and Leander, *Historische Grammatik*   **B-M**: Beer, *Grammatik*   **Berg**: Bergsträsser, *Grammatik*
Brock: Brockelmann, *Syntax*   **Dav**: Davidson, *Syntax*   **GAHG**: Richter, *Grammatik*
Gib: Gibson, *Davidson's Syntax, 4th ed.*   **GKC**: *Gesenius' Grammar*   **IBHS**: Waltke and O'Connor, *Syntax*
Jen: Jenni, *Lehrbuch*   **J-M**: Joüon and Muraoka, *Grammar*   **Ros**: Rosenthal, *Grammar*
Sch: Schneider, *Grammatik*   **Wms**: Williams, *Syntax*

24.4	Berg 2.129i
24.7	GKC §115a; 115c; IBHS 600
24.8	Berg 2.35i; Brock §111h
24.9	J-M §112i n 3
25.3	GKC §53k, 113k; J-M §123r n 3; Gib 50 □ B-L 333g'; Berg 2.65h, 2.105i, 2.105 n k
25.4	Dav §87R1; GKC §112dd; J-M §123r n 3 □ Berg 1.127cc
25.5	Dav §64; GKC §110f; J-M §116f; Gib 105 □ Berg 2.48f, 2.50k
25.6	GKC §109g
25.9	J-M §143k; IBHS 309, 313 n 21; Gib 95 □ Berg 2.112c
25.11	IBHS 313 n 21
25.12	GKC §74h □ B-L 375; Berg 1.124w, 2.158e
25.13	GKC §76h, 117w; J-M §143k; IBHS 309, 313 □ Berg 2.17d, 2.148k
25.14	GKC §135g; IBHS 663 n 73
25.15	GKC §131k; J-M §119l; Gib 94
25.16	GKC §55b; IBHS 426 □ B-L 283t; GAHG 1.72 n 134; Berg 2.108 n b
25.26	Dav §20R4; GKC §127g; Wms §29 □ Brock §62a, 73c
25.27	GKC §76h □ B-L 445p; Berg 2.122c, 2.152 n t
25.28	Berg 2.160a
25.29	Dav §121; GKC §16b, 150a; J-M §161a; IBHS 582 n 12; Gib 183 □ B-L 323b'; B-M 2.161; GAHG 3.204 n 771; Berg 2.92i, 2.137k, 2.160a
25.30	Dav §67R3; Gib 115
25.31	Berg 2.71g
25.34	Dav §96R5; GKC §91l; J-M §124s; Gib 133 □ B-L 253x, 599h'; Berg 2.56f
25.36	GKC §24e; J-M §162e
25.37	Berg 2.136h, 2.171 n d
26.5	Dav §87R1; GKC §113k; J-M §123r n 3; IBHS 590; Gib 126 □ Berg 2.65h
26.6	GKC §8k, 34b; IBHS 307 n 5 □ B-L 261b; B-M 2.12; Berg 1.45e
26.7	GAHG 3.102 n 289

26.9	GKC §75qq; J-M §78g □ B-L 440c; Berg 2.158d
26.14	IBHS 676 n 9 □ Berg 2.49i
26.15	Gib 154, 187
26.17	J-M §147b
26.18	Dav §71R4; J-M §16f n 3, 97Eb, 121f, 128c; Gib 138 □ B-L 518c', 564
26.19	B-L 111k'; Berg 2.148l; Gib 124
26.20	B-L 581; Gib 138
26.21	Berg 2.54d*
27.2	B-L 122r
27.3	Dav §32R2, 99R1; GKC §126w; IBHS 622; Gib 44, 135, 144
27.4	GKC §49k □ Brock §108a
27.6	Brock §34b
27.7	Dav §1; GKC §135f; J-M §146d; Gib 2 □ GAHG 1.186 n 640
27.8	Dav §72R4, 91R4; GKC §152x
27.9	J-M §158e □ Berg 1.113 n e; Brock §152a
27.10	J-M §169g; IBHS 440
27.11	Berg 2.40b
27.12	Gib 105
27.15	J-M §125c, 169g; IBHS 639
27.16	Dav §69R2; GKC §90e; Wms §64; IBHS 186; Gib 145 □ Jen §25.3.2.7
27.18	Dav §69a, 149R2; GKC §72o, 76g; J-M §160l; Gib 143 □ GAHG 3.173 n 561; Berg 2.143 n b
27.20	GKC §53q □ B-L 228a'; Berg 2.105k
27.21	Gib 143
27.22	Berg 2.112c
28.1	GKC §134p; IBHS 284 □ Brock §60a
28.3	GKC §131d
28.4	GKC §132g
28.6	GKC §75t; J-M §79m □ GAHG 3.177 n 600; Berg 2.49h, 2.125b, 2.161b
28.7	Gib 176 □ GAHG 3.170 n 521, 3.215 n 815
28.8	GKC §111h; J-M §125c
28.9	Dav §9b, 146; GKC §127a, 157c, 157c n 3; J-M §145a, 157c; IBHS 334; Gib 9, 110 □ B-M 3.30, 3.99

B-L: Bauer and Leander, *Historische Grammatik*   **B-M:** Beer, *Grammatik*   **Berg:** Bergsträsser, *Grammatik*
Brock: Brockelmann, *Syntax*   **Dav:** Davidson, *Syntax*   **GAHG:** Richter, *Grammatik*
Gib: Gibson, *Davidson's Syntax, 4th ed.*   **GKC:** *Gesenius' Grammar*   **IBHS:** Waltke and O'Connor, *Syntax*
Jen: Jenni, *Lehrbuch*   **J-M:** Joüon and Muraoka, *Grammar*   **Ros:** Rosenthal, *Grammar*
Sch: Schneider, *Grammatik*   **Wms:** Williams, *Syntax*

28.10	GKC §93pp	31.1	Dav §29R7; GKC §75hh; Gib
28.11	GKC §131d		42 □ B-L 423; Berg 2.161b
28.16	Dav §21R1; GKC §61h, 126b;	31.2	GKC §113dd, 131m; J-M
	J-M §126i, 155o n 2; IBHS 171,		§125ba n 2 □ B-L 362a'
	246; Gib 28 □ B-M 2.61	31.3	GKC §117x □ Brock §122s
29.1	GKC §53p; IBHS 93	31.4	GAHG 3.170 n 533; Berg
29.5	GKC §66c, 91c		2.157b
29.7	B-L 438; Berg 1.142f, 2.100h	31.5	Dav §41a; Gib 13, 68 □ GAHG
29.8	GKC §53o □ B-L 534; Berg		3.170 n 533
	2.104 n h	31.6	Dav §41a; Gib 68
29.10	GKC §74h	31.7	Dav §67R2; GKC §67ff, 118q □
29.11	J-M §130a		Berg 2.97h
29.14	GKC §49k; J-M §112i □ B-L	31.8	GKC §118q, 119q; J-M §126c;
	374m, 606k; Berg 2.17d		Gib 56 □ Brock §103a
29.15	GKC §90d; J-M §93e □ Berg	31.9	Dav §116R6; IBHS 197; Gib 24
	2.113f	31.12	B-L 354g; Berg 2.83p, 2.172 n e
29.17	GKC §132e □ Berg 2.35i,	31.14	Berg 2.17d
	2.96 n f	31.15	Dav §116R1, 127b; GKC §145m
29.18	J-M §112i		□ B-L ‡132d; Brock §39bα
29.19	GKC §113k, 144p; J-M	31.16	B-L ‡132d
	§123r n 3; IBHS 641; Gib 126 □	31.18–19	IBHS 665
	Jen §20.3.3; Berg 2.65h	31.18	Dav §143; GKC §51c; IBHS
29.23	GKC §74e; J-M §177n; IBHS		419 n 4; Gib 11 □ GAHG
	298 n 30 □ B-M 2.131; Berg		3.102 n 289
	2.115a	31.21	GKC §44h, 126y; J-M §138g;
29.25	GKC §16b, 91d; 124b n 1; Gib		Gib 6 □ B-L 385g', 637s;
	18 □ Berg 1.70b; Brock §34b		GAHG 1.87 n 233; Berg 2.15a;
29.26	Berg 2.41f		Brock §23d, 60b
29.27	GAHG 3.206 n 786	31.22	GKC §47o; IBHS 516 □ Berg
29.28	GKC §66c, 91c □ B-L 578l'		2.19a, 2.109d
29.32	J-M §155o n 2	31.25	Dav §143; Gib 10 □ Berg
30.3	GAHG 3.204 n 771		2.172 n e
30.6	Dav §98R1, 125, 140; GKC	31.26	B-L 402r''; Berg 1.66q, 2.148k
	§156b; J-M §156b; Gib 18, 134	31.27	J-M §119n
30.10	GKC §116p; J-M §121k n 1 □	31.28	GKC §45g □ Berg 1.122t,
	Berg 2.72h, 2.107a		2.137k
30.11	GKC §113n, 113v □ Berg 2.62c;	31.30	Brock §122o
	Gib 77, 176	31.31	J-M §119n □ Berg 2.72h
30.12	Dav §32R5; Gib 44	31.32	GKC §63o, 138b n 1; J-M §9c,
30.13	GKC §152o; Gib 57		54c n 3, 158h n 1 □ B-L 351;
30.14	Dav §96R2; GKC §117q; Gib		Berg 2.106l
	115	31.33	GKC §10h, 60a; Gib 93 □ B-L
30.15	Dav §96R2		111m', 346x''; Berg 1.124w
30.16	GKC §67s; Gib 77 □ B-L 439p';		(bis), 1.126bb, 2.28 n e, 2.79g
	Berg 2.133 n b, 2.174 n k; Brock	31.34	GKC §9o, 133g; J-M §6b n 6 □
	§38b, 49c		Berg 1.45e
30.21	Dav §41R2; GKC §136c; J-M	31.35	GKC §65d; J-M §129l □ Brock
	§144a n 1; Gib 68		§42c
30.23	Berg 2.99e	31.38	GKC §17b; J-M §119n □ B-L
			77m

B-L: Bauer and Leander, *Historische Grammatik* **B-M**: Beer, *Grammatik* **Berg**: Bergsträsser, *Grammatik*
Brock: Brockelmann, *Syntax* **Dav**: Davidson, *Syntax* **GAHG**: Richter, *Grammatik*
Gib: Gibson, *Davidson's Syntax, 4th ed.* **GKC**: *Gesenius' Grammar* **IBHS**: Waltke and O'Connor, *Syntax*
Jen: Jenni, *Lehrbuch* **J-M**: Joüon and Muraoka, *Grammar* **Ros**: Rosenthal, *Grammar*
Sch: Schneider, *Grammatik* **Wms**: Williams, *Syntax*

31.40	GKC §127g; IBHS 231	33.5	GKC §116t □ Berg 2.97h,
32.1	GKC §134p; Gib 51		2.158e
32.3	J-M §158j	33.6	GKC §49k
32.4	Dav §86a, 111, 140; GKC §51k;	33.7	J-M §133h
	Gib 124 □ B-L 323z; Berg 2.92i	33.8	B-L 268j, 563v
32.5	GKC §118f; J-M §125n, 155s □	33.10	GAHG 3.170 n 533; Berg
	Brock §122k		1.129b
32.7–9	Berg 1.111c	33.11	J-M §133h; Gib 56
32.9	GKC §10g □ B-L 301u; Berg	33.12	GAHG 3.170 n 533
	1.124w, 2.23f, 2.79g	33.13	J-M §103n
32.10	Dav §21e; GKC §126s; J-M	33.16	B-L 303a'
	§137m; IBHS 245 n 13; Gib 27	33.18	GKC §131h
	□ Berg 2.21d	33.19	J-M §48b n 1
32.11	B-L 77m	33.20	Dav §29R4; GKC §128d, 131r;
32.12	Dav §20R4; GKC §127h □ Berg		J-M §129a n 4 □ B-M 2.147;
	1.111c; Brock §73d		Berg 1.129b, 2.137k
32.14	Dav §32R2, 55a; GKC	33.21	J-M §121k n 1 □ Brock §111f
	§124b n 1, 126x; J-M §123u,	33.22	Dav §28R1; GKC §116g, 130a;
	168d; Gib 44, 94 □ Berg 2.66k		J-M §121k n 1, 129m; IBHS
32.15	GAHG 3.170 n 533; Gib 58		155 n 34; Gib 34 □ Berg 2.136i
32.17	GKC §152b; IBHS 266 n 24;	33.24	GKC §111h, 143d
	Gib 45 □ Brock §111g	33.26	Wms §303
32.19	GKC §128x, 138d □ Berg	34.2	Berg 2.66k
	1.134a	34.3	Dav §86a, 111; J-M §123p;
32.20	Dav §136; J-M §177p; Gib 37 □		IBHS 582; Gib 124
	Berg 2.161b	34.9	GKC §132d; J-M §148a
32.21	GKC §85b, 116g n 1 □ B-L	34.10	B-M 3.80; Berg 2.59n
	487oε; B-M 2.32	34.16	Brock §80c
32.22	GKC §116g n 1	34.18–20	J-M §176b n 2
32.27	GKC §152b; IBHS 266 n 24;	35.2	J-M §43b
	Gib 45	35.4	Berg 2.21d
32.29	IBHS 595 n 57	35.5	GAHG 2.24 n 93; Berg 1.89b
32.33	Dav §88R1; GKC §113k, 113ff;	35.8	Berg 2.58n
	J-M §136h; Gib 126 □ Berg	35.10	Berg 2.163g
	2.65h	35.14	Dav §79; J-M §123r n 3, 128b;
32.35	GKC §74k; J-M §123r n 3 □		Gib 118, 126 □ Brock §35d
	B-L 375; Berg 2.158d	35.15	GKC §110i; J-M §116f,
32.36	GAHG 3.206 n 786		123r n 3; IBHS 590 n 41; Gib
32.37	J-M §112i		126 □ Berg 1.131e
32.38	J-M §103c n 4	35.17	GKC §150m n 2
32.40	J-M §136l	36	IBHS 16
32.43	GKC §138b; J-M §158i	36.2	GKC §130d, 155l; J-M §119l;
32.44	Dav §88R1; GKC §113y; J-M		Gib 12 □ Jen §9.3.3.2
	§103n, 123x; Gib 126, 127 □	36.3	J-M §169g
	B-M 3.64; Berg 2.67m; Brock	36.4–5	J-M §154fa n 2
	§46c	36.5	Berg 2.161b
33.1	Gib 137	36.6	Berg 2.16d
33.2	J-M §79k, 121k n 1	36.10	Gib 143
33.3	J-M §116b	36.13	B-M 2.132; Berg 2.117a
		36.14	B-L 340c'

B-L: Bauer and Leander, *Historische Grammatik*   **B-M**: Beer, *Grammatik*   **Berg**: Bergsträsser, *Grammatik*
Brock: Brockelmann, *Syntax*   **Dav**: Davidson, *Syntax*   **GAHG**: Richter, *Grammatik*
Gib: Gibson, *Davidson's Syntax, 4th ed.*   **GKC**: *Gesenius' Grammar*   **IBHS**: Waltke and O'Connor, *Syntax*
Jen: Jenni, *Lehrbuch*   **J-M**: Joüon and Muraoka, *Grammar*   **Ros**: Rosenthal, *Grammar*
Sch: Schneider, *Grammatik*   **Wms**: Williams, *Syntax*

36.15	J-M §64a □ B-L 340c'; B-M 2.166	38.9	GKC §111l; IBHS 558; Gib 97□ GAHG 3.174 n 564, 3.175 n 594, 3.175 n 596
36.18	Dav §44R1; GKC §107b; J-M §113f; IBHS 416; Gib 74 □ Berg 2.32d	38.10	J-M §43b □ Berg 2.17d, 2.112c
36.20	J-M §166j	38.11–12	GKC §93x
36.22	Dav §72R4; GKC §117l; J-M §128b; IBHS 419 n 4; Gib 117 □ Berg 1.152a; Brock §96*	38.11	GKC §8k □ B-L 534; Berg 1.45e, 1.102n
		38.12	GKC §93x □ B-L 534; Berg 1.102n, 1.144d
36.23	Dav §88R1; GKC §97c, 107e, 113z, 134s, 135p; J-M §123x, 166m; IBHS 303; Gib 48, 127 □ Berg 2.32d, 2.32e	38.14	Dav §32R2; GKC §126w; J-M §138c, 154fe; IBHS 260; Gib 44
		38.15	GKC §48g
36.25	GKC §160b; IBHS 606 □ B-M 3.59	38.16	Dav §99R2; GKC §17b; Gib 135 □ B-L 132c; Berg 1.3g, 2.71g; Brock §31b
36.27	Sch §49.3.4.1		
36.28	J-M §119l	38.19	Brock §133e
36.30	J-M §121e; Gib 138	38.21	J-M §52c
36.32	Dav §38R5; GKC §103l; Gib 21, 51, 118 □ B-L 651z; Brock §50a	38.22	J-M §150ia □ Berg 2.151q
		38.23	Dav §108; GKC §116t, 144i; IBHS 71; Gib 14 □ B-M 3.22; GAHG 3.177 n 606; Berg 2.72h*
37.3	GKC §53q □ B-L 229g'		
37.7	GKC §61a; Wms §110		
37.9	Dav §9R3, 11c, 51R4; GKC §139f; J-M §146k; Gib 13	38.24–25	GKC §109g
		38.24	Gib 107
37.10	Wms §453; Gib 153 □ Berg 2.40d; Brock §165a	38.26	GKC §115a; J-M §154fe □ Berg 2.58n
37.11	GKC §112uu; J-M §119z □ Berg 2.43 n b-k	38.27	Jen §11.4.10
		38.28	GKC §112qq
37.12	GKC §53q □ B-L 228a'; Berg 2.82 n m	39.2	IBHS 448
		39.4	B-L 516q, 598
37.13	IBHS 149 n 27 □ Jen §8.3.2.2	39.7	GKC §53q, 72z; J-M §80r □ B-L 228a'; B-M 1.95; Berg 2.105k
37.14	Jen §6.5.2.1; Gib 188		
37.15	GKC §112f, 112tt □ Berg 1.147d, 2.43 n b-k	39.9	J-M §137r; IBHS 240
		39.11	Dav §48R2; Gib 96
37.16	GKC §87i □ Berg 1.97e	39.12	GKC §17b, 22s □ B-L 127a', 222s, 340c'; Berg 1.66q
37.17	Dav §126; GKC §133c, 150n; J-M §161l		
37.20	GKC §109g; Gib 107 □ GAHG 3.215 n 815	39.14	Dav §91R4; GKC §115c; IBHS 600; Gib 130 □ Berg 2.54c
		39.15	Berg 2.74l
37.21	Dav §88R1; GKC §113z; J-M §123x n 2 □ Berg 2.67m	39.16	B-L 445p; Berg 2.66k, 2.158d
38.1	GKC §53q □ B-L 229g'	39.17	Berg 2.85r
38.4	Dav §79; GKC §75rr □ B-L 426; GAHG 3.120 n 330; Berg 1.132e, 2.168q; Brock §35d	39.18	B-L 368
		40.1	GKC §35d □ B-L 563x; Berg 1.91d, 1.101m
38.5	J-M §75i	40.2	GKC §117n; Gib 118
38.6	GKC §127f	40.3	GKC §112qq, 126x
38.7	J-M §131b □ Brock §63a		

B-L: Bauer and Leander, *Historische Grammatik*   **B-M**: Beer, *Grammatik*   **Berg**: Bergsträsser, *Grammatik*
Brock: Brockelmann, *Syntax*   **Dav**: Davidson, *Syntax*   **GAHG**: Richter, *Grammatik*
Gib: Gibson, *Davidson's Syntax, 4th ed.*   **GKC**: *Gesenius' Grammar*   **IBHS**: Waltke and O'Connor, *Syntax*
Jen: Jenni, *Lehrbuch*   **J-M**: Joüon and Muraoka, *Grammar*   **Ros**: Rosenthal, *Grammar*
Sch: Schneider, *Grammatik*   **Wms**: Williams, *Syntax*

40.4	GKC §35d, 106m; J-M §112g; IBHS 489 □ B-L 263f, 563x; B-M 3.59, 3.114; GAHG 3.204 n 772; Berg 1.91d, 2.28e, 2.52o, 2.58m; Brock §15g	42.19	Dav §40b; GKC §72x; J-M §80m; Gib 61
40.5	GKC §72s □ B-L 398c″; Berg 2.146e; Brock §147	42.20	J-M §139e n 1 □ Berg 2.167o; Brock §106e
		42.21	J-M §158i n 1
40.7	J-M §133e; Wms §326; Gib 18 □ Brock §16f	43.1	J-M §158i n 1
		43.10	GKC §84^{b}m □ B-L 483vδ
40.9	B-L 132c	44.3	J-M §124l, 124o; Gib 9, 11
40.14	GKC §115c	44.4	J-M §112a, 123r n 3; IBHS 493
40.15	GKC §10g, 108c; J-M §114d, 116b; IBHS 650; Gib 93 □ B-L 345q″; Berg 1.124w, 1.131e, 2.47e, 2.53q; Brock §173	44.5	Berg 2.59n
		44.6	IBHS 392 n 33
		44.7	GKC §114o; J-M §124o; IBHS 607 □ Berg 2.57k
40.16	GKC §75hh; J-M §79n □ Berg 2.161b	44.8	GKC §8k □ Berg 1.45e, 2.60p
		44.9	GKC §91k
41.3	J-M §146e	44.12	Berg 2.17e
41.4	Dav §96R5; Gib 133	44.14	Berg 1.129b
41.5	GKC §116k; J-M §121o	44.15	Berg 2.71f
41.6	Dav §86R4; GKC §113u, 115e n 1; J-M §123n; Gib 125 □ Berg 2.65 n h; Brock §93g	44.16	Jen §27.3.2
		44.17	GKC §113e; J-M §123x, 124r; IBHS 660 □ B-L 367; B-M 3.16; Berg 2.62b, 2.62 n b, 2.105i*; Brock §34b
41.7	GKC §119gg		
41.8	GKC §48g		
41.10	GKC §75q	44.18	GKC §67c, 67e, 67dd, 102b; J-M §82j; Gib 157 □ B-L 367, 439p′, 642p′; B-M 2.145; Berg 2.62b, 2.134c
41.12	GKC §119g; IBHS 193		
41.14	J M §82h □ Berg 2.134 n d		
41.15	Jen §25.3.3; Brock §106b	44.19	Dav §86R1, 96R4; GKC §53k, 58g, 91e, 144u, 145u; J-M §61i, 124p, 148c; IBHS 598; Gib 132 □ B-L 353v; B-M 3.19; Berg 2.62b, 2.62 n b; Brock §28bα
41.16	GKC §124q, 127e, 164d □ Brock §145bζ		
42.1	Gib 36		
42.2	GKC §75ff. □ Berg 2.65h*		
42.4	IBHS 214 n 99 □ Jen §14.5.6.1	44.21	GKC §52o; J-M §79m □ Berg 2.96 n f, 2.161b
42.5	J-M §158i n 1 □ Berg 2.49h		
42.6	Dav §149; GKC §17a, 32d; J-M §39a, 168d; Wms §175, 521; Gib 39, 159 □ B-L 248h; B-M 2.8; Jen §11.4.10; Berg 1.3g, 2.71g; Brock §169b	44.23	GKC §74g; J-M §170i; Wms §534
		44.25	Dav §84R1, 114; GKC §72k, 111h, 146g; Gib 21 □ B-L 404; Berg 2.62 n b, 2.105i, 2.149m(bis); Brock §124b
42.8	J-M §133j □ Brock §119b		
42.10	Dav §86R2, 149R2; GKC §19i, 69g □ B-L 384c′; Berg 2.64 n f, 2.125 n b	44.26	Dav §119; J-M §165d; IBHS 679; Gib 186
		44.28	Dav §11Rf; GKC §137b; Wms §326; IBHS 213; Gib 14 □ Brock §111b
42.12	IBHS 107 n 39		
42.15	GKC §73d		
42.16–17	Brock §123d	44.29	GKC §72r; J-M §143a □ Berg 2.147g
42.16	Dav §57R3; GKC §112y; Gib 91	45.1	GKC §61a; J-M §65b □ B-L 344e″; Berg 2.82n
42.17	GKC §112y; Dav §57R3; Gib 91		
42.18	IBHS 392 n 33	45.3	GAHG 2.34 n 145, 3.170 n 525

B-L: Bauer and Leander, *Historische Grammatik*　**B-M**: Beer, *Grammatik*　**Berg**: Bergsträsser, *Grammatik*
Brock: Brockelmann, *Syntax*　**Dav**: Davidson, *Syntax*　**GAHG**: Richter, *Grammatik*
Gib: Gibson, *Davidson's Syntax, 4th ed.*　**GKC**: *Gesenius' Grammar*　**IBHS**: Waltke and O'Connor, *Syntax*
Jen: Jenni, *Lehrbuch*　**J-M**: Joüon and Muraoka, *Grammar*　**Ros**: Rosenthal, *Grammar*
Sch: Schneider, *Grammatik*　**Wms**: Williams, *Syntax*

45.4	J-M §125i; IBHS 300	48.19	B-L 511y, 548z; Berg 2.165l;
45.5	GKC §150a; J-M §161a; IBHS		Brock §16f
	169	48.20	GKC §10g
46.1	GKC §138e n 2	48.21	Berg 1.145 n e
46.2	GKC §134p	48.22	GKC §88c
46.3	Berg 2.114k	48.26	GKC §112r; IBHS 440 n 17 □
46.5	Dav §1R1, 86R3; GKC §117q;		Berg 2.55e
	J-M §82b; IBHS 375 n 32; Gib	48.27	J-M §161d □ Berg 1.68v,
	125 □ B-L 286m′; Berg 2.84p,		2.55 n e; Brock §54f
	2.88c, 2.147i	48.28	J-M §112i
46.6	Dav §128R2; J-M §114k □	48.31	GKC §70d □ B-L 382; Berg
	GAHG 2.36 n 154, 3.218 n 826;		2.128 n h
	Berg 2.51l; Brock §52a	48.32	Dav §20R4; GKC §127f; Gib 26
46.8	GKC §68i; J-M §73f □ B-L		□ Brock §81a
	370m, 372x; B-M 2.137; Berg	48.34	J-M §101b
	2.108 n b, 2.121d	48.35	J-M §130g
46.9	Dav §28R6; GKC §130e; Gib 36	48.36	Dav §25, 115; GKC §80g, 130d,
46.11	B-L 426; Berg 2.15a, 2.167o;		155h; J-M §89n; Gib 12, 22 □
	Brock §16f		B-L 511v
46.16	Dav §32R2, 99R1; GKC §126w;	48.37	Gib 170
	IBHS 574; Gib 44, 82, 175 □	48.38	Dav §29e; Gib 42
	Berg 2.47e; Brock §60a	48.39	Berg 2.55e
46.18	Gib 12	48.41	GKC §44m, 145k; J-M §150g,
46.20	GKC §23k n 1, 84^{b}n □ Berg		150h □ B-M 2.104; Berg 2.15b,
	1.44d		2.138l, 2.138m
46.27	Berg 2.107a	48.42	GKC §119y; IBHS 440 n 17 □
47.1	GKC §138e n 2		Brock §111f
47.2	Brock §71d	48.44	GKC §131n n 1
47.4	GKC §45g, 67cc; J-M §82k □	48.45	Dav §24R3, 101Rc; GKC §55f,
	B-L 210f; Berg 1.122t		119w; Wms §321; IBHS 214
47.5	J-M §155nd □ B-L 581; Berg	49.1	GAHG 3.175 n 581
	1.157o	49.2	Berg 2.130m
48.1	Berg 2.139p; Gib 188	49.3	GKC §54b; IBHS 424 n 2 □ B-L
48.2	Dav §101; GKC §67t; GKC		351, 405; B-M 2.121; Berg
	§119y; J-M §61f □ GAHG		1.112d, 2.96g, 2.99e
	3.175 n 593; Berg 2.139 n o,	49.4	GKC §144p □ B-L 436, 581;
	2.171 n d		Berg 1.157o, 2.99g
48.5	GKC §43a n 1	49.5	Berg 2.140 n q
48.6	GKC §75w	49.7	GKC §10h, 73a n 1 □ GAHG
48.7	J-M §70d; IBHS 28 n 79 □ B-L		3.175 n 593, 3.175 n 595; Berg
	361x; Berg 2.82n		1.126aa, 2.153t; Brock §21cγ
48.9	Dav §86R2; Gib 125 □ Berg	49.8	GKC §46a n 2, 63o, 130d; J-M
	2.64 n f, 2.168 n q		§48a; IBHS 452 n 6 □ Berg
48.11	GKC §72dd; J-M §112a □ B-L		2.59n*, 2.106l
	381l, 403; Berg 2.150p	49.9	Gib 153
48.12	Berg 2.115a	49.10	GKC §75pp □ B-L 375; Berg
48.15	GKC §145u; Gib 24		2.158e, 2.167o
48.16	Berg 2.57k	49.11	GKC §47k, 48i, 60a n 1 □ Berg
48.17	B-L 195a′		2.20 n a, 2.81i

B-L: Bauer and Leander, *Historische Grammatik* **B-M**: Beer, *Grammatik* **Berg**: Bergsträsser, *Grammatik*
Brock: Brockelmann, *Syntax* **Dav**: Davidson, *Syntax* **GAHG**: Richter, *Grammatik*
Gib: Gibson, *Davidson's Syntax, 4th ed.* **GKC**: *Gesenius' Grammar* **IBHS**: Waltke and O'Connor, *Syntax*
Jen: Jenni, *Lehrbuch* **J-M**: Joüon and Muraoka, *Grammar* **Ros**: Rosenthal, *Grammar*
Sch: Schneider, *Grammatik* **Wms**: Williams, *Syntax*

49.12	Dav §106R2; GKC §141h, 150a; J-M §123p, 161a; IBHS 582 □ Berg 2.58m, 2.160a	50.20	GKC §74k, 121b; J-M §128b □ GAHG 120 n 330; Berg 2.157c; Brock §80e
49.13	J-M §165b	50.21	Gib 181, 182
49.15	GAHG 3.204 n 771	50.24	GKC §75z
49.16	GKC §90l, 144p, 147c; J-M §93n, 129m, 167i, 171b; Wms §448 □ B-L 495mŋ, 549a′; B-M 2.71	50.26	GKC §67n □ Berg 2.46c, 2.49h, 2.135e
		50.27	B-L 352; Berg 2.80i; Gib 188
		50.28	J-M §129e, 162e; IBHS 104, 147; Gib 31
49.17	GKC §91k; 122i; J-M §134g; IBHS 104	50.29	B-L 77m; Berg 2.49h, 2.174 n h
49.19	GKC §108h; IBHS 318, 518 □ Berg 2.139p	50.30	Berg 2.171 n d
		50.31	GKC §130d
49.20	GKC §67y, 132c; J-M §82n, 96Ce □ B-L 439p′; Berg 2.139 n o	50.33	Berg 2.54d*
		50.34	Dav §86R3; GKC §53l, 73d, 113x; J-M §81e, 123q, 125u n 1; IBHS 581 n 10 □ B-L 362a′, 393c′; Berg 2.106 n l, 2.152s
49.21	B-L 368t; Berg 2.82n, 2.88d		
49.23	GKC §75pp, 113d; IBHS 597 n 63 □ B-L 332t; Berg 2.61b		
		50.36	Berg 2.17e
49.24	GKC §59g, 145k; J-M §150g □ B-L 197b; B-M 1.107; Berg 2.18f	50.37	IBHS 374 □ B-L 386n′; B-M 2.145; Berg 2.87c
		50.40	J-M §124j □ Berg 2.84p; Brock §99b
49.25	GKC §80g; IBHS 374 n 30 □ B-L 287n′, 599h′; Berg 2.88c		
		50.43	Berg 2.44l
49.26	B-M 2.146; Berg 2.136i, 2.171 n d	50.44	GKC §108h
		50.45	GKC §67y □ B-L 439p′; Berg 2.139 n o
49.28	GKC §20b, 67cc □ B-L 439p′; Berg 2.80i, 2.133b		
49.30	GKC §20g, 63o □ Berg 1.66t, 2.43 n b-k, 2.59n*, 2.106l, 2.140 n q	50.46	Dav §113; GKC §145u; J-M §129p, 150k; IBHS 156 n 37; Gib 21
		51.3	GKC §17b, 152h n 1 □ B-L 77m; Berg 2.164i
49.31	J-M §159oa □ B-L 557f′; Berg 2.168p		
49.34	GKC §138e n 2	51.5	Wms §323
49.36	Dav §21c; GKC §20m; Gib 27 □ B-M 1.116; Berg 1.142 n f	51.6	J-M §125i □ Berg 2.171 n d
		51.8	Gib 141
49.37	GKC §67w, 67aa, □ B-L 437; Berg 2.133 n b	51.9	GKC §75qq, 75oo; IBHS 194 □ B-L 376r; Berg 2.159g(bis)
50.3	Berg 2.140 n q	51.10	Berg 2.47e
50.5	GKC §51o □ Berg 2.92 n gh	51.11	B-M 2.147; Berg 2.137k
50.6	GKC §44m □ Berg 2.15b	51.13	GKC §80d, 90n; J-M §89j, 93o □ B-L 612z, 614; Berg 1.137 n g, 2.15a, 2.82n
50.8	Berg 2.140 n q		
50.9	GKC §141d n 4; J-M §133h		
50.10	Dav §69b; GKC §122i; Gib 144	51.14	GKC §163d; J-M §146k, 164c, 165c, 165e, 173c; IBHS 679
50.11	GKC §80h; J-M §171b133h □ B-L 511x, 598; Berg 2.113f		
		51.16	IBHS 501
50.14	B-M 2.140; Berg 2.127e	51.17	J-M §159oa
50.17	IBHS 413	51.18	Berg 2.109c
		51.21	GKC §111w n 1
		51.24	Dav §69b; Gib 144
		51.25	B-L 282o; Berg 2.108c; Gib 144

B-L: Bauer and Leander, *Historische Grammatik*   **B-M**: Beer, *Grammatik*   **Berg**: Bergsträsser, *Grammatik*
Brock: Brockelmann, *Syntax*   **Dav**: Davidson, *Syntax*   **GAHG**: Richter, *Grammatik*
Gib: Gibson, *Davidson's Syntax, 4th ed.*   **GKC**: *Gesenius' Grammar*   **IBHS**: Waltke and O'Connor, *Syntax*
Jen: Jenni, *Lehrbuch*   **J-M**: Joüon and Muraoka, *Grammar*   **Ros**: Rosenthal, *Grammar*
Sch: Schneider, *Grammatik*   **Wms**: Williams, *Syntax*

51.29–32	Berg 2.29h	51.58	GKC §20i; IBHS 582 ☐ B-L
51.29	GKC §111w n 1, 145k; J-M		218c, 383, 425; Berg 1.69 n b,
	§150h ☐ Berg 2.140 n q, 2.152t		2.62c, 2.64f, 2.109c, 2.126d,
51.30	IBHS 386		2.172d
51.31	Gib 164	51.59	GKC §134p
51.32	B-L 599i′	51.62	B-M 3.59; Berg 2.57k, 2.58n;
51.33	GKC §53l; J-M §54c n 3 ☐ Berg		Brock §119b
	2.17e, 2.106 n l; Brock §13a	52	IBHS 17 ☐ B-L 73d
51.34	GKC §75oo; J-M §78g ☐ B-M	52.1	GKC §90k ☐ B-L 524h
	2.155; Berg 2.148l, 2.156b	52.3	B-L 346x″
51.35	Dav §69b; GKC §135m; IBHS	52.4	GKC §134p
	303	52.7	Dav §44R2, 50a; Gib 74 ☐
51.37	J-M §15m ☐ Berg 1.78m		Brock §20b
51.39	GKC §117r n 4 ☐ Berg 2.136f,	52.8	J-M §162e
	2.171c	52.10	GKC §90e
51.45	J-M §125i	52.12	GKC §155d
51.46	Dav §127c; GKC §145o; J-M	52.13	GKC §128w
	§168g n 3; Gib 160	52.15	Berg 1.111 n c; Gib 18
51.47	J-M §112a n 5	52.16	Gib 18
51.48	GKC §145o; J-M §150j	52.18	Berg 2.31d
51.49	Dav §94; GKC §114i; J-M	52.20	Dav §29R4; GKC §128d; J-M
	§154d; IBHS 610; Gib 132 ☐		§142m
	GAHG 76 n 201; Berg 2.60o	52.21	J-M §142m
51.50	GKC §69x ☐ Berg 2.131 n o	52.22	GAHG 3.161 n 480
51.52	Berg 2.15 n b	52.25	GKC §127g ☐ Brock §61
51.53	J-M §167i, 171b; Wms §530	52.33	B-L 426; Berg 2.45n
51.54	J-M §162e	52.34	J-M §140b n 1
51.56	GKC §20h, GKC §44m, 52k;		
	J-M §146e; Gib 181 ☐ B-L 437;		
	Berg 1.68v; Brock §68b		

B-L: Bauer and Leander, *Historische Grammatik*   **B-M**: Beer, *Grammatik*   **Berg**: Bergsträsser, *Grammatik*
Brock: Brockelmann, *Syntax*   **Dav**: Davidson, *Syntax*   **GAHG**: Richter, *Grammatik*
Gib: Gibson, *Davidson's Syntax, 4th ed.*   **GKC**: *Gesenius' Grammar*   **IBHS**: Waltke and O'Connor, *Syntax*
Jen: Jenni, *Lehrbuch*   **J-M**: Joüon and Muraoka, *Grammar*   **Ros**: Rosenthal, *Grammar*
Sch: Schneider, *Grammatik*   **Wms**: Williams, *Syntax*

EZEKIEL

B-L: Bauer and Leander, *Historische Grammatik* **B-M**: Beer, *Grammatik* **Berg**: Bergsträsser, *Grammatik*
Brock: Brockelmann, *Syntax* **Dav**: Davidson, *Syntax* **GAHG**: Richter, *Grammatik*
Gib: Gibson, *Davidson's Syntax, 4th ed.* **GKC**: Gesenius' *Grammar* **IBHS**: Waltke and O'Connor, *Syntax*
Jen: Jenni, *Lehrbuch* **J-M**: Joüon and Muraoka, *Grammar* **Ros**: Rosenthal, *Grammar*
Sch: Schneider, *Grammatik* **Wms**: Williams, *Syntax*

5.2	GKC §74h; IBHS 408 □ B-L 70 n 2; Berg 2.158e	7.14	GKC §72z, 113z n 2; J-M §80n □ B-L 403; Berg 2.67 n m, 2.149 n m
5.3	Berg 2.140 n q		
5.4	GAHG 3.170 n 533	7.17	GKC §88f; J-M §91e, 150d; IBHS 117 □ B-L 516s; Brock §18a
5.5	J-M §16f n 2; Gib 5		
5.6	GKC §75gg □ Berg 2.165k		
5.7	B-L 538i	7.19	B-L 588l; Berg 1.147d
5.8	Gib 38	7.20	B-L 227s, 402s"
5.9	Wms §363; IBHS 202; Gib 149	7.22	B-M 2.147
5.10	Berg 2.17d	7.23	Berg 1.145d
5.11	GKC §72r, 109d; J-M §80k; IBHS 664; Gib 38 □ Berg 2.51l, 2.145d, 2.157c	7.24	Dav §32R5; GKC §93oo, 132c; J-M §82i, 141d; IBHS 261, 262; Gib 44 □ B-L 434k'; Berg 2.17d, 2.139p
5.12	GKC §52n, 75hh, 91e; J-M §52c; IBHS 408 □ B-L 251j, 629x; Berg 2.95e, 2.161b	7.25	B-L 328a'
		7.27	GKC §54k
5.13	GKC §29v, 54c; IBHS 360 n 30 □ B-L 355m, 367; Berg 1.109 n c, 2.99 n d	7.44	GKC §72r
		8.2	GKC §90f; J-M §93i; Wms §267 □ B-L 511y, 528t, 547
5.16	Dav §63R3; GKC §109d; J-M §114g; Gib 82 □ B-L 279 n 1, 301 n 4; Berg 2.79h	8.3	GKC §75qq □ B-L 376r; Berg 2.158 n e
6.3	GKC §93v, 135e; J-M §146d; IBHS 300 n 40 □ B-L 582v'; B-M 2.71; Berg 1.102o	8.6	Dav §91R1; GKC §37c, 45d □ IBHS 317 n 5; Gib 130 □ B-L 266e, 354g; B-M 2.14; Berg 2.84 n p
6.5	Berg 2.17d	8.7	Berg 2.70e
6.6	GKC §67p n 2, 67dd; J-M §82h □ B-L 439p'; Berg 2.134 n d	8.8	GKC §125b; J-M §137u
		8.10	Berg 1.78m, 2.70e, 2.173 n f
6.7	J-M §112a n 5	8.12	GKC §116s; J-M §154c, 160i, 161b □ Berg 2.71g
6.8	GKC §91l □ B-L 253b', 423		
6.9	Dav §11c; GKC §72dd; J-M §80o; Gib 13 □ B-L 404; Berg 2.150p	8.13	GAHG 3.170 n 533
		8.14	Dav §69R2; GKC §90e; J-M §93f
6.10	GKC §119ii; IBHS 221	8.15	GAHG 3.170 n 533
6.11	Dav §28R3; GKC §128c; J-M §105b, 129a n 4; IBHS 683; Gib 188 □ Berg 2.165k	8.16	GKC §75kk □ B-L 426, 588l; Berg 2.15 n a; Brock §112
		8.17	J-M §141i □ B-L 77l
6.12	GKC §91e	8.18	GKC §72r; J-M §125s; IBHS 167 □ Berg 2.51l
6.13	J-M §129q □ Brock §162		
6.14	GKC §133l	9.1–2	GKC §135n
7.2	Dav §36R3; GKC §97c; Gib 48 □ B-L 623d	9.1	J-M §125s □ B-L 534
		9.2	Dav §32R2, 98R1, 99R2, 100R4; GKC §116k, 121d, 126w, 156c; J-M §121o, 138b; IBHS 260 n 13, 616; Gib 44, 133, 135 □ B-M 2.162; GAHG 2.24 n 94
7.4	J-M §80k □ Berg 2.19a, 2.51l(bis)		
7.5	GAHG 3.203 n 766		
7.7	GKC §127g; J-M §155nd		
7.8	B-L 302a'	9.3	Dav §98R1; GKC §49e, 116k, 121d n 1; J-M §121o, 138a n 2; IBHS 616 n 22; Gib 133 □ GAHG 2.24 n 95
7.9	J-M §80k		
7.10	Berg 2.152t		
7.11	Berg 2.161 n c		

B-L: Bauer and Leander, *Historische Grammatik*   **B-M**: Beer, *Grammatik*   **Berg**: Bergsträsser, *Grammatik*
Brock: Brockelmann, *Syntax*   **Dav**: Davidson, *Syntax*   **GAHG**: Richter, *Grammatik*
Gib: Gibson, *Davidson's Syntax, 4th ed.*   **GKC**: *Gesenius' Grammar*   **IBHS**: Waltke and O'Connor, *Syntax*
Jen: Jenni, *Lehrbuch*   **J-M**: Joüon and Muraoka, *Grammar*   **Ros**: Rosenthal, *Grammar*
Sch: Schneider, *Grammatik*   **Wms**: Williams, *Syntax*

9.4	J-M §119l n 2	11.25	B-L 426; Berg 2.106l
9.6	B-M 2.147	12.4	Berg 2.17d
9.7	GKC §112tt; Gib 104 □ B-L 375	12.5	Berg 2.17d
9.8	GKC §64i □ B-L 344e", 357;	12.12	Dav §147; GKC §107q,
	B-M 2.167; Berg 2.23f, 2.82n,		107q n 2
	2.92 n gh	12.14	GKC §52n; J-M §52c
9.9	IBHS 268; Gib 45	12.15	Berg 2.17d
9.10	GKC §72r; J-M §80k □ B-L	12.19	GKC §67p, 128h; J-M §82h □
	352; Berg 2.51l		Berg 1.127cc
9.11	Dav §98R1; GKC §116k; J-M	12.22	B-M 2.128; Berg 2.111c
	§121o; IBHS 617	12.25	GKC §144b □ Brock §156a
10.2	B-M 3.68	12.27	IBHS 210
10.3	Dav §29R7; GKC §130a n 3,	13.2	Dav §28R1; GKC §93oo, 130a;
	131n, 131n n 2; J-M §146e;		J-M §129n; Gib 34
	Wms §71; IBHS 233; Gib 42 □	13.3	Dav §149R2; GKC §152b, 152x,
	B-L 525i; Berg 2.71f; Brock		155n; Wms §362
	§68b	13.6	IBHS 536; Gib 88 □ B-L 423;
10.4	GAHG 3.120 n 330		Jen §27.4.1; Berg 2.41e, 2.151r,
10.7	J-M §103n n 3		2.166n
10.9	Dav §32R2; GKC §84ᵃr, 126z,	13.7	Dav §108; GKC §116t, 144i;
	134l;J-M §143m; Gib 44 □ Berg		IBHS 384 n 16 □ B-L 232j
	1.140c; Brock §60b	13.9	IBHS 124
10.11	Berg 2.136 n i	13.10ff.	GKC §117ee, 158b
10.12	GKC §91c	13.10	J-M §170f n 2 □ Brock §145bβ
10.15	Dav §1R2; GKC §72dd □ B-L	13.11	GKC §32i, 35m, 65e □ B-L
	404; Jen §25.3.3; Berg 2.140 n q		248i; Jen §8.4.2; Berg 1.153c
10.16	Berg 2.136 n i, 2.145d	13.12	Dav §132R2; Gib 156
10.17	GKC §72q, 72dd; J-M §80k,	13.14	Brock §94b
	80o □ B-L 399h", 404k	13.17	GKC §91c □ B-L 252p, 564;
10.19	B-L 404; Berg 2.140 n q,		B-M 2.54
	2.145d(bis)	13.18	GKC §87f, 103f n 2; IBHS 416
10.21	B-L 516s		□ B-M 2.11
10.22	GKC §117m n 3; IBHS 183; Gib	13.19	GKC §72k, 93r; J-M §52c,
	117		80b n 3 □ B-L 436; B-M 2.120;
11.1	Gib 49		Berg 2.95d, 2.146f
11.3	GKC §150a n 1	13.20	GKC §32i, 91l, 93l, 117c; J-M
11.6	J-M §134c □ Berg 2.45n,		§39a, 94i, 149c n 1 □ B-L 248i,
	2.167o; Brock §17		253y, 614; Jen §8.4.2
11.7	Dav §86R3	13.21	B-L 547
11.10	B-L 302a'	13.22	Dav §29R4, 96R4; IBHS 72;
11.12	Dav §9R1		Gib 41, 132 □ Berg 2.57k
11.13	Dav §67R3; GKC §117b,	13.23	B-L 547; Berg 2.76 n b
	150a n 1; J-M §125s; Gib 115	14.1	GKC §145s; J-M §150j
11.15	Gib 42	14.3	Dav §86a; GKC §51c, 51k, 51p,
11.16	J-M §171b; IBHS 663; Gib 142		113w; Wms §138; IBHS 390;
11.17	GKC §72v □ Berg 2.41g, 2.147i;		Gib 124 □ B-L 323z, 323a', 357;
	Brock §153b; Gib 90		B-M 2.118; Berg 1.111 n c,
11.23	Brock §119a		2.92h, 2.92i
11.24	Dav §60b; GKC §90c; J-M	14.5	Gib 42
	§93d; Gib 144	14.4	Berg 2.111b*

B-L: Bauer and Leander, *Historische Grammatik* **B-M**: Beer, *Grammatik* **Berg**: Bergsträsser, *Grammatik*
Brock: Brockelmann, *Syntax* **Dav**: Davidson, *Syntax* **GAHG**: Richter, *Grammatik*
Gib: Gibson, *Davidson's Syntax, 4th ed.* **GKC**: *Gesenius' Grammar* **IBHS**: Waltke and O'Connor, *Syntax*
Jen: Jenni, *Lehrbuch* **J-M**: Joüon and Muraoka, *Grammar* **Ros**: Rosenthal, *Grammar*
Sch: Schneider, *Grammatik* **Wms**: Williams, *Syntax*

14.7	Dav §65R6; Gib 104 □ B-L 131; Berg 2.111b*; Brock §17, 116e
14.8	Berg 2.152 n t
14.9	Berg 2.167o; Gib 155
14.11	J-M §168d; Wms §524; IBHS 639 n 26 □ GAHG 3.171 n 539
14.13	GKC §49m, 112c, 112hh; IBHS 521; Gib 155
14.14	GKC §112ll, 112tt
14.15	GKC §59g, Wms §459; Gib 155 □ B-L 342p'; GAHG 3.178 n 618; Berg 2.18f; Brock §31a
14.17	J-M §167q
14.19	J-M §167q □ B-M 2.116
14.21	IBHS 664 □ GAHG 3.177 n 605
14.22	Dav §72R4, 132R2; GKC §117l, 126w; J-M §125j; Gib 117, 135, 156 □ Berg 2.137i
15.3	B-M 2.117
15.4	Dav §132R2; Gib 156 □ Berg 2.136h
15.5	IBHS 664 □ GAHG 3.177 n 605; Berg 2.136i
16.3	IBHS 144 □ B-L 598
16.4–5	GKC §121b
16.4	Dav §86R2; GKC §22s, 52q, 53s, 63d, 63q, 64e, 71, 113w; J-M §23a, 57b, 69a, 123p; IBHS 374 n 30, 447 n 1, 448 n 2, 452, 582, 586; Gib 125 □ B-L 127a', 222s, 287n', 355p, 357, 379t, 565x; B-M 2.67, 2.121, 2.130, 2.132; GAHG 3.122 n 332; Berg 1.152a(bis), 2.54d, 2.62c, 2.64f, 2.87c, 2.96g, 2.106n, 2.115a, 2.118c; Brock §35d
16.5	GKC §45d, 71; J-M §49d □ B-L 348i, 379t; B-M 2.106; GAHG 3.122 n 332; Berg 2.54d, 2.83p, 2.106n, 2.130m
16.6	GKC §123d n 2 □ Berg 2.21d, 2.115l
16.7	Dav §34R4; GKC §133i; J-M §141l □ Berg 2.117a
16.8	Berg 2.70e, 2.92h
16.10	GKC §49c, 107b n 2 □ B-L 354c, 424; Berg 2.22e, 2.113g
16.11	Berg 2.23f; Gib 109
16.12	Berg 2.123d

16.13	GKC §76f □ B-L 370l; B-M 2.139; Berg 2.15a, 2.126d
16.14	Berg 2.110e
16.15	GKC §75ii, 911; J-M §94j □ B-L 253b', 606k; Berg 2.163g
16.18	GKC §44h □ B-L 368t; Berg 2.15a
16.19	GAHG 1.78 n 169; Berg 2.18f, 2.163g
16.20	GKC §91l; J-M §94j □ B-L 253b', 606k; Berg 2.15a
16.22	B-L 310k; Berg 2.15a
16.23	GKC §122l n 5 □ Berg 1.137g
16.27	Dav §29R4; GKC §128d, 131r; Gib 41
16.28	J-M §170i □ Berg 2.56h, 2.83p, 2.118c
16.29	J-M §93d □ Berg 2.118c
16.31	GKC §91l □ B-L 253b', 422t", 423, 425; Berg 2.15a
16.32	GKC §117d
16.33	GKC §20l, 64c □ B-L 354b, 357, 579q'; Berg 1.103q, 1.156l, 2.15a, 2.116c
16.34	Dav §109; GKC §121a; J-M §88La*, 128ba; IBHS 374 n 30 □ B-L 287n', 423; B-M 3.83; Berg 1.140c, 2.87c; Brock §35c
16.36	Berg 2.15a, 2.161b
16.37	Berg 1.128dd
16.38	Dav §67R2
16.41	Berg 1.140c
16.43	IBHS 664, 684 □ B-L 310k; Berg 2.15a; Brock §4
16.44	GKC §91e; J-M §94h, 164a □ B-L 563x
16.45	GKC §96
16.47	GKC §103m, 152z □ B-L 425, 644y'; Berg 2.15a
16.48	GKC §75m
16.50	GKC §471 □ B-L 361a'; Berg 2.15a, 2.20 n a, 2.21d
16.51	GKC §96; IBHS 404 □ B-L 425, 616c; Berg 2.15a
16.52	GKC §52p, 91n, 95p, 96 (p. 284); J-M §52c, 94g □ B-L 253s, 345m", 59al, 616c, 644y'; Berg 2.96f

B-L: Bauer and Leander, *Historische Grammatik*　B-M: Beer, *Grammatik*　Berg: Bergsträsser, *Grammatik*
Brock: Brockelmann, *Syntax*　Dav: Davidson, *Syntax*　GAHG: Richter, *Grammatik*
Gib: Gibson, *Davidson's Syntax, 4th ed.*　GKC: *Gesenius' Grammar*　IBHS: Waltke and O'Connor, *Syntax*
Jen: Jenni, *Lehrbuch*　J-M: Joüon and Muraoka, *Grammar*　Ros: Rosenthal, *Grammar*
Sch: Schneider, *Grammatik*　Wms: Williams, *Syntax*

16.53	GKC §91c, 91e, 91f; J-M §94h □ B-L 252p, 253b′, 583w′, 606k; B-M 2.57	18.7	GKC §131r; J-M §112d n 2
16.54	GKC §103b □ B-L 441c, 642n′	18.8	J-M §112d n 2
16.55	GKC §47l, 72k; J-M §80b □ B-L 303c′, 405; Berg 2.19a, 2.146f(bis)	18.9	J-M §112d n 2, 123e
		18.10	Dav §35R2; GKC §96c, 119w n 2, 139d; IBHS 683 n 39 □ B-L 618k
16.56	GKC §96	18.11	Jen §6.3.4
16.57	GKC §72k, 72p; J-M §80k □ B-L 405; Berg 1.44c, 2.146 n g	18.12	Berg 2.128h
		18.14	GKC §103l; J-M §103c n 3 □ B-L 651z
16.59	GKC §44i □ B-L 425; Berg 2.15a	18.17	J-M §123e
		18.18	Dav §130R5; Gib 155
16.60	GKC §8l □ Berg 1.45e, 2.16c	18.19	Dav §41R2; J-M §79m; Gib 68 □ Berg 2.161b
16.61	GKC §96		
16.63	Berg 1.144d	18.20	Dav §101Ra; GKC §119m
17.3	Berg 1.134a, 2.151q	18.21	J-M §125q
17.5	GKC §19i, 66g □ B-L 366t; GAHG 1.55 n 56; Berg 2.124 n f	18.22	B-L 636j
		18.23	Dav §86a; Gib 124 □ Berg 2.42g
17.6	GKC §75rr		
17.7	GKC §52d; J-M §142ba □ B-L 221p, 362a′, 582u′; Berg 1.134a, 1.152a, 2.97h	18.24	Berg 2.39 n a-f, 2.41f; Gib 181
		18.25	GKC §145u; GAHG 1.72 n 135
		18.26	GKC §135p; J-M §149a □ B-L 583w′; Berg 2.41f
17.9–10	IBHS 684 n 46		
17.9	Dav §91R3; GKC §45e, 93m, 115d, 150a n 1; J-M §96Ad □ B-L 441c, 556e′; Berg 1.122t(bis), 2.84 n p	18.27	Berg 2.39 n a-f
		18.28	GKC §75t □ B-L 405; Berg ‡2.145c
		18.29	Dav §116R6; GKC §145u □ GAHG 1.72 n 135; Berg 1.68v
17.10	Dav §91a; Gib 129 □ Berg 2.123c, 2.126d	18.32	Dav §136R1; GKC §139d, 144e, 154b; J-M §155h, 177m
17.13	Berg 2.26c		
17.14	Berg 2.100i	19.1	GKC §124e □ B-L 323 n 1
17.15	GKC §29i n 1, 93rr; J-M §96Ce □ Berg 1.101l, 1.160a	19.2	GKC §80h □ B-L 511x; Berg 1.93 n h
17.18	IBHS 678	19.5	Berg 2.128 n g
17.19	GKC §67v; J-M §82n; IBHS 680 □ B-L 438; Berg 2.140q	19.7	GKC §67p; J-M §82h □ Berg 2.135d
		19.9	Dav §149; IBHS 639 n 26; Gib 160 □ B-L 323 n 1; GAHG 3.171 n 539
17.21	Dav §72R4; GKC §117m; J-M §125j; Gib 117		
17.22	GKC §49m □ Berg 2.41g; Gib 90	19.12	GKC §53u; J-M §57a; IBHS 375 n 32 □ B-L 286m′; Berg 1.150n, 2.88c, 2.106n, 2.43 n b-k
17.23	GKC §44o, 60a □ B-L 303d′, 346x″; B-M 1.109; Berg 2.79g		
		20.4	B-L 302a′
17.24	IBHS 437 n 13, 438, 532, 540 □ Berg 2.41g, 2.43 n b-k	20.5	Berg 2.116d, 2.128g
		20.6	J-M §130a n 2
18.2	GKC §117r □ J-M §161i	20.8	GKC §67t, 114m n 1
18.3	GAHG 3.171 n 539	20.9	Dav §149R2; GKC §67t □ Berg 2.137i
18.4	J-M §174j	20.11	Berg 2.40b
18.5	Dav §130R5; Gib 155		
18.6	Dav §29e; GKC §131c; J-M §112d n 2; Gib 41		

B-L: Bauer and Leander, *Historische Grammatik*   **B-M**: Beer, *Grammatik*   **Berg**: Bergsträsser, *Grammatik*
Brock: Brockelmann, *Syntax*   **Dav**: Davidson, *Syntax*   **GAHG**: Richter, *Grammatik*
Gib: Gibson, *Davidson's Syntax, 4th ed.*   **GKC**: *Gesenius' Grammar*   **IBHS**: Waltke and O'Connor, *Syntax*
Jen: Jenni, *Lehrbuch*   **J-M**: Joüon and Muraoka, *Grammar*   **Ros**: Rosenthal, *Grammar*
Sch: Schneider, *Grammatik*   **Wms**: Williams, *Syntax*

20.13	Berg 2.40b		21.20	Dav §96R1, 149R1; GKC §45c,
20.14	GKC §67t			75ff, 102f; J-M §105b; IBHS 683
20.16	GKC §117m; J-M §125j; IBHS			□ B-L 638u; Berg 2.161c
	183; Gib 117		21.21	GKC §73a; IBHS 104 n 37 □
20.18	B-L 564; Berg 1.45e			B-L 357; B-M 2.127; Berg
20.22	GKC §67t, 112tt; J-M §172a;			2.110e, 2.152 n t, 2.173 n f;
	Gib 103			Brock §16g
20.25	GKC §152a n 1		21.24	IBHS 607 □ Berg 2.57l
20.26	Dav §146; GKC §157c; J-M		21.25	Dav §72R3; GKC §102f; J-M
	§157c			§125bb □ B-L 638u; Berg 2.57l
20.27	B-L 354e; GAHG 3.170 n 533;		21.26	Berg 2.109c
	Berg 2.116d		21.28	J-M §96Ce
20.29	GKC §116q		21.29	GKC §53l, 61e; J-M §54c □ B-L
20.30–31	GKC §93oo			345o"; B-M 2.168; Berg 2.91g,
20.30	J-M §102m □ B-L 541j; Berg			2.118d
	1.68v, 1.92e		21.30	IBHS 77 n 15
20.31	GKC §150a, 150h; J-M §161a;		21.31	Dav §88R2; GKC §80k,
	IBHS 390; Gib 183 □ Berg			113bb n 3, 113dd; Gib 127 □
	1.92e			B-L 511y, 557e'; Berg 2.66 n k,
20.33	B-L 302a'			2.149 n m
20.34	GKC §72v □ B-L 193q; Jen		21.32	GKC §133l
	§13.4.3		21.33	GKC §45c, 68i
20.36	GKC §51p □ Berg 2.92h		21.35	GKC §72y, 130c; J-M §129q □
20.37	GKC §3b n 1, 23f, 63o; J-M			B-L 127a', 405, 598; Berg
	§16a n 2 □ B-L 72b; Berg 1.3d,			2.149m, 2.157c
	1.91 n bd, 1.157n		22.2	J-M §136b
20.38	Dav §116R6; GKC §145u; Gib		22.3	GKC §102f, 116x
	24		22.4	Dav §116R6; GKC §47k, 145t □
20.39	GKC §110a; J-M §177e			B-L 444p; Berg 2.20 n a, 2.157c
20.40	B-L 357, 614; Gib 42		22.5	GKC §35b □ B-L 221p
20.41	GKC §72v, 119i		22.7	GKC §35g □ B-L 263g; Berg
20.43	GKC §72v □ B-L 375; B-M			2.137k
	2.152; Berg 2.147i; Gib 13		22.8	B-L 582u'
21.11	GKC §65e □ B-L 361w; Berg		22.12	Berg 1.154e, 2.118c
	1.153c, 2.117a		22.14	J-M §150d; IBHS 532 □ Berg
21.12	GKC §67t, 88f; J-M §91e; IBHS			2.41g
	117 □ B-L 431t, 516s; Berg		22.15	Berg 2.138l
	2.165l		22.16	GKC §67u; J-M §82i □ B-L
21.14	Berg 2.138n			434k'
21.15	GKC §75n; IBHS 375 n 31 □		22.18	Dav §29c; GKC §131d; IBHS
	B-L 287n', 357, 423; B-M 2.160;			26 n 73; Gib 41
	Berg 2.88c, 2.138n, 2.161c		22.20	GKC §66f □ B-L 199l, 368t;
21.16	GKC §45d; IBHS 375 n 31 □			Berg 2.123c
	B-L 287n', 357; Berg 2.84 n p,		22.22	B-L 481yγ; Berg 1.151b
	2.88c, 2.138n		22.24	Dav §100R3; GKC §93q,
21.17	GKC §130a; J-M §129m			152a n 1; IBHS 419, 422; Gib
21.18	GKC §64d			138 □ B-L 567i
21.19	Dav §32R2; GKC §126z; J-M		22.25	GKC §29f □ Berg 1.71e
	§138c □ B-L 628x		22.26	GKC §67t; J-M §82m □ Berg
				2.136i

B-L: Bauer and Leander, *Historische Grammatik*   **B-M**: Beer, *Grammatik*   **Berg**: Bergsträsser, *Grammatik*
Brock: Brockelmann, *Syntax*   **Dav**: Davidson, *Syntax*   **GAHG**: Richter, *Grammatik*
Gib: Gibson, *Davidson's Syntax, 4th ed.*   **GKC**: *Gesenius' Grammar*   **IBHS**: Waltke and O'Connor, *Syntax*
Jen: Jenni, *Lehrbuch*   **J-M**: Joüon and Muraoka, *Grammar*   **Ros**: Rosenthal, *Grammar*
Sch: Schneider, *Grammatik*   **Wms**: Williams, *Syntax*

22.28	Berg 2.145e		23.47	GKC §103b; J-M §119p □ B-L
22.29	GKC §152a n 1			642n'; B-M 2.155
22.30	Berg 1.129b		23.48–49	GKC §91f
23.3	Berg 2.172d		23.48	GKC §55k; J-M §59f, 94h □
23.4–5	B-M 3.9			B-L 252n, 283s, 383, 598; Berg
23.5	GKC §63c, 63m □ B-L 352;			2.108 n b, 2.129 n l
	Berg 2.110b, 2.156a		23.49	GKC §74k, 76b, 144a; J-M
23.6	J-M §121o			§94h; IBHS 124 □ B-L 252n,
23.7	GKC §91l; J-M §94j □ B-L			441c, 598; B-M 3.21; Berg 1.92f,
	253b', 606k			2.157c
23.8	Berg 2.172d		24.2	Dav §11c; GKC §139g □ J-M
23.13	B-L 622c			§143k; IBHS 190; Gib 13 □ B-L
23.14	Berg 2.173 n f			306j
23.15	GKC §122h n 5		24.3	GKC §69f □ Berg 2.127e
23.16	Dav §69b; GKC §48d; J-M		24.6	GKC §91e, 123d; J-M §94h,
	§45a n 1, 93d; Gib 144 □ B-L			162d; IBHS 682; Gib 188 □ B-L
	352; Berg 2.23f(bis), 2.110b			603g; Berg 2.23g; Brock §11a
23.17	Berg 2.174 n h		24.7	Berg 2.18f(bis)
23.18	Berg 2.174 n h		24.9	IBHS 682 □ Brock §11a
23.19	Berg 2.161b		24.10	B-M 2.162; Berg 1.148g, 2.136i,
23.20	GKC §48d; J-M §45a n 1			2.137k, 2.165k
23.21	Berg 2.172d		24.11	GKC §67q, 67bb □ B-L 439p';
23.24	B-L 547; GAHG 3.161 n 480			Berg 2.17e, 2.23g, 2.138o
23.25	B-L 368t; Berg 1.154e		24.12	GKC §75m; IBHS 259 n 8 □
23.28	Dav §10; GKC §91e, 138e; J-M			B-L 424; Berg 1.157o, 2.165 n l
	§94h; IBHS 331, 335 □ B-L		24.13	GKC §115a, 131r; J-M §124g
	346s'', 549a'; B-M 3.99		24.14	Berg 2.41g
23.30	Dav §88R2; GKC §113f, 113dd,		24.17	J-M §113m □ B-L 436; Berg
	113ff; J-M §123w; Gib 127			2.135e
23.31	B-L 385g'; Berg 2.44n		24.19	Berg 2.118b
23.32	Dav §116R6; GKC §47k, 145t □		24.23	Berg 2.134c, 2.136h
	B-L 423; Berg 2.20 n a, 2.55e		24.24	Berg 2.42g
23.36	B-M 3.9		24.26	GKC §53e, 54k, 86k, 126r; J-M
23.39	J-M §69b □ B-L 354e; Berg			§54c, 88Mj, 137n □ B-L 362a',
	2.116d			505rι; Berg 2.39 n a-f, 2.106m
23.40	Dav §9R3; J-M §158m n 2 □		25.3	Dav §117; GKC §67u; J-M §82i;
	GAHG 3.177 n 605; Berg 2.45n			Gib 188 □ B-L 434k'
23.41	Berg 2.45n		25.4	GKC §91e; J-M §94h; IBHS 402
23.42	Dav §113; GKC §21c □ B-L			□ B-L 346s'', 549a'
	556e'; Berg 1.106b, 2.168p		25.6	GKC §23c, 61c, 74e; J-M §69b,
23.43	Dav §1; J-M §93g n 3			70d □ B-L 535f; Berg 2.82n,
23.44	GKC §96 (p. 285), 96			2.146 n g, 2.156a, 2.157b
	(p. 285) n 1 □ B-L 617g; B-M		25.7	GKC §155f □ Berg 2.112c
	2.81, 3.9		25.8	GKC §63i □ Berg 2.114i
23.45ff.	GKC §135o		25.10	IBHS 639 n 26
23.45	GKC §103b □ B-L 642n'		25.12	Dav §67b; Gib 115 □ Berg
23.46–47	GKC §112u			2.38g, 2.124f
23.46	Dav §88R2; GKC §113cc,		25.13	GKC §90i; J-M §93c □ B-L
	113dd; J-M §119p □ Berg			529v, 534
	2.66k, 2.160a			

B-L: Bauer and Leander, *Historische Grammatik*   **B-M**: Beer, *Grammatik*   **Berg**: Bergsträsser, *Grammatik*
Brock: Brockelmann, *Syntax*   **Dav**: Davidson, *Syntax*   **GAHG**: Richter, *Grammatik*
Gib: Gibson, *Davidson's Syntax, 4th ed.*   **GKC**: *Gesenius' Grammar*   **IBHS**: Waltke and O'Connor, *Syntax*
Jen: Jenni, *Lehrbuch*   **J-M**: Joüon and Muraoka, *Grammar*   **Ros**: Rosenthal, *Grammar*
Sch: Schneider, *Grammatik*   **Wms**: Williams, *Syntax*

25.15	GKC §72p, 117q; IBHS 382 ☐ Berg 1.144c, 2.146 n g	27.29	B-L 114b
26	IBHS 148 n 25	27.30	Dav §70b; Gib 144
26.1–28.10	J-M §112h n 1	27.31	GKC §80h
26.2	GKC §44m, 51p, 67t; Wms §23;	27.32	GKC §23k
	Gib 188 ☐ B-L 431t; Berg	27.33	Berg 2.118c
	2.15 n b, 2.136h	27.34	Dav §100R6; GKC §116g n 1
26.3–4	J-M §158n n 1	27.35	GKC §117q
26.3	GKC §117n	27.36	Dav §29e; J-M §154k; Gib 42
26.5	B-L 546x	28.2	J-M §112a
26.6	IBHS 375 n 31; Gib 119	28.3	GKC §133a, 145d; Wms §317 ☐
26.7	GKC §133i; J-M §141l		Berg 1.93h, 2.132a
26.8	J-M §132a	28.7	Dav §32R5; GKC §133h; J-M
26.9	B-L 582u'; Berg 1.135d, 1.136d		§96As; Gib 44 ☐ B-L 577i'
26.10	Dav §28R1; GKC §130b; J-M	28.8	J-M §125q n 2 ☐ Berg 2.146f
	§129s; IBHS 448	28.9	GKC §113q ☐ Berg 2.97h,
26.11	J-M §150i		2.63d, 2.140 n r
26.14	Dav §116R6; GKC §47k, 51l ☐	28.10	Brock §72b
	B-L 423, 546x; Berg 2.20 n a	28.12–19	J-M §112h n 1
26.15	GKC §51l, 117q; IBHS 375 n 31	28.13	GKC §74e ☐ B-L 373d, 511v;
	☐ B-L 228z, 351; Berg 2.92 n i		Berg 1.127cc, 2.156a
26.16	J-M §137i; IBHS 402 ☐ B-M	28.14	GKC §32g ☐ J-M §39a n 1 ☐
	2.112		B-L 248e
26.17	Dav §22R4; GKC §52s, 138k;	28.15	GKC §90g; IBHS 643 ☐ B-L
	J-M §145e, 158n; Gib 29 ☐ B-L		345p'', 528t, 604g
	265e; Berg 2.96 n f	28.16	Dav §101; GKC §23d, 68k,
26.18	J-M §90c, 130f; IBHS 118 ☐		75qq, 111w n 1; J-M §24e, 24fa
	B-L 517t, 563x		☐ B-L 370m, 375; B-M 1.94,
26.19	J-M §112a, 119o ☐ Berg 2.112c		2.155, 2.168; Berg 1.113 n e,
26.20	Dav §149; IBHS 639 n 26		2.121d, 2.156 n a
26.21	GKC §10g ☐ B-L 208s, 328a';	28.17	GKC §75n, 111w n 1 ☐ B-L
	Berg 1.124w		426; Berg 2.84 n p, 2.167 n p
27.3	GKC §90m, 90n; J-M §93o;	28.18	GKC §93u; J-M §146a n 4;
	IBHS 132 n 17 ☐ Berg 2.15a;		IBHS 213 ☐ B-L 583w'
	Brock §73b	28.22	J-M §158n n 1
27.4	Berg 2.132a, 2.171c	28.23	GKC §55d; J-M §112a n 5 ☐
27.5	B-L 516q, 534		B-L 368t; Berg 2.107 n a
27.6	B-L 538i	28.24	GKC §72p; J-M §80k ☐ B-L
27.7	GKC §121b		405; Berg 1.44c, 2.146 n g
27.8	J-M §146a n 4	28.26	GKC §72p; J-M §80k ☐ B-L
27.9	GAHG 2.67 n 288, 2.67 n 291		405; Berg 1.44c, 2.146 n g
27.10	J-M §129h	29.2	Brock §62f
27.11	Berg 2.171c	29.3	GKC §117x, 124e; J-M
27.12ff.	GKC §93uu		§125ba n 1, 158n; IBHS 458 ☐
27.12	J-M §112d n 3 ☐ B-L 517v		B-L 335c
27.15	Dav §3R2; Gib 3	29.4	B-L 564
27.19	GKC §20i ☐ B-L 218c, 365o;	29.5	J-M §112a n 5 ☐ B-L 368t
	Berg 1.69y	29.7	Dav §54a; GKC §127c; Gib 94
27.26	GKC §58g; IBHS 408		☐ B-L 438; Berg 1.128dd,
27.27	J-M §88Mb		2.136i
		29.12	J-M §141j n 1 ☐ Berg 2.19a

B-L: Bauer and Leander, *Historische Grammatik* **B-M**: Beer, *Grammatik* **Berg**: Bergsträsser, *Grammatik*
Brock: Brockelmann, *Syntax* **Dav**: Davidson, *Syntax* **GAHG**: Richter, *Grammatik*
Gib: Gibson, *Davidson's Syntax, 4th ed.* **GKC**: *Gesenius' Grammar* **IBHS**: Waltke and O'Connor, *Syntax*
Jen: Jenni, *Lehrbuch* **J-M**: Joüon and Muraoka, *Grammar* **Ros**: Rosenthal, *Grammar*
Sch: Schneider, *Grammatik* **Wms**: Williams, *Syntax*

29.13	J-M §112i	32.6	Berg 2.17d, 2.165 n l
29.15	B-L 441c; Berg 2.156b	32.7	GKC §49k; Gib 181
29.16	Gib 20	32.10	J-M §137i
29.18	J-M §155nd	32.11	GKC §118f; J-M §125ba □ B-M
30.2	Dav §117; GKC §105a; J-M		3.75
	§105b; Gib 188	32.12	J-M §158n n 1 □ Berg 2.132a*
30.4	Berg 2.17e, 2.108c	32.14	IBHS 445 □ Brock §122q
30.7	J-M §141j n 1 □ B-L 614; Berg	32.15	GKC §133l; J-M §119o
	2.112c	32.16	GKC §44o □ B-L 303d', 404
30.8	J-M §119o	32.18	GKC §66c, 53s
30.9	GKC §93y, 118q □ GAHG	32.19	GKC §46a n 2, 53s; J-M §48a;
	3.204 n 771; Berg 1.102n,		IBHS 452 □ B-L 333k'; Berg
	2.108c		2.106n
30.10	Berg 2.41g	32.20	GKC §46d; J-M §48c □ B-L
30.12	GKC §124e		306l; B-M 2.114; Berg 2.80i
30.14	Berg 2.16c	32.21	B-L 582v'
30.16	Dav §24R4; GKC §73c; IBHS	32.22	IBHS 104 □ B-M 3.18; Berg
	610 n 35; Gib 34 □ Berg 2.16c,		1.145d
	2.60o, 2.118b, 2.146 n g, 2.151s,	32.23	Berg 1.161d
	2.152t	32.24	GAHG 3.146 n 382, 3.152 n 417
30.17	B-L 232j	32.25	Dav §108R2; GKC §144g
30.18	GKC §61b; J-M §65b, 119o; Gib	32.26	B-L 547; Berg 2.97h, 2.140 n r
	181 □ B-L 232j, 343b''	32.28	J-M §51b □ B-L 320g
30.21	J-M §124o	32.30	GKC §20m, 72n □ Berg 1.142f,
30.22	Berg 2.40c		2.144b
30.25	J-M §119o	32.32	GKC §53s □ Berg 2.106n
30.26	Berg 2.17d	33.2	GKC §143b; Gib 155
31.2	Berg 2.28g; Gib 63	33.4	Dav §108R1; GKC §111w,
31.3	GKC §67v; J-M §130f □ B-M		112ll; J-M §155d; Gib 13
	2.147; Berg 2.137k	33.5	GKC §52l □ Berg 2.95d, 1.161d
31.4	B-L 221p, 362a'; Berg 2.97h	33.6	GAHG 3.102 n 289; Gib 155
31.5–6	GKC §85w	33.7	Berg 2.44k
31.5	GKC §44f, 75rr □ B-L 361a';	33.9	Brock §164cβ; Gib 155
	B-M 2.128; Berg 2.14a, 2.111c	33.10	Berg 2.136h
31.6	J-M §150e □ Berg 2.97h	33.11	Brock §168
31.7	GKC §76f □ B-M 1.106; Berg	33.12	GKC §51n, 74h □ B-L 321j,
	2.126d, 2.163g		375; B-M 2.118/2; Berg 2.91g,
31.8	GKC §75rr; 85w □ Berg 2.132a		2.114l, 2.158e
31.9	B-L 376r	33.13	B-L 583w'; Gib 182
31.11	GKC §75n □ B-L 582v'; Berg	33.17	GKC §135f, 143a n 3; J-M
	2.33 n b-h		§146e, 156b □ GAHG
31.15	Berg 2.167o		1.72 n 135
31.16	Dav §28R4; GKC §128a n 1;	33.18	Dav §14R2; GKC §135p; J-M
	J-M §129a n 5; Wms §29; IBHS		§149a □ Berg 2.39 n a-f, 2.41f
	139; Gib 35	33.19	GKC §135p □ Berg 2.39 n a-f,
31.18	GKC §91e □ Berg 2.28g; Gib 63		2.41f, 2.134d
32	IBHS 148 n 25	33.20	B-L 302a'; GAHG 1.72 n 135
32.1	GKC §97d	33.21	GKC §126r □ J-M §137n
32.2	Berg 1.129b (bis), 2.149m	33.22	IBHS 215, 383 □ Berg 2.112d
32.5	B-L 506st	33.24	Berg 1.152a

B-L: Bauer and Leander, *Historische Grammatik*   **B-M**: Beer, *Grammatik*   **Berg**: Bergsträsser, *Grammatik*
Brock: Brockelmann, *Syntax*   **Dav**: Davidson, *Syntax*   **GAHG**: Richter, *Grammatik*
Gib: Gibson, *Davidson's Syntax, 4th ed.*   **GKC**: *Gesenius' Grammar*   **IBHS**: Waltke and O'Connor, *Syntax*
Jen: Jenni, *Lehrbuch*   **J-M**: Joüon and Muraoka, *Grammar*   **Ros**: Rosenthal, *Grammar*
Sch: Schneider, *Grammatik*   **Wms**: Williams, *Syntax*

33.26	GKC §44k; J-M §42f □ B-L 425; Berg 2.15 n a; Brock §122o	35.10	Dav §72R4; GKC §117m; J-M §125j; IBHS 182; Gib 117 □
33.27	GKC §35k		B-M 3.11; GAHG 3.177 n 606;
33.28–29	GKC §133l		Berg 2.78e, 2.82n; Brock §31b
33.30	GKC §96c; J-M §100b n 1 □ B-L 622b; B-M 2.85	35.11	GKC §91l; J-M §94j □ B-L 253b', 604g; Berg 2.42g
33.32	IBHS 602 □ Berg 2.55d*	35.12	GKC §84^{b}e □ B-L 600i'
33.33	Dav §109R2 □ GAHG 3.203 n 766	35.13	IBHS 440 n 17 □ Berg 2.43 n b-k
34.2	GKC §57 n 4, 135k; J-M §113m, 146k	35.15	J-M §150m □ Berg 2.132a
34.4	GKC §72i, 72w, 117n; Gib 18 □ Berg 2.69c, 2.111b*, 2.150n	36.3	Dav §72R1, 147R2; GKC §67r, 75y, 113e, 113g; J-M §123x, 124r, 170f n 2, 170o; Gib 116 □
34.5–6	IBHS 393		B-L 425, 439p'; Berg 1.154e,
34.5	Berg 2.146f		2.38g, 2.135 n f; Brock §145bβ
34.8	GKC §57 n 4, 114r, 135k; J-M §146k □ Berg 2.38g	36.4	J-M §170o
		36.5	Dav §22R3; GKC §91e; J-M
34.10	GKC §57 n 4, 135k, 149c, 167b; J-M §146k; IBHS 300 n 40 □ Berg 2.19a		§94h □ B-L 252l, 268j; Berg 1.95e, 2.84 n p, 2.146 n g
		36.7	Dav §40b; Gib 61
34.11	Dav §56; GKC §135e; J-M §146d; IBHS 300, 300 n 40 □ Berg 2.42g	36.8	B-L 557e'; B-M 2.63; Berg 1.122t, 1.148g
		36.9	GKC §117m n 3; Wms §301;
34.12	Dav §32R2; GKC §126z; Gib 44 □ Berg 1.143a		IBHS 194 □ Berg 2.113f
34.14	GKC §93ss; J-M §96Ce	36.11	GKC §70e □ B-L 403; Berg 2.128 n h
34.15	GKC §135a; J-M §146a	36.12	GKC §69s □ B-L 383
34.16	Berg 2.69c	36.13	GKC §32b, 116t; J-M §155f □
34.17	GKC §32i □ B-L 248i; Jen §8.4.2		B-L 248f; GAHG 3.192 n 698
		36.14	B-L 329e'; GAHG 3.171 n 539
34.18	Berg 1.134c	36.19	Berg 1.50g, 2.21d
34.19	Berg 1.134c	36.23	Berg 1.142f
34.20	GKC §135e; J-M §146d; IBHS 300 n 40 □ B-L 598	36.27	Dav §150 □ Brock §161bβ
34.21	GKC §103b □ B-L 642n'	36.28	Brock §107g
34.25	B-L 581	36.29	GKC §49l
34.27	J-M §65b □ B-L 343b''	36.30	Brock §17
34.29	Berg 1.144d	36.31	GKC §72v; Gib 13
34.31	GKC §32i; J-M §39a, 149c n 1 □ B-L 248i; Jen §8.4.2	36.32	GKC §152d; J-M §160l
		36.35	GKC §34f, 35k, 118p; J-M
35.3	GKC §133l □ Berg 2.16c		§36b; IBHS 307 □ B-L 261f;
35.6	GKC §10h, 60a, 149b □ B-L 111m', 353v; Berg 1.124w, 1.126z, 1.126bb, 1.134c, 2.79g		GAHG 3.146 n 382
		36.36	GKC §122q □ Berg 2.41g
		36.38	GKC §35k; J-M §129f; IBHS 153; Gib 32 □ B-L 582u'
35.7	GKC §133l □ Berg 1.124w	37.1	B-M 3.7
35.9	GKC §69b n 1, 72k □ B-L 384c, 405; Berg 1.124w, 2.125b, 2.146f	37.2	GKC §112pp; J-M §119z □ Berg 1.78m, 2.45n
		37.5	Berg 2.114l

B-L: Bauer and Leander, *Historische Grammatik*   **B-M**: Beer, *Grammatik*   **Berg**: Bergsträsser, *Grammatik*
Brock: Brockelmann, *Syntax*   **Dav**: Davidson, *Syntax*   **GAHG**: Richter, *Grammatik*
Gib: Gibson, *Davidson's Syntax, 4th ed.*   **GKC**: *Gesenius' Grammar*   **IBHS**: Waltke and O'Connor, *Syntax*
Jen: Jenni, *Lehrbuch*   **J-M**: Joüon and Muraoka, *Grammar*   **Ros**: Rosenthal, *Grammar*
Sch: Schneider, *Grammatik*   **Wms**: Williams, *Syntax*

37.7	GKC §60a n 1, 112pp; J-M §44da, 119z; IBHS 497 n 2 □ Berg 2.20 n a, 2.45n	39.14	Dav §24R4
37.8	GKC §9u, 29i n 1 □ Berg 1.160a, 2.45n	39.15	J-M §112i
		39.23–24	GKC §53n
37.9	IBHS 360 n 30 □ Berg 2.122c	39.25	Berg 2.17d
		39.26	GKC §75qq □ B-L 441c; Berg 2.156a
37.10	GKC §112pp; J-M §119z; IBHS 360 n 30, 426, 660 □ B-L 440c; Berg 2.45n, 2.99 n d, 2.157c	39.27	Dav §32R2; GKC §112v, 126z; IBHS 260; Gib 44
37.11	GKC §116t, 119s; J-M §133d; IBHS 209 n 79 □ Berg 2.43 n b-k	39.28	GKC §112kk
		40.1	GKC §164d; IBHS 644 □ B-M 2.92, 3.110; Jen §18.3.4.2; Brock §163b
37.13	J-M §70d □ Berg 2.82n	40.2	Dav §139; IBHS 164, 660; Gib 168
37.15	GKC §135m		
37.16	GKC §66g, 119u; J-M §137u; IBHS 206 n 65 □ Jen §27.3.3; Berg 1.102 n o, 2.124 n f	40.3	GKC §74l □ B-L 444p; B-M 2.165; Berg 2.149m
		40.4	GKC §74d □ B-L 372a; Berg 2.157c
37.17	GKC §52n, 64h; J-M §52c, 119m □ B-L 358v; Berg 2.117e; Brock §83a	40.5	Dav §37R4; GKC §134n □ Berg 2.135d
37.19	GKC §117m n 3 □ Brock §83a, 107g	40.6	B-L 598
		40.7	B-L 563x
37.22	Berg 2.166n	40.9	J-M §91ea n 1 □ B-L 582v'
38.4	J-M §121o	40.10	GAHG 2.26 n 103; Berg 1.153c; Gib 51
38.5	GKC §141c		
38.7	B-L 403; Berg 2.147 n i	40.16	GKC §91l, 94a; J-M §94i □ B-L 253z, 582v'; B-M 2.57
38.8	Berg 2.129i		
38.11	Dav §69R4; GKC §118f, 130a; J-M §129m; IBHS 155 n 34; Gib 34	40.17	GKC §94a, 121d □ B-L 603f; Berg 1.135c
		40.18	Berg 1.135c
38.12	J-M §82k	40.19	GKC §80k; J-M §93k □ B-L 511y, 535f
38.13	J-M §82k		
38.14	IBHS 684 n 48 □ Berg 1.161d	40.24	Berg 2.43 n b-k
38.16	Dav §93; Gib 131	40.27	GKC §134g □ Brock §84c
38.17	Dav §11Ra, 29d; Gib 14	40.28	Dav §32R2; GKC §126w; J-M §138c; Wms §73; IBHS 260 n 14; Gib 44 □ Brock §60a
38.21	GKC §49l		
38.22	GKC §35m □ Berg 1.134c		
38.23	GKC §27s, 54k; J-M §53f; IBHS 431 □ B-L 328c'; B-M 2.122; Jen §15.4; Berg 2.99e(bis)	40.31	Dav §32R2; GKC §93ss; IBHS 260 n 14; Gib 44 □ B-L 588l
		40.34	B-L 588l
39.2	GKC §55f	40.35	GKC §35n □ Berg 2.43 n b-k
39.3	B-L 535f	40.37	B-L 588l
39.4	GKC §119hh	40.39	B-L 354e
39.7	GKC §67y; J-M §82i	40.43	GKC §20m, 88f; J-M §91e □ B-L 212k, 516s; Berg 1.135c
39.8	Berg 2.165l		
39.9	GKC §66e □ B-L 368u; Berg 1.169b, 2.124 n g	40.45	GKC §136d n 2
		40.48	GKC §92g □ B-L 582v'
39.11	GAHG 2.18.61, 3.199 n 745; Brock §116a, 144, 162	41.3	B-L 582v'
39.13	Wms §136	41.6	GKC §134r; IBHS 280, 287

B-L: Bauer and Leander, *Historische Grammatik* **B-M**: Beer, *Grammatik* **Berg**: Bergsträsser, *Grammatik*
Brock: Brockelmann, *Syntax* **Dav**: Davidson, *Syntax* **GAHG**: Richter, *Grammatik*
Gib: Gibson, *Davidson's Syntax, 4th ed.* **GKC**: *Gesenius' Grammar* **IBHS**: Waltke and O'Connor, *Syntax*
Jen: Jenni, *Lehrbuch* **J-M**: Joüon and Muraoka, *Grammar* **Ros**: Rosenthal, *Grammar*
Sch: Schneider, *Grammatik* **Wms**: Williams, *Syntax*

41.7	GKC §67dd; J-M §82j; IBHS 9 □ B-L 431t; B-M 2.147; Berg 2.138n, 2.139p		44.6	GKC §133c; J-M §141i
41.8	B-L 534		44.7	Dav §29R7; Gib 42
41.9	B-M 2.153; Berg 2.151q; Gib 142		44.8	GKC §49d n 1, 58g; J-M §44e; IBHS 516 □ B-L 582u'
41.12	Berg 1.129b		44.9	GKC §93hh, 143e; J-M §125l; IBHS 211
41.15	GKC §91l; J-M §94i; Wms §359 □ B-L 253w, 533f		44.10	Berg 2.44i
41.18	GKC §121d		44.12	GKC §112e n 1 □ Berg 2.31d, 2.32d, 2.43i*
41.20	GKC §5n □ B-L 79s; Berg 1.5l		44.13	GKC §115b
41.22	Dav §69c; GKC §141b; J-M §131a, 154e; Gib 144 □ B-M 3.8; Brock §14bα		44.15	Gib 182
			44.19	Dav §73R4
			44.20	Berg 1.110b
41.25	GKC §131m n 1, 131n n 1		44.30	GKC §115b □ IBHS 271 n 30
41.26	B-L 534		45.1	Dav §36R3; J-M §133c, 142d n 3
42.2	Gib 49		45.2	GKC §52s, 65d □ B-L 362a'
42.3	Berg 1.135c		45.3	Dav §36R3; Gib 48 □ B-L 437; Berg 2.134d
42.5	GKC §68h, 131n □ Berg 1.71e, 2.121 n e		45.9–10	Berg 2.46c
42.6	IBHS 423 □ B-M 1.76		45.9	Wms §72
42.9	B-L 640f'		45.11–12	Brock §21dδ
42.12	B-L 444p		45.11	GKC §126n □ J-M §137o
42.13	Wms §75		45.12	J-M §137o; Gib 49 □ B-L 626q; B-M 2.89
42.14	Dav §29R7; GKC §103g, 131n; J-M §146e; IBHS 127 n 8; Gib 42 □ B-L 525i, 640f'; B-M 2.50; Brock §68b		45.13	GKC §97e; IBHS 414
			45.16	Dav §20R4, 29R5; GKC §127g □ Brock §73c
42.15	GKC §133k		45.18	Berg 2.17d
42.17	GKC §134g □ Berg 1.71e		45.21	GAHG 3.121 n 330
43.6	GKC §102b □ J-M §121g; IBHS 628 □ B-L 642p'; B-M 2.178; GAHG 3.102 n 289; Berg 2.73i		45.23	Gib 3
			46.1	IBHS 386
			46.6	GKC §132g n 1
43.7	Dav §72R4; GKC §117m; J-M §125j		46.9	GKC §93q □ B-L 215k
			46.14	Berg 2.136f
43.8	Berg 2.164i		46.16	J-M §133c
43.10	Dav §78R8; GKC §117c		46.17	GKC §72o; J-M §42f, 176 □ B-L 405; Berg 2.14a
43.16	B-L 629a'; B-M 2.90			
43.17	Dav §72R4; GKC §91l, 103o, 117k; J-M §94i □ B-L 253v, 598, 629a'; Berg 1.129b		46.19	Dav §20R4; GKC §127f; J-M §131d n 1; Wms §82
			46.20	Berg 2.60p
43.19	Dav §9R2 □ Berg 2.43i*		46.22	GKC §5n, 53q, 53s □ B-L 79s, 229h', 362a'; Berg 1.5l, 2.105 n k
43.20	J-M §62e □ B-L 340h'			
43.26	B-L 375			
43.27	GKC §75rr □ B-L 426; Berg 2.168q		46.23	GKC §121d
			46.24	GKC §124r; J-M §136n
44.2	Berg 2.117a		47.2	Berg 2.138l
44.3	Dav §72R4; GKC §117m; Gib 117		47.3	GKC §128n, 134n; J-M §127b
44.5	IBHS 210		47.4	Dav §29R3; GKC §131e; Wms §48, 69

B-L: Bauer and Leander, *Historische Grammatik*   **B-M**: Beer, *Grammatik*   **Berg**: Bergsträsser, *Grammatik*
Brock: Brockelmann, *Syntax*   **Dav**: Davidson, *Syntax*   **GAHG**: Richter, *Grammatik*
Gib: Gibson, *Davidson's Syntax, 4th ed.*   **GKC**: *Gesenius' Grammar*   **IBHS**: Waltke and O'Connor, *Syntax*
Jen: Jenni, *Lehrbuch*   **J-M**: Joüon and Muraoka, *Grammar*   **Ros**: Rosenthal, *Grammar*
Sch: Schneider, *Grammatik*   **Wms**: Williams, *Syntax*

47.5	GKC §93x; J-M §26d, 88Ce □ B-M 2.71; Jen §14.4.6; Berg 1.103q, 2.36k
47.6	J-M §161b
47.7	GKC §91e □ B-L 251h, 405
47.8	GKC §75oo □ B-L 376r; Berg 2.72h*, 2.159g
47.9	GKC §104g
47.10	GKC §91e; J-M §94h □ B-L 534
47.11	B-L 598
47.12	GKC §67g; IBHS 412
47.14	GKC §109d; J-M §133c
47.15	Dav §20R4; GKC §127f, 127f n 1 □ Berg 2.57 n k

47.16	Dav §32R2
47.17ff.	GKC §117m
47.17–19	Dav §72R4; GKC §117m
47.19	GKC §90i
47.20	Berg 2.57 n k
47.22	GKC §35n; J-M §133c □ B-L 227x; Berg 1.124w
48.1	GKC §127f n 1 □ Berg 2.57 n k
48.14	Dav §63R2; GKC §72dd, 109d; J-M §114l; IBHS 567; Gib 82 □ Berg 2.52 n n
48.16	B-L 77m
48.18	GKC §91e
48.28	GKC §9a

B-L: Bauer and Leander, *Historische Grammatik* **B-M**: Beer, *Grammatik* **Berg**: Bergsträsser, *Grammatik*
Brock: Brockelmann, *Syntax* **Dav**: Davidson, *Syntax* **GAHG**: Richter, *Grammatik*
Gib: Gibson, *Davidson's Syntax, 4th ed.* **GKC**: *Gesenius' Grammar* **IBHS**: Waltke and O'Connor, *Syntax*
Jen: Jenni, *Lehrbuch* **J-M**: Joüon and Muraoka, *Grammar* **Ros**: Rosenthal, *Grammar*
Sch: Schneider, *Grammatik* **Wms**: Williams, *Syntax*

HOSEA

1.1	IBHS 648 ☐ B-L 501aι	2.15	Dav §72R1, 73R3, 145; J-M
1.2	Dav §25, 68; GKC §52o, 93m,		§118n; Gib 116, 157 ☐ Berg
	130d; J-M §129p; Wms §489;		2.34h, 2.163g
	IBHS 121, 156, 645; Gib 12,	2.16	Dav §75, 100e; J-M §79k; Gib
	144, 161 ☐ Jen §22.4.5, 25.3.3;		137 ☐ GAHG 3.204 n 771
	Sch §45.5	2.17	Dav §101Rd; GKC §118u; Gib
1.4	Dav §56; GKC §112x; Gib 87 ☐		128 ☐ Berg 2.16c
	Brock §13a	2.20	Dav §101
1.5	Dav §57R2	2.21	GKC §133l; J-M §132g; Wms
1.6	Dav §83, 100R3; GKC §120c,		§238; Gib 36
	120h, 152a n 1; J-M §177c;	2.23	Dav §57R2, 105; Gib 90
	Wms §225; IBHS 657; Gib 120,	2.24	Gib 36
	138 ☐ B-M 3.82; Berg 2.115a;	2.25	GKC §152a n 1; J-M §119d
	Brock §143a	3.1	Dav §91c, 98b; GKC §115d,
1.7	Dav §101, 101Ra, 111; GKC		115f, 125c; Gib 128, 129, 137
	§119o; J-M §132g; IBHS 649	3.2	Dav §24b, 101; GKC §20h ☐
1.9	Dav §128R1; IBHS 93, 206 n 64		Berg 1.68v, 2.79 n g; Brock
2.1	Dav §25, 44a; GKC §130c; J-M		§106e
	§119c; Gib 12	3.4	Dav §68, 140; IBHS 171; Gib
2:2	Berg 2.17e		144
2.3	GKC §96 (p. 284) ☐ B-L 616c	3.5	Dav §101; GKC §2v n 1; Gib
2.4	B-L 483wð; Gib 107		147
2.5	Dav §22R2, 53c, 90, 101Rd;	4.1–2	Sch §49.2.3
	GKC §72w, 118u; J-M	4.2	Dav §88; GKC §113ff.; Gib 127
	§125w n 2; Gib 28, 93, 128, 150		☐ B-L 422t"; Berg 2.67l, 2.160a
	☐ B-L 403; Berg 2.148k	4.3	GKC §112m, 119i ☐ GAHG
2.6	GKC §52n ☐ Berg 1.161e, 2.95d		3.120 n 330; Berg 2.107a
2.7	Dav §14, 98b; J-M §114c; IBHS	4.4	Dav §63; GKC §118x; IBHS
	617, 648GKC §52n; Gib 18, 36,		568; Gib 81 ☐ Berg 2.153t;
	134 ☐ Berg 1.69x, 2.171 n d		Brock §76b
2.8	Dav §3R2; Gib 2, 3 ☐ Berg	4:5	Berg 2.42g
	2.72h, 2.172d	4.6	Dav §41b, 101Rc, 107; Gib 22,
2.9	Dav §33, 52, 62; J-M §114c;		38, 68, 175 ☐ Brock §111f, 176a
	IBHS 265; Gib 45, 150 ☐ B-L	4.7	Dav §28R1, 151; J-M §174c;
	346x"		IBHS 641; Gib 161 ☐ B-L 771
2.10	IBHS 648	4.8	Dav §44a, 116R1; GKC §145m;
2.11	Dav §14, 83; GKC §120e; J-M		Gib 23, 75
	§124d, 177b; Gib 18, 92, 120	4.9	Dav §151R2; GKC §161c ☐
2.12	Dav §11Rb; Gib 14		Brock §109d
2.13	IBHS 648	4:10	Berg 2.44k
2.14	Dav §10R2; GKC §59g; Gib 10	4.11	Dav §114; J-M §150p; Gib 21 ☐
	☐ Berg 1.111 n c, 2.18f		Brock §133b
		4.12	GKC §29w ☐ B-L 235u; Gib 31

B-L: Bauer and Leander, *Historische Grammatik*   **B-M**: Beer, *Grammatik*   **Berg**: Bergsträsser, *Grammatik*
Brock: Brockelmann, *Syntax*   **Dav**: Davidson, *Syntax*   **GAHG**: Richter, *Grammatik*
Gib: Gibson, *Davidson's Syntax, 4th ed.*   **GKC**: *Gesenius' Grammar*   **IBHS**: Waltke and O'Connor, *Syntax*
Jen: Jenni, *Lehrbuch*   **J-M**: Joüon and Muraoka, *Grammar*   **Ros**: Rosenthal, *Grammar*
Sch: Schneider, *Grammatik*   **Wms**: Williams, *Syntax*

4.13	Dav §44a; J-M §52c; Gib 75 □ B-L 328b', 512f'; B-M 2.131; Berg 2.115a	6.10	Brock §158
		7.1–3	Dav §44a
4.14	Dav §11b, 44R3; GKC §155f; J-M §52c; Gib 13, 76 □ B-L 302a'; Berg 2.115a	7.1–2	Gib 75
		7.1	GKC §114q; Gib 170
		7.2	Dav §11c, 146R1; GKC §152t, 157a; Gib 13 □ Brock §144
4.15	Dav §63	7.4	Dav §81, 83R2; GKC §45d, 80k; J-M §93k; Gib 121 □ B-L 302a', 348i, 511y, 548a'; Berg 2.83p
4.16	Dav §22R2; GKC §150a		
4.17	Dav §98b; Gib 134		
4.18	Dav §88R4; GKC §55e, 113w; J-M §59d □ Berg 2.126 n c, 2.160a	7.5	Dav §68; GKC §93ss, 130a; J-M §129n; IBHS 155 n 35, 450; Gib 144 □ Berg 2.150p
4:19	Berg 1.113 n e	7.6	Dav §68; GKC §91c, 91c n 1; J-M §96Ce; Gib 144
5.1	Dav §21f; Gib 27		
5.2	GKC §64a □ B-L 354e, 500tθ; Berg 2.84 n p	7.7	Dav §54a; GKC §112m; J-M §119q; IBHS 527; Gib 93
5.3	GKC §135a □ Berg 2.167o	7.8	Dav §100R3, 128R5; GKC §152t; J-M §160m; Gib 138 □ Brock §125b
5.5	Dav §41b; Gib 68 □ Berg 2.24g		
5.6	Dav §110		
5.8	Dav §117R3; GKC §147c; Gib 164	7.9	Gib 38
		7.10	B-L 346x"; Gib 5
5.9	Dav §14; Gib 17	7.11	Dav §140; GKC §152u; J-M §160o
5.10	GKC §118x; IBHS 203 n 52; Gib 134		
5.11	GKC §120g; J-M §177d; Gib 121 □ Berg 2.88 n d	7.12	GKC §24f n 2, 70b □ B-L 358v, 383; Berg 1.98 n h, 2.128 n h
5.13	Dav §29R1 □ Berg 2.157b	7.13	Brock §11c
5.14	Dav §59; GKC §135a; Gib 137	7.14–16	Dav §44a; Gib 75
5.15	Dav §53b, 83R4; GKC §60e; J-M §63e, 112i n 5; Gib 93 □ B-L 338p	7.14	GKC §70d □ B-L 382
		7.16	GKC §34b n 3; J-M §103a □ B-L 261b
6.1	Dav §51R5, 59, 83R4; GKC §108d; 109k; J-M §119y □ Berg 2.34h, 2.47e, 2.113g, 2.165k	8.1	Dav §117R3; Gib 188
		8.2	GKC §65h □ GAHG 2.18 n 61; B-L 360t; Berg 2.118c
6.2	GKC §96 n 1 (p. 286), 119y n 3, 134s; J-M §119y; Wms §316; IBHS 213; Gib 48 □ Berg 2.162d	8.3	GKC §60d □ B-L 338n; Berg 2.24 n g
		8.4	Dav §149R3; GKC §67v, 117ii; J-M §5m n 5, 82n, 125w, 169g; Gib 159 □ Berg 2.140 n q
6.3	Dav §59, 62, 143; GKC §155g □ Berg 2.174 n h		
6.4	Dav §22R2, 83, 138a; GKC §120g; J-M §177g; Gib 28, 168	8.5	Dav §96Obs, 145R3 □ GAHG 3.161 n 480; Berg 2.84p
6.6	Dav §34R2; GKC §119w, 133b; IBHS 214 n 99, 266; Gib 46, 148	8.6	Dav §71R4, 136R1; IBHS 665 n 81; Gib 141
		8.7	Dav §69R2; GKC §29w, 53g n 1, 90f; Gib 145 □ B-L 528t; Brock §52bβ
6.8	Gib 134		
6.9	Dav §20R4; GKC §23l, 75aa, 93s; IBHS 140; Gib 141 □ B-L 424; B-M 2.68; GAHG 2.18 n 61; Berg 2.62 n b, 2.97h, 2.161 n c	8.9	GKC §119s; IBHS 208 n 78 □ Berg 1.148g
		8.10	GKC §20g, 111w n 1; J-M §171c □ GAHG 3.177 n 605; Berg 1.66t, 2.39 n a-f, 2.137 n k

B-L: Bauer and Leander, *Historische Grammatik*   **B-M**: Beer, *Grammatik*   **Berg**: Bergsträsser, *Grammatik*
Brock: Brockelmann, *Syntax*   **Dav**: Davidson, *Syntax*   **GAHG**: Richter, *Grammatik*
Gib: Gibson, *Davidson's Syntax, 4th ed.*   **GKC**: Gesenius' *Grammar*   **IBHS**: Waltke and O'Connor, *Syntax*
Jen: Jenni, *Lehrbuch*   **J-M**: Joüon and Muraoka, *Grammar*   **Ros**: Rosenthal, *Grammar*
Sch: Schneider, *Grammatik*   **Wms**: Williams, *Syntax*

8.11	Dav §96Obs	10.9	B-L 604g
8.12	Dav §132R2; GKC §159c; Gib	10.10	Dav §96R5; GKC §60a, 171;
	156 □ B-L 302a', 627s; B-M		J-M §77a n 2; Gib 133 □ B-L
	2.88		383; Berg 2.79g, 2.97h,
8.13	Dav §51R4, 59; GKC §111t;		2.129 n m
	IBHS 559; Gib 101	10.11	GKC §90l, 135a; J-M §93n □
8.14	GKC §112x □ Berg 2.42g		B-L 613d'
9.2	Dav §114; GKC §29g; J-M	10.12	Dav §64, 92, 96Obs; GKC
	§150p; Gib 21 □ Berg 2.116b		§110a; Gib 80 □ Berg 2.174 n h;
9.4	Dav §116R2; Gib 23		Brock §3, 1071δ
9.6	Dav §115, 132R2; GKC §130a;	10.13	GKC §90g; Gib 145
	Gib 22, 156 □ GAHG	10.14	Dav §101Rd, 116R2; GKC §9b,
	3.204 n 771		23g, 53u, 72p, 156c; J-M §7b,
9.7	Dav §96R2; J-M §155nd; Gib		80k; IBHS 374 n 29 □ B-L
	43		286m', 404; Berg 1.44c, 2.42g,
9.8–9	Brock §33		2.87c, 2.147g
9.8	Dav §106b	10.15	Dav §41b; GKC §133i
9.9	Dav §82, 83, 101Rd; GKC	11.1	Dav §50b, 145; GKC §68f,
	§118u, 120g, 120h, 130a; J-M		111b; IBHS 498 n 8, 553; Gib
	§177g; Gib 120, 121 □ B-L		96, 157 □ Sch §53.3.3.2; Berg
	302a'; Brock §133b		2.120b
9.11	Dav §101Rc, 106b; GKC §69m,	11.2	Dav §151, 108; J-M §174e □
	143b, 159m □ Berg 2.126c		B-L 328w
9.12	Dav §101, 101Rc; GKC §159m;	11.3	GKC §19i, 55h, 66g; J-M §59e
	Gib 141 □ B-L 404		□ B-L 366t; GAHG 1.72 n 136;
9.13	Dav §94; GKC §114k; IBHS		Berg 2.108 n b, 2.124 n f
	610 n 35; Gib 132	11.4	Dav §50a, 101Ra; GKC §68c;
9.14	Dav §113; GKC §145n; J-M		J-M §90e; Gib 134 □ B-L 370l,
	§134j; IBHS 103; Gib 21 □ Berg		372x; B-M 2.137; Berg
	2.102d		1.101 n m, 2.21 n c, 2.33 n b-h,
9.15	Dav §63R3; GKC §109d; J-M		2.34h, 2.120 n d, 2.165k
	§114g; Gib 82 □ B-L 279 n 1,	11.5	GAHG 3.218 n 825
	301 n 4; Berg 2.79h	11.6	Dav §101Rc
9.16	J-M §171c; Gib 154 □ GAHG	11.7	Dav §108; GKC §75rr, 145c;
	3.177 n 605; Berg 2.20b1; Brock		J-M §103a; Gib 22 □ B-L
	§52bβ		427t''; Berg 2.168q
9.17	Berg 2.140 n q; Gib 78, 138	11.8	Dav §101 n 1, 117 □ Berg
10.1	Dav §73R7, 109; IBHS 104; Gib		1.139b
	118 □ B-L 294d'''	11.9	GKC §114n n 2 □ Berg 2.59n*
10.2	Berg 2.141r	11.10	Dav §44R3, 143; Gib 11
10.4	Dav §84, 87R1, 88R1; GKC	12.1	Dav §16; GKC §124h; Gib 19
	§75n, 113ff; Gib 23, 123, 127 □	12.3	Dav §96R4; J-M §124p; Gib
	B-L 422t''; Berg 2.67 n l,		132
	2.161 n c; Brock §46b	12.4–5	Berg 2.34h
10.5	Dav §115; Gib 22	12.5	Dav §69a; GKC §58k, 118g;
10.6	Dav §79, 111; GKC §121b; Gib		J-M §126h; Gib 143 □ B-L
	118 □ GAHG 3.120 n 330		401n''; Berg 2.174 n k
10.7	Dav §41b; Gib 68	12.6	J-M §177n
10.8	Dav §113; J-M §97Eb, 150p □	12.9	GKC §144f; J-M §155b; Gib 176
	B-L 339z	12.10	Dav §101Rd; GKC §118u

B-L: Bauer and Leander, *Historische Grammatik*   **B-M**: Beer, *Grammatik*   **Berg**: Bergsträsser, *Grammatik*
Brock: Brockelmann, *Syntax*   **Dav**: Davidson, *Syntax*   **GAHG**: Richter, *Grammatik*
Gib: Gibson, *Davidson's Syntax, 4th ed.*   **GKC**: *Gesenius' Grammar*   **IBHS**: Waltke and O'Connor, *Syntax*
Jen: Jenni, *Lehrbuch*   **J-M**: Joüon and Muraoka, *Grammar*   **Ros**: Rosenthal, *Grammar*
Sch: Schneider, *Grammatik*   **Wms**: Williams, *Syntax*

12.11	GKC §112dd, 135a, 142f □ Berg 2.43 n b-k	13.14	GKC §93q, 126e □ B-L 582u'; B-M 2.56; Berg 1.135d
12.12	GKC §159v; J-M §96Al □ B-M 1.101, 2.70; Berg 1.102o	13.15	GKC §75rr; J-M §79l; IBHS 200 □ B-L 425; Berg 2.126 n d, 2.168q
12.14	GKC §119o; IBHS 380 □ Jen §11.3.1.2	14.1	Dav §116R5; GKC §84ᵃg, 145u; IBHS 421; Gib 24
12.15	Dav §71R2; GKC §118q; Gib 145 □ B-L 367	14.2	B-L 135i; Berg 1.107e; Gib 149
13.2	Dav §24a, 44a; GKC §91e, 128l □ B-L 599h'	14.3	Dav §28R3; GKC §128e; Wms §30 □ GAHG 2.18 n 61; Brock §144
13.3	GKC §55b, 120g; J-M §177g □ B-L 281j; Berg 2.108 n b	14.4	Dav §9R1; GKC §121f, 158b; J-M §132e
13.4	B-L 644c''; Brock §118		
13.6	Dav §50b; Gib 97 □ Berg 2.84 n p	14.5	Dav §70b; GKC §68f, 118q; Gib 144 □ Berg 2.120b
13.8	Dav §12; GKC §122e; J-M §134c, 137i; IBHS 107; Gib 16 □ Brock §16a	14.7	Dav §65R6, 113; GKC §145p □ Berg 2.50l
13.9	B-L 355n; Berg 2.116e; Brock §159a	14.9	Dav §8R3 □ Berg 1.148g
13.10	Dav §10R2; GKC §150l; Gib 10, 185	14.10	Dav §65d, 150; GKC §69b n 1, 109i, 141a, 166a, 166a n 3; J-M §167m n 1; IBHS 320; Gib 160 □ B-M 3.16, 3.103; Brock §157
13.12	Dav §104a □ B-L 147 n 2		
13.13	Dav §128R1; GKC §152a n 1; Wms §400; Gib 138, 142 □ B-M 1.105; Brock §13b		

B-L: Bauer and Leander, *Historische Grammatik* **B-M**: Beer, *Grammatik* **Berg**: Bergsträsser, *Grammatik*
Brock: Brockelmann, *Syntax* **Dav**: Davidson, *Syntax* **GAHG**: Richter, *Grammatik*
Gib: Gibson, *Davidson's Syntax, 4th ed.* **GKC**: *Gesenius' Grammar* **IBHS**: Waltke and O'Connor, *Syntax*
Jen: Jenni, *Lehrbuch* **J-M**: Joüon and Muraoka, *Grammar* **Ros**: Rosenthal, *Grammar*
Sch: Schneider, *Grammatik* **Wms**: Williams, *Syntax*

JOEL

1–4	Brock §97c	2.16	B-L 574y
1.1	Jen §6.3.5	2.17	GKC §150e; IBHS 199 n 38 □
1.2	Dav §21f; GKC §110n, 126e,		Jen §19.4.4; Brock §112, 173
	150g; J-M §137g, 161e; Gib 27,	2.18	J-M §112h n 1
	184 □ B-L 632j; B-M 2.173;	2.19	GKC §117z □ Brock §90d
	Brock §169c	2.20	Dav §65R6; GKC §145k n 2 □
1.5	GKC §126e; J-M §137g □ B-L		Berg 2.59n*
	99o	2.21	GKC §46e □ B-L 362a', 398e'';
1.6	GKC §152v; J-M §160o □ B-L		Berg 2.59n*, 2.81k
	600i'; Berg 1.112d	2.22	GKC §144a; J-M §150a; Wms
1.7	GKC §113n; J-M §123j; IBHS		§234
	588 n 33	2.23	GKC §111w; J-M §118s
1.8	Dav §98R1; GKC §63l, 116k;	2.24	GKC §93r; J-M §96Ag □ B-L
	J-M §121o		581; Berg 2.172d
1.9	Berg 2.28g	2.26	Dav §83R5; GKC §113s, 114o □
1.10	B-L 285f'; B-M 2.126; Berg		Berg 2.60p
	2.107a	3.1	J-M §125a; IBHS 167
1.12	GKC §102b □ B-L 198l; Berg	3.3	Berg 1.124w
	2.107a	3.4	Dav §27; Gib 35
1.13	Dav §114; J-M §137g; Gib 22	4.1	GKC §125k □ GAHG
1.15	Dav §117; GKC §147d; IBHS		3.204 n 771
	683; Gib 188	4.2	Berg 1.128dd, 2.42g
1.17	GKC §20h □ Berg 1.68v, 1.149g	4.3	GKC §69u □ Berg 2.129 n k,
1.18	GKC §148a		2.172 n e
1.19	Gib 63	4.4	GKC §133k n 1 □ Berg 1.68v,
1.20	Dav §116; GKC §145k,		1.161d, 2.72h*
	145k n 2; J-M §150g; Gib 23 □	4.10	J-M §169g □ Berg 2.135e
	B-M 3.20	4.11	GKC §51o, 64h □ B-L 322v,
2.1	Gib 170		367; B-M 2.130; Berg 2.92 n gh,
2.2	GKC §106c, 109d; J-M §75f;		2.116e
	IBHS 567; Gib 82 □ Berg 2.79h	4.13	Berg 2.172d, 2.174 n h
2.4	GKC §72u, 126p, 161c	4.14	Dav §29R8; GKC §123e, 147c;
2.5	B-L 539i; B-M 2.129; Berg		J-M §135e; IBHS 119; Gib 42 □
	1.148g, 1.156l, 2.20b		Berg 1.79m
2.6	GKC §23d	4.18	Dav §73R2; GKC §117z; J-M
2.7	GKC §126p □ Berg 2.20b;		§119c, 119u, 125d □ Brock
	Brock §122o		§90d
2.8	Berg 2.20b; Brock §122o	4.19	B-L 564; Berg 1.44c
2.9	Berg 2.135d	4.21	GKC §49k, 75x □ B-M 2.163;
2.13	GKC §152g		Berg 2.17d, 2.167o
2.14	Dav §43R1; Gib 80		

B-L: Bauer and Leander, *Historische Grammatik* **B-M**: Beer, *Grammatik* **Berg**: Bergsträsser, *Grammatik*
Brock: Brockelmann, *Syntax* **Dav**: Davidson, *Syntax* **GAHG**: Richter, *Grammatik*
Gib: Gibson, *Davidson's Syntax, 4th ed.* **GKC**: *Gesenius' Grammar* **IBHS**: Waltke and O'Connor, *Syntax*
Jen: Jenni, *Lehrbuch* **J-M**: Joüon and Muraoka, *Grammar* **Ros**: Rosenthal, *Grammar*
Sch: Schneider, *Grammatik* **Wms**: Williams, *Syntax*

AMOS

1.1	Wms §371; IBHS 221, 242; Gib 26, 31	2.11	Dav §123, 123R1; Gib 183, 184 □ Berg 2.21d; Brock §107g
1.3–15	Gib 48	2.12	GKC §51n □ B-L 440c; Berg
1.3–4	Gib 87		2.92g
1.3	Dav §36b, 91c; GKC §134s, 158c; J-M §170h; Gib 47, 129, 159	2.13	Dav §98a, 101Rb; Gib 133
		2.14	Gib 56
		2.15	Dav §24R5, 71R3; Gib 34
1.4	GKC §49m □ Berg 2.16c	2.16	Dav §24d, 70a; GKC §118n,
1.5	GKC §145c; Gib 22 □ Berg 1.70b		128y; Gib 33
		3.2	GKC §153
1.6	Dav §36b, 91c; GKC §158c; Gib 47, 159	3.3–4	IBHS 642 n 32
		3.3	Dav §154; 130b; Wms §422;
1.7	Berg 2.16c		IBHS 389, 642 n 31; Gib 79,
1.8	GKC §145e; IBHS 109		154, 176
1.9	Dav §36b, 91c; 96; GKC §114r, 158c; J-M §124q; Wms §535; Gib 47, 131, 159	3.4–6	Dav §138a
		3.4	Dav §130b; GKC §163c; J-M §173a; Wms §422, 557; IBHS
1.10	Berg 2.16c		642; Gib 154, 168
1.11	Dav §55b, 92, 96; GKC §58g, 112i, 114r; J-M §61i, 119v, 150e; IBHS 537, 555, 600; Gib 23, 94, 131, 159 □ B-L 303g′, 346t″; Berg 2.43 n b-k	3.5	Dav §86b; GKC §113q; Gib 124, 149, 168 □ B-L 302a′; Berg 2.62c
		3.6	Dav §122; J-M §161d; Gib 168
		3.7	Dav §44a, 154; GKC §107g, 163c; J-M §133b, 173b; Wms §556; IBHS 642, 642 n 31; Gib 74, 141, 176
1.12	Berg 2.16c		
1.13	J-M §65a, 70d, 158c; IBHS 408 □ B-L 361x; Berg 2.82n		
		3.8	Dav §132R2; GKC §159h; Gib 79 □ B-M 3.113
2.1–6	Gib 48		
2.1	GKC §158c	3.9	GKC §124e; J-M §136j
2.2	Dav §116R5; Gib 24	3.10	Dav §14; J-M §134n, 138e; Wms §72, 276; Gib 17, 120, 128 □ Berg 2.54d*
2.3	Dav §116R5; Gib 24 □ Berg 2.112c		
2.4	B-L 354e; Berg 2.116d	3.11	Dav §136R1; GKC §67t, 154 n 1b; J-M §82m; Gib 37 □ B-L 431t; B-M 2.146; GAHG 3.161 n 480; Berg 2.136h
2.6	Dav §22d; GKC §61b, 158c; J-M §65b, 91c; Wms §535; IBHS 245 n 12; Gib 28, 130 □ B-L 343b″; Berg 2.82n		
		3.12	Dav §22c, 44a; GKC §88f, 126r; Gib 28, 74
2.7	Dav §44a, 149R3; GKC §126b; J-M §138e, 169g; Wms §198; IBHS 639 n 25; Gib 159, 160	3.13	Dav §24R6; GKC §125h
		3.14	Berg 2.42g
2.8	Dav §44a; Wms §489	4.1–2	GKC §135o
2.9–12	IBHS 498	4.1	Dav §1R3, 99; GKC §135o, 144a; J-M §138e, 150a; Wms §234; Gib 135 □ B-L 538i
2.9	GKC §53n; Gib 2		
2.10	GKC §69x; Gib 2 □ B-L 385g′; Berg 2.21d		

B-L: Bauer and Leander, *Historische Grammatik*   **B-M**: Beer, *Grammatik*   **Berg**: Bergsträsser, *Grammatik*
Brock: Brockelmann, *Syntax*   **Dav**: Davidson, *Syntax*   **GAHG**: Richter, *Grammatik*
Gib: Gibson, *Davidson's Syntax, 4th ed.*   **GKC**: *Gesenius' Grammar*   **IBHS**: Waltke and O'Connor, *Syntax*
Jen: Jenni, *Lehrbuch*   **J-M**: Joüon and Muraoka, *Grammar*   **Ros**: Rosenthal, *Grammar*
Sch: Schneider, *Grammatik*   **Wms**: Williams, *Syntax*

4.2	Dav §79, 109; GKC §75oo, 112x; J-M §165b; Wms §59; IBHS 679; Gib 59, 91 ☐ GAHG 3.204 n 771; Jen §17.3.4; Berg 2.72h, 2.156b	5.6	Dav §53c, 64; GKC §110f, 112p; J-M §116f; Gib 93, 105, 137
4.3	GKC §44k; J-M §147d; Wms §55 ☐ B-L 332p; B-M 2.105; Berg 2.15 n a	5.7–12	Dav §100e; Gib 137
		5.7	Dav §100R4; GKC §126b; J-M §138e
4.4	Dav §64, 82; GKC §110a, 113z, 114n n 2; Wms §103; IBHS 572; Gib 81, 105, 120 ☐ Jen §27.3.3; Berg 2.59n*	5.8–9	IBHS 618 n 28
		5.8	Dav §40c, 49a; 98a; GKC §111u, 117ii; J-M §112l, 118r, 125w, 125w n 2; IBHS 174 n 22, 561 n 21; Gib 101, 133 ☐ B-L 294d‴; Berg 2.38e, 2.69c
4.5	J-M §123x		
4.6	Gib 173, 175	5.9	Dav §98a; Gib 133 ☐ Berg 1.161e, 2.34h
4.7–8	IBHS 534; Gib 90 ☐ Berg 2.42g*		
		5.10	Berg 2.115a
4.7	Dav §54b, 109; GKC §112h n 3, 112s, 144c; J-M §152e; Wms §241, 499; Gib 172, 175 ☐ Brock §35a	5.11	GKC §61e; Gib 131, 158 ☐ B-L 346x″; Berg 2.95d
		5.12	Dav §146R3; J-M §157b; Gib 111
4.8	Dav §54b, 109; GKC §134s; Gib 48 ☐ B-L 398f″	5.13	GKC §67g; Gib 135
4.9	Dav §22R1; GKC §126n; IBHS 246 n 14; Gib 29 ☐ Berg 2.65 n h	5.14	GKC §109k, 152g; J-M §168a n 2, 169g; Gib 25 ☐ Brock §43
4.10	Dav §136R1; GKC §154a n 1, 154a n 1b; Wms §435; IBHS 649; Gib 37 ☐ GAHG 3.161 n 480	5.15	Dav §43b; GKC §63l, 67cc; J-M §82k; Gib 25, 79 ☐ B-L 347g, 371v, 437; B-M 2.144; Berg 2.114k, 2.133b
4.11	Dav §91R3; GKC §115d, 115f ☐ B-M 2.107; Berg 2.84p	5.16	Dav §117; GKC §105a; Gib 25, 188
4.12	GKC §158b; Gib 159, 179	5.18	GKC §152d; Gib 133
4.13	Dav §98R1; GKC §29e n 1, 116g n 1; J-M §97Eb; IBHS 618 n 28; Gib 55 ☐ GAHG 3.204 n 771; Berg 1.131d	5.19	Dav §22c, 54a; GKC §112c, 112m, 126r; J-M §119q; Wms §92; Gib 28, 94 ☐ Brock §41k
		5.21	GKC §20h, 106g, 154a n 1; J-M §112a; Wms §163; Gib 63 ☐ B-L 212k, 614; Berg 1.68v, 2.28g; Brock §41c, 133b
5.2	Dav §41b, 140; GKC §128k; IBHS 153; Gib 137 ☐ B-M 3.50, 3.58; Jen §29.3.2		
5.3	Dav §28R5, 71R1; GKC §117z, 129g ; Gib 135	5.22	Gib 154
		5.24	J-M §82m ☐ B-M 2.146; Berg 2.136i
5.4	Dav §64; GKC §110f; J-M §116f, 168a n 2; Gib 105 ☐ B-M 3.112; Berg 2.50k	5.25	J-M §161b; IBHS 685 ☐ Berg 1.68v
5.5	Dav §63; GKC §113n, 122h; J-M §123e, 123u n 1, 134g; IBHS 104 ☐ Berg 2.52n	5.26	Dav §57R1; GKC §112x, 112rr ☐ Berg 2.43 n b-k
		5.27	Dav §57R1; Gib 11, 88
5.6–7	GKC §144p	6.1	Dav §34R5, 144R4; GKC §112n; J-M §119r; IBHS 271; Gib 12, 46

B-L: Bauer and Leander, *Historische Grammatik*   **B-M**: Beer, *Grammatik*   **Berg**: Bergsträsser, *Grammatik*
Brock: Brockelmann, *Syntax*   **Dav**: Davidson, *Syntax*   **GAHG**: Richter, *Grammatik*
Gib: Gibson, *Davidson's Syntax, 4th ed.*   **GKC**: *Gesenius' Grammar*   **IBHS**: Waltke and O'Connor, *Syntax*
Jen: Jenni, *Lehrbuch*   **J-M**: Joüon and Muraoka, *Grammar*   **Ros**: Rosenthal, *Grammar*
Sch: Schneider, *Grammatik*   **Wms**: Williams, *Syntax*

6.2	Dav §24R6; GKC §125h, 126y, 133a; J-M §96Dd, 131n; Gib 44, 184 □ B-L 510v	7.12	Dav §45R4, 101Rb; J-M §133d; Wms §491; Gib 150 □ Jen §27.3.3
6.3	Dav §19R2, 49a, 100R5; GKC §49d n 1; J-M §44e, 125k, 138e; IBHS 516 n 48; Gib 101, 118, 138 □ Berg 2.21b, 2.172 n e	7.13	Dav §22R3, 104; Gib 29
		7.14	Dav §104; GKC §128v; J-M §160c, 172c; Wms §555, 562; IBHS 615 n 17, 671 n 100 □ B-M 3.33
6.4	IBHS 622; Gib 135		
6.6	GKC §63e, 93k, 119m n 1; J-M §41a; IBHS 392; Gib 46 □ Brock §106a	7.15	GKC §119b; Wms §358; IBHS 221
6.7	Gib 95	7.17	Dav §105; GKC §113n; J-M §123e; IBHS 420; Gib 118
6.8	Dav §11c; Wms §130; Gib 13 □ Berg 2.115a	8.3	B-L 652b; Gib 6
6.10	Dav §95, 126, 127d; GKC §114l, 145m, 147d n 1, 152s; Wms §196, 397; IBHS 610, 683; Gib 132, 184, 188 □ B-L 652b; Berg 2.58m	8.4	Dav §96R4; GKC §53q; J-M §54b, 124p; Gib 132 □ B-L 228a'; Berg 2.105 n k
		8.5	Dav §65d; GKC §108d; J-M §116c; IBHS 575; Gib 106, 185 □ Brock §91, 176c
6.11	Dav §146R4; Gib 111, 114 □ GAHG 3.204 n 771	8.6	J-M §91c
6.12	Dav §17R6, 108; GKC §123a n 1, 144d; J-M §155e; Gib 13 □ B-L 352	8.8	GKC §19k n 2, 112p, 125e; J-M §119f; Gib 27 □ Brock §23e
		8.9	Dav §57R2, 73R7; GKC §49l, 112y; Wms §273; Gib 6, 118
6.13	Dav §128R1; GKC §152a n 1; J-M §138e; Gib 142	8.10	GKC §128h, 135p; J-M §129e; IBHS 147; Gib 31 □ Brock §77e
6.14	GKC §112t, 125c; J-M §119n □ Berg 2.57 n k	8.11–14	Gib 90
7.1	Dav §100a; GKC §86i, 147b; Wms §587; Gib 136, 137 □ B-L 512d'; Berg 2.70e	8.11	Berg 2.72h; Gib 91, 137
		8.12	B-L 398f'
		8.13	GKC §54k, 146g; J-M §150q; Gib 90 □ Berg 2.99e
7.2	Dav §8R1, 130b; GKC §112uu; J-M §119z; Wms §123; IBHS 320 n 10; Gib 8, 120, 154 □ B-M 2.13; GAHG 3.170 n 523, 3.215 n 815; Berg 1.132e, 2.43 n b-k	8.14	Dav §119; GKC §93aa n 1; IBHS 631; Gib 34, 137, 186
		9.1	Dav §28R5, 108R1; GKC §61g, 144e; J-M §130g, 155d; Wms §222; IBHS 555; Gib 100 □ B-L 361a'; B-M 2.128; GAHG 3.102 n 289; Berg 2.82 n n; Brock §37, 49a, 122q
7.3	Gib 5		
7.4	Dav §57R1; GKC §112tt; IBHS 498 n 4; Gib 103, 137 □ Berg 2.43 n b-k, 2.70e	9.2ff.	GKC §159r
		9.2–4	Dav §130a; Wms §454, 529; Gib 87, 154
7.5	Dav §8R1; Wms §123; IBHS 320 n 10; Gib 8 □ B-M 2.13; GAHG 3.170 n 523, 3.215 n 815	9.2	J-M §171d; Gib 153 □ B-M 3.114
7.6	Dav §4R1; GKC §156b; J-M §152c; Gib 3	9.3	GKC §112p; J-M §119c, 177j
		9.4	GKC §61g
7.7	Dav §139; GKC §156b; Gib 137, 168 □ Berg 2.70e	9.5–6	IBHS 618 n 28

B-L: Bauer and Leander, *Historische Grammatik*   **B-M**: Beer, *Grammatik*   **Berg**: Bergsträsser, *Grammatik*
Brock: Brockelmann, *Syntax*   **Dav**: Davidson, *Syntax*   **GAHG**: Richter, *Grammatik*
Gib: Gibson, *Davidson's Syntax, 4th ed.*   **GKC**: *Gesenius' Grammar*   **IBHS**: Waltke and O'Connor, *Syntax*
Jen: Jenni, *Lehrbuch*   **J-M**: Joüon and Muraoka, *Grammar*   **Ros**: Rosenthal, *Grammar*
Sch: Schneider, *Grammatik*   **Wms**: Williams, *Syntax*

9.5	Dav §49a, 51R4, 100R4; GKC §19k n 2; J-M §118r, 177n; IBHS 393; Gib 101, 137 □ B-L 399h″, 403; Berg 2.38 n e, 2.145c
9.6	J-M §118r; IBHS 561; Gib 55 □ B-L 598; Berg 2.38e
9.7	Dav §126R4; GKC §150e □ B-M 3.87
9.8	Dav §86b, 86R1, 154; GKC §53k, 113n, 113v; J-M §123o, 173a; Wms §205, 558; IBHS 673; Gib 124, 176 □ GAHG 2.64 n 271; Berg 2.42h, 2.63c, 2.105i

9.9	Dav §109, 146R4; Gib 111 □ B-M 2.151; GAHG 3.204 n 771; Berg 2.16c, 2.148k
9.10	B-L 644c‴
9.11	Dav §101Rd; GKC §116d, 118u; J-M §121i □ Berg 2.69 n c
9.13	GKC §54k, 112x; J-M §119d □ Berg 2.72h, 2.99e
9.14	GKC §91c; J-M §119f □ B-L 578l′
9.15	J-M §112i; Gib 101

B-L: Bauer and Leander, *Historische Grammatik*   **B-M**: Beer, *Grammatik*   **Berg**: Bergsträsser, *Grammatik*
Brock: Brockelmann, *Syntax*   **Dav**: Davidson, *Syntax*   **GAHG**: Richter, *Grammatik*
Gib: Gibson, *Davidson's Syntax, 4th ed.*   **GKC**: *Gesenius' Grammar*   **IBHS**: Waltke and O'Connor, *Syntax*
Jen: Jenni, *Lehrbuch*   **J-M**: Joüon and Muraoka, *Grammar*   **Ros**: Rosenthal, *Grammar*
Sch: Schneider, *Grammatik*   **Wms**: Williams, *Syntax*

OBADIAH

1	Berg 1.47e
3	GKC §90l, 93x
4	GKC §73f; J-M §167i □ B-L 405, Berg 1.151 n s
5	Dav §130b; Gib 153 □ B-M 2.161
8	Dav §56
9–10	Dav §101Rc
9	J-M §169g; Gib 119 □ B-M 2.219
10	Dav §23; GKC §128h; J-M §129e; Wms §38; IBHS 147; Gib 32 □ B-M 3.33
11	GKC §9v, 61d, 61f n 1, 69u, 118x; J-M 133g; IBHS 204 n 57 □ B-L 353v, Berg 1.83n, 2.129 n k, 2.172 n e
12–14	Dav §63
12	GKC §53n □ Berg 1.163f
13	GKC §47k; IBHS 517 n 63 □ Berg 1.20 n a
15	GKC §161b □ Berg :128dd
16	J-M §174d
18	B-L 123 n 1
20	GKC §29q □ B L 510v, Berg 1.139 n o

B-L: Bauer and Leander, *Historische Grammatik* **B-M**: Beer, *Grammatik* **Berg**: Bergsträsser, *Grammatik*
Brock: Brockelmann, *Syntax* **Dav**: Davidson, *Syntax* **GAHG**: Richter, *Grammatik*
Gib: Gibson, *Davidson's Syntax, 4th ed.* **GKC**: *Gesenius' Grammar* **IBHS**: Waltke and O'Connor, *Syntax*
Jen: Jenni, *Lehrbuch* **J-M**: Joüon and Muraoka, *Grammar* **Ros**: Rosenthal, *Grammar*
Sch: Schneider, *Grammatik* **Wms**: Williams, *Syntax*

JONAH

1.2	J-M §138a, 141c; IBHS 258	2.3	J-M 119y n 2 □ Brock §82b
1.3	Dav §14; GKC §116d, 122t, 135p; Gib 18 □ GAHG 3.102 n 288, 3.102 n 289, Berg 2.69c	2.6	IBHS 215 n 103
		2.7	Dav §106b
		2.8	Dav 143 n 1
		2.9	J-M 141m; IBHS 267
1.4	Dav §14; IBHS 381; Gib 18	2.10	GKC §90g □ B-L 528t
1.5	GKC §51m □ B-L 320g, Berg 2.27d, 2.91g, 2.137k	2.11	Dav §146R4; GKC §122s; Gib 111 □ Berg 2.157b
1.6	Dav §8R3, 70a; GKC §120b; J-M §127a, 161i; Gib 8, 179 □ Berg 2.119a	3.3	Dav §34R6; J-M 159f; Wms §81; IBHS 268; Gib 46
1.7–8	GKC §150k	3.4	Dav §69c; J-M 111d n 1; Gib 144 □ Berg 2.72h*
1.7	GKC §36, 150k; IBHS 335 n 15 □ B-M 2.13, Berg 2.47e	3.5	GKC §133g; J-M 128ba, 141j; Wms §79; IBHS 270; Gib 45 □ Brock §60c
1.8	Dav §8R4; J-M 143h; IBHS 328 □ B-M 2.15	3.9	Dav §43R1; Gib 80
1.9	GKC §2b; J-M §121l □ B-L 13c, 71a′; B-M 1.12	4.1	GKC §117q; IBHS 377
		4.2	Dav §82; GKC §16f, 114n n 2; Gib 120 □ Berg 2.59n*
1.10	Dav §67b; GKC §117q; J-M §143g; Gib 115	4.3	GAHG 3.215 n 815
1.11	Dav §65d; GKC §113u, 165a; J-M §113m, 116e,g, 123s, 161m, 169i; Gib 106 □ Berg 2.71f	4.4	J-M 161b; Gib 63 □ Berg 2.28g; Brock §93d
		4.5	GKC §107k; J-M 113k □ Sch §48.4.3.5
1.12	J-M 169i; IBHS 335 n 15 □ Berg 2.149l	4.6	GKC §117q
		4.9	GKC §113k; IBHS 269, 269 n 28; Gib 63 □ Berg 2.28g; 2.65h*; Brock §93d
1.14	Dav §62; GKC §16f, 105a, 108c; J-M 114f; Gib 82, 105 □ B-L 564; GAHG 3.216 n 815, Berg 1.44c, 2.49h	4.10	Dav §24R3; GKC §96 (p. 285), 128v; IBHS 335 n 14; Gib 12 □ B-L 618j
1.15	GKC §61c, Berg 2.82n	4.11	Dav §121; GKC §20m, 97b, 150a; IBHS 282; Gib 49, 183 □ B-L 627s; B-M 2.88, 3.87; Jen §18.4.8, Berg 2.65h*
1.16	J-M 125u n 1, Berg 2.122b		
2.1	GKC §122s □ B-L 361x, Berg 2.164i		
2.2	GKC §122s		

B-L: Bauer and Leander, *Historische Grammatik* **B-M**: Beer, *Grammatik* **Berg**: Bergsträsser, *Grammatik*
Brock: Brockelmann, *Syntax* **Dav**: Davidson, *Syntax* **GAHG**: Richter, *Grammatik*
Gib: Gibson, *Davidson's Syntax, 4th ed.* **GKC**: *Gesenius' Grammar* **IBHS**: Waltke and O'Connor, *Syntax*
Jen: Jenni, *Lehrbuch* **J-M**: Joüon and Muraoka, *Grammar* **Ros**: Rosenthal, *Grammar*
Sch: Schneider, *Grammatik* **Wms**: Williams, *Syntax*

MICAH

1.2	Dav §21f; GKC §109k, 135r, 144p; J-M §146j; IBHS 77, 247 n 17; Gib 28 □ Berg 2.49h; Brock §10, 153c	2.7	Dav §32R2; GKC §100n, 118n; IBHS 645 n 36; Gib 44
1.3	B-L 597h'; GAHG 3.204 n 771; Berg 1.131d	2.8	Dav §98R1; GKC §72p, 116h; J-M §121n; IBHS 442; Gib 134 □ B-L 333x; Berg 2.146 n g
1.4	IBHS449	2.9	J-M §136n
1.5	GKC §23c, 37a, 137a; J-M §144b; IBHS 320; Gib 8	2.10	Dav §143; Gib 10
1.6	IBHS 209, 437; Gib 114	2.11	Dav §131; GKC §159x; Gib 155 □ GAHG 3.178 n 618; Berg 1.147b, 2.41d
1.7	GKC §52l, 67y, 117ii; IBHS 375 n 32 □ B-L 286m', 329i'; Berg 2.88c, 2.96 n g	2.12	Dav §20R4, 29R6; GKC §72k, 127i; 80b n 3, 80i n 1; IBHS 127 n 5, 249 n 21; Gib 26, 42 □ B-L 251i, 268j, 370f, 581; B-M 2.137; Berg 1.89a, 2.120b, 2.173 n f
1.8	GKC §69b n 1, 118n; J-M §114c □ B-L 385g'; GAHG 3.152 n 417, 215 n 812; Berg 2.131o		
1.9	Dav §109R2, 116, 116R6; Gib 23, 24	2.13	Dav §49b, 50b; GKC §111w; IBHS 557; Gib 102 □ Berg 2.29h
1.10	Dav §86b; GKC §113v; J-M §123o; Gib 124 □ GAHG 2.35 n 148, 2.64 n 270, 3.168 n 505; Brock §90d	3.1	GKC §114l, 150e; Wms §284; IBHS 208 □ Jen §27.3.3
1.11	GKC §122s, 131c, 145m	3.2–5	Dav §99
1.12	Berg 2.173 n f	3.2	Gib 128, 135
1.13	GKC §110k; J-M §97Eb □ Berg 2.20 n a	3.3	Gib 135
		3.4	Dav §65R6; GKC §107c n 3, 109k; J-M §170k □ Berg 2.51l
1.15	GKC §74k □ B-L 444p; Berg 1.90c, 2.158d	3.5	Dav §55c, 99R2, 100R4, 132R2; IBHS 221 n 119, 631 n 55; Gib 135, 137, 156 □ B-M 3.54; Berg 2.41e
1.16	B-L 362a'; Berg 2.80i, 2.134c		
2.1–2	Dav §54a		
2.1	Gib 94		
2.3	Dav §71R2; GKC §118q; J-M §129d; IBHS 172; Gib 145 □ B-M 3.78; Berg 1.145d, 2.173 n g; Brock §104, 122d	3.6	Dav §101Rc; GKC §119w, 144c; J-M §152e □ Berg 2.17e; Brock §35d
		3.8	Dav §109; Gib 63, 174 □ B-L 375
2.4	Dav §108; GKC §67u, 117r, 144d, 148b; J-M §123p, 125p; IBHS 582; Gib 13 □ B-L 439p'; Berg 2.63f, 2.132a*, 2.134c, 2.168 n q	3.9	Dav §14, 100R4; J-M §134n; Gib 17, 137 □ B-L 549a'
		3.11	Dav §44a; Gib 75 □ Berg 2.76 n b
2.6	GKC §72dd, 150o; IBHS 438 □ B-L 404; Berg 2.150 n o	3.12	Dav §80; GKC §44k, 87e, 121d; J-M §90c, 97Eb, 128c; IBHS 118; Gib 27, 118 □ B-L 517t, 564
		4.1–3	IBHS 17

B-L: Bauer and Leander, *Historische Grammatik*   **B-M**: Beer, *Grammatik*   **Berg**: Bergsträsser, *Grammatik*
Brock: Brockelmann, *Syntax*   **Dav**: Davidson, *Syntax*   **GAHG**: Richter, *Grammatik*
Gib: Gibson, *Davidson's Syntax, 4th ed.*   **GKC**: *Gesenius' Grammar*   **IBHS**: Waltke and O'Connor, *Syntax*
Jen: Jenni, *Lehrbuch*   **J-M**: Joüon and Muraoka, *Grammar*   **Ros**: Rosenthal, *Grammar*
Sch: Schneider, *Grammatik*   **Wms**: Williams, *Syntax*

4.1	J-M §121e □ B-L 73d; Berg 2.42g*	6.5	GKC §117gg □ GAHG 3.215 n 815
4.2	IBHS 654; Gib 77 □ Berg 2.47d, 2.47e	6.6	B-L 637p; Berg 2.136i
4.3	GKC §91n, 145c □ B-L 563x	6.7	Dav §76; GKC §134g
4.5	B-L 158 n 2	6.8	Dav §91R3; GKC §163d; J-M §173c; IBHS 325, 592; Gib 8, 129, 148, 176 □ Berg 2.55d*, 2.67 n l; Brock §99b
4.6–7	GKC §122s □ Berg 2.53q		
4.6	Dav §14, 63R3, 99; GKC §68h, 84ªs, 122s; J-M §119j; Gib 18, 135 □ Berg 2.120b		
4.7	J-M §119j □ Berg 2.112c	6.9	GKC §146b; J-M §162e; IBHS 664
4.8	GKC §68f; J-M §73g; IBHS 22 □ B-M 2.164; Berg 1.91d, 1.92f, 1.148g, 2.17e, 2.120c	6.10	GKC §47b n 1, 118g; J-M §126h □ B-L 634u; Berg 1.104 n t
4.9	Dav §67b, 86R3; GKC §117q; Gib 115, 125 □ Brock §93d	6.11	GKC §47b □ Berg 1.104 n t
		6.12–13	IBHS 664
4.10	GKC §10k, 73b, 76g □ B-L 398h″; Berg 2.145 n d, 2.152t	6.13	Dav §87; GKC §67ee, 115c; J-M §82k; Gib 126 □ B-L 439p′; Berg 2.133 n b
4.11	Dav §116; GKC §119dd, 145n; J-M §150d; Gib 21, 23 □ Berg 1.161d, 2.49h, 2.163g; Brock §43	6.14	Dav §65R6 □ B-L 581; Berg 1.149g, 2.51l
		6.15	B-L 302a′; Berg 1.129b, 1.150m, 2.84q
4.12	Dav §22e; GKC §90i; Gib 28 □ Berg 1.142f	6.16	Dav §51R4, 149R3; J-M §169g; IBHS 559; Gib 160 □ B-M 1.114
4.13	Dav §76; GKC §44h, 44h n 1, 72q, 117ii; J-M §80k, 103b; Gib 114 □ B-L 352, 398h″; B-M 2.147; Berg 2.15 n a, 2.138l, 2.145d	7.1	Dav §117, 128R6, 143; GKC §93p; J-M §96Ad, 105b; IBHS 682; Gib 188 □ B-L 210f, 581; Berg 1.122t, 2.57l
4.14	Dav §24R3, 101Ra; GKC §3g, 119o; Wms §243; IBHS 197	7.2	Dav §77, 127b; GKC §117ff., 119i, 152k; IBHS 175; Gib 57, 144
5.1	GKC §90g n 1, 135g, 142g; J-M §134g; IBHS 104 □ Berg 1.90c; Brock §19b	7.3	Dav §49a, 106d; GKC §135f; J-M 146d; IBHS 299 n 35; Gib 101
5.2	Dav §41c, 108R1; GKC §106o, 155l; Gib 13, 67	7.4	Dav §34R3; GKC §133e, 133g; Wms §79; IBHS 265, 271; Gib 45 □ B-M 3.37; Brock §60c
5.4	Dav §24a, 29e; GKC §72i, 128l, 134s; IBHS 338; Gib 42, 48 □ Berg 2.150n		
		7.6	Jen §10.4.11; Gib 52
5.5	Berg 2.174 n h	7.8	Dav §130R4, 132R2; GKC §72b n 1, 122s; J-M §97Fb, 134o □ B-L 231b, 613d′; Berg 2.146f
5.7	Dav §130b; Gib 153 □ Berg 2.40d		
5.8	Dav §65R6 □ Berg 2.51l		
5.11	Berg 1.113 n e	7.9	B-L 636j
5.13	B-L 600j′	7.10	Dav §65R6, 113; GKC §75p, 75w, 75hh, 122s, 145n; J-M §97Fh, 150d, 167a; Gib 185 □ B-L 426, 613d′; B-M 2.158, 3.36; Jen §25.3.3; Berg 1.158q, 2.50l, 2.163f, 2.167o
6.1	GKC §138e		
6.2	J-M §113c n 1 □ Berg 2.129l		
6.3	GKC §53p, 75ee, 163b □ B-L 266e, 424; Berg 2.106l, 2.167o		

B-L: Bauer and Leander, *Historische Grammatik*   **B-M**: Beer, *Grammatik*   **Berg**: Bergsträsser, *Grammatik*
Brock: Brockelmann, *Syntax*   **Dav**: Davidson, *Syntax*   **GAHG**: Richter, *Grammatik*
Gib: Gibson, *Davidson's Syntax, 4th ed.*   **GKC**: *Gesenius' Grammar*   **IBHS**: Waltke and O'Connor, *Syntax*
Jen: Jenni, *Lehrbuch*   **J-M**: Joüon and Muraoka, *Grammar*   **Ros**: Rosenthal, *Grammar*
Sch: Schneider, *Grammatik*   **Wms**: Williams, *Syntax*

7.11	GKC §126x	7.18	GKC §148c □ GAHG
7.12	Dav §6R1; GKC §126aa		3.181 n 636
7.14	GKC §90m; J-M §93n	7.19	Dav §83; GKC §129g; J-M
7.16	Dav §22R3; Gib 29		§177b; Gib 120 □ GAHG
7.17	Dav §101; GKC §116h; Gib		3.218 n 825
	147, 148		

B-L: Bauer and Leander, *Historische Grammatik*   **B-M**: Beer, *Grammatik*   **Berg**: Bergsträsser, *Grammatik*
Brock: Brockelmann, *Syntax*   **Dav**: Davidson, *Syntax*   **GAHG**: Richter, *Grammatik*
Gib: Gibson, *Davidson's Syntax, 4th ed.*   **GKC**: *Gesenius' Grammar*   **IBHS**: Waltke and O'Connor, *Syntax*
Jen: Jenni, *Lehrbuch*   **J-M**: Joüon and Muraoka, *Grammar*   **Ros**: Rosenthal, *Grammar*
Sch: Schneider, *Grammatik*   **Wms**: Williams, *Syntax*

NAHUM

B-L: Bauer and Leander, *Historische Grammatik*　**B-M**: Beer, *Grammatik*　**Berg**: Bergsträsser, *Grammatik*
Brock: Brockelmann, *Syntax*　**Dav**: Davidson, *Syntax*　**GAHG**: Richter, *Grammatik*
Gib: Gibson, *Davidson's Syntax, 4th ed.*　**GKC**: *Gesenius' Grammar*　**IBHS**: Waltke and O'Connor, *Syntax*
Jen: Jenni, *Lehrbuch*　**J-M**: Joüon and Muraoka, *Grammar*　**Ros**: Rosenthal, *Grammar*
Sch: Schneider, *Grammatik*　**Wms**: Williams, *Syntax*

HABAKKUK

1.2–3	Dav §41R2	2.14	Dav §73R7, 90, 143; GKC
1.2	GKC §106h; J-M §125b		§116f n 2, 155g; Gib 11 □ Berg
1.5	Dav §88R4; GKC §116s; J-M		2.55d*, 2.59n
	§154c □ Jen §14.4.5	2.15	Dav §88R1; GKC §113z, 116g;
1.6	Dav §143; GKC §13c, 155e; Gib		Gib 127
	11 □ Berg 1.67u	2.16	Dav §34R2; Gib 46, 128 □ B-L
1.7	B-L 583y'		437
1.8	GKC §67ee □ Berg 2.132a*,	2.17	Dav §23; GKC §20n, 60d, 67v;
	2.134c(bis)		Gib 32 □ B-L 338n, 437; Berg
1.9–10	GKC §111t		1.141 n a, 2.23g, 2.140q
1.9	J-M §118q, 146j □ Berg	2.18	Dav §41R2; GKC §37d; Gib 68
	2.39 n a-f		□ B-L 266e
1.10	Dav §51R4; J-M §118q □ Berg	2.19	Dav §24R4, 117; GKC
	2.39 n a-f		§100g n 2, 152p; J-M §160k;
1.11	Dav §6R1; GKC §102d, 138h;		Gib 34
	J-M §103b □ Berg 2.34g	2.20	GKC §147d; Gib 188 □ B-M
1.12	B-L 771, 382; Berg 2.118b		2.145; Berg 2.135c, 2.164n;
1.13	Dav §34R2; GKC §65e; Gib 45	3	IBHS 14, 681
	□ B-L 538i; B-M 2.132	3.1	IBHS 207 n 70; Gib 35
1.14	Dav §100R3; GKC §152u; Gib	3.2	Dav §45R4; GKC §75mm □
	138 □ Berg 2.161b		B-L 302a', 423; B-M 2.171;
1.15	GKC §63p □ B-L 174m, 425;		Berg 2.55d*, 2.162d
	Berg 1.154e, 2.135d	3.3	J-M §93d n 2; Gib 71
1.16	GKC §65e, 103g □ B-L 361a',	3.5	Brock §107lα
	640f'; Berg 1.153c, 2.117a	3.6	GKC §67k, 67ee; J-M §82k □
1.17	GKC §114k, 114p n 2, 156g □		Berg 1.123v, 2.109d, 2.134c
	B-L 352; Berg 2.59 n mop	3.8	Dav §29R4; GKC §131r; IBHS
2.1	Dav §65R5; GKC §37b; Gib 172		140; Gib 41
2.2	Berg 2.115a	3.9	Dav §67b, 78R3, 86R3; GKC
2.3	GKC §65f, 72dd, 113n; J-M		§65e, 117q; J-M §93d n 2,
	§123e □ B-L 404; GAHG		125w, 128c; IBHS 382 n 10; Gib
	3.175 n 589; Berg 2.51l, 2.117a;		125 □ B-L 425; Berg 1.153c,
	Brock §93a		2.84 n p, 2.117a, 2.171 n d
2.5	GAHG 3.177 n 605; Berg	3.10	Dav §45R2; GKC §91l; J-M
	2.153u		§94i □ B-L 253v, 547
2.6	GKC §13c, 147c □ Berg 1.67u	3.11	GKC §90d
2.7	Berg 2.108c	3.13	Dav §91R3; GKC §22s, 75aa,
2.8	J-M §82g □ Berg 2.135d		75n, 113h; J-M §49ca, 79p,
2.10	GKC §116s, 118p □ Berg		93d n 2; IBHS 140 □ B-L 127a',
	2.174 n h		222s, 425; GAHG 2.18 n 61;
2.12	GKC §112n; J-M §119r, 121l;		Berg 1.66q, 2.84 n p, 2.161 n c,
	IBHS 631; Gib 95 □ Berg 2.41e;		2.171 n d
	Brock §44c	3.15	Dav §109R3; GKC §144m
2.13	GAHG 3.205 n 780	3.16	B-L 435p'; Berg 2.140q

B-L: Bauer and Leander, *Historische Grammatik* **B-M**: Beer, *Grammatik* **Berg**: Bergsträsser, *Grammatik*
Brock: Brockelmann, *Syntax* **Dav**: Davidson, *Syntax* **GAHG**: Richter, *Grammatik*
Gib: Gibson, *Davidson's Syntax, 4th ed.* **GKC**: *Gesenius' Grammar* **IBHS**: Waltke and O'Connor, *Syntax*
Jen: Jenni, *Lehrbuch* **J-M**: Joüon and Muraoka, *Grammar* **Ros**: Rosenthal, *Grammar*
Sch: Schneider, *Grammatik* **Wms**: Williams, *Syntax*

3.17–19   Berg 2.29i   3.19   GKC §86i; IBHS 560; Gib 97 ☐
3.17   Dav §116; GKC §95f, 145u;   B-L 203q Nachtr.; Berg 2.37b
          J-M §150l; Gib 23 ☐ B-L 547
3.18   Berg 2.84q, 2.113f

B-L: Bauer and Leander, *Historische Grammatik*   **B-M**: Beer, *Grammatik*   **Berg**: Bergsträsser, *Grammatik*
Brock: Brockelmann, *Syntax*   **Dav**: Davidson, *Syntax*   **GAHG**: Richter, *Grammatik*
Gib: Gibson, *Davidson's Syntax, 4th ed.*   **GKC**: *Gesenius' Grammar*   **IBHS**: Waltke and O'Connor, *Syntax*
Jen: Jenni, *Lehrbuch*   **J-M**: Joüon and Muraoka, *Grammar*   **Ros**: Rosenthal, *Grammar*
Sch: Schneider, *Grammatik*   **Wms**: Williams, *Syntax*

ZEPHANIAH

1.2–3	GKC §72aa		2.14	Dav §136; GKC §90o; J-M §93r; Gib 37
1.2	Dav §86R2; GKC §113w n 3; Gib 125 □ Berg 2.64 n f, 2.173 n g		2.15	Dav §127d; GKC §90l, 152s; J-M §160n
1.3	Berg 2.173 n g		3.1	GKC §75rr □ B-L 424; Berg 2.168q
1.6	Berg 2.97h			
1.7	GKC §147d; Gib 188		3.2	IBHS 367 □ Berg 2.77c
1.8	Dav §57R2; J-M §121o n 1		3.3	GKC §87m
1.9	Dav §98a; J-M §52d n 5; IBHS 415; Gib 133		3.4	Dav §14, 24c, 24R3; J-M §97Ca; Gib 17, 33
1.12	Dav §57R2 □ Berg 2.137k		3.5	Dav §100R3; GKC §152a n 1; Gib 138
1.14	Dav §70b; GKC §52s; J-M §52c, 102c; Gib 52, 144 □ B-L 217d, 356v; Berg 1.112 n e		3.7	Dav §83; GKC §120g; J-M §177g; Wms §225; Gib 121 □ GAHG 2.33 n 133; Brock §133b
1.15	GKC §133l			
1.17	B-L 263g, 287n'; Berg 1.139b, 2.16c		3.8	IBHS 385 □ Brock §25eβ; Gib 118
1.18	GKC §162b		3.9	GKC §107k n 3, 118q, J-M §126d; IBHS 172; Gib 144 □ Berg 2.112e; Brock §93m, 102
2.1	Dav §88R4, 100R3, 145; GKC §152a n 1 □ Berg 2.135 n e			
2.2	Dav §91R1, 128; GKC §152y; J-M §160p; Wms §394; Gib 130 □ Brock §52bε		3.10	Brock §120a
			3.11	Dav §24R2; GKC §135n; Gib 33 □ Berg 2.118c
2.3	Berg 2.97h		3.14	GKC §67ff □ B-L 353v; Berg 2.80i
2.5	Berg 2.112c			
2.6	B-L 215h, 588l; B-M 1.101; Berg 1.102 n o		3.16	GKC §145p, J-M §150d
			3.17	Dav §44R3, 143; IBHS 217; Gib 10, 76
2.7	GKC §135p; J-M §149a □ Berg 2.166m			
2.9	GKC §8k; Jou §82g □ Berg 1.45e		3.18	GKC §69t □ B-L 443k; Berg 2.128 n g
			3.19	Dav §14; GKC §84ªs; Gib 18, 172
2.12	Dav §21f; Gib 28			
2.13	Dav §65R6; GKC §109k; J-M §114l; Gib 104 □ GAHG 3.218 n 826; Berg 2.50l, 2.51l, 2.163g		3.20	Dav §96R3; GKC §91l; J-M §94j □ B-L 253b', 606k

B-L: Bauer and Leander, *Historische Grammatik* **B-M**: Beer, *Grammatik* **Berg**: Bergsträsser, *Grammatik*
Brock: Brockelmann, *Syntax* **Dav**: Davidson, *Syntax* **GAHG**: Richter, *Grammatik*
Gib: Gibson, *Davidson's Syntax, 4th ed.* **GKC**: *Gesenius' Grammar* **IBHS**: Waltke and O'Connor, *Syntax*
Jen: Jenni, *Lehrbuch* **J-M**: Joüon and Muraoka, *Grammar* **Ros**: Rosenthal, *Grammar*
Sch: Schneider, *Grammatik* **Wms**: Williams, *Syntax*

HAGGAI

1.1	GKC §129f; J-M §130d, 142b, 142c, 142o; IBHS 286 □ B-M 3.32; Brock §60a	2.6	GKC §116p □ Berg 2.72h*; Brock §13a
1.2	GKC §152d; J-M §155m, 155nd □ B-M 2.161; Brock §29b	2.7	Dav §115; GKC §145e; J-M §155nd; Gib 22 □ Berg 2.17d
1.4	Dav §32R2, 70a; GKC §118p, 126z, 131h n 1, 135g; J-M §127a, 138a n 2, 146d; IBHS 262, 299; Gib 2, 44 □ Brock §81f	2.8	J-M §154f, 154ff. □ GAHG 3.77 n 205
		2.9	J-M §139a, 155nd, 170c
		2.12	Dav §126; GKC §152c, 159w; J-M §160j, 161l, 167l; Gib 184
1.6	Dav §109; GKC §45d, 113z; J-M §123x, 152d; IBHS 72, 425; Gib 127 □ B-L 217a, 316d; B-M 1.114, Berg 2.57k; 2.67m, 2.83p(bis), 2.136f; Brock §46c	2.13	J-M §129i; Gib 184
		2.14	J-M §170c □ Berg 1.129b
		2.15	Dav §96R5; Gib 133 □ GAHG 3.170 n 522, 215 n 815, Berg 2.56f; Brock §145bα
1.8	J-M §155nd	2.16	GKC §63i; J-M §68e □ B-L 348h, Berg 1.147d, 1.156k
1.9	Dav §88R2; GKC §37f; J-M §37d, 123w, 155i, 158e; IBHS 595; Gib 127 □ Berg 2.65h*; 2.67l; Brock §152a	2.17	Dav §22R1, 28R1, 72R4, 128R3; GKC §117m n 3, 152n; IBHS 183, 246 n 14; Gib 29, 117 □ B-L 633t
1.10	B-L 375, Berg 2.159g	2.18	GAHG 3.170 n 522
1.14	GKC §131g □ Berg 2.149m	2.19	Dav §101Rb; J-M §161b
2.1	B-M 2.94	2.21	J-M §92b
2.3	J-M §141j n 2; Gib 7 □ Berg 2.37a	2.23	IBHS 489 n 17
2.5	GKC §44o, 91d, 117l; J-M §125j; IBHS 177 n 30 □ Berg 2.71g		

B-L: Bauer and Leander, *Historische Grammatik*   **B-M**: Beer, *Grammatik*   **Berg**: Bergsträsser, *Grammatik*
Brock: Brockelmann, *Syntax*   **Dav**: Davidson, *Syntax*   **GAHG**: Richter, *Grammatik*
Gib: Gibson, *Davidson's Syntax, 4th ed.*   **GKC**: *Gesenius' Grammar*   **IBHS**: Waltke and O'Connor, *Syntax*
Jen: Jenni, *Lehrbuch*   **J-M**: Joüon and Muraoka, *Grammar*   **Ros**: Rosenthal, *Grammar*
Sch: Schneider, *Grammatik*   **Wms**: Williams, *Syntax*

ZECHARIAH

1.2–3	Berg 2.52o	3.7	GKC §53o, 117r □ B-L 385g',
1.2	Dav §67b; GKC §117q; Gib 115		557h'; Berg 2.104 n h, 2.131 n o
1.3	J-M §116b □ Berg 2.43i	3.8	Dav §21f; GKC §116p, 126e;
1.4	Berg 1.131e		J-M §137g; IBHS 247; Gib 27 □
1.5	Jen §27.3.2		Jen §6.3.5; Berg 2.72h; Brock
1.6	Gib 176		§10
1.8	GKC §132d; J-M §92c □ B-M	3.9	GKC §88f, 97c, 122n; J-M §91e,
	3.29		134a n 2; IBHS 104, 117 □ B-L
1.9	IBHS 441 n 22		516s; Berg 2.72h; Brock §18a
1.10	B-M 2.122	4.2	GKC §91e, 97c □ B-L 598
1.12	GKC §136d	4.7	Dav §32R2; GKC §126x; Gib 44
1.13	Dav §29e; GKC §131c; J-M	4.10	Dav §29c; GKC §72dd, 106n,
	§131a; Gib 41 □ B-M 3.35;		127h; J-M §80o, 134a n 2; IBHS
	Berg 1.139b; Brock §62g		104; Gib 41□ B-L 402u"; Berg
1.14	Dav §67b; GKC §117q; J-M		2.150p
	§125bc; Gib 115	4.12	GKC §10g □ B-L 614; Berg
1.15	GKC §117q, 158b; Gib 115		1.124w, 126bb
1.16	IBHS 512 □ GAHG 1.93 n 265;	4.14	GKC §119cc
	Berg 2.28e(bis)	5.1	Berg 2.21d
1.17	GKC §72k	5.2	GKC §134n □ GAHG
2.2	Gib 54		3.102 n 288, 3.102 n 289
2.5	Dav §139; Gib 168	5.4	GKC §73d, 75mm, 80i; J-M
2.6	J-M §121d, 121h n 1; IBHS 613;		§81e □ B-L 403; Berg 2.14a,
	Gib 185 □ Jen §8.3.2.2; Berg		2.17e, 2.165l
	2.136f	5.7	GKC §74i, 136d n 2 □ Berg
2.8	Dav §71R1; GKC §34f, 118r;		1.90b
	J-M §126e; IBHS 440 n 17	5.9	GKC §74k □ B-L 441c, 640f';
2.10	GKC §154b; IBHS 440 n 17		Berg 2.158d
2.11	GKC §29o n 2 □ Berg 2.92g	5.10	GKC §32n; J-M §149c □ B-L
2.12	B-L 771		248j
2.13	GKC §116p □ Berg 2.72h	5.11	Dav §116R6; J-M §25a, 103f;
2.14	GKC §67ff □ Berg 2.72h		Gib 24 □ B-L 403, 598, 640f';
2.17	GKC §72v, 72ee, 147d; J-M		Berg 1.95e, 2.150 n o
	§80p; Gib 188 □ Berg 2.151q	6.1	Berg 2.21d
3.1	Dav §21c; GKC §61b, 115c,	6.5	Gib 47
	125f; J-M §65b; Gib 27 □ B-L	6.7	GKC §54k □ Berg 2.99e; Gib
	343b"; Berg 2.82n		18, 21, 24
3.3	Dav §100R2; J-M §116r,	6.10	Dav §88R2; GKC §49l; J-M
	121f n 1, 121o; IBHS 620; Gib		§33, 43b, 123u; Gib 127 □ Berg
	138 □ Berg 2.73i, 2.74l		2.16d, 2.66k
3.4	Dav §88R1; GKC §113z; J-M	6.12	Dav §144R3; GKC §155e; J-M
	§21i; IBHS 489 n 17; Gib 127 □		§158b; Gib 11
	Berg 1.157n	6.14	Dav §113; Gib 21
3.5	J-M §137f	6.15	J-M §123g □ Berg 2.20b

B-L: Bauer and Leander, *Historische Grammatik* **B-M**: Beer, *Grammatik* **Berg**: Bergsträsser, *Grammatik*
Brock: Brockelmann, *Syntax* **Dav**: Davidson, *Syntax* **GAHG**: Richter, *Grammatik*
Gib: Gibson, *Davidson's Syntax, 4th ed.* **GKC**: *Gesenius' Grammar* **IBHS**: Waltke and O'Connor, *Syntax*
Jen: Jenni, *Lehrbuch* **J-M**: Joüon and Muraoka, *Grammar* **Ros**: Rosenthal, *Grammar*
Sch: Schneider, *Grammatik* **Wms**: Williams, *Syntax*

7.1	GKC §134p; Gib 50 □ Sch §47.3.5	9.5	Dav §65R6; GKC §75p, 75hh, 107n, 109k; J-M §167a; Gib 73 □ B-L 426, 547; Berg 1.148g, 1.158q, 2.50l, 2.163f
7.2	Dav §48R2; Gib 96		
7.3	GKC §113h, 136d; Gib 126, 185 □ B-L 323b′, 651w; Berg 2.65h*, 2.92i		
		9.9	Dav §17R3, 136R1; GKC §72s, 124o, 154a n 1b; J-M §137j; IBHS 122; Gib 20, 37 □ B-L 398e″; B-M 3.18; Berg 2.145e; Brock §16f
7.5–6	IBHS 300		
7.5	Dav §73R4, 88R1, 113q, 113z, 136R1; GKC §59a, 113z, 117x, 135e; J-M §62a n 2, 123x, 125ba n 2, 146d; IBHS 169, 305, 596; Gib 4, 124, 127 □ B-L 217e; B-M 1.114; Berg 2.18f, 2.63d, 2.67m, 2.147g; Brock §97a		
		9.10	Jen §11.4.10; Berg 2.16c
		9.11ff.	Berg 2.29i
		9.11	GKC §135f, 152a, 153
		9.12	GKC §116s; J-M §154c
		9.15	B-L 606i; Berg 2.79h
		9.17	J-M §162a □ Brock §12
7.6	GKC §116q, 126k; J-M §137l	10.1	J-M §147d
7.7	Dav §72R4; GKC §117l; J-M §125j; Gib 51, 117	10.2	GKC §124h □ B-L 423
		10.3	B-L 302a′; Berg 2.44l
7.9	Dav §67b; Gib 115	10.5	GKC §72p; J-M §80d n 1 □ B-L 398h″; Berg 2.143 n b
7.10	GKC §139c, 139c n 1; J-M §147d; Gib 14		
		10.6	GKC §72x; J-M §112a, 119y n 2, 174d n 2 □ B-L 405; Berg 2.128 n h
7.11	Dav §101Rc		
7.14	Dav §17R5; GKC §52n; J-M §52c □ B-L 357; Berg 1.156m, 2.95e		
		10.7	Dav §65R6; Gib 73 □ Berg 2.51l, 2.117a; Brock §109e
8.2	Dav §67R2; GKC §117q; Gib 115	10.9	Berg 1.148g
		11.2	Dav §32R2; GKC §126w; Gib 44, 158
8.3	Berg 2.28e(bis)		
8.5	GKC §132d; J-M §148a	11.4	Dav §24c; Gib 33
8.6	GKC §150a; J-M §171b	11.5	Dav §116R1; GKC §19k, 60h; Gib 23 □ B-L 226q, 337j; Berg 1.93 n h
8.9	J-M §121r, 150d		
8.10	Dav §51R6; GKC §146a□ Berg 2.22e; Gib 105		
8.13	Dav §29e; J-M §150d; Gib 42	11.6	IBHS 678 n 16
8.14–15	GKC §67aa	11.7	Dav §35R2; GKC §96, 130g, 132c, 133h; J-M §129o □ B-L 353v
8.14	B-L 430m; B-M 2.145; Berg 2.133b		
		11.8	Berg 2.21d
8.15	Dav §83; GKC §120g; Gib 121 □ B-L 430m; Berg 2.133b	11.9	GKC §68c, 116d; J-M §121i n 1; IBHS 69 □ B-L 622b; Berg 2.69c
8.17	Dav §72R4; GKC §117l, 139c n 1; Gib 14		
		11.10	GKC §67w □ B-L 278l′; Berg 2.137k
8.19	GKC §63l		
8.20	Brock §159b	11.13	Berg 1.93 n h, 2.21d, 2.23f
8.21	J-M §114e	11.14	B-M 2.80
8.23	Dav §146R3; GKC §157a; J-M §114e, 176b n 2; Gib 111 □ Berg 2.47e	11.15	GAHG 3.171 n 535
		11.16	B-M 2.126, 3.13; GAHG 3.171 n 539
9.3	Berg 2.162f	11.17	GKC §90l, 113n; J-M §93n; IBHS 128 □ B-L 438; GAHG 1.126 n 403
9.4	B-M 2.53 □ B-L 534		

B-L: Bauer and Leander, *Historische Grammatik* **B-M**: Beer, *Grammatik* **Berg**: Bergsträsser, *Grammatik*
Brock: Brockelmann, *Syntax* **Dav**: Davidson, *Syntax* **GAHG**: Richter, *Grammatik*
Gib: Gibson, *Davidson's Syntax, 4th ed.* **GKC**: *Gesenius' Grammar* **IBHS**: Waltke and O'Connor, *Syntax*
Jen: Jenni, *Lehrbuch* **J-M**: Joüon and Muraoka, *Grammar* **Ros**: Rosenthal, *Grammar*
Sch: Schneider, *Grammatik* **Wms**: Williams, *Syntax*

12.1	GKC §116d □ Berg 2.69c
12.3	J-M §123p; IBHS 582
12.4	IBHS 246; Gib 28
12.6	Brock §114b
12.8	Berg 2.79h
12.10	Dav §9R3, 88R1; GKC §113z, 138e n 1; J-M §123x; IBHS 597; Gib 127 □ Berg 2.67m, 2.137k; Brock §46c
12.11	GKC §85v □ B-L 525j, 549a'
12.12	GKC §123d
13.1	J-M §129s □ B-L 503gı
13.3	B-L 440c
13.4	GKC §74h □ B-L 440c; Berg 2.158e
13.6	GKC §121b
13.7	GKC §72s, 110k, 144a □ B-L 398e''; Berg 2.19a, 2.20 n a, 2.145e
13.8	J-M §101b
13.9	Dav §91R1, 91R3; Gib 130 □ Berg 2.56f
14.1	IBHS 421
14.2	IBHS 375 n 31 □ B-L 232j; B-M 3.19; Berg 2.136h, 2.174 n k
14.4	Dav §32R5; GKC §93v, 121d, 128w n 1; J-M §128c; Gib 44 □ B-L 203p, 582v'
14.5	GKC §156c □ B-L 557f'
14.9	IBHS 274
14.10	Dav §32R2; GKC §72p, 126w; J-M §138b; IBHS 260; Gib 44 □ B-L 404, 437; Berg 1.44c, 1.113 n e, 2.136i, 2.147g; Brock §119b
14.12	Dav §88, 116R1; GKC §67dd, 113b, 145m; Gib 23 □ B-L 431q; B-M 2.146; Berg 2.67l, 2.134c, 2.137k
14.15	Berg 1.147d
14.16	Berg 2.136f

B-L: Bauer and Leander, *Historische Grammatik*   **B-M**: Beer, *Grammatik*   **Berg**: Bergsträsser, *Grammatik*
Brock: Brockelmann, *Syntax*   **Dav**: Davidson, *Syntax*   **GAHG**: Richter, *Grammatik*
Gib: Gibson, *Davidson's Syntax, 4th ed.*   **GKC**: *Gesenius' Grammar*   **IBHS**: Waltke and O'Connor, *Syntax*
Jen: Jenni, *Lehrbuch*   **J-M**: Joüon and Muraoka, *Grammar*   **Ros**: Rosenthal, *Grammar*
Sch: Schneider, *Grammatik*   **Wms**: Williams, *Syntax*

MALACHI

B-L: Bauer and Leander, *Historische Grammatik* **B-M**: Beer, *Grammatik* **Berg**: Bergsträsser, *Grammatik*
Brock: Brockelmann, *Syntax* **Dav**: Davidson, *Syntax* **GAHG**: Richter, *Grammatik*
Gib: Gibson, *Davidson's Syntax, 4th ed.* **GKC**: *Gesenius' Grammar* **IBHS**: Waltke and O'Connor, *Syntax*
Jen: Jenni, *Lehrbuch* **J-M**: Joüon and Muraoka, *Grammar* **Ros**: Rosenthal, *Grammar*
Sch: Schneider, *Grammatik* **Wms**: Williams, *Syntax*

PSALMS

1–150	Brock §84a	2.10	Dav §22R3; GKC §126h, 154b; J-M §177m; Gib 91
1	IBHS 472		
1.1ff.	Berg 2.29i	2.12	Dav §28R1, 53R1; GKC §118g n 1, 130a; J-M §119y, 129m; IBHS 155, 155 n 34; Gib 34, 93 □ Berg 1.155f; Brock §99a
1.1	Dav §21e, 39b; J-M §97Eb, 112d n 2; IBHS 681; Gib 27, 32, 62, 188 □ Jen §22.3.3; Brock §7a		
1.2	GKC §163a; J-M §112d n 2; Wms §555; IBHS 658, 671 n 101; Gib 62, 174	3.1	GKC §129c; J-M §130b; IBHS 157, 209 □ B-M 3.30; Jen §6.3.5; Sch §47.2.2; Brock §74a
1.3–6	Dav §44a; Gib 74	3.2	GKC §67ee; J-M §112a n 1, 162a; IBHS 263; Gib 61, 63, 134, □ Berg 2.28g
1.3	Dav §101Rd; GKC §16g, 107g, 119cc; IBHS 216 n 106, 472, 473; Gib 149 □ B-L 184n'; B-M 1.78; Jen §26.3.3		
		3.3	Dav §69R2, 101Rb; GKC §90g, 152n n 1; J-M §93d n 2, 93j; Gib 145, 150 □ B-M 2.50; Jen §25.3.2.7
1.4–6	Gib 28		
1.4	Dav §9b, 22R2; IBHS 245, 334; Gib 9, 174		
		3.5	Dav §50a, 109R3; GKC §144m; J-M §151c; IBHS 559 □ B-M 3.21; Berg 1.131 n d, 2.34h; Brock §93n*
1.6	GKC §68c; Gib 173 □ Berg 2.71g		
2.1	Dav §39b; GKC §106l; Gib 62, 164	3.6	Dav §51R7; GKC §49e; Gib 102 □ B-L 402r"; Berg 2.23f
2.2	Dav §19R4, 22R3; GKC §107f, 119dd, 126h; IBHS 250; Gib 29 □ Berg 2.128 n g; Brock §20b, 41i	3.8	Dav §71, 71R3; GKC §72s, 72s n 1, 117ll; J-M §126g; IBHS 172, 494 n 26, 495, 665; Gib 69, 145 □ B-L 398c"; Berg 1.127cc, 2.145e; Brock §94c
2.3	GKC §48c, 91l, 108b; J-M §45a, 114e; IBHS 574; Gib 82 □ B-L 184n', 253z, 274n		
		3.9	Dav §133; Gib 185
2.4	GKC §126h	4.1	GKC §124f
2.5	GKC §58g, 103p n 2	4.2	IBHS 150, 494 n 26, 495 n 27, 517 n 61; Gib 69 □ Berg 2.135e
2.6	Dav §3, 24R2, 155; GKC §135a, 135n, 154b; J-M §140b; Wms §41; IBHS 150, 296, 304, 489 n 17; Gib 4, 33, 173		
		4.3	GKC §37e, 47m, 156d; IBHS 9, 147, 325, 516 □ B-L 328a'; Berg 2.20b
2.7	GKC §44d, 69s; IBHS 145, 487; Gib 53, 61, 64, 147, 179 □ B-L 193v; B-M 1.104, 2.115; Berg 2.25b, 2.78e	4.4	GKC §154b
		4.7	Dav §135; GKC §76b; Gib 151, 186 □ B-L 441c; Berg 1.71e, 1.72f, 2.122 n c
2.8	Dav §22R3; IBHS 250; GKC §108d; Gib 29	4.8	Dav §25, 28R1; GKC §133e n 4, 155l; Wms §584; IBHS 338; Gib 12 □ Brock §144
2.9	Dav §24b; GKC §128o; IBHS 151; Gib 32, 78 □ B-M 3.34; Berg 2.135d; Brock §76c		
		4.9	IBHS 250 □ Berg 2.52o, 2.158 n e

B-L: Bauer and Leander, *Historische Grammatik*   **B-M:** Beer, *Grammatik*   **Berg:** Bergsträsser, *Grammatik*
Brock: Brockelmann, *Syntax*   **Dav:** Davidson, *Syntax*   **GAHG:** Richter, *Grammatik*
Gib: Gibson, *Davidson's Syntax, 4th ed.*   **GKC:** *Gesenius' Grammar*   **IBHS:** Waltke and O'Connor, *Syntax*
Jen: Jenni, *Lehrbuch*   **J-M:** Joüon and Muraoka, *Grammar*   **Ros:** Rosenthal, *Grammar*
Sch: Schneider, *Grammatik*   **Wms:** Williams, *Syntax*

5.2	GKC §73a; J-M §48d	7.7	Dav §41R5; GKC §72s, 119gg,
5.3	IBHS 506 □ B-L 205d', 362a',		156d; IBHS 494 n 26; Gib 69 □
	405; B-M 1.100		B-L 398c''', 604g; Berg 1.157o,
5.4	Dav §68; GKC §118i; Gib 144 □		2.145e, 2.146e
	B-L 184n'	7.8	GKC §72s
5.5	Dav §73; GKC §107s, 116f,	7.10	Dav §31; GKC §124g, 132h,
	117bb; J-M §121l; IBHS 170,		158a; IBHS 122, 257; Gib 43 □
	616; Gib 79 □ Berg 2.35i, 2.85r;		Brock §19c, 59c
	Brock §90a	7.11	Dav §22R3; Gib 29
5.6	Berg 2.28g; Gib 63	7.12–17	Berg 2.29i
5.7	Dav §24c, 28R4; GKC §128a,	7.12	GKC §127b; IBHS 289 □ B-L
	128t; IBHS 162; Gib 33, 35 □		268h
	Berg 2.115a	7.13	GKC §111w, 120g □ B-L 302a';
5.8	GKC §107s □ Berg 1.154f, 2.35i		Berg 2.37b
5.9	GKC §24f n 2, 70b □ B-L 384c';	7.16	GKC §155h
	Berg 1.99h, 2.128 n h	7.17	GKC §10h; Gib 172 □
5.10	GKC §122q, 124e, 145m, 152o;		Berg1.126bb
	IBHS 121	7.18	IBHS 573 □ Berg 1.106b; Brock
5.11	GKC §29e, 58g; Gib 180 □ B-L		§109c
	339v; Berg 1.130c, 2.112d	8.2–4	Sch §52.2.3
5.12	GKC §103p n 2, 116g, 156d;	8.2	GKC §66h, 148b; J-M §144e,
	J-M §121m, 177l □ B-M 3.66;		162a; IBHS 123, 216, 326; Gib
	Sch §49.1.3; Berg 1.154e,		19 □ B-L 368t; Brock §12
	1.155i, 2.80 n h, 2.113f	8.3	GKC §128a; Gib 31 □ B-L 228a'
5.13	Dav §78R2; GKC §117ee □	8.4	GKC §150dd, 164d; IBHS 643
	Berg 2.113f		□ B-M 3.109; Jen §18.3.4.2
6.1	GKC §124f	8.5	Dav §19R4, 43b, 150; GKC
6.2	GKC §152h; J-M §160f; IBHS		§107v, 111m, 150h; J-M §169e;
	567		IBHS 322 n 15, 326, 518, 639;
6.3	Sch §53.3.3.1; Berg 1.113ne,		Gib 8, 79, 97, 160 □ Jen §19.3.4
	1.147 n d	8.6	Dav §51R4, 75, 78R2; GKC
6.4	GKC §32g, 147c; Gib 185 □		§117cc; J-M §113h; IBHS 176,
	B-L 248e		404; Gib 113, 173 □ Jen §13.3.3;
6.5	B-M 2.120		Berg 2.39 n a-f
6.6	GKC §152o; Gib 179 □ B-L	8.7	Dav §51R5 □ B-L 405; Berg
	443k		2.146f
6.7	GKC §106g □ Berg 2.28g; Gib	8.8	Dav §19R4; IBHS 122 n 14 □
	63, 179		B-L 456m'; Berg 1.100 n k
6.8	GKC §67bb	8.10	IBHS 123
6.9	Dav §41a; GKC §93x; Gib 68	9–10	Berg 1.5h
6.10	Dav §41a; GKC §142f; Gib 68	9	GKC §5h □ B-L 66s
6.11	Dav §68; Gib 144	9.2	GKC §13c □ B-L 268g
7.2	Berg 2.28g; Gib 63	9.3	GKC §5h
7.3	GKC §118p, 152l □ B-L 303g'	9.5	Brock §107a
7.4	GKC §159m □ Berg 2.158e	9.6	IBHS 222
7.5	Dav §98c; GKC §49e; J-M	9.7	Dav §1; GKC §126m, 135f; J-M
	§121k; Gib 134 □ Berg 2.23f		§146d; IBHS 299
7.6	GKC §63n; J-M §16g □ B-L	9.8	J-M §75c
	209d, 353v; Berg 2.49h, 2.79 n g	9.9	Berg 1.129b
		9.10	Berg 2.50l

B-L: Bauer and Leander, *Historische Grammatik*   **B-M**: Beer, *Grammatik*   **Berg**: Bergsträsser, *Grammatik*
Brock: Brockelmann, *Syntax*   **Dav**: Davidson, *Syntax*   **GAHG**: Richter, *Grammatik*
Gib: Gibson, *Davidson's Syntax, 4th ed.*   **GKC**: *Gesenius' Grammar*   **IBHS**: Waltke and O'Connor, *Syntax*
Jen: Jenni, *Lehrbuch*   **J-M**: Joüon and Muraoka, *Grammar*   **Ros**: Rosenthal, *Grammar*
Sch: Schneider, *Grammatik*   **Wms**: Williams, *Syntax*

9.11	GKC §106k; J-M §112d ☐ Berg 2.28f		10.17	Gib 69
			10.18	IBHS 567 n 6 ☐ GAHG 3.171 n 537
9.13	GKC §5h; IBHS 184 n 38			
9.14–15	IBHS 575		11.1	GKC §118r, 129c, 148b; Gib 63, 79 ☐ Sch §44.4; Berg 2.28g, 2.140 n q
9.14	GKC §20b, 63l, GKC §67cc ☐ B-L 437; Berg 2.81i, 2.133 n b			
9.15	GKC §5h, 91l, 108d; J-M §94j ☐ B-L 253b', 599h'		11.2	Dav §41R3; GKC §47m ☐ B-L 300q, 443k; B-M 2.100, 2.140; Jen §8.4.8; Berg 2.29i, 2.127e, 2.168q
9.16	Dav §6R3, 143; GKC §138g; J-M §145c; Wms §129, 536; IBHS 332, 333; Gib 11			
			11.3	Dav §41R2; Gib 68 ☐ B-L 321h, 549a'
9.17	GKC §5h ☐ Berg 2.170 n c		11.4	Dav §102, 106b; GKC §143b, 145u, 155e ☐ GAHG 3.10 n 22; Jen §9.3.5
9.18	Dav §69R2; GKC §90e, 116b, J-M §50b ☐ Jen §25.3.2.7; Berg 2.85r			
			11.5	GKC §142f
9.19	Dav §128R6; GKC §68c, 152z; J-M §160q; Gib 164		11.6	Dav §65R6; GKC §109k; J-M §114l; Gib 73 ☐ B-L 274l, 598, 599i'; Berg 2.51l
9.20	Berg 2.135d			
9.21	Dav §146R3; GKC §157a; J-M §157b; Gib 111 ☐ B-L 547		11.7	GKC §91l, 103f n 3; J-M §94i; Gib 52 ☐ B-L 253 n 1
10	B-L 66s; Berg 1.5h; Gib 75		12.2	GKC §123b; IBHS 115
10.1	GKC §5h (bis)		12.3	Dav §29R8, 67R3; GKC §117t, 123f; J-M §135d; IBHS 116; Gib 42, 115 ☐ B-L 649l
10.2	GKC §138g; Wms §129			
10.3	GKC §5h, 106k; Gib 62 ☐ Berg 2.95d, 2.115a; Brock §41g			
			12.4	Dav §65R6; GKC §53n, 122q; J-M §152h ☐ B-M 2.102, 2.124; Berg 2.51l
10.4	Dav §146R1 ☐ B-L 633t			
10.5	Dav §29e, 69R1, 106b; GKC §5h, 141c; Gib 42, 182 ☐ B-L 404		12.6	Dav §40b, 144; Gib 11, 78
			12.7	GKC §10g, 10g n 3, 97h, 134r; J-M §100o; Gib 51 ☐ Berg 1.124w; Brock §126a
10.6	Dav §146R2; J-M §160m; Wms §413; Gib 37 ☐ Berg 2.92h			
10.8	J-M §136g ☐ B-L 583v'		12.8	Dav §6; GKC §126y; IBHS 337 ☐ Berg 2.121a
10.9	GKC §91e ☐ B-L 252k			
10.10	GKC §93x, 154a n 1 ☐ B-L 583v'; Berg 1.103o, 2.134d, 2.159f		12.9	GKC §54k ☐ B-L 328w; Berg 2.140q
			13.2	Gib 79
10.11	Dav §146R1; GKC §106g; Wms §162; IBHS 491; Gib 111 ☐ B-M 3.12; Brock §52bβ		13.3	Gib 79
			13.4	Dav §67R2; GKC §117r, 117r n 4; Gib 115
10.12–17	GKC §5h			
10.12	GKC §66c, 76b ☐ B-L 441c; B-M 2.135; Berg 2.122 n c		13.5	Dav §73; GKC §44e, 59i, 152z; J-M §125b; IBHS 166; Gib 164 ☐ B-L 312u, 340e'; Berg 2.78e; Brock §90a
10.13	Dav §146R1; GKC §37f, 157a; Gib 62, 68, 111			
10.14	J-M §121f n 1; Gib 62 ☐ B-L 583v'; GAHG 3.229 n 879		13.6	Berg 2.28g, 2.46c, 2.47d; Gib 63
			14	IBHS 17 ☐ B-L 73d
10.15	GKC §104g ☐ B-L 357, 649k; Berg 1.129b, 1.132f		14.1	GKC §129c, 154a n 1a ☐ Brock §133b
			14.2–2	Gib 62
10.16	Dav §41R5; Gib 69 ☐ Berg 1.161e		14.2	Dav §65R5 ☐ Berg 1.127cc

B-L: Bauer and Leander, *Historische Grammatik* **B-M**: Beer, *Grammatik* **Berg**: Bergsträsser, *Grammatik*
Brock: Brockelmann, *Syntax* **Dav**: Davidson, *Syntax* **GAHG**: Richter, *Grammatik*
Gib: Gibson, *Davidson's Syntax, 4th ed.* **GKC**: *Gesenius' Grammar* **IBHS**: Waltke and O'Connor, *Syntax*
Jen: Jenni, *Lehrbuch* **J-M**: Joüon and Muraoka, *Grammatik* **Ros**: Rosenthal, *Grammatik*
Sch: Schneider, *Grammatik* **Wms**: Williams, *Syntax*

14.3	GKC §152o
14.5	Dav §67b; GKC §117p; J-M §125q; Wms §51; IBHS 167; Gib 115
14.7	Dav §135R3; GKC §151b; Gib 186 □ Berg 2.511
15.1	IBHS 508 □ B-L 580u'
15.2-3	Gib 137
15.2	GKC §117r n 4, 118n □ GAHG 3.152 n 417
15.3	B-M 1.70
15.4	GKC §72dd; J-M §121l
15.5	IBHS 512
16.1	GKC §9v, 48i n 2, 61f n 1; Gib 63 □ B-L 339v; Berg 1.71e, 2.28g, 2.81i
16.2	GKC §44i, 152t; J-M §160m □ B-L 370q
16.3	GKC §130d, 143e; J-M §158g
16.4	GKC §93m, 145p, 155f; J-M §158a; IBHS 164 □ Brock §91
16.5	GKC §50e; Gib 52 □ B-L 318n; Berg 2.85 n r
16.6	Dav §14; GKC §80g, 122q; J-M §89n; Wms §386; IBHS 101 n 29; Gib 17, 38 □ B-L 603g
16.7	J-M §136b
16.8	GKC §116s; J-M §154c; Gib 143
16.9	Dav §51R2; GKC §111r; J-M §118p; IBHS 556; Gib 63, 102, 175 □ Berg 2.28g, 2.37b
16.10	GKC §114m; Gib 75, 150 □ Berg 2.59n
16.11	Dav §17R2; GKC §122q, 124e; Gib 17, 20
17.1	GAHG 2.63
17.3	Dav §90R1; GKC §59h, 67ee; IBHS 601 n 12, 644 n 35 □ B-L 233l, 340f', 430m; B-M 3.145; Berg 2.18f, 2.135 n f
17.4	GKC §143e
17.5	Dav §88R5; GKC §113gg; Wms §210; IBHS 595 n 55; Gib 127 □ Berg 2.67 n l
17.6	Berg 2.165k; Gib 69
17.7	B-L 376r; Berg 2.158e
17.8	Dav §45R4; J-M §113m; Gib 5
17.9	Dav §6R3; GKC §138g; J-M §145c; IBHS 336 □ Berg 2.132a*; Brock §150b
17.10-11	Gib 63
17.10	Dav §17R4, 109R3; GKC §91f, 91l, 96q, 124s, 144m; J-M §94h, 136l; IBHS 25 n 72 □ B-L 251d, 252o; B-M 2.54; Jen §25.3.2.5
17.11	Dav §71; Gib 145 □ B-L 538i; Berg 1.139b
17.12	GKC §126p; J-M §136g □ B-L 302a'
17.13-14	GKC §144m
17.13	Dav §109R3; IBHS 445
17.14	Dav §109R3; Gib 5 □ Berg 1.124w
17.15	J-M §114c
18	IBHS 14, 17, 498; Gib 71, 116 □ B-L 73d; GAHG 2.39 n 164
18.1	Dav §25; GKC §2r, 53l, 130d, 154 n 1b; J-M §54c n 3; IBHS 207; Gib 12 □ Berg 2.106 n l
18.2	GKC §135m n 3 □ B-L 581; Berg 1.157o
18.3	GKC §93pp, 155i □ Brock §148
18.4	Dav §97R1; GKC §116e, 132b; J-M §121i; Gib 133 □ Berg 2.69d, 2.117a, 2.128g; Brock §123f
18.5	Gib 5
18.6	J-M §129u; IBHS 269 □ Berg 2.132a*
18.7-23	Berg 2.34h
18.7	Dav §45R2; GKC §10g n 3, 107b; IBHS 498 □ GAHG 3.218 n 827; Berg 1.135c
18.9	IBHS 364; Gib 151
18.10	GKC §69p
18.11	Berg 2.163f
18.12	Dav §51R5; GKC §109k; IBHS 298, 546 □ GAHG 3.218 n 827; Berg 2.34h, 2.149m
18.14-15	Gib 100
18.14	GKC §107b; J-M §113h; IBHS 225 n 132, 498 □ Berg 2.34h
18.15	Berg 2.174 n h
18.16	IBHS 159; Gib 24
18.17ff.	GKC §107b
18.17	GKC §117g □ Berg 2.173 n g
18.18	Dav §32R2; GKC §126z; Gib 44

B-L: Bauer and Leander, *Historische Grammatik*   B-M: Beer, *Grammatik*   Berg: Bergsträsser, *Grammatik*
Brock: Brockelmann, *Syntax*   Dav: Davidson, *Syntax*   GAHG: Richter, *Grammatik*
Gib: Gibson, *Davidson's Syntax, 4th ed.*   GKC: *Gesenius' Grammar*   IBHS: Waltke and O'Connor, *Syntax*
Jen: Jenni, *Lehrbuch*   J-M: Joüon and Muraoka, *Grammar*   Ros: Rosenthal, *Grammar*
Sch: Schneider, *Grammatik*   Wms: Williams, *Syntax*

18.19	B-L 215l	18.44	GKC §87f; J-M §158c; Wms
18.22	Dav §101; GKC §119ff.; Wms		§540; IBHS 498; Gib 11 □
	§323		GAHG 3.218 n 827
18.23	Berg 1.161e	18.45	Brock §74c
18.24	IBHS 425	18.46	GKC §91n; J-M §94g □ B-L
18.26	GKC §93h, 93s; IBHS 425; Gib		591l; B-M 1.58
	172 □ B-L 573x; B-M 1.108	18.48	GKC §103d; J-M §103e n 1 □
18.27	GKC §67l; Gib 173 □ B-L		B-M 1.982
	329e'; Berg 2.136 n h, 2.136 n i	18.49	GKC §102b, 116i; Gib 175 □
18.28	Dav §31; GKC §132f, 145n; J-M		B-L 642p'
	§148a; Gib 43	18.50	GKC §107n
18.30	GKC §67q, 119o; J-M §52c n 6	18.51	J-M §136g; IBHS 121, 440
	□ B-L 328y; Berg 2.140 n q	19.1	Gib 30
18.31	Dav §106; GKC §126c, 140d,	19.2	B-M 3.7; Jen §29.3.2
	143a; IBHS 76; Gib 182 □ B-M	19.3	GKC §20f; IBHS 505; Gib 170 □
	1.58, 1.96, 2.66; GAHG		Berg 1.66r
	2.24 n 93	19.4	GKC §152t; J-M §160m; Wms
18.33	Dav §78R2, 98c, 99; GKC		§419; Gib 179
	§116f, 116x, 117cc, 126b n 1,	19.5	GKC §135p; Gib 170
	131r; J-M §66a, 118r, 121k;	19.6	GKC §122o; Gib 150
	Wms §82; IBHS 408 n 34, 561;	19.8ff.	GKC §5h
	Gib 134, 135, 137 □ B-L 344g",	19.8-11	IBHS 621 n 38; Gib 179
	345m"; B-M 2.22, 2.68, 2.168,	19.8-10	Gib 53
	3.46, 3.66, 3.68; GAHG	19.8-9	GKC §116g
	2.10 n 15; Berg 2.38e, 2.68a;	19.8	Dav §98b; GKC §116g; Gib 31,
	Brock §73b, 99a		134
18.34	J-M §133h; Wms §583 □ B-L	19.9-11	Gib 179
	203q Nachtr.; B-M 1.94	19.9	Dav §98b; Gib 134
18.35	Dav §116; GKC §44m, 145k;	19.10-11	IBHS 622
	J-M §150g; Gib 23 □ B-L 367;	19.10	Dav §29e, 98b; GKC §126b,
	Berg 2.15b, 2.122a		141c; J-M §97Be, 131c, 154e;
18.36-46	Berg 2.32e		Gib 42, 135 □ Brock §14bε
18.36	Dav §90R1; IBHS 150	19.11	Dav §97R1, 99; GKC §116e;
18.37	GKC §103d; J-M §103e n 1		IBHS 37 n 25, 248, 265; Gib
18.38ff.	GKC §107b, 107b n 2, 108e		133, 135 □ B-L 538i; Berg
18.38	GKC §107b n 2; IBHS		1.154f, 2.113h
	576 n 28; Gib 105 □ Berg 2.50l	19.12	Gib 179
18.39	IBHS 498, 507 n 28 □ B-M	19.14	GKC §49k, 67p; J-M §82h □
	2.113, 3.50ll.135; GAHG		B-L 439p'; Berg 1.72f, 2.17d,
	3.218 n 827		2.135d
18.40	Dav §98R1; GKC §23f, 68k,	19.15	B-M 2.55; Berg 1.107e, 1.157o
	103d, 116i; J-M §103e n 1,	20.3	GKC §135m; J-M §129h □ Berg
	121n; IBHS 618; Gib 134 □		1.135d
	B-M 2.70; Berg 1.91e	20.4	Dav §63R1; GKC §27n, 48d;
18.41	Dav §78R7; GKC §116w,		Gib 83 □ B-L 329d'; Berg
	117ii n 1; J-M §39a n 4, 156aa		2.23 n f, 2.29i
	□ B-M 2.22, 2.105; Berg	20.6	B-L 438; Berg 1.127cc, 2.97h
	1.13 n g, 1.142f, 2.123 n d	20.7	Dav §41a; Gib 68 □ Berg 2.28g
18.42	Gib 164	20.8	Dav §5; Gib 6 □ B-L 158 n 2
18.43	Brock §110k; Gib 105		

B-L: Bauer and Leander, *Historische Grammatik* **B-M**: Beer, *Grammatik* **Berg**: Bergsträsser, *Grammatik*
Brock: Brockelmann, *Syntax* **Dav**: Davidson, *Syntax* **GAHG**: Richter, *Grammatik*
Gib: Gibson, *Davidson's Syntax, 4th ed.* **GKC**: *Gesenius' Grammar* **IBHS**: Waltke and O'Connor, *Syntax*
Jen: Jenni, *Lehrbuch* **J-M**: Joüon and Muraoka, *Grammar* **Ros**: Rosenthal, *Grammar*
Sch: Schneider, *Grammatik* **Wms**: Williams, *Syntax*

20.9	Dav §58a; Gib 68, 102 □ Berg 2.45n	22.32	Dav §97R1, 100R1; GKC §116e; IBHS 620; Gib 133, 137 □ B-M 3.67; Berg 2.69d
21.2	Dav §65R6; GKC §109k, 126h, 148b □ Berg 2.48f, 2.53q, 2.149m	23.1	IBHS 513; Gib 52
21.3	IBHS 487	23.2	Dav §24c; GKC §124e, 128p; IBHS 74; Gib 33
21.4	GKC §117ff.; IBHS 226	23.3	GKC §21d □ Berg 1.106c, 1.106cN
21.6	IBHS 216 n 105, 437		
21.7	GKC §117ii, 124e	23.4	Dav §19R4; GKC §107x, 159bb; J-M §171c; Wms §174; IBHS 638; Gib 109, 154 □ GAHG 3.177 n 605; Berg 1.160b
21.10	GKC §58g		
21.11	GKC §91l □ B-L 252o; B-M 2.54; Jen §25.3.2.5		
21.13	Dav §78R7; GKC §58g, 117ii n 1, 156d □ Berg 1.161d	23.5	GKC §126n, 141c, 141d
		23.6	Dav §101; GKC §69m n 1 □ Berg 2.126 n c
22.2	GKC §59h; J-M §102c, 148b □ Berg 2.28g	24.1	GKC §129c, 130a; J-M §154f, 154ff.
22.3	GKC §152d; Gib 75		
22.4	GKC §117bb	24.2	GKC §107b, 124e □ Berg 2.34h
22.5	GKC §58g	24.3	GKC §63n, 107t □ Berg 1.145d
22.6	GKC §112h □ Berg 2.45n	24.4–5	IBHS 512
22.7	GKC §116l, 152d	24.4	Dav §24d; GKC §128y; Gib 33 □ B-M 3.34
22.8	Dav §73R6; GKC §119q; J-M §125m; Wms §244; Gib 75, 110	24.6	IBHS 311; Gib 5
22.9	GKC §144p; Gib 132 □ B-L 429j, 436; B-M 2.145; Berg 2.135e	24.8	Dav §7c; GKC §136c; IBHS 318; Gib 8
		24.10	GKC §136c; J-M §144a n 1 □ Brock §30a
22.10	B-L 398h″; Berg 2.145 n d; Gib 173	25	GKC §5h □ B-L 66s; Berg 1.5h
22.11	J-M §57a □ Berg 1.150n, 2.106n, 2.172 n e	25.1	GKC §5h; Gib 75
		25.2	Dav §62; GKC §105c; J-M §114c; Gib 63, 82 □ Berg 1.104r, 1.155i, 2.28g, 2.46c, 2.49h, 2.113f
22.13	Gib 63, 172		
22.14	GKC §118r; J-M §126e		
22.15	GKC §67t □ Berg 2.136h		
22.16	GKC §121c, 122n; IBHS 450 □ Brock §16g	25.3	IBHS 512
		25.7	Gib 31
22.17	Berg 1.50g	25.8	Gib 52
22.18–19	Gib 75	25.9	Dav §65R6; J-M §114l; IBHS 567; Gib 73, 104, 170 □ Berg 2.51l
22.18	GKC §107s □ Brock §106a		
22.22	Dav §41R5, 51R5, 101; GKC §23f, 119ff.; IBHS 495; Gib 147 □ B-L 583y′; Berg 1.89b	25.10	Dav §29e; GKC §141c; Gib 42 □ Berg 1.149i
		25.11	Dav §56; GKC §112nn; Gib 69, 88 □ Berg 2.43i
22.23	B-L 436; Berg 1.152a		
22.24	B-L 436	25.12	GKC §136c, 155h; J-M §121l
22.25	B-L 362a′; Berg 1.145d	25.14	Dav §94; GKC §114i; Gib 131 □ Berg 2.59 n mop
22.27	IBHS 570 □ B-L 436		
22.29	Dav §100a; GKC §116s; J-M §154c	25.16	Gib 52
		25.19	J-M §96Cb
22.30	Dav §41R1, 49b; IBHS 557; Gib 68, 102	25.20	B-L 306m; B-M 2.114; Berg 1.71e, 2.52o, 2.81i

---

B-L: Bauer and Leander, *Historische Grammatik*   **B-M**: Beer, *Grammatik*   **Berg**: Bergsträsser, *Grammatik*
Brock: Brockelmann, *Syntax*   **Dav**: Davidson, *Syntax*   **GAHG**: Richter, *Grammatik*
Gib: Gibson, *Davidson's Syntax, 4th ed.*   **GKC**: *Gesenius' Grammar*   **IBHS**: Waltke and O'Connor, *Syntax*
Jen: Jenni, *Lehrbuch*   **J-M**: Joüon and Muraoka, *Grammar*   **Ros**: Rosenthal, *Grammar*
Sch: Schneider, *Grammatik*   **Wms**: Williams, *Syntax*

25.21	Berg 2.122a	28.9	GKC §10g □ B-M 2.10, 2.69
26.1	Dav §44R3; GKC §156g; IBHS	29	IBHS 470 n 75
	512; Gib 76	29.1	GKC §124q, 128v; J-M §129j □
26.2	GKC §48i, 61g □ B-L 306o,		B-L 649l
	358v; Berg 2.81k(bis)	29.2	J-M §129g
26.3	GKC §112rr	29.3	J-M §162d n 1 □ B-M 1.97,
26.4–5	Berg 2.32e		2.124
26.4–4	Gib 63	29.4	GKC §141c n 2; Wms §564 □
26.4	Dav §45R3; GKC §128t □ B-M		Jen §25.3.3
	3.80; Berg 2.112c, 2.113f	29.5–6	Berg 2.38 n d
26.5	Dav §45R3; Gib 170	29.5	IBHS 499; Gib 164
26.6	Dav §62; Gib 75, 104, 170	29.6	B-L 583y'; B-M 2.181; Gib 24
26.7	GKC §53q □ B-L 228a', 268g;	29.8–9	Gib 75
	Berg 2.105k	29.9	J-M §68b n 2; IBHS 499 □ B-L
26.10	GKC §20f		347b, 581; B-M 2.17; Berg
26.12	GKC §93qq □ Berg 1.106c		2.39 n a–f, 2.110b
27.1	Dav §7a; IBHS 213, 512; Gib 7,	29.10	GKC §111r; IBHS 206 n 61,
	52, 148		498 n 4
27.2	Dav §58a; GKC §135m n 3; J-M	29.11	J-M §137k; IBHS 250
	§146f; IBHS 304; Gib 36 □ Berg	30	Dav §39R1
	2.441	30.1	Dav §21c; Gib 27 □ B-M 2.82
27.3	J-M §89b n 2	30.2	GKC §60f; J-M §61d n 3; IBHS
27.4	Berg 2.28g		408 □ B-M 2.133; Berg 2.95d
27.5	GKC §91e □ B-L 252k	30.4	GKC §69m □ B-L 383; B-M
27.6	Dav §62		1.94, 2.178; Berg 2.126 n c,
27.7	GKC §144m; J-M §151c; IBHS		2.167o
	506	30.7	B-M 2.71; Berg 2.27d
27.8	Berg 2.97h	30.8	GKC §90n, 93aa; J-M §52c n 5
27.9	Dav §65R3; GKC §109c; Gib		□ B-L 356v, 564; B-M 1.118,
	107 □ Berg 2.28g, 2.48g, 2.165k		2.10, 2.56, 2.124; Berg 2.27d,
27.10	Dav §51R5; Gib 173 □ Jen		2.74l
	§29.3.2	30.10	Dav §8R2; J-M §18h n 1,
27.12	B-L 552o; Berg 2.85r, 2.172d		61f n 1; IBHS 323 n 16; Gib 8 □
27.13	GKC §5n, 159dd, 167a □ B-L		B-L 383
	79s; GAHG 3.179 n 618; Berg	30.11	J-M §121e n 2, 121f n 1
	1.5l	30.12	J-M §96An □ B-M 2.105, 2.120
27.14	Berg 2.51 n l, 2.80 n h	30.13	Dav §149R3; J-M §160g; Gib
28.1	Dav §101; GKC §29f, 119ff.,		160 □ B-M 2.144, 2.165
	161a n 1; J-M §27d, 31c, 168h;	31.2	GKC §106g, 108c; J-M §114c;
	Wms §334; Gib 75 □ Berg		Gib 63 □ B-M 2.177; Berg
	1.107e, 1.130c, 2.16c		2.28g, 2.49h
28.2	GKC §66b □ B-L 205d', 362a',	31.3	GKC §128p
	405, 441c; Berg 2.123c, 2.157b	31.4	J-M §6d n 3
28.3	GKC §141e	31.5–6	IBHS 495
28.7	GKC §53q □ B-L 197m', 443k;	31.5	Dav §6R3; GKC §29f, 138g □
	B-M 1.106, 1.117, 2.65f, 2.112;		B-L 188p, 193q
	Berg 2.43 n b-k, 2.105k,	31.6	Dav §41R5; Gib 69 □ B-M
	2.111b*, 2.113f		2.159; Jen §24.3.3.5
28.8	J-M §61i n 3, 136g; IBHS 121 □	31.7	GKC §106g; Gib 63 □ B-M
	Berg 1.71e		2.71; Berg 2.28g(bis)

B-L: Bauer and Leander, *Historische Grammatik*   **B-M**: Beer, *Grammatik*   **Berg**: Bergsträsser, *Grammatik*
Brock: Brockelmann, *Syntax*   **Dav**: Davidson, *Syntax*   **GAHG**: Richter, *Grammatik*
Gib: Gibson, *Davidson's Syntax, 4th ed.*   **GKC**: *Gesenius' Grammar*   **IBHS**: Waltke and O'Connor, *Syntax*
Jen: Jenni, *Lehrbuch*   **J-M**: Joüon and Muraoka, *Grammar*   **Ros**: Rosenthal, *Grammar*
Sch: Schneider, *Grammatik*   **Wms**: Williams, *Syntax*

31.8	GKC §108b; J-M §114c	33.10	GKC §67v; J-M §82n; Gib 62 □
31.9	B-M 1.97, 1.105		B-L 438; Berg 2.140q
31.10	Berg 2.132a	33.12	GKC §155h; J-M §158c
31.11	GKC §67bb □ Berg 2.132a	33.15	GKC §126b; J-M §138e
31.16	J-M §154f, 154ff.	33.16	J-M §113c n 1 □ B-L 562v
31.18	J-M §114c □ Berg 2.46c, 2.49h,	33.17	Dav §22c; IBHS 244; Gib 28
	2.171 n d	33.20	J-M §112a
31.20	Dav §32R1; Gib 44 □ B-M	33.22	Berg 2.48g
	2.177; Berg 1.65p	34	GKC §5h, 5h n 3 □ B-L 66s;
31.21	GKC §93r □ B-L 582u'		Berg 1.5h
31.22	GKC §119i	34.1	GKC §5h □ B-L 131
31.23	J-M §6d n 3 □ B-L 205d',	34.2	GKC §21d □ Berg 1.107d
	362a', 405; GAHG 2.33 n 133;	34.4	IBHS 403 □ Berg 2.46c
	Berg 1.112 n d	34.5	J-M §119y n 2 □ B-L 598; Berg
31.24	Dav §101Rd; J-M §6e3; Wms		1.145d, 2.45n
	§290; IBHS 218 n 111 □ B-L	34.6	Dav §128R2; GKC §109e □
	347g, 371v; B-M 2.66f, 2.129;		Berg 2.111c
	Brock §90c	34.7	J-M §143i; IBHS 338
31.25	B-M 2.112, 2.114; Berg 2.51 n l,	34.8	Dav §49a; GKC §111u; J-M
	2.80 n h		§118r; IBHS 562; Gib 101 □
32.1	Dav §98R1; GKC §75qq, 116k;		Berg 2.38 n d
	J-M §121o; IBHS 617 □ B-L	34.9	GKC §155f; J-M §158a □
	441c; Berg 2.158e		GAHG 2.52 n 245; Berg 1.65p,
32.2	Dav §143; GKC §152o, 155i;		2.80i
	Gib 11	34.10	GKC §75oo □ Berg 1.93g
32.3–5	Berg 2.34h	34.11	IBHS 492 □ Berg 2.145e
32.4–5	GKC §107b	34.12	GKC §60f, 126o □ Berg 1.72f
32.4	J-M §113a	34.14	B-L 368t; Berg 2.122c
32.5	Dav §51R5 □ Berg 2.167o	34.15	Berg 1.52k
32.6	GKC §143e, 153 □ B-L 574y;	34.22	GKC §142ff; J-M §155nd □
	B-M 2.56, 2.82		B-L 135h
32.7	B-L 199l, 368t; B-M 2.22, 2.134;	34.23	B-L 135h
	Berg 2.122a, 2.122b; Gib 134	35.1	GKC §73d, 117w □ Berg 2.145e
32.8	Dav §109R3; GKC §107q, 138g,	35.2	Dav §101Ra; GKC §119i; J-M
	155h, 156c; J-M §75c; Gib 104		§133c □ B-L 131
	□ B-M 1.110, 2.139	35.6	GKC §141c n 2 □ Berg 2.49h
32.9	Dav §94, 128R5; GKC §114a,	35.8	Dav §69R4, 139; GKC §60d,
	114k, 114s; Wms §416 □ B-M		156g; IBHS 332; Gib 168, 182 □
	2.175; Berg 2.54d, 2.60o		B-L 337n; B-M 3.92; Berg 2.23g
32.10	Dav §32R1; J-M §141b; IBHS	35.10	GKC §9u □ B-L 268j
	518; Gib 44 □ B-M 1.94, 1.96;	35.11–12	Gib 75
	Brock §58	35.12	Dav §78R1; GKC §117ff □ B-L
32.11	B-L 131; B-M 2.66, 2.133		461i"
33.1	IBHS 212 □ B-L 438; Berg	35.13	Berg 2.167o
	2.97h	35.14	Dav §101Rd; GKC §93hh; J-M
33.3	GKC §114n; J-M §124n n 1 □		§96Bd □ Berg 1.149h
	Berg 2.55d*	35.15	Dav §144; GKC §113h □ B-L
33.5	GKC §116s; J-M §154c		465d'''; B-M 2.145
33.7	GKC §118w, 126o	35.16	Dav §28R6; GKC §91l, 113h,
33.8	GKC §145e; IBHS 570; Gib 82		119q, 130e, 133h; J-M §61i n 3

B-L: Bauer and Leander, *Historische Grammatik*   **B-M**: Beer, *Grammatik*   **Berg**: Bergsträsser, *Grammatik*
Brock: Brockelmann, *Syntax*   **Dav**: Davidson, *Syntax*   **GAHG**: Richter, *Grammatik*
Gib: Gibson, *Davidson's Syntax, 4th ed.*   **GKC**: *Gesenius' Grammar*   **IBHS**: Waltke and O'Connor, *Syntax*
Jen: Jenni, *Lehrbuch*   **J-M**: Joüon and Muraoka, *Grammar*   **Ros**: Rosenthal, *Grammar*
Sch: Schneider, *Grammatik*   **Wms**: Williams, *Syntax*

35.17	B-L 651w; B-M 1.94; Berg 1.98g; Gib 185
35.18	B-L 436
35.19	Dav §29R4; GKC §131q n 3, 152z; J-M §121k, 160q; Gib 41 □ B-M 2.155, 3.35
35.20–21	IBHS 559
35.20	GKC §93ii □ B-M 1.110, 2.62, 2.120; Berg 2.113h
35.21	Berg 2.37a; Gib 188
35.22	J-M §112a □ B-L 233j, 352
35.23	GKC §135q; Gib 20
35.25	J-M §70b; IBHS 683 □ B-M 2.136; Berg 2.118c
35.26	IBHS 440, 440 n 17 □ B-M 2.112; GAHG 2.24 n 92; Berg 1.147d
35.27	J-M §121l □ B-M 1.105, 2.112
35.28	B-M 2.22
36.3	J-M §52c n 5
36.5	Wms §400
36.6	GKC §35n; Gib 146 □ B-L 227x; B-M 1.94
36.7	Dav §34R6; Wms §81; IBHS 268, 655; Gib 46, 164 □ B-L 77m; Berg 1.123v
36.8	GKC §75u'; J-M §144e; IBHS 326 □ Berg 2.166m
36.9	GKC §75u □ Berg 2.21b, 2.166m
36.12	J-M §125ba □ Berg 2.140 n q
36.13	Dav §41a; GKC §64d; IBHS 375 n 31 □ B-L 286n', 354j; Berg 2.88c; Brock §76d
37	GKC §5h □ B-L 66s; Berg 1.5h
37.1	GKC §5h, 35b, 75bb □ B-L 221p; Berg 2.164i
37.2	B-L 366t; Berg 2.139p
37.3	Dav §73 □ B-L 305j
37.4	GKC §54k □ Berg 1.129b, 2.99e
37.5	GKC §67n □ B-L 429j, 436; B-M 2.145; Berg 2.80 n h, 2.135e
37.6	GKC §116i
37.7–8	Berg 2.51m
37.7	GKC §29f □ B-L 436; Berg 1.71e, 2.109d, 2.171c
37.9	GKC §20f □ B-L 321h; Berg 2.20b
37.10	GKC §159g □ Brock §13a

37.12	B-L 971
37.14	Dav §22R3; GKC §45g; Gib 62
37.15	GKC §20h □ Berg 1.68v
37.16	GKC §129b
37.20	GKC §29o, 75m, 119i; Wms §449; IBHS 492 □ B-L 424; Berg 1.161f, 2.166n
37.21	Berg 2.132a*
37.22	GKC §116l
37.23	GKC §121f; J-M §132d; IBHS 448 □ Berg 2.77c; Brock §36b
37.24	GKC §159bb; Wms §448; Gib 154
37.25	GAHG 3.102 n 289
37.27	Dav §64; GKC §110f; J-M §116f, 171b; Gib 105 □ Berg 2.50k
37.28	IBHS 384 □ B-M 1.97, 1.117, 2.128
37.30	Gib 74, 170
37.31	Dav §116; GKC §145k, 145k n 12; J-M §150g; Gib 23
37.33	GKC §61e
37.34	GKC §60f □ B-L 405; Berg 2.95d; Brock §106a
37.35	IBHS 487
37.36	B-L 346x''; Berg 2.97h
37.38	Dav §41a; Gib 68 □ Berg 2.28f
37.40	Dav §49b; Gib 102 □ Berg 2.39 n a-f, 2.166n
38.2	GKC §152h, 152z; J-M §160f, 160q; IBHS 567 □ B-L 574y; Berg 1.148g
38.3	B-L 198k; B-M 1.109; Berg 2.122a, 2.122 n a, 2.173 n f
38.5	GKC §133c; J-M §141i
38.9	Dav §58a; Gib 103 □ Berg 2.45n, 2.147i, 2.159f
38.11	GKC §55e, 135f, 145n; J-M §59d, 146d □ B-L 282n; B-M 2.126; GAHG 1.186 n 640; Jen §28.3.2.1; Berg 2.107a
38.12–13	IBHS 559
38.12	J-M §113h; IBHS 498 n 4
38.13	GKC §124e □ B-M 2.119; Berg 2.97h, 2.171c
38.14	Dav §143; IBHS 507; Gib 11
38.15	Dav §100R3; J-M §160c; Gib 138

B-L: Bauer and Leander, *Historische Grammatik*   **B-M**: Beer, *Grammatik*   **Berg**: Bergsträsser, *Grammatik*
Brock: Brockelmann, *Syntax*   **Dav**: Davidson, *Syntax*   **GAHG**: Richter, *Grammatik*
Gib: Gibson, *Davidson's Syntax, 4th ed.*   **GKC**: *Gesenius' Grammar*   **IBHS**: Waltke and O'Connor, *Syntax*
Jen: Jenni, *Lehrbuch*   **J-M**: Joüon and Muraoka, *Grammar*   **Ros**: Rosenthal, *Grammar*
Sch: Schneider, *Grammatik*   **Wms**: Williams, *Syntax*

38.17	GKC §72q, 152w; J-M §80k; IBHS 440 n 17 □ B-M 2.151; Berg 2.145d	41.3	Dav §128R2; GKC §109e; J-M §114k; IBHS 422 □ GAHG 3.218 n 826; Berg 2.50l, 2.162d
38.20	Dav §29R4; GKC §131q n 3; Gib 41 □ Berg 2.43 n b-k, 2.77c	41.4	B-L 587k
38.21	GKC §61c □ B-L 343c″, 353v; B-M 2.167; Berg 2.82n	41.5	GKC §30m, 74h □ B-L 376r; Berg 1.72f, 2.81k
39.2	B-M 2.113	41.6	GKC §112p
39.5	J-M §114c, 154i □ B-L 266g; Brock §176c	41.7	Dav §130b; J-M §167g; Gib 154
		41.8	GKC §54f
39.6	Dav §28R3; Gib 29	41.10	GKC §135n
39.7	Dav §101Ra; GKC §75u, 119i	41.11	Berg 2.149l
39.8	Dav §41R2; Gib 68, 91	41.13	GKC §111r; J-M §118p; IBHS 555
39.9	GKC §117ii		
39.11	GKC §135a	42.1	Gib 35
39.12	Dav §132, 132R2; Gib 156 □ Berg 2.165k	42.2	Dav §143; GKC §122f, 155g; J-M §158a* n 2, 174d; Gib 11
39.13	GKC §10h □ B-L 352; Berg 1.126aa	42.3	Gib 185
39.14	GKC §75gg, 108d □ B-L 427t″; Berg 2.164 n	42.4	Dav §91R1, 96R5; GKC §115e n 1; J-M §124s; Gib 130 □ Berg 2.56f
40.2–4	IBHS 548	42.5	Dav §65R5, 73R4; GKC §30m, 107e, 117x; IBHS 503 n 20; Gib 4, 74, 83 □ Berg 2.31d
40.2	GKC §52o, 75aa □ B-L 327p; Berg 2.63e, 2.96f, 2.160a		
40.5	GKC §93oo; Gib 62, 63 □ Berg 2.174 n k	42.6	Dav §51R4, 101 n 1 (p.143); GKC §111t; J-M §118q, 136g; IBHS 121, 425; Gib 58, 101, 149 □ B-L 443k; Berg 1.155f, 2.39 n a-f, 2.111b*, 2.113e
40.6	Dav §95, 132R2; GKC §108f, 114l, 133c, 159e; J-M §167a; Gib 132 □ B-M 3.112; Berg 2.54d		
		42.7	Dav §101 n 1 (p.143); J-M §136k; Gib 149
40.7	B-M 1.94	42.9	IBHS 151
40.8	Berg 2.34g	42.10	GKC §68g, 102l, 107n □ B-L 370p, 639a′; B-M 2.136; Berg 2.36i, 2.119a
40.9	GKC §106g; J-M §112a; Gib 63 □ B-L 276w; Berg 2.28g; Brock §41c		
		42.11	Gib 130
40.10	Berg 2.159g	42.12	Dav §51R4, 101 n 1 (p.143); GKC §111t; J-M §118q □ Berg 2.113e
40.11	Gib 151		
40.13	GKC §106l, 122t □ Brock §145a	43.1	Dav §128R1; GKC §72s, 152a n 1; J-M §113m; Gib 142, 148 □ B-L 398d″; Berg 1.131 n d, 2.146e; Brock §13b
40.14ff.	GKC §3g		
40.14–18	IBHS 17		
40.14	B-L 73d		
40.15	GKC §29o n 2; J-M §121l □ Berg 2.92g	43.2	GKC §102l, 107n □ B-L 639a′; Berg 2.36i
40.16	IBHS 683; Gib 188 □ Berg 2.134d	43.3	GKC §124b □ B-M 3.31; Berg 1.127cc
40.18	GKC §29q, 65e □ B-L 207i, 233j, 371s; Berg 1.161e, 2.113h, 2.119e	43.4	J-M §141m; IBHS 268
		43.5	Dav §101 n 1 (p.143); GKC §111t □ Berg 2.111b*, 2.113e
41.2–3	IBHS 570	44.2	Berg 2.25b

B-L: Bauer and Leander, *Historische Grammatik*   **B-M**: Beer, *Grammatik*   **Berg**: Bergsträsser, *Grammatik*
Brock: Brockelmann, *Syntax*   **Dav**: Davidson, *Syntax*   **GAHG**: Richter, *Grammatik*
Gib: Gibson, *Davidson's Syntax, 4th ed.*   **GKC**: *Gesenius' Grammar*   **IBHS**: Waltke and O'Connor, *Syntax*
Jen: Jenni, *Lehrbuch*   **J-M**: Joüon and Muraoka, *Grammar*   **Ros**: Rosenthal, *Grammar*
Sch: Schneider, *Grammatik*   **Wms**: Williams, *Syntax*

B-L: Bauer and Leander, *Historische Grammatik* **B-M**: Beer, *Grammatik* **Berg**: Bergsträsser, *Grammatik* **Brock**: Brockelmann, *Syntax* **Dav**: Davidson, *Syntax* **GAHG**: Richter, *Grammatik* **Gib**: Gibson, *Davidson's Syntax, 4th ed.* **GKC**: *Gesenius' Grammar* **IBHS**: Waltke and O'Connor, *Syntax* **Jen**: Jenni, *Lehrbuch* **J-M**: Joüon and Muraoka, *Grammar* **Ros**: Rosenthal, *Grammar* **Sch**: Schneider, *Grammatik* **Wms**: Williams, *Syntax*

49.7	Dav §99; GKC §126b; Gib 135 □ B-M 1.96	50.18	Dav §130b; Gib 154 □ B-M 2.158; Berg 2.162f
49.8–10	Dav §65c; Gib 106	50.19–21	Berg 2.32e
49.8	Dav §86b; GKC §113v; J-M §123o; Wms §205; Gib 124 □ Berg 2.63c	50.19–20	Gib 75
		50.20	Dav §83, 141R3
49.9	GKC §69f □ B-L 383; B-M 2.128; Berg 2.126 n d	50.21	Dav §86R3, 146R1; GKC §112cc, 113x, 157a; J-M §123q; Gib 111 □ Berg 2.16c
49.10	B-M 1.105, 2.157; GAHG 3.171 n 536	50.22	GKC §116b; J-M §50b □ Berg 2.85r
49.11	Dav §118 □ B-M 2.136, 2.175	50.23	GKC §58i; J-M §61h; IBHS 518 □ B-L 338r, 339s; B-M 2.166
49.12	GKC §91l; J-M §61i n 3 □ B-L 617i; B-M 2.22, 2.154	51.2	J-M §166n; IBHS 604; Gib 129 □ Jen §10.3.1.3
49.13	Dav §22R2, 143; GKC §152t, 155g; Gib 11	51.3	Dav §28; J-M §113m; Wms §259; IBHS 203; Gib 32, 179
49.14	Dav §143; GKC §155e; J-M §61i n 3, 143i, 158a n 1	51.4	Dav §83; GKC §75gg, 120g; J-M §113m; Gib 120 □ B-M 2.162; Berg 2.165k
49.15	Dav §94; GKC §10g n 3, 67ee, 111t, 114k n 2, 126o; Gib 102, 131 □ B-L 405; B-M 1.94, 2.177; Berg 1.71e, 2.174 n k	51.5	GKC §142f
		51.6	Dav §149R3; GKC §107q, 165b; J-M §169g; Gib 160 □ Berg 2.85r; Brock §138
49.16	J-M §164b	51.7	GKC §64h □ B-L 382; Berg 1.152a, 2.115a, 2.125 n a-e
49.18	GKC §152e; J-M §160e, 160k □ Berg 1.106c	51.9–11	Gib 179
49.21	GKC §155g	51.9	GKC §165a; J-M §113m; Wms §146; IBHS 509
50.1ff.	Berg 2.29i		
50.2–3	IBHS 570	51.10	GKC §155h; J-M §113m; IBHS 338 □ Berg 2.149m, 2.159f
50.3	Dav §109, 128R2; GKC §109e, 144c; J-M §103n, 114k, 152e □ B-L 645d″; B-M 3.12; GAHG 2.36 n 154, 2.41 n 175, 3.218 n 826; Berg 2.50l; Brock §35a, 52a	51.11–14	IBHS 509 n 30
		51.13	Gib 140
		51.14	Dav §75; GKC §117ff.; Gib 5, 113
		51.18	Dav §65c; GKC §108f; Gib 106
50.4	GKC §115b; IBHS 460; Gib 129	51.19	GKC §128h; J-M §129g; Gib 179 □ Berg 2.159f
50.5	Dav §101Rd; J-M §115c n 3; Gib 149	51.20	Gib 179
50.6	IBHS 460 □ Berg 2.39 n a-f	51.21	GKC §107c n 3
50.10–11	IBHS 655	52.2	Jen §6.3.1.5; Berg 2.38g
50.10	Dav §22R3; GKC §90n; J-M §93i; Gib 29 □ Berg 1.123v	52.5	Dav §34R2; GKC §22s, 119w; IBHS 214 n 99, 265; Gib 46 □ B-L 127a′
50.12	GKC §159m, 159r; Wms §453, 517; Gib 154 □ B-M 2.136; Berg 2.119a	52.7	IBHS 413; Gib 78
		52.9	Dav §45R3, 50a, 51R4; Gib 101 □ Berg 2.34h
50.15	GKC §61g □ Berg 2.81k	52.10	J-M §112a
50.16	Dav §50a; J-M §118r, 161i; IBHS 323, 562, 609; Gib 8, 102 □ Berg 2.38d, 2.58m	53	IBHS 17 □ B-L 73d
50.17–18	Berg 2.52o	53.1	B-L 511v
50.17	GKC §142d	53.4	J-M §146j

B-L: Bauer and Leander, *Historische Grammatik*   **B-M**: Beer, *Grammatik*   **Berg**: Bergsträsser, *Grammatik*
Brock: Brockelmann, *Syntax*   **Dav**: Davidson, *Syntax*   **GAHG**: Richter, *Grammatik*
Gib: Gibson, *Davidson's Syntax, 4th ed.*   **GKC**: *Gesenius' Grammar*   **IBHS**: Waltke and O'Connor, *Syntax*
Jen: Jenni, *Lehrbuch*   **J-M**: Joüon and Muraoka, *Grammar*   **Ros**: Rosenthal, *Grammar*
Sch: Schneider, *Grammatik*   **Wms**: Williams, *Syntax*

B-L: Bauer and Leander, *Historische Grammatik* **B-M**: Beer, *Grammatik* **Berg**: Bergsträsser, *Grammatik* **Brock**: Brockelmann, *Syntax* **Dav**: Davidson, *Syntax* **Gib**: Gibson, *Davidson's Syntax, 4th ed.* **GKC**: *Gesenius' Grammar* **IBHS**: Waltke and O'Connor, *Syntax* **Jen**: Jenni, *Lehrbuch* **J-M**: Joüon and Muraoka, *Grammar* **Ros**: Rosenthal, *Grammar* **Sch**: Schneider, *Grammatik* **Wms**: Williams, *Syntax*

59.7	GKC §120g		62.10	Dav §34R3, 132R2; IBHS
59.8	GKC §151a			265 n 22; Gib 46
59.10	GKC §48c; J-M §45a □ B-M		62.11	Gib 155
	2.113		62.12	GKC §134s, 138g □ Gib 48
59.12	GKC §58g □ B-L 339v		63.2	GKC §132d; IBHS 258 □
59.13	GKC §91l, 96q □ B-L 251d			GAHG 2.68 n 295
59.14	GKC §91l, 165a		63.3	GKC §114o; IBHS 225 □ B-L
59.16	Dav §50b, 130R4; GKC §111t,			197m'
	159s; Gib 97 □ Berg 2.39 n a-f		63.4	GKC §60e, 145u □ B-L 338p;
59.17–18	GKC §107n			Berg 2.24g
59.17	Dav §25; GKC §130d; Gib 12		63.6–7	GKC §159n n 1
60.2	GKC §16t		63.6	GKC §117t; J-M §136o; Gib 115
60.3	GKC §59h; IBHS 491 □ Berg		63.7	Dav §17R2; GKC §124b; Gib 20
	2.109d		63.8	GKC §90g □ B-L 528t
60.4	GKC §44g, 75pp; J-M §78g;		63.9	IBHS 129
	IBHS 392 n 31 □ B-L 315n',		63.11	GKC §144g
	376r; Berg 2.159g		64.2	J-M §113m; Gib 81, 179
60.5	Dav §29e; GKC §130c n 2,		64.4–11	Berg 2.29i
	131c; Wms §66; IBHS 230; Gib		64.4	J-M §82a n 4
	41		64.5	GKC §69r; J-M §136g □ B-L
60.6	Berg 1.137g; Gib 69			443k
60.7ff.	GKC §3g		64.6	Dav §146R1; Gib 111 □ Berg
60.7–14	IBHS 17			1.129 n b
60.7	GKC §144m; J-M §151c □		64.7	Dav §27; GKC §67e; IBHS 420;
	Brock §93m*			Gib 35 □ B-L 439p', 604g; Berg
60.8	Berg 2.52o, 2.112c			1.110 n b
60.10	Dav §23; J-M §140b; Gib 31		64.8ff.	GKC §111w
60.11	Dav §41R2		64.8–10	Dav §49b; Gib 102
60.12	Dav §51R5		64.8	GKC §117ff.; IBHS 175; Gib
60.13	Dav §139; GKC §80g, 158a;			144 □ B-L 93c; Berg 2.37b,
	J-M §89n, 170c □ B-L 604g;			2.127e
	GAHG 3.199 n 743; Sch		64.9	Dav §116R1; GKC §103p n 2,
	§53.1.2.3; Brock §135b			130a; Gib 78 □ Berg 2.37b
61.1	GKC §80f □ B-L 511v		64.10	Berg 2.37b
61.3	GKC §51l, 133c; J-M §51b;		64.11	J-M §119k □ B-L 436
	IBHS 266, 505; Gib 75		65.4	Dav §17R3; GKC §133c, 143b;
61.5	J-M §114c □ Jen §13.4.9			IBHS 266
61.6	Gib 69		65.5	Dav §25, 32R5, 144; GKC
61.7	GKC §107n □ Berg 2.51m			§10g n 3, 130d, 155n; J-M
61.8	Dav §65R4; GKC §66f, 75cc;			§114e; IBHS 151 n 31, 261 n 19;
	Gib 107 □ B-L 199l, 368t; Berg			Gib 11, 45, 164 □ B-M 3.102;
	2.122a, 2.164i			Jen §22.3.3; Brock §147
62.3	Brock §93k		65.6	GKC §92g □ B-L 564; Berg
62.4	Dav §32R2, 99R1; GKC §52q,			1.120 n o, 1.145d
	126x; J-M §97Be; Gib 44, 135 □		65.7	Berg 2.112d
	B-L 362a'; Berg 2.96g, 2.97h		65.8–9	IBHS 561
62.5	Dav §116R1; GKC §145m, 156d		65.9	GKC §111l
	□ B-L 438; Berg 2.97h			
62.6	Berg 2.135e			
62.8	GKC §13c □ Berg 1.69x			

B-L: Bauer and Leander, *Historische Grammatik*   **B-M**: Beer, *Grammatik*   **Berg**: Bergsträsser, *Grammatik*
Brock: Brockelmann, *Syntax*   **Dav**: Davidson, *Syntax*   **GAHG**: Richter, *Grammatik*
Gib: Gibson, *Davidson's Syntax, 4th ed.*   **GKC**: *Gesenius' Grammar*   **IBHS**: Waltke and O'Connor, *Syntax*
Jen: Jenni, *Lehrbuch*   **J-M**: Joüon and Muraoka, *Grammar*   **Ros**: Rosenthal, *Grammar*
Sch: Schneider, *Grammatik*   **Wms**: Williams, *Syntax*

B-L: Bauer and Leander, *Historische Grammatik*   **B-M**: Beer, *Grammatik*   **Berg**: Bergsträsser, *Grammatik*
Brock: Brockelmann, *Syntax*   **Dav**: Davidson, *Syntax*   **GAHG**: Richter, *Grammatik*
Gib: Gibson, *Davidson's Syntax, 4th ed.*   **GKC**: *Gesenius' Grammar*   **IBHS**: Waltke and O'Connor, *Syntax*
Jen: Jenni, *Lehrbuch*   **J-M**: Joüon and Muraoka, *Grammar*   **Ros**: Rosenthal, *Grammar*
Sch: Schneider, *Grammatik*   **Wms**: Williams, *Syntax*

69.15	Dav §62, 65R3; GKC §108c, J-M §114c, 116j; Gib 107 □ Berg 2.46c, 2.47d	72.14	GKC §69b n 1, 69f □ B-L 383, 563v; Berg 2.126 n d
69.16	Berg 2.112d	72.15–17	Berg 2.50l
69.18	GKC §109c □ Berg 2.48g	72.15	GKC §58i; J-M §139g, 167f, 177l; IBHS 518 □ B-L 339s
69.19	GKC §48i; J-M §48d □ B-L 306n; Berg 2.23g, 2.81i	72.16–17	GKC §109k
69.21	Berg 1.142f	72.16	Dav §65R6
69.22	Dav §51R5	72.17	GKC §10g; IBHS 250, 413; Gib 29 □ Berg 2.152 n t
69.24	GKC §64h □ Berg 2.116e	72.19	Dav §81R2; GKC §121d; J-M §128c n 1; Gib 118 □ B-M 3.84
69.25	Berg 1.150m		
69.26	Berg 2.49h(bis)	72.20	GKC §52q; J-M §56a; IBHS 419 n 4 □ B-L 424; Berg 2.96g
69.31	B-L 436		
69.32	IBHS 443 □ Berg 2.103d*	73.2	Dav §116; GKC §44m, 75u, 106p, 145k; J-M §150h; Gib 23 □ B-L 287n′, 316r′, 411v, 441e; Berg 2.15b, 2.88c, 2.166m
69.33	Dav §45R2		
69.35	B-L 436		
69.36	GKC §69s; Gib 104		
70	GKC §3g; IBHS 17 □ B-L 73d	73.3	Berg 2.30b
70.3	J-M §121l	73.4	B-L 583w′
70.4	IBHS 621 n 38; Gib 188 □ Jen §8.3.2.2	73.5–9	Gib 75
		73.5	GKC §91l; IBHS 662
71.1	GKC §108c; J-M §114c □ Berg 2.49h	73.6	GKC §58g □ Berg 2.75a
		73.7	GKC §91l, 145o; IBHS 25
71.2	J-M §113m	73.9	GKC §63n, 67ee, 69x; J-M §75g □ B-L 385g′, 405; Berg 2.131o, 2.134c, 1.154e, 2.174 n k
71.6	Berg 2.145 n d, 2.172 n e		
71.7	GKC §131r; IBHS 173, 256; Gib 41		
		73.10	Dav §32R5; GKC §103f n 3, 121f, 128w; Gib 44
71.9	Gib 5		
71.12	B-L 399h″; Berg 2.152 n t	73.11	GKC §106p □ Berg 1.129b
71.13	Berg 2.113f	73.12	B-L 376r; Berg 2.159f; Gib 5
71.16	J-M §146d n 1; IBHS 442	73.13	Dav §71R2 □ Berg 2.167o; Gib 145
71.18	GKC §155f; J-M §158a □ B-M 3.96		
		73.14	GKC §123c; J-M §137i; IBHS 245 □ Berg 2.74l
71.20	GKC §120g □ Berg 2.162d		
71.21	Dav §63R2; J-M §79i n 3, 114g □ Berg 2.50l, 2.165k	73.15	Dav §131R1; GKC §159n, 159y; Gib 155
		73.16	GKC §32l, 49e, 108e; IBHS 301; Gib 3 □ Berg 2.22e, 2.23f
71.23	GKC §44o □ B-L 303d′; Berg 2.20a		
72.1	Gib 31	73.17	Dav §45, 65R5; GKC §107c, 108h; J-M §114c n 2; Gib 83
72.2	GKC §107n □ Berg 1.106c, 2.51 n m		
		73.18ff.	Berg 2.29i
72.4	Brock §74c	73.18	GKC §117n; Gib 118
72.5	J-M §177l; Gib 148 □ Brock §113	73.19	GKC §148b; J-M §162b
		73.20	GKC §53q, 119y n 3; Wms §316; IBHS 213 □ B-L 228a′; Berg 2.105 n k
72.7	Berg 1.129b		
72.8	J-M §177l □ Berg 2.50l		
72.11	J-M §177l	73.27	Dav §98R1, 101; GKC §119ff.; Gib 134 □ Berg 2.85r
72.12	GKC §152u, 152v; J-M §159oa		
72.13	Dav §65R6; GKC §62r; J-M §80k n 2; Gib 73 □ Berg 2.51l	73.28	GKC §63d; Gib 44, 129 □ B-L 405, 614; Berg 2.54d, 2.146f

B-L: Bauer and Leander, *Historische Grammatik*   **B-M**: Beer, *Grammatik*   **Berg**: Bergsträsser, *Grammatik*
Brock: Brockelmann, *Syntax*   **Dav**: Davidson, *Syntax*   **GAHG**: Richter, *Grammatik*
Gib: Gibson, *Davidson's Syntax, 4th ed.*   **GKC**: *Gesenius' Grammar*   **IBHS**: Waltke and O'Connor, *Syntax*
Jen: Jenni, *Lehrbuch*   **J-M**: Joüon and Muraoka, *Grammar*   **Ros**: Rosenthal, *Grammar*
Sch: Schneider, *Grammatik*   **Wms**: Williams, *Syntax*

74.1	Berg 2.113f; Gib 63	76.7	Dav §67R2; GKC §104g,
74.2	GKC §138g; J-M §145c; IBHS		154a n 1b, 162b; J-M §177p ☐
	313, 337; Gib 7, 114		B-L 649l; Gib 37
74.3–8	Gib 71	76.8	Dav §136; GKC §116e; J-M
74.3	Brock §144		§121i; Gib 133
74.4–8	Gib 180	76.9	Berg 2.45n
74.5	GKC §10g, 93t ☐ B-L 208s,	76.10	GKC §115g; J-M §103i; Gib 129
	580r'; Berg 1.124w	76.11	Dav §97R1, 143; GKC §124e;
74.6	J-M §93g n 3 ☐ Berg 2.112c		Gib 141
74.7	Dav §91R3, 116R3; GKC	77.2–7	Berg 2.29i
	§119gg ☐ Berg 2.97h	77.2	GKC §63o; Gib 75 ☐ B-L 348k;
74.8	GKC §60d, 76f ☐ B-L 338n;		B-M 2.130; Berg 2.112c
	Berg 2.23g	77.3	Berg 2.54d*
74.9	GKC §137b, 147c; J-M §112a,	77.4	Dav §65R5; GKC §75l, 75u;
	160c		J-M §79o; Gib 83 ☐ B-L 409l;
74.10	GKC §64e; Gib 185 ☐ Berg		B-M 2.158; Berg 2.22f, 2.166m,
	2.115a, 2.116b		2.168p
74.11	Dav §101; Gib 37	77.6	Berg 2.50l
74.12–17	Gib 180	77.7	Dav §65R5; GKC §108g; Gib 83
74.12–15	Gib 71		☐ Berg 2.39 n a-f, 2.50l
74.12	IBHS 160; Gib 52	77.10	GKC §67r ☐ B-L 437; Berg
74.13–14	IBHS 122		2.135 n f
74.13	J-M §136f; Gib 19	77.11	GKC §67r ☐ B-L 436; Berg
74.14	Berg 2.34h		2.54d, 2.135 n f
74.15	Dav §136R1; GKC §128w; Gib	77.12	J-M §164b; Gib 141
	44	77.16	GKC §20g, 125c ☐ Berg 1.67t
74.17	GKC §143b; J-M §156aa ☐ B-L	77.18	GKC §55b, 93bb; J-M §90e,
	649l		96Ao, 125b ☐ B-L 564; Berg
74.19	GKC §80f		2.108 n b
74.21	B-L 436; Berg 2.49h	77.20	GKC §20h ☐ B-L 557f'; B-M
74.22	GKC §72s ☐ B-L 398d''; Berg		2.64; Berg 1.68v
	2.145e	78	Gib 67, 180
74.23	Dav §98R1; Gib 134	78.2	Berg 1.106c
75.3	Dav §71R2; GKC §118q; Gib	78.6	Dav §44R3; GKC §107k, 107q,
	145, 154		155f; J-M §158a; Gib 77, 104 ☐
75.4	GKC §116w, 146g ☐ B-M 2.11;		B-L 274g; GAHG 3.122 n 332
	Berg 2.72h, 2.147i	78.8	B-L 424
75.5	Berg 2.135d	78.9	Dav §28R6; GKC §130e; Gib 36
75.6	GKC §152z; J-M §160q	78.10	Jen §7.1
75.8	GKC §34c ☐ B-L 267e; B-M	78.12	Gib 180
	2.17; Brock §23b; Gib 6	78.13	IBHS 363; Gib 66, 180
75.9	IBHS 449	78.14	Gib 71
76.4	GKC §93m; J-M §96Ad ☐ B-L	78.15–72	Berg 2.34h
	582u'; Berg 1.122t	78.15	Dav §51R5; GKC §107e,
76.5	Berg 1.123v, 2.143 n b		132h n 1, 132h n 2; IBHS
76.6	GKC §54a n 2, 72l, 154a n 1 ☐		101 n 29, 363; Gib 180
	B-L 398e'', 439p'; B-M 2.122,	78.16	GKC §74l; J-M §78i ☐ Berg
	3.67; Berg 2.99d, 2.145e		2.157b
		78.17	Dav §45R2; GKC §53q ☐ B-L
			228a'; Berg 2.105 n k

B-L: Bauer and Leander, *Historische Grammatik* **B-M**: Beer, *Grammatik* **Berg**: Bergsträsser, *Grammatik*
Brock: Brockelmann, *Syntax* **Dav**: Davidson, *Syntax* **GAHG**: Richter, *Grammatik*
Gib: Gibson, *Davidson's Syntax, 4th ed.* **GKC**: *Gesenius' Grammar* **IBHS**: Waltke and O'Connor, *Syntax*
Jen: Jenni, *Lehrbuch* **J-M**: Joüon and Muraoka, *Grammar* **Ros**: Rosenthal, *Grammar*
Sch: Schneider, *Grammatik* **Wms**: Williams, *Syntax*

78.18	GKC §114o		80.11	Dav §34R6, 80; GKC §52q,
78.20	Dav §45R2			121d; J-M §128c; Wms §81; Gib
78.21	GKC §66e; IBHS 431 □ B-L			46, 118 □ B-L 424; Berg 2.96g;
	368u; Berg 2.122b, 2.124 n g			Brock §98b
78.23	IBHS 384 n 15		80.13	GKC §112h; J-M §119e, 119t,
78.24	Gib 67			161m
78.25	B-M 3.51; Gib 67		80.14	GKC §5n, 56; J-M §60 □ B-L
78.26	Dav §51R5; Gib ‡71, 100 □			80u, 281i; B-M 2.127; Jen
	Berg 2.34h			§28.3.2.1; Berg 1.5l, 1.110b,
78.29–30	IBHS 91			2.110e; Brock §138
78.30	Berg 2.145e; Gib 180		80.15	Dav §6R1; GKC §125h, 131s;
78.34	J-M §167g □ B-M 3.54; Berg			J-M §131o; Gib 7, 25 □ GAHG
	2.41d			3.215 n 815
78.35	Gib 110		80.16	B-L 429j; Berg 2.135 n e
78.38	GKC §114n n 2 □ Berg 2.59n*		80.18	Berg 2.48g
78.40	GKC §107e; IBHS 326; Gib 185		80.19	GKC §72t □ B-L 399h"; Berg
	□ B-L 651w			2.21 n c, 2.162d
78.44	GKC §75u, 124e □ B-L 409k;		80.20	GKC §131s; J-M §131o; Gib 25
	Berg 2.166m		81.4	B-L 579q'; Berg 1.103q, 1.137g
78.47	B-L 485gε		81.6	Dav §25, 144; GKC §53q, 130d,
78.49	Dav §32R5, 51R5; GKC §128w;			155n; J-M §129q(3); IBHS 218;
	J-M §141f; Gib 44			Gib 12 □ GAHG 2.52 n 246
78.50	Dav §51R5		81.7–8	Berg 2.34h
78.52	Gib ‡71		81.7	Dav §51R5 □ Berg 2.148k
78.54	GKC §138g; J-M §145c; Gib 7		81.8	Dav §51R5; IBHS 225 □ Berg
78.55	J-M §133c			2.162d
78.57	Berg 1.155i, 2.113e		81.9	Dav §134; GKC §109b, 151e;
78.63	Berg 2.96g			J-M §163c; IBHS 680; Gib 107,
78.68	Gib 173			186 □ B-M 3.117; Sch §53.5.1.3
79.1	B-L 564		81.11	GKC §116f; Gib 107, 134 □ B-L
79.2	GKC §90o; J-M §93r			375; Berg 2.68a
79.5	IBHS 325		81.14	Dav §131, 134; GKC §159z; Gib
79.7	Berg 2.137k			155, 186 □ GAHG 3.178 n 618;
79.8	J-M §137i			Brock §39bβ
79.10	Dav §99; GKC §150e; Gib 135		82	IBHS 470 n 75
	□ Brock §173		82.1	J-M §113c n 1; IBHS 505
79.11	Brock §15a		82.2	Gib 185
79.12	GKC §97h, 134r; J-M §100o		82.3	IBHS 571
80.2	B-L 383		82.5	IBHS 505, 512
80.3	GKC §90g		82.6	GKC §131s, 135a
80.5	Dav §41R2; GKC §106h, 131s;		82.7	GAHG 2.33 n 133, 3.176 n 599
	Gib 25, 68		82.8	IBHS 572 □ B-L 398c"; Berg
80.6–13	Berg 2.34h			2.145e
80.6	GKC §131c n 2; IBHS 442 □		83	GKC §131s
	B-L 93c; Berg 2.112c		83.2	GKC §152g □ B-M 3.9; Brock
80.8	GKC §131s; Gib 25			§7b
80.9–13	Gib 71		83.3–6	Gib 75
80.9	Dav §45R2; IBHS 558		83.3	GKC §75u
			83.4	GKC §63n □ B-M 2.141; Berg
				2.115a, 2.129l

B-L: Bauer and Leander, *Historische Grammatik*   B-M: Beer, *Grammatik*   Berg: Bergsträsser, *Grammatik*
Brock: Brockelmann, *Syntax*   Dav: Davidson, *Syntax*   GAHG: Richter, *Grammatik*
Gib: Gibson, *Davidson's Syntax, 4th ed.*   GKC: *Gesenius' Grammar*   IBHS: Waltke and O'Connor, *Syntax*
Jen: Jenni, *Lehrbuch*   J-M: Joüon and Muraoka, *Grammar*   Ros: Rosenthal, *Grammar*
Sch: Schneider, *Grammatik*   Wms: Williams, *Syntax*

B-L: Bauer and Leander, *Historische Grammatik* B-M: Beer, *Grammatik* Berg: Bergsträsser, *Grammatik*
Brock: Brockelmann, *Syntax* Dav: Davidson, *Syntax* GAHG: Richter, *Grammatik*
Gib: Gibson, *Davidson's Syntax, 4th ed.* GKC: *Gesenius' Grammar* IBHS: Waltke and O'Connor, *Syntax*
Jen: Jenni, *Lehrbuch* J-M: Joüon and Muraoka, *Grammar* Ros: Rosenthal, *Grammar*
Sch: Schneider, *Grammatik* Wms: Williams, *Syntax*

89.34	GKC §67v; J-M §82n ☐ B-L 438; Berg 2.140q	90.15	Dav §25; GKC §87n, 96m, 130d; J-M §98f, 158c; IBHS 338; Gib 12 ☐ B-L 618n; B-M 2.83, 3.96; Brock §144
89.36	J-M §165d; IBHS 275; Gib 187		
89.38	J-M §177n ☐ B-M 2.118, 2.129		
89.39	J-M §39a n 4 ☐ B-M 1.105	91.1	Berg 2.151s
89.40	Dav §101; GKC §64e, 119gg; J-M §52c n 5 ☐ Berg 2.115a	91.3	B-L 538i
		91.4	GKC §67p, 84^{a}s, 109k; Gib 104 ☐ Berg 2.80 n h, 2.137l
89.41	Berg 1.127cc, 1.147d		
89.42	B-M 2.22; Berg 2.174 n k	91.6	Dav §68; GKC §67q, 118i; Gib 144 ☐ B-L 439p'; Berg 2.140q
89.43	J-M §80m; IBHS 446		
89.44	GKC §72w; J-M §80m ☐ Berg 2.150n	91.7	Gib 170
		91.9	GKC §117ii
89.45	J-M §52a n 4 ☐ B-M 2.120; Berg 1.126aa, 2.119e	91.11	GKC §20c ☐ B-L 199n; Berg 1.66s
89.46	J-M §136h; IBHS 121	91.12	GKC §60e ☐ B-L 131, 338p; Berg 2.24g
89.47	B-M 2.131		
89.48	Dav §1R1; GKC §135f; IBHS 218; Gib 8 ☐ B-M 2.105, 2.155	91.14	Dav §59; J-M §119y n 2
		91.15	J-M §119y n 2; Gib 150
89.50	B-M 2.175	92.2–3	Berg 2.58m
89.51	Dav §1R1, 32R1; GKC §132b; J-M §141b; IBHS 160; Gib 44 ☐ B-L 441c; B-M 2.68, 2.54 Anm 5	92.2	IBHS 605
		92.3	J-M §136b
		92.6	IBHS 434; Gib 63, 164 ☐ B-M 3.50; Berg 1.66s, 2.28g; Brock §41b
89.52	GKC §20h; J-M §52c n 1 ☐ B-L 557f'; B-M 2.64; Berg 1.68v		
		92.8	GKC §111v; IBHS 562; Gib 102 ☐ Berg 2.38g
90.1	B-M 2.105; GAHG 3.229 n 879; Berg 1.65q, 1.71e		
		92.9	Dav §29e, 69R1; Gib 42
90.2	Dav §145; GKC §107c, 152r; J-M §113j; Gib 157 ☐ B-M 3.111; GAHG 3.122 n 332; Berg 2.109d; Brock §145bα	92.11	Dav §19R4; GKC §67ee; Wms §583 ☐ B-L 430m, 583y'; Berg 2.37a, 2.134c
		92.12	Dav §32R2; GKC §132b; Gib 44
90.3–6	Gib 75	92.13–15	Gib 75
90.3	Dav §65R6; GKC §109k, 111t; IBHS 558, 567; Gib 73, 95 ☐ Berg 2.39 n a-f, 2.51l	92.13	J-M §130f ☐ B-L 376r; Berg 2.159f
		92.14	GKC §65e, 118p ☐ B-L 361a'; Berg 2.80 n h
90.4	GKC §118r, 134g		
90.5–9	Gib 62	92.15	B-L 557h'; B-M 1.100; GAHG 3.170 n 533; Berg 1.139b
90.5	GKC §155g		
90.6–9	Gib 179	92.16	GKC §90g; J-M §93j ☐ B-L 131, 604g; Jen §25.3.2.7; Berg 1.65q
90.6	GKC §112m; J-M §119q; Wms §268; Gib 94 ☐ Berg 2.140 n r		
		93	IBHS 470 n 75
90.8	GKC §73d; J-M §33 ☐ B-L 405; Berg 1.158q, 2.146f	93.1	GKC §156g; J-M §111h, 155nd; IBHS 367, 567 n 6; Gib 64, 113, 175 ☐ B-L 312t; Berg 2.77c, 2.77 n c
90.9	B-L 131; Berg 1.103q		
90.10	GKC §49e; J-M §47e; Gib 179 ☐ B-L 119 n 2; Berg 2.23f		
		93.2	Gib 157
90.13	GKC §147c; Gib 179	93.3	IBHS 501
90.14	B-L 438; Berg 1.142f, 2.97h; Gib 107	93.4	Brock §58

B-L: Bauer and Leander, *Historische Grammatik*   **B-M**: Beer, *Grammatik*   **Berg**: Bergsträsser, *Grammatik*
Brock: Brockelmann, *Syntax*   **Dav**: Davidson, *Syntax*   **GAHG**: Richter, *Grammatik*
Gib: Gibson, *Davidson's Syntax, 4th ed.*   **GKC**: *Gesenius' Grammar*   **IBHS**: Waltke and O'Connor, *Syntax*
Jen: Jenni, *Lehrbuch*   **J-M**: Joüon and Muraoka, *Grammar*   **Ros**: Rosenthal, *Grammar*
Sch: Schneider, *Grammatik*   **Wms**: Williams, *Syntax*

93.5	GKC §75x ☐ B-L 422t'', 599h'; Berg 1.66q, 2.107 n a	96.8	J-M §129g ☐ B-L 552r
94.1	GKC §53m, 69v; J-M §54c ☐ B-L 383; Berg 2.104i	96.9	GKC §145e ☐ Berg 2.152t
		96.10	Gib 64
94.6–7	IBHS 559	96.11–12	Gib 82
94.7	Berg 1.66q	96.11	IBHS 570; Gib 105, 170 ☐ Berg
94.9	Dav §126R2; GKC §65d, 93qq; J-M §96Cc ☐ Brock §54d		2.48f
		96.12	Wms §9 ☐ Berg 1.107d
94.10	Brock §54d	96.13	Berg 1.129b
94.12	GKC §13c, 20g ☐ Berg 1.67t	97.1	Dav §39R1; J-M §155nd; IBHS
94.13	Berg 1.67u		570; Gib 82 ☐ Berg 2.48f
94.14	B-L 367	97.2	J-M §103n ☐ B-L 645d''
94.16	Wms §332	97.4	Berg 2.149m
94.17	Dav §73, 131; GKC §90g, 106p; Gib 155 ☐ B-L 528t; Berg 1.65q	97.5	B-M 2.146; Berg 2.136h
		97.6–9	Gib 62
94.18	GKC §164d; J-M §166p	97.8	Berg 2.149m
94.19	Berg 2.108c	98.1	IBHS 210 ☐ Berg 1.65q, 1.67u
94.20	GKC §60b, 63m; J-M §63b ☐ B-L 351; Berg 2.79 n g	98.2	IBHS 442
		98.3	Berg 1.156k
94.21–22	IBHS 559	98.7–8	IBHS 570; Gib 82
94.21	B-L 435p'; Berg 2.135d	98.7	GKC §130a
94.22–23	Gib 102	98.8	IBHS 570
94.22	Dav §49b; GKC §111w	99.3	GKC §126h
94.23	Dav §49b ☐ Berg 2.34h	99.4	IBHS 644 n 35 ☐ Berg 1.66r
95.1	IBHS 574; Gib 83 ☐ B-L 438; Berg 2.47e	99.5	Berg 2.114i
		99.6–7	Berg 2.32d, 2.32e
95.2	Berg 1.67u	99.6	Dav §101Ra; GKC §74i, 75oo,
95.3–5	Sch §44.2.2		119i ☐ B-L 549a'; Berg 1.92e,
95.3	GKC §133i		2.156a
95.4	Berg 1.154e	99.9	Berg 1.145d
95.5	Jen §27.3.3	100.3	GKC §29l, 103g, 141b; J-M
95.6	IBHS 574; Gib 83, 105 ☐ B-L 131; Berg 2.47e		§154j; IBHS 205 n 59; Gib 179
		100.4	B-L 552r; Berg 1.67u; Gib 109,
95.7	Dav §134; GKC §151e; J-M §163c; Gib 186 ☐ Berg 1.67u; Brock §170a		134, 144
		100.5	Gib 37
		101.1	Gib 5
95.8	Dav §101Rd; J-M §133h; Gib 150	101.2	B-L 131; Berg 2.52o; Gib 185
		101.3	Dav §91R3; GKC §75n; Gib 128
95.9–10	Berg 2.34h		☐ Berg 1.50g, 2.52o, 2.55d*,
95.9	GKC §160b; Wms §382; Gib 157 ☐ Jen §13.3.2.4		2.161c
		101.5	Dav §22R3; GKC §55b, 55c,
95.10	Dav §22R3, 50a; GKC §72r; IBHS 480, 558; Gib 100		64i, 90m, 115b; J-M §93n ☐
			B-L 281j, 557f'; Berg 2.108 n b
95.11	Dav §150; GKC §149b, 149c; J-M §165d; Gib 161	101.8	GKC §114o; J-M §137i ☐ Berg
			1.129 n b
96	IBHS 17	101.24	IBHS 27 (LXX)
96.1	GKC §145e; IBHS 210	102	Gib 63
96.4	Dav §97R1; Gib 133	102.1	B-L 353v
96.5	Gib 53, 172	102.3	GKC §130d; Gib 12, 75 ☐ Berg
96.7	GKC §104g		2.48g; Brock §145a

B-L: Bauer and Leander, *Historische Grammatik*   **B-M:** Beer, *Grammatik*   **Berg:** Bergsträsser, *Grammatik*
Brock: Brockelmann, *Syntax*   **Dav:** Davidson, *Syntax*   **GAHG:** Richter, *Grammatik*
Gib: Gibson, *Davidson's Syntax, 4th ed.*   **GKC:** *Gesenius' Grammar*   **IBHS:** Waltke and O'Connor, *Syntax*
Jen: Jenni, *Lehrbuch*   **J-M:** Joüon and Muraoka, *Grammar*   **Ros:** Rosenthal, *Grammar*
Sch: Schneider, *Grammatik*   **Wms:** Williams, *Syntax*

102.4	GKC §67u, 119i; J-M §82i □ B-L 434k'; Berg 1.161d, 2.139o	103.15	Gib 172
		103.16	Berg 1.66q; Brock §80e
102.5	Dav §101Rc; GKC §63l, 90 □ Berg 1.45e, 2.114i	103.17	Gib 172
		103.19	IBHS 448 □ Jen §9.3.5
102.6–8	Gib 63	103.20	GKC §114o
102.7	Berg 2.28g; Gib 63	104.1	GKC §106g; J-M §112a; Gib 61, 63 □ Jen §11.3.3; Berg 2.28g(bis)
102.8	Berg 1.107d		
102.9–10	Gib 63		
102.9	Dav §98R1; GKC §116i; Gib 63, 134	104.2	GKC §117y; J-M §138e
		104.3	GKC §20m n 2, 35b, 126b □ B-L 221p
102.10	B-L 535f; Berg 1.97 n c, 1.111 n c, 1.144d, 1.145d	104.4	J-M §125w, 138e; Gib 63
102.11	Berg 1.148g	104.5	IBHS 392 n 31
102.12	Gib 75	104.6ff.	GKC §107b
102.14	Dav §83, 141R3; GKC §67a, 67cc; Gib 121 □ B-L 437; Berg 2.57l, 2.133b	104.6–9	Gib 71
		104.6–8	Dav §45R2
		104.6–7	Berg 2.34h
102.16	J-M §177l	104.6	Dav §78R2; IBHS 184 n 41
102.19	GKC §116e; J-M §116i; Gib 133, 137 □ Berg 1.107d, 2.69d	104.7	GKC §72u, 102b □ B-L 321h, 642p'
102.24–25a	IBHS 512	104.8	GKC §138g; J-M §129q, 145c; IBHS 313 n 20, 336; Gib 7, 12 □ B-M 3.97
102.24	IBHS 27		
102.25	Berg 1.156k		
102.27	Gib 172	104.10–13	Gib 75
102.28	Dav §106R2; GKC §67g, 135a n 1; J-M §154j ; Gib 3 □ B-M 2.144	104.11	GKC §90n; J-M §93r; Gib 29
		104.12	GKC §93z □ B-L 215g, 215h, 302a', 579p'; B-M 2.72
102.29	B-L 303a'; Berg 2.84q	104.13	Gib 114
103.1	GKC §10g; J-M §9c3	104.14	Dav §96; GKC §29e, 114o; Gib 131 □ Berg 1.130c, 2.60p
103.2	J-M §121r		
103.3	GKC §91e, 91l; J-M §94h, 94i □ B-L 535f, 538i	104.15	Dav §75, 96; Gib 131 □ Berg 2.60p
103.4	GKC §35b, 58g; J-M §61i, 94i □ B-L 253u, 344g'', 548a', 564; Berg 1.142f, 2.68a	104.16	Dav §34R6
		104.17	GKC §143a
		104.18	Dav §32R2; GKC §20m, 126x; Gib 44
103.5	Dav §116; GKC §145k, 145k n 2, 156d; J-M §94i, 150g; Wms §233; IBHS 512; Gib 23, 107 □ B-L 534	104.19	GKC §122o; IBHS 570
		104.20	Dav §22R3, 75R6, 132b; GKC §109h, 159d; J-M §93r, 114g, 167a; Gib 29, 104 □ B-L 274k; B-M 3.112; GAHG 1.143 n 464; Sch §51.4.1.2; Brock §135b
103.7	Gib 30		
103.8	Gib 52, 55		
103.9	GKC §117g; Gib 110, 170 □ B-L 367; Brock §127b		
103.10–13	Gib 62	104.21	Dav §96R4; GKC §114p, 114p n 2; Gib 132 □ Berg 2.60p
103.10	GKC §152e □ Berg 1.49d		
103.11	B-L 360p; Gib 174	104.22	Dav §132R2; Gib 156 □ B-L 321h
103.13	J-M §112a; Gib 74		
103.14	Dav §100R7; GKC §50f; J-M §50e; Gib 138 □ Berg 2.88d	104.23	IBHS 215 □ B-L 582u'
103.15–16	Gib 74, 75	104.24	GKC §67ee; Gib 63 □ Berg 2.28g(bis)

B-L: Bauer and Leander, *Historische Grammatik*   **B-M**: Beer, *Grammatik*   **Berg**: Bergsträsser, *Grammatik*
Brock: Brockelmann, *Syntax*   **Dav**: Davidson, *Syntax*   **GAHG**: Richter, *Grammatik*
Gib: Gibson, *Davidson's Syntax, 4th ed.*   **GKC**: *Gesenius' Grammar*   **IBHS**: Waltke and O'Connor, *Syntax*
Jen: Jenni, *Lehrbuch*   **J-M**: Joüon and Muraoka, *Grammar*   **Ros**: Rosenthal, *Grammar*
Sch: Schneider, *Grammatik*   **Wms**: Williams, *Syntax*

104.25	Dav §6R1; GKC §136d n 2, 152u; J-M §143i
104.26	GKC §138g; J-M §145c; Wms §129; IBHS 313 n 20, 336 □ B-M 3.97
104.27–30	Dav §132R2; Gib 156
104.27	B-L 328w
104.28–30	GKC §159c n 3
104.28	GKC §47m, 159c; J-M §44e, 167a; IBHS 637 □ B-L 300q; B-M 2.100; Jen §16.3.4; Brock §134c
104.29	GKC §68h, 159d; J-M §73f, 167a □ B-L 321h, 371u; B-M 2.137, 3.112; Berg 2.120b
104.30	B-L 321h; B-M 3.112; Gib 104, 170
104.31	GKC §109k □ Berg 2.50l
104.32	Dav §51R4, 51R6; Gib 101, 104, 170 □ Berg 2.38 n e, 2.113f
104.33	Dav §3R1; Gib 4, 58
104.34	IBHS 371
104.35	J-M §156m
105	Gib 67
105.3	B-L 436
105.4	Berg 2.97h
105.12	GKC §118x; IBHS 204
105.22	B-L 348h; Berg 1.156k, 2.114i
105.24	GKC §75gg □ Berg 2.165k
105.25	IBHS 383
105.28	GKC §53n □ B-L 352; Berg 2.104i
105.37	J-M §132g n 1
105.43	GKC §78l; J-M §78i □ Berg 2.157b
105.44	Berg 2.34h
105.45	IBHS 639 □ Jen §19.3.4
106	Gib 67
106.1	IBHS 17
106.6	Gib 66
106.7	Berg 1.106c
106.8	Gib 173
106.9	GKC §125g
106.13	Dav §83; GKC §120g; Wms §225; Gib 121
106.14	Dav §67b; J-M §125q; IBHS 91; Gib 115
106.15	J-M §97Bd
106.18–43	Berg 2.34h
106.18	Dav §51R5
106.19	GKC §107b
106.20	B-L 77l
106.23	Dav §91R4; Gib 130, 155
106.24	B-L 131
106.25	B-L 131
106.26	Dav §91R4; Gib 130
106.27	Dav §91R4; Gib 130
106.32	J-M §152d
106.33	B-L 422t″; Berg 2.158e
106.43	Dav §44R1 □ Berg 2.134 n d
106.45	B-L 131; Berg 2.91g
106.47–48	IBHS 17
106.47	IBHS 425 □ Berg 2.118b
107	Gib 67, 71
107.2	Gib 66
107.3	Berg 1.127cc
107.4	Gib 66
107.5	GKC §118n; Gib 175
107.6	Dav §51R5
107.7	B-L 131
107.13–14	Berg 2.34h
107.13	Dav §51R5
107.16	Berg 2.117a; Gib 172
107.18	GKC §107b □ Berg 1.130c
107.19–20	Berg 2.34h
107.20	Gib 5, 105
107.21–22	Gib 105
107.23ff.	Berg 1.3l, 1.5l
107.23	GKC §5n, 17e □ B-L 79s
107.24	B-L 131
107.26–29	Dav §51R6
107.26–28	Berg 2.35h
107.27	B-L 436; Berg 2.140 n q; Gib 105
107.28	B-L 79s
107.29	Dav §65R6; GKC §107b, 109k; IBHS 567; Gib 71 □ Berg 2.34h
107.30	J-M §129g; IBHS 144; Gib 31
107.32	B-L 436; Berg 1.128dd
107.33–35	Berg 2.34h
107.35	B-L 619p
107.40	GKC §5n □ B-L 79s; Berg 1.5l
107.42	Gib 69, 104
107.43	GKC §93m; J-M §167m n 1 □ B-L 210f, 581; Berg 1.122t
108.2–6	IBHS 17
108.2	Dav §109R3; GKC §144m
108.3	Berg 2.145e
108.7–14	IBHS 17
108.7	Dav §109R3; GKC §144m

108.13	GKC §80g □ B-L 604g	111.1	GKC §5h □ Berg 2.97h
109.1	B-L 233j, 352	111.2	J-M §121e n 1, 121i, 132f; IBHS
109.2–3	Gib 63		434, 620 □ B-L 553 n 2; Berg
109.2	Dav §32R5, 67R3; GKC §117t;		2.69d
	IBHS 164; Gib 44, 115	111.4–5	Gib 62
109.3	Dav §73R4; GKC §57 n 2; IBHS	111.6	GKC §114o
	165, 304 □ B-L 344h"; Jen	111.7	Dav §29e; Gib 42
	§11.3.1.2	111.8	Dav §32R5; GKC §141b; IBHS
109.4	Dav §29e; GKC §141d; J-M		215; Gib 44
	§154e; Gib 42 □ GAHG	112	GKC §5h □ B-L 66s; Berg 1.5h
	3.82 n 221; Brock §14bε	112.1	GKC §5h
109.7	Dav §70a; GKC §109a n 2; J-M	112.2	GAHG 3.229 n 879
	§114g n 1; Gib 56	112.3	GKC §141b □ B-M 3.8; GAHG
109.10	GKC §64e, 112q; J-M §119k;		3.76 n 200;
	Wms §143; IBHS 530 □ Berg	112.7	GKC §50f □ Berg 2.88d
	2.53q, 2.115a	112.8	GKC §164f
109.11	Berg 2.69 n c, 2.170 n c; Gib	112.9	GKC §120g
	105	112.10	Berg 2.136h
109.12	GKC §116r; Gib 105 □ Berg	113.1	B-L 436
	2.49h, 2.74 n l	113.2	Berg 2.49h, 2.74l
109.13–14	GKC §75y	113.4	Gib 146
109.13	GKC §114k; IBHS 196, 610 n 35	113.5ff.	GKC §90m
	□ B-L 424; Sch §49.3.2; Berg	113.5–7	Gib 135
	2.49h, 2.59o, 2.164 n	113.5–6	Brock §71d, 73b; Gib 120
109.14	Berg 2.49h	113.5	J-M §93n; Gib 7 □ Berg 2.59n*
109.15	Gib 105	113.6	J-M §93n □ B-L 526l, 534
109.16	Berg 2.55d*	113.7	GKC §90m; J-M §93n
109.18	B-L 564	113.8	GKC §90n; J-M §93p
109.19	Dav §143; Gib 11, 108 □ Berg	113.9	GKC §90l, 90m
	2.49h	114.1	GKC §128a n 1, 128a n 2
109.22	Berg 2.133 n a	114.2	B-L 614; Berg 1.148g
109.23	IBHS 360 n 27, 382 n 9 □ Berg	114.3–6	IBHS 570
	2.97h, 2.131 n o	114.3	Dav §51R5
109.24	Dav §101Rc	114.5	GKC §107v
109.25	Gib 156	114.7–8	IBHS 570
109.28	Dav §49b; J-M §146a; IBHS	114.8	Dav §76, 78R3; GKC §90m,
	557; Gib 69 □ B-L 438		90o; J-M §93n, 93r, 125w; Gib
109.29	GKC §117y; Gib 113		114, 164 □ B-L 525i, 547, 548a'
109.30	GKC §144m n 4 □ B-L 436	115.2	GKC §150e □ Brock §173
110.1	GKC §164f; Gib 158	115.4	J-M §154e
110.2	Dav §60R2; GKC §110c; J-M	115.5	GKC §140a □ GAHG
	§114p; IBHS 572; Gib 81		3.76 n 200
110.3	Dav §29e; GKC §141c; J-M	115.7	Dav §3R2; GKC §143d, 147e;
	§129u, 154e; Gib 42 □ Brock		J-M §82o, 154o □ B-L 437;
	§14bε		B-M 3.9; GAHG 1.86, 3.24 n 76;
110.4	GKC §90l; J-M §93m; IBHS		Berg 2.140q; Brock §13b
	127 n 6, 128; Gib 24 □ B-L	115.8	Dav §99R2; Gib 135
	526k, 603g	115.14	Berg 2.49h
110.5ff.	Berg 2.29i	115.15	GKC §116l, 121f; J-M §132f
111	GKC §5h □ B-L 66s; Berg 1.5h	116	GAHG 1.190 n 680

B-L: Bauer and Leander, *Historische Grammatik*   **B-M**: Beer, *Grammatik*   **Berg**: Bergsträsser, *Grammatik*
Brock: Brockelmann, *Syntax*   **Dav**: Davidson, *Syntax*   **GAHG**: Richter, *Grammatik*
Gib: Gibson, *Davidson's Syntax, 4th ed.*   **GKC**: *Gesenius' Grammar*   **IBHS**: Waltke and O'Connor, *Syntax*
Jen: Jenni, *Lehrbuch*   **J-M**: Joüon and Muraoka, *Grammar*   **Ros**: Rosenthal, *Grammar*
Sch: Schneider, *Grammatik*   **Wms**: Williams, *Syntax*

116.1	GKC §90n; J-M §93p	118.16	GKC §84ªs □ B-L 405; Berg
116.2	GAHG 3.161 n 480		1.113ne
116.3–4	Gib 71	118.17	Berg 2.114l
116.3	J-M §113h	118.18	GKC §20g, 52o, 59f, 113p; J-M
116.4	GKC §16f n 1, 105a		§62c, 123i; IBHS 517 n 64 □
116.5	Dav §104		B-L 327p, 383; Berg 1.67t,
116.6	GKC §53q, 67ee; J-M §54b □		2.62c, 2.96f
	B-L 229f′, 384c′, 430m, 579p′;	118.19	Dav §65R4; Gib 107
	B-M 2.145; Berg 2.105 n k,	118.20	Dav §28R5; J-M §143i; Gib 36
	2.134c	118.22	Gib 11
116.7	GKC §72s, 91l; J-M §94i □ B-L	118.23	GKC §74g, 122q □ B-L 375;
	398e″, 538i, 641i′; B-M 2.56;		B-M 2.155; Berg 2.158 n e
	Berg 1.133h, 1.145d, 2.145c	118.25	GKC §20f, 53m □ B-L 199p,
116.12	GKC §91l; J-M §94i □ B-L		362a′, 384c′; GAHG
	253v, 535f		3.170 n 521, 3.215 n 815; Berg
116.13	GKC §128q		2.22f
116.14–18	Berg 2.52o	118.26	GKC §59e; J-M §61a n 1 □ B-L
116.14–15	GKC §90f		342s′; Sch §48.6.3.2; Berg 2.27e
116.14	Dav §69R2; GKC §93i; J-M	118.27	IBHS 560; Gib 97
	§93c; Gib 145 □ B-L 567g; B-M	119	GKC §5h □ B-L 66s; Berg 1.5h
	2.68	119.1	GKC §5h, 128x; J-M §129i
116.15	Dav §28R5, 69R2; GKC §90f;	119.5	Dav §135R2; GKC §151e; J-M
	J-M §93i; Gib 36, 145 □ B-L		§105b n 2, 163c; Wms §549;
	528t; B-M 2.70		Gib 186 □ B-M 3.117; GAHG
116.16	GKC §117n □ B-L 235u		3.178 n 617; Brock §8b
116.18	Dav §69R2; GKC §90f, 93i; J-M	119.9	IBHS 609 □ Berg 2.35i, 2.60p
	§93c; Gib 145 □ B-L 567g	119.11	Dav §149; IBHS 640; Gib 160
116.19	GKC §91e; J-M §94h □ B-L	119.13	Berg 2.119e
	583w′	119.14	GKC §95u, 118s n 2, 118s n 2 □
118.2	Berg 1.132e; Gib 19		B-M 2.77
118.5	GKC §20g, 59f, 119gg □ Berg	119.16	IBHS 426 □ Berg 2.108c
	1.67t, 2.162d	119.17	Dav §65R4; J-M §116i; Gib 107
118.7	GKC §119i; J-M §133c, 136f;		□ Berg 2.114l
	IBHS 123	119.18	GKC §75cc □ Berg 2.164i
118.8–9	Gib 128	119.19	Berg 2.48g
118.8	Dav §33, 104; J-M §68; Gib 45	119.21	Dav §99R1; GKC §126w; Gib
	□ B-L 361x; GAHG 3.78 n 209;		69, 135
	Berg 2.58m, 2.114i; Brock §15g	119.22	GKC §67p, 75cc; J-M §82l; Gib
118.9	Dav §33, 104; J-M §68e; Gib 45		140 □ B-L 429j, 436; B-M
	□ B-L 361x; Berg 2.114i		2.145; Berg 2.135 n e
118.10ff.	GKC §60d	119.25	GKC §32c
118.10	GKC §60d; J-M §164b □ B-L	119.26	J-M §119y n 2
	338n, 403; Berg 2.23g	119.28	GKC §72m; J-M §80h □ Jen
118.11	Dav §88R4; GKC §67cc □ B-L		§27.4.1; Berg 2.151r
	403; Berg 2.23g, 2.132a*	119.33–39	Gib 81
118.12	B-L 338n, 403; Berg 2.23g,	119.33	GKC §60a □ B-L 368t; Berg
	2.132a*		2.79g
118.13	GKC §45g, 113p; J-M §49f,	119.34	Berg 2.122b
	123i □ Berg 2.63e	119.36	B-L 631c
118.14	GKC §80g; J-M §89n	119.37	GKC §91k; J-M §94j

B-L: Bauer and Leander, *Historische Grammatik*   **B-M**: Beer, *Grammatik*   **Berg**: Bergsträsser, *Grammatik*
Brock: Brockelmann, *Syntax*   **Dav**: Davidson, *Syntax*   **GAHG**: Richter, *Grammatik*
Gib: Gibson, *Davidson's Syntax, 4th ed.*   **GKC**: *Gesenius' Grammar*   **IBHS**: Waltke and O'Connor, *Syntax*
Jen: Jenni, *Lehrbuch*   **J-M**: Joüon and Muraoka, *Grammar*   **Ros**: Rosenthal, *Grammar*
Sch: Schneider, *Grammatik*   **Wms**: Williams, *Syntax*

119.40	GKC §106k; Gib 63 □ Berg 2.28g	119.126	J-M §132f n 2 □ B-M 3.60; Berg 2.571
119.41	Dav §69R4; GKC §91k; J-M §125ba	119.128	GKC §130f n 4
		119.129	Gib 52
119.43	GKC §91k □ Berg 2.48g	119.130	B-L 579p'; Berg 1.101m
119.46	Berg 2.52o	119.131	Berg 2.171d
119.47	IBHS 426 □ Berg 2.108c	119.133	B-L 333z
119.49	J-M §158m	119.136	Dav §73R2; GKC §117z, 155n,
119.50	Berg 2.165l		158b; Wms §534; Gib 159 □
119.51	Berg 2.148l		B-M 3.106
119.52	B-L 355m; Berg 2.115a	119.137	Dav §116R3; GKC §145r; J-M
119.55	GKC §49e □ B-L 302z; Berg 2.23f		§148b n 1; Wms §75; IBHS 261; Gib 1, 44, 52 □ B-M 3.19
119.57	Berg 2.58m	119.142	J-M §131c n 2
119.60	Berg 2.109c	119.145	GKC §145r
119.61	GKC §72m; J-M §80h	119.148	Berg 2.152t
119.62	Dav §68; Gib 144	119.151	Gib 53
119.66	Berg 1.106c	119.152	J-M §126i n 1
119.67	J-M §113j; Gib 73 □ B-M 3.108	119.154	B-L 398d"
119.70	IBHS 25 n 72 □ Berg 2.108c	119.155	Dav §116R3; J-M §102c, 148b; Gib 44
119.72	Dav §116R3; GKC §134n; Gib 44	119.156	Berg 1.79m
119.75	Dav §71R2; Gib 145	119.162	IBHS 596 n 60 □ B-L 375; Berg 2.158e
119.76	Berg 2.48g	119.163	GKC §108g □ Berg 2.22e, 2.23f
119.77	Dav §69R4	119.167–168	Jen §7.1
119.78	Dav §71R2; Gib 145	119.167	GKC §48i n 2, 61f n 1 □ Berg
119.80	Dav §149; Gib 160 □ Berg 2.49h		2.120b
		119.170	Berg 2.46c
119.86	Dav §29R4, 71R2; Gib 41, 53, 145	119.172	Berg 2.47d, 2.163g
		119.173	Berg 2.48g
119.87	GKC §106p; IBHS 225 □ B-M 3.52	119.175	B-L 436; Berg 2.113f
119.90	J-M §118o n 1; IBHS 556	120.1	GKC §90g, 127e; J-M §119y n 2 □ B-L 528t
119.91	GKC §143e	120.2	J-M §131c; IBHS 227, 256
119.92	Dav §131; Gib 72, 155 □ Berg 2.34g; Brock §176b	120.3	Wms §66 □ Brock §62g
119.98	GKC §91k, 91n	120.5	Dav §73, 117; GKC §105a, 117bb; J-M §105b; IBHS
119.99	Berg 1.127cc		682 n 35; Gib 188
119.101	GKC §75oo; J-M §78g □ B-L 375; Berg 2.159g	120.6	GKC §80f, 119s; J-M §102c; IBHS 209; Gib 150
119.102	Berg 2.167o(bis)	120.7	Dav §29e; GKC §141c n 3; Gib
119.103	Dav §115; Gib 22		42 □ GAHG 3.82 n 221
119.105	Gib 52	121.1	GKC §127e; J-M §113d, 161g; Gib 185
119.106	GKC §72m; J-M §80h □ Jen §27.4.1; Berg 2.151r	121.3	Dav §19R2, 128R2; GKC §107p, 109e; IBHS 569; Gib 82
119.108	GAHG 3.170 n 519, 3.216 n 815		□ GAHG 3.218 n 826; Berg
119.113	Gib 172		2.50l, 2.51l
119.117	GKC §75l; J-M §79o □ B-L 354c, 409l; B-M 2.158; Berg 2.22f, 2.116e		

B-L: Bauer and Leander, *Historische Grammatik*   **B-M**: Beer, *Grammatik*   **Berg**: Bergsträsser, *Grammatik*
Brock: Brockelmann, *Syntax*   **Dav**: Davidson, *Syntax*   **GAHG**: Richter, *Grammatik*
Gib: Gibson, *Davidson's Syntax, 4th ed.*   **GKC**: *Gesenius' Grammar*   **IBHS**: Waltke and O'Connor, *Syntax*
Jen: Jenni, *Lehrbuch*   **J-M**: Joüon and Muraoka, *Grammar*   **Ros**: Rosenthal, *Grammar*
Sch: Schneider, *Grammatik*   **Wms**: Williams, *Syntax*

121.4	J-M §164a ☐ GAHG 3.203 n 760	126.2	Jen §14.3.3; Berg 2.33g, 2.55e
121.5	GKC §124k; Gib 52	126.3	Berg 2.59n*(bis)
121.6	B-L 345q"	126.5	Berg 2.69c
121.7	Gib 164	126.6	Dav §86c; GKC §113p, 113u;
121.8	Berg 1.130b, 1.150m		J-M §90e, 123i, 123m; IBHS
122.1	GKC §127e; Gib 63 ☐ Berg 2.28g		586 n 29, 590; Gib 125 ☐ B-L 471qα; Berg 2.65h
122.2	IBHS 628 n 51; Gib 138	127.1	Dav §130R4; J-M §112i; Gib
122.3	Gib 12		140, 143, 153 ☐ Sch §49.1.1
122.4	IBHS 335; Gib 12	127.2	Dav §68, 90; GKC §80h, 114n,
122.6	GKC §75u ☐ B-L 409k; B-M 2.157; Berg 1.104r, 2.166m, 2.168p		118i, 231; J-M §7b, 31c, 89k, 121m, 124n n 1; Gib 144 ☐ B-L 511x, 600i'; B-M 2.42; Berg 1.44c, 2.55d*
122.7	Berg 2.49h	127.3	GKC §96 (p. 285); J-M
122.9	B-L 328a'; B-M 2.120		§140c n 3
123.1	GKC §90m, 127e; J-M §93n, 112e, 113d ☐ B-L 526l, 548a'; B-M 2.51; Jen §25.3.2.3; Brock §73b	127.4	GKC §161c
		128.1	GKC §127e
123.2	Dav §151; J-M §174c; IBHS 336, 642; Gib 161 ☐ B-M 2.170; Berg 1.150n	128.3	GKC §75v, 96 (p. 285); J-M §89n, 99c n 1 ☐ B-L 590h, 617g; B-M 2.81; Berg 1.157o
123.4	Dav §20R4, 28R5; GKC §80f, 119s, 127g; J-M §102c; Wms §82; IBHS 209 n 79 ☐ B-L 500pθ; Brock §101	128.5	Dav §65d; GKC §110i; J-M §116f; Gib 105 ☐ Berg 2.46c, 2.49h; Brock §3
		128.6	J-M §130g
124.1–5	IBHS 668 n 88	129.1–2	GKC §80f
124.1	Dav §131R1; GKC §127e ☐ Berg 1.132e	129.1	GKC §127e; J-M §102c ☐ Berg 2.132a*, 1.132e
124.2–3	IBHS 668	129.2	Wms §530 ☐ Berg 2.132a*; Brock §101
124.2	Dav §131R1; J-M §103c		
124.3	Dav §70a; IBHS 172 n 19; Gib 114 ☐ B-L 631a; Berg 2.34g	129.3	Dav §108R1; GKC §117n; IBHS 165
124.4	Dav §69R2; GKC §90f; J-M §93i; Gib 145 ☐ B-L 132c, 528t; Berg 1.154e, 2.34g	129.4	GKC §521 ☐ Berg 2.95d; Gib 69
		129.5	J-M §139i
		129.6	Dav §145R2; GKC §164d
124.5	GKC §145o; J-M §150j ☐ B-L 631a; Berg 2.34g	129.7	B-L 581
		129.8	Dav §40b; Gib 61 ☐ Jen §24.3.3.3; Berg 2.27e
124.6	IBHS 335		
124.8	Gib 12	130.1	Dav §40b; GKC §127e; Gib 61, 69, 75
125.1	Dav §143; GKC §127e, 155g; Gib 11		
		130.2	Dav §31; Gib 43
125.2	GKC §143a; J-M §103n; Gib 181	130.3	Gib 7
		130.4	GKC §76e; J-M §169g
125.3	GKC §90g; J-M §93j; Gib 145	130.5	GKC §106g; J-M §112a; Gib 63 ☐ Berg 2.28g
125.4	Dav §24R5		
125.5	Dav §22R3, 106c; J-M §155nd	130.7	Berg 1.104r; Gib 148
126.1	GKC §127e	131.1	GKC §72l, 127e; J-M §80j, 134 ☐ B-L 398e", 404; Berg 2.145e
126.2–3	Wms §226		
		131.2	Dav §101 n 1 (p. 143n), 120R3; J-M §161d

B-L: Bauer and Leander, *Historische Grammatik*   **B-M**: Beer, *Grammatik*   **Berg**: Bergsträsser, *Grammatik*
Brock: Brockelmann, *Syntax*   **Dav**: Davidson, *Syntax*   **GAHG**: Richter, *Grammatik*
Gib: Gibson, *Davidson's Syntax, 4th ed.*   **GKC**: *Gesenius' Grammar*   **IBHS**: Waltke and O'Connor, *Syntax*
Jen: Jenni, *Lehrbuch*   **J-M**: Joüon and Muraoka, *Grammar*   **Ros**: Rosenthal, *Grammar*
Sch: Schneider, *Grammatik*   **Wms**: Williams, *Syntax*

132.1	Dav §90; GKC §52r, 75aa, 127e; IBHS 419 n 2; Gib 128 □ Berg 1.4b, 1.150m, 2.55d*, 2.96f	136.8–9	GKC §130a
132.3	GKC §128m; IBHS 153; Gib 187	136.10–11	GKC §116x
		136.10	J-M §121j
		136.11	J-M §121j □ Berg 2.38e
132.4	GKC §80g; J-M §89n; Gib 187 □ B-L 511v, 600i'	136.13ff.	GKC §116x
		136.14	J-M §121j; Gib 104 □ Berg 2.45n
132.5	Dav §17R2; GKC §107l, 124b; Gib 20	136.15	Gib 104
		136.19–20	GKC §117n
132.6	GKC §65h □ B-L 360t; Berg 1.154e, 2.118c	136.19	Dav §73R7; Gib 118
		136.20	Dav §73R7; Gib 118
132.11	Dav §6R3, 28R5; J-M §102d, 140b	136.21	Berg 2.45n; Gib 104
		137.1	GKC §124e
132.12	Dav §6R3, 28R5; GKC §34b, 34b n 3, 91n, 138g; J-M §94g, 130g, 145c; Wms §129; IBHS 336; Gib 7 □ B-L 253s, 265d, 591l; B-M 3.97; Brock §150b	137.3	Dav §11Ra, 75, 101Rc; GKC §64f, 117gg; IBHS 174; Gib 14, 112 □ B-L 496vη; Berg 2.77c
		137.4	GKC §107t, 148b
132.15	Dav §75; IBHS 176; Gib 113	137.5	GKC §159m, 159r; Gib 87
132.16	Dav §75; IBHS 176 n 25; Gib 112	137.6	GKC §58g, 159n n 1; J-M §61i; IBHS 450 □ B-L 346s''
132.18	Dav §75; IBHS 176 n 25; Gib 112	137.7	GKC §65cc, 116d; IBHS 621 n 38; Gib 150 □ B-L 425; Berg 2.69c, 2.166n, 2.171 n d
133.1	Dav §7b; GKC §115f, 127e; Gib 8 □ Berg 2.54d	137.8	Dav §25, 97R1; J-M §158ha; IBHS 138 n 5, 336, 620; Gib 12, 133
133.2	GKC §126x; J-M §158e		
133.3	J-M §136j □ Berg 1.123v	137.9	Dav §25; IBHS 336 n 17; Gib 12
134.1	GKC §127e; J-M §136b	138.1	B-M 2.168
134.2	Dav §69R2; GKC §91k, 118f □ B-L 252r; B-M 2.130	138.2	GKC §16f; J-M §14c(7); IBHS 437 □ B-L 183i', 268i
135.2	Sch §13.2.2	138.3	Dav §25, 50b, 51R5; IBHS 553; GKC §130d; Gib 12, 97
135.5	B-L 538i		
135.7	GKC §53o; J-M §112l, 138e □ B-L 443i; Berg 1.155f, 2.104h, 2.156 n b	138.6	GKC §69b n 1, 69p; J-M §75c n 3 □ B-L 382; Berg 2.125b, 2.126 n c
		138.7	Gib 75, 170
135.9	GKC §91e; J-M §94h □ B-L 583w'	138.8	B-L 413f'
135.10–11	GKC §117n	139.1–6	Gib 63
135.10	Berg 2.43 n b-k	139.1	GKC §59h □ Berg 2.18f
135.12	Berg 2.43 n b-k	139.2	GKC §73a, 73a n 1, 135a □ Berg 2.151s
135.14	GKC §29v □ B-L 355m		
135.17	Dav §128R3; Wms §569 □ GAHG 3.174 n 575	139.3	IBHS 420 n 7 □ Berg 2.82n
		139.4	Gib 108
136.1	GKC §2r, 141b; J-M §141a; IBHS 256	139.5	GKC §91e; J-M §94h □ B-L 251i
136.2–3	GKC §133i	139.6	GKC §133c
136.3	GKC §102m, 133i; IBHS 123; Gib 19	139.7	B-L 631f
		139.8–11	Gib ‡101
136.4–7	Dav §98b; Gib 134	139.8–9	GKC §108e; IBHS 510 n 31
136.6	GKC §65d □ Jen §10.4.5		

B-L: Bauer and Leander, *Historische Grammatik*   **B-M**: Beer, *Grammatik*   **Berg**: Bergsträsser, *Grammatik*
Brock: Brockelmann, *Syntax*   **Dav**: Davidson, *Syntax*   **GAHG**: Richter, *Grammatik*
Gib: Gibson, *Davidson's Syntax, 4th ed.*   **GKC**: *Gesenius' Grammar*   **IBHS**: Waltke and O'Connor, *Syntax*
Jen: Jenni, *Lehrbuch*   **J-M**: Joüon and Muraoka, *Grammar*   **Ros**: Rosenthal, *Grammar*
Sch: Schneider, *Grammatik*   **Wms**: Williams, *Syntax*

139.8   Dav §132R2; GKC §66e, 100o, 111x, 159m, 159t; J-M §167a, 167d; IBHS 575; Gib 58, 83, 154, 156 □ B-L 368u; Berg 1.110 n e, 2.124g

139.9   Dav §132R2; J-M §114b n 1, 167a, 167d; IBHS 565 n 3; Gib 156

139.10 J-M §167d

139.11 Dav §48d, 132R2; GKC §103d, 111x, 159f; J-M §103e n 1; Gib 156 □ B-L 644c″

139.12 Dav §34R2; GKC §133b n 2; J-M §141i; IBHS 441; Gib 45, 150 □ B-L 600j′

139.13 Dav §51R5; GKC §107b □ B-M 2.219; Berg 2.135d, 2.173 n g

139.14 Dav §71R2; GKC §75qq, 118p; IBHS 173; Gib 145, 159 □ B-L 541j, 632m; Berg 2.158d

139.15 GKC §75z; IBHS 374 n 30 □ B-L 287n′, 574y; B-M 2.160; Berg 2.88c

139.16 IBHS 374 n 30 □ B-L 287n′; Berg 2.87c

139.18 Dav §3R1, 132R2; GKC §159c, 159c n 2; J-M §167a; Gib 4, 156 □ B-L 402r″, 409i; Brock §134c

139.19 Dav §134; GKC §39e, 151e; J-M §40a n 3, 163c; Wms §458, 550; Gib 186 □ B-L 334b; B-M 1.79; Berg 1.78m; Brock §170a

139.20 GKC §23i, 68h, 75oo □ B-L 441c; Berg 2.15 n a, 2.173 n g

139.21 GKC §72cc; J-M §113m □ B-L 404, 497zη; Berg 1.79m, 1.113ne, 2.99 n f

139.22 Dav §67b; GKC §117q, 128r; J-M §113m, Gib 115 □ Brock §93h

139.24 Gib 31

140.2   GKC §66f; J-M §113m □ B-L 198l, 368t; B-M 2.134; Jen §20.4.2; Berg 2.121a

140.3   Berg 2.171 n d

140.4   GKC §91l; J-M §8a n 4, 82a n 4

140.5   GKC §66f □ B-L 198l, 368t; Jen §20.4.2; Berg 2.121a

140.8   Gib 69

140.9   Dav §65R4 □ Berg 1.120 n o

140.10 GKC §58g, 66f, 75mm □ B-L 215j, 424; Berg 2.162d, 2.166m

140.12 Dav §24R3; GKC §128t; IBHS 149 n 28

140.13 GKC §44i; J-M §42f □ B-L 382; Berg 2.15a

141.1   Gib 75

141.3   GKC §20h, 48i □ B-L 368t, 449f; B-M 2.20; Berg 1.68v, 2.81i

141.4   GKC §76c, 96 (p. 285); J-M §99b n 1; Wms §415; IBHS 199 □ B-L 616d; Berg 1.78m

141.5   Dav §128R2, 132R2; GKC §74k □ B-L 445p; Berg 2.112c, 2.157b, 2.158d

141.7   IBHS 381

141.8   GKC §75bb, 103g □ B-L 640f′; Berg 2.48g, 2.164i

141.9   GKC §119hh

141.10 Dav §116R1; GKC §145m; Gib 23

142.2–8 Gib 75

142.2   GKC §144m; J-M §113d, 151c

142.4   Dav §101 n 1 (p. 143); GKC §138g; Wms §288; Gib 129 □ B-M 3.97

142.5   GKC §53m, 113bb □ B-L 366t; Berg 2.105i

142.7   B-L 430m; Berg 2.134c

143.2   Gib 14

143.3–4 IBHS 549

143.3   GKC §75oo □ Berg 1.106c, 2.156b, 2.159f

143.4   IBHS 217, 425; Gib 149 □ B-M 1.108

143.6   GKC §106g; J-M §112e; Wms §162; IBHS 488

143.7   Dav §65R2; GKC §161a n 1; Gib 107 □ Berg 2.48g

143.8   GKC §138g

143.10 GKC §126z □ J-M §138f □ Berg 2.58n

144.2   Dav §144; GKC §87f; J-M §146f; Gib 11 □ B-L 517w, 564; Berg 2.174 n h

144.3   Dav §51R3; GKC §111m, 111v; J-M §118h n 1, 161m n 2, 169e; IBHS 560; Gib 97

144.4   Berg 2.28g; Gib 63

B-L: Bauer and Leander, *Historische Grammatik* **B-M**: Beer, *Grammatik* **Berg**: Bergsträsser, *Grammatik*
Brock: Brockelmann, *Syntax* **Dav**: Davidson, *Syntax* **GAHG**: Richter, *Grammatik*
Gib: Gibson, *Davidson's Syntax, 4th ed.* **GKC**: *Gesenius' Grammar* **IBHS**: Waltke and O'Connor, *Syntax*
Jen: Jenni, *Lehrbuch* **J-M**: Joüon and Muraoka, *Grammar* **Ros**: Rosenthal, *Grammar*
Sch: Schneider, *Grammatik* **Wms**: Williams, *Syntax*

144.5	GKC §109f □ Berg 2.113f, 2.122c	147.2	GKC §20m; J-M §121l □ Berg 1.142 n f, 2.171 n d
144.6	GKC §117q; J-M §125p; IBHS 167; Gib 115 □ Brock §35a	147.3	J-M §121q; IBHS 648 n 2
		147.4	Gib 172
144.8	GKC §124s	147.5	B-M 3.19
144.10	Berg 2.69c	147.7	GKC §63l; J-M §68a n 1 □ Berg
144.12	GKC §118r □ B-L 606i		2.114i
144.13	Dav §116; Gib 22 □ B-L 534, 577g'; B-M 2.71; Berg 2.171c	147.10	Berg 2.110b
		147.11	Berg 1.127cc, 1.142f
144.14	GKC §122e □ Brock §16a	147.12	B-L 436
144.15	J-M §154f □ Jen §22.3.3	147.14–16	Gib 137
145.1	GKC §5h, 60f; J-M §61d n 3 □ Berg 2.95d	147.14–15	IBHS 630 n 54
		147.15	B-L 603g; B-M 1.105
145.2	B-L 436	147.18	Dav §132b
145.6	GKC §68c; J-M §156aa	147.20	Wms §413
145.7	GKC §132b; Gib 44	148	Gib 81
145.8	Berg 1.134a(bis)	148.5	Berg 2.45n
145.10	B-L 345q"	148.13	Dav §22R3; Gib 29
145.11	GKC §68c	149.1	Sch §51.4.6.4
145.13	GKC §123c	149.2	Dav §16; GKC §122h n 5, 124k;
145.14	GKC §117n		J-M §136e; IBHS 123; Gib 19 □
145.18	GKC §60c		Berg 1.106c
145.20	J-M §113c n 1, 121h n 1; Gib 173	149.3	Berg 1.106c
		149.5	B-L 438; Berg 2.97h, 2.113f
146.1	B-L 436	149.6	Dav §139; GKC §96 (p. 286);
146.2	Dav §3R1; Gib 4 □ B-L 436		J-M §98e □ B-L 620s
146.4	Dav §132R2; J-M §167a □ B-L 499 n 2, 636k	149.8	B-L 348h; Berg 1.140c, 1.156k, 2.114i
146.5	Dav §101Ra; J-M §133c, 154f, 154fa; IBHS 336	150.1	GKC §135n
		150.2	J-M §96Ag □ B-L 567i
146.4	Gib 156	150.3	B-L 574y
146.8	GKC §117n	150.4	GKC §84^{a}t □ B-L 517w, 564
146.9	J-M §121h n 1	150.5	B-L 549a'; Berg 1.149g
147.1	Dav §116R3; GKC §52p; J-M §52c; Gib 44 □ B-L 329j'; Berg 2.96f	150.6	GKC §145c; J-M §150o

B-L: Bauer and Leander, *Historische Grammatik* **B-M**: Beer, *Grammatik* **Berg**: Bergsträsser, *Grammatik*
Brock: Brockelmann, *Syntax* **Dav**: Davidson, *Syntax* **GAHG**: Richter, *Grammatik*
Gib: Gibson, *Davidson's Syntax, 4th ed.* **GKC**: *Gesenius' Grammar* **IBHS**: Waltke and O'Connor, *Syntax*
Jen: Jenni, *Lehrbuch* **J-M**: Joüon and Muraoka, *Grammar* **Ros**: Rosenthal, *Grammar*
Sch: Schneider, *Grammatik* **Wms**: Williams, *Syntax*

JOB

B-L: Bauer and Leander, *Historische Grammatik*   **B-M**: Beer, *Grammatik*   **Berg**: Bergsträsser, *Grammatik*
Brock: Brockelmann, *Syntax*   **Dav**: Davidson, *Syntax*   **GAHG**: Richter, *Grammatik*
Gib: Gibson, *Davidson's Syntax, 4th ed.*   **GKC**: *Gesenius' Grammar*   **IBHS**: Waltke and O'Connor, *Syntax*
Jen: Jenni, *Lehrbuch*   **J-M**: Joüon and Muraoka, *Grammar*   **Ros**: Rosenthal, *Grammar*
Sch: Schneider, *Grammatik*   **Wms**: Williams, *Syntax*

B-L: Bauer and Leander, *Historische Grammatik*   **B-M**: Beer, *Grammatik*   **Berg**: Bergsträsser, *Grammatik*
Brock: Brockelmann, *Syntax*   **Dav**: Davidson, *Syntax*   **GAHG**: Richter, *Grammatik*
Gib: Gibson, *Davidson's Syntax, 4th ed.*   **GKC**: *Gesenius' Grammar*   **IBHS**: Waltke and O'Connor, *Syntax*
Jen: Jenni, *Lehrbuch*   **J-M**: Joüon and Muraoka, *Grammar*   **Ros**: Rosenthal, *Grammar*
Sch: Schneider, *Grammatik*   **Wms**: Williams, *Syntax*

5.1	GKC §61h, 91d; J-M §61f n 3, 66b □ B-L 588l; Berg 1.132e, 2.68a	6.2	Dav §108R2, 134; GKC §113w, 144g, 151e; J-M §123g, 123p, 163c; Wms §174, 205, 548; IBHS 393, 511, 582, 587, 680; GAHG 3.178 n 618; Berg 1.90 n bd, 2.63e, 2.64f; Gib 13, 124, 186
5.2	GKC §117n; J-M §125k; Wms §273, 449; IBHS 165, 184; Gib 118		
5.3	GKC §135a □ B-L 438; GAHG 3.102 n 289; Berg 1.72f, 2.138o	6.3	Dav §17R2; Gib 79 □ Berg 2.133 n a
5.4	B-L 198e	6.4	Dav §73R4; IBHS 169; Gib 4
5.5	GKC §119e	6.5	GKC §150h; J-M §161e □ B-L 155h'; Berg 1.107e
5.7	Dav §24R3, 151; GKC §9o, 128v, 161a; Wms §437; Gib 161 □ B-M 3.101; Berg 1.45e		
		6.6	B-L 118 n 3; Gib 79
5.8	GKC §107x, 159c; Gib 174	6.7	GKC §66b, 106g; Gib 120 □ B-L 113q', 587k
5.9ff.	Berg 2.29i		
5.9	IBHS 618 n 28	6.8	Dav §135, 135R3; GKC §95h, 151d; J-M §97Bd, 163d; Wms §547; Gib 186 □ GAHG 3.210 n 793; Brock §9, 143a
5.10	GKC §126b; Gib 135 □ B-L 113q'		
5.11	Dav §51R5, 69R2; IBHS 392 n 31		
5.12	GKC §166a □ Berg 2.137k	6.9	Dav §65b, 83; GKC §120d; J-M §116h; Gib 120 □ Berg 2.49h
5.13	GKC §91e □ B-L 131, 604g		
5.14	GKC §118u □ B-L 437; Berg 2.97h	6.10	Dav §3R2, 65b; GKC §108f, 156g; J-M §116h □ Brock §80d
5.15	Dav §49b; GKC §111t; Gib 102 □ Berg 2.37b	6.11	Dav §150; GKC §107u; Gib 79, 160
5.16	Dav §49b; GKC §90g; Gib 102 □ B-L 604g; B-M 1.100; Berg 2.37b	6.12	Dav §122; GKC §141d, 141l, 150f; J-M §154fa, 161d; Gib 183 □ B-M 3.88 Anm 1
5.18	GKC §75qq; GKC §63d; J-M §29f, 32c, 78g, 118q n 1 □ B-L 376r; Berg 1.161e, 2.110b, 2.113g, 2.159g	6.13	Dav §126R2; GKC §150g n 1
		6.14	B-L 110i', 352
		6.16	GKC §103p n 2, 126b □ B-M 2.122
5.19–22	Gib 48		
5.19	GKC §134s	6.17	Dav §45R2, 109R1; GKC §130d, 144c, 155l; Gib 12
5.20	Dav §41b; GKC §106n; Gib 68		
5.21	Gib 151	6.19–21	Gib 62
5.22	Dav §60R2, 128R2; GKC §109e; J-M §114k; Gib 81 □ Berg 2.35i	6.19	GKC §93r, 119s □ B-L 597h'
		6.20	GKC §135p, 145u □ Berg 2.77d
5.23	Dav §41b; J-M §129h; IBHS 451; Gib 68	6.21	Dav §51R4; GKC §75t, 152a; J-M §31c; IBHS 560; Gib 101 □ Berg 1.67u
5.24	Dav §29e; GKC §141l, 159g; Gib 42 □ B-L 315k'; B-M 3.113; Berg 2.16c	6.22	GKC §22p, 64a, 69o, 150d; J-M §157a n 2, 161j; Wms §451; Gib 141 □ B-L 357, 653f; Berg 1.156k, 2.125c
5.27	GKC §20g □ B-L 340c'; Berg 1.67t		
		6.23	GKC §107n; J-M §113m □ Berg 2.52n
		6.25	Dav §84; GKC §113b, 154a; Wms §202; IBHS 591; Gib 123 □ B-L 113q'; Berg 2.62 n b; Brock §38a, 49b

B-L: Bauer and Leander, *Historische Grammatik*   **B-M**: Beer, *Grammatik*   **Berg**: Bergsträsser, *Grammatik*
Brock: Brockelmann, *Syntax*   **Dav**: Davidson, *Syntax*   **GAHG**: Richter, *Grammatik*
Gib: Gibson, *Davidson's Syntax, 4th ed.*   **GKC**: *Gesenius' Grammar*   **IBHS**: Waltke and O'Connor, *Syntax*
Jen: Jenni, *Lehrbuch*   **J-M**: Joüon and Muraoka, *Grammar*   **Ros**: Rosenthal, *Grammar*
Sch: Schneider, *Grammatik*   **Wms**: Williams, *Syntax*

6.26	GKC §65f, 69v □ B-L 382, 598; Berg 2.118b	8.3	Dav §124; J-M §150h, 161e; Gib 184
6.27	Dav §73R5; GKC §91d; Wms §589; Gib 110	8.4	Dav §130b; GKC §159o; Gib 154 □ B-M 3.115; Brock §166
6.28	Dav §122; GKC §120g, 149e; J-M §177d; Gib 183	8.5	GKC §159r
6.29	GAHG 3.171 n 535	8.6	Dav §131R2; GKC §112p, 159t; J-M §167s; Gib 155
7.2	Dav §44R3, 143; GKC §155g; Gib 11, 74, 76, 109 □ GAHG 3.210 n 793	8.7	GKC §145u; J-M §150k □ Berg 2.159f
7.3	Dav §108R2; GKC §121c, 144g; J-M §128c, 155c; IBHS 176 n 24; Gib 13 □ B-M 2.134, 3.83; Brock §98b	8.8	Dav §73R5; IBHS 146 n 20; Gib 110 □ B-L 628w; B-M 2.90; GAHG 3.215 n 815
7.4	Dav §130b; GKC §122gg, 124f, 159o; Gib 153, 185 □ Berg 2.16c, 2.41g	8.9	Dav §29e; GKC §141d; Gib 42 □ B-M 3.8; GAHG 2.16 n 44; Brock §25cα
7.5	B-L 131; Berg 1.145d, 2.133 n b; Gib 113	8.10	GKC §125c
		8.11–19	Gib 75
7.6	GKC §133b; Wms §426; Gib 63	8.11	GKC §75rr, 150h, 152a n 1; J-M §103n; Wms §400, 420; Gib 142 □ GAHG 3.210 n 793; Berg 2.159f; Brock §125b
7.7	Berg 1.144d; Gib 110		
7.8	J-M §121k; IBHS 618; Gib 134		
7.9	Dav §40c, 49a; J-M §112d; IBHS 488, 555; Gib 62, 101□ B-M 3.96	8.12	Dav §44R3
		8.13	Berg 2.85r
7.10	Gib 185	8.14	GKC §72r, 93oo □ Berg 1.145d, 2.145 n d
7.11	Berg 2.52o		
7.12	Dav §150; Gib 79, 160, 184	8.18	GKC §29g, 64g; J-M §31d □ B-L 188p, 356s; Berg 1.130c
7.13–14	GKC §159aa □ B-M 3.115		
7.13	Dav §101Ra; GKC §112hh, 119m; Gib 154	8.19	Dav §115; GKC §145d; Gib 22
		8.20	GAHG 3.204 n 768
7.14	Dav §81; GKC §58i, 60d; Wms §320; IBHS 518; Gib 119 □ B-L 338r; B-M 2.166; Berg 2.42g*	8.21	GKC §23e, 75pp; J-M §78g □ B-L 375; Berg 2.55e, 2.158e
		9.2	Dav §7b, 118; GKC §106g; Gib 8 □ Brock §55c
7.15	GKC §133b; IBHS 266; Gib 46 □ Berg 2.33 n e	9.3	GKC §159r □ Brock §90b
7.16	Berg 2.27e; Gib 61, 63, 79	9.4	Dav §24d, 48b, 73R5; Gib 33, 101, 110
7.17–18	Gib 101	9.5	Dav §139
7.17	Dav §43b, 51R4; J-M §169e; Gib 79	9.6	GKC §54k
		9.7	GKC §109g, 165a
7.18	GKC §111t, 123c; J-M §118q, 137i; Wms §281; IBHS 206 n 62 □ Berg 2.39 n a-f	9.8	GKC §87s; J-M §97Eb □ Berg 1.131d
		9.9–10	IBHS 618 n 28
7.19	B-L 361x, 651w; Berg 2.82n	9.11–13	Dav §44a
7.20	Dav §101Rd, 132R2; GKC §102l, 111t, 119aa, 159h; Gib 156 □ B-L 771, 639a′	9.11–12	Gib 59
		9.11	GKC §117n, 159w; J-M §167l; Gib 5 □ B-M 3.114
7.21	GKC §37f, 159g □ GAHG 3.210 n 793; Berg 1.155f	9.12	J-M §167l; IBHS 321; Gib 7
8.2	Berg 1.107e	9.13	J-M §82k; Gib 179 □ Berg 2.132a*

B-L: Bauer and Leander, *Historische Grammatik*   **B-M**: Beer, *Grammatik*   **Berg**: Bergsträsser, *Grammatik*
Brock: Brockelmann, *Syntax*   **Dav**: Davidson, *Syntax*   **GAHG**: Richter, *Grammatik*
Gib: Gibson, *Davidson's Syntax, 4th ed.*   **GKC**: *Gesenius' Grammar*   **IBHS**: Waltke and O'Connor, *Syntax*
Jen: Jenni, *Lehrbuch*   **J-M**: Joüon and Muraoka, *Grammar*   **Ros**: Rosenthal, *Grammar*
Sch: Schneider, *Grammatik*   **Wms**: Williams, *Syntax*

9.14	Wms §387; Gib 175 ☐ GAHG 3.177 n 605; Berg 1.135d	9.35	J-M §116i; Wms §337; Gib 107 ☐ Berg 2.52o
9.15	Dav §130b; GKC §§55b, 55c, 159n, 160a; J-M §59a; Wms §156, 529; IBHS 75; Gib 79, 154 ☐ B-L 281j; B-M 3.105; Sch §53.5.1.2; Berg 2.35i, 2.108 n b; Brock §167	10.1	Dav §101 n 1 (p. 143); GKC §72dd; J-M §80o n 2; Gib 149 ☐ B-L 404; Berg 2.150p
		10.4	GKC §150h; J-M §161e
		10.6	B-L 357
9.16	Dav §130b; GKC §111x; IBHS 557; Gib 79, 101, 154 ☐ B-L 371x; B-M 2.137; Brock §165a	10.7	Dav §101Rd; GKC §119aa n 2; J-M §171e; Wms §288, 531; IBHS 605; Gib 149 ☐ B-M 3.58; Brock §110b
9.17	Gib 18	10.8	Dav §51R4; GKC §111e, 145n
9.18	GKC §20h, 60d, 113d, 114m; J-M §123b, 136g; Wms §203; IBHS 121; Gib 123 ☐ B-L 212k, 338n, 493eη; Berg 1.68v, 2.23g, 2.62b	10.9–13	Berg 2.35h
		10.9	GKC §150a; Wms §261
		10.10–11	GKC §107b
		10.11	GKC §60g ☐ B-L 437; B-M 1.76Jb; Berg 2.173 n g
9.19	Dav §117; GKC §147b	10.13	GKC §106g; Wms §337 ☐ Berg 2.28g; Brock §113
9.20	GKC §53c, 53n, 159r, 107x; Wms §174, IBHS 510, 655 n 28; Gib 79 ☐ B-L 353v; Berg 2.39 n a-f, 2.104 n h, 2.113f		
		10.14	Dav §130b, 131R1; Gib 153 ☐ Berg 2.36k, 2.41d
		10.15	GKC §159ff.; J-M §105b, 167p; IBHS 402 n 24, 682; Gib 188 ☐ Berg 2.36k, 2.41d
9.21	B-L 131; Gib 179		
9.22	GKC §106i; Gib 3		
9.23	B-L 454a′	10.16	Dav §65R6, 83; GKC §74b, 109h, 120g, 159c; J-M §114l; IBHS 426; Gib 120, 156 ☐ Berg 2.36k, 2.51l, 2.156b
9.24	GKC §150l n 1		
9.25–26	Gib 63		
9.25	Gib 171		
9.26	Dav §44R3, 101Rd; GKC §155g, 161a n 1; Wms §334; IBHS 220; Gib 76, 148, 171 ☐ GAHG 3.210 n 793; Berg 1.156m	10.17	Dav §65R6; GKC §154a n 1b; J-M §114l ☐ Berg 2.36k, 2.50l, 2.165k
		10.18–19	GKC §107n
		10.18	GKC §107n ☐ Berg 2.36k
9.27	Dav §96R3; GKC §159u ☐ Berg 2.79g	10.19	GKC §107n; J-M §174d n 2 ☐ Berg 2.36k
9.29	Dav §43b; GKC §107n	10.20	GKC §107n, 108d
9.30–31	B-M 3.116	10.21	GKC §107c; Wms §72
9.30	GKC §64d, 159n; J-M §167f ☐ B-L 354j, 423; B-M 2.147; Berg 1.152a, 2.40d, 2.138l	10.22	Dav §51R4, 128R3; GKC §90g, 111v, 152a n 1; Gib 96 ☐ B-L 528t; Berg 2.129h
9.31	GKC §126r	11.2	Dav §24R3; GKC §128t, 150h; J-M §161e; IBHS 149 n 28; Gib 33, 184
9.32	Dav §65c, 65R4; GKC §116s, 135r, 152d, 166a; J-M §116i, 154c; Wms §399; Gib 106, 107 ☐ B-M 3.103		
		11.3	GKC §111t; J-M §118h n 1 ☐ Berg 2.39 n a-f
9.33	Dav §65c, 65R4; GKC §109i, 152d, 166a n 3; J-M §116i; Gib 106, 107 ☐ Berg 2.51l	11.4	Berg 2.37a
		11.5	Dav §135R3; GKC §151b; Gib 174, 186 ☐ Brock §143a
9.34	GKC §70d; IBHS 518 ☐ Berg 2.49h	11.6	Dav §65d, 73R7; GKC §110i, 134r n 2; J-M §100o; Gib 118

B-L: Bauer and Leander, *Historische Grammatik*   **B-M**: Beer, *Grammatik*   **Berg**: Bergsträsser, *Grammatik*
Brock: Brockelmann, *Syntax*   **Dav**: Davidson, *Syntax*   **GAHG**: Richter, *Grammatik*
Gib: Gibson, *Davidson's Syntax, 4th ed.*   **GKC**: *Gesenius' Grammar*   **IBHS**: Waltke and O'Connor, *Syntax*
Jen: Jenni, *Lehrbuch*   **J-M**: Joüon and Muraoka, *Grammar*   **Ros**: Rosenthal, *Grammar*
Sch: Schneider, *Grammatik*   **Wms**: Williams, *Syntax*

11.7	GKC §150h, J-M §161e; Gib 79	12.18	Dav §49a; Gib 101 □ Berg
11.9	GKC §91e; J-M §127b □ B-L		2.112d, 2.117a
	598; Brock §81e	12.22–25	Dav §49a; Gib 101
11.10	GAHG 3.210 n 793	12.22–24	Berg 2.38 n d
11.11	GKC §128t; J-M §118p	12.22	GKC §111u; J-M §118r □ B-L
11.12	GKC §51g, 67cc, 131c n 2; J-M		599h'; Berg 1.139 n b
	§82m; IBHS 391 □ B-L 437;	12.23	GKC §117n; J-M §118r □ Berg
	Berg 2.91f, 2.133b		2.159f
11.13	Dav §130b; GKC §159n; IBHS	12.24	Dav §138R3; GKC §128a, 152u;
	406; Gib 153 □ Berg 2.40d		J-M §118r; IBHS 140
11.15	Dav §101Rc, 131R2; GKC	12.25	GKC §111t □ B-L 437; Berg
	§119w, 159n, 159ee; J-M §167s;		2.97h
	Gib 149, 155	13.1	GKC §135i
11.16	Dav §41R3, 143; GKC §155g;	13.3	GKC §53k, 113d; J-M §123b;
	Gib 11, 155		IBHS 597; Gib 123, 174 □ Berg
11.17	Dav §34R3, 63R1, 109; GKC		2.61b
	§48d, 108e, 133e, 144c; J-M	13.4	Gib 174
	§45a n 1, 152e; Wms §584;	13.5	Dav §65b, 135; GKC §109h,
	IBHS 265; Gib 46 □ B-L 404;		113n, 151d; J-M §123j; IBHS
	Berg 2.20 n a		587; Gib 106, 124, 186 □ Berg
11.19	GKC §142f		2.63e
11.20	GKC §103i, 103m □ B-L 644y'	13.7	Dav §126R1; GKC §150h
12.2	Dav §118; Gib 141 □ GAHG	13.9	GKC §53q, 67g; Gib 130 □ B-L
	3.177 n 605		95 n 4, 229f', 439p'; Berg
12.3	Dav §100R3; GKC §152d; J-M		2.105 n k(bis), 2.113h
	§160c; Wms §347; Gib 138 □	13.10	Berg 2.63e
	B-L 118 n 3, 651z	13.12	Wms §283 □ Brock §31a
12.4	GKC §107n, 111u, 116d; Gib	13.13	Dav §8; GKC §119ff., 137c; J-M
	102 □ Berg 2.38e, 2.55e		§115c n 3, 144f; Gib 8, 107 □
12.5	GKC §95t □ B-L 605f; B-M		B-M 2.16; Brock §55c*
	2.77	13.14	Gib 184
12.6	GKC §29t, 75u, 124e; J-M	13.15	GKC §39e n 1, 153, 159w; J-M
	§136g; IBHS 121 □ B-L 409k;		§40a n 3 □ B-L 334b
	Berg 1.104r	13.16	GKC §152e; IBHS 661 n 59
12.7	Dav §116; GKC §145k; J-M	13.17	GKC §113r; J-M §123l □ B-L
	§150g; Gib 23 □ GAHG		277d'; Berg 2.64g
	3.215 n 815	13.18	GAHG 3.170 n 524
12.9	Dav §41R2; Gib 68	13.19	Dav §131R2, 144R1; Gib 7, 11,
12.11	Dav §151; GKC §135i, 161a;		156 □ Berg 2.35i
	J-M §174h; Wms §437; Gib 161	13.20	Berg 2.48g
12.12	GKC §141d	13.21	GKC §29q, 60d, 64h □ B-L
12.14	GKC §159w; J-M §167l □ B-L		232j; B-M 2.130; Berg 1.161e,
	351		2.116e
12.15	GKC §15c; J-M §167l □ Berg	13.22	Wms §589 □ Brock §127b
	1.130c	13.23	B-L 651w; Gib 185
12.17ff.	Berg 2.29i	13.24	B-M 3.66; Gib 114
12.17	Dav §70a, 71R1; GKC §116s,	13.25	GKC §117c; IBHS 181 □ B-L
	116x, 118o; J-M §126a, 154c;		353v
	Gib 114	13.26	GKC §124e

B-L: Bauer and Leander, *Historische Grammatik*   **B-M**: Beer, *Grammatik*   **Berg**: Bergsträsser, *Grammatik*
Brock: Brockelmann, *Syntax*   **Dav**: Davidson, *Syntax*   **GAHG**: Richter, *Grammatik*
Gib: Gibson, *Davidson's Syntax, 4th ed.*   **GKC**: *Gesenius' Grammar*   **IBHS**: Waltke and O'Connor, *Syntax*
Jen: Jenni, *Lehrbuch*   **J-M**: Joüon and Muraoka, *Grammar*   **Ros**: Rosenthal, *Grammar*
Sch: Schneider, *Grammatik*   **Wms**: Williams, *Syntax*

13.27	Dav §65R6; GKC §54f, 93r, 109k; IBHS 430; Gib 104 □ B-L 220j, 302a'; Berg 1.141e, 2.51l, 2.173 n f	15.8	Gib 71
		15.9	GAHG 3.210 n 793
		15.10	Dav §24R5; GKC §131q; J-M §127b; IBHS 173; Gib 34 □ Brock §81e
13.28	GKC §144p, 155h; Gib 11		
14.1	Dav §98b; GKC §10g, 116l; Gib 31, 134 □ B-L 208r, 557f'; Berg 1.124w	15.11	GKC §133c □ Brock §111g
		15.13	GKC §125c □ B-L 374m; Berg 2.17d
14.2–12	Berg 2.29i	15.14	GKC §116l; IBHS 322 n 15
14.2	Dav §49a; GKC §111s; Gib 101 □ Berg 2.37b	15.15	GKC §67ee; J-M §150l □ B-L 423; Berg 2.134c
14.3	GKC §153; Wms §385; Gib 38, 175	15.16	Dav §97R1; GKC §116e; Wms §387; Gib 133, 175 □ GAHG 3.177 n 605; Berg 2.69d
14.4	Dav §135R3; GKC §151b; Gib 186		
14.6	GKC §109f, 156g	15.17	GKC §65bb, 138h, 143d; J-M §145c; IBHS 337; Gib 7 □ B-L 423; Berg 1.72f, 2.97h
14.7	GKC §159r; Wms §449; Gib 57		
14.9	GKC §53g n 1, 65e, 112m □ B-L 361a'; Berg 2.80 n h	15.18	GKC §156g
		15.19	Berg 2.27d
14.10	Dav §51R4; GKC §47i, 111t; J-M §118q; Gib 101 □ Berg 2.37b, 2.110b	15.20	GKC §146a □ Brock §124a
		15.21	Dav §60R4; GKC §118f; J-M §125ba, 137k; IBHS 250
14.11	Dav §151; GKC §161a; J-M §174h; Gib 161	15.22	GKC §75v, 114c □ B-L 425; Berg 1.97c, 2.168p
14.12	B-M 3.111; Gib 161	15.23	GKC §147c □ Berg 2.140 n q
14.13	Dav §135R3; GKC §151d, Wms §547; Gib 186 □ GAHG 3.210 n 793; Brock §143a	15.24	B-L 476wβ
		15.26	GKC §128r □ B-L 577i', 583v'; GAHG 3.210 n 793
14.14–15	GKC §107x	15.27	GKC §53g n 1
14.14	GKC §150d □ B-M 3.87	15.28	J-M §133d □ B-L 302a'
14.16	B-L 302a'	15.30	B-M 2.140
14.17	IBHS 557 □ B-M 3.45; Berg 2.38d	15.31–32	GKC §144b
		15.31	J-M §88Cf; GKC §109c □ B-L 583w'; B-M 2.71
14.18–22	Gib 75		
14.18	Gib 174	15.32	GKC §152a n 1 □ B-L 131, 281l; B-M 2.126; Berg 2.107a
14.19–20	Berg 2.29i		
14.19	Dav §116; GKC §145k; J-M §68f, 150g; Gib 23 □ B-L 233j; Berg 1.112d, 1.127cc, 1.129b, 1.150m	15.33	Dav §65R6; GKC §109k; J-M §114l □ B-L 215k, 581; Berg 2.51l
		15.35	GKC §113ff; J-M §123w; IBHS 594 □ Berg 2.67l, 2.160a; Brock §46b
14.22	Dav §101 n 1 (p. 143); GKC §153		
15.3	Dav §101; GKC §113h, 119hh □ B-L 302a'; Berg 2.65h*	16.3	Dav §126R1; GKC §150g; J-M §161e; Gib 177 □ Brock §169c
15.4	GKC §153; Wms §385	16.4–5	GKC §108f
15.6	GKC §145u	16.4	Dav §131; GKC §103l, 108f, 119q; J-M §125m, 167k n 1; Wms §244; Gib 155 □ GAHG 3.175 n 579
15.7–8	GKC §107b		
15.7	Dav §45R1, 71R1; GKC §121d; J-M §113h; Gib 71 □ B-L 628w; Berg 2.35h; Brock §58		

B-L: Bauer and Leander, *Historische Grammatik*   **B-M**: Beer, *Grammatik*   **Berg**: Bergsträsser, *Grammatik*
Brock: Brockelmann, *Syntax*   **Dav**: Davidson, *Syntax*   **GAHG**: Richter, *Grammatik*
Gib: Gibson, *Davidson's Syntax, 4th ed.*   **GKC**: *Gesenius' Grammar*   **IBHS**: Waltke and O'Connor, *Syntax*
Jen: Jenni, *Lehrbuch*   **J-M**: Joüon and Muraoka, *Grammar*   **Ros**: Rosenthal, *Grammar*
Sch: Schneider, *Grammatik*   **Wms**: Williams, *Syntax*

16.5	GKC §60f □ B-L 351; B-M 2.168; Berg 2.95d	17.8	GKC §72m □ Berg 2.134d
16.6	GKC §63f, 108e, 159ff.; J-M §167p; Wms §128; IBHS 575; Gib 83, 154 □ B-L 265c; B-M 3.114; GAHG 3.216 n 819; Berg 2.79g, 2.112c; Brock §164bγ	17.9	GKC §10h, 128y □ B-L 538i; Berg 1.126aa, 1.134a(bis)
		17.10	GKC §120e, 135r; J-M §113m, 146j □ B-L 504kι, 518 n 2, 529y; Brock §153c
16.7	GKC §53p, 75ee, 144p, 153 □ B-L 424; Berg 2.106l	17.11	GAHG 2.18 n 61
		17.13	GKC §124b
16.8	Dav §141R3; GKC §120c	17.15	GKC §150l; Gib 185
16.9–11	Berg 2.35h	17.16	GKC §47k; IBHS 517 n 63 □ Berg 2.125b
16.9	Dav §73R6; GKC §118q, 119q; Gib 110	18.2	GKC §130a; J-M §113m
16.10	Dav §73R6; GKC §54k, 119q; J-M §125m; Wms §244; Gib 110 □ B-L 328w; B-M 2.156	18.3	GKC §75qq □ Berg 2.158 n e, 2.173 n f
		18.4	GKC §51n, 139f; J-M §146k □ B-L 352; B-M 2.118; Berg 2.91g
16.11	Berg 2.125 n a-e	18.5ff.	Berg 2.29i
16.12	GKC §78b, 112tt; Gib 104 □ Berg 2.43 n b-k, 2.109c	18.5–20	Gib 75
		18.7	Dav §24R2; GKC §67dd, 135n; Gib 33 □ B-L 438; Berg 2.139p
16.13	GKC §72w, 95h, 156g □ Berg 2.174 n h	18.8	GKC §29q, 54k
16.14	GKC §126p; J-M §137i; IBHS 505	18.9	Dav §65R6; GKC §109k; J-M §114l; Gib 73 □ Berg 2.51l
		18.10	J-M §129h
16.15	Berg 2.43 n b-k	18.11	Berg 2.43 n b-k
16.16	Dav §116R4; GKC §44m, 55e, 145h; J-M §59d; Gib 23 □ B-L 285g', 352; Berg 2.107a	18.12	Dav §65R6; GKC §109k; J-M §114l □ Berg 2.50l
		18.14–15	GAHG 1.113 n 324
		18.14	Dav §109, 109R2
16.17	Dav §101Rd; GKC §104b, 152a n 1, 160c; J-M §171e; Wms §489, 531; IBHS 645 □ B-M 3.105; Brock §145a	18.15	Dav §109, 109R2; GKC §144b; IBHS 420
		18.16	B-M 2.144; Berg 2.139o
		18.17	GKC §152d; J-M §159oa □ B-M 2.178
16.18	Berg 2.49h	18.18	GKC §144g; J-M §155b □ Berg 2.138l
16.19	GKC §124b; Gib 91 □ GAHG 3.60 n 163, 3.204 n 771; Berg 2.85 n r	18.19	J-M §159oa; Wms §72
		18.21	GKC §130d; J-M §129q, 158d □ Brock §147
16.20	Dav §65b; Gib 106	19.2	GKC §21d, 60e, 75gg, 75oo; J-M §63e; IBHS 516 □ B-L 338p, 375, 412a'; B-M 2.171; Berg , 2.24g, 2.104 n h, 2.156a, 2.166m
16.21	Dav §65b; Wms §437; Gib 106		
16.22	GKC §69x, 75u, 145u □ Berg 2.131o		
17.1	Dav §17R3; GKC §124c; Gib 20 □ Brock §19d*		
17.2	Dav §65R6; GKC §20h, 73e, 75ff.; J-M §161d; Gib 73 □ B-L 212k, 403, 424; Berg 1.68v, 2.106m, 2.149m	19.3	Dav §6R2, 83; GKC §53n, 120c, 136d; Gib 6, 51, 120 □ Berg 2.104 n h
		19.4	Dav §132R2; 159h; Gib 156
17.3	Berg 2.117a	19.5	IBHS 440 n 17
17.4	GKC §72cc □ Berg 2.151 n r	19.6	IBHS 663 n 72 □ B-L 538i
17.5	GKC §75w; Gib 185		
17.7	GKC §75p □ Berg 2.163g		

B-L: Bauer and Leander, *Historische Grammatik* **B-M**: Beer, *Grammatik* **Berg**: Bergsträsser, *Grammatik*
Brock: Brockelmann, *Syntax* **Dav**: Davidson, *Syntax* **GAHG**: Richter, *Grammatik*
Gib: Gibson, *Davidson's Syntax, 4th ed.* **GKC**: *Gesenius' Grammar* **IBHS**: Waltke and O'Connor, *Syntax*
Jen: Jenni, *Lehrbuch* **J-M**: Joüon and Muraoka, *Grammar* **Ros**: Rosenthal, *Grammar*
Sch: Schneider, *Grammatik* **Wms**: Williams, *Syntax*

19.7	Dav §81R4; GKC §63h n 1, 159w; J-M §125b; IBHS 415
19.10	GKC §69p, 69x; J-M §113o □ B-L 233j
19.11	Berg 2.165k; Gib 114
19.12	J-M §113o □ B-M 2.144; Berg 2.135d
19.15	GKC §60a; J-M §44da, 63a □ Berg 2.23g
19.16	GKC §107n, 144m n 4 □ Berg 2.36i
19.17	GKC §67ee □ B-L 131; Berg 2.135 n f, 2.143 n b
19.18	Dav §65R5, 108e, 130R4, 132R2; GKC §159e; J-M §167a; IBHS 575; Gib 83, 156 □ B-M 3.112; Berg 2.50l; Brock §135b
19.19	Dav §6R3; GKC §138h, 145d; J-M §145c; Wms §129, 536; IBHS 337; Gib 7 □ Berg 2.113e; Brock §150b
19.20	B-L 328x; Berg 1.160b, 2.23f
19.21	Gib 27
19.23	Dav §21e, 135R3; GKC §53u, 67y, 126s, 151d; J-M §137m, 163d; IBHS 245 n 13, 375; Gib 27, 118, 185, 186 □ B-L 286m', 320h; Berg 2.88c; Brock §9
19.24	GKC §51m; IBHS 375 □ B-L 320h; Berg 2.20b
19.25	Dav §70a, 71R1, 146R3; GKC §118n; J-M §157b; Gib 56, 111 □ B-M 3.66
19.26	Dav §101Rc, 108R2; GKC §119w, 144g
19.27	Berg 2.29i
19.28–29	Gib 87
19.28	Dav §146R1; GKC §117n
19.29	GKC §36; J-M §38 n 6 □ B-L 264b; Brock §150c
20.2	Berg 1.45e
20.4	Dav §96R5; GKC §150e; J-M §58c; Gib 130, 133 □ B-L 399h''; B-M 3.87; Berg 2.152t
20.6	Gib 172
20.7	B-L 556e'; Berg 1.124w, 1.149g; Brock §80e
20.9	GKC §122l; J-M §134m
20.10	GKC §72k, 145n; J-M §80i □ B-M 2.152, 3.21; Berg 2.149m
20.11	Dav §116; J-M §136h, 150g; Gib 23
20.12	GKC §159q □ Berg 2.102d
20.14	Dav §130R4; Gib 153
20.15	Berg 2.39 n a-f
20.17	Dav §28R6, 61, 128R2; GKC §109e, 130e, 130f; Gib 36 □ GAHG 3.218 n 826; Berg 2.50l; Brock §70d
20.18	Berg 2.50l
20.19–20	GAHG 1.113 n 324
20.19	GKC §154a n 1a
20.22	GKC §74h, 118c, 118f; J-M §125ba, 152d; IBHS 377 □ B-L 428f; Berg 2.135d, 2.158e; Brock §35b
20.23	Dav §65R6; GKC §103f n 3 (p. 302p n 2), 109k; J-M §103m; Gib 104 □ B-L 253 n 1; Berg 1.139b
20.24	GKC §159c
20.26	Dav §65R6; GKC §68f, 109k, 145u, 156f; J-M §63b; IBHS 374 n 30, 419 n 3; Gib 21, 73 □ B-L 223e, 287n; B-M 2.158; Berg 1.92f, 2.50l, 2.87c, 2.119a, 2.163g
20.27	B-L 131
20.28	Dav §65R6, 113; GKC §109k; Gib 73 □ B-M 2.157; Berg 2.139 n o, 2.162f
20.29	GKC §131c, 135m □ B-L 581
21.2	GKC §113r; J-M §123l □ Berg 1.127cc, 2.64g
21.3	GKC §107s; J-M §115c n 3; Wms §170 □ Berg 2.36i, 2.122c
21.4	GKC §100n, 135f, 143a, 150g; J-M §156b, 161e; Gib 184 □ B-L 632j; B-M 3.14; Berg 1.128dd; Brock §169c
21.5	Dav §22R3; GKC §67v; J-M §116f □ B-L 432b'; Berg 2.137 n k
21.6	Berg 2.40d; Gib 153
21.7	Dav §71; GKC §117z; Wms §380; Gib 145
21.9	Dav §101Rc; GKC §119w, 141c n 3, 152d; J-M §159oa; IBHS 214 □ Jen §28.3.3
21.11	GKC §52n

B-L: Bauer and Leander, *Historische Grammatik* **B-M**: Beer, *Grammatik* **Berg**: Bergsträsser, *Grammatik*
Brock: Brockelmann, *Syntax* **Dav**: Davidson, *Syntax* **GAHG**: Richter, *Grammatik*
Gib: Gibson, *Davidson's Syntax, 4th ed.* **GKC**: *Gesenius' Grammar* **IBHS**: Waltke and O'Connor, *Syntax*
Jen: Jenni, *Lehrbuch* **J-M**: Joüon and Muraoka, *Grammar* **Ros**: Rosenthal, *Grammar*
Sch: Schneider, *Grammatik* **Wms**: Williams, *Syntax*

21.12	Gib 74	22.18	GKC §106n n 2; J-M §112k;
21.13	GKC §20i, 66f □ B-L 233j, 367;		Gib 69
	Berg 1.69 n b, 2.173 n f	22.20	Dav §14R2; GKC §91f, 149e;
21.14	Berg 2.55d*		IBHS 394 □ B-L 252m
21.15	GKC §107u	22.21	GKC §48d, 53m, 76h, 110f,
21.16	Dav §41R5; GKC §20f,		135p; J-M §149a; IBHS 451 □
	106n n 2; Gib 69 □ GAHG		B-L 333z, 444p; Berg 2.48f,
	3.204 n 768		2.50k, 2.105i*
21.17	GKC §103p n 2, 150h; Gib 185	22.23	GKC §159ff. □ GAHG
	□ B-L 651w		3.210 n 793
21.18	B-M 1.107; Berg 2.18f	22.27	GKC §63o; J-M §119y n 2;
21.19	Berg 1.127cc, 1.150m		IBHS 563
21.21	Dav §116R2, 145R1; GKC	22.28	Dav §65b, 65R6; GKC §29e,
	§37d, 146a; Gib 23, 158 □ B-L		109h □ Berg 1.130c, 2.119e
	266f; B-M 2.124; GAHG	22.29	GKC §23f, 147c, 159aa □ Berg
	1.72 n 136, 3.180 n 628		1.91d, 2.132a*
21.22	Dav §105; GKC §142d	22.30	Dav §128R3; GKC §152q; J-M
21.23	GKC §84^{a}g, 139g; J-M §146j,		§102j n 2; Gib 142
	147a □ B-L 485hε, 557f'; Berg	23.2	GKC §119aa, 141c
	2.168p	23.3–5	Dav §65b; Gib 106
21.25	GKC §119m	23.3	Dav §135R3; GKC §120e, 151c;
21.27	GKC §155k; Gib 11		Wms §547; Gib 186 □ GAHG
21.29	GKC §44d, 64f; J-M §42d □		3.210 n 793; Brock §9
	Berg 2.78e	23.4	GKC §108f; J-M §114b n 1,
21.31	GKC §159h		116i; Gib 5
21.32	GKC §124c □ B-L 302a'	23.6	GKC §100l, 152c, 153 □ Berg
21.33	B-L 302a'		1.68v
21.34	Dav §71R2; Gib 145	23.7	GKC §108f
22.2	GKC §103f n 3, 103p n 2; J-M	23.8	GKC §159w; J-M 167l
	§103m □ B-L 253 n 1	23.9–11	Dav §65R6
22.3	Dav §124; GKC §67y; J-M	23.9	GKC §109k □ GAHG
	§161e, 163d; Wms §544; Gib		3.218 n 826; Berg 2.21c, 2.50l,
	184 □ Berg 2.139o		2.163g
22.4	GKC §150h □ B-L 118 n 3	23.10	Dav §132R2;p GKC §106p,
22.6–9	Berg 2.32e		107x, 159h; Gib 156 □ B-M
22.6–7	GKC §107e		3.113; Brock §134c
22.7	GKC §152e	23.11	GKC §76c, 107e, 109k; J-M
22.8	Gib 181		§114l □ B-M 2.162; GAHG
22.9	GKC §121b, 121e; J-M		3.218 n 826; Berg 2.21c, 2.165k
	§112d n 2	23.12	GKC §143d
22.12	Dav §69R1; GKC §20i, 117h,	23.13	Dav §48d, 101Ra, 132R2; 119i;
	141c, 158a □ B-L 404; Berg		GKC §159h; Gib 156 □ Berg
	1.69y, 2.140 n q; Brock §14bγ		2.163g
22.13	IBHS 224; Gib 8 □ Berg 2.16c	23.14	GKC §135m
22.14	Brock §89	23.15	B-M 2.118; Berg 2.92h
22.15	GKC §128t	23.16	GKC §67v; IBHS 394 n 37 □
22.16	GKC §121d, 152d; J-M §17,		Berg 2.137k
	121r □ Brock §29b, 89	23.17	Dav §11c; Gib 13
22.17	Dav §146R1	23.28	J-M §167l

B-L: Bauer and Leander, *Historische Grammatik* **B-M**: Beer, *Grammatik* **Berg**: Bergsträsser, *Grammatik*
Brock: Brockelmann, *Syntax* **Dav**: Davidson, *Syntax* **GAHG**: Richter, *Grammatik*
Gib: Gibson, *Davidson's Syntax, 4th ed.* **GKC**: *Gesenius' Grammar* **IBHS**: Waltke and O'Connor, *Syntax*
Jen: Jenni, *Lehrbuch* **J-M**: Joüon and Muraoka, *Grammar* **Ros**: Rosenthal, *Grammar*
Sch: Schneider, *Grammatik* **Wms**: Williams, *Syntax*

B-L: Bauer and Leander, *Historische Grammatik*   **B-M**: Beer, *Grammatik*   **Berg**: Bergsträsser, *Grammatik*
Brock: Brockelmann, *Syntax*   **Dav**: Davidson, *Syntax*   **GAHG**: Richter, *Grammatik*
Gib: Gibson, *Davidson's Syntax, 4th ed.*   **GKC**: *Gesenius' Grammar*   **IBHS**: Waltke and O'Connor, *Syntax*
Jen: Jenni, *Lehrbuch*   **J-M**: Joüon and Muraoka, *Grammar*   **Ros**: Rosenthal, *Grammar*
Sch: Schneider, *Grammatik*   **Wms**: Williams, *Syntax*

28.4	GKC §126b, 154a n 1a; J-M §82k ☐ B-L 398e"; Berg 2.133 n a	29.21	GKC §20i, 24e, 67g; J-M §82h n 3 ☐ B-L 382; Berg 1.69y; Brock §107k
28.5	Dav §101Rd; GKC §118w ☐ Brock §109e	29.22	GKC §103p n 2; IBHS 438
28.6	GKC §124l; Wms §9	29.23	GKC §118w; Wms §244
28.8	Dav §24R3	29.24	Dav §141R3
28.11	GKC §119x	29.25	GKC §10g n 3, 126p, 142f ☐ B-L 302a'; Berg 1.135c
28.12	GKC §119ff.; J-M §137j	30.1	Dav §24R5; Gib 34
28.14	GKC §152d; J-M §160c; Wms §399	30.2	GKC §103p n 2; Gib 151
28.16	B-L 375; B-M 2.161; Berg 2.158e	30.3	GKC §126b, 133l
		30.4	Berg 2.139 n p
28.17	GKC §152z ☐ B-L 512e'	30.5	GKC §103p n 2
28.19	B-L 375, 603f; Berg 2.158e	30.6	Dav §34, 94; GKC §114k, 133h; Gib 132 ☐ Berg 2.59 n mop
28.21	Berg 2.43 n b-k, 2.113f	30.8	B-L 442e; Berg 2.168q
28.25	Dav §51R5; GKC §114r	30.10	GKC §106g
28.27	GKC §60d; J-M §166l n 2 ☐ Berg 2.23g, 2.34g	30.11	IBHS 556 ☐ Berg 2.117a
28.28	IBHS 124	30.12	GKC §145e
29.2–25	Berg 2.32e	30.13	GKC §152u, 155n
29.2	Dav §101Rd, 135R3; GKC §118u, 130d, 151b; J-M §129p, 133h, 163d; Gib 186 ☐ Brock §9	30.14	GKC §75u, 126p ☐ B-L 283v; B-M 2.146; Berg 1.50g, 2.108c
		30.15	GKC §121b ☐ B-M 2.130; Berg 2.113e
		30.16–22	Gib 75
29.3	Dav §73R1; GKC §67p, 109k, 118h, 131o ☐ B-L 436, 525i; Berg 2.31b, 2.80h, 2.135 n f; Brock §68b	30.16	Dav §101 n 1 (p. 143); IBHS 425
		30.17	GKC §119ff; IBHS 420 ☐ Berg 2.20b
29.6	GKC §23f ☐ B-L 459e"; Berg 1.93g, 2.31b, 2.173 n h	30.18	Brock §117a
		30.19	GKC §59f, 75ll ☐ B-M 2.141; Berg 2.127 n e, 2.162d
29.7	GKC §107e, 118f		
29.8	GKC §120g n 4, 154a n 1a	30.20	GKC §72bb ☐ Berg 2.109d
29.9	GKC §107e	30.21	IBHS 208 n 73
29.10	Dav §116R2; GKC §44c, 146a; Gib 23 ☐ Berg 2.77c	30.25	Dav §22R3; J-M §161d
		30.26	GKC §40e, 108e ☐ Berg 2.22e, 2.23f
29.11	GKC §159h; J-M §125b	30.28	Dav §141R3; GKC §118n, 120c ☐ Brock §106m
29.12–13	GKC §107e		
29.12	Dav §100R3; GKC §152u, 155n; J-M §159oa; Gib 138 ☐ B-M 3.97	30.30	GKC §119ff ☐ B-L 131; Berg 2.134c
29.13	B-L 438; Berg 2.69c	31	Gib 153
29.14	GKC §60c	31.1	GKC §148a, 150d n 2; Wms §428; Gib 8
29.15	GKC §141d	31.2	GKC §48l
29.16	GKC §130d, 155n; J-M §129q	31.4	B-L 302a'
29.17	IBHS 577 ☐ B-L 600i'; Berg 2.23f	31.5–39	Berg 2.32e
		31.5	Dav §130b; GKC §72ff.; Gib 154 ☐ B-L 402u"; Berg 2.68a, 2.149m, 2.173 n f
29.18	GAHG 2.18 n 61		

B-L: Bauer and Leander, *Historische Grammatik* **B-M**: Beer, *Grammatik* **Berg**: Bergsträsser, *Grammatik*
Brock: Brockelmann, *Syntax* **Dav**: Davidson, *Syntax* **GAHG**: Richter, *Grammatik*
Gib: Gibson, *Davidson's Syntax, 4th ed.* **GKC**: *Gesenius' Grammar* **IBHS**: Waltke and O'Connor, *Syntax*
Jen: Jenni, *Lehrbuch* **J-M**: Joüon and Muraoka, *Grammar* **Ros**: Rosenthal, *Grammar*
Sch: Schneider, *Grammatik* **Wms**: Williams, *Syntax*

B-L: Bauer and Leander, *Historische Grammatik* **B-M**: Beer, *Grammatik* **Berg**: Bergsträsser, *Grammatik*
Brock: Brockelmann, *Syntax* **Dav**: Davidson, *Syntax* **GAHG**: Richter, *Grammatik*
Gib: Gibson, *Davidson's Syntax, 4th ed.* **GKC**: *Gesenius' Grammar* **IBHS**: Waltke and O'Connor, *Syntax*
Jen: Jenni, *Lehrbuch* **J-M**: Joüon and Muraoka, *Grammar* **Ros**: Rosenthal, *Grammar*
Sch: Schneider, *Grammatik* **Wms**: Williams, *Syntax*

33.19	B-L 563v
33.20	IBHS 91
33.21	Dav §65R6; GKC §14d, 64e, 109k; J-M §20a n 1, 114l; IBHS 571 n 18 □ B-L 126z, 287n', 426; Berg 1.64n, 1.93h, 2.50l, 2.87 n c, 2.115a, 2.163f
33.22	IBHS 439, 600 n 10
33.24	Berg 1.150n
33.25	GKC §10g, 56; J-M §9c(5), 136h □ B-L 353v; GAHG 3.218 n 825; Berg 1.124w, 2.110e
33.27	Dav §32R5, 65R6; Gib 44 □ B-L 399h"; Berg 2.34h, 2.152t
33.29	J-M §102f
33.30	GKC §51l, 72v □ B-L 228z; Berg 2.92 n i, 2.143 n b
33.31	J-M §48d
33.32	GKC §61d; J-M §61f n 3, 65d □ B-L 345m"; Berg 2.54c, 2.55d*
33.33	Berg 2.121d
34.3	GKC §161a; J-M §174h
34.4	B-L 646i"
34.5	GKC §106g □ Berg 2.28g
34.6	GKC §135m; IBHS 218
34.7	GAHG 3.210 n 793
34.8	Dav §96R4; GKC §114p, 128t; IBHS 611; Gib 132 □ Berg 2.60p
34.10	GKC §119hh, 128t
34.13	GKC §90f □ B-L 528t
34.17	GKC §150g; Wms §385 □ B-L 351; Berg 2.165k
34.18	GKC §113ee n 5, 150d □ Berg 2.114i
34.19	GKC §29g □ Berg 1.130c
34.20	GKC §144f, 144g; J-M §155b
34.22	GKC §115g; Gib 129 □ Berg 2.57l
34.23	GKC §152e; GAHG 3.171 n 539
34.24	GKC §111t, J-M §118q □ Berg 2.39 n a-f
34.25	B-M 2.60
34.27	GKC §158b n 1
34.29	Dav §65R6, 136; GKC §109h, 162b; Gib 37
34.31	Dav §110; GKC §100n, 142g
34.32	Dav §144; Gib 11, 154
34.35	GKC §53k; IBHS 598 □ Berg 2.104h, 2.105i
34.36	GKC §159cc; J-M §105f, 163c; IBHS 680 n 26 □ B-M 3.117; Brock §8b
34.37	Dav §65R6; GKC §109k; J-M §114l □ B-L 302a'; Berg 2.50l
35.3	Dav §146R1
35.5	Berg 2.28g
35.6	GKC §64c, 159h □ B-L 354b; Berg 2.40d, 2.116e
35.10	Dav §16; GKC §124k; J-M §136e; IBHS 123, 618; Gib ‡19 □ Brock §19c
35.11	GKC §68k □ B-L 548a'; B-M 2.137; Berg 2.121d
35.14	Dav §146R1; Gib 111 □ GAHG 3.177 n 605; Berg 2.109d, 2.171c
35.15	Dav §128R3; GKC §152k □ GAHG 3.174 n 576, 3.206 n 786
36.2	GKC §65e, 86g n 1 □ B-L 329f'; GAHG 3.175 n 589; Berg 2.119e
36.4	Dav §17R2; J-M §136g; IBHS 121, 663
36.7–10	Berg 2.39 n a-f
36.7	Dav §49b; GKC §111b n 2; Gib 102
36.8–9	Gib 97
36.8	B-L 320h; Brock §139a
36.9	Dav §50b
36.10	Berg 2.20b
36.14	Dav §65R6; GKC §109k; J-M §136h; Gib 73 □ Berg 2.51l
36.15	Dav §65R6 □ Berg 2.50l
36.16	Berg 2.149l
36.18	GKC §145u; J-M §150k; IBHS 518
36.21	GKC §51n
36.24	Berg 2.159f
36.25	B-L 423
36.26	GKC §143d, 152d
36.32	GKC §122o
37.2	GKC §113r; J-M §123l □ B-L 93c, 579q'; Sch §50.4.2; Berg 1.103q, 2.64g
37.4	Dav §65R6; Gib 73

B-L: Bauer and Leander, *Historische Grammatik*   **B-M**: Beer, *Grammatik*   **Berg**: Bergsträsser, *Grammatik*
Brock: Brockelmann, *Syntax*   **Dav**: Davidson, *Syntax*   **GAHG**: Richter, *Grammatik*
Gib: Gibson, *Davidson's Syntax, 4th ed.*   **GKC**: *Gesenius' Grammar*   **IBHS**: Waltke and O'Connor, *Syntax*
Jen: Jenni, *Lehrbuch*   **J-M**: Joüon and Muraoka, *Grammar*   **Ros**: Rosenthal, *Grammar*
Sch: Schneider, *Grammatik*   **Wms**: Williams, *Syntax*

37.5	Dav §65R6, 71R2; GKC §118p; Gib 73, 145 ☐ B-L 632m; B-M 2.173	38.26	Dav §128R3, 143; GKC §152u, 155e; J-M §160o; Gib 11 ☐ Brock §13b, 32c, 35a
37.6	GKC §75hh ☐ B-L 423; Berg 2.153u, 2.168q	38.27	GKC §133l
37.7	Dav §91R2; Gib 130 ☐ B-L 352	38.28	Dav §126R1; GKC §150g; J-M §161e ☐ Brock §169c
37.8	GKC §111l ☐ Berg 2.39 n a-f	38.30	GKC §54k, 118w
37.11	GKC §24b ☐ Berg 1.97f	38.31	Dav §126R1; J-M §161e ☐ Brock §169c
37.12	GKC §90f; J-M §93i ☐ B-L 528t; Berg 1.144d	38.32	Dav §126R1; GKC §145m
37.14	GKC §117w	38.33	GKC §63i
37.16	GKC §124e, 128x	38.34	GKC §109f, 165a; J-M §115c n 3
37.18	GKC §150b ☐ GAHG 3.210 n 793	38.35	Dav §126R4; J-M §115c n 3; Gib 59
37.22	J-M §113o	38.38	Berg 2.127e
37.23	B-L 118 n 3, 563v	38.39	Brock §138
37.24	GKC §59i	38.40	GKC §35b
38.2	GKC §136c; J-M §143g	39.2	GKC §91f; J-M §94h ☐ B-L 252p, 382
38.3–4	GKC §110a	39.3	GKC §135o
38.3	GKC §126p; J-M §116f ☐ Berg 1.106c	39.5	B-L 469fad
38.4	GKC §69n, 159o; J-M §125q ☐ B-M 3.115; Berg 2.126d	39.8	IBHS 193 ☐ B-L 357, 488sε; Berg 2.142 n a
38.5	GKC §159dd ☐ Berg 1.65q	39.9	GKC §22s, 114m ☐ B-L 127a', 222s, 583y'; Berg 1.44c, 1.66q, 1.89b, 1.156m, 2.54d*; Brock §52bζ
38.6	GKC §135n, 137b		
38.7	GKC §67n, 114r, 128v ☐ B-M 2.145; Berg 2.38g, 2.136f		
38.8	B-L 405; Berg 2.80 n h, 2.153t	39.10	B-L 583y'; Berg 1.44c
38.9ff.	GKC §114r	39.13	GKC §150f; Gib 183
38.10	Berg 2.21d, 2.38g	39.15	GKC §111l, 135p; Gib 110 ☐ Berg 2.39 n a-f
38.12	Dav §1R1; GKC §119w n 2; IBHS 413; Gib 148	39.16	Berg 2.39 n a-f
38.13	GKC §5n, 114r ☐ B-L 80u; Berg 1.5l	39.17	GKC §119m
		39.18	Berg 1.135c
38.14	GKC §118w, 134r ☐ Brock §109e	39.19	IBHS 683
38.15	GKC §5n ☐ B-L 80u; Berg 1.5l	39.21	GAHG 3.210 n 793; Gib 104
38.16	GKC §150h	39.23	GKC §47k ☐ Berg 2.174 n h
38.17	J-M §113o	39.24	GKC §75oo ☐ B-L 374r; Berg 2.158e
38.18	GKC §122q, 150b; J-M §152b	39.25	Dav §117; IBHS 683; Gib 188
38.19	GKC §143a, 155k; J-M §143g; IBHS 327 n 26; Gib 181 ☐ B-M 3.96; Brock §148	39.26	Dav §65R6; GKC §53n ☐ B-L 333z; Berg 2.51l, 2.105i*
38.20	GKC §128h; Wms §450; Gib 5	39.28	B-L 562v
38.21	Dav §116R2; GKC §107c, 146a; Gib 23 ☐ Berg 2.33g	39.30	GKC §30m, 55f ☐ B-L 437; Berg 1.110 n b; Brock §152e
38.24	Dav §65R6; GKC §109k, 155k, 165a; IBHS 327 n 26; Gib 73 ☐ Berg 2.51l		

B-L: Bauer and Leander, *Historische Grammatik*   **B-M**: Beer, *Grammatik*   **Berg**: Bergsträsser, *Grammatik*
Brock: Brockelmann, *Syntax*   **Dav**: Davidson, *Syntax*   **GAHG**: Richter, *Grammatik*
Gib: Gibson, *Davidson's Syntax, 4th ed.*   **GKC**: Gesenius' *Grammar*   **IBHS**: Waltke and O'Connor, *Syntax*
Jen: Jenni, *Lehrbuch*   **J-M**: Joüon and Muraoka, *Grammar*   **Ros**: Rosenthal, *Grammar*
Sch: Schneider, *Grammatik*   **Wms**: Williams, *Syntax*

40.2	Dav §88R2, 88R5; GKC §73d, 113ee, 113gg, 150d; IBHS 595 n 55; Gib 127 □ B-L 479jγ; B-M 3.64; Berg 2.671; Brock §46a	41.2	GKC §72cc, 152d □ B-L 368t; Berg 2.151r
40.4	Brock §107k; Gib 63	41.3	Dav §65e; Gib 106
40.5	GKC §134r (bis), 134s; IBHS 276; Gib 48, 51 □ B-L 629c'; Brock §88	41.4	GKC §103g, 124e
		41.7	GKC §118r
		41.8	J-M §72g n 1 □ B-L 233j, 367
40.7	GKC §126p; J-M §116f	41.10	GKC §145k; J-M §150g
40.8	Dav §123R1; GKC §150g; Wms §385; Gib 73, 184 □ Berg 1.52k	41.11	B-L 475tβ
		41.12	GKC §154a n 1b
40.9	Dav §65R6; Gib 73, 134 □ Berg 1.107e	41.15	GKC §44c, 156g □ Berg 2.77c
40.10ff.	GKC §110a	41.17	GKC §76b □ B-L 583y'; B-M 2.25; Berg 1.90b, 2.123c, 2.158d
40.10	Dav §73R3; J-M §113m, 125d; Wms §72; Gib 109 □ B-L 135h	41.18	GKC §116w, 152t; J-M §160m □ B-L 490bζ; Berg 2.68a; Brock §52bβ
40.11	B-L 604g	41.19	GKC §128p
40.14	J-M §113b	41.20	GKC §128v □ Berg 2.113e
40.15	J-M §136f; IBHS 122; Gib 19 □ GAHG 3.170 n 524	41.22	GKC §133h □ Berg 1.139 n b
		41.23	GAHG 3.210 n 793; Berg 1.148g
40.16	IBHS 122 □ GAHG 3.170 n 524; Berg 1.107e	41.25	GKC §24b, 75v, 126b; J-M §79p □ B-L 425; Berg 1.97c, 2.168p
40.17	Berg 1.107e	41.26	GKC §16f, 117a n 4; J-M §14c(7) □ B-L 183i'; Berg 1.71e
40.18	Berg 1.149i; Gib 52		
40.19	Dav §65R6, 98c; GKC §109k, 116g n 1, 127l; J-M §121k; IBHS 122 □ B-L 251g, 588l	42.2	GKC §44i □ B-L 382; Berg 2.15a
		42.3	GKC §133d, 156f □ B-M 2.129
		42.4	J-M §115c n 3
40.20	Berg 1.107e	42.5	GKC §75mm; Gib 64, 101 □ Berg 2.25b, 2.27d, 2.165l
40.22	GKC §67n □ B-L 565x; Berg 2.135d(bis)	42.6	B-L 232j
40.23	GKC §159w □ B-L 352; Berg 2.153t	42.7	GKC §164d; Wms §360 □ B-M 3.109; Brock §145bζ
40.24	GKC §66f; Gib 5 □ B-L 197b, 199l, 368t; B-M 1.107, 2.134; Berg 2.122 n a	42.8	GKC §163d; J-M §119l
		42.10	GKC §91k □ B-L 438
40.25ff.	GKC §150a n 1	42.11	J-M §121k; Wms §131; IBHS 618 □ B-L 616c
40.29	B-L 135h; Gib 150	42.12	Dav §37d; GKC §134g; Gib 49
40.31	Berg 1.107e	42.13	GKC §80k, 97c □ B-L 624i
40.32	GKC §69v; J-M §116i □ B-L 333a'; Berg 1.107e, 2.50k	42.15	GKC §135o, 145o n 1
		42.16	GKC §75t, 87m
41.1	GKC §93ss	42.17	B-L 557f'

B-L: Bauer and Leander, *Historische Grammatik* **B-M**: Beer, *Grammatik* **Berg**: Bergsträsser, *Grammatik*
Brock: Brockelmann, *Syntax* **Dav**: Davidson, *Syntax* **GAHG**: Richter, *Grammatik*
Gib: Gibson, *Davidson's Syntax, 4th ed.* **GKC**: *Gesenius' Grammar* **IBHS**: Waltke and O'Connor, *Syntax*
Jen: Jenni, *Lehrbuch* **J-M**: Joüon and Muraoka, *Grammar* **Ros**: Rosenthal, *Grammar*
Sch: Schneider, *Grammatik* **Wms**: Williams, *Syntax*

1.1	Berg 1.5l	2.5	Dav §131R2; Wms §511; Gib
1.3	Dav §84; GKC §113e; J-M		140, 155
	§123c; IBHS 591; Gib 123 □	2.7	GKC §116h
	B-M 3.62; Berg 2.61b	2.8	GKC §114i n 1, 114r □ Berg
1.5	GKC §69v □ Berg 2.127e		2.60p
1.7	Dav §40c; Gib 32, 62 □ Brock	2.10	GKC §145u; J-M §150k □ B-M
	§122r		1.109
1.9	Dav §24c; GKC §91n; Gib 33	2.11	GKC §58k, 66f □ B-L 345q'',
1.10	GKC §68h, 75hh □ B-L 442g;		368t
	Berg 2.51m, 2.121e, 2.168q	2.12	IBHS 121
1.11	Berg 2.47d	2.13	GKC §35g; J-M §35d □ B-L
1.12	Dav §70a		263g
1.16	GKC §145u	2.14	GKC §116x, 128w □ Berg 2.58n
1.17	GKC §128u □ Berg 1.99i	2.17	J-M §35d, 35g, 116x, 121j □
1.18	Gib 13		B-L 263g
1.19	GKC §29f; J-M §31c □ Berg	2.18	Berg 2.140 n q; Gib 32
	1.71e	2.19	Dav §98R1; GKC §116i; J-M
1.20–33	IBHS 100		§121n; Gib 32, 134
1.20–21	Gib 74	2.21	Gib 109, 170
1.20	GKC §47k, 86l, 124e; J-M	2.22	GKC §144g; J-M §155c; IBHS
	§88Mk □ B-L 438, 506tι; B-M		393 □ Berg 2.122b
	2.39; Berg 2.20 n a, 2.134c;	3.2	GKC §145u
	Brock §19b	3.3–4	GKC §110f
1.21	GKC §68c, 75v, 145u □ Brock	3.3	J-M §64a, 116f; Gib 179 □ B-L
	§122g		339u
1.22	GKC §63m, 93t n 1, 106h, 106l;	3.4	J-M §116f; Gib 35 □ Berg 2.50k
	J-M §137g; Gib 185 □ B-L	3.6	Berg 2.125c
	223e, 371u, 583x'; B-M 2.137;	3.7	GKC §109c; Gib 179 □ B-L
	Berg 1.92f, 1.101m, 2.120c		274j; Berg 2.51m, 2.127d
1.23	GKC §159c, 159d □ Brock §4	3.8	GKC §22s; J-M §116i □ B-L
1.26	Gib 38		127a', 222s, 565x; B-M 2.67;
1.27	Dav §91a; GKC §114r, 135m;		Berg 1.45e, 1.152a
	Gib 129 □ Berg 2.120c	3.10	Dav §73R2; GKC §117z; J-M
1.28	GKC §60e □ B-L 338p; B-M		§125d; Gib 113
	2.171; Berg 2.24g	3.11	Berg 2.51m
1.29	GKC §158b; Wms §534 □ B-M	3.12	GKC §16b, 154a n 1b; J-M
	3.106		§113a □ B-M 2.137; GAHG
1.31	Gib 114		3.161 n 480
1.32	GKC §145u □ Berg 1.101m	3.13	Jen §22.3.3; Gib 62, 170
2.1	Gib 148	3.14	B-L 581
2.2	GKC §114o □ Berg 2.60p	3.16	Gib 179
2.4–5	B-M 3.114	3.17	Dav §29e; GKC §141c, 141d;
2.4	B-L 346x''; Berg 1.127cc		J-M §131c n 2, 154e; Gib 42,
			170 □ Brock §14bε

B-L: Bauer and Leander, *Historische Grammatik* **B-M**: Beer, *Grammatik* **Berg**: Bergsträsser, *Grammatik*
Brock: Brockelmann, *Syntax* **Dav**: Davidson, *Syntax* **GAHG**: Richter, *Grammatik*
Gib: Gibson, *Davidson's Syntax, 4th ed.* **GKC**: *Gesenius' Grammar* **IBHS**: Waltke and O'Connor, *Syntax*
Jen: Jenni, *Lehrbuch* **J-M**: Joüon and Muraoka, *Grammar* **Ros**: Rosenthal, *Grammar*
Sch: Schneider, *Grammatik* **Wms**: Williams, *Syntax*

3.18	Dav §116R1; GKC §145l; Wms §104; IBHS 289; Gib 23, 53, 172, 179 □ Brock §28bγ	5.6	Dav §139; GKC §72l, 156g; Gib 168 □ B-L 398e″; Berg 2.145e
3.19–20	Gib 179	5.7	B-M 2.181, 3.26
3.21	Gib 179	5.8	Gib 170
3.23	Dav §67R2 □ B-L 367	5.13	GKC §75ee □ Berg 2.167o
3.24	Dav §132a; Gib 156, 179	5.14	GKC §106p □ Jen §24.3.3.1
3.25	Dav §128R2; GKC §109e; J-M §114k	5.16	GKC §150a
		5.17	GKC §152o
3.26	Dav §101Ra; GKC §119i	5.18	Berg 2.49h
3.27–31	Gib 179	5.19	Dav §24c; GKC §128p; J-M §129g; IBHS 149; Gib 33
3.28	Dav §139	5.20	B-M 3.26; Gib 104
3.30	GKC §73e □ B-L 399h″; Berg 2.152 n t; Brock §90c	5.22	Dav §29R7; GKC §60e, 131m n 3; J-M §146e; Gib 42 □ B-L 338p; B-M 2.166; Berg 2.24 n g; Brock §68b
3.31	Gib 180		
3.35	Dav §116R1; GKC §145l		
4.1	J-M §124q	5.23	Wms §411
4.2	GKC §106n □ Berg 2.27e	6.2	Berg 1.107e
4.4	GKC §75n, 110f □ Berg 1.129b, 1.150m, 1.161e, 2.50k, 2.161b	6.5	B-L 538i
		6.6	J-M §137g; IBHS 247
4.5	Berg 1.107e, 1.129b, 2.51m	6.8	Berg 2.29i; Gib 75
4.6	J-M §64a □ B-L 368t; Berg 2.23g, 2.122a	6.9	Gib 185
		6.10	J-M §136j
4.8	GKC §60f, 67l □ B-L 345k″; B-M 2.127; Berg 2.23g, 2.95d, 2.109c	6.11	Dav §57R1; Gib 88
		6.12	GKC §131c
		6.13	Dav §73R6; GKC §119q; Wms §244; Gib 110
4.11	GKC §75ee □ Berg 2.27e, 2.167o	6.16–19	Gib 48
4.12	B-L 428f; B-M 2.144; Berg 2.135d	6.16	Dav §106R2; GKC §134s; J-M §152g □ B-L 624h
4.13	GKC §20h □ B-L 368t, 413f′; Berg 1.68v, 2.51m, 2.81i	6.17	Dav §31; GKC §132f; Gib 43
		6.18	Dav §31; Gib 43
4.14	Gib 172	6.21	GKC §135o; J-M §149b
4.16	Dav §54a; J-M §14c; Gib 94 □ B-L 303a′; Berg 2.84q	6.22	Dav §132a; Gib 156 □ B-L 344d″; Berg 2.16c, 2.82m, 2.148k
4.18	Dav §86R4; GKC §113u, J-M §123s; Gib 126 □ Berg 2.71g, 2.144b		
		6.23–24	Sch §45.4.5
		6.23	Gib 53, 172
4.21	GKC §72ee □ B-L 400i″; Berg 2.151q	6.24	GKC §114i n 1, 128w □ B-M 3.34; Berg 2.59 n mop
4.24	GKC §64h □ B-L 231d, 506sι; B-M 2.130; Berg 1.115c, 2.117e	6.27	GKC §63m
		6.30	B-L 302a′
4.25	GKC §70b □ B-L 384c′; Berg 1.99 n h, 2.80 n h, 2.128 n h	6.35	J-M §171b
		7.1	J-M §113m
4.27	Berg 2.51m	7.2	GKC §29q, 75n, 110f; J-M §116f □ Berg 2.50k
5.1	B-M 3.26		
5.2	GKC §114r, 145u; J-M §124q	7.3	J-M §64a □ B-L 339u
5.4	GKC §96 (p. 286); J-M §98e □ B-L 620s; B-M 2.81	7.4	IBHS 100 □ Berg 2.129 n i
		7.5	GKC §114i n 1 □ Berg 2.59 n mop

B-L: Bauer and Leander, *Historische Grammatik*   **B-M**: Beer, *Grammatik*   **Berg**: Bergsträsser, *Grammatik*
Brock: Brockelmann, *Syntax*   **Dav**: Davidson, *Syntax*   **GAHG**: Richter, *Grammatik*
Gib: Gibson, *Davidson's Syntax, 4th ed.*   **GKC**: *Gesenius' Grammar*   **IBHS**: Waltke and O'Connor, *Syntax*
Jen: Jenni, *Lehrbuch*   **J-M**: Joüon and Muraoka, *Grammar*   **Ros**: Rosenthal, *Grammar*
Sch: Schneider, *Grammatik*   **Wms**: Williams, *Syntax*

B-L: Bauer and Leander, *Historische Grammatik* **B-M**: Beer, *Grammatik* **Berg**: Bergsträsser, *Grammatik*
Brock: Brockelmann, *Syntax* **Dav**: Davidson, *Syntax* **GAHG**: Richter, *Grammatik*
Gib: Gibson, *Davidson's Syntax*, 4th ed. **GKC**: *Gesenius' Grammar* **IBHS**: Waltke and O'Connor, *Syntax*
Jen: Jenni, *Lehrbuch* **J-M**: Joüon and Muraoka, *Grammar* **Ros**: Rosenthal, *Grammar*
Sch: Schneider, *Grammatik* **Wms**: Williams, *Syntax*

10.23	Gib 128 ☐ B-L 636m; Berg 2.55e	12.18	GKC §75qq; Gib 57 ☐ B-L
10.24	GKC §118f; J-M §125ba ☐ B-L		119 n 4; Berg 2.158e
	598; Berg 1.145d	12.19	Dav §65R5; GKC §108h
10.25	Dav §132R2; GKC §164g; Gib	12.21	GKC §152b; Gib 63
	157	12.22	Gib 172
10.26	Dav §16; GKC §35g, 124k; J-M	12.24	B-L 303a'
	§136e ☐ B-L 263g	12.25	GKC §145u; IBHS 361 n 35 ☐
10.27	Berg 2.77 n c		Berg 2.170 n c
10.30	GKC §152t	12.26	Dav §65R6; Gib 73
10.31	GKC §117zz; J-M §125o	12.28	Dav §128R2; GKC §91e, 152g;
11.2	Dav §48d, 132R2; GKC §111s,		J-M §94h; IBHS 661 n 59
	159h; IBHS 556; Gib 148, 156,	13.1	Berg 2.28f
	171 ☐ B-M 3.113	13.3	IBHS 407; Gib 181
11.3	GKC §67n, 67cc; J-M §82g ☐	13.4	GKC §131n, 152k
	B-L 439p'; GAHG 3.161 n 480;	13.5	Gib 74
	Berg 2.133b, 2.135d	13.6	GKC §142f
11.4	Gib 182	13.7	IBHS 431; Gib 57 ☐ Berg 2.98c
11.6	Gib 31	13.10	Dav §109R1; GKC §153
11.7	IBHS 498 n 4, 500	13.13	B-L 350r
11.10	B-L 399h"; Berg 2.114i(bis),	13.16	Brock §122r
	2.143 n b	13.18	IBHS 419 n 4
11.14	GKC §123b; IBHS 115	13.19	Gib 128
11.15	GKC §67t; J-M §82m ☐ B-L	13.20	GKC §67t, 110f; J-M §82m,
	438; Berg 2.136i		116f ☐ B-L 438; Berg 2.136i
11.16	Dav §24R3, 151; Gib 161	13.21	Dav §72R4; GKC §117c, 117ff;
11.18	J-M §96Bb		Gib 116
11.21	Dav §22R3; GKC §22s ☐ B-L	13.23	GKC §23g, 72p; Gib 57 ☐ B-L
	127a', 222s; Berg 1.66q		405; Berg 1.44c, 2.147g
11.24	IBHS 623; Gib 57	13.24	Dav §77; GKC §117ff.;
11.25	GKC §60w ☐ B-L 444k; Berg		Gib 144
	2.129 n i, 2.168q, 2.174 n h	14.1	GKC §86l, 145k n 3 ☐ B-L
11.26	GKC §29f, 145c; Gib 181 ☐		506tι
	Berg 1.71e, 2.139p	14.2	Dav §98R1; GKC §116k, 128y;
11.31	Wms §387, 514; Gib 175 ☐		Gib 54, 134 ☐ GAHG 2.24 n 92
	GAHG 3.177 n 605	14.3	GKC §47g; J-M §44c ☐ B-L
12.1	GKC §16f ☐ B-L 175u, 184k';		337m; Berg 2.79 n g
	B-M 1.77, 1.87	14.5	GKC §128p
12.2	Gib 74	14.6	B-L 564; Berg 2.136h
12.4	Dav §24R3; Gib 172	14.7	GKC §152u n 1
12.5	Gib 52, 179	14.9	Dav §116R1; Gib 23
12.6	Berg 2.54d	14.10	GKC §22s; J-M §23a ☐ B-L
12.7	Dav §132R2; GKC §113ff; J-M		128a', 222s, 356s, 598; Berg
	§123w ☐ Berg 2.67l; Brock		1.152a, 2.99e, 2.116b, 2.117e
	§13b, 80e	14.11	GKC §65e ☐ B-L 361a'; B-M
12.8	Brock §117a		3.21; Berg 2.80 n h
12.10	GKC §145h ☐ Brock §28bγ	14.12	Gib 57
12.11	GKC §117z, 122q ☐ Berg	14.13	GKC §131n n 1; Gib 174 ☐
	1.129b, 2.28g		Berg 2.55e
12.16	Gib 181	14.14	GKC §72p
12.17	GKC §159c	14.16	IBHS 69, 492

B-L: Bauer and Leander, *Historische Grammatik*   **B-M**: Beer, *Grammatik*   **Berg**: Bergsträsser, *Grammatik*
Brock: Brockelmann, *Syntax*   **Dav**: Davidson, *Syntax*   **GAHG**: Richter, *Grammatik*
Gib: Gibson, *Davidson's Syntax, 4th ed.*   **GKC**: *Gesenius' Grammar*   **IBHS**: Waltke and O'Connor, *Syntax*
Jen: Jenni, *Lehrbuch*   **J-M**: Joüon and Muraoka, *Grammar*   **Ros**: Rosenthal, *Grammar*
Sch: Schneider, *Grammatik*   **Wms**: Williams, *Syntax*

14.19	Dav §40c; Gib 62, 170	16.12	Gib 128
14.20	GKC §121f □ Sch §50.3.1.2	16.13	GKC §124e; J-M §113a
14.21	B-L 581; Gib 181	16.15	B-L 534; Gib 171
14.24	Gib 5, 52	16.16	GKC §75n, 115b; Gib 128 □
14.26	B-L 564		B-L 425; Berg 2.54d, 2.161c
14.28	Wms §426	16.19	Dav §32R5; IBHS 601 n 12 □
14.30	GKC §124d		Berg 2.54d, 2.82m
14.32	IBHS 375 n 31	16.20	B-L 581; Gib 181
14.34	GKC §72bb □ Berg 2.109d(bis)	16.21	B-L 565b; Gib 171
14.35	Dav §116R2; GKC §114i n 1;	16.29	Dav §54a
	Gib 23	16.30	GKC §114i n 1 □ B-L 348h;
15.1	GKC §20c, 22s; Gib 74 □ B-L		Berg 2.59 n mop
	127a′; Berg 1.66s	16.33	GKC §121b □ B-L 131; GAHG
15.3	B-L 590h		3.120 n 330; Brock §35d
15.5	GKC §63n □ B-L 353v; Berg	17.1	Dav §116R3; IBHS 266; Gib 44
	2.80 n h	17.3	Dav §151; GKC §161a; J-M
15.8	IBHS 107 n 39; Gib 53		§174h; Gib 161 □ B-M 3.101;
15.9	J-M §113a		GAHG 3.199 n 743; Brock
15.10	Brock §15c		§135b
15.11	GAHG 3.177 n 605; Gib 175	17.4	GKC §68i □ B-L 350v; B-M
15.12	Dav §84; GKC §113d, 113f; J-M		2.137; Berg 1.91d, 2.121d,
	§113a; IBHS 597; Gib 123 □		2.121e
	B-L 382; Berg 2.61b	17.5	Dav §40b
15.16	B-M 3.7	17.7	GAHG 3.177 n 605; Gib 175
15.18	GKC §128t	17.8	GKC §128p □ Brock §76d
15.19	Gib 53	17.10	GKC §66f □ B-L 367; Berg
15.20	Dav §24a; GKC §107f, 128l;		2.173 n f
	J-M §113c; Wms §168; IBHS	17.11	GKC §153
	153; Gib 32 □ Jen §24.3.3.4	17.12	Dav §88R2, 88R5; GKC §113cc,
15.21	Berg 2.55d*, 2.131o		113gg, 133b n 2, 152g; Wms
15.22	GKC §113ff, 145k; J-M §123w,		§212; IBHS 594; Gib 127 □
	150g; IBHS 594; Gib 127 □		Berg 2.66k; Brock §45
	Berg 2.67l	17.13	Dav §132R2; J-M §156g; Gib
15.24	Gib ‡142		157 □ Berg 2.69c
15.25	Dav §65R6; GKC §109k; J-M	17.14	GKC §116w □ B-L 367; Berg
	§114l; Gib 104 □ Berg 2.51l		2.118b, 2.122 n c
15.27	GKC §117p □ B-M 3.75	17.15	GKC §154a n 1c; IBHS
15.30	Berg 1.72f		402 n 24, 439
16.2	GKC §146c; J-M §150o; Gib 53	17.16	Berg 2.58m
16.3	B-L 436	17.17	IBHS 196 □ Berg 2.61b
16.4	Dav §20R4; GKC §127i; J-M	17.20	Dav §24R5; Gib 34
	§140c □ Brock §73d	17.21	GKC §114i n 1
16.5	Dav §22R3	17.22	B-M 2.140
16.6	Wms §72; Gib 128 □ Berg	17.25	J-M §88Le; Gib 170
	2.54d	17.26	GKC §114a, 153; J-M §124b;
16.7	Gib 175		IBHS 601 n 12 □ Berg 2.54d
16.10	GKC §107o □ B-L 354b; B-M	17.28	Gib 56
	2.131; Berg 2.116e	18.3	Dav §48d
16.11	GKC §128a n 1; J-M §129a n 5;	18.5	GKC §152d □ Berg 2.54d
	IBHS 139 n □ Berg 1.107e	18.6	GKC §145u; J-M §96Cb

B-L: Bauer and Leander, *Historische Grammatik*   **B-M**: Beer, *Grammatik*   **Berg**: Bergsträsser, *Grammatik*
Brock: Brockelmann, *Syntax*   **Dav**: Davidson, *Syntax*   **GAHG**: Richter, *Grammatik*
Gib: Gibson, *Davidson's Syntax, 4th ed.*   **GKC**: *Gesenius' Grammar*   **IBHS**: Waltke and O'Connor, *Syntax*
Jen: Jenni, *Lehrbuch*   **J-M**: Joüon and Muraoka, *Grammar*   **Ros**: Rosenthal, *Grammar*
Sch: Schneider, *Grammatik*   **Wms**: Williams, *Syntax*

18.7	Gib 170
18.8	Berg 1.107e(bis)
18.9	Dav §24R3; GKC §128u
18.10	Dav §54a; IBHS 392 n 31; Gib 94
18.11	Gib 52
18.13	Dav §132R2; Gib 157
18.14	IBHS 518 □ Brock §16g
18.16	GKC §92g; J-M §15nd □ B-L 547
18.17	Dav §54a; Gib 94
18.19	Gib 171
18.21	GKC §145l
18.22	Dav §132R2, 48d; GKC §159h; J-M §167a; Gib 156 □ B-M 3.112f; GAHG 3.202 n 758; Brock §134c
18.24	GKC §47b, 114i, 117a n 4 □ Berg 1.103 n t, 2.59 n mop
19.1	GKC §128y; Wms §252
19.2	GKC §114s □ Berg 2.56h
19.5	Gib 170
19.6	GKC §128t □ Gib 171
19.7	GKC §9u, 59c; Gib 175 □ B-L 268j, 534; GAHG 3.177 n 605; Berg 1.147 n d
19.8	Dav §94; GKC §114i, 139f; J-M §146k; IBHS 610; Gib 131 □ B-L 294f‴; Berg 2.60o
19.9	Gib 170
19.10	GKC §139f □ GAHG 3.177 n 605; B-L 422t;
19.14	GKC §53o
19.16	J-M §146k □ Jen §12.3.3
19.18	J-M §146k
19.19	Berg 1.134a
19.23	GKC §121d □ Berg 2.35i
19.25	Dav §108R3; GKC §63n, 144h; Gib 14 □ B-L 353v, 382; Berg 2.80 n h
19.26	GKC §116x
19.27	Berg 2.82m
20.2	GKC §128h; J-M §129e; IBHS 147 □ Brock §77e
20.3	Dav §101Rc; GKC §119w
20.6	Gib 7
20.7	Dav §145R1; Gib 158
20.9	GKC §107t; Gib 63 □ Berg 2.28g, 2.35i
20.10	Dav §29R8; GKC §123f; J-M §135d; IBHS 116 n 8; Gib 42 □ Brock §129d
20.11	GKC §153; Gib 39
20.12	GKC §75v
20.13	Dav §64; GKC §110h; J-M §116i □ Berg 2.50k, 2.112d, 2.174 n h
20.14	GKC §118p; J-M §142k
20.16	GKC §63l, 66g □ B-L 351; Berg 2.114k, 2.124 n f
20.18	GKC §145k; J-M §150g
20.20	B-L 473aβ
20.22	GKC §22s, 109f; J-M §116d □ Berg 1.66s
20.23	Gib 44, 53
20.24	Brock §52bγ
20.25	GKC §114i □ Berg 2.58m, 2.59 n mop, 2.134 n d
20.26	GKC §111u; J-M §118r; IBHS 407 □ Berg 2.39 n a-f
20.28	GKC §66f; IBHS 360 n 27 □ GAHG 3.219 n 836, 3.219 n 837; Berg 2.122a
21.1	Jen §11.3.4
21.2	Gib 53
21.3	Dav §33, 91R3; IBHS 387; Gib 45 □ Berg 2.54d, 2.161c
21.6	Dav §28R3; GKC §128c; Gib 35
21.7	B-L 436; Berg 2.135d
21.8	GKC §24a n 1 □ B-L 192i; B-M 1.98
21.9	Dav §33, 91R3; GKC §114a; Gib 45, 128 □ Berg 2.58m
21.10	IBHS 375 n 32 □ B-L 286m′; Berg 2.88c
21.12	GKC §125c
21.13	Dav §81R4
21.14	IBHS 256; Gib 146 □ Berg 2.173 n f
21.15	GKC §115b; J-M §124i
21.16	Dav §84; GKC §113e; J-M §123c; Wms §207; IBHS 591; Gib 123 □ Berg 2.61b
21.19	Dav §24R3 □ Berg 2.54d
21.20	GKC §128l □ Berg 2.69d
21.22	Dav §49a; GKC §91e; J-M §94h; Gib 101 □ B-L 564
21.26	GKC §117q; J-M §125q; IBHS 167 n 12

B-L: Bauer and Leander, *Historische Grammatik*   **B-M**: Beer, *Grammatik*   **Berg**: Bergsträsser, *Grammatik*
Brock: Brockelmann, *Syntax*   **Dav**: Davidson, *Syntax*   **GAHG**: Richter, *Grammatik*
Gib: Gibson, *Davidson's Syntax, 4th ed.*   **GKC**: *Gesenius' Grammar*   **IBHS**: Waltke and O'Connor, *Syntax*
Jen: Jenni, *Lehrbuch*   **J-M**: Joüon and Muraoka, *Grammar*   **Ros**: Rosenthal, *Grammar*
Sch: Schneider, *Grammatik*   **Wms**: Williams, *Syntax*

21.27	GKC §145l		23.15	Dav §1; GKC §106o, 135f; J-M
21.28	IBHS 412			§146d; Gib 2 □ GAHG
21.29	GKC §134s; J-M §125b □ Berg			1.186 n 640, 2.65 n 279
	2.137k		23.20	GKC §103f n 3 □ B-L 253 n 1;
22.3	Berg 1.102o			Berg 2.51m
22.6	IBHS 221 n 119; Gib 175 □		23.21	Berg 2.174 n h
	GAHG 3.177 n 605		23.22	GKC §138g; J-M §145c; IBHS
22.7	B-L 302a′, 405			336; Gib 7 □ Brock §150b
22.11	GKC §155e □ B-L 538i; Berg		23.24	GKC §73b, 116w, 159i □ B-L
	1.134a(bis)			398h″; B-M 3.112; Berg 2.63e,
22.12	Dav §40c			2.151s, 2.152t; Brock §123g
22.13	Dav §40c □ Berg 2.117a		23.25	Dav §65R6; GKC §109k □ Berg
22.14	J-M §19d			2.48f
22.17	GKC §107n; J-M §113m; IBHS		23.27	GKC §93kk □ Berg 1.139 n b
	509 □ Berg 2.52n		23.28	Wms §386
22.18	Brock §159a		23.29	GKC §131q; IBHS 682 □
22.19	Dav §1; GKC §135e; IBHS 442;			GAHG 2.49 n 225, 2.51 n 240
	Gib 2 □ Berg 2.28e		23.30	B-L 348h; Berg 2.114i
22.20	GKC §106u		23.31	Berg 1.65q, 2.51m
22.21	Dav §29e; GKC §10k, 93p,		23.32	J-M §32c □ Berg 2.76 n b
	124k, 131c; J-M §131c, 154e;		23.35	GKC §120c □ B-L 346x″
	Wms §66; IBHS 230; Gib 41 □		24.1	GKC §5h, 75bb □ Berg 1.5h,
	Berg 1.137g; Brock §62g			2.51m
22.22	B-L 299j		24.3	GKC §5h □ Berg 1.5h
22.23	Dav §71; GKC §117ff; Gib 112		24.4	GKC §29o, 51n □ B-L 375;
22.24	Dav §24R3; GKC §75bb, 128u;			Berg 2.92g
	J-M §136g □ B-M 3.80; Berg		24.5	GKC §5h, 128t □ B-L 563v;
	2.164i; Brock §19b			Berg 1.5h
22.25	Brock §80c		24.6	Berg 1.66s
22.26	Berg 1.107e, 2.51m		24.8	Dav §24R3; GKC §128u
22.27	GKC §119c n 2 □ B-M 3.60;		24.9	GKC §130a □ GAHG
	Berg 2.57l			2.51 n 243
22.28	J-M §113m □ Berg 2.51m		24.10	GKC §75z, 91e; J-M §94h
22.29	B-L 233j, 368t; Berg 2.35i		24.11	Dav §134; GKC §151e; Wms
23.1–2	Berg 2.53q			§458; Gib 186 □ B-L 352
23.1	Dav §86R3; GKC §73a, 73d,		24.12	B-L 582u′; GAHG 3.204 n 768
	107n, 113x; J-M §81e, 123q □		24.14	GKC §27u, 48l, 69o, 159p; J-M
	B-L 393c′; Berg 2.51m, 2.63e,			§29f □ B-L 382; B-M 3.115; Jen
	2.151s			§16.3.4; Sch §53.1.2.4; Berg
23.2	Dav §24R3; GKC §128u; Gib 33			2.23f, 2.126 n c; Brock §166
23.3	GKC §75bb □ B-M 2.161; Berg		24.16	GKC §134r
	2.51m, 2.164i		24.17	GKC §51l; IBHS 382 □ B-L
23.6	GKC §75bb; J-M §125h □ Berg			228z; B-M 1.95, 2.119; Berg
	2.51m			2.48f, 2.92 n i
23.7	GKC §152t; J-M §160m; Wms		24.18	GKC §152w
	§414 □ B-L 427t″; Berg 1.124w;		24.19	Berg 2.51m
	Brock §32a		24.22	GKC §135m, 151a; Gib 7
23.8	Berg 2.16c		24.23	Dav §84; J-M §123b, 160m;
23.15–16	Gib 104			Wms §202, 414; Gib 123 □ B-L
				367; Berg 2.54d; Brock §32a

B-L: Bauer and Leander, *Historische Grammatik*   **B-M:** Beer, *Grammatik*   **Berg:** Bergsträsser, *Grammatik*
Brock: Brockelmann, *Syntax*   **Dav:** Davidson, *Syntax*   **GAHG:** Richter, *Grammatik*
Gib: Gibson, *Davidson's Syntax, 4th ed.*   **GKC:** *Gesenius' Grammar*   **IBHS:** Waltke and O'Connor, *Syntax*
Jen: Jenni, *Lehrbuch*   **J-M:** Joüon and Muraoka, *Grammar*   **Ros:** Rosenthal, *Grammar*
Sch: Schneider, *Grammatik*   **Wms:** Williams, *Syntax*

24.24	B-L 353b; Berg 2.116e	25.24	Dav §24R3; GKC §114a; J-M
24.25	IBHS 377		§124b; IBHS 149 n 28; Gib 33,
24.27	Dav §57R1; GKC §112oo □		128 □ Berg 2.54d
	Berg 2.23g	25.25	Dav §151; GKC §161a n 1;
24.28	GKC §128w □ Berg 2.51m		Wms §437; IBHS 651; Gib 161
24.29	J-M §147d □ B-L 582u'		□ Brock §11b
24.30	B-L 232j	25.26	GKC §53s; Gib 161, 172 □ Berg
24.31	Dav §80; GKC §117z; J-M		2.106n
	§125o; Gib 118 □ B-L 231d,	25.27	GKC §113b; J-M §123b, 123t,
	424, 517v, 538i; Berg 2.96g		154b; IBHS 69, 591; Gib 123 □
24.32	Dav §107R1; Gib 2		B-L 277g'; B-M 3.62; Berg
24.33	Dav §57R1; GKC §152t; J-M		2.61b
	§136j	25.28	Gib 161
24.34	Dav §57R1	26.1	J-M §174c; Gib 161
25.1	GKC §127e	26.2	Dav §93; GKC §114o, 128w;
25.2	GKC §53k □ B-L 332t; B-M		J-M §129l; Gib 131 □ Berg
	2.125; Berg 2.104h		2.60p
25.3	Dav §151; GKC §29i n 1; 161a;	26.3	GKC §161a; J-M §174h
	J-M §174h; IBHS 651 n 13; Gib	26.4	Berg 2.51m; Brock §133e
	161 □ Berg 1.151a, 1.160a	26.6	Berg 2.174 n h
25.4–5	Berg 2.67l	26.7	Dav §151; GKC §75u; Gib 161
25.4	Dav §50b,84,88R2,132R2;		□ B-L 423; Berg 2.166 n m
	GKC §113ff; J-M §123w; IBHS	26.8	Dav §151; GKC §67cc; Gib 161
	26 n 73; Gib 97, 123, 127, 157 □		□ Berg 2.133b
	Berg 2.39 n a-f, 2.160a	26.9	GKC §161a; J-M §174h; Gib
25.5	Dav §84,88R2,132R2; GKC		161
	§126n; IBHS 246; Gib 123, 127,	26.10	B-L 402u''; Berg 2.109d(bis),
	157 □ B-M 3.28; Berg 2.160a		2.174 n h
25.6	Berg 2.119e	26.12	Dav §108R3, 132R2; Gib 14,
25.7	GKC §63i, 114a; J-M §124b □		156
	B-L 349q; Berg 2.54d, 2.56f,	26.13	J-M §112d; IBHS 200
	2.114i(bis)	26.14	Dav §151; GKC §161a; J-M
25.8	GKC §115k; Gib 129		§174h; IBHS 651; Gib 161 □
25.9	GKC §75bb □ B-L 413d'; Berg		B-L 220j, 437; Berg 1.141e
	2.51m, 2.164i	26.15	IBHS 386 □ Berg 2.59n
25.11	GKC §93r □ Brock §110h	26.17	Dav §143; GKC §155e; Gib 11
25.12	GKC §161a n 1		□ Berg 1.67u
25.13	GKC §124k; J-M §136e	26.18	Dav §99R1; GKC §126w; J-M
25.14	GKC §152k		§138c; Gib 135, 161 □ Berg
25.16	GKC §76h, 91d □ B-L 251i,		1.140 n a, 2.109c
	563x; Berg 2.148k, 2.150n;	26.19	Gib 161
	Brock §164a	26.20	Brock §145a; Gib 74
25.17	Dav §73; GKC §69v; Gib 113 □	26.21	GKC §128t, 161a n 1; Gib 161
	B-L 383; Berg 2.119e, 2.129h		□ B-L 437; B-M 2.146; Berg
25.19	GKC §52s, 67s, 92g; J-M §96Cb		2.108c
	□ B-L 357, 564; Berg 2.96 n f,	26.22	Berg 1.107e(bis)
	1.120 n o, 2.133 n a	26.23	GKC §145u; J-M §148c; IBHS
25.20	Dav §151; Gib 161 □ Berg		26 n 73
	2.113f	26.25	IBHS 413 □ Berg 2.51m
25.23	GKC §72bb □ Berg 2.109d		

B-L: Bauer and Leander, *Historische Grammatik*   **B-M**: Beer, *Grammatik*   **Berg**: Bergsträsser, *Grammatik*
Brock: Brockelmann, *Syntax*   **Dav**: Davidson, *Syntax*   **GAHG**: Richter, *Grammatik*
Gib: Gibson, *Davidson's Syntax, 4th ed.*   **GKC**: *Gesenius' Grammar*   **IBHS**: Waltke and O'Connor, *Syntax*
Jen: Jenni, *Lehrbuch*   **J-M**: Joüon and Muraoka, *Grammar*   **Ros**: Rosenthal, *Grammar*
Sch: Schneider, *Grammatik*   **Wms**: Williams, *Syntax*

26.26	Dav §132R2; GKC §54c; J-M §53e; IBHS 360 n 30, 426; Gib 156 □ B-L 424; GAHG 3.218 n 825; Berg 1.109 n c, 2.99 n d	28.21	Dav §84; J-M §13d, 123b; Gib 123 □ B-L 367; Berg 2.54d
26.28	GKC §122n	28.22	GKC §10h, 118f; J-M §125ba □ B-L 212j, 356v, 547; B-M 1.118
27.1	Berg 2.125b	28.26	J-M §154j
27.2	Dav §65R3	28.28	J-M §103c
27.6	GKC §63c □ Berg 2.112c	29.1	Dav §24R3; GKC §128t
27.7	GKC §143a	29.2	B-L 95 n 2; Berg 2.117a
27.8	GKC §126p	29.6	GKC §67q; J-M §82l □ B-L 438; Berg 2.117a, 2.140q
27.9	GKC §146e; J-M §150p □ B-L 565b	29.8	Dav §24R3
		29.9	GKC §116w, 162b □ Berg 2.69c
27.10	B-L 465d'''	29.12	GKC §127a; IBHS 157
27.11	B-L 362a'; B-M 2.132; Berg 2.117a	29.13	B-L 565x
		29.14	J-M §121k n 1
27.13	B-L 351	29.18	GKC §91h □ B-L 253v, 581
27.14	GKC §113k; J-M §123r; IBHS 593; Gib 56, 157 □ Berg 2.65h*, 2.105i	29.21	Dav §132R2; J-M §136h; Gib 157
		29.24	GKC §139f; J-M §146k
27.15	GKC §55k, 75x, 128t; J-M §88Ja □ B-L 426; Berg 2.108 n b, 2.165 n l	29.25	GKC §145u; J-M §150n □ B-L 600j'; Berg 1.122t, 2.54d
27.16	Dav §116R1; GKC §145l; Gib 23	30.1	GKC §96 (p. 285) □ B-L 618j
		30.2	Brock §111g; Gib 141
27.17	Berg 2.138 n l	30.3	Dav §16,128R6; GKC §124h, 166a; J-M §136d; Gib 19
27.18	IBHS 419 n 4		
27.20	GKC §85v □ B-L 499hθ	30.4	B-M 2.143; Berg 1.160a, 2.132a*
27.21	GKC §161a, 161a n 1; J-M §174h □ B-L 491kζ	30.6	GKC §10k, 69v □ B-L 175s, 383; Berg 2.51m, 2.127 n e
27.22	B-L 302a'	30.9	GKC §29l □ Berg 2.16c(bis), 2.128g, 2.174 n h
27.23	J-M §123j; IBHS 588 n 33; Gib 5	30.10	Wms §151; IBHS 443 □ Berg 2.51m, 2.104g
27.24	GKC §150g n 1; Gib 184	30.12	Berg 1.152a
27.25	GKC §20h □ B-L 212k, 582u'; Berg 1.68v	30.13	GKC §72l □ B-L 398e''', 404; B-M 2.14; Berg 2.145c
27.27	GAHG 3.177 n 605	30.14	GKC §114i n 1 □ Berg 2.59 n mop
28.1	Dav §116R1, 139; GKC §145l; Gib 23, 168	30.15–16	Gib 48, 62
28.6	GKC §88e n 1	30.15	Dav §106R2; GKC §134s; J-M §152g □ B-L 653f; Berg 2.126 n c
28.7	Brock §14c		
28.11	Gib 52	30.16	B-L 619q
28.12	J-M §103c	30.17	GKC §10g n 3, 20h n 2, 155f; J-M §158a; Gib 104 □ B-L 600j'; Berg 1.105t, 1.135c
28.14	GKC §52k		
28.15	IBHS 429 n 18	30.18–19	Gib 48
28.16	GKC §145l	30.18	GKC §133c, 134s; J-M §152g
28.18	GKC §88e n 1 □ Berg 2.113f	30.20	Gib 62
28.19	GKC §122q	30.21	J-M §152g; Gib 48
28.20	Dav §17R2; J-M §136g; IBHS 121 □ Brock §19b		

B-L: Bauer and Leander, *Historische Grammatik*   B-M: Beer, *Grammatik*   Berg: Bergsträsser, *Grammatik*
Brock: Brockelmann, *Syntax*   Dav: Davidson, *Syntax*   GAHG: Richter, *Grammatik*
Gib: Gibson, *Davidson's Syntax, 4th ed.*   GKC: *Gesenius' Grammar*   IBHS: Waltke and O'Connor, *Syntax*
Jen: Jenni, *Lehrbuch*   J-M: Joüon and Muraoka, *Grammar*   Ros: Rosenthal, *Grammar*
Sch: Schneider, *Grammatik*   Wms: Williams, *Syntax*

30.22	B-L 302a		31.5	Gib 104
30.23	B-M 2.78		31.6	Berg 2.69c
30.24	Dav §106R2; GKC §133g		31.9	Dav §71R2; GKC §118q; Gib 145
30.25ff.	GKC §111e		31.10–31	GKC §5h □ Berg 1.5h
30.25–26	GKC §152a n 1		31.10	GKC §2r, 5h; Gib 7, 33 □ B-L 66s
30.25	Dav §128R1; GKC §152a n 1; J-M §118r; IBHS 560; Gib 97, 142		31.11	Berg 1.129b
30.28	Dav §108R3; GKC §144h; Gib 14		31.13	Gib 62
			31.17	B-L 563v
30.29	Dav §106R2; J-M §152g □ Berg 2.55d*		31.19	B-L 362a'; Berg 1.107e
			31.20	B-L 362a'
30.30	GKC §152b □ Berg 1.107e; Gib 171		31.21	J-M §121o
			31.22	Berg 1.134c
30.31	GKC §35m		31.25	B-L 67s, 562v
30.32	GKC §67aa □ Brock §103b		31.27	GKC §75u □ B-L 590h
31	Berg 1.5h		31.28	J-M §119za □ B-L 436; Berg 2.23g
31.1	Dav §29R1; GKC §128h; IBHS 127, 143 □ B-L 525h; Berg 1.144d		31.29	Dav §32R1; GKC §91f; J-M §94h, 141b; IBHS 259; Gib 44 □ B-L 252p, 268j
31.2	GKC §37f □ B-L 546z; Berg 1.119o		31.30	GKC §54g; IBHS 432 □ Berg 2.98b; Brock §39dδ
31.3	GKC §53q, 87e; J-M §90c; IBHS 118 □ B-L 228a', 517t, 581; Berg 2.105 n k		31.31	B-L 66s, 436
31.4	GKC §75n; Wms §404 □ B-L 427t", 525h; Berg 1.144d, 2.161c			

B-L: Bauer and Leander, *Historische Grammatik* **B-M**: Beer, *Grammatik* **Berg**: Bergsträsser, *Grammatik*
Brock: Brockelmann, *Syntax* **Dav**: Davidson, *Syntax* **GAHG**: Richter, *Grammatik*
Gib: Gibson, *Davidson's Syntax, 4th ed.* **GKC**: *Gesenius' Grammar* **IBHS**: Waltke and O'Connor, *Syntax*
Jen: Jenni, *Lehrbuch* **J-M**: Joüon and Muraoka, *Grammar* **Ros**: Rosenthal, *Grammar*
Sch: Schneider, *Grammatik* **Wms**: Williams, *Syntax*

RUTH

1–3	Jen §10.4.11	1.14	GKC §74k, 76b; J-M §78f, 118f;
1.1–2	IBHS 242		Gib 58 □ B-L 441c; GAHG
1.1	Dav §136R1; GKC §49b n 1,		1.85 n 216; Berg 2.158d
	111g; J-M §118c n 2, 146c;	1.16	GKC §138e; J-M §158m; Gib 29
	IBHS 554, 613 □ B-L 588l; Jen	1.17	Dav §120R4; J-M §165a n 1;
	§8.3.2.2; Berg 2.37a		IBHS 332 n 4; Gib 188 □ Jen
1.2–4	Gib 55		§11.1; Berg 2.51m, 2.92h
1.2	J-M §136l, 137f	1.19	GKC §91f; J-M §94h, 155h n 1,
1.3	J-M §146c; IBHS 240 □ Berg		155e n 1, 161b; Gib 5 □ B-L
	2.91g		252p, 444p, 622c; B-M 2.172;
1.4	Dav §38R1; J-M §133g; Wms		Berg 2.172 n f
	§257; IBHS 203; Gib 12, 150 □	1.20	GKC §46f, 74h, 80h; J-M §89k
	B-M 2.91; GAHG 1.85 n 216;		□ B-L 376r, 511x, 598; GAHG
	Jen §26.3.3; Brock §109b		1.85 n 216; Berg 2.19a, 2.157c
1.5	GAHG 1.85 n 216; Berg 2.91g;	1.21	Dav §70a, 138c; GKC §100g,
	Brock §111c		118n; J-M §126a, 133c; Gib 56,
1.6	J-M §146c; IBHS 294; Gib 2 □		168 □ GAHG 3.146 n 382
	GAHG 1.85 n 216	1.22	Dav §22R4; GKC §32n, 138k;
1.8–9	Brock §124b		J-M §118k, 127i n 2, 145e,
1.8	GKC §135o, 144a; J-M §149b,		149c; IBHS 170 n 15, 340; Gib
	150a; Wms §234; Gib 3 □ Jen		3, 29 □ B-L 248j
	§9.4.6; Berg 2.49h, 2.131o,	2.1	J-M §89b; IBHS 209, 652 □
	2.146f		B-M 2.140; Berg 2.129 n i
1.9	Dav §65d; GKC §46f, 74h, 110i;	2.2	GKC §10h, 64i; J-M §114d,
	J-M §133c, 136l, 149b, 177h;		114n, 119j, 122c; Berg 1.126aa;
	Gib 3, 106 □ B-L 441c; GAHG		Gib 10
	1.85 n 216; Berg 2.19a, 2.49h,	2.3	Dav §28R5; GKC §129d; J-M
	2.157c(bis)		§118k; IBHS 158, 551; Gib 36 □
1.10	Sch §53.3.1.2		B-M 3.32; GAHG 2.50 n 233;
1.11	GKC §112p; J-M §113n,		Berg 2.162f
	119i n 2; IBHS 534; Gib 88, 92	2.4	J-M §163b □ GAHG
	□ GAHG 1.85 n 216		1.85 n 216, 3.89 n 236
1.12	Dav §34R2, 130b; GKC §46f;	2.6	GKC §138k; J-M §145e
	106p; J-M §15e; Wms §446,	2.7	Dav §55a, 69a, 145; GKC §10h,
	517; Gib 45, 63, 153 □ Jen		64i, 112q; J-M §119j, 122c;
	§9.4.6; Berg 2.19a, 2.28g,		IBHS 530; Gib 94, 157 □ B-L
	2.131o; Brock §111g		353v; B-M 3.53; Berg 2.53q;
1.13	Dav §109; GKC §51m, 103f n 4,		Brock §111e
	107x, 152g; J-M §141i, 152d,	2.8	GKC §47g, 47o; J-M §44c, 44f,
	160j, 161l; Wms §403, 595;		112a, 168c; IBHS 516, 516 n 51;
	IBHS 267 □ B-L 352, 640f';		Gib 140 □ B-L 300q, 352; Berg
	B-M 2.177 Anm 1; GAHG		2.19a, 2.79g
	1.85 n 216 □ Jen §28.3.3; Berg		
	2.20a, 2.60p, 2.91g; Brock §35b		

B-L: Bauer and Leander, *Historische Grammatik*   **B-M**: Beer, *Grammatik*   **Berg**: Bergsträsser, *Grammatik*
Brock: Brockelmann, *Syntax*   **Dav**: Davidson, *Syntax*   **GAHG**: Richter, *Grammatik*
Gib: Gibson, *Davidson's Syntax, 4th ed.*   **GKC**: *Gesenius' Grammar*   **IBHS**: Waltke and O'Connor, *Syntax*
Jen: Jenni, *Lehrbuch*   **J-M**: Joüon and Muraoka, *Grammar*   **Ros**: Rosenthal, *Grammar*
Sch: Schneider, *Grammatik*   **Wms**: Williams, *Syntax*

2.9	GKC §47m, 75qq, 112kk; J-M §4e, 78g, 112g, 125b, 166b, 167b □ B-L 300q, 363h, 376r; B-M 1.106; Berg 2.20b, 2.158e	3.6	GKC §59g □ Berg 2.18f, 2.165l
		3.8	Dav §69a; J-M §126h; Wms §135; IBHS 170; Gib 143
2.10	GKC §115c; J-M §124l, 124s; Wms §198; IBHS 607; Gib 129, 131 □ Berg 2.57k	3.9	Dav §57R1; J-M §15k, 119w; IBHS 318; Gib 88 □ B-M 3.89; Berg 2.43i
2.11	J-M §158f □ B-L 77m; Berg 2.63e	3.10	J-M §132f □ Jen §27.3.3
2.12	J-M §68e; Gib 9 □ Sch §51.4.7; Berg 2.114i	3.11	Dav §24R3; J-M §125i □ Brock §76d
2.13	IBHS 275 □ Berg 2.52o	3.12	GKC §163d; J-M §16e; Wms §568; IBHS 72; Gib 57, 141 □ B-L 77m; GAHG 3.177 n 605
2.14	GKC §53n, 66c, 69v, 103g; J-M §15k, 25a, 103f, 114m, 119l n 2; IBHS 571 □ B-L 135h, 333a', 367, 640f'; Berg 1.95e, 1.132f, 2.119e, 2.122c, 2.129h	3.13	J-M §113n, 167r; Wms §56 □ Berg 2.116d
		3.14	Dav §69a; GKC §107c; Gib 143 □ Berg 2.36k
2.15	GKC §35k; J-M §113l □ Berg 1.107e	3.15	Dav §37R4; GKC §64c, 69o, 134n; J-M §69b, 142n; Wms §590; IBHS 279; Gib 50 □ B-L 347g, 354c, 371v, 653f; Berg 1.156k, 2.114k, 2.157 n d; Brock §6a, 85e
2.16	Dav §86R3; GKC §67o, 113x; J-M §123q □ B-L 135h, 439p'; Berg 2.62c, 2.64f, 2.132a*		
2.17	Dav §29d; J-M §133g, 137u n 1; IBHS 231 n 9; Gib 41 □ Brock §109a	3.16	J-M §125i; IBHS 320
		3.17	J-M §114j; Wms §590 □ B-L 77m
2.18	Gib 151	3.18	Dav §154; GKC §103f n 4, 163c, 163c n 1; J-M §44f, 137p n 2, 173b; IBHS 516 n 51; Gib 176, 185 □ B-L 300q; Berg 2.19a
2.19	IBHS 329, 628 □ Berg 2.74l		
2.20	GKC §121f; J-M §132f; IBHS 207		
2.21	Dav §28R5, 41c; GKC §47o, 122g, 135m n 3; J-M §44f, 112i, 130e, 157a n 2; Wms §378, 457; IBHS 516; Gib 36, 67 □ B-L 300q	4.1	GKC §69p, 72t; J-M §147f, 158i, 177e; Gib 14 □ B-M 2.16; Berg 1.153c, 2.70e, 2.125b; Brock §24c
2.22	J-M §141g	4.3	Dav §22R4, 41; GKC §129h, 138k; J-M §145e; IBHS 489; Gib 29, 61
3.1	J-M §113m		
3.2	GKC §91f, 141c; J-M §89b, 94h, 102k; Gib 58 □ B-L 614; Berg 2.129 n i	4.4	GKC §29i n 1, 114l n 5, 152o; J-M §112f, 113n, 132g; IBHS 488 n 15, 610 □ Berg 2.36i, 2.52o, 2.57l
3.3–4	GKC §44h, 112aa		
3.3	GKC §104g, 112c; J-M §16e, 42f, 132c n 2; IBHS 390 □ B-L 383, 405; Berg 2.15a, 2.43i	4.5	IBHS 648 n 2
		4.6–8	IBHS 652
		4.6	B-M 2.131
3.4	GKC §47o, 109k, 112z; J-M §42f, 44f, 65b, 113m, 119z; IBHS 516 n 51; Gib 18 □ B-L 310k, 344d'', 409i; B-M 2.101, 157; Berg 2.15a, 2.19a, 2.48f, 2.53q, 2.82m, 2.166m	4.7	GKC §112h; J-M §80h; Wms §105 □ Jen §27.4.1; Berg 2.44l; Brock §78
		4.9	J-M §112f; IBHS 488
3.5	J-M §125i □ B-L 77m		

B-L: Bauer and Leander, *Historische Grammatik*   B-M: Beer, *Grammatik*   Berg: Bergsträsser, *Grammatik*
Brock: Brockelmann, *Syntax*   Dav: Davidson, *Syntax*   GAHG: Richter, *Grammatik*
Gib: Gibson, *Davidson's Syntax, 4th ed.*   GKC: *Gesenius' Grammar*   IBHS: Waltke and O'Connor, *Syntax*
Jen: Jenni, *Lehrbuch*   J-M: Joüon and Muraoka, *Grammar*   Ros: Rosenthal, *Grammar*
Sch: Schneider, *Grammatik*   Wms: Williams, *Syntax*

4.11	GKC §110i; J-M §145e; Gib 106	4.18	IBHS 652
	□ B-L 622c; GAHG 1.85 n 216;	4.21–22	IBHS 652
	Berg 2.49h		
4.15	Dav §9R2; GKC §59g; J-M		
	§31c, 158g □ Berg 2.18f,		
	2.108c; Brock §152a		

B-L: Bauer and Leander, *Historische Grammatik*   **B-M**: Beer, *Grammatik*   **Berg**: Bergsträsser, *Grammatik*
Brock: Brockelmann, *Syntax*   **Dav**: Davidson, *Syntax*   **GAHG**: Richter, *Grammatik*
Gib: Gibson, *Davidson's Syntax, 4th ed.*   **GKC**: *Gesenius' Grammar*   **IBHS**: Waltke and O'Connor, *Syntax*
Jen: Jenni, *Lehrbuch*   **J-M**: Joüon and Muraoka, *Grammar*   **Ros**: Rosenthal, *Grammar*
Sch: Schneider, *Grammatik*   **Wms**: Williams, *Syntax*

CANTICLES

B-L: Bauer and Leander, *Historische Grammatik*   B-M: Beer, *Grammatik*   Berg: Bergsträsser, *Grammatik*
Brock: Brockelmann, *Syntax*   Dav: Davidson, *Syntax*   GAHG: Richter, *Grammatik*
Gib: Gibson, *Davidson's Syntax, 4th ed.*   GKC: *Gesenius' Grammar*   IBHS: Waltke and O'Connor, *Syntax*
Jen: Jenni, *Lehrbuch*   J-M: Joüon and Muraoka, *Grammar*   Ros: Rosenthal, *Grammar*
Sch: Schneider, *Grammatik*   Wms: Williams, *Syntax*

B-L: Bauer and Leander, *Historische Grammatik*   **B-M**: Beer, *Grammatik*   Berg: Bergsträsser, *Grammatik*
Brock: Brockelmann, *Syntax*   **Dav**: Davidson, *Syntax*   **GAHG**: Richter, *Grammatik*
Gib: Gibson, *Davidson's Syntax, 4th ed.*   **GKC**: *Gesenius' Grammar*   **IBHS**: Waltke and O'Connor, *Syntax*
Jen: Jenni, *Lehrbuch*   **J-M**: Joüon and Muraoka, *Grammar*   **Ros**: Rosenthal, *Grammar*
Sch: Schneider, *Grammatik*   **Wms**: Williams, *Syntax*

8.6	Dav §34R6; GKC §93m; J-M §96Ad, 137i n 3, 141n; IBHS 269; Gib 46, 170 □ B-L 503iι, 582u'; Berg 1.122t	8.9	Berg 2.140 n q
		8.10	GKC §74i □ B-L 612y; Berg 1.92f, 2.34g
8.7	GKC §139d; J-M §147b □ Berg 2.63e, 2.147g	8.11	J-M §97Ca, 155g
		8.12	J-M §97Ca, 146f
8.8	IBHS 335, 421 n 9; Gib 12	8.13	B-L 339y
		8.14	GKC §119s

B-L: Bauer and Leander, *Historische Grammatik*   **B-M**: Beer, *Grammatik*   **Berg**: Bergsträsser, *Grammatik*
Brock: Brockelmann, *Syntax*   **Dav**: Davidson, *Syntax*   **GAHG**: Richter, *Grammatik*
Gib: Gibson, *Davidson's Syntax, 4th ed.*   **GKC**: *Gesenius' Grammar*   **IBHS**: Waltke and O'Connor, *Syntax*
Jen: Jenni, *Lehrbuch*   **J-M**: Joüon and Muraoka, *Grammar*   **Ros**: Rosenthal, *Grammar*
Sch: Schneider, *Grammatik*   **Wms**: Williams, *Syntax*

QOHELET

1.1	GKC §122r □ Berg 1.5l
1.2	Dav §34.R4; GKC §133i; Wms §80; IBHS 267; Gib 46 □ B-L 573x
1.3	J-M §158ha
1.4	GKC §116l; J-M §121d; IBHS 626 □ B-M 3.67; Berg 2.71g
1.5	Berg 1.72f
1.6	GKC §113u
1.7	J-M §129q n 2; Gib 12 □ B-M 3.56; Berg 2.45n, 2.59n*, 2.71g; Brock §162
1.8	Gib 53
1.9	Dav §8; GKC §106c, 137c, 152p; J-M §111i, 113a, 144g, 160k; Wms §471, 537; Gib 8, 12, 62 □ B-M 2.16; Berg 2.26b; Brock §155a
1.11	Gib 182
1.13	Dav §32R5; GKC §112pp n 2; Wms §182; Gib 44, 103 □ Berg 2.45n
1.14	Wms §129
1.16	Dav §107R1; GKC §135b; J-M §146b; IBHS 296; Gib 2, 148, 181 □ GAHG 3.203 n 766; Brock §34b, 51
1.17	Dav §106R2; GKC §6k, 86l, 112pp n 2; J-M §88Mk, 119za, 154j □ Berg 2.23f, 2.45n
1.18	GKC §50e, 159c □ GAHG 3.218 n 825; Brock §134c
2.1	Dav §107R1; GKC §135b; J-M §146b; IBHS 296; Gib 2, 13
2.2	Berg 2.55e
2.3	GKC §107k; J-M §113k, 143g; IBHS 327 n 25
2.4	J-M §129h
2.5	GKC §112pp n 2; IBHS 541 □ Berg 2.45n
2.7	GKC §145u; J-M §150l; Gib 23
2.8	GKC §122v
2.9	GKC §112pp n 2; IBHS 541; Gib 103

2.11	Dav §107R1; GKC §112pp n 2, 135b; J-M §158ha; Gib 2 □ Berg 2.60p
2.12–13	Wms §182
2.12	GKC §37d; J-M §37c □ B-L 266d, 266e; B-M 2.14
2.13	GKC §24e, 112pp n 2, 133b; Wms §472; Gib 103, 172
2.14	GKC §143a; Wms §472; Gib 181
2.15	Dav §107R1; GKC §93rr, 112pp n 2, 135b, 135e; Gib 2, 72, 103, 140 □ GAHG 1.186 n 640; Berg 1.101
2.16	Dav §101Rd; J-M §102n; Wms §472; Gib 148
2.17	Gib 53
2.18	Wms §474
2.19	Dav §126R1; GKC §150g, 150i; J-M §102n, 161e, 161f; Wms §544; IBHS 365 □ B-M 3.95; Berg 2.76b*; Brock §131, 169c
2.20	GKC §64e □ Berg 2.16c, 2.115a
2.21	GKC §131m; Gib 57
2.22	GKC §36; J-M §38 n 6 □ B-L 264c, 423; Berg 2.153u
2.24	GKC §117h; J-M §157d □ B-L 426; Berg 2.106l
2.25	Brock §120a
2.26	GKC §75oo; J-M §78g □ Berg 2.158e
3.2	Dav §96R5; GKC §2s, 66b; Gib 133 □ Berg 2.56f, 2.123c
3.3	Berg 2.157b
3.4	GKC §114b; J-M §124d □ Berg 2.54d, 2.55e
3.5	B-L 354g; Berg 2.114i
3.8	GKC §63i; J-M §49d □ B-L 354g; Berg 2.83p
3.11	GKC §152y; J-M §158m n 2
3.12	Berg 2.58m
3.14	Dav §95; GKC §114l, 165b; J-M §160j; IBHS 609; Gib 132 □ B-M 3.102; Berg 2.58m

B-L: Bauer and Leander, *Historische Grammatik* **B-M**: Beer, *Grammatik* **Berg**: Bergsträsser, *Grammatik*
Brock: Brockelmann, *Syntax* **Dav**: Davidson, *Syntax* **GAHG**: Richter, *Grammatik*
Gib: Gibson, *Davidson's Syntax, 4th ed.* **GKC**: Gesenius' *Grammar* **IBHS**: Waltke and O'Connor, *Syntax*
Jen: Jenni, *Lehrbuch* **J-M**: Joüon and Muraoka, *Grammar* **Ros**: Rosenthal, *Grammar*
Sch: Schneider, *Grammatik* **Wms**: Williams, *Syntax*

3.15	Dav §94; GKC §114i, 137c; J-M §144g; IBHS 325, 610 n 35; Gib 131, 180 □ Berg 2.60o; Brock §155a	5.5	Dav §126R5; GKC §53q, 107t, 150e; J-M §113m; IBHS 324; Gib 184 □ B-L 228a'; Berg 2.105k; Brock §173
3.17–18	GKC §135b	5.6	GKC §143d
3.17	GKC §126m; Wms §92; IBHS 244 □ B-M 3.28; Brock §21cβ	5.7	GKC §124h
		5.8	GKC §32l □ Berg 2.113f
3.18	GKC §36, 67p; J-M §38 n 6, 82l □ B-L 264c, 430o; Berg 2.135 n f	5.11	GKC §69n; J-M §75h □ B-M 2.139; Berg 2.127d, 2.151q
3.19	GKC §93rr, 152k □ Berg 1.101	5.13	GKC §152p; Gib 103 □ Berg 2.45n
3.21	GKC §100m, 150i n 4	5.14	GKC §109i, 118n □ Berg 2.51l
3.22	GKC §102k □ B-L 638z; Brock §155a	5.15	Dav §28R3; GKC §161b □ B-M 3.101
4.1	Dav §88R1; GKC §112pp n 2, 120e; J-M §119za, 158e; IBHS 595 n 57; Gib 127 □ B-L 119 n 2; Berg 2.45n(bis), 2.69d	5.16	GKC §147e □ Brock §13b
		5.18	GKC §112pp n 2, 141h
		6.1	GKC §155h; Gib 57
4.2	Dav §88R1, 88R5; GKC §113ff, 113gg; J-M §123x n 1; Wms §210; IBHS 596 n 60, 658 n 45; Gib 127 □ B-M 3.64, 2.65	6.2	GKC §112pp □ B-M 3.16; Berg 2.85r
		6.3	B-L 574y
		6.4	Berg 2.96g
4.3	Dav §72R4; GKC §117l; IBHS 658 n 45; Gib 117 □ B-M 3.73; Berg 1.128dd; Brock §96*	6.6	GKC §159l; Wms §516 □ B-L 423, 652b'; B-M 3.117; Brock §165d
4.7	GKC §112pp n 2, 120e; J-M §119za; IBHS 595 n 57	6.8–9	GKC §69x, 159z
		6.10	Dav §146; J-M §157c; Gib 110 □ Brock §155a
4.8	Gib 57		
4.10	GKC §124o, 131n; J-M §105a, 105b; IBHS 682 □ B-L 652a; Sch §13.2.1; Berg 2.56f, 2.57l	6.12	Brock §106f
		7.1	Gib 170
		7.2	J-M §170j □ Berg 2.58m
4.11	GKC §112ff	7.3	Berg 2.55e, 2.136f; Gib 52
4.12	GKC §60d; IBHS 423 □ B-L 337n; Berg 2.23g	7.4	Gib 172
		7.5	Berg 2.58m
4.13–16	Gib 179	7.6	Berg 2.55e
4.13	GAHG 3.171 n 539	7.7	GKC §117c, 145o; Gib 141 □ B-M 2.146
4.14	GKC §35d, 160b □ B-L 263f, 538i; Berg 1.91d; Brock §167	7.10	Wms §473
		7.12	Dav §24R3; IBHS 123; Gib 19
4.15	GKC §35b □ B-M 2.18; Berg 2.36k	7.14	GKC §165b □ B-M 3.103
		7.15	GAHG 3.173 n 554; Gib 57
4.16	Gib 141	7.16	GKC §54c, 54k, 131q; J-M §53e; IBHS 426 □ B-L 439p'; B-M 1.108; Berg 1.109 n c, 2.99e, 2.99 n d, 2.136 n i; Brock §173
4.17	GKC §113b, 133e □ Berg 2.62 n b		
5.3	J-M §113m		
5.4	Dav §146; J-M §157a; Wms §488; IBHS 644; Gib 56 □ B-L 367; B-M 3.93; Brock §159b	7.17	GKC §150e
		7.18	J-M §103c n 1; Wms §488 □ B-L 353b, 371u; Berg 2.51m, 2.112d, 2.120b, 2.151q
		7.19	IBHS 239

B-L: Bauer and Leander, *Historische Grammatik*   B-M: Beer, *Grammatik*   Berg: Bergsträsser, *Grammatik*
Brock: Brockelmann, *Syntax*   Dav: Davidson, *Syntax*   GAHG: Richter, *Grammatik*
Gib: Gibson, *Davidson's Syntax, 4th ed.*   GKC: *Gesenius' Grammar*   IBHS: Waltke and O'Connor, *Syntax*
Jen: Jenni, *Lehrbuch*   J-M: Joüon and Muraoka, *Grammar*   Ros: Rosenthal, *Grammar*
Sch: Schneider, *Grammatik*   Wms: Williams, *Syntax*

7.20	Gib 141
7.21	B-M 2.61; GAHG 3.102 n 289
7.22	J-M §157d n 2 □ B-L 248e
7.23	J-M §45a
7.24	GKC §133k; J-M §142k; IBHS 233; Gib 42
7.25	Dav §78R6; GKC §117ii
7.26	Dav §9R2, 22c; GKC §75oo, 126m; IBHS 248 n 18; Gib 28 □ B-L 375; B-M 2.155, 3.28; Berg 1.147d, 2.158e; Brock §31b
7.27	GKC §122r
7.28	B-M 2.120 □ B-L 328a'; GAHG 3.171 n 539
7.29	J-M §157c; Gib 110 □ B-L 538i
8.1	GKC §35n, 75rr; IBHS 239 □ B-L 426; B-M 2.19; Berg 2.168q
8.2	Dav §136R1; IBHS 68– n 28
8.3	Berg 2.52n
8.4	J-M §170j
8.5	GKC §139d
8.6	GAHG 3.173 n 559
8.7	IBHS 325 n 18
8.8	J-M §160i □ Berg 2.59n, 2.157b, 2.159g
8.9	GKC §113z; J-M §123x □ Berg 2.67m
8.10	Dav §32R5; GKC §54g, 119ii, 128w n 1; IBHS 221, 425, 432; Gib 44 □ GAHG 3.102 n 289; Berg 2.98b; Brock §39dδ
8.11	Berg 2.59n
8.12	GKC §75oo □ Berg 2.158e
8.17	GKC §117h; J-M §157d □ Berg 1.128dd
9.1	Dav §96R4, 146; GKC §67q, 93ww, 114p; J-M §82l, 157c; Gib 110, 132 □ B-L 435p'; Berg 2.60 n p, 2.140 n q
9.2	GKC §75oo; J-M §174i □ Berg 2.158e
9.4	GKC §16b, 145e; IBHS 212 □ B-M 3.15; GAHG 3.173 n 559; Berg 1.70b; Brock §31a
9.7	GKC §10g □ B-L 208r, 427t''; Berg 1.124w
9.11	Dav §88R1; GKC §113z; J-M §88Lf, 123x; IBHS 595 n 57; Gib 127 □ B-L 491jζ; Berg 2.67m

9.12	GKC §52s; J-M §121q, 158e; Wms §262, 472; IBHS 197 n 27 □ B-L 287o', 383, 491iζ; Berg 1.141 n a, 2.69d(bis), 2.96 n f, 2.129 n i; Brock §163b
9.14ff.	Berg 2.45n
9.14	GKC §112pp n 2
9.15	GKC §52l, 126d □ Berg 2.95d
9.18	GKC §75oo □ Berg 2.158e
10.3	Wms §472 □ Berg 2.40d
10.4	Berg 2.51m
10.5	GKC §75qq, 155h □ B-L 511x, 598; Berg 2.156a
10.7	J-M §137g □ GAHG 3.102 n 289
10.8	Berg 2.122b; Gib 181
10.10	GKC §53k, 152e □ B-L 332t; Berg 2.105i, 2.109c
10.11	Berg 2.76 n b
10.13	GKC §86l; J-M §88Mk □ B-L 505oι
10.15	GKC §145m □ Berg 2.59n
10.16–17	GKC §138d
10.16	GKC §105a; J-M §105b; IBHS 682 □ B-L 652a; Brock §11c, 153c
10.17	GKC §91l □ B-L 253u, 581; B-M 2.56; Brock §153c
10.18	GKC §20m n 2, 88b □ Berg 2.76b*, 2.136i
10.19	Berg 2.55 n e
10.20	GKC §53n □ Berg 2.51l
11.2	GKC §134s; J-M §144d; IBHS 318 n 6; Gib 48
11.3	GKC §23i, 75s; J-M §137f n 2 □ B-L 423; Berg 2.163 n g; Brock §162, 169b
11.6	GKC §29i n 1; J-M §143g; IBHS 327 n 25 □ Berg 2.51m
11.7	GKC §35g □ B-L 263g; Berg 2.58m
11.8	Berg 2.65h*
11.9	GKC §126c; J-M §136h, 137g; IBHS 247; Gib 80 □ B-M 2.58
12.1–2	Brock §174
12.1	GKC §124k, 164d; J-M §136h □ B-M 3.110
12.2	GKC §164d
12.3	GKC §52k; Gib 12 □ B-L 315k

B-L: Bauer and Leander, *Historische Grammatik* **B-M**: Beer, *Grammatik* **Berg**: Bergsträsser, *Grammatik* **Brock**: Brockelmann, *Syntax* **Dav**: Davidson, *Syntax* **GAHG**: Richter, *Grammatik* **Gib**: Gibson, *Davidson's Syntax, 4th ed.* **GKC**: Gesenius' *Grammar* **IBHS**: Waltke and O'Connor, *Syntax* **Jen**: Jenni, *Lehrbuch* **J-M**: Joüon and Muraoka, *Grammar* **Ros**: Rosenthal, *Grammar* **Sch**: Schneider, *Grammatik* **Wms**: Williams, *Syntax*

12.4	Dav §24R3; GKC §45c, 72t, 128v □ B-L 317f; B-M 3.33; Berg 2.82m, 2.144c	12.7	Dav §65R6; GKC §109k; J-M §114l □ Berg 1.144d, 2.51l
12.5	GKC §73g; IBHS 425 □ B-L 217a, 437; B-M 1.114; Berg 2.133 n b	12.8	GKC §122v □ B-L 573x
		12.9	GKC §52l, 145h; IBHS 109, 404 n 28; Gib 58 □ Berg 1.129b, 2.45n
12.6	GKC §67q, 67t, 164d; J-M §82m □ B-L 321j, 431t, 438; B-M 2.146; Berg 2.80 n h, 2.91g, 2.136h, 2.140 n q; Brock §174	12.11	J-M §132d □ B-L 534, 548a; Berg 1.144c'
		12.12	GKC §103m; IBHS 389 □ B-L 644y'
		12.13	B-L 306j
		12.14	Berg 1.128dd

B-L: Bauer and Leander, *Historische Grammatik*   **B-M**: Beer, *Grammatik*   **Berg**: Bergsträsser, *Grammatik*
Brock: Brockelmann, *Syntax*   **Dav**: Davidson, *Syntax*   **GAHG**: Richter, *Grammatik*
Gib: Gibson, *Davidson's Syntax, 4th ed.*   **GKC**: *Gesenius' Grammar*   **IBHS**: Waltke and O'Connor, *Syntax*
Jen: Jenni, *Lehrbuch*   **J-M**: Joüon and Muraoka, *Grammar*   **Ros**: Rosenthal, *Grammar*
Sch: Schneider, *Grammatik*   **Wms**: Williams, *Syntax*

LAMENTATIONS

1–4	GKC §5h		1.20	GKC §55e, 118x; J-M §59d □
1	B-L 66s			B-L 285g', 285 n 1; Berg 1.70b,
1.1	Dav §24d, 117; GKC §5h, 90l,			2.107a, 2.160a; Brock §138
	122h n 5, 148b; J-M §93m,		1.21	Dav §41R5; GKC §155h; Gib 69
	112a, 129n, 162b; IBHS 128,			□ B-L 651z
	329; Gib 24, 33 □ B-L 526k,		1.22	Berg 1.107e
	526l, 599h'; Jen §25.3.2.3; Brock		2–4	GKC §5h
	§12		2	B-L 67s
1.2	J-M §123k; Gib 57 □ Berg		2.1	GKC §148b; Gib 185
	1.67u		2.4	GKC §118x □ B-L 650p
1.3	GKC §122i; IBHS 104		2.5	IBHS 184 n 40 □ B-L 650p
1.4	Dav §109; GKC §69t, 87c, 116h;		2.6	IBHS 409 n 35
	J-M §96Cc, 121n, 152d; IBHS		2.7	GKC §64e □ Berg 1.107e,
	118, 148 □ B-L 443k, 517t,			2.115a
	549a'; Berg 2.85r, 2.128 n g		2.8	GKC §65e □ Berg 2.107a,
1.5	Dav §71R2; Gib 145 □ Berg			2.118b
	2.128h		2.11	GKC §51l, 55e, J-M §51b, 59d
1.6	IBHS 119			□ B-L 93c, 228z, 285g', 285 n 1;
1.7	B-L 493zζ			Berg 2.92 n i, 2.107a
1.8	Dav §67b; GKC §67y, 72ee,		2.13	Dav §20R4, 65d; J-M §116c;
	117p; J-M §125q; Wms §51;			Gib 8, 26, 106
	IBHS 386; Gib 115 □ B-L 436;		2.14	B-L 423, 547
	Berg 1.141 n a, 2.139p		2.15	B-L 981; Berg 1.107e, 1.132f,
1.9	Dav §71R2; GKC §118q, 124f;			1.133f; Gib 12
	IBHS 440 n 17, Gib 145		2.16	Dav §41R4; GKC §15c □ B-L
1.10	Dav §1R1, 28R5, 41R3, 83R1,			971, 981; Berg 1.130c
	98R1; GKC §120c, 155f; J-M		2.17	Wms §492; Gib 179 □ B-L
	§130g, 158a; Gib 36, 120			603g; B-M 1.105; Berg 1.157o
1.11	Dav §65R1; Gib 107 □ B-L		2.18	GKC §80f; J-M §129n
	493zζ; B-M 2.35		2.19	GKC §67ee □ B-L 429j; Berg
1.14	Dav §144; GKC §130d, 155n;			2.134c; Brock §116e
	Gib 11		2.20	Dav §122; IBHS 375 n 31; Gib
1.16	GKC §75v, 117z, 133l n 2; J-M			183
	§79p, 96Cc □ B-L 549a', 590h;		2.22	Dav §58a; Gib 103 □ Berg
	Berg 1.66q, 1.102o, 2.85r,			2.17d
	2.119e; Brock §90d		3	GKC §5h □ B-L 67s
1.17	Dav §73R6; GKC §119q; J-M		3.1	Dav §143; GKC §144p; Gib 11
	§103n, 125m; IBHS 201; Gib		3.2	Dav §75; GKC §29q □ B-L
	110 □ B-L 645d"			333a'; Berg 1.162g, 2.131o
1.18	Dav §106R2; J-M §154j; IBHS		3.5	GKC §53n □ B-L 333a', 368t;
	299 □ GAHG 3.164 n 498; Berg			Berg 2.104i
	1.132e; Brock §30a		3.7	J-M §97Fd
1.19	Dav §65R1; GKC §107q, 165a;		3.10	J-M §136g
	J-M §116b n 1, 116e; Gib 107		3.11	Berg 2.85r

B-L: Bauer and Leander, *Historische Grammatik*   **B-M**: Beer, *Grammatik*   **Berg**: Bergsträsser, *Grammatik*
Brock: Brockelmann, *Syntax*   **Dav**: Davidson, *Syntax*   **GAHG**: Richter, *Grammatik*
Gib: Gibson, *Davidson's Syntax, 4th ed.*   **GKC**: *Gesenius' Grammar*   **IBHS**: Waltke and O'Connor, *Syntax*
Jen: Jenni, *Lehrbuch*   **J-M**: Joüon and Muraoka, *Grammar*   **Ros**: Rosenthal, *Grammar*
Sch: Schneider, *Grammatik*   **Wms**: Williams, *Syntax*

3.12	GKC §80h; J-M §89k □ B-L 511x, 599i'	3.63	B-L 452q; Berg 1.119o
		4ʹ	B-L 66s, 67s
3.13	GKC §128v	4.1	GKC §54k, 75rr, 148b; Gib 185
3.14	GKC §87f □ B-L 517w; Berg 2.55e		□ B-L 426; Berg 2.87 n c, 2.99e, 2.168q
3.15	Dav §75, 78R5; Gib 113, 114	4.2	GKC §75rr □ Berg 2.158e
3.20	Dav §101 n 1 □ B-L 77l, 399h″; Berg 2.140 n q	4.3	GKC §35b, 87e □ B-L 221p, 565x
3.22	GKC §20o; J-M §164b; Gib 141 □ B-L 439p'; Berg 1.110 n b	4.5	GKC §117n □ B-L 533f
		4.6	Brock §109e
3.23	J-M §137i	4.7	Berg 2.132a*, 2.134c
3.26	Dav §136R1; GKC §100g n 2, 107q; Gib 37 □ Berg 2.173 n f	4.10	B-L 501yθ
		4.12	Gib 110
3.27	Dav §146; Gib 56	4.14	Dav §83; GKC §51h, 72l, 120g; Gib 120 □ B-L 356v, 398e″; Berg 2.92 n gh, 2.145e
3.28	B-M 2.144		
3.33	GKC §69u □ B-L 443k; Berg 2.128 n h, 2.129 n k, 2.168q		
		4.15	B-L 398e″; Gib 111
3.38	GKC §150a □ Brock §54a	4.16	Berg 2.132a*
3.41	Dav §101Rb □ Brock §82a	4.17	GKC §100o □ B-L 634v; B-M 2.174; Brock §108a
3.42	GKC §32d □ B-L 248h; Jen §8.4.2; Brock §34b		
		4.18	GKC §72l □ B-L 398e″; Berg 2.145e
3.43–66	Gib 180		
3.44	Dav §28R5; Gib 36	4.19	Brock §97a
3.45	Dav §84R1; GKC §113d; IBHS 592; Gib 123 □ Berg 2.61b	4.21	GKC §90n, 110a; J-M §93o □ Berg 1.70b, 2.15a
3.48	Dav §73R2; GKC §29q, 69p, 117z; Gib 113 □ B-L 383; Berg 2.125c; Brock §90d	4.22	Berg 2.29i
		5	GKC §5h
		5.1	GKC §53m □ B-L 366t; Berg 2.105i
3.49	Berg 2.172d		
3.50	Dav §65R5; GKC §109k; J-M §114l; Gib 83 □ Berg 2.50l	5.4	B-L 235u; Brock §122q
		5.5	GKC §72ee n 1, 121a; J-M §128ba □ Berg 2.150o, 2.151q; Brock §35c
3.52	B-M 3.66		
3.53	GKC §69u □ B-L 220n, 443k; Berg 2.129k		
		5.6	Dav §69R2
3.54	J-M §112g	5.7	Brock §80e
3.55	Gib 69	5.16	GAHG 2.34 n 145, 3.170 n 525
3.56	Dav §41R5	5.10	Dav §116R6; GKC §145u; Gib 24
3.58	GKC §73a □ B-L 392w; B-M 2.15; Berg 2.151s		
		5.17	Berg 2.168p; Brock §110e
3.59	J-M §112a	5.21	J-M §133h □ Berg 2.46c, 2.52o

B-L: Bauer and Leander, *Historische Grammatik* **B-M**: Beer, *Grammatik* **Berg**: Bergsträsser, *Grammatik*
Brock: Brockelmann, *Syntax* **Dav**: Davidson, *Syntax* **GAHG**: Richter, *Grammatik*
Gib: Gibson, *Davidson's Syntax, 4th ed.* **GKC**: *Gesenius' Grammar* **IBHS**: Waltke and O'Connor, *Syntax*
Jen: Jenni, *Lehrbuch* **J-M**: Joüon and Muraoka, *Grammar* **Ros**: Rosenthal, *Grammar*
Sch: Schneider, *Grammatik* **Wms**: Williams, *Syntax*

ESTHER

1.1	GKC §49l n 1, 134g; J-M §118c n 2, 176f; IBHS 554; Gib 50 □ B-M 3.45; Berg 2.37a	3.2	J-M §121f
		3.4	Dav §146; GKC §123c, 157c; J-M §135d, 157c, 157ca; IBHS 116; Gib 110
1.4	GKC §93ww; J-M §142g		
1.5	GKC §74h □ Berg 2.158e	3.7	IBHS 284 n 25
1.6	B-L 603f; Berg 1.135c	3.8	GKC §100o n 2; J-M §102k □ B-L 268h; B-M 2.17; Brock §80e
1.7	J-M §123q □ Berg 2.54d, 2.161 n c		
1.8	Dav §29R8; GKC §104g, 123c; J-M §104d, 135d; IBHS 116; Gib 42 □ B-L 649l	3.9	J-M §133f □ B-L 302a'; Jen §29.3.3; Brock §110d
		3.11	Berg 2.57k
1.11	GAHG 2.24 n 91	3.13	GKC §67n, 113z, 113gg; J-M §123x, 123y; Wms §210; IBHS 596 n 60 □ B-L 435p'; B-M 3.64f; Berg 2.62b, 2.67m, 2.136f
1.12	J-M §131k		
1.17	GKC §93m □ Berg 1.156k		
1.19	J-M §133f, 140a; Wms §296; IBHS 218 n 113		
1.20	B-M 3.20; Berg 1.156k	3.14	Wms §196 □ B-L 135h; Berg 1.52k, 1.132f
1.22	Dav §29R8; IBHS 116 n 7; Gib 42		
2.1	Berg 2.136f	4.2	Dav §95; GKC §114l; J-M §124b, 124l, 160j; Wms §196, 410; Gib 132 □ Berg 2.58m; Brock §15g
2.2–3	IBHS 596		
2.2	GKC §144f; J-M §155b □ GAHG 2.60 n 261		
		4.3	J-M §129q □ Berg 2.71f; Brock §162
2.3	GKC §113z; J-M §123x; IBHS 596 n 60 □ B-L 131; GAHG 2.60 n 261; Berg 2.67m		
		4.4	GKC §55g □ B-L 283v; Berg 2.99e, 2.108c
2.5	Berg 1.126bb	4.8	GKC §9u, 93ww
2.6	J-M §16f n 3, 132c □ B-L 518c'	4.11	J-M §157c; Gib 110 □ Berg 1.134c, 2.129h, 2.157c
2.7	GAHG 2.24 n 91; Berg 2.73i	4.13	J-M §126h
2.8	GKC §10g □ Berg 2.118b	4.14	Dav §43R1; GKC §85e, 150i; J-M §88Lb; Gib 7, 80 □ B-L 486jε; B-M 3.95; Berg 1.107d, 2.71g, 2.118c, 2.119a
2.9	GKC §75v □ B-L 599i'; Berg 1.119o		
2.11–14	Berg 2.32d		
2.11	Dav §29R8; GKC §123c; J-M §121f; Gib 42 □ B-L 534; Berg 2.30a		
		4.16	Dav §114, 130R4; GKC §106o, 119ii; J-M §151a, 176o n 1; Gib 21
2.13	J-M §103c n 1, 121f		
2.14	GKC §10h, 107e; J-M §9d, 121f □ Berg 2.32d	5.2	J-M §176f □ GAHG 3.102 n 289; Berg 1.75g
2.15	Dav §100R2; GKC §74i; Gib 138 □ B-L 328a'; Berg 1.89b	5.3	Dav §65d
		5.6	Dav §65d; IBHS 215 □ Berg 2.50k, 2.164h
2.18	GKC §72z, 85c; J-M §88Lb □ B-L 403, 486jε; Berg 2.106m	5.10	GKC §54k
		5.12	J-M §121q
3.1	GKC §52l □ Berg 2.95d	5.13	GAHG 3.102 n 289

B-L: Bauer and Leander, *Historische Grammatik*   **B-M**: Beer, *Grammatik*   **Berg**: Bergsträsser, *Grammatik*
Brock: Brockelmann, *Syntax*   **Dav**: Davidson, *Syntax*   **GAHG**: Richter, *Grammatik*
Gib: Gibson, *Davidson's Syntax, 4th ed.*   **GKC**: *Gesenius' Grammar*   **IBHS**: Waltke and O'Connor, *Syntax*
Jen: Jenni, *Lehrbuch*   **J-M**: Joüon and Muraoka, *Grammar*   **Ros**: Rosenthal, *Grammar*
Sch: Schneider, *Grammatik*   **Wms**: Williams, *Syntax*

5.14	J-M §116f □ GAHG 3.152 n 417	8.17	J-M §129q; IBHS 431 □ B-M 2.141; Berg 2.98c, 2.129l
6.1	J-M §121q; IBHS 630 □ Berg 2.69d, 2.73i*	9.1	Dav §88R5; GKC §63c; 113gg, 135a n 1; J-M §123y, 146c;
6.2	J-M §157c; Gib 56, 110		Wms §210; IBHS 596 n 60; Gib
6.3	J-M §144d; IBHS 318 n 6		127 □ B-M 2.129, III,64ff.; Jen
6.8	IBHS 222 □ B-M 3.80		§18.4.4; Berg 2.62b, 2.67m,
6.9	GKC §113z; J-M §123x □ Berg 2.67m		2.92i, 2.111b*, 2.113e; Brock §67b
6.10	GKC §120g	9.2	GKC §106f n 1
6.13	GKC §20g, 67w; J-M §82n □ B-L 436; Berg 1.67t	9.4	Dav §86R4; GKC §113n; J-M §123s; Gib 126 □ Berg 2.71f
6.14	Jen §27.3.2	9.5	J-M §88Mb □ B-L 499hθ; Berg
7.2	GKC §109f □ Berg 2.50k		1.134c
7.4	GKC §159l, 159x; J-M §167k n 1; Wms §516; IBHS	9.6	Dav §88R1; GKC §113z; J-M §123x; Gib 127 □ Berg 2.67m
	603; Gib 133 □ B-L 652b'; B-M	9.7	GKC §2s
	3.117; Berg 2.56f; Brock §165d	9.12	Dav §88R1; GKC §142g; Gib
7.5	GKC §74g, 137a; J-M §78j		127 □ GAHG 3.171 n 538; Berg
7.8	GKC §114i; J-M §132a, 154d, 166h □ Berg 2.58m		2.50k, 2.67m
8.1	GKC §137c □ B-L 266e	9.13	B-L 534
8.5	IBHS 376 n 42	9.16ff.	GKC §113z
8.6	Dav §83; GKC §120o; J-M §177h; Gib 120 □ B-L 499mθ,	9.16	Dav §88R1; J-M §123x; Gib 127 □ Berg 2.67m
	546z; GAHG 3.185 n 656; Berg	9.17	Dav §88R1; Gib 127
	1.134c, 1.144c; Brock §143a	9.19	GKC §45e; J-M §49e □ B-L
8.8	Dav §88R1, 95; GKC §63c,		362a'; Berg 2.71g, 2.83p
	113z, 114l; IBHS 597; Gib 127,	9.21–32	Jen §27.4.1
	132 □ B-M 2.129; Berg 2.58m,	9.21	GKC §72m; J-M §80h; IBHS
	2.67m, 2.92i, 2.111b*		630 n 53 □ Berg 2.74k
8.9	GKC §123c; J-M §143j; IBHS 284 n 25	9.22	Berg 2.83p
8.10	Berg 1.136e	9.23	GKC §145o n 1; Gib 103 □ Brock §50a
8.11	GKC §67n □ B-L 435p'; Berg 2.136f, 2.140 n q	9.26	B-L 266e
8.14	Berg 1.136e	9.27	GKC §72m; IBHS 630 n 53 □ B-M 2.148; Berg 2.74k
8.15	GKC §132a; J-M §130h; IBHS 226 □ B-L 496wη; B-M 3.20	9.31	GKC §72m □ Berg 2.151r
		10.2	Dav §123R2; Gib 184 □ Berg 1.134c

B-L: Bauer and Leander, *Historische Grammatik*   **B-M**: Beer, *Grammatik*   **Berg**: Bergsträsser, *Grammatik*
Brock: Brockelmann, *Syntax* **Dav**: Davidson, *Syntax*   **GAHG**: Richter, *Grammatik*
Gib: Gibson, *Davidson's Syntax, 4th ed.*   **GKC**: *Gesenius' Grammar*   **IBHS**: Waltke and O'Connor, *Syntax*
Jen: Jenni, *Lehrbuch*   **J-M**: Joüon and Muraoka, *Grammar*   **Ros**: Rosenthal, *Grammar*
Sch: Schneider, *Grammatik*   **Wms**: Williams, *Syntax*

DANIEL

1–12	Brock §85a	2.10	GKC §142f n 2; Ros §33
1.1	GKC §49b n 1 □ Berg 2.26c	2.11	Ros §95, 176
1.2	B-L 599h′	2.12	Ros §88
1.3	GKC §154a n 1b	2.13	Dav §146R4; J-M §124s n 2;
1.4	GKC §23c, 128a n 1, 152p; J-M		Gib 111
	§129a n 5, 160k; Wms §29;	2.14	GKC §126q n 1
	IBHS 139 n 6; Gib 35 □ GAHG	2.16	Dav §96R4, 111R2
	2.60 n 261, 2.67; Berg 1.92e,	2.17	Ros §79
	2.57l; Brock §70c	2.18	Dav §96R4, 111R2; Ros §16, 82,
1.5	Dav §36c; GKC §135o; J-M		86
	§124l; Gib 3, 47 □ Berg 2.36k	2.19	Ros §10, 75
1.7	GKC §143b	2.20	Ros §31, 81
1.8	Dav §146; J-M §157c; Gib 110	2.22	Ros §44
	□ B-L 355m; Berg 2.115a,	2.24–25	Ros §20
	2.117e	2.24	Ros §164
1.10	GKC §72m, 93ss, 150e; J-M	2.25	Ros §86, 117, 164
	§80h, 161h; IBHS 324 □ Berg	2.26	Dav §144R3; Ros §10, 95
	2.153u, 2.158e	2.28	Ros §33, 57
1.12	Dav §36c; GKC §75cc; J-M	2.30	Dav §108R2; Ros §10, 80, 86,
	§116b n 1; Gib 47 □ Berg 2.164i		95
1.13	GKC §75hh; J-M §114m; IBHS	2.31	Ros §46
	571 □ B-L 425; Berg 2.161b	2.32	Ros §32, 34, 54
1.15	Dav §36c; GKC §93ss; J-M	2.34	Ros §117, 164
	§96Ce; Gib 47, 56	2.35	Ros §59, 64, 79, 145, 158
1.16	Dav §100R2; GKC §93ss; Gib	2.37	Dav §9R1; Ros §36
	138 □ Berg 2.73i*	2.38	GKC §141h n 2 □ Ros §30
1.17	Dav §36R4; IBHS 592; Gib 48	2.39	Ros §13, 80 □ B-L 176a
	□ Berg 2.26c, 2.61b	2.40	J-M §82h; Ros §20, 96, 159, 164
1.18	Brock §152d	2.41	Ros §76, 80
1.20	Dav §38R5; J-M §142q; IBHS	2.42	Ros §80
	287; Gib 51	2.43	Ros §76(bis), 86
1.21	Gib 51	2.44	Ros §32, 164
2.1	GKC §64g, 106e, 124o, J-M	2.45	Ros §117, 124
	§136j; Gib 51 □ B-L 355q; Berg	2.46	B-L 118 n 3, 119 n 2
	2.26c, 2.115a	2.47	Ros §80, 86(bis)
2.3	B-L 321k	2.48	Ros §76
2.4–7.28	Ros §1 □ B-M 1.11; Berg 1.1d	2.49	Ros §15, 48
2.4	GKC §1c; Ros §2 □ B-L 4f	3.2–3	Ros §17, 22
2.5	Ros §10, 57, 62, 86	3.2	GKC §126q n 1; Ros §16
2.6	Ros §25, 62, 153	3.3–4	Ros §177
2.7	GKC §142f n 2; Ros §72, 88	3.3	Ros §16
2.8–9	Ros §86	3.4	Ros §23, 25
2.8	Ros §88	3.5	Ros §16, 19, 46, 57, 86
2.9	Ros §30, 114, 147	3.6	Ros §59

B-L: Bauer and Leander, *Historische Grammatik* B-M: Beer, *Grammatik* Berg: Bergsträsser, *Grammatik*
Brock: Brockelmann, *Syntax* Dav: Davidson, *Syntax* GAHG: Richter, *Grammatik*
Gib: Gibson, *Davidson's Syntax, 4th ed.* GKC: *Gesenius' Grammar* IBHS: Waltke and O'Connor, *Syntax*
Jen: Jenni, *Lehrbuch* J-M: Joüon and Muraoka, *Grammar* Ros: Rosenthal, *Grammatik*
Sch: Schneider, *Grammatik* Wms: Williams, *Syntax*

3.7	Ros §46, 57, 191	4.31	Ros §82, 83, 178
3.8	Ros §58	4.32	Ros §27, 87, 149
3.10	Ros §16, 19, 46, 57	4.33	Ros §10, 27, 130
3.12	J-M §103k n 1; Ros §31, 48, 58, 84, 95	4.34	Ros §36, 143
3.13	Ros §167	5.1	Ros §46, 51
3.14	Ros §93, 95, 140	5.2	GKC §119m n 1; Ros §77
3.15	GKC §167a; Ros §19, 25, 30, 46, 57, 86(bis), 95, 175	5.3–4	Ros §145
3.16	Ros §142	5.3	Ros §77
3.17	Ros §49(bis)	5.5	J-M §133b n 4, 158e; Ros §51, 177
3.18	Ros §49, 95	5.6	GKC §117x; Ros §33
3.19	Ros §70, 82, 121, 149	5.7	Ros §13, 71, 86
3.20	Ros §27	5.8	Ros §162
3.21	Ros §10(bis) □ B-M 2.127; Berg 2.110e	5.9	Ros §20, 88
3.22	Ros §86, 88, 123, 184	5.10	Ros §47, 108(bis), 117, 120, 152, 158
3.23	J-M §98f; Ros §73	5.11	J-M §42f n 1; Ros §16, 117
3.24	Ros §5, 88	5.12	J-M §42f n 1; Ros §36, 89, 108, 111(bis), 152
3.25	Ros §47, 91	5.13	Ros §26, 30, 164
3.26	Ros §119, 148	5.14	J-M §42f n 1
3.27	Dav §17R4; Ros §59(bis), 76	5.15	Ros §164
3.28	Ros §85, 86	5.16	GKC §135h; Ros §71
3.29	Ros §57	5.17	Ros §62, 129
3.32	Ros §83	5.19	Dav §100R2; Ros §10, 23, 37, 170; IBHS 629; Gib 138
3.33	Ros §83, 92	5.20	GKC §72z, 85c; J-M §80n, 155c; Ros §76, 116, 133, 142 □ B-L 403
4.1	Ros §51		
4.3	J-M §18b n 4		
4.4	Ros §23, 162		
4.5	Dav §144R3; Ros §89, 120	5.21	J-M §144g; Ros §23, 76, 83
4.6	Dav §9R1; Ros §23	5.22	Ros §86
4.9	Ros §10, 59, 96, 138, 157	5.23	Ros §36, 77, 84, 117, 143
4.11	Ros §10, 160	5.27	Ros §13, 117
4.12	Ros §76, 186	5.29	Ros §10, 71
4.13	Ros §66	5.30	Ros §89
4.14	Ros §42, 86, 118	6.1	Ros §74, 78
4.15	Ros §34, 86	6.3	Ros §64, 80(bis)
4.16	Ros §13, 46, 78, 108, 126, 157	6.4	J-M §143e n 2; Ros §82, 142
4.18	Ros §59, 96	6.5–6	Ros §76
4.19	Ros §145	6.5	J-M §42f n 1; Ros §44, 84, 124
4.20	Ros §76, 160	6.6	J-M §143e n 2; Ros §86
4.22	Dav §108R2; GKC §144i n 1; Ros §76, 86, 118, 181	6.8	Ros §48, 81, 85, 86
4.23	Ros §10	6.9	Ros §78
4.24	J-M §90c; Ros §14, 25, 161	6.11	Ros §57(bis), 61, 76, 84, 177
4.25	Ros §96	6.13	Ros §10(bis), 48, 78, 81, 85
4.27	Ros §10(bis), 30, 36, 59, 79	6.14	Ros §80, 86
4.28	Dav §108R2; Ros §76, 90	6.15	Ros §13, 82(bis), 159
4.29	Dav §108R2; Ros §118	6.16	Ros §87, 129
4.30	Ros §76	6.17	Ros §36, 48
		6.18	Ros §46, 77, 86, 133, 167

B-L: Bauer and Leander, *Historische Grammatik*   **B-M**: Beer, *Grammatik*   **Berg**: Bergsträsser, *Grammatik*
Brock: Brockelmann, *Syntax*   **Dav**: Davidson, *Syntax*   **GAHG**: Richter, *Grammatik*
Gib: Gibson, *Davidson's Syntax, 4th ed.*   **GKC**: *Gesenius' Grammar*   **IBHS**: Waltke and O'Connor, *Syntax*
Jen: Jenni, *Lehrbuch*   **J-M**: Joüon and Muraoka, *Grammar*   **Ros**: Rosenthal, *Grammar*
Sch: Schneider, *Grammatik*   **Wms**: Williams, *Syntax*

B-L: Bauer and Leander, *Historische Grammatik*   **B-M**: Beer, *Grammatik*   **Berg**: Bergsträsser, *Grammatik*
Brock: Brockelmann, *Syntax*   **Dav**: Davidson, *Syntax*   **GAHG**: Richter, *Grammatik*
Gib: Gibson, *Davidson's Syntax, 4th ed.*   **GKC**: *Gesenius' Grammar*   **IBHS**: Waltke and O'Connor, *Syntax*
Jen: Jenni, *Lehrbuch*   **J-M**: Joüon and Muraoka, *Grammar*   **Ros**: Rosenthal, *Grammar*
Sch: Schneider, *Grammatik*   **Wms**: Williams, *Syntax*

9.15	GKC §29w	11.1	Dav §96R3
9.16	J-M §105c n 4 □ GAHG	11.4	Dav §65R6; Gib 104 □ Berg
	3.213 n 803, 3.216 n 815; Berg		2.50l
	2.48g	11.6	GKC §116f, 127i, 139h; J-M
9.17	B-L 156k′		§121k □ B-L 563v; GAHG
9.18	GKC §10g; J-M §154fe □ B-L		3.161 n 480
	208r; Berg 2.71g	11.8	GKC §131d, 139h
9.19	GKC §48i □ Berg 1.135c, 2.81k,	11.10	Dav §65R6, 86c; GKC §113r;
	2.106m		J-M §123l; Gib 104, 124 □
9.20–21	GKC §116u □ Berg 2.70e*		GAHG 3.218 n 825; Berg 2.51l
9.21	GAHG 3.102 n 289; Berg	11.11	Dav §29R7; GKC §55g, 131n;
	2.150 n o		J-M §146e; IBHS 426; Gib 42 □
9.23	Dav §29e; GKC §73a, 124e,		B-L 283v; Berg 2.108c
	141c; J-M §136g; IBHS 121 □	11.12	GKC §97g; IBHS 282 □ B-L
	Berg 2.153t		437; Berg 1.93h, 2.135d
9.24	GKC §75aa, 121b □ B-L 348h,	11.13	Dav §86c; Gib 124 □ Berg
	424, 539i; Berg 2.114i, 2.161c,		1.130c
	2.168q	11.14	Dav §28R6; GKC §54c; J-M
9.25	Dav §8g; GKC §120e; J-M		§17, 119zb; IBHS 360 n 30; Gib
	§177b; Gib 120 □ Berg 2.45a,		36 □ B-L 441c; Berg 1.109 n c,
	2.53q		2.99 n d
9.26	Dav §99R1; GKC §134h; Wms	11.16–19	Dav §65R6; Gib 104
	§97; IBHS 281, 283, 622; Gib	11.16	Berg 2.50l
	135 □ B-M 3.38; Brock §85b	11.17	Berg 2.51l
9.27	Berg 1.113 n e	11.18	Berg 2.51l
10.1	Dav §144R3; GKC §73a; J-M	11.19	B-L 240t′; Berg 2.51l
	§81d □ B-L 392w; B-M 2.149;	11.20	GKC §93dd □ B-M 2.63
	Berg 1.112 n d	11.22	IBHS 375 n 31
10.2–3	GKC §131d	11.23	GKC §53l, 54k, 86k; J-M §53f,
10.2	Berg 2.73i*		88Mj □ B-L 351, 505rι; B-M
10.3	IBHS 588; Gib 124 □ Berg		2.123; Jen §28.3.3; Berg 2.99f
	2.62c, 2.146f, 2.147g	11.25	Dav §65R6 □ Berg 2.51l
10.5	J-M §121o, 136b, 137u □ Berg	11.26	B-L 302a′
	2.138 n n	11.27	Dav §29R7; Gib 42 □ GAHG
10.6	B-L 156k′		3.175 n 589
10.7	IBHS 672; Gib 141 □ B-L 375;	11.28	Dav §65R6 □ Berg 2.51l
	GAHG 3.176 n 598; Brock §56b	11.29	J-M §133h, 174i
10.8	IBHS 216 n 105	11.30	Dav §65R6 □ B-L 582u′; Berg
10.9	Dav §100R2; Gib 138		1.102n, 2.51l
10.11	GKC §111b □ B-L 581	11.31	Dav §32R2 □ Berg 1.113 n e;
10.12	GKC §126w; IBHS 482, 486;		Brock §127a
	Gib 62 □ Jen §25.3.3	11.32	J-M §148a □ B-L 219g, 600j′;
10.13	Berg 2.71f		Berg 1.139b
10.14	GKC §75rr	11.35	GKC §53q □ B-L 228a′, 332t;
10.16	Berg 2.23f, 2.70e		GAHG 3.175 n 589; Berg
10.18	Brock §109d		2.105 n k; Brock §34a
10.20–21	IBHS 672	11.36	J-M §112i; IBHS 491 □ Berg
10.20	GAHG 3.206 n 785,		2.111b*
	3.214 n 808; Berg 2.72h(bis)	11.37	GKC §152b □ B-M 2.122
10.21	GAHG 3.176 n 598; Brock §56b	11.38	GKC §117n

B-L: Bauer and Leander, *Historische Grammatik*   **B-M**: Beer, *Grammatik*   **Berg**: Bergsträsser, *Grammatik*
Brock: Brockelmann, *Syntax*   **Dav**: Davidson, *Syntax*   **GAHG**: Richter, *Grammatik*
Gib: Gibson, *Davidson's Syntax, 4th ed.*   **GKC**: *Gesenius' Grammar*   **IBHS**: Waltke and O'Connor, *Syntax*
Jen: Jenni, *Lehrbuch*   **J-M**: Joüon and Muraoka, *Grammar*   **Ros**: Rosenthal, *Grammar*
Sch: Schneider, *Grammatik*   **Wms**: Williams, *Syntax*

11.39	Wms §336		12.7	GKC §93aa n 1 □ B-L 132c;
11.40	Berg 2.117a			Berg 2.173 n g
11.45	Berg 1.39i		12.8	Berg 2.23f
12.2	Dav §5; GKC §102b, 124e; J-M		12.11	Dav §96R4; GKC §134g; J-M
	§103d n 3, 136g; IBHS 121; Gib			§125p; Gib 132 □ Berg
	6 □ B-L 643s′; B-M 2.178; Berg			1.113 n e; Brock §127a
	1.142f		12.13	GKC §87e; J-M §90c; IBHS 118
12.3	IBHS 444 □ Berg 2.103d*			□ B-L 517t, 618n; B-M 2.83 □
12.4	GAHG 3.218 n 825			GAHG 3.218 n 825; Jen
12.6	J-M §121o			§25.3.2.2

B-L: Bauer and Leander, *Historische Grammatik*   **B-M**: Beer, *Grammatik*   **Berg**: Bergsträsser, *Grammatik*
Brock: Brockelmann, *Syntax*   **Dav**: Davidson, *Syntax*   **GAHG**: Richter, *Grammatik*
Gib: Gibson, *Davidson's Syntax, 4th ed.*   **GKC**: *Gesenius' Grammar*   **IBHS**: Waltke and O'Connor, *Syntax*
Jen: Jenni, *Lehrbuch*   **J-M**: Joüon and Muraoka, *Grammar*   **Ros**: Rosenthal, *Grammar*
Sch: Schneider, *Grammatik*   **Wms**: Williams, *Syntax*

EZRA

1–10	Brock §84a	4.4	GKC §145c
1.1	GKC §49b n 1; J-M §130d, 131k	4.5	GKC §6k □ B-L 549a'
1.3	B-M 2.101, 2.157; Berg 2.49h; 2.49i, 2.162f	4.7	GKC §29q, 55h; Ros §2; IBHS 4 □ B-M 2.127; Jen §28.3.2.1; Berg 2.110e
1.5	Dav §144R5; GKC §155d, 155n; J-M §125l; IBHS 211 n 89; Gib 12 □ Brock §31a	4.8–6.18	Ros §1 □ B-M 1.11; Berg 181.1d
		4.8	GKC §1c; Ros §19, 46 □ B-L 4f
1.6	IBHS 602 □ Berg 2.55e	4.9	Ros §35,58, 191
1.7	Dav §39R1; J-M §131k	4.10	Ros §23, 25, 62, 89
1.9	J-M §136l □ B-L 485hε	4.11	Ros §82, 89
1.11	GKC §143e	4.12	Ros §13, 15(bis), 49, 84, 178
2	Dav §37R3	4.13	Ros §42, 93, 99, 118
2.12	J-M §100m	4.14	Ros §49, 82
2.48	B-L 511x	4.15	Ros §10, 21, 27, 62(bis), 80, 111 □ B-M 2.81
2.55	GKC §122r □ B-L 511x		
2.57	GKC §122r	4.16 (= 15)	Ros §82
2.59	Dav §125; J-M §161f	4.16	Ros §177
2.62	Dav §29R4, 101; GKC §119y, 131r □ B-M 2.130; Berg 2.116c, 2.129l	4.17	Ros §25, 89
		4.18	Ros §10, 49 □ Berg 2.117e
		4.19	Ros §27, 62, 80, 82, 126, 177
2.64	IBHS 283; Gib 49 □ B-L 627s; B-M 2.88	4.21	Ros §86, 87
		4.22	Dav §91R3; Ros §82, 86, 111, 148
2.65	Dav §32R3		
2.69	GKC §97g; J-M §100n □ B-L 627s; Berg 1.93h	4.23	Ros §10, 25
		4.24	Ros §10, 177
3.3	GKC §124q, 147a; J-M §136o □ Berg 2.23 n f	5.2	Ros §20
		5.3	Ros §149
3.4	Wms §254	5.4	J-M §144b n 1; Ros §30, 34, 38; IBHS 320 n 9
3.6	GKC §134p; Gib 50 □ Brock §86		
		5.5	Ros §86, 89, 141, 178
3.7	Dav §24R6	5.7	Ros §96
3.8	Dav §83R2 □ B-L 360p	5.8	Dav §80; J-M §29e; Ros §11, 15(bis), 51, 111
3.9	Dav §116R3 □ B-M 2.132; Berg 2.118b		
		5.9	Ros §149
3.10	GKC §88f; Gib 103 □ B-L 516s; Berg 2.45n	5.10	Ros §62, 86, 111
		5.11	GKC §141h n 1; Ros §29(bis), 30, 47, 61, 121, 177
3.11	GKC §158b □ Berg 2.129 n i		
3.12	Dav §6R1, 29R7; GKC §69n, 126aa, 131n; J-M §143i; IBHS 197, 611; Gib 6, 42 □ Berg 2.60p	5.12	Dav §1R1; GKC §135a n 1; Ros §19(bis), 49, 75, 84, 184; Gib 3
		5.13	Ros §149; Gib 51
4.1	Berg 1.72g	5.14	GKC §155n; Ros §36, 46, 130
4.2	GKC §103l	5.15	Ros §32, 34, 119, 122, 126, 184
4.4–5	Berg 2.73i*	5.16	Ros §81

B-L: Bauer and Leander, *Historische Grammatik*   **B-M**: Beer, *Grammatik*   **Berg**: Bergsträsser, *Grammatik*
Brock: Brockelmann, *Syntax*   **Dav**: Davidson, *Syntax*   **GAHG**: Richter, *Grammatik*
Gib: Gibson, *Davidson's Syntax, 4th ed.*   **GKC**: *Gesenius' Grammar*   **IBHS**: Waltke and O'Connor, *Syntax*
Jen: Jenni, *Lehrbuch*   **J-M**: Joüon and Muraoka, *Grammar*   **Ros**: Rosenthal, *Grammar*
Sch: Schneider, *Grammatik*   **Wms**: Williams, *Syntax*

B-L: Bauer and Leander, *Historische Grammatik* **B-M**: Beer, *Grammatik* **Berg**: Bergsträsser, *Grammatik*
Brock: Brockelmann, *Syntax* **Dav**: Davidson, *Syntax* **GAHG**: Richter, *Grammatik*
Gib: Gibson, *Davidson's Syntax, 4th ed.* **GKC**: *Gesenius' Grammar* **IBHS**: Waltke and O'Connor, *Syntax*
Jen: Jenni, *Lehrbuch* **J-M**: Joüon and Muraoka, *Grammar* **Ros**: Rosenthal, *Grammar*
Sch: Schneider, *Grammatik* **Wms**: Williams, *Syntax*

10.8	GKC §134o n 1 □ Jen §27.3.3; Berg 2.30a	10.16	GKC §45g; J-M §142o □ B-L 357
10.9	J-M §126b	10.17	Dav §22R4; GKC §127c n 2, 138i; J-M §145d; Wms §91, 539; IBHS 248 n 19; Gib 29
10.12	Dav §67R3; GKC §145e; J-M §125s; Gib 115 □ Berg 2.58m	10.23	B-L 511x
10.13	Dav §29e, 82; GKC §141d; J-M §154e; IBHS 274; Gib 42, 120, 141 □ GAHG 3.176 n 598; Brock §14bε, 56b		
10.14	Dav §20R4, 22R4, 28R5, 29R8; GKC §123c, 127i, 138i; J-M §140b n 1, 145d; Wms §91, 442; IBHS 116 n 7, 248 n 19, 339, 422; Gib 29, 42 □ B-L 649l; Brock §73d		

B-L: Bauer and Leander, *Historische Grammatik*   **B-M**: Beer, *Grammatik*   **Berg**: Bergsträsser, *Grammatik*
Brock: Brockelmann, *Syntax*   **Dav**: Davidson, *Syntax*   **GAHG**: Richter, *Grammatik*
Gib: Gibson, *Davidson's Syntax, 4th ed.*   **GKC**: *Gesenius' Grammar*   **IBHS**: Waltke and O'Connor, *Syntax*
Jen: Jenni, *Lehrbuch*   **J-M**: Joüon and Muraoka, *Grammar*   **Ros**: Rosenthal, *Grammar*
Sch: Schneider, *Grammatik*   **Wms**: Williams, *Syntax*

NEHEMIAH

1–13	Brock §84a, 85a		3.5	B-L 548z
1.1	Dav §38; GKC §49b n 1; J-M		3.8	GKC §124o, 128v □ Brock §74c
	§118c n 2; IBHS 554; Gib 51 □		3.13	GKC §35d □ B-L 263f, 487oε,
	Berg 2.37a			533f; Berg 1.93 n h
1.4–5	Jen §15.7.3		3.14	B-L 263f, 533f; Berg 2.33 n b-h,
1.4	Dav §100R2; GKC §116r; J-M			2.39 n i
	§121f, 121g, 176f; Gib 138 □		3.15	B-L 437; Berg 2.33 n b-h, 2.97h
	Jen §26.3.3; Berg 2.23f, 2.73i*		3.16–31	Wms §358
1.7	Dav §86R3; GKC §113x □ Jen		3.20	GKC §120h
	§7.1; Berg 2.64 n f		3.26	Berg 2.73i; Brock §119c
1.8	GKC §159c; J-M §167a, 167d □		3.28	GKC §119c
	B-L 354b; Berg 2.116e		3.31	GKC §128v
1.9	J-M §167d; Gib 3 □ Berg		3.34	B-L 483rδ; Berg 1.113 n e,
	2.118d			1.147 n d
1.11	B-L 362a' □ GAHG 3.216 n 815		3.37	Berg 2.48g, 2.164i
2.1	Dav §38R2; IBHS 284 n 25; Gib		4.1	B-L 564
	51 □ Berg 2.23f		4.3	GKC §49e n 2, 53n □ B-L 353v;
2.3	Dav §147; GKC §67dd,			Berg 2.104i
	109a n 2; IBHS 375 n 36; Gib		4.4	Dav §17; GKC §119m; IBHS
	158 □ B-L 286n'; Berg 2.139p			115; Gib 19
2.5	GKC §165a		4.6	Gib 51
2.7	GKC §68g; J-M §155b □ B-L		4.7	GKC §20h □ B-L 93c; Berg
	599h'; Berg 2.120a			1.68v
2.8	Berg 1.154e		4.8	Berg 2.21d
2.9	Dav §48R2; Gib 96 □ B-L 599h'		4.9	GKC §49e n 2, 67x □ B-L 405;
2.10	Dav §67b; J-M §157a; Gib 115			Berg 2.138l, 2.145c
	□ Brock §38a, 49b		4.10	J-M §176f
2.11	Gib 47		4.11–12	Berg 2.71f
2.12	Dav §29d, 114; GKC §131e,		4.11	Dav §35R1
	137c; J-M §131f; IBHS		4.12	Dav §98R1; GKC §116k n 2,
	325 n 19; Gib 22, 41 □ B-M			121d; J-M §121o; IBHS 194;
	2.16, 3.35; GAHG 2.49 n 225;			Gib 133
	Berg 1.78m, 2.21d		4.13	IBHS 592 n 46
2.13	Dav §100R2; GKC §5n, 49e;		4.14	J-M §129q
	J-M §114b n 1, 121g; IBHS		4.17	Dav §1R1; GKC §152n; J-M
	375 n 36; Gib 138 □ B-L 286n',			§160i; Gib 3 □ B-L 633t; Jen
	533f; Berg 1.5l, 2.73i*			§27.3.2
2.15	Dav §100R2; J-M §121g; Gib		5.2–4	GKC §139h n 1
	138 □ Berg 2.21d, 2.73i*		5.3	J-M §116c
2.16	Dav §116R3; IBHS 221		5.4	B-L 512b'
2.18	J-M §157d n 1		5.5	Dav §101Rc
2.19	B-M 2.51 □ B-L 525h		5.7–8	GKC §49e
2.20	GKC §72aa; J-M §80n □ Berg		5.7	Dav §101R1 n 1; □ Berg 2.23f,
	2.21d			2.159g(bis)

B-L: Bauer and Leander, *Historische Grammatik*   **B-M:** Beer, *Grammatik*   **Berg:** Bergsträsser, *Grammatik*
Brock: Brockelmann, *Syntax*   **Dav:** Davidson, *Syntax*   **GAHG:** Richter, *Grammatik*
Gib: Gibson, *Davidson's Syntax, 4th ed.*   **GKC:** *Gesenius' Grammar*   **IBHS:** Waltke and O'Connor, *Syntax*
Jen: Jenni, *Lehrbuch*   **J-M:** Joüon and Muraoka, *Grammar*   **Ros:** Rosenthal, *Grammar*
Sch: Schneider, *Grammatik*   **Wms:** Williams, *Syntax*

5.10	Berg 2.69 n c, 2.159g
5.11	J-M §35e; IBHS 288, 648 n 2; Gib 51 □ Berg 2.69 n c; Brock §109b
5.13	GKC §49e □ Brock §50e*
5.14	Dav §38R2, 114; GKC §91e; J-M §129d, 151a; IBHS 147; Gib 21, 51 □ B-L 599h'
5.15	J-M §133c; Wms §96
5.18	Dav §84R1; Wms §332; IBHS 200 □ Berg 2.65h*; Brock §113
5.19	IBHS 488; Gib 62 □ Berg 2.81i
6.1	Dav §81; GKC §90k; J-M §51c n 4; IBHS 385 n 19; Gib 119
6.2	Dav §17R3; GKC §124o; Gib 20
6.3	Berg 2.23f, 2.76 n b
6.4	Berg 2.21d
6.5	B-M 2.91; Brock §88
6.6	Dav §100R6; GKC §90k; J-M §93s; Gib 138 □ B-L 423, 525h; B-M 2.51; Berg 2.153u
6.7	Berg 2.27d
6.8	GKC §23c, 74i □ B-L 548a'; Berg 1.92e, 2.156a
6.9	GKC §109g; J-M §150d
6.10	GKC §144i; J-M §155f; Gib 14 □ Berg 2.52o
6.11	GKC §49e, 100m □ Brock §82c
6.12	Dav §127a; Gib 141
6.14	Berg 2.81i
6.17	GKC §116c □ Berg 2.71f
6.18	GKC §128u; Dav §24R3
6.19	Berg 2.73i
7.2	GKC §53g; 118x; J-M §133g; Wms §261; IBHS 203 □ B-L 351; Brock §109c
7.3	GKC §64c; J-M §69b, 166i □ B-L 354c, 371v; Berg 2.67m, 2.105i
7.5	Berg 2.23f, 2.55e
7.48	Berg 1.161d
7.57	B-L 511x
7.60	Berg 1.52k, 1.132f
7.64	Dav §29R4; GKC §64i
7.66	GKC §23i, 97g; J-M §100n □ B-L 627s; Berg 1.44c
7.70–71	GKC §97g
7.70	B-M 2.88 □ B-L 627s; Berg 1.93h; Brock §105b

7.71	GKC §23i; J-M §100n □ B-L 627s; B-M 2.88; Berg 1.44c
7.72	J-M §100n
8.2	GKC §74l; J-M §78i □ B-L 444p; Berg 2.157b
8.5	Berg 1.132 n f, 2.82n
8.6	Berg 1.52k; Gib 111
8.7	B-L 581; Berg 1.50g, 1.52k, 1.144d
8.8	Dav §88R1; GKC §2t, 113z; J-M §123x □ Berg 1.2m, 1.52k, 1.132 n f, 2.66h*
8.9	J-M §125l
8.10	Dav §144R5; GKC §85g n 1, 128p, 152v, 155n; J-M §158d; Gib 12 □ B-L 240t', 538i
8.11	Dav §117; GKC §105a; J-M §105b; IBHS 683 □ B-L 653b; B-M 2.145; Berg 2.135e
8.13	Dav §96R4, 136R1; GKC §114p, 154a n 1b; Gib 132 □ Berg 2.60 n p
8.14–15	GKC §165b
8.14	J-M §113m, 157c; Gib 110 □ GAHG 3.102 n 289
8.15	B-L 588i; Gib 110
8.17	Berg 2.69c
8.18	Wms §254 □ Brock §129c
9.1	J-M §143k
9.3	Dav §100a, 100R6; GKC §116s; J-M §154c; IBHS 624 n 41; Gib 138 □ Berg 2.71f
9.5	Dav §100a, 100R6; Gib 138
9.6	Dav §106R2; Gib 2, 55 □ B-L 248e
9.7	J-M §119za □ Berg 2.45n
9.8	GKC §113z; J-M §119za, 123x □ GAHG 3.102 n 289; Berg 2.45n, 2.67m; Brock §46c
9.10	Berg 2.153t
9.11	Brock §109e
9.13	GKC §113z, 132d; J-M §123x; 148a; IBHS 258 □ B-M 3.29; Sch §45.4.5; Berg 2.67m
9.17	Berg 1.149g
9.18	GAHG 3.177 n 605; Berg 2.162d

B-L: Bauer and Leander, *Historische Grammatik*   **B-M**: Beer, *Grammatik*   **Berg**: Bergsträsser, *Grammatik*
Brock: Brockelmann, *Syntax*   **Dav**: Davidson, *Syntax*   **GAHG**: Richter, *Grammatik*
Gib: Gibson, *Davidson's Syntax, 4th ed.*   **GKC**: *Gesenius' Grammar*   **IBHS**: Waltke and O'Connor, *Syntax*
Jen: Jenni, *Lehrbuch*   **J-M**: Joüon and Muraoka, *Grammar*   **Ros**: Rosenthal, *Grammar*
Sch: Schneider, *Grammatik*   **Wms**: Williams, *Syntax*

9.19	Dav §72R4; GKC §35n, 117m; J-M §125j(7); IBHS 182; Gib 117 □ B-L 228a'; Brock §31b, 51	12.30	Berg 2.115a
		12.31	B-L 533f; Berg 2.23f
		12.36	J-M §8a n 4
		12.38	GKC §35n □ B-L 635b
9.20	B-L 547	12.44	GKC §95n □ B-L 598; B-M 2.65; Berg 1.103o
9.21	IBHS 371		
9.22	GKC §63m □ B-L 564	12.45	J-M §177p □ Berg 2.84 n p
9.24	GKC §93aa □ B-L 564	12.46	GKC §114b; J-M §124d, 129b
9.25	Berg 1.129b, 2.103d*	12.47	GKC §95n; J-M §129b □ B-L 598; Berg 1.102o
9.27–29	Berg 2.32e		
9.27	Berg 2.137k	13.1	Berg 2.45n
9.28	Dav §73R4, 109; J-M §141b, 152d; IBHS 169; Gib 4, 44 □ Berg 2.33 n e, 2.145d; Brock §88, 100b	13.2	B-L 438
		13.3	Jen §15.7.4
		13.5	IBHS 630 □ Berg 2.73i*
		13.6	GKC §51e
9.31	Dav §78R7	13.7–11	GKC §49e
9.32	Dav §72R4; GKC §117k, 117l, 117aa; J-M §125j; Wms §59, 72; Gib 117 □ GAHG 3.92 n 244; Brock §35c, 102	13.8	B-L 333y
		13.9	GKC §165a
		13.10	Dav §116; GKC §44m, 95n; Gib 23 □ B-L 368t, 598; Berg 1.102o
9.34	Dav §72R4; GKC §72x, 117m; J-M §125j; IBHS 182; Gib 117 □ B-L 404; Brock §51	13.13	GKC §53g, 53n, 68i □ B-L 333c', 351, 372x; Berg 2.15b, 2.82 n m, 2.104 n h, 2.120 n d
9.35	Dav §32R2; GKC §126x; Gib 44	13.14	GKC §75ii; J-M §125b □ B-L 424; Berg 2.48g, 2.164 n
9.37	J-M §154fe		
10.1	GKC §91h □ Berg 2.71g	13.15	B-L 343b''; Berg 1.113 n e, 2.21d, 2.82n
10.29	Dav §83R2; Gib 121		
10.30	Berg 2.71g	13.16	GKC §9b □ B-L 547, Berg 1.44c
10.33	Berg 2.112c	13.17	Dav §47; Gib 96
10.37	Dav §17R6; GKC §123a n 1; J-M §135b n 2	13.18	GKC §114o □ Berg 2.60p
		13.20	GKC §134r; J-M §102f, 137u n 1; Gib 51, 103
10.38	J-M §146e; IBHS 414		
10.39	Dav §84R1; GKC §53k, 53q □ B-L 228a', 332t, 353v, 468w'''; B-M 2.26; Berg 2.82 n m	13.21–22	GKC §49e
		13.21	Dav §22R3; GKC §73f; J-M §14c; Gib 29 □ B-L 399h''; Berg 2.144b; Brock §116d
11.1	GKC §134r n 3		
11.2	B-M 3.33	13.22	J-M §125b; IBHS 630 □ Berg 2.74k
11.17	GKC §53q; J-M §54b □ B-L 229f', 443k; Berg 2.31b, 2.105k		
		13.23	Dav §1R1, 41R3; GKC §155d □ B-L 231d; Berg 1.113 n e
11.21	Berg 2.73i		
11.24	Berg 1.127cc, 2.54d	13.24	Dav §29R8; GKC §2a, 2w; IBHS 116 n 7; Gib 42 □ B-L 13a, 27s; Berg 1.2e
11.35	B-L 547		
12.7	Berg 2.23f		
12.14	J-M §93s □ B-L 525h	13.25	B-L 438; Berg 2.97h
12.22	J-M §129b	13.27	GKC §100n
12.26	J-M §129b	13.29	B-L 213p
12.27	J-M §91e	13.30	Berg 2.45n
12.28	J-M §177p		
12.29	J-M §177p		

B-L: Bauer and Leander, *Historische Grammatik*   **B-M**: Beer, *Grammatik*   **Berg**: Bergsträsser, *Grammatik*
Brock: Brockelmann, *Syntax*   **Dav**: Davidson, *Syntax*   **GAHG**: Richter, *Grammatik*
Gib: Gibson, *Davidson's Syntax, 4th ed.*   **GKC**: *Gesenius' Grammar*   **IBHS**: Waltke and O'Connor, *Syntax*
Jen: Jenni, *Lehrbuch*   **J-M**: Joüon and Muraoka, *Grammar*   **Ros**: Rosenthal, *Grammar*
Sch: Schneider, *Grammatik*   **Wms**: Williams, *Syntax*

1 CHRONICLES

B-L: Bauer and Leander, *Historische Grammatik*   B-M: Beer, *Grammatik*   Berg: Bergsträsser, *Grammatik*
Brock: Brockelmann, *Syntax*   Dav: Davidson, *Syntax*   GAHG: Richter, *Grammatik*
Gib: Gibson, *Davidson's Syntax, 4th ed.*   GKC: *Gesenius' Grammar*   IBHS: Waltke and O'Connor, *Syntax*
Jen: Jenni, *Lehrbuch*   J-M: Joüon and Muraoka, *Grammar*   Ros: Rosenthal, *Grammatik*
Sch: Schneider, *Grammatik*   Wms: Williams, *Syntax*

B-L: Bauer and Leander, *Historische Grammatik* **B-M**: Beer, *Grammatik* **Berg**: Bergsträsser, *Grammatik*
Brock: Brockelmann, *Syntax* **Dav**: Davidson, *Syntax* **GAHG**: Richter, *Grammatik*
Gib: Gibson, *Davidson's Syntax, 4th ed.* **GKC**: *Gesenius' Grammar* **IBHS**: Waltke and O'Connor, *Syntax*
Jen: Jenni, *Lehrbuch* **J-M**: Joüon and Muraoka, *Grammar* **Ros**: Rosenthal, *Grammar*
Sch: Schneider, *Grammatik* **Wms**: Williams, *Syntax*

B-L: Bauer and Leander, *Historische Grammatik*   **B-M**: Beer, *Grammatik*   **Berg**: Bergsträsser, *Grammatik*
Brock: Brockelmann, *Syntax*   **Dav**: Davidson, *Syntax*   **GAHG**: Richter, *Grammatik*
Gib: Gibson, *Davidson's Syntax, 4th ed.*   **GKC**: *Gesenius' Grammar*   **IBHS**: Waltke and O'Connor, *Syntax*
Jen: Jenni, *Lehrbuch*   **J-M**: Joüon and Muraoka, *Grammar*   **Ros**: Rosenthal, *Grammar*
Sch: Schneider, *Grammatik*   **Wms**: Williams, *Syntax*

B-L: Bauer and Leander, *Historische Grammatik*   **B-M**: Beer, *Grammatik*   **Berg**: Bergsträsser, *Grammatik*
Brock: Brockelmann, *Syntax*   **Dav**: Davidson, *Syntax*   **GAHG**: Richter, *Grammatik*
Gib: Gibson, *Davidson's Syntax, 4th ed.*   **GKC**: Gesenius' *Grammar*   **IBHS**: Waltke and O'Connor, *Syntax*
Jen: Jenni, *Lehrbuch*   **J-M**: Joüon and Muraoka, *Grammar*   **Ros**: Rosenthal, *Grammar*
Sch: Schneider, *Grammatik*   **Wms**: Williams, *Syntax*

29.3	Dav §144R5; GKC §155d, 155n; Gib 12		29.17	Dav §22R4; GKC §138i; J-M §145d, 146a; IBHS 248; Gib 29 □ Berg 2.60p
29.4	Dav §29R3; J-M §136o			
29.6	J-M §125l; IBHS 185 □ Brock §31a		29.18	B-M 2.114 □ B-L 199p, 306m, 306p
29.7	Gib 49 □ Berg 1.136e		29.20	GKC §117n; J-M §125k n 1
29.8	Dav §22R4; GKC §138i; J-M §145d; Gib 29		29.21	Berg 1.122t(bis)
			29.22	Dav §73R7; GKC §117n; J-M §125k
29.9	GKC §117q □ Berg 2.117a			
29.11	Berg 1.78m		29.23	GKC §65f □ Berg 2.117a
29.14	Dav §146R2; Gib 111		29.25	IBHS 216 n 105
29.16	GKC §32l; J-M §80m □ B-L 217c; Berg 2.148k		29.29	Dav §123R2; Gib 184
			29.30	J-M §136o □ Berg 1.135d

B-L: Bauer and Leander, *Historische Grammatik* **B-M**: Beer, *Grammatik* **Berg**: Bergsträsser, *Grammatik*
Brock: Brockelmann, *Syntax* **Dav**: Davidson, *Syntax* **GAHG**: Richter, *Grammatik*
Gib: Gibson, *Davidson's Syntax, 4th ed.* **GKC**: *Gesenius' Grammar* **IBHS**: Waltke and O'Connor, *Syntax*
Jen: Jenni, *Lehrbuch* **J-M**: Joüon and Muraoka, *Grammar* **Ros**: Rosenthal, *Grammar*
Sch: Schneider, *Grammatik* **Wms**: Williams, *Syntax*

2 CHRONICLES

B-L: Bauer and Leander, *Historische Grammatik* **B-M**: Beer, *Grammatik* **Berg**: Bergsträsser, *Grammatik*
Brock: Brockelmann, *Syntax* **Dav**: Davidson, *Syntax* **GAHG**: Richter, *Grammatik*
Gib: Gibson, *Davidson's Syntax, 4th ed.* **GKC**: *Gesenius' Grammar* **IBHS**: Waltke and O'Connor, *Syntax*
Jen: Jenni, *Lehrbuch* **J-M**: Joüon and Muraoka, *Grammar* **Ros**: Rosenthal, *Grammar*
Sch: Schneider, *Grammatik* **Wms**: Williams, *Syntax*

6.39	J-M §99f n 2; IBHS 170 n 16	9.28	Dav §108; Gib 14
6.40	GKC §145n; J-M §148c, 150c,	9.29	J-M §149a
	150r □ GAHG 3.216 n 815	10.4	Berg 2.137k
6.41	B-L 534	10.5	Brock §50e*
6.42	J-M §125k □ Berg 2.48g	10.6	GKC §117n
7.1	GKC §111b; J-M §176l	10.7	GKC §35n; J-M §35e
7.3	GKC §76f, 113z, 115f; J-M	10.8	Dav §116R1
	§123q, 123x □ Berg 1.135c	10.9	GKC §117n □ Berg 2.137k
7.7	B-L 382	10.10	GKC §93q □ B-L 582u'; Berg
7.8	Berg 2.57 n k		1.135d
7.9	J-M §97Bc	10.11	Wms §591; Gib 42
7.10	J-M §126a	10.14	Wms §591
7.12	Berg 2.45n	10.16	GKC §147c □ B-L 771
7.13	GKC §159w; J-M §167l	11.4	GKC §47m n 1 (p. 129); J-M
7.17	Dav §96R4; GKC §114p; Gib		§44e n 1 □ Berg 2.21b
	132 □ Berg 2.60 n p	11.12	Dav §29R8; GKC §123c; IBHS
7.18	Dav §73R5; Wms §589; Gib 110		116 n 7; Gib 42 □ Berg 2.65h*
7.19	J-M §44e n 1	11.17	Wms §268
7.20	Berg 2.39i	11.18	B-L 510v
7.21	GKC §143e; J-M §125l; IBHS	11.22	GKC §114i, 114k, 147a; J-M
	184; Gib 118		§154d □ Berg 2.59 n mop
8.3	B-L 510v	12.2	J-M §176f
8.5	GKC §126y, 128c; J-M §131m	12.3	Berg 1.124w
8.7	J-M §177o n 1	12.5	J-M §112g □ Berg 2.28e
8.10	Gib 36	12.7	GKC §111b
8.11	Dav §28R5; Gib 36	12.10	J-M §119za □ Berg 2.45n
8.12	Berg 2.34g	12.11	J-M §176f □ Berg 2.32e
8.13	Dav §96R4; GKC §114k; Gib	12.12	GKC §114i; J-M §154d; IBHS
	132 □ Berg 2.59 n mop		603 n 19 □ Berg 2.56h
8.14	IBHS 116 n 7; Gib 42	12.13	GKC §131h; IBHS 227 □ B-L
8.15	Berg 1.113 n e		624i; B-M 3.35
8.16	Dav §20R4; GKC §127g □	13.3	Berg 2.112d
	Brock §73c	13.5	GKC §114l; Wms §284 □ Berg
8.17	Berg 2.34g		2.58m
8.18	Dav §29R3; GKC §93r □ B-L	13.7	GKC §54k □ B-M 2.122
	597h'	13.9	GKC §152a n 1; J-M §111i □
9.5	J-M §154m; Gib 42		Berg 2.42g*
9.8	Berg 2.49h	13.10	B-L 158 n 2, 614
9.9	Dav §29R3	13.11	Brock §129c
9.10–11	GKC §35m	13.15	J-M §176l
9.10	Berg 1.112d	13.21	Gib 48
9.11	Berg 1.112d	14.2	Berg 2.117a
9.13	Dav §29R3	14.6	Berg 2.137k
9.15	GKC §134g; Gib 75	14.9	GKC §90i; J-M §150j n 1
9.20	Dav §128	14.10	GKC §44o, 107p □ B-L 348h;
9.21	Dav §44b; J-M §126b; Gib 73 □		Berg 2.50k
	B-L 444p	14.12	Brock §145a
9.22	Brock §107iα	15.1	Gib 182
9.25	B-M 2.76 □ B-L 603g; Berg	15.3	GKC §147a
	1.102m	15.4	B-L 346x''

B-L: Bauer and Leander, *Historische Grammatik*   **B-M**: Beer, *Grammatik*   **Berg**: Bergsträsser, *Grammatik*
Brock: Brockelmann, *Syntax*   **Dav**: Davidson, *Syntax*   **GAHG**: Richter, *Grammatik*
Gib: Gibson, *Davidson's Syntax, 4th ed.*   **GKC**: *Gesenius' Grammar*   **IBHS**: Waltke and O'Connor, *Syntax*
Jen: Jenni, *Lehrbuch*   **J-M**: Joüon and Muraoka, *Grammar*   **Ros**: Rosenthal, *Grammar*
Sch: Schneider, *Grammatik*   **Wms**: Williams, *Syntax*

15.7	GKC §145p; J-M §150d	19.2	GKC §114k; J-M §113l; IBHS
15.8	GKC §54k, 111b, 127f		508 □ B-L 348h; Berg 1.65q,
15.11	GKC §155d; J-M §145d n 1		2.58m, 2.112d
15.15	GKC §52d □ B-L 346x''	19.4	Berg 1.142f
15.16	Berg 2.138l, 2.148l	19.5	Dav §29R8; IBHS 116 n 7; Gib
15.18	B-L 582u'		42
16.1	Berg 2.143 n b	19.6	GKC §147a
16.4	GKC §125h; J-M §131n	19.7	GKC §45e; J-M §49e; Gib 128
16.7	Berg 2.91g		□ B-L 366t; Berg 1.132f, 2.46c,
16.8	Berg 2.65h*, 2.91g		2.48f, 2.83p(bis)
16.9	Dav §113, 144, 144R5; GKC	19.9	Berg 1.141f
	§155n; J-M §158d; IBHS	19.11	Berg 2.49h
	87 n 13; Gib 11, 12, 21	20.1	GKC §102b; J-M §176f □ Berg
16.10	GKC §147a		1.78m
16.11	Dav §123R2; IBHS 16; Gib 184	20.2	Brock §120a
16.12	Dav §71R3; GKC §75rr, 118q,	20.3	J-M §125k
	147a; J-M §79l, 125b, 126g n 2	20.6	Dav §95, 106R2; Wms §410;
	□ B-L 424; GAHG 3.147 n 390,		IBHS 609; Gib 2, 132 □ Berg
	3.156 n 445, 3.156 n 446; Berg		2.58m
	2.161b, 2.168q	20.7	J-M §88Fb □ Berg 1.157o
16.14	GKC §124c, 154a n 1 □ B-L	20.9	IBHS 169, 563 □ Berg 2.47d,
	547; Berg 1.119o; Brock §19d*		2.52o
17.3	J-M §125k	20.11	J-M §103d n 3, 125u □ B-L
17.4	GKC §150d; J-M §125k		643s'; Berg 1.142f; Brock §94a
17.7	GKC §117n	20.15	Dav §155
17.11	GKC §03x □ B-L 564; Berg	20.17	Dav §95; IBHS 609; Gib 132 □
	1.102n, 2.71f		Berg 2.58m
17.12	Dav §86R4; GKC §113u; J-M	20.18	J-M §118f
	§123s; Gib 126 □ B-L 597h';	20.19	GKC §128v
	Berg 2.73i*	20.20	GKC §110f □ Berg 2.50k
17.13	GKC §117n; J-M §150k	20.22	Dav §144R5; GKC §155l; Gib
17.14	Dav §116R6		12
18.3	Dav §151R2; GKC §147a	20.25	J-M §49e; IBHS 603 n 21, 629 □
18.11	Berg 2.50k		Berg 2.56h, 2.73i*, 2.83p
18.12	J-M §142ba □ Berg 2.53q	20.29	Berg 1.135d
18.14	J-M §152fa □ Berg 2.50k	20.34	GKC §63p; J-M §68f, 149a □
18.15	Gib 185		B-L 425; Berg 1.154e
18.16	GAHG 3.102 n 289	20.35	GKC §54a n 2; J-M §53a n 2;
18.18	GAHG 3.102 n 289		Gib 120 □ B-L 351; B-M 2.122;
18.23	GKC §155d; IBHS 327 n 26		Berg 2.59n*, 2.99d
18.24	B-L 375; Berg 2.158e; Brock	20.36	GKC §118f
	§129c	20.37	GKC §106n □ Berg 2.29h
18.26	GKC §131c; J-M §127b □ B-L	21.4	GKC §119w n 2
	135h	21.10	J-M §113h; Gib 72 □ Berg
18.29	GKC §113dd n 4; IBHS 594 □		2.33g
	Berg 2.66 n k	21.11	Berg 2.165k
18.30	Berg 1.52k	21.12	Brock §163b
18.32	B-L 135h	21.13	Berg 2.161b
18.33	B-L 135h; Berg 1.160b		

B-L: Bauer and Leander, *Historische Grammatik*   **B-M**: Beer, *Grammatik*   **Berg**: Bergsträsser, *Grammatik*
Brock: Brockelmann, *Syntax*   **Dav**: Davidson, *Syntax*   **GAHG**: Richter, *Grammatik*
Gib: Gibson, *Davidson's Syntax, 4th ed.*   **GKC**: *Gesenius' Grammar*   **IBHS**: Waltke and O'Connor, *Syntax*
Jen: Jenni, *Lehrbuch*   **J-M**: Joüon and Muraoka, *Grammar*   **Ros**: Rosenthal, *Grammar*
Sch: Schneider, *Grammatik*   **Wms**: Williams, *Syntax*

21.17	GKC §133g; J-M §129f, 141e, 141j; Wms §78; IBHS 154, 261, 270; Gib 45 □ B-M 3.37; Brock §60c	25.9	GKC §154b; J-M §177m; Wms §480; IBHS 592 n 46, 609; Gib 50 □ Berg 2.58m(bis)
21.18	B-L 637p; Brock §145a	25.10	GKC §35n, 117n; J-M §35e
21.19	J-M §176f; IBHS 91	25.14–15	Sch §48.4.3.3, 54.2.2.1
22.5	GKC §35d □ B-L 263f, 563x; Berg 1.91d	25.14	Berg 2.31d
		25.16	Dav §108, 126R5; GKC §150e; IBHS 208 n 78; Gib 13, 184
22.6	Dav §44R2; IBHS 432; Gib 75 □ Berg 2.33 n b-h	25.17	GKC §48i, 69x, 75l, 156c n 1 □ B-L 385g', 409m; Berg 2.131o
22.8	GAHG 3.102 n 289	25.19	Berg 2.45n
22.9	GKC §116o; J-M §121f; Gib 132 □ B-L 348h; Berg 2.57l	25.20	Dav §22R3
		25.21	GKC §156c n 1
22.12	Berg 2.74 n l	25.23	IBHS 215 n 101
23.1	Dav §73R7; GKC §117n; J-M §125l; Gib 118	25.24	GKC §112pp
		26.5	GKC §114c; IBHS 446 □ Berg 2.60o
23.4	GKC §47m n 1 (p. 129); J-M §121n □ Berg 2.21b	26.6	J-M §79m
23.6	Gib 182	26.7	GKC §93x □ B-L 564
23.10	GKC §154a n 1, 156c; GKC §154a n 1b	26.8	IBHS 440 □ Berg 2.57k
		26.10	GKC §22s; J-M §177p □ B-L 127a'; Berg 1.66s
23.11	Berg 2.49h		
23.12	GKC §35b	26.13	Dav §17; Gib 19 □ B-L 348h
23.18	Brock §110i	26.14	GKC §124q, 131n; J-M §125l, 146e
23.19	GAHG 3.152 n 417		
24.4	J-M §176f	26.15	GKC §75rr, 114n, 126z; J-M §79l □ B-L 443k, 538i; B-M 2.140; Berg 2.59n*, 2.127e, 2.168q
24.6	J-M §129d; IBHS 143		
24.8	GKC §35o		
24.10	GKC §75aa; J-M §79p n 1, 123c □ Berg 2.61b		
		26.16	GKC §64c □ B-L 354b; Berg 2.57k, 2.116e
24.11–14	Berg 2.32e		
24.11	GKC §75cc, 155l; J-M §118b, 166q □ B-L 425; Berg 2.32e(bis), 2.166n	26.18	GKC §114l; IBHS 609 □ Berg 2.58m
		26.19	J-M §176l □ Berg 2.116d
24.12	GKC §117n; J-M §121g, 125l □ B-L 549a'; Berg 2.73i*	26.21	J-M §126c
		27.4	GKC §35k □ B-L 597h'
24.14	GKC §114b; J-M §124d, 129b n 3; IBHS 602 n 16; Berg 2.54d, 2.55e	27.5	J-M §177p
		27.7	Dav §123R2; GKC §150e; J-M §161c; Gib 184
24.15	B-M 2.112	28.3	J-M §158h
24.17	Berg 2.34g	28.4	GKC §65e □ B-L 361a'; Berg 2.117a
24.18	Gib 6		
24.21	Gib 145	28.6	J-M §170j
24.22	B-M 2.158; Berg 2.49h, 2.163f	28.8	J-M §155oa
24.23	J-M §176f	28.9	Dav §101Rb; GKC §155f
24.25	IBHS 91	28.10	GKC §45g, 135g, 142f n 2; J-M §156d
24.26	B-L 510v		
25.1	J-M §16f n 3 □ B-L 518c'	28.13	J-M §141b
25.5	Wms §14	28.15	GKC §72l, 93pp, 117n; IBHS 465 □ B-L 493zz; Berg 1.140c
25.8	B-L 348h		

B-L: Bauer and Leander, *Historische Grammatik*   **B-M**: Beer, *Grammatik*   **Berg**: Bergsträsser, *Grammatik*
Brock: Brockelmann, *Syntax*   **Dav**: Davidson, *Syntax*   **GAHG**: Richter, *Grammatik*
Gib: Gibson, *Davidson's Syntax, 4th ed.*   **GKC**: *Gesenius' Grammar*   **IBHS**: Waltke and O'Connor, *Syntax*
Jen: Jenni, *Lehrbuch*   **J-M**: Joüon and Muraoka, *Grammar*   **Ros**: Rosenthal, *Grammar*
Sch: Schneider, *Grammatik*   **Wms**: Williams, *Syntax*

28.16	B-L 348h
28.18	GKC §129b
28.19	Dav §88R1; GKC §113z; J-M §123x; Gib 127 □ Berg 2.67m
28.20	Dav §73R4; GKC §67x; IBHS 367 □ B-L 438; Berg 1.112d, 2.138l
28.21	GKC §147a; J-M §93j
28.22	J-M §146e □ Berg 2.137k
28.23	GKC §53o □ B-L 361a', 534; Berg 2.104 n h, 2.117a
29.3	J-M §130d
29.6	GKC §67y
29.7	J-M §155oa
29.10	GKC §165a
29.11	Berg 1.104r
29.17	GKC §134p; Wms §268; Gib 50
29.18	GKC §117n; J-M §155oa
29.19	GKC §29l, 44o, 72w; J-M §155oa, 80m □ B-L 217c; Berg 2.148k
29.21	Berg 1.129b
29.22	J-M §93e
29.27	Dav §25, 136R1; GKC §35n, 155l; Gib 12
29.28	Berg 2.57k
29.29	J-M §125s; IBHS 608
29.31	GKC §66c □ B-L 367; Berg 2.122c
29.34	GKC §107c, Wms §167 □ Berg 1.128dd
29.36	Dav §22R4; GKC §100h, 138i; J-M §145d; IBHS 249, 339
30.9	GKC §114p, 147a □ Berg 2.60 n p
30.10	Dav §100R2; J-M §121g; Gib 138 □ Berg 2.73i*
30.11	Berg 1.113 n e
30.16	J-M §159b
30.17	GKC §152a n 1, 155d
30.18	GKC §64d, 130d n 2 □ B-L 216n, 355m; Berg 2.115a
30.19	Dav §144R5; GKC §155n; J-M §129q(3); Gib 12
30.21	Wms §254; IBHS 199
30.22	J-M §126b
31.1	GKC §75aa; J-M §79p n 1, 123c, 124s □ Berg 2.61b
31.7	Dav §111R2; GKC §69n, 71, 142f n 2; J-M §75l, 77a n 2 □ B-L 383; Berg 2.130m
31.10	Dav §111R2; GKC §53q, 72z, 113ee, 121d n 1; J-M §54b, 80r, 123w, 155i; IBHS 594 □ B-L 228a'; Berg 2.67l, 2.105k
31.12	GKC §10h □ Berg 1.126bb
31.16	J-M §146e
31.17	GKC §117m
31.19	GKC §155d □ Berg 2.55e
31.21	J-M §125k
32.1	GKC §119gg; J-M §65a □ B-L 361x; Berg 2.82n
32.4	GKC §150m
32.9	GKC §101a; J-M §16f n 3 □ B-L 518c'
32.12	J-M §146e
32.13	GKC §8k □ Berg 1.45e
32.14	B-L 382
32.15	GKC §74l, 152b; J-M §78i □ B-L 441c; GAHG 3.177 n 605
32.19	GKC §118s n 2
32.23	IBHS 360 n 30 □ B-L 441c; Berg 1.109 n c, 2.99 n d
32.28	B-L 603g; Berg 1.102 n o
32.30	GKC §69u; J-M §146e □ B-L 33c', 384c'; Berg 2.117a, 2.129 n k
32.32	Dav §123R2; GKC §150e; J-M §161c; Gib 184
33.4	Berg 2.45n
33.6	Berg 2.45n, 2.59n*
33.8	J-M §125l □ GAHG 3.191 n 681; Berg 2.140 n q
33.9	GKC §75gg □ Berg 2.165k
33.14	Berg 2.45n
33.19	Berg 2.54d
33.20	Dav §69R1; GKC §118g; J-M §126h
33.22	Berg 1.127cc
33.23	J-M §146e
34.3	J-M §125k
34.4	J-M §155oa □ Berg 1.2f
34.7	B-L 436; Berg 2.117a, 2.137 n k
34.10	GKC §45g □ B-L 210f; Berg 1.122t
34.11	GKC §16f
34.12	GKC §10h □ Berg 1.78m
34.21	J-M §158g

B-L: Bauer and Leander, *Historische Grammatik*   **B-M**: Beer, *Grammatik*   **Berg**: Bergsträsser, *Grammatik*
Brock: Brockelmann, *Syntax*   **Dav**: Davidson, *Syntax*   **GAHG**: Richter, *Grammatik*
Gib: Gibson, *Davidson's Syntax, 4th ed.*   **GKC**: *Gesenius' Grammar*   **IBHS**: Waltke and O'Connor, *Syntax*
Jen: Jenni, *Lehrbuch*   **J-M**: Joüon and Muraoka, *Grammar*   **Ros**: Rosenthal, *Grammar*
Sch: Schneider, *Grammatik*   **Wms**: Williams, *Syntax*

34.22	Dav §144R5	36.13	Berg 2.165k
34.31	B-L 581	36.15	GKC §113k; J-M §123r n 3 □
35.3	J-M §49e □ Berg 2.54d, 2.83p		Berg 2.65h
35.4	GKC §93ww	36.16	Dav §100R2; J-M §121g; IBHS
35.13	J-M §96Al, 102g □ B-L 614;		426; Gib 138 □ Berg 2.73i*,
	Berg 1.141 n a		2.109c
35.15	Berg 2.58m, 2.65h	36.19	GKC §114k; 142f n 2 □ Berg
35.17	GKC §93oo n 1 (p. 273)		2.60p
35.21	GKC §109g, 119s, 135g, 147a;	36.21	GKC §67y; IBHS 448 n 2
	J-M §116j, 146d □ GAHG	36.23	GKC §137c □ B-M 2.158; Berg
	3.172 n 542		2.49i, 2.163g
35.23	GKC §69r □ B-L 444k; Berg		
	2.127e, 2.127 n e		

B-L: Bauer and Leander, *Historische Grammatik*   **B-M**: Beer, *Grammatik*   **Berg**: Bergsträsser, *Grammatik*
Brock: Brockelmann, *Syntax*   **Dav**: Davidson, *Syntax*   **GAHG**: Richter, *Grammatik*
Gib: Gibson, *Davidson's Syntax, 4th ed.*   **GKC**: *Gesenius' Grammar*   **IBHS**: Waltke and O'Connor, *Syntax*
Jen: Jenni, *Lehrbuch*   **J-M**: Joüon and Muraoka, *Grammar*   **Ros**: Rosenthal, *Grammar*
Sch: Schneider, *Grammatik*   **Wms**: Williams, *Syntax*